Readings in the Philosophy of Law

Readings in the Philosophy of Law

FOURTH EDITION

edited by

KEITH C. CULVER and MICHAEL GIUDICE

broadview press

BROADVIEW PRESS
Peterborough, Ontario, Canada

Founded in 1985, Broadview Press is a fully independent academic publishing house owned by approximately twenty-five shareholders—almost all of whom are either Broadview employees or Broadview authors. Broadview is supported by a collaboration with Trent University, a liberal arts university located in Peterborough, Ontario—the city where Broadview was founded and continues to operate. Broadview is committed to environmentally responsible publishing and fair business practices.

Library and Archives Canada Cataloguing in Publication

Title: Readings in the philosophy of law / edited by Keith C. Culver and Michael Giudice.
Names: Culver, Keith, 1969- editor | Giudice, Michael, editor
Description: Fourth edition. | Includes bibliographical references.
Identifiers: Canadiana (print) 2025031696X | Canadiana (ebook) 20250316978 | ISBN 9781554816606 (softcover) | ISBN 9781460408629 (EPUB) | ISBN 9781770489387 (PDF)
Subjects: LCSH: Law—Philosophy—Textbooks. | LCSH: Common law—Textbooks. | LCGFT: Textbooks.
Classification: LCC K235 .R422 2026 | DDC 340/.1—dc23

Broadview Press handles its own distribution in Canada and the United States:
PO Box 1243, Peterborough, Ontario K9J 7H5, Canada
555 Riverwalk Parkway, Tonawanda, NY 14150, USA
Tel: (705) 482-5915
email: customerservice@broadviewpress.com

Broadview Press books are imported and distributed in the United Kingdom and European Union by:
Gazelle Book Services Ltd.
White Cross Mills, Hightown, Lancaster, Lancashire, LA1 4XS
sales@gazellebookservices.co.uk

European Union – Responsible Person (for official use only):
eucomply OÜ
Pärnu mnt 139b14
11317 Tallinn, Estonia
hello@eucompliancepartner.com
+33757690241

Canada Broadview Press acknowledges the financial support of the Government of Canada for our publishing activities.

Copy-edited by Michel Pharand
Book Design by Em Dash Design

PRINTED IN THE UNITED STATES

1 2 3 4 5 6 7 8 9 10   26 27 28 29 30

Contents

Acknowledgments

The first edition of this textbook was published in 1999, motivated by the need for an affordable philosophy of law textbook useable everywhere the common law tradition is at the foundation of state legal systems. That edition's inclusion of work on international law was slightly unusual at the time, yet was received positively by readers whose response to the volume started a dialogue between editors and users enabling subsequent editions to present what a reader community regarded as enduringly valuable argument along-side selections encouraging readers to explore new issues arising. This fourth edition aims to preserve what readers have found useful, while looking forward again, now including work on Indigenous law, a topic important in its own right and as an example of the increasing complexity of the legal life world in which state legal systems are just one source of legality. We are grateful to anonymous reviewers and colleagues who have approached us directly to offer their views on the last edition, and we promise to keep listening as you use this fourth edition of a textbook whose life has now spanned the end of one century and the first quarter of the next.

Preface

Why use this textbook in philosophy of law?

Accessibility: This textbook is designed to be used by readers with no prior experience of philosophy of law. Brief, easily understood introductions explain the context and key features of the readings, giving readers enough background to enable them to take on the real work of developing their own views regarding the arguments contained in each reading. The introductions are supplemented by a clearly written glossary, study questions, and further readings, providing readers with tools for evaluating their own understanding, and a path toward more readings and perspectives on issues introduced in this textbook.

A real debate: Philosophy of law is a living discipline, inhabited by real people thinking about ideas and practices with real consequences for our everyday lives. These ideas have histories, and there are many points of view regarding those histories, so it is sometimes difficult to see the contemporary relevance of philosophy of law when it seems to be preoccupied with its history and diversity. This textbook takes seriously the importance of understanding the interaction between arguments which are in direct conflict, or offer incompatible points of view. Each section of this book is organized to present arguments which clearly compete and conflict with each other in trying to provide the best answer to shared questions and issues. It is up to you, the reader, to decide which arguments are the winners, or whether there is no winner and further investigation is needed.

Understanding what authors themselves said: A sound understanding of the issues and arguments of philosophy of law requires first-hand experience of philosophy of law. This textbook recognizes the importance of each reader coming to his or her own conclusions about what authors in philosophy of law have actually said. There is no substitute for the original text when trying to reach a fair understanding of the best available arguments regarding issues in philosophy of law. The readings contained in this textbook have been edited very lightly, and authors' original references have been left intact wherever possible, to allow this book to serve as a useful resource for further exploration of these arguments. We look forward to your reaction to this fourth edition, and hope you find in philosophy of law a rich trove of arguments and insights to contribute to your life as a student, citizen, and perhaps Prime Minister or President.

Keith C. Culver and Michael Giudice

Introduction

Why read this introduction? And while we are asking questions, why has the course you're taking assigned a textbook? And why is it so long—if the ideas it introduces can be summarized in an introduction, why is there both an introduction and then long readings? Taking the first question first, this introduction makes it easier for new students of philosophy of law to approach and understand arguments using possibly unfamiliar terms, and addressing possibly unfamiliar ideas, in possibly unfamiliar contexts. That is not to say that this introduction makes philosophy of law easy, but this introduction will provide you with an overview of what philosophy of law is and how it is represented in this textbook, so as you proceed in classes and in readings to consider particular arguments you have a "big picture" sense of the place of those arguments in the philosophy of law. This introduction will also offer you some tips regarding how to approach reading philosophy of law. It is entirely possible for anyone skilled in reading in the English language to begin reading the selections in this textbook; but much as it is generally easier to drive a car or ride a bike or cook a recipe new to you with the benefit of advice in advance from an experienced person, reading philosophy of law is best approached with a plan and some advice about what to do when feeling stuck.

Turning to the second question, this textbook provides a course instructor and students with a broad overview of key ideas and issues in philosophy of law, together with guidance as to how to approach philosophy of law, all in an inexpensive paperback volume providing everyone in a class with a common basis for turning to a particular argument located on the same page for everyone. Readers will also benefit from the editors' having selected especially important or representative parts of work written by various authors, steering readers straight to the heart of what generations of readers have found enduringly valuable, or recent readers think positively provocative and in need of greater attention.

This overall introduction and introductions to individual sections may seem long by contemporary standards, in a time when consumption of information online has driven emergence of an expectation that anything important will be provided to us very briefly, and in the simplest possible terms. This expectation comes to life in so-called online attempts to draw eyes to sales pitches or political views by promising solutions to problems with a 'hack' or a 'simple trick.' Some important ideas can be provided simply, and some hacks or simple tricks may work to solve simple problems of laundry stains or shoes that always come undone. Yet humanity's biggest problems, the ones we aim to use law to help resolve, are not the sort of problems quickly solved by hacks, and the ideas creating and eventually solving those big problems can be simplified only so far. Much as humans did not solve the problem of how to travel to the moon by demanding that it be closer, when the problems are difficult we should not be dismissive of the possibility that answers might be time-consuming to construct and large and complex when they arrive, even while we remain open to quick, simple, break-through solutions if we can have them. If you work through the introductions to excerpts or portions of important arguments provided in this textbook, and work in class and with peers to extend your understanding, you will certainly add understanding of philosophy of law to your accomplishments, and you will improve your readiness to tackle and solve the problems that cannot be solved with hacks or tricks.

What we cannot supply in a textbook is your own choice to give yourself a chance to work with those questions and arguments to determine how they inform your judgment and choices as a student, a citizen, and perhaps a future employee, employer, or parent. We observe that as we write, understanding the nature and limits of law as a means of social organization and dispute resolution has gained new importance. At the close of the Cold War between the US and its allies, and the Soviet Union and its allies, the world appeared to be moving toward ever greater integration and shared mechanisms for dispute resolution. Among other important events following the Cold War, the European Union attempted to foster greater cohesion by considering development of a European Constitution, Russia joined the G7 group of economic powers making the G8 a venue for negotiation through disputes, and China joined the World Trade Organization and agreed to use its dispute resolution mechanisms. These and other developments contributed to what politicians call the "international rules-based order" committed to using law rather than force to resolve disputes. In recent years that rules-based order has been challenged by war in Europe and in the Middle East, and by rising tensions in the Indo-Pacific region. The role law can play in resolving underlying disputes and preventing new disputes has yet to be determined. Whatever role law plays, its effectiveness relies in part on its users holding a sound understanding of what law can do and cannot do. Study of the philosophy of law will contribute to your understanding of the options available for maintenance of peaceful relations among states, whose citizens need their states to attend to many other current challenges to our societies, including the operation of legal systems providing justice for all. Whether you use your understanding to contribute to preserving some dimension of law you think important or instead to advocate change or simply to understand a predicament, studying philosophy of law can help you to understand your options.

1. What Is "Philosophy of Law"?

Philosophy of law is concerned with the nature and conceptual foundations of law as a distinctive mode of social organization. Philosophy of law asks a wide and widening range of questions about law and legal practices. Some of these questions continue an ancient debate, asking "What is law?" and "What is legal obligation?" Other questions probe the links among law, authority, and morality, asking "What is legitimate authority?" and "Are immoral laws really laws?" Still other questions explore responsibility, restitution, crime, punishment, race, and the border between literary, economic, and political understandings of law. Answers to these questions come from lawyers, philosophers, and others concerned with law and social life. These questions and answers are variously called philosophy of law, legal theory, legal philosophy, or jurisprudence (from the Latin *juris*, meaning law, and *prudentia*, meaning knowledge). We will use these terms interchangeably since they all refer to the same range of questions.

2. How Are These Questions Answered?

Traditionally, philosophy of law has been divided into "analytical" and "normative" areas of inquiry. Analytical jurisprudence has been concerned with *analysis* and *explanation* of legal concepts, asking such general questions as "What is law?" and "What is legal obligation?" Normative jurisprudence has been concerned with *evaluation* and *justification* of law and legal practices, asking such questions as "What is the nature of legitimate legal authority?" and "What justifies legal punishment?" This traditional distinction has recently come under extensive criticism from several directions, some of them represented in this book. Some writers charge that the traditional distinction ought to be abandoned as unfounded or, at best, seriously misleading. Influential writers such as Ronald Dworkin suppose that meaningful legal analysis and evaluation must be carried out simultaneously and focused on interpretation of a particular legal culture—American, or Canadian, or British, and so forth. Writers from feminist, Critical Legal Studies, Critical Race Theory, and other perspectives are skeptical of the traditional distinction between analytical and normative investigations and argue that it promotes a dangerously distorted understanding of law and legal practices in which important social forces such as gender, race, and class are not properly accounted for. Law is fundamentally political and fundamentally attached to particular societies, according to these writers, so broad and general analytical and normative investigations are pointless and misleading. Yet those who are skeptical of the traditional distinction have not succeeded in persuading all legal theorists that the division between analytical and normative investigations ought to be given up as an unfortunate mistake. Many writers continue to defend the value of distinguishing analytical from normative philosophy of law.

As you consider analytical, normative, and other approaches to philosophy of law, it is also important to think about what each approach tries to accomplish. Some are contributions to understanding of what it is to be a human living in a society. Others ask us to take immediate, practical action to fix problems in our legal systems. There is probably a place for a range of approaches to philosophy of law, but they will sometimes conflict and it will not always be an option to try to find a compromise or common ground. Philosophy of law is open to alternative views and new approaches, yet it is not simply a collection of all that has been said about the core questions of philosophy of law. Philosophy of law is above all an attempt to work toward better understanding of life under law, even when that means rejecting particular arguments or entire approaches to law. This book tries to give a concise picture of some of the main contenders in the debate over what philosophy of law is and what it should try to accomplish, and a picture of the results of different theorists' philosophical investigations into law. This book also tries to give you the resources to decide for yourself which perspectives are likely to give the most helpful answers to questions of philosophy of law. You may not arrive at final answers to these questions, but at least you will have some of the tools needed to work toward answers.

3. What Am I Going to Get from Philosophy of Law?

Law pervades our daily lives whether we like it or not, so we all share an immediate practical interest in understanding law. In the longer run, law plays a role in shaping the general structure of our societies, so we also have a longer-term stake in understanding law. A course in philosophy of law will acquaint you with some of the best answers to date regarding immediate, practical questions with philosophical dimensions, such as the way we ought to understand the wrongdoing involved in an unsuccessful attempt to commit a crime. You will also have an opportunity to examine more abstract yet equally important philosophical issues regarding the relation between law and justice—issues which may become especially important as you choose how to vote, where you will volunteer your skills in your community, or where you will lend your voice to a protest. As you study some of the arguments philosophers of law have offered in response to questions of philosophy of law, your instructor will show you how to demonstrate understanding of those arguments by explaining them, criticizing them, finding further support for their key claims, and assessing their strength relative to other arguments. Skills in critical analysis and evaluation of arguments in philosophy of law can be an excellent part of preparation for study of law, public service, journalism, business, and life as a private citizen.

4. Am I Ready for This Unfamiliar Discipline?

A new area of study can seem more challenging than it really is. To understand this book, you do not need any background in either philosophy or law. In philosophy of law, as in many other areas of study, the main requirement for success at the introductory level and beyond is a willingness to encounter new ideas. It is also important to be prepared to learn about philosophers' and lawyers' special use of certain terms and concepts, and to be ready to read critically and thoroughly. Sometimes this means reading an argument more than once, but this is an ordinary and expected part of reading arguments which have been very carefully and precisely assembled.

Here is some time-tested advice regarding reading philosophy of law and making the most out of your class.

You ought to try to complete an assigned reading before a lecture, then re-read it again soon after the lecture, taking notes at each stage. Since you know in advance that reading philosophy of law might be uncomfortable, as it requires sustained attention to complex arguments, you know before you start reading that you may need to coach yourself through momentary discomfort. Much of what you probably already know about self-coaching through an exercise program or even tasks such as doing laundry can be helpful here. Do you feel as though the reading is so long that you will never be able to complete it? Think of the reading like the challenge of a pile of clean laundry, or your commitment to cardio exercise for twenty minutes. Focus on reading the introduction to the article, promising yourself a brief, timed rest when you do, thinking of this just like getting going on folding laundry by telling yourself that you can at least fold your shirts then pause, because anyone can fold a few shirts, or exercise for the first five minutes of a twenty-minute session. Re-set after you achieve the first step, pausing to clear your head with a breath of fresh air—or maybe even folding an actual shirt! If you are still having difficulty getting started, think about making a deal with a friend or a classmate, promising to hold each other accountable for completing a task, checking in after a set time to celebrate completion or to encourage continued work to completion. It can help a great deal to feel that you are not the only human alive working on a difficult task. Even 'programmed' recognition from a friend can be rewarding!

If while you are reading you come across terms that are unfamiliar to you, pause, find your phone or computer, which you have put out of reach while you are committed to completing your reading, and use online general or legal dictionaries to find the meaning of the term. Try to treat unfamiliar terms or ideas as puzzles to be solved rather than reasons to stop reading. You can solve the vast majority of these puzzles by yourself prior to class. As you read, try taking handwritten notes if you can. You may find that knowing how time-consuming it is to write notes by hand leads you to think carefully about what you write. By thinking carefully to create better quality notes, you are likely to understand a reading better because you have thought about it in different ways as you have read, then created a summary or recorded a question. Your notes should focus less on summarizing what you read, and more on identifying the author's thesis or central organizing idea, and the structure and organization of the argument presented—how the author thinks one reason hangs together with the next and perhaps another to support the big idea the author wants you to accept. Make special note of areas you find unclear, and consider keeping a record of what questions you have about an author's argument.

If you prepare for class using the approaches we have suggested, you may find it much easier to take notes in class. Since you will have already created a picture of the structure of an author's argument, you will be ready to listen or participate, then add to your existing notes. If further attention to difficult areas still leaves you uncertain whether you understand an argument, asking a question in class at an appropriate moment will give you an opportunity to extend your understanding, and to do shy classmates a favor since many others are likely to share your question. If the right moment for your question does not arise in class, it is a very good idea to visit your instructor or teaching assistant. Contrary to popular rumor, instructors do not actually eat students for breakfast and are very happy to help you. Short emails to instructors can be helpful, but when working to get clear about an idea it is usually best to be face to face for discussion requiring more than very brief answers. Some instructors have a "drop in any time" policy, while others need to schedule specific office hours conducted in person or online. Office hours are usually listed on the course outline, on the instructor's office door, or at the main office of your instructor's department.

5. The Structure of This Book: What to Expect

This book focuses on questions which have concerned legal theorists in the "common law societies" that inherited the structure of the English legal system, as well as in the emerging world of international law. These questions include, but are not limited to, "What is law?"; "What limits may justifiably be imposed by law on individual liberty?"; "How can law justifiably determine what it is to be responsible for legal wrongdoing?"; and "What is international law?"

For each section there are four tools to help you. *Introductions* aimed at first-time readers of legal philosophy discuss some of the main ideas of the section. Each section concludes with recommendations for *Further Reading*, and *Study Questions* to help you refine your understanding of the arguments you have read. Both the further readings and the study questions will make it possible for you to find more perspectives on the arguments you read, and provide new ways into the debates we examine. Finally, a *glossary* of legal and philosophical terms forms the last part of the book. This glossary is intended to help you to move between philosophy and law, and to account for the different contexts in which different writers make their arguments. This glossary is designed to be useful to readers of this textbook and does not aim to be comprehensive. You may find it useful to have a credible online law dictionary available as an additional resource.

6. The Content of This Book: An Overview

In the remainder of this general introduction, we will explore very briefly the main ideas of the book. We will do this so that you can begin reading already knowing how the book hangs together as a whole, and how the questions and arguments contained in the book represent an extended exchange of arguments and replies.

6.1 SECTION 1: NATURAL LAW THEORY AND THE DUTY TO OBEY

The first section begins with natural law theory, a *normative* approach to law. Natural lawyers have traditionally argued that laws must meet certain moral standards if they are to generate genuine obligations. So-called laws which do not meet these standards cannot justifiably demand obedience. Our selections present both a classical natural law theory and a modified, contemporary natural law theory which claims that genuine laws which ought to be obeyed must at least *aim* at morally good goals. We will encounter in this contemporary view the very interesting claim that even immoral laws must sometimes be obeyed if they are only a small part of a system of laws which generally pursues morally justified goals. Since natural law is traditionally thought to set moral standards which laws must meet in order to be real laws, it is perhaps surprising to see a natural law theorist making a purely *analytical* claim that what is treated as a law is in fact a law, even if it does not pursue a morally acceptable goal. Can a natural law theory make this claim and still maintain natural lawyers' ability to distinguish genuine, binding laws from defective laws which ought to be disobeyed? This will be for you to decide. We also include in this section a famously skeptical view about the obligation to obey the law, that even the best available accounts fail to establish a general reason to do as the law says because the law says so. The consequences of this view, if accurate, raise interesting and important questions for the success of natural law theory.

6.2 SECTION 2: LEGAL POSITIVISM

In the second section we turn to what has long been regarded as the view most plainly opposed to natural law theory. Legal positivism traditionally argues that while laws often are morally justified, it is *not necessary* for the existence of law that it have moral merit or even aim at morally justified goals. Legal positivists have instead explained laws as social practices such as "commands," "social rules," or other norms which are not necessarily moral norms. This *analytical* theory of law allows legal positivists to explain easily how legal systems which pursue different goals in different ways at different times—even systems of morally bad law, such as the law of Nazi-era Germany—are all systems of law. Yet legal positivism has been criticized on several grounds. How, some critics ask, can an entire system of laws pursue morally bad aims and still provide any reason for judges to apply law or for citizens to obey it? Some critics suppose that legal positivists' insistence that laws need not aim at morally good goals is a terrible distortion of what distinguishes life under law from tyranny or a war of all against all. Other critics have objected in a variety of ways to the broad and general scope of legal positivism's picture of law, arguing that this sort of picture has very little value. We include a selection from one of legal positivism's strongest critics in this section.

6.3 SECTION 3: LEGAL REALISM AND LEGAL REASONING

In this section we encounter a theory of law quite different from natural law and legal positivist theories of law. "Legal realist" writers of the first half of the twentieth century tried to break free of earlier attempts to develop a "scientific" understanding of law as a set of rationally ordered rules whose meaning and proper application could be determined with scientific certainty. Legal realists recognized that there is much more to law than written rules stored in law libraries, and argued that a realistic understanding of law must use a wide array of social scientific approaches and disciplines, from psychology to economics, history and political science, to take account of what courts in fact do with laws. The legal realists' emphasis on the activities of courts reminded legal theorists that law is a living thing which exists in practice as well as in statutes, codes, and other written documents. We include again a selection from an important critic, Ronald Dworkin. Like the legal realists, Dworkin engages in close investigation of the nature of judicial reasoning to show that law is composed of more than just rules. But unlike the legal realists, he finds that law also involves an underlying web of moral "principles." To understand the law as it is, he argues, requires a kind of practically-oriented philosophical interpretation properly attuned to law's purpose of morally justifying the use of coercive force. According to Dworkin, focusing on law's social, economic, and political conditions, as legal realists advocate, distorts the very essence of law, since it turns attention away from law's moral nature. Which account better explains the nature of law and judicial reasoning: legal realism or Dworkin's theory of "law as integrity"? Or do these views raise different but complementary questions? This will be for you to judge.

6.4 SECTION 4: FEMINIST JURISPRUDENCE AND CRITICAL RACE THEORY

In the fourth section we consider some influential contemporary criticisms of the dominant analytical and normative theories of law. Feminist and Critical Race theorists argue from insights similar to those of legal realists that much orthodox legal theory proceeds on assumptions which must be challenged. These assumptions range from one we noted above—that jurisprudence is either analytical or normative—to assumptions about human nature and the shared experiences, values, and goals of persons living together under law. Many of the critics from these movements are concerned that legal theory's abstract worries about the nature of law have taken attention away from important practical questions of the actual effect of law on social life, and of the strategies required for reform of unjust laws and legal systems. Many feminist legal theorists, for example, have focused on normative evaluation of the way women are and have been treated in law, and analysis of the ways law and theories of law bear a male bias. Critical Race Theory writers, departing from some insights of the Critical Legal Studies movement, whose members express largely moral concerns about the way law affects members of ethnic groups historically distinguished from elites on the basis of the slippery idea of "race." We also include a selection from Professor Kimberlé Crenshaw, who shows the importance of 'intersectional' analysis, namely, how the lenses of feminist and Critical Race theorists must be combined. All approaches included in this section examine the promise and appearance of law, and ask us to look more deeply and critically at its real nature beyond mere appearance.

6.5 SECTION 5: LEGAL PLURALISM AND INDIGENOUS LAW

The first four sections of this textbook offer four different kinds of answers to the question "What is law?" These accounts of law are sometimes clearly at odds with one another, as analytical, normative, and skeptical approaches appear to pursue entirely different goals. At other points, it seems possible to borrow the insights of at least parts of analytical and normative theories, while abandoning their weaknesses, to arrive at an acceptable single, comprehensive theory. There are difficulties in either an "all-star" theory made up of analytical and normative insights, or a defense of one particular analytical or normative answer to the question of the nature of law. There are also difficulties with skeptical approaches which deny the traditional distinction between analytical and normative approaches, yet do not offer a better, comprehensive replacement for understanding what law is or what law should become. The ideas provided here and in the suggested further readings can provide a great deal of insight into what the best understanding of law might look like. There is, of course, much more to be said about the nature of law, so it is well worth pursuing answers to the question "What is law?" in the large and rich literature beyond this book.

The fifth section takes up questions about the existence and operation of legal pluralism, the idea that more than one legal order can operate in a given social situation. Legal pluralists, of all kinds, argue that too much legal theory has proceeded on the assumption that the only law that does and can exist in some social situation is the official, formal law of the state. According to legal pluralists, this view ignores and overlooks the many ways in which non-state legal orders not only exist but also play an important role in organizing social life. Examples of non-state legal orders include religious law, customary law, transnational law, and possibly even the law of various sub-cultures and voluntary associations such as sports clubs and universities. The first chapter in this section provides one account of a legal pluralist approach to understanding and categorizing the various kinds of legal phenomena visible in social life. The next two chapters explore more deeply an example of state law's operation alongside Indigenous law, an increasingly prominent instance of non-state law emerging from lengthy suppression and in some instances near eradication in colonial and post-colonial states such as Canada and the United States. The selections we provide investigate the similarities and differences between Indigenous law and law rooted in European traditions. The selections make the case for the revival of Indigenous law as an essential contribution to Indigenous peoples' self-determination. Such revival is not without its challenges, however. To what extent must states reconceive their practices to form better relations with Indigenous peoples and governments and address historical and continuing injustices? Must we go even further, and rethink the very concept of law, to properly understand and appreciate the prevalence and need for legal orders to co-exist in the same space? If legal pluralists are right, the task for the philosophy of law is fundamental, and raises in a new light the need to revisit the question 'what is law?'

6.6 SECTION 6: LAW AND INDIVIDUAL LIBERTY

The sixth section of the book turns to one important aspect of life under law: personal freedom and its limits. When you think of law, what images immediately come to mind? Courts, police, and criminals probably appear in the first few thoughts. This is not surprising, given that our lives are filled with fictional TV cops, judges, bad guys, and "reality TV" capitalizing on our fascination with the worst dimensions of human behavior, from robberies to car-jacking and more. We are intrigued by the interaction between these groups, and often shocked by what the bad guys have done: in acting "against the law" or "breaking the law" they have used their personal freedom in ways prohibited by law. Here we find an important issue in philosophy of law. In constitutional documents, declarations, and human rights legislation, common law societies are committed to the preservation of the widest possible range of human freedom. Yet we all recognize that freedom needs limits. What should those limits be?

We begin with John Stuart Mill's expression of the classical liberal view that the good of individuals and the good of societies require that laws leave as wide as possible a range of freedoms to individual persons. On this view, society is justified in legislating against only that conduct which harms others. Private conduct which is harmless to others cannot justifiably be limited by law. This view can explain and justify many laws, especially much of the criminal law, yet Mill's arguments have encountered criticism nonetheless. Some of these criticisms are identified in the lengthier introduction to this section of the book.

In the next two chapters in this section we examine a famous debate over the amount and type of liberty a society can tolerate. In the Hart-Devlin debate presented here, the English judge Lord Devlin argued against legalization of homosexual conduct in private between consenting adults, on grounds including the need for a society to have a shared set of values in order to exist. Hart responded with a modified version of Mill's liberal understanding of freedom, and argued in favor of legalization of private homosexual conduct. In this debate some crucial issues of public policy are intertwined with philosophy, and philosophy can be seen as a useful practical tool for resolving some of these issues.

6.7 SECTION 7: CRIMINAL RESPONSIBILITY AND PUNISHMENT

From our consideration of liberty and its limits, we move to the ideas of responsibility and punishment. Many readers have heard the saying that "with freedom comes responsibility," meaning that our freely chosen actions are ours and ours alone, and we must bear the brunt of criticism or praise for those actions because they are ours—sometimes in the form of suffering significant liberty-limiting punishments. Philosophically interesting questions arrive when we have to say precisely and unambiguously *how* actions are "our own responsibility" in a way worth punishing. This section explores the idea of responsibility specifically in the context of the criminal law.

The first chapter examines the role of *intention* and *action* in criminal wrongdoing, in an attempt to determine how to characterize the wrongdoing committed in crimes people "meant to do." The difficulty and importance of arriving at a clear and unambiguous understanding of criminal wrongdoing is then illustrated in the second chapter with close consideration of responsibility for hate crimes. Finally the third chapter raises the crucial question of whether punishment can ever be justified when applied by societies bearing the hallmarks of widespread injustice, often occurring despite the sincere intentions of the framers of institutional arrangements and rules to produce justice in those societies.

6.8 SECTION 8: THE NATURE OF INTERNATIONAL LAW

Most of us have a sense of what international law does. It governs such matters as basic human rights which exist in all countries, international borders, and rules of international trade. But does this add up to a *law of nations*, something binding all or nearly all states always or nearly always? What are we to make of the fact that international human rights law is frequently ignored, typically with little repercussion against those who ignore it? Does international law really provide binding obligations in the same way the law of individual countries is binding within those countries? There is more than a surface resemblance between these questions and the questions we encountered in the first four sections. Here we ask "What is international law?" and rejoin the debate over the value of analytical and normative approaches to questions in philosophy of law. Our selections include works from analytical and normative perspectives, and an argument from an author who is skeptical both about the existence of international law and about the value of analytical and normative perspectives on international law.

Our selections begin with Hugo Grotius's natural law theory, which argues that certain standards of conduct hold universally among all peoples and all countries. This view captures the widespread sense that there are shared standards which all decent, civilized societies ought to recognize as the basis of international legal order. The second article presents H.L.A. Hart's legal positivist argument that an international legal system remains a possibility which does not yet exist. Hart's argument points to the absence of a settled way to test the validity of what are claimed to be international laws and reminds us that there is an important difference between our aspirations for international law as a way to guide international life and the actual fact of the matter.

The third article in this section, by Martti Koskenniemi, rejects both normative and analytical approaches to understanding international law, arguing that both approaches lack sensitivity to the actual political context of international relations. According to this skeptical argument, there are strong political reasons against the existence of international law in the form theorists have traditionally expected it to take. This skeptical argument claims that purely normative theories of international law lack realism about international relations, and purely analytical theories of law attempt awkwardly to understand international law within the inadequate concepts of domestic law. Koskenniemi's approach goes beyond analytical and normative approaches to law in order to understand law in a broader social and political context, much as the Feminist and Critical Race Theory approaches examined in Section 4 attempt to go beyond the traditional conception of jurisprudence.

In the final article of this section, we explore a set of arguments designed to show the limits of thinking that only states, or organizations of states, make law at regional or global levels. Roger Cotterrell argues that we ought to adopt a legal pluralist framework for viewing law beyond states, so as not to miss the distinctive character of overlapping and competing legal orders created and maintained by transnational communities of non-state actors. While such transnational law is not meant to replace international law, transnational law forces us to reflect on whether an understanding of law built up from experience of state law is sufficiently sensitive to detect and explain the various forms which law can take. In many ways this final article brings us full circle to the issues and questions raised in earlier sections of the book about what law is, and whether analytical or normative approaches, or perhaps something else entirely new, might be needed as life under law changes as our societies change.

Further Readings

Brian H. Bix, *Jurisprudence: Theory and Context*. 9th ed. Durham, NC: Carolina Academic Press, 2023.

Jules Coleman and Scott Shapiro, eds., *The Oxford Handbook of Jurisprudence and Philosophy of Law*. Oxford: Oxford UP, 2002.

Martin Golding and William Edmundson, eds., *The Blackwell Guide to the Philosophy of Law and Legal Theory*. Oxford: Blackwell, 2004.

Dennis Patterson, ed., *A Companion to Philosophy of Law and Legal Theory*. 2nd ed. Oxford: Wiley-Blackwell, 2010.

Andreas Philippopoulous-Mihalopoulos, ed., *Routledge Handbook of Law and Theory*. London: Routledge, 2021.

Raymond Whacks, *Philosophy of Law: A Very Short Introduction*. Oxford: Oxford UP, 2014.

SOME ACADEMIC JOURNALS

Canadian Journal of Law and Jurisprudence
Criminal Law and Philosophy
Jurisprudence
Law and Philosophy
Legal Theory
Oxford Journal of Legal Studies
Ratio Juris
Res Publica
The Journal of Legal Philosophy

SECTION 1

Natural Law Theory and the Duty to Obey

Introduction

This section explores the idea of natural law. The range of ideas associated with natural law theory is so wide that it is nearly impossible to avoid excluding one important understanding of natural law while trying to explain another. Here we will explore a general description of natural law theories before discussing the work of two authors whose ideas have been particularly influential.

It is reasonably safe to say that all natural law theorists suppose that certain facts about humans and their world provide the right basis for laws with which to guide human conduct. Natural law theorists differ significantly, however, in their understanding of exactly which facts about the world must be taken as guides to law. Some theorists depend on the existence of God and religious texts, inspiration, or divine revelation as the basis for laws. Others rely on an understanding of human nature, human capacity to reason, or human social or biological needs. Yet no matter which facts a particular natural law theorist thinks especially relevant to the basis of law, all natural law theorists argue that their particular set of facts shows that laws cannot have just any content. What we might call "real" laws are those laws which meet certain standards—usually moral standards. Those standards are found by looking at the right facts, and using practical reasoning to determine how those facts ought to guide human conduct.

This section presents readings from two influential natural law theorists. The first, St. Thomas Aquinas, is the best-known writer of the Roman Catholic natural law tradition. The second, Professor John Finnis, is the best-known contemporary defender of natural law theory. It might seem at first glance that there can be little in common between a Catholic theologian who studied and wrote in various European centers of learning in the thirteenth century, and a professor of jurisprudence teaching at Oxford University in England in the late twentieth and early twenty-first centuries. In fact, the two share several views, and Finnis makes clear his debt to Aquinas. It is a mark of the persuasiveness of natural law theory that many of its central ideas have survived substantially unchanged from the thirteenth to the twenty-first centuries and still appear relevant and compelling. Here we will examine just three of the many areas of agreement between Aquinas and Finnis before turning to the specific features of each author's argument.

1. The Purpose of Law and Legal Theory

Aquinas and Finnis (and many other natural law theorists) agree on the answer to the question "What is the purpose of philosophical investigation of law?" Both authors suppose that the philosophy of law ought to determine how best to order social interaction for the common good—the good of all. Aquinas does not leap out and say explicitly that this is the purpose of the philosophy of law, but we will not have to dig very deeply into his work to find this view. Finnis takes time at the beginning of his book *Natural Law and Natural Rights* (from which our selection is taken) to make clear why he thinks a philosophical investigation of law must do more than simply describe certain features of law. Aquinas and Finnis agree that description is not enough: an adequate philosophy of law must contain the means to distinguish between real laws which impose genuine obligations, and laws which do not impose genuine obligations and are best regarded as defective or degenerate. As Professor Neil MacCormick describes the natural law view, it supposes that "... laws, like other social institutions, are fully intelligible only by reference to the ends or values they ought to realise, and thus by reference to the intentions that those who participate in making them or implementing them must at least purport to have. This does not entail any acceptance of substantive moral criteria as criteria of legal validity, but it does involve acknowledging the moral quality of the relevant ends and values, namely justice and the public good."[1]

2. The Self-Evidence of Basic Goods

Aquinas and Finnis share a further understanding of the way in which we can determine which facts about the world are appropriate guides to the formation of laws. Both writers argue that certain goods (values) are self-evident. Aquinas, writing from a Christian perspective, supposes that certain Christian values are self-evidently good and valuable. Finnis does not appeal to Christian theology. Rather, he argues that careful attention to the requirements of social life and individual fulfilment show that at least some values are good in and of themselves. Laws must advance these values to best serve the goal of human flourishing. Despite their slightly different starting points, both writers are sympathetic to the famous ancient Greek philosopher Aristotle's view of human flourishing as involving happiness. This sort of happiness is rather more than a warm and fuzzy feeling of contentment. It involves a deeper sense of fulfilment in several areas of life such as self-development and treating others fairly. Happiness of this sort is self-evidently good, according to Aquinas and Finnis, and laws ought to contribute to this happiness.

3. Practical Reasoning

Aquinas and Finnis both recognize that laws do not make or interpret themselves. Even if it is possible to arrive at a set of general principles which all persons will recognize as the correct basis for laws of human conduct, these general principles must be interpreted and applied by humans to provide specific guidance in specific situations. Consider, for example, the principle that one ought not to harm others. This principle does not contain in itself any guidance regarding its application. Are police officers to be exempt from this principle? If so, under what conditions? To determine how to put this principle into practice in a particular situation, we must use skills of *practical reasoning* to arrive at a law which will guide human conduct in the best possible way.

4. St. Thomas Aquinas

St. Thomas Aquinas (1224–74) is one of the great thinkers of Western philosophy, and a central figure of Catholic philosophy and theology. Aquinas was born near Naples, Italy, and spent his adult life in several cities in Europe. The source of the selection included in this book is Aquinas's *Summa Theologica*. His *Summa*, as it is called, is a sort of systematic working out of a *theological* view of the world. A theological view of the world accepts the existence of God and asks what sort of world God has created. Aquinas's concern with the nature of law is understandably influenced by the fact that he views the discussion of law as only part of his larger discussion of the nature of a God-created world. It is worth noting, however, that Aquinas's theory of law is persuasive to

1 D. Neil MacCormick, "The Separation of Law and Morals," in R.P. George, ed., *Natural Law Theory: Contemporary Essays* (Oxford: Clarendon P, 1992), p. 113.

many non-Christians as well: much of his argument can be accepted on rational grounds alone without reference to faith.

Much of the rational, non-religious appeal of Aquinas's arguments can be traced to his philosophical debt to Aristotle. Although Aquinas was certainly a powerful and important original thinker in his own right, his understanding of metaphysics, physics, politics, and ethics is thoroughly Aristotelian. In the thirteenth century, when Aquinas wrote, Aristotle was taken so seriously that he was referred to simply as "The Philosopher." Authors commonly wrote "The Philosopher says ..." in support of their arguments. This was done not simply on the blind assumption that what Aristotle said was true, but on the reasoned, sincerely held belief that Aristotle's views were the most sophisticated, best available views, regardless of the fact that he was not a Christian. To the extent that Aquinas examined law using Aristotle's map of the basic foundations of logical thought, Aquinas's views appeal to both Christians and non-Christians.

In a moment we shall discuss some of Aquinas's main arguments, but first we must examine their packaging. If you have never read the work of a medieval philosopher, Aquinas's style of organization may seem quite odd. Aquinas's discussion of law is given in a form called a "disputatio"—an imitation of a verbal dispute. His work looks a bit like a screenplay with too few indications as to which character should say which line. Yet once the structure of his writing is exposed, we will be able to see that it is actually very carefully and logically organized. The framework is as follows:

1. Aquinas begins by asking a question or series of questions whose answers are a matter of dispute. He encounters each question in turn, each in a unit he calls an "Article."
2. At the beginning of each Article, Aquinas lists a series of objections or possible arguments *against* the view he intends to defend, sometimes mentioning the name of the person known for offering this objection, and sometimes not. Sometimes he does not bother to identify an author of an objection because the view contained in the objection is very well known, or the view is so widely held that there is no need to point to specific persons.
3. After the question and the objections, Aquinas often quotes an authority whose argument disputes the claims of the objections and generally supports Aquinas's own view. He begins this section by saying "on the contrary," to mark the fact that the authority's argument runs contrary to the objection Aquinas has noted. It is worth mentioning again that authorities such as Aristotle are often cited not simply in the blind belief that if an authority said it then it must be true, but in the same way that we rely today on a scientist's expert testimony in court or a physician's expert advice about how to remain healthy.
4. Following his citation of an expert opinion in support of his view, Aquinas offers his own argument. He begins the body or "corpus" of his own argument with the words, "I answer that ..."
5. Aquinas completes consideration of the question by returning to the objections with which he began. He replies to them one by one, restating and expanding parts of the main body of his argument.

It may be tempting to rush past the objections in order to get at the meat of Aquinas's own views. If you do so, you risk misunderstanding precisely why he offers the arguments he does. Aquinas's methodical examination of a question offers in an admittedly artificial format the give-and-take which actually occurs when we attempt to defend a view. Only very rarely will an audience collapse in stunned silence at a speaker's feet, in awe of the speaker's shining intelligence and awesome reasoning. Usually even the most persuasive arguments are met with reasonable objections which must be answered. A full understanding of a speaker's view includes both the body of the speaker's argument and the speaker's responses to objections.

The selections presented here from Aquinas's *Summa Theologica* have been limited to the Questions and Articles most useful to a new reader of Aquinas's philosophy of law. However, in order to leave the door open for your further reading, where Articles have been omitted, their titles have been included for your reference. The selections explore four particular aspects of Aquinas's natural law theory. In this introduction we will begin with (1) his definition of law, and (2) his explanation of what natural law is. We will conclude our discussion of Aquinas with (3) his explanation of the difference between real laws and defective laws and (4) his explanation of how laws bind their subjects.

4.1 AQUINAS'S DEFINITION OF LAW

Aquinas's definition of law states the essence, or fundamental nature, of laws. It is important to recognize that Aquinas was concerned mainly with defining the nature of *laws* rather than the nature of a *legal system*, unlike writers such as Finnis who are concerned as much with the way laws operate in a system as with the nature of *law* more generally. (As you will see in other introductions and readings in this book, there are important differences between explanations of law and of legal systems made up of many laws, much as there are important differences between explanations of a person and of a society, composed of many persons.) Aquinas's definition of law may seem immediately familiar, and that is perhaps a good indication of how thoroughly it has penetrated thought in the Western world. In the body or "corpus" of Question 90, Article 4, Aquinas summarizes the investigation of the question. He writes, "Thus from the four preceding articles, the definition of law may be gathered; and it is nothing else than an ordinance of reason for the common good, made by him who has care of the community, and promulgated." A law, according to Aquinas, is a result of reasoning about how to reach the common good (the good for everyone). A law is made by a person in authority, and made public or "promulgated" so the law's requirements can be known.

4.2 NATURAL LAW

Armed with an understanding of what Aquinas supposes a law is, we can now ask what makes such a law part of natural law? To understand the answer to this question we must first examine Aquinas's understanding of humans. Aquinas accepts that humans were created by God in God's own image, and that God gave humans certain characteristics. The defining characteristic of humans, according to Aquinas, is our possession of *reason*, or *rationality*. We tend naturally to attempt to do good things, mirroring in a limited way God's characteristics as a supremely rational, wholly good being who has created a rationally ordered universe. When we use our God-given powers of reasoning we can see that certain things are self-evidently good, and worth pursuing. Consider, for example, the claim that what is good is to be pursued, and what is bad is to be avoided. Aquinas supposes that this claim is self-evidently true: as rational humans we can see that it is true simply by looking at it. When we use our reasoning correctly as we pursue self-evidently good things and attempt to make laws to achieve the common good, we are said to be using "right reason" and participating or sharing in God's reasoning and rational ordering of the world. So the natural law is in each person and is discovered by applying reason to general principles whose truth is self-evidently clear. This process results in practical rules for living that best fit our nature as rational persons who are generally good. As Aquinas explains the natural law in the body of Article 2, Question 91, "Wherefore it [the rational creature] has a share of the Eternal Reason, whereby it has a natural inclination to its proper act and end: and this participation of the eternal law in the rational creature is called the natural law."

4.3 REAL AND DEFECTIVE LAWS

It might seem from this sketch of natural law that there can only be one right way to make a law: either a man-made or "positive" law discovers correctly the reasonable way to achieve the common good, or it doesn't. This is not Aquinas's view. His understanding of natural law is much more subtle and complex. Aquinas recognizes that there may be more than one way to solve a particular social problem and he can accept that different cultures may choose to place different limits on behavior, as required by different social situations. What is important is that any particular solution meet the general requirements set by the principles which all rational persons must accept. Aquinas divides man-made or positive law into two types: "real" law and "defective" law. (These are not the precise words of Aquinas or his translators, but they represent ideas recognizable in any translation.) Real laws meet the requirements of right reason: they are reasonable standards of conduct which aim at serving the common good. Real laws are "just," because they meet the requirements of justice. Aquinas recognizes, however, that some so-called laws fail in some way to meet the requirements of natural law—they may be unjust, or perhaps they are not promulgated properly. What are we to make of these so-called laws? According to Aquinas, while these failed attempts at laws may in fact be accepted and followed in some particular situation, "such laws do not bind in conscience." These defective laws are justifiably disobeyed. It is arguable, for example, that acts of civil disobedience committed by persons such as Dr. Martin Luther King were justified because the laws Dr. King disobeyed were not binding in conscience, and therefore were not real laws genuinely deserving of obedience.

4.4 HOW LAWS BIND THEIR SUBJECTS

We may now face the last of our four topics in consideration of the ideas of Aquinas. In his discussion of legal obligations, Aquinas notes that the Latin word for law (*lex*) comes from a word which means "to bind." Many of us in the modern world may feel that this is exactly what our huge and complex bodies of law do to us—laws leave us tightly tied and restrict our options, sometimes for good reasons, and at other times for bad reasons or for reasons which are no longer relevant. Often we continue to obey some law only to avoid being arrested or sued if we ignore that law. For Aquinas, however, police action or other sanctions against disobedience are a last resort and the least important reason to obey the law. According to Aquinas, if a law is real and meets the requirements of natural law, it is *morally* binding. If you are subject to that law, you ought to obey it because the law is for the common good. As a rational person you ought to realize that the common good is a worthwhile goal and you ought to respect law as a reasonable way of achieving that worthwhile goal. You ought also to obey the law because the law is part of God's will, and you are a subject of God. With these weighty considerations supporting the law, police action is left as a tool of last resort. Police action is to be applied to those few persons who for whatever reason fail to realize what they are reasonably required to do or withhold from doing.

You may, after reading all of this, find yourself impressed by the organization of Aquinas's argument and yet still suppose it is not relevant to you. You might, for example, reject the existence of God. Or you might suppose that Aquinas's understanding of God is somehow defective. It may seem that if Aquinas's idea of God is rejected, Aquinas's theory of natural law must be rejected also. It is worth considering, however, whether at least some of the elements of Aquinas's theory can be used in a more modern theory of natural law that does not rely on the existence of God as part of its justification.

5. Professor Finnis and Natural Law as Practical Reasonableness

The selections included here from Finnis's book *Natural Law and Natural Rights* are limited to four important topics. We begin with some of Finnis's remarks from his introductory discussion of the purposes of theorizing about law. We will then jump to Finnis's discussion of how we know what is good for humans. In the third part of our selection Finnis discusses "practical reasonableness." The fourth and final part of our excerpt contains Finnis's response to the question of whether an immoral law ought to be obeyed. Throughout these selections, you will find strong similarities between the views of Aquinas and Finnis. Is this evidence that Finnis is not an original thinker? It is likely better to see Finnis as an active participant and developer of an idea and argument which has been refined gradually over several centuries. Far from lacking originality as a philosopher, Finnis is faced with the difficult task of improving arguments which have already benefited from the close attention of some of the best philosophers.

In an earlier section of this introduction, we noted that Aquinas and Finnis agree on the purpose of philosophizing about law. A complete philosophy of law, both agree, is one which helps humans to guide their conduct in a way which promotes the common good. Finnis, with the benefit of several centuries of hindsight, goes further. To simply describe what happens when people make or use laws is not useful at all, according to Finnis. A theory of law which consists merely of a series of descriptions is seriously incomplete. A theorist who lacks an understanding of the *purpose* of law will not know which phenomena to observe or which observations to include in the theory. For Finnis, the key to understanding law is to see law as a *purposeful* activity conducted by generally reasonable humans. To reach this understanding, the theorist must stand inside the law, and understand and participate in achieving the purposes of law. As Finnis puts it, "... A theorist cannot give a theoretical description and analysis of social facts unless he also participates in the work of evaluation, of understanding what is really good for human persons, and what is really required by practical reasonableness."

In our discussion of Aquinas, we noted that theology supplied him with a picture of what is really good for humans. Finnis does not appeal to theology. Instead, Finnis supposes that there are certain basic goods for humans, and that these goods are self-evident upon rational consideration of them. (While Aquinas supposes we are rational and able to perceive goods because God made us rational, Finnis leaves the origin of our rationality largely untreated. What is important for Finnis's theory is that we are rational, not whether we are rational because we evolved to be this way or because God made us so.) According to Finnis, there are seven basic forms of good: life, knowledge, play, aesthetic experience, sociability (friendship), practical reasonableness, and "religion," or a desire for a larger explanation of our nature and origin.

Finnis's list of basic goods answers the question "What is really good for humans?" The list does not, however, explain what moral or legal rules must be enacted to help us to achieve these goods. *How* we are to achieve the good for humans is a question of practical reasoning, and Finnis suggests that practical reasoning cannot proceed in just any way. This is the crucial second part of his argument. According to Finnis, proposed moral or legal rules must meet standards of "practical reasonableness" (which is itself a basic human good). Practical reasonableness can be seen as a sort of blend of pure rationality and perception of basic goods. Practical reasonableness is not simply rationality, because what is rationally possible may sometimes be prohibited as unreasonable. Nor is practical reasonableness simply a composite of the six other basic goods. Practical reasonableness is about rationally balancing our pursuit of different goods, while respecting the basic value of each of those goods as necessary ingredients in a good individual and a good society. We shall discuss here just two aspects of practical reasonableness, to give a sense of the sort of procedural standards Finnis thinks are self-evidently good.

Practical reasonableness requires that our attempts to achieve human goods proceed fairly. For example, when we treat persons differently, we must do so for good reasons, and not arbitrarily. Practical reasonableness also requires a certain degree of foresight: we cannot sacrifice certain basic goods simply to achieve consequences which promote some other basic good. So, for example, the basic good of play is not worth having at the cost of life and friendship, as might happen if we ask our friends to stand with apples on their heads as we practice archery. It is important to recognize that the sort of balanced pursuit of human goods which emerges from the requirements of practical reasonableness is simply a weighing of consequences in which achievement of two basic goods outweighs the loss of failing to achieve one basic good. Rather, basic goods are *fundamental* in our thinking about how we ought to conduct ourselves, and we are never justified in sacrificing these goods entirely.

Finnis argues that morality and law are the result of applying the standards of practical reasonableness to questions of how we ought to conduct ourselves, keeping in mind always what is really good for humans—the seven basic goods. Notice that we have said that *both* morality and law are the result of this process of practical reasoning. For Finnis, and for Aquinas and many other natural law theorists, law just *is* a special sort of morality. It is part of the nature of a law that it is morally justified. If a law does not aim at the common good, or fails to meet the requirements of practical reasonableness, that law must be rejected.

Finnis is careful to note that he does not suppose individual citizens are always right to disobey laws which lack moral justification. He observes that there is considerable value in the stability of the rule of law, and allows that there may be an obligation in a larger sense to obey an immoral law for the sake of the rule of law. There is no quick and simple answer to the question "Should I obey this law?"

6. M.B.E. Smith and the Obligation to Obey

Is there a general obligation to obey the law? In a classic essay on this question, M.B.E. Smith offers arguments intended to show that there is indeed always what Smith calls a 'prima facie' obligation to obey at least *particular* laws, but no larger *general* prima facie obligation to obey all laws. 'Prima facie' is a Latin term meaning 'at first face' or 'at first sight.' Smith uses the term in this context to propose that laws always aim to carry a moral obligation of obedience. This is not to say, Smith points out, that such a moral obligation is final or absolute. There might be competing and weightier moral reasons not to obey particular laws, which might become apparent for various reasons, including changing social circumstances showing particular laws to be defective in ways depriving them of their authority. But it does mean that laws always carry a standing claim to moral obligation as the reason why they deserve obedience. Demonstration of the binding nature of law *in general* appears to be much more difficult than the task of demonstrating how particular laws demand our obedience, at least in part because individual laws address specific circumstances, while by contrast it is difficult to say just what law in general demands of us.

Smith explores several arguments that might support a general, prima facie obligation to obey the law. Arguments of gratitude claim that since the law provides benefits to its subjects, subjects ought to obey out of gratitude or thanks. Closely related to gratitude arguments are 'fair play' arguments, which suppose that it would be unfair if only some were to abide by the restraints of the law and not others, so we all ought to obey. Implicit or tacit consent theories are also often invoked, claiming that by living and remaining in a society, we have in our conduct demonstrated a choice to accept or promise to abide by its laws. Finally, there are arguments based on the general principle of utility, a principle which claims the rightness of some decision is to be measured by the net positive value of the consequences it brings about. These arguments maintain that since social life is on the whole better when we all obey the law, there is such a general obligation. Each of the arguments Smith explores is intended to show that the subjects of a given political community ought to obey not just particular laws of that community, but rather law in general as it is found in that community.

Smith assesses each argument, and finds each to fall short of the goal of establishing a general obligation to obey law. Are his arguments convincing? If so, what are the implications for how subjects ought to relate to law? If there is no general moral obligation to obey the law as it stands, what might this mean for natural law theory, which maintains that law and morality are essentially connected?

1

St. Thomas Aquinas

"Treatise on Law," from *Summa Theologica*

Question 90: Of the Essence of Law (In Four Articles)

... [T]here are four points of inquiry (1) Whether law is something pertaining to reason? (2) Concerning the end of law, (3) Its cause, (4) The promulgation of law.

FIRST ARTICLE: WHETHER LAW IS SOMETHING PERTAINING TO REASON?

We proceed thus to the First Article:—

Objection 1. It would seem that law is not something pertaining to reason. For the Apostle says (Rom. Vii. 23): *I see another law in my members*, etc. But nothing pertaining to reason is in the members; since the reason does not make use of a bodily organ. Therefore law is not something pertaining to reason.

Obj. 2. Further, in the reason there is nothing else but power, habit, and act. But law is not the power itself of reason. In like manner, neither is it a habit of reason: because the habits of reason are the intellectual virtues of which we have spoken above (Q. 57). Nor again is it an act of reason: because then law would cease, when the act of reason ceases, for instance, while we are asleep. Therefore law is nothing pertaining to reason.

Obj. 3. Further, the law moves those who are subject to it to act aright. But it belongs properly to the will to move to act, as is evident from what has been said above (Q. 9, A. 1). Therefore law pertains, not to the reason, but to the will; according to the words of the Jurist (*Lib.* i. *ff.*, *De Const. Prin.* Leg. I): *Whatsoever pleaseth the sovereign, has force of law.*

On the contrary, It belongs to the law to command and to forbid. But it belongs to reason to command, as stated above (Q. 17, A. 1). Therefore law is something pertaining to reason.

I answer that, Law is a rule and measure of acts, whereby man is induced to act or is restrained from acting: for *lex* (law) is derived from *ligare* (to bind), because it binds one to act. Now the rule and measure of human acts is the reason, which is the first principle of human acts, as is evident from what has been stated above (Q. 1, A. 1 *ad* 3); since it belongs to the reason to direct to the end, which is the first principle in all matters of action, according to the Philosopher (*Phys.* Ii). Now that which is the principle in any genus, is the rule and measure of that genus: for instance, unity in the genus of numbers, and the first movement in the genus of movements. Consequently it follows that law is something pertaining to reason.

Reply Obj. 1. Since law is a kind of rule and measure, it may be in something in two ways. First, as in that which measures and rules: and since this is proper to reason, it follows that, in this way, law is in the reason alone.—Secondly, as in that which is measured and ruled. In this way, law is in all those things that are inclined to something by reason of some law: so that any inclination arising from a law, may be called a law, not essentially but by participation as it were. And thus the inclination of the members to concupiscence is called the *law of the members.*

Reply Obj. 2. Just as, in external action, we may consider the work and the work done, for instance the work of building and the house built; so in the acts of reason, we may consider the act itself of reason, i.e., to understand and to reason, and something produced by this act. With regard to the speculative reason, this is first of all the definition; secondly, the proposition; thirdly, the syllogism or argument. And since also the practical reason makes use of a syllogism in respect of the work to be done, as stated above (Q. 13, A. 3; Q. 76, A. 1) and as the Philosopher teaches (*Ethic.* Vii, 3); hence we find in the practical reason something that holds the same position in regard to operations, as, in the speculative intellect, the proposition holds in regard to conclusions. Such like universal propositions of the practical intellect that are directed to actions have the nature of law. And these propositions are sometimes under our actual consideration, while sometimes they are retained in the reason by means of a habit.

Reply Obj. 3. Reason has its power of moving from the will, as stated above (Q. 17, A. 1): for it is due to the fact that one wills the end, that the reason issues its commands as regards things ordained to the end. But in order that the volition of what is commanded may have the nature of law, it needs to be in accord with some rule of reason. And in this sense is to be understood the saying that the will of the sovereign has the force of law; otherwise the sovereign's will would savor of lawlessness rather than of law.

SECOND ARTICLE: WHETHER THE LAW IS ALWAYS SOMETHING DIRECTED TO THE COMMON GOOD?

We proceed thus to the Second Article:—

Objection 1. It would seem that the law is not always directed to the common good as to its end. For it belongs to law to command and to forbid. But commands are directed to certain individual goods. Therefore the end of the law is not always the common good.

Obj. 2. Further, the law directs man in his actions. But human actions are concerned with particular matters. Therefore the law is directed to some particular good.

Obj. 3. Further, Isidore says (*Etym.* V. 3): *If the law is based on reason, whatever is based on reason will be a law*. But reason is the foundation not only of what is ordained to the common good, but also of that which is directed to private good. Therefore the law is not only directed to the good of all; but also to the private good of an individual.

On the contrary, Isidore says (Etym. V. 21) that *laws are enacted for no private profit, but for the common benefit of the citizens*.

I answer that, As stated above (A. 1), the law belongs to that which is a principle of human acts, because it is their rule and measure. Now as reason is a principle of human acts, so in reason itself there is something which is the principle in respect of all the rest: wherefore to this principle chiefly and mainly law must needs be referred.—Now the first principle in practical matters, which are the object of the practical reason, is the last end: and the last end of human life is bliss or happiness, as stated above (Q. 2, A. 7; Q. 3, A. 1). Consequently the law must needs regard principally the relationship to happiness. Moreover, since every part is ordained to the whole, as imperfect to perfect; and since one man is a part of the perfect community, the law must needs regard properly the relationship to universal happiness. Wherefore, the Philosopher, in the above definition of legal matters mentions both happiness and the body politic: for he says (*Ethic.* V.1) that we call those legal matters *just, which are adapted to produce and preserve happiness and its parts for the body politic*: since the state is a perfect community, as he says in *Polit.* i. 1.

Now in every genus, that which belongs to it chiefly is the principle of the others, and the others belong to that genus in subordination to that thing: thus fire, which is chief among hot things, is the cause of heat in mixed bodies, and these are said to be hot in so far as they have a share of fire. Consequently, since the law is chiefly ordained to the common good, any other precept in regard to some individual work, must needs be devoid of the nature of a law, save in so far as it regards the common good. Therefore every law is ordained to the common good.

Reply Obj. 1. A command denotes an application of a law to matters regulated by the law. Now the order to the common good, at which the law aims, is applicable to particular ends. And in this way commands are given even concerning particular matters.

Reply Obj. 2. Actions are indeed concerned with particular matters: but those particular matters are referable to the common good, not as to a common genus or species, but as to a common final cause, according as the common good is said to be the common end.

Reply Obj. 3. Just as nothing stands firm with regard to the speculative reason except that which is traced back to the first indemonstrable principles, so nothing stands firm with regard to the practical reason, unless it be directed to the last end which is the common good: and whatever stands to reason in this sense, has the nature of a law.

THIRD ARTICLE: WHETHER THE REASON OF ANY MAN IS COMPETENT TO MAKE LAWS?

We proceed thus to the Third Article:—

Objection 1. It would seem that the reason of any man is competent to make laws. For the Apostle says (Rom. Ii. 14) that *when the Gentiles, who have not the law, do by nature those things that are of the law, ... they are a law to themselves*. Now he says this of all in general. Therefore anyone can make a law for himself.

Obj. 2. Further, as the Philosopher says (*Ethic.* Ii. 1), *the intention of the lawgiver is to lead men to virtue*. But every man can lead another to virtue. Therefore the reason of any man is competent to make laws.

Obj. 3. Further, just as the sovereign of a state governs the state, so every father of a family governs his household. But the sovereign of a state can make laws for the state. Therefore every father of a family can make laws for his household.

On the contrary, Isidore says (*Etym.* V.10): *A law is an ordinance of the people, whereby something is sanctioned by the Elders together with the Commonalty.*

I answer that, A law, properly speaking, regards first and foremost the order to the common good. Now to order anything to the common good, belongs either to the whole people, or to someone who is the viceregent of the whole people. And therefore the making of a law belongs either to the whole people or to a public personage who has care of the whole people: since in all other matters the directing of anything to the end concerns him to whom the end belongs.

Reply Obj. 1. As stated above (A. 1 *ad* 1), a law is in a person not only as in one that rules, but also by participation as in one that is ruled. In the latter way each one is a law to himself, in so far as he shares the direction that he receives from one who rules him. Hence the same text goes on: *Who show the work of the law written in their hearts.*

Reply Obj. 2. A private person cannot lead another to virtue efficaciously: for he can only advise, and if his advice be not taken, it has no coercive power, such as the law should have, in order to prove an efficacious inducement to virtue, as the Philosopher says (*Ethic.* X. 9). But this coercive power is vested in the whole people or in some public personage, to whom it belongs to inflict penalties, as we shall state further on (Q. 92, A. 2 *ad* 3; II–II, Q. 64, A. 3). Wherefore the framing of laws belongs to him alone.

Reply Obj. 3. As one man is a part of the household, so a household is a part of the state: and the state is a perfect community, according to *Polit.* i. 1. And therefore, as the good of one man is not the last end, but is ordained to the common good; so too the good of one household is ordained to the good of a single state, which is a perfect community. Consequently he that governs a family, can indeed make certain commands or ordinances, but not such as to have properly the force of law.

FOURTH ARTICLE: WHETHER PROMULGATION IS ESSENTIAL TO A LAW?

We proceed thus to the Fourth Article:—

Objection 1. It would seem that promulgation is not essential to a law. For the natural law above all has the character of law. But the natural law needs no promulgation. Therefore it is not essential to a law that it be promulgated.

Obj. 2. Further, it belongs properly to a law to bind one to do or not to do something. But the obligation of fulfilling a law touches not only those in whose presence it is promulgated, but also others. Therefore promulgation is not essential to a law.

Obj. 3. Further, the binding force of a law extends even to the future, since *laws are binding in matters of the future,* as the jurists say (*Cod.* 1., tit. *De lege et constit.* Leg. Vii). But promulgation concerns those who are present. Therefore it is not essential to a law. *On the contrary,* It is laid down in the *Decretals,* dist. 4, *that laws are established when they are promulgated.*

I answer that, As stated above (A. 1), a law is imposed on others by way of a rule and measure. Now a rule or measure is imposed by being applied to those who are to be ruled and measured by it. Wherefore, in order that a law obtain the binding force which is proper to a law, it must needs be applied to the men who have to be ruled by it. Such application is made by its being notified to them by promulgation. Wherefore promulgation is necessary for the law to obtain its force.

Thus from the four preceding articles, the definition of law may be gathered; and it is nothing else than an ordinance of reason for the common good, made by him who has care of the community, and promulgated.

Reply Obj. 1. The natural law is promulgated by the very fact that God instilled it into man's mind so as to be known by him naturally.

Reply Obj. 2. Those who are not present when a law is promulgated, are bound to observe the law, in so far as it is notified or can be notified to them by others, after it has been promulgated.

Reply Obj. 3. The promulgation that takes place now, extends to future time by reason of the durability of written characters, by which means it is continually promulgated. Hence Isidore says (*Etym.* V.3; ii. 10) that *lex* (law) *is derived from legere* (to read) *because it is written.*

Question 91: Of the Various Kinds of Law (In Six Articles)

We must now consider the various kinds of law: under which head there are six points of inquiry: (1) Whether there is an eternal law? (2) Whether there is a natural law? (3) Whether there is a human law? (4) Whether there is a Divine law? (5) Whether there is one Divine law, or several? (6) Whether there is a law of sin? [*Ed. Note*: Articles 4–6 are omitted here.]

FIRST ARTICLE: WHETHER THERE IS AN ETERNAL LAW?

We proceed thus to the First Article:—

Objection 1. It would seem that there is no eternal law. Because every law is imposed on someone. But there was not someone from eternity on whom a law could be imposed: since God alone was from eternity. Therefore no law is eternal.

Obj. 2. Further, promulgation is essential to law. But promulgation could not be from eternity: because there was no one to whom it could be promulgated from eternity. Therefore no law can be eternal.

Obj. 3. Further, a law implies order to an end. But nothing ordained to an end is eternal: for the last end alone is eternal. Therefore no law is eternal.

On the contrary, Augustine says (*De Lib. Arb.* i. 6): *That Law which is the Supreme Reason cannot be understood to be otherwise than unchangeable and eternal.*

I answer that, As stated above (Q. 90, A. 1 *ad* 2; AA. 3, 4), a law is nothing else but a dictate of practical reason emanating from the ruler who governs a perfect community. Now it is evident, granted that the world is ruled by Divine Providence, as was stated in the First Part (Q. 22, AA. 1, 2), that the whole community of the universe is governed by Divine Reason. Wherefore the very Idea of the government of things in God the Ruler of the universe, has the nature of a law. And since the Divine Reason's conception of things is not subject to time but is eternal, according to Prov. Viii. 23, therefore it is that this kind of law must be called eternal.

Reply Obj. 1. Those things that are not in themselves, exist with God, inasmuch as they are foreknown and preordained by Him, according to Rom. Iv. 17: *Who calls those things that are not, as those that are.* Accordingly the eternal concept of the Divine law bears the character of an eternal law, in so far as it is ordained by God to the government of things foreknown by Him.

Reply Obj. 2. Promulgation is made by word of mouth or in writing; and in both ways the eternal law is promulgated: because both the Divine Word and the writing of the Book of Life are eternal. But the promulgation cannot be from eternity on the part of the creature that hears or reads.

Reply Obj. 3. The law implies order to the end actively, in so far as it directs certain things to the end; but not passively,—that is to say, the law itself is not ordained to the end,—except accidentally, in a governor whose end is extrinsic to him, and to which end his law must needs be ordained. But the end of the Divine government is God Himself, and His law is not distinct from Himself. Wherefore the eternal law is not ordained to another end.

SECOND ARTICLE: WHETHER THERE IS IN US A NATURAL LAW?

We proceed thus to the Second Article:—

Objection 1. It would seem that there is no natural law in us. Because man is governed sufficiently by the eternal law: for Augustine says (*De Lib. Arb.* I) that *the eternal law is that by which it is right that all things should be most orderly*. But nature does not abound in superfluities as neither does she fail in necessaries. Therefore no law is natural to man.

Obj. 2. Further, by the law man is directed, in his acts, to the end, as stated above (Q. 90, A. 2). But the directing of human acts to their end is not a function of nature, as is the case in irrational creatures, which act for an end solely by their natural appetite; whereas man acts for an end by his reason and will. Therefore no law is natural to man.

Obj. 3. Further, the more a man is free, the less is he under the law. But man is freer than all the animals, on account of his free-will, with which he is endowed above all other animals. Since therefore other animals are not subject to a natural law, neither is man subject to a natural law.

On the contrary, A gloss on Rom. Ii. 14: *When the Gentiles, who have not the law, do by nature those things that are of the law, comments as follows: Although they have no written law, yet they have the natural law, whereby each one knows, and is conscious of, what is good and what is evil.*

I answer that, As stated above (Q. 90, A. 1 *ad* 1), law, being a rule and measure, can be in a person in two ways: in one way, as in him that rules and measures; in another way, as in that which is ruled and measured, since a thing is ruled and measured, in so far as it partakes of the rule or measure. Wherefore, since all things subject to Divine providence are ruled and measured by the eternal law, as was stated above (A. 1); it is evident that all things partake somewhat of the eternal law, in so far as, namely, from its being imprinted on them, they derive their respective inclinations to their proper acts and ends. Now among all others, the rational creature is subject to Divine providence in the most excellent way, in so far as it partakes of a share of providence, by being provident both for itself and for others. Wherefore it has a share of the Eternal Reason, whereby it has a natural inclination to its proper act and end: and this participation of the eternal law in the rational creature is called the natural law. Hence the Psalmist after saying (Ps. Iv. 6): *Offer up the sacrifice of justice*, as though someone asked what the works of justice are, adds: *Many say, Who showeth us good things?* In answer to which question he says: *The light of Thy countenance, O Lord, is signed upon us*: thus implying that the light of natural reason, whereby we discern what is good and what is evil, which is the function of the natural law, is nothing else than an imprint on us of Divine light. It is therefore evident that the natural law is nothing else than the rational creature's participation of the eternal law.

Reply Obj. 1. This argument would hold, if the natural law were something different from the eternal law: whereas it is nothing but a participation thereof, as stated above.

Reply Obj. 2. Every act of reason and will in us is based on that which is according to nature, as stated above (Q. 10, A. 1): for every act of reasoning is based on principles that are known naturally, and every act of appetite in respect of the means is derived from the natural appetite in respect of the last end. Accordingly the first direction of our acts to their end must needs be in virtue of the natural law.

Reply Obj. 3. Even irrational animals partake in their own way of the Eternal Reason, just as the rational creature does. But because the rational creature partakes thereof in an intellectual and rational manner, therefore the participation of the eternal law in the rational creature is properly called a law, since a law is something pertaining to reason, as stated above (Q. 90, A.

1). Irrational creatures, however, do not partake thereof in a rational manner, wherefore there is no participation of the eternal law in them, except by way of similitude.

THIRD ARTICLE: WHETHER THERE IS A HUMAN LAW?

We proceed thus to the Third Article:—

Objection 1. It would seem that there is not a human law. For the natural law is a participation of the eternal law, as stated above (A. 2). Now through the eternal law *all things are most orderly*, as Augustine states (*De Lib. Arb.* i. 6). Therefore the natural law suffices for the ordering of all human affairs. Consequently there is no need for a human law.

Obj. 2. Further, a law bears the character of a measure, as stated above (Q. 90, A. 1). But human reason is not a measure of things, but vice versa, as stated in *Metaph.* X, text. 5. Therefore no law can emanate from human reason.

Obj. 3. Further, a measure should be most certain, as stated in *Metaph.* X, text. 3. But the dictates of human reason in matters of conduct are uncertain, according to Wis. Ix. 14: *The thoughts of mortal men are fearful, and our counsels uncertain.* Therefore no law can emanate from human reason.

On the contrary, Augustine (*De Lib. Arb.* 1.6) distinguishes two kinds of law, the one eternal, the other temporal, which he calls human.

I answer that, As stated above (Q. 90, A. 1 *ad* 2), a law is a dictate of the practical reason. Now it is to be observed that the same procedure takes place in the practical and in the speculative reason: for each proceeds from principles to conclusions, as stated above (*ibid.*). Accordingly we conclude that just as, in the speculative reason, from naturally known indemonstrable principles, we draw the conclusions of the various sciences, the knowledge of which is not imparted to us by nature, but acquired by the efforts of reason, so too it is from the precepts of the natural law, as from general and indemonstrable principles, that the human reason needs to proceed to the more particular determination of certain matters. These particular determinations, devised by human reason, are called human laws, provided the other essential conditions of law be observed, as stated above (Q. 90, AA. 2, 3, 4). Wherefore Tully says in his *Rhetoric* (*De Invent. Rhet.* Ii) *that justice has its source in nature; thence certain things came into custom by reason of their utility; afterwards these things which emanated from nature and were approved by custom, were sanctioned by fear and reverence for the law.*

Reply Obj. 1. The human reason cannot have a full participation of the dictate of the Divine Reason, but according to its own mode, and imperfectly. Consequently, as on the part of the speculative reason, by a natural participation of Divine Wisdom, there is in us the knowledge of certain general principles, but not proper knowledge of each single truth, such as that contained in the Divine Wisdom; so too, on the part of the practical reason, man has a natural participation of the eternal law, according to certain general principles, but not as regards the particular determinations of individual cases, which are, however, contained in the eternal law. Hence the need for human reason to proceed further to sanction them by law.

Reply Obj. 2. Human reason is not, of itself, the rule of things: but the principles impressed on it by nature, are general rules and measures of all things relating to human conduct, whereof the natural reason is the rule and measure, although it is not the measure of things that are from nature.

Reply Obj. 3. The practical reason is concerned with practical matters, which are singular and contingent: but not with necessary things, with which the speculative reason is concerned. Wherefore human laws cannot have that inerrancy that belongs to the demonstrated conclusions of sciences. Nor is it necessary for every measure to be altogether unerring and certain, but according as it is possible in its own particular genus.

...

Question 94: Of the Natural Law (In Six Articles)

We must now consider the natural law; concerning which there are six points of inquiry: (1) What is the natural law? (2) What are the precepts of the natural law? (3) Whether all acts of virtue are prescribed by the natural law? (4) Whether the natural law is the same in all? (5) Whether it is changeable? (6) Whether it can be abolished from the heart of man? [*Ed. Note*: Article 3 is omitted here.]

FIRST ARTICLE: WHETHER THE NATURAL LAW IS A HABIT?

We proceed thus, to the First Article:—

Objection 1. It would seem that the natural law is a habit. Because, as the Philosopher says (*Ethic.* Ii. 5), *there are three things in the soul, power, habit, and passion.* But the natural law is not one of the soul's powers: nor is it one of the passions; as we may see by going through them one by one. Therefore the natural law is a habit.

Obj. 2. Further, Basil says that the conscience or *synderesis is the law of our mind*; which can only apply to the natural law. But the *synderesis* is a habit, as was shown in the First Part (Q. 79, A. 12). Therefore the natural law is a habit.

Obj. 3. Further, the natural law abides in man always, as will be shown further on (A. 6). But man's reason, which the law regards, does not always think about the natural law. Therefore the natural law is not an act, but a habit.

On the contrary, Augustine says (*De Bono Conjug.* Xxi) that *a habit is that whereby something is done when necessary.* But such is not the natural law: since it is in infants and in the damned who cannot act by it. Therefore the natural law is not a habit.

I answer that, A thing may be called a habit in two ways. First, properly and essentially: and thus the natural law is not a habit. For it has been stated above (Q. 90, A. 1 *ad* 2) that the natural law is something appointed by reason, just as a proposition is a work of reason. Now that which a man does is not the same as that whereby he does it: for he makes a becoming speech by the habit of grammar. Since then a habit is that by which we act, a law cannot be a habit properly and essentially.

Secondly, the term habit may be applied to that which we hold by a habit: thus faith may mean that which we hold by faith. And accordingly, since the precepts of the natural law are sometimes considered by reason actually, while sometimes they are in the reason only habitually, in this way the natural law may be called a habit. Thus, in speculative matters, the indemonstrable principles are not the habit itself whereby we hold these principles, but are the principles the habit of which we possess.

Reply Obj. 1. The Philosopher proposes there to discover the genus of virtue; and since it is evident that virtue is a principle of action, he mentions only those things which are principles of human acts, viz., powers, habits and passions. But there are other things in the soul besides these three: there are acts; thus to will is in the one that wills; again, things known are in the knower; moreover its own natural properties are in the soul, such as immortality and the like.

Reply Obj. 2. *Synderesis* is said to be the law of our mind, because it is a habit containing the precepts of the natural law, which are the first principles of human actions.

Reply Obj. 3. This argument proves that the natural law is held habitually; and this is granted.

To the argument advanced in the contrary sense we reply that sometimes a man is unable to make use of that which is in him habitually, on account of some impediment: thus, on account of sleep, a man is unable to use the habit of science. In like manner, through the deficiency of his age, a child cannot use the habit of understanding of principles, or the natural law, which is in him habitually.

SECOND ARTICLE: WHETHER THE NATURAL LAW CONTAINS SEVERAL PRECEPTS, OR ONE ONLY?

We proceed thus to the Second Article:—

Objection 1. It would seem that the natural law contains, not several precepts, but one only. For law is a kind of precept, as stated above (Q. 92, A. 2). If therefore there were many precepts of the natural law, it would follow that there are also many natural laws.

Obj. 2. Further, the natural law is consequent to human nature. But human nature, as a whole, is one; though, as to its parts, it is manifold. Therefore, either there is but one precept of the law of nature, on account of the unity of nature as a whole; or there are many, by reason of the number of parts of human nature. The result would be that even things relating to the inclination of the concupiscible faculty belong to the natural law.

Obj. 3. Further, law is something pertaining to reason, as stated above (Q. 90, A. 1). Now reason is but one in man. Therefore there is only one precept of the natural law.

On the contrary, The precepts of the natural law in man stand in relation to practical matters, as the first principles to matters of demonstration. But there are several first indemonstrable principles. Therefore there are also several precepts of the natural law.

I answer that, As stated above (Q. 91, A. 3), the precepts of the natural law are to the practical reason, what the first principles of demonstrations are to the speculative reason; because both are self-evident principles. Now a thing is said to be self-evident in two ways: first, in itself; secondly, in relation to us. Any proposition is said to be self-evident in itself, if its predicate is contained in the notion of the subject: although, to one who knows not the definition of the subject, it happens that such a proposition is not self-evident. For instance, this proposition, *Man is a rational being*, is, in its very nature, self-evident, since who says *man*, says a *rational being*: and yet to one who knows not what a man is, this proposition is not self-evident. Hence it is that, as Boethius says (*De Hebdom.*), certain axioms or propositions are universally self-evident to all; and such are those propositions whose terms are known to all, as, *Every whole is greater than its part, and, Things equal to one and the same are equal to one another*. But some propositions are self-evident only to the wise, who understand the meaning of the terms of such propositions: thus to one who understands that an angel is not a body, it is self-evident that an angel is not circumscriptively in a place: but this is not evident to the unlearned, for they cannot grasp it.

Now a certain order is to be found in those things that are apprehended universally. For that which, before aught else, falls under apprehension, is *being*, the notion of which included in all things whatsoever a man apprehends. Wherefore the first indemonstrable principle is that the *same thing cannot be affirmed and denied at the same time*, which is based on the notion of *being* and *not-being*: and on this principle all others are based, as is stated in *Metaph.* Iv, text 9. Now as *being* is the first thing that falls under the apprehension simply, so *good* is the first thing that falls under the apprehension of the practical reason, which is directed to action: since every agent acts for an end under the aspect of good. Consequently the first principle in the practical reason is one founded on the notion of good, viz., *that good is that which all things seek after.* Hence this is the first precept of law, that good is to be done and pursued, and evil is to be avoided. All other precepts of the natural law are based upon this: so that whatever the practical reason naturally apprehends as man's good, (or evil) belongs to the precepts of the natural law as something to be done or avoided.

Since, however, good has the nature of an end, and evil, the nature of a contrary, hence it is that all those things to which man has a natural inclination, are naturally apprehended by reason as being good, and consequently as objects of pursuit, and their contraries as evil, and objects of avoidance. Wherefore according to the order of natural inclinations, is the order of the precepts of the natural law. Because in man there is first of all an inclination to good in accordance with the nature which he has in common with all substances: inasmuch as every substance seeks the preservation of its own being, according to its nature: and by reason of this inclination, whatever a means of preserving human life, and warding off its obstacles, belongs to the natural law. Secondly, there is in man an inclination to things that pertain to him more specially, according to that nature which he has in common with other animals: and in virtue of this inclination, those things are said to belong to the natural law, *which nature has taught to all animals*, such as sexual intercourse, education of offspring and so forth. Thirdly, there is in man an inclination to good, according to the nature of his reason, which nature is proper to him: thus man has a natural inclination to know the truth about God, and to live in society: and in this respect, whatever pertains to this inclination belongs to the natural law; for instance, to shun ignorance, to avoid offending those among whom one has to live, and other such things regarding the above inclination.

Reply Obj. 1. All these precepts of the law of nature have the character of one natural law, inasmuch as they flow from one first precept.

Reply Obj. 2. All the inclinations of any parts whatsoever of human nature, e.g., of the concupiscible and irascible parts, in so far as they are ruled by reason, belong to the natural law, and are reduced to one first precept, as stated above: so that the precepts of the natural law are many in themselves, but are based on one common foundation.

Reply Obj. 3. Although reason is one in itself, yet it directs all things regarding man; so that whatever can be ruled by reason, is contained under the law of reason.

...

FOURTH ARTICLE: WHETHER THE NATURAL LAW IS THE SAME IN ALL MEN?

We proceed thus to the Fourth Article:—

Objection 1. It would seem that the natural law is not the same in all. For it is stated in the Decretals (*Dist.* I) that *the natural law is that which is contained in the Law and the Gospel.* But this is not common to all men; because, as it is written (Rom. X. 16), *all do not obey the gospel.* Therefore the natural law is not the same in all men.

Obj. 2. Further, *Things which are according to the law are said to be just*, as stated in *Ethic.* V. But it is stated in the same book that nothing is so universally just as not to be subject to change in regard to some men. Therefore even the natural law is not the same in all men.

Obj. 3. Further, as stated above (AA. 2, 3), to the natural law belongs everything to which a man is inclined according to his nature. Now different men are naturally inclined to different things; some to the desire of pleasures, others to the desire of honors, and other men to other things. Therefore there is not one natural law for all.

On the contrary, Isidore says (*Etym.* V. 4): *The natural law is common to all nations.*

I answer that, As stated above (AA. 2, 3), to the natural law belongs those things to which a man is inclined naturally: and among these it is proper to man to be inclined to act according to reason. Now the process of reason is from the common to the proper, as stated in *Phys.* i. The speculative reason, however, is differently situated in this matter, from the practical reason. For, since the speculative reason is busied chiefly with necessary things, which cannot be otherwise than they are, its proper conclusions, like the universal principles, contain the truth without fail. The practical reason, on the other hand, is busied with contingent matters, about which human actions are concerned: and consequently, although there is necessity in the general principles, the more we descend to matters of detail, the more frequently we encounter defects. Accordingly then in speculative matters truth is the same in all men, both as to principles and as to conclusions: although the truth is not known to all as regards the conclusions, but only as regards the principles which are called common notions. But in matters of action, truth or practical rectitude is not the same for all, as to matters of detail, but only as to the general principles: and where there is the same rectitude in matters of detail, it is not equally known to all.

It is therefore evident that, as regards the general principles whether of speculative or of practical reason, truth or rectitude is the same for all, and is equally known by all. As to the proper conclusions of the speculative reason, the truth is the same for all, but is not equally known to all: thus it is true for all that the three angles of a triangle are together equal to two right angles, although it is not known to all. But as to the proper conclusions of the practical reason, neither is the truth or rectitude the same for all, nor, where it is the same, is it equally known by all. Thus it is right and true for all to act according to reason: and from this principle it follows as a proper conclusion, that goods entrusted to another should be restored to their owner. Now this is true for the majority of cases: but it may happen in a particular case that it would be injurious, and therefore unreasonable, to restore goods held in trust; for instance if they are claimed for the purpose of fighting against one's country. And this principle will be found to fail the more, according as we descend further into detail, e.g., if one were to say that goods held in trust should be restored with such and such a guarantee, or in such and such a way; because the greater the number of conditions added, the greater the number of ways in which the principle may fail, so that it be not right to restore or not to restore.

Consequently we must say that the natural law, as to general principles, is the same for all, both as to rectitude and as to knowledge. But as to certain matters of detail, which are conclusions, as it were, of those general principles, it is the same for all in the majority of cases, both as to rectitude and as to knowledge; and yet in some few cases it may fail, both as to rectitude, by reason of certain obstacles (just as natures subject to generation and corruption fail in some few cases on account of some obstacle), and as to knowledge, since in some the reason is perverted by passion, or evil habit, or an evil disposition of nature; thus formerly, theft, although expressly contrary to the natural law, was not considered wrong among the Germans, as Julius Cæsar relates (*De Bello Gall.* vi).

Reply Obj. 1. The meaning of the sentence quoted is not that whatever is contained in the Law and the Gospel belongs to the natural law, since they contain many things that are above nature; but that whatever belongs to the natural law is fully contained in them. Wherefore Gratian, after saying that *the natural law is what is contained in the Law and the Gospel*, adds at once, by way of example, *by which everyone is commanded to do: to others as he would be done by.*

Reply Obj. 2. The saying of the Philosopher is to be understood of things that are naturally just, not as general principles, but as conclusions drawn from them, having rectitude in the majority of cases, but failing in a few.

Reply Obj. 3. As, in man, reason rules and commands the other powers, so all the natural inclinations belonging to the other powers must needs be directed according to reason. Wherefore it is universally right for all men, that all their inclinations should be directed according to reason.

FIFTH ARTICLE: WHETHER THE NATURAL LAW CAN BE CHANGED?

We proceed thus to the Fifth Article:—

Objection 1. It would seem that the natural law can be changed. Because on Ecclus, xvii. 9, *He gave them instructions, and the law of life, the gloss says: He wished the law of the letter to be written, in order to correct the law of nature.* But that which is corrected is changed. Therefore the natural law can be changed.

Obj. 2. Further, the slaying of the innocent, adultery, and theft are against the natural law. But we find these things changed by God: as when God commanded Abraham to slay his innocent son (Gen. xxii. 2); and when he ordered the Jews to borrow and purloin the vessels of the Egyptians (Exod. xii. 35); and when He commanded Osee to take to himself a *wife of fornications* (Osee i. 2). Therefore the natural law can be changed.

Obj. 3. Further, Isidore says (*Etym.* V. 4) that *the possession of all things in common, and universal freedom, are matters of natural law.* But these things are seen to be changed by human laws. Therefore it seems that the natural law is subject to change.

On the contrary, It is said in the Decretals (Dist. v): *The natural law dates from the creation of the rational creature. It does not vary according to time, but remains unchangeable.*

I answer that, A change in the natural law may be understood in two ways. First, by way of addition. In this sense nothing hinders the natural law from being changed: since many things for the benefit of human life have been added over and above the natural law both by the Divine law and by human laws.

Secondly, a change in the natural law may be understood by way of subtraction, so that what previously was according to the natural law ceases to be so. In this sense, the natural law is altogether unchangeable in its first principles but in its secondary principles, which as we have said (A. 4), are certain detailed proximate conclusions drawn from the first principles, the natural law is not changed so that what it prescribes be not right in most cases. But it may be changed in some particular cases of rare occurrence, through some special causes hindering the observance of such precepts, as stated above (A. 4).

Reply Obj. 1. The written law is said to be given for the correction of the natural law, either because it supplies what was wanting to the natural law; or because the natural law was perverted in the hearts of some men, as to certain matters, so that they esteemed those things good which are naturally evil; which perversion stood in need of correction.

Reply Obj. 2. All men alike, both guilty and innocent, die the death of nature which is inflicted by the power of God on account of original sin, according to 1 Kings ii. 6: *The Lord killeth and maketh alive.* Consequently by the command of God, death can be inflicted on any man, guilty or innocent, without any injustice whatever.—In like manner adultery is intercourse with another's wife; who is allotted to him by the law emanating from God. Consequently intercourse with any woman, by the command of God, is neither adultery nor fornication.—The same applies to theft, which is the taking of another's property. For whatever is taken by the command of God, to Whom all things belong, is not taken against the will of its owner, whereas it is in this that theft consists.—Nor is it only in human things, that whatever is commanded by God is right; but also in natural things, whatever is done by God, is, in some way, natural, as stated in the First Part (Q. 105, A. 6 *ad* 1).

Reply Obj. 3. A thing is said to belong to the natural law in two ways. First, because nature inclines thereto: e.g., that one should not do harm to another. Secondly, because nature did not bring in the contrary: thus we might say that for man to be naked is of the natural law, because nature did not give him clothes, but art invented them. In this sense; *the possession of all things in common and universal freedom* are said to be of the natural law, because, to wit, the distinction of possessions and slavery were not brought in by nature, but devised by human reason for the benefit of human life. Accordingly the law of nature was not changed in this respect, except by addition.

SIXTH ARTICLE: WHETHER THE LAW OF NATURE CAN BE ABOLISHED FROM THE HEART OF MAN?

We proceed thus to the Sixth Article:—

Objection 1. It would seem that the natural law can be abolished from the heart of man. Because on Rom. Ii. 14, *When the Gentiles who have not the law*, etc., a gloss says that *the law of righteousness, which sin had blotted out, is graven on the heart of man when he is restored by grace.* But the law of righteousness is the law of nature. Therefore the law of nature can be blotted out.

Obj. 2. Further, the law of grace is more efficacious than the law of nature. But the law of grace is blotted out by sin. Much more therefore can the law of nature be blotted out.

Obj. 3. Further, that which is established by law is made just. But many things are enacted by men, which are contrary to the law of nature. Therefore the law of nature can be abolished from the heart of man.

On the contrary, Augustine says (*Conf.* ii): *Thy law is written in the hearts of men, which iniquity itself effaces not.* But the law which is written in men's hearts is the natural law. Therefore the natural law cannot be blotted out.

I answer that, As stated above (AA. 4, 5), there belong to the natural law, first, certain most general precepts, that are known to all; and secondly, certain secondary and more detailed precepts; which are, as it were, conclusions following closely from first principles. As to those general principles, the natural law, in the abstract, can nowise be blotted out from men's hearts. But it is blotted out in the case of a particular action, in so far as reason is hindered from applying the general principle to a particular point of practice, on account of concupiscence or some other passion, as stated above (Q. 77, A. 2).—But as to the other, i.e., the secondary precepts, the natural law can be blotted out from the human heart, either by evil persuasions, just as in speculative matters errors occur in respect of necessary conclusions; or by vicious customs and corrupt habits, as among some men, theft, and even unnatural vices, as the Apostle states (Rom. I), were not esteemed sinful.

Reply Obj. 1. Sin blots out the law of nature in particular cases, not universally, except perchance in regard to the secondary precepts of the natural law, in the way stated above.

Reply Obj. 2. Although grace is more efficacious than nature, yet nature is more essential to man, and therefore more enduring.

Reply Obj. 3. This argument is true of the secondary precepts of the natural law, against which some legislators have framed certain enactments which are unjust.

Question 95: Of Human Law (In Four Articles)

We must now consider human law; and (1) this law considered in itself; (2) its power; (3) its mutability. Under the first head there are four points of inquiry: (1) Its utility. (2) Its origin. (3) Its quality. (4) Its division. [*Ed. Note*: only Article 2 is included here.]

SECOND ARTICLE: WHETHER EVERY HUMAN LAW IS DERIVED FROM THE NATURAL LAW?

We proceed thus to the Second Article:—

Objection 1. It would seem that not every human law is derived from the natural law. For the Philosopher says (*Ethic.* V. 7) *that the legal just is that which originally was a matter of indifference.* But those things which arise from the natural law are not matters of indifference. Therefore the enactments of human laws are not all derived from the natural law.

Obj. 2. Further, positive law is contrasted with natural law, as stated by Isidore (*Etym.* V. 4) and the Philosopher (*Ethic.* V, *loc. cit.*). But those things which flow as conclusions from the general principles of the natural law belong to the natural law, as stated above (Q. 94, A. 4). Therefore that which is established by human law does not belong to the natural law.

Obj. 3. Further, the law of nature is the same for all; since the Philosopher says (*Ethic.* V. 7) that *the natural just is that which is equally valid everywhere.* If therefore human laws were derived from the natural law, it would follow that they too are the same for all: which is clearly false.

Obj. 4. Further, it is possible to give a reason for things which are derived from the natural law. But *it is not possible to give the reason for all the legal enactments of the law-givers*, as the jurist says. Therefore not all human laws are derived from the natural law.

On the contrary, Tully says (*Rhetor.* Ii): Things which emanated from nature and were approved by custom, were sanctioned by fear and reverence for the laws.

I answer that, As Augustine says (*De Lib. Arb.* i. 5), *that which is not just seems to be no law at all*: wherefore the force of a law depends on the extent of its justice. Now in human affairs a thing is said to be just, from being right, according to the rule of reason. But the first rule of reason is the law of nature, as is clear from what has been stated above (Q. 91, A. 2 *ad* 2). Consequently every human law has just so much of the nature of law, as it is derived from the law of nature. But if in any point it deflects from the law of nature, it is no longer a law but a perversion of law.

But it must be noted that something may be derived from the natural law in two ways: first, as a conclusion from premises, secondly, by way of determination of certain generalities. The first way is like to that by which, in sciences, demonstrated conclusions are drawn from the principles: while the second mode is likened to that whereby, in the arts, general forms are particularized as to details: thus the craftsman needs to determine the general form of a house to some particular shape. Some things are therefore derived from the general principles of the natural law, by way of conclusions; e.g., that *one must not kill* may be derived as a conclusion from the principle that *one should do harm to no man*: while some are derived therefrom by way of determination; e.g., the law of nature has it that the evil-doer should be punished; but that he be punished in this or that way, is a determination of the law of nature.

Accordingly both modes of derivation are found in the human law. But those things which are derived in the first way, are contained in human law not as emanating therefrom exclusively, but have some force from the natural law also. But those things which are derived in the second way, have no other force than that of human law.

Reply Obj. 1. The Philosopher is speaking of those enactments which are by way of determination or specification of the precepts of the natural law.

Reply Obj. 2. This argument avails for those things that are derived from the natural law, by way of conclusions.

Reply Obj. 3. The general principles of the natural law cannot be applied to all men in the same way on account of the great variety of human affairs: and hence arises the diversity of positive laws among various people.

Reply Obj. 4. These words of the Jurist are to be understood as referring to decisions of rulers in determining particular points of the natural law: on which determinations the judgment of expert and prudent men is based as on its principles; in so far, to wit, as they see at once what is the best thing to decide.

Hence the Philosopher says (Ethic. Vi. 11) that in such matters, we ought to pay as much attention to the undemonstrated sayings and opinions of persons who surpass us in experience, age and prudence, as to their demonstrations.

...

Question 96: Of the Power of Human Law (In Six Articles)

We must now consider the power of human law. Under this head there are six points of inquiry: (1) Whether human law should be framed for the community? (2) Whether human law should repress all vices? (3) Whether human law is competent to direct all acts of virtue? (4) Whether it binds man in conscience? (5) Whether all men are subject to human law? (6) Whether those who are under the law may act beside the letter of the law? [*Ed. Note*: only Article 4 is included here.]

FOURTH ARTICLE: WHETHER HUMAN LAW BINDS A MAN IN CONSCIENCE?

We proceed thus to the Fourth Article:—

Objection 1. It would seem that human law does not bind a man in conscience. For an inferior power has no jurisdiction in a court of higher power. But the power of man, which frames human law, is beneath the Divine power. Therefore human law cannot impose its precept in a Divine court, such as is the court of conscience.

Obj. 2. Further, the judgment of conscience depends chiefly on the commandments of God. But sometimes God's commandments are made void by human laws, according to Matth. Xv. 6: *You have made void the commandment of God for your tradition.* Therefore human law does not bind a man in conscience.

Obj. 3. Further, human laws often bring loss of character and injury on man, according to Isa. X. 1 et seq.: Woe to them that make wicked laws, and when they write, write injustice; to oppress the poor in judgment, and do violence to the cause of the humble of My people. But it is lawful for anyone to avoid oppression and violence. Therefore human laws do not bind man in conscience.

On the contrary, It is written (1 Pet. Ii. 19): *This is thankworthy, if for conscience ... a man endure sorrows, suffering wrongfully.*

I answer that, Laws framed by man are either just or unjust. If they be just, they have the power of binding in conscience, from the eternal law whence they are derived, according to Prov. Viii. 15: *By Me kings reign; and lawgivers decree just things.* Now laws are said to be just, both from the end, when, to wit, they are ordained to the common good;—and from their author, that is to say, when the law that is made does not exceed the power of the lawgiver,—and from their form, when, to wit, burdens are laid on the subjects, according to an equality of proportion and with a view to the common good. For, since one man is a part of the community, each man in all that he is and has, belongs to the community; just as a part, in all that it is, belongs to the whole; wherefore nature inflicts a loss on the part, in order to save the whole: so that on this account, such laws as these, which impose proportionate burdens, are just and binding in conscience, and are legal laws.

On the other hand laws may be unjust in two ways: first, by being contrary to human good, through being opposed to the things mentioned above:—either in respect of the end, as when an authority imposes on his subjects burdensome laws, conducive, not to the common good, but rather to his own cupidity or vainglory;—or in respect of the author, as when a man makes a law that goes beyond the power committed to him;—or in respect of the form, as when burdens are imposed unequally on the community, although with a view to the common good. The like are acts of violence rather than laws; because, as Augustine says (*De Lib. Arb.* i. 5), *a law that is not just, seems to be no law at all.* Wherefore such laws do not bind in conscience, except perhaps in order to avoid scandal or disturbance; for which cause a man should even yield his right, according to Matth. V. 40, 41: *If a man take away thy coat, let go thy cloak also unto him; and whosoever will force thee one mile, go with him another two.*

Secondly, laws may be unjust through being opposed to the Divine good: such are the laws of tyrants inducing to idolatry, or to anything else contrary to the Divine law: and laws of this kind must nowise be observed, because, as stated in Acts v. 29, *we ought to obey God rather than men.*

Reply Obj. 1. As the Apostle says (Rom. Xiii, 1, 2), all human power is from God ... *therefore he that resisteth the power*, in matters that are within its scope, *resisteth the ordinance of God*; so that he becomes guilty according to his conscience.

Reply Obj. 2. This argument is true of laws that are contrary to the commandments of God, which is beyond the scope of (human) power. Wherefore in such matters human law should not be obeyed.

Reply Obj. 3. This argument is true of a law that inflicts unjust hurt on its subjects. The power that man holds from God does not extend to this: wherefore neither in such matters is man bound to obey the law, provided he avoid giving scandal or inflicting a more grievous hurt.

2
John Finnis
from *Natural Law and Natural Rights**†

I. Evaluation and the Description of Law

I.1 THE FORMATION OF CONCEPTS FOR DESCRIPTIVE SOCIAL SCIENCE

There are human goods that can be secured only through the institutions of human law, and requirements of practical reasonableness that only those institutions can satisfy. It is the object of this book to identify those goods, and those requirements of practical reasonableness, and thus to show how and on what conditions such institutions are justified and the ways in which they can be (and often are) defective.

It is often supposed that an evaluation of law as a type of social institution, if it is to be undertaken at all, must be preceded by a value-free description and analysis of that institution as it exists in fact. But the development of modern jurisprudence suggests, and reflection on the methodology of any social science confirms, that a theorist cannot give a theoretical description and analysis of social facts, unless he also participates in the work of evaluation, of understanding what is really good for human persons, and what is really required by practical reasonableness.

---

* *Ed. note*: In his argument Finnis frequently refers to parts of his book which are not included in this excerpt; however, these references have been left in the excerpted text in the interest of its completeness as a resource for further exploration of the full text of *Natural Law and Natural Rights*.

† Finnis, John. From *Natural Law and Natural Rights, First Edition*, Oxford University Press, 1980. Copyright © J.M. Finnis 1980. Reproduced with the permission of Oxford Publishing Limited through PLSclear (pp. 3–4, 18–19, 23–26, 59–60, 100–12, 118–19, 351–62).

A social science, such as analytical or sociological jurisprudence, seeks to describe, analyse, and explain some object or subject-matter. This object is constituted by human actions, practices, habits, dispositions and by human discourse. The actions, practices, etc., are certainly influenced by the "natural" causes properly investigated by the methods of the natural sciences, including a part of the science of psychology. But the actions, practices, etc., can be fully understood only by understanding their point, that is to say their objective, their value, their significance or importance, as conceived by the people who performed them, engaged in them, etc. And these conceptions of point, value, significance, and importance will be reflected in the discourse of those same people, in the conceptual distinctions they draw and fail or refuse to draw. Moreover, these actions, practices, etc., and correspondingly these concepts, vary greatly from person to person, from one society to another, from one time and place to other times and places. *How, then, is there to be a general descriptive theory of these varying particulars?*

A theorist wishes to describe, say, law as a social institution. But the conceptions of law (and of *jus, lex, droit, nomos*, ...) which people have entertained, and have used to shape their own conduct, are quite varied. The subject-matter of the theorist's description does not come neatly demarcated from other features of social life and practice. Moreover, this social life and practice bears labels in many languages. The languages can be learned by speakers of other languages, but the principles on which labels are adopted and applied—i.e., the practical concerns and the self-interpretations of the people whose conduct and dispositions go to make up the theorist's subject-matter—are not uniform. Can the theorist do more, then, than list these varying conceptions and practices and their corresponding labels? Even a list requires some principle of selection of items for inclusion in the list. And jurisprudence, like other social sciences, aspires to be more than a conjunction of lexicography with local history, or even than a juxtaposition of all lexicographies conjoined with all local histories....

...

I.5 THE THEORY OF NATURAL LAW

Bentham, Austin, Kelsen, Weber, Hart, and Raz all published stern repudiations of what they understood to be the theory of natural law; and Fuller carefully dissociated himself from that theory in its classical forms. But the theoretical work of each of these writers was controlled by the adoption, on grounds left inexplicit and inadequately justified, of some practical viewpoint as the standard of relevance and significance in the construction of his descriptive analysis. A sound theory of natural law is one that explicitly, with full awareness of the methodological situation just described, undertakes a critique of practical viewpoints, in order to distinguish the practically unreasonable from the practically reasonable, and thus to differentiate the really important from that which is unimportant or is important only by its opposition to or unreasonable exploitation of the really important. A theory of natural law claims to be able to identify conditions and principles of practical right-mindedness, of good and proper order among men and in individual conduct. Unless some such claim is justified, analytical jurisprudence in particular and (at least the major part of) all the social sciences in general can have no critically justified criteria for the formation of general concepts, and must be content to be no more than manifestations of the various concepts peculiar to particular peoples and/or to the particular theorists who concern themselves with those people.

A theory of natural law need not be undertaken primarily for the purpose of thus providing a justified conceptual framework for descriptive social science. It may be undertaken, as this book is, primarily to assist the practical reflections of those concerned to act, whether as judges or as statesmen or as citizens. But in either case, the undertaking cannot proceed securely without a knowledge of the whole range of human possibilities and opportunities, inclinations and capacities, a knowledge that requires the assistance of descriptive and analytical social science. There is thus a mutual though not quite symmetrical interdependence between the project of describing human affairs by way of theory and the project of evaluating human options with a view, at least remotely, to acting reasonably and well. The evaluations are in no way deduced from the descriptions (see II.4); but one whose knowledge of the facts of the human situation is very limited is unlikely to judge well in discerning the practical implications of the basic values. Equally, the descriptions are not deduced from the evaluations; but without the evaluations one cannot determine what descriptions are really illuminating and significant.

...

II. Images and Objections

II.1 NATURAL LAW AND THEORIES OF NATURAL LAW

What are *principles of natural law*? The sense that the phrase "natural law" has in this book can be indicated in the following rather bald assertions, formulations which will seem perhaps empty or question-begging until explicated in Part Two: There is (i) a set of basic practical principles which indicate the basic forms of human flourishing as goods to be pursued and realized, and which are in one way or another used by everyone who considers what to do, however unsound his conclusions; and (ii) a set of basic methodological requirements of practical reasonableness (itself one of the basic forms of human flourishing) which distinguish sound from unsound practical thinking and which, when all brought to bear, provide the criteria for distinguishing between acts that (always or in particular circumstances) are reasonable-all-things-considered (and not merely relative-to-a-particular purpose) and acts that are unreasonable-all-things-considered, i.e., between ways of acting that are morally right or morally wrong thus enabling one to formulate (iii) a set of general moral standards.

To avoid misunderstandings about the scope of our subject-matter in this book, I should add here that the principles of natural law, thus understood, are traced out not only in moral philosophy or ethics and "individual" conduct, but also in political philosophy and jurisprudence, in political action, adjudication, and the life of the citizen. For those principles justify the exercise of authority in community. They require, too, that that authority be exercised, in most circumstances, according to the manner conveniently labelled the Rule of Law, and with due respect for the human rights which embody the requirements of justice, and for the purpose of promoting a common good in which such respect for rights is a component. More particularly, the principles of natural law explain the obligatory force (in the fullest sense of "obligation") of positive laws, even when those laws cannot be deduced from those principles. And attention to the principles, in the context of these explanations of law and legal obligation, justifies regarding certain positive laws as radically defective, *precisely as laws*, for want of conformity to those principles.

My present purpose, however, is not to anticipate later chapters, but to make some preliminary clarifications. A first essential distinction is that between a theory, doctrine, or account and the subject-matter of that theory, doctrine, or account. There can be a history of theories, doctrines, and accounts of matters that have no history. And principles of natural law, in the sense formulated in the two preceding paragraphs, have no history.

Since I have yet to show that there are indeed any principles of natural law, let me put the point conditionally. Principles of this sort would hold good, as principles, however extensively they were overlooked, misapplied, or defied in practical thinking, and however little they were recognized by those who reflectively theorize about human thinking. That is to say, they would "hold good" just as the mathematical principles of accounting "hold good" even when, as in the medieval banking community, they are unknown or misunderstood. So there could be a history of the varying extent to which they have been used by people, explicitly or implicitly, to regulate their personal activities. And there could be a history of the varying extent to which reflective theorists have acknowledged the sets of principles as valid or "holding good." And there could be a history of the popularity of the various theories offered to explain the place of those principles in the whole scheme of things. But of natural law itself there could, strictly speaking, be no history.

Natural law could not rise, decline, be revived, or stage "eternal returns." It could not have historical achievements to its credit. It could not be held responsible for disasters of the human spirit or atrocities of human practice.

But there is a history of the opinions or set of opinions, theories, and doctrines which assert that there are principles of natural law, a history of origins, rises, declines and falls, revivals and achievements, and of historical responsibilities. Anyone who thinks there really are no such principles will consider that a book about natural law must be a book about mere opinions, and that the principal interest of those opinions is their historical causes and effects. But anyone who considers that there are principles of natural law, in the sense already outlined, ought to see the importance of maintaining a distinction between discourse about natural law and discourse about a doctrine or doctrines of natural law. Unhappily, people often fail to maintain the distinction.[1]

This is a book about natural law. It expounds or sets out a theory of natural law, but is not *about* that theory. Nor is it about other theories. It refers to other theories only to illuminate the theory expounded here, or to explain why some truths about natural law have at various times and in various ways been overlooked or obscured. The book does not enter into discussions about whether natural law doctrines have exerted a conservative or radical influence on Western politics, or about the supposed psychological (infantile)[2] origins of such doctrines, or about the claim that some or all specific natural law doctrines are asserted hypocritically,[3] arrogantly,[4] or as a disguise or vehicle for expressions of ecclesiastical faith. For none of these discussions has any real bearing on the question whether there is a natural law and, if so, what its content is. Equally irrelevant to that question is the claim that disbelief in natural law yields bitter fruit. Nothing in this book is to be interpreted as either advancing or denying such claims; the book simply prescinds from all such matters.

II.2 LEGAL VALIDITY AND MORALITY

The preceding section treated theories of natural law as theories of the rational foundations for moral judgment, and this will be the primary focus of subsequent sections of this chapter. But in the present section I consider the more

1 Notable examples of this failure include A.P. D'Entrèves, *Natural Law* (London: 1951, rev. ed. 1970), e.g., pp. 13, 18, 22, etc.; Julius Stone, *Human Law and Human Justice* (London: 1965), chs. 2 and 7.

2 See Alf Ross, *On Law and Justice* (London: 1958), pp. 258, 262–63.

3 See Wolfgang Friedmann, letter (1953) 31 *Canadian Bar Rev.* 1074 at 1075.

4 See Wolfgang Friedmann, review (1958) 3 *Nat. L.F.* 208 at 210; also Hans Kelsen, *Allgemeine Staatslehre* (Berlin: 1925), p. 335, on "natural law naivety or arrogance" (in the passage, omitted from the 1945 English translation (*General Theory*, cf. p. 300), about the fully legal character of despotism).

restricted and juristic understanding of "natural law" and "natural law doctrine(s)."

Here we have to deal with the image of natural law entertained by jurists such as Kelsen, Hart, and Raz. This image should be reproduced in their own words, since they themselves scarcely identify, let alone quote from, any particular theorist as defending the view that they describe as the view of natural law doctrine. Joseph Raz usefully summarizes and adopts Kelsen's version of this image:

> Kelsen correctly points out that according to natural law theories there is no specific notion of legal validity. The only concept of validity is validity according to natural law, i.e., moral validity. Natural lawyers can only judge a law as morally valid, that is, just or morally invalid, i.e., wrong. They cannot say of a law that it is legally valid but morally wrong. If it is wrong and unjust, it is also invalid in the only sense of validity they recognise.[5]

In his own terms, Raz later defines "Natural Law theorists" as "those philosophers who think it a criterion of adequacy for theories of law that they show ... that it is a necessary truth that every law has moral worth."[6]

For my part, I know of no philosopher who fits, or fitted, such a description, or who would be committed to trying to defend that sort of theoretical or meta-theoretical proposal.

...

[*Ed. note*: Having rejected Raz's characterization of natural law theory, Finnis explains his understanding of natural law. The next excerpt demonstrates the style of his reasoning about the basic good of "knowledge." What is important here is that Finnis supposes "knowledge" is *self-evidently* good and so is a "given" in deliberations about conduct. We will not examine Finnis's full discussion of the seven basic forms of the human good: life, knowledge, play, aesthetic experience, friendship, practical reasonableness, and "religion." We will turn instead to Finnis's discussion of what "practical reasonableness" requires us to do as we pursue these basic goods.]

III. A Basic Form of Good: Knowledge

III.1 AN EXAMPLE

Neither this chapter nor the next makes or presupposes any moral judgments. Rather, these two chapters concern the evaluative substratum of all moral judgments. That is to say, they concern the acts of practical understanding in which we grasp the basic values of human existence and thus, too, the basic principles of all practical reasoning.

The purpose of this chapter, in particular, is to illustrate (i) what I mean by "basic value" and "basic practical principle," (ii) how such values and principles enter into any consideration of good reasons for action and any full description of human conduct, and (iii) the sense in which such basic values are obvious ("self-evident"), and even unquestionable. For this purpose, I discuss only one basic value, leaving to the next chapter the identification of the other forms of human good that, so far as I can see, are likewise irreducibly basic.

---

5 Raz, "Kelsen's Theory of the Basic Norm" (1974) 19 *Am. J. Juris.* 94 at p. 100.

6 *Practical Reason*, p. 162. This formulation corresponds to the contradictory of the characterization of "Legal Positivism" constructed by Hart in order to define "the issue between Natural Law and Legal Positivism": *Concept of Law*, p. 181. See also *Practical Reason*, pp. 155, 162; all these formulations seem to be intended by Raz to apply equally to "definitional" and "derivative" approach theories of natural law. (Since no one uses the "definitional" approach, there is no need to inquire into the value of the supposed distribution between "definitional" and "derivative" approaches.)

The example of a basic value to be examined now is: knowledge. Perhaps it would be more accurate to call it "speculative knowledge," using the term "speculative" here, not to make the Aristotelian distinction between the *theoretike* and the *praktike*, but to distinguish knowledge as sought for its own sake from knowledge as sought only instrumentally, i.e., as useful in the pursuit of some other objective, such as survival, power, popularity, or a money-saving cup of coffee. Now "knowledge," unlike "belief," is an achievement-word; there are true beliefs and false beliefs, but knowledge is of truth. So one could speak of truth as the basic good with which we are here concerned, for one can just as easily speak of "truth for its own sake" as of "knowledge for its own sake." In any event, truth is not a mysterious abstract entity; we want the truth when we want the judgments in which we affirm or deny propositions to be true judgments, or (what comes to the same) want the propositions affirmed or denied, or to be affirmed or denied, to be true propositions. So, to complete the explanation of what is meant by the knowledge under discussion here, as distinct from instrumental knowledge, I can add that the distinction I am drawing is not between one set of propositions and another. It is not a distinction between fields of knowledge. Any proposition, whatever its subject-matter, can be inquired into (with a view to affirming or denying it) in either of the two distinct ways, (i) instrumentally or (ii) out of curiosity, the pure desire to know, to find out the truth about it simply out of an interest in or concern for truth and a desire to avoid ignorance or error as such.

This chapter, then, is an invitation to reflect on one form of human activity, the activity of trying to find out, to understand, and to judge matters correctly. This is not, perhaps, the easiest activity to understand; but it has the advantage of being the activity which the reader himself is actually engaged in. But if it seems too abstruse and tricky to try to understand this form of activity reflectively (i.e., by reflecting on one's attempt to understand and assess the truth of this chapter itself), one can reflect on any other exercise of curiosity. One could consider, for example, the wide-ranging effort of historical inquiry involved in discovering the actual intentions of the principal authors of the Statute of Uses (1536) or of the Fourteenth Amendment of the US Constitution (1866). Or something more humble (like weighing the truth of some gossipy rumour), or more "scientific"—it makes no difference, for present purposes.

...

V. The Basic Requirements of Practical Reasonableness

V.1 THE GOOD OF PRACTICAL REASONABLENESS STRUCTURES OUR PURSUIT OF GOODS

There is no reason to doubt that each of the basic aspects of human well-being is worth seeking to realize. But there are many such basic forms of human good; I identified seven. And each of them can be participated in, and promoted, in an inexhaustible variety of ways and with an inexhaustible variety of combinations of emphasis, concentration, and specialization. To participate thoroughly in any basic value calls for skill, or at least a thoroughgoing commitment. But our life is short.

By disclosing a horizon of attractive possibilities for us, our grasp of the basic values thus creates, not answers, the problem for intelligent decision: What is to be done? What may be left undone? What is not to be done? We have, in the abstract, no reason to leave any of the basic goods out of account. But we do have good reason to choose commitments, projects, and actions, knowing that choice effectively rules out many alternative reasonable or possible commitment(s), project(s), and action(s).

To have this choice between commitment to concentration upon one value (say, speculative truth) and commitment to others, and between one intelligent and reasonable project (say, understanding this book) and other eligible projects for giving definite shape to one's participation in one's selected value, and between one way of carrying out that project and other appropriate ways, is the primary respect in which we can call ourselves both free and responsible. For amongst the basic forms of good that we have no good reason to leave out of account is the good of practical reasonableness, which is participated in precisely by shaping one's participation in the other basic goods, by guiding one's commitments, one's selection of projects, and what one does in carrying them out.

The principles that express the general ends of human life do not acquire what would nowadays be called a "moral" force until they are brought to bear upon definite ranges of project, disposition, or action, or upon particular projects, dispositions, or actions. How they are thus to be brought to bear is the problem for practical reasonableness. "Ethics," as classically conceived, is simply a recollectively and/or prospectively reflective expression of this problem and of the general lines of solutions which have been thought reasonable.

How does one tell that a decision is practically reasonable? This question is the subject-matter of the present chapter. The classical exponents of ethics (and of theories of natural law) were well aware of this problem of criteria and standards of judgment. They emphasize that an adequate response to that problem can be made only by one who has experience (both of human wants and passions and of the conditions of human life) and intelligence and a desire for reasonableness stronger than the desires that might overwhelm it. Even when, later, Thomas Aquinas clearly distinguished a class of practical principles which he considered self-evident to anyone with enough experience and intelligence to understand the words by which they are formulated, he emphasized that moral principles such as those in the Ten Commandments are *conclusions from* the primary self-evident principles, that reasoning to such conclusions requires good judgment, and that there are many other more complex and particular moral norms to be followed and moral judgments and decisions to be made, all requiring a degree of practical wisdom which (he says) few men in fact possess: II.3, above.

Now, you may say, it is all very well for Aristotle to assert that ethics can be satisfactorily expounded only by and to those who are experienced and wise and indeed of good habits,[1] and that these characteristics are only likely to be found in societies that already have sufficiently sound standards of conduct,[2] and that the popular morality of such societies (as crystallized and detectable in their language of praise and blame, and their lore) is a generally sound pointer in the elaboration of ethics.[3] He may assert that what is right and morally good is simply *seen* by the man (the *phronimos*, or again the *spoudaios*) who is right minded and morally good,[4] and that what such a man thinks and does *is* the criterion of sound terminology and correct conclusions in ethics (and politics).[5] Such assertions can scarcely be denied. But they are scarcely helpful to those who are wondering whether their own view of what is to be done is a reasonable view *or not*. The notion of "the mean," for which Aristotle is perhaps too well known, seems likewise to be

1 *Nic. Eth.* I, 3: 1095a7–11; 4: 1095b5–13; X, 9: 1179b27–30.
2 *Nic. Eth.* X, 9: 1179b27–1180a5.
3 See *Nic. Eth.* VI, 5: 1140a24–25; II, 5: 1105b30–31; III, 6: 1115a20; III, 10:1117b32; cf. X, 2: 1173a1.
4 *Nic. Eth.* VI, 11: 1143a35–1143b17.
5 *Nic. Eth.* X, 10: 1176a17–18; cf. III, 6: 1113a33; IX, 4: 1166a12–13: see also I.4, above.

accurate but not very helpful (though its classification of value-words doubtless serves as a reminder of the dimensions of the moral problem). For what is "the mean and best, that is characteristic of virtue"? It is "to feel [anger, pity, appetite, etc.] when one ought to, and in relation to the objects and persons that one ought to, and with the motives and in the manner that one ought to...."[6] Have we no more determinate guide than this?

In the two millennia since Plato and Aristotle initiated formal inquiry into the content of practical reasonableness, philosophical reflection has identified a considerable number of requirements of *method* in practical reasoning. Each of these requirements has, indeed, been treated by some philosopher with exaggerated respect, as if it were the exclusive controlling and shaping requirement. For, as with each of the basic forms of good, each of these requirements is fundamental, underived, irreducible, and hence is capable when focused upon of seeming the most important.

Each of these requirements concerns what one *must* do, or think, or be if one is to participate in the basic value of practical reasonableness. Someone who lives up to these requirements is thus Aristotle's *phronimos*; he has Aquinas's *prudentia*; they are requirements of reasonableness or practical wisdom, and to fail to live up to them is irrational. But, secondly, reasonableness both *is* a basic aspect of human well-being and *concerns* one's participation in all the (other) basic aspects of human well-being. Hence its requirements concern fullness of well-being (in the measure in which any one person can enjoy such fullness of well-being in the circumstances of his lifetime). So someone who lives up to these requirements is also Aristotle's *spoudaios* (mature man), his life is *eu zen* (well-living) and, unless circumstances are quite against him, we can say that he has Aristotle's *eudaimonia* (the inclusive all-round flourishing or well-being—not safely translated as "happiness"). But, thirdly, the basic forms of good are opportunities of *being*; the more fully a man participates in them the more he is what he can be. And for this state of being fully what one can be, Aristotle appropriated the word *physis*, which was translated into Latin as *natura* (cf. XIII.1, below). So Aquinas will say that these requirements are requirements not only of reason, and of goodness, but also (by entailment) of (human) nature: II.4, above.

Thus, speaking very summarily, we could say that the requirements to which we now turn express the "natural law method" of working out the (moral) "natural law" from the first (pre-moral) "principles of natural law." Using only the modern terminology (itself of uncertain import) of "morality," we can say that the following sections of this chapter concern the sorts of reasons why (and thus the ways in which) there are things that morally ought (not) to be done.

V.2 A COHERENT PLAN OF LIFE

First, then, we should recall that, though they correspond to urges and inclinations which can make themselves felt prior to any intelligent consideration of what is worth pursuing, the basic aspects of human well-being are discernible only to one who thinks about his opportunities, and thus are realizable only by one who intelligently directs, focuses, and controls his urges, inclinations, and impulses. In its fullest form, therefore, the first requirement of practical reasonableness is what John Rawls calls a rational plan of life.[7] Implicitly or explicitly one must have a harmonious set of purposes and orientations, not as the "plans" or

6 *Nic. Eth.* II, 6: 1106b21–24.
7 *Theory of Justice*, pp. 408–23, adopting the terminology of W.F.R. Hardie, "The Final Good in Aristotle's Ethics" (1965) 60 *Philosophy* 277.

"blueprints" of a pipe-dream, but as effective commitments. (Do not confuse the adoption of a set of basic personal or social commitments with the process, imagined by some contemporary philosophers, of "choosing basic values"!) It is unreasonable to live merely from moment to moment, following immediate cravings, or just drifting. It is also irrational to devote one's attention exclusively to specific projects which can be carried out completely by simply deploying defined means to defined objectives. Commitment to the practice of medicine (for the sake of human life), or to scholarship (for the sake of truth), or to any profession, or to a marriage (for the sake of friendship and children) ... all require both direction and control of impulses, and the undertaking of specific projects; but they also require the redirection of inclinations, the reformation of habits, the abandonment of old and adoption of new projects, as circumstances require, and, overall, the harmonization of all one's deep commitments for which there is no recipe or blueprint, since basic aspects of human good are not like the definite objectives of particular projects, but are *participated in* (see III.3, above).

As Rawls says, this first requirement is that we should "see our life as one whole, the activities of one rational subject spread out in time. Mere temporal position, or distance from the present, is not a reason for favouring one moment over another."[8] But since human life is in fact subject to all manner of unforeseeable contingencies, this effort to "see" our life as one whole is a rational effort only if it remains on the level of general commitments, and the harmonizing of them. Still, generality is not emptiness (as one can confirm for oneself by contrasting any of the basic forms of good, which as formulated in the "substantive" practical principles are quite general, with their opposites). So, in every age, wise men have counselled "in whatever you do remember your last days" (Ecclesiasticus 7:36), not so much to emphasize the importance of the hour of death in relation to a life hereafter, but rather to establish the proper perspective for choosing how to live one's present life. For, from the imagined and heuristically postulated standpoint of the still unknown time of one's death, one can see that many sorts of choices would be irrational, a waste of opportunities, meaningless, a failure, a shame. So the Christian parable of the man who devoted all his energies to gathering riches, with a view to nothing more than drinking and eating them up, makes its "moral" point by appealing to the intelligence by which we discern folly: "*You fool!* This night your life shall be required of you. Then whose shall that wealth be which you have heaped together?" (Luke 12:20).

The content and significance of this first requirement will be better understood in the light of the other requirements. For indeed, all the requirements are interrelated and capable of being regarded as aspects one of another.

V.3 NO ARBITRARY PREFERENCES AMONGST VALUES

Next, there must be no leaving out of account, or arbitrary discounting or exaggeration, of any of the basic human values. Any commitment to a coherent plan of life is going to involve some degree of concentration on one or some of the basic forms of good, at the expense, temporarily or permanently, of other forms of good: IV.4. But the commitment will be rational only if it is on the basis of one's assessment of one's capacities, circumstances, and even of one's tastes. It will be unreasonable if it is on the basis of a devaluation of any of the basic forms of human excellence, or if it is on the basis of an overevaluation of such merely derivative and supporting or instrumental goods as wealth or "opportunity" or of such merely secondary and conditionally valuable goods as

8 *Theory of Justice*, p. 420.

reputation or (in a different sense of secondariness) pleasure.

A certain scholar may have little taste or capacity for friendship, and may feel that life for him would have no savour if he were prevented from pursuing his commitment to knowledge. None the less, it would be unreasonable for him to deny that, objectively, human life (quite apart from truthseeking and knowledge) and friendship are good in themselves. It is one thing to have little capacity and even no "taste" for scholarship, or friendship, or physical heroism, or sanctity; it is quite another thing, and stupid or arbitrary, to think or speak or act as if these were not real forms of good.

So, in committing oneself to a rational plan of life, and in interacting with other people (with their own plans of life), one must not use Rawls's "thin theory of the good." For the sake of a "democratic"[9] impartiality between differing conceptions of human good, Rawls insists that, in selecting principles of justice, one must treat as primary goods only liberty, opportunity, wealth, and self-respect, and that one must not attribute intrinsic value to such basic forms of good as truth, or play, or art, or friendship. Rawls gives no satisfactory reason for this radical emaciation of human good, and no satisfactory reason is available: the "thin theory" is arbitrary. It is quite reasonable for many men to choose not to commit themselves to any real pursuit of knowledge, and it is quite unreasonable for a scholar-statesman or scholar-father to demand that all his subjects or children should conform themselves willy-nilly to the modes and standards of excellence that he chooses and sets for himself. But it is even more unreasonable for anyone to deny that knowledge *is* (and is to be treated as) a form of excellence, and that error, illusion, muddle, superstition, and ignorance are evils that no one should wish for, or plan for, or encourage in himself or in others. If a statesman (VIII.5) or father or any self-directing individual treats truth or friendship or play or any of the other basic forms of good as of no account, and never asks himself whether his life-plan(s) makes reasonable allowance for participation in those intrinsic human values (and for avoidance of their opposites), then he can be properly accused both of irrationality and of stunting or mutilating himself and those in his care.

V.4 NO ARBITRARY PREFERENCES AMONGST PERSONS

Next, the basic goods are human goods, and can in principle be pursued, realized, and participated in by any human being. Another person's survival, his coming to know, his creativity, his all-round flourishing, may not interest me, may not concern me, may in any event be beyond my power to affect. But have I any *reason* to deny that they are really good, or that they are fit matters of interest, concern, and favour by that man and by all those who have to do with him? The questions of friendship, collaboration, mutual assistance, and justice are the subject of the next chapters. Here we need not ask just who is responsible for whose well-being: see VII.4. But we can add, to the second requirement of fundamental impartiality of recognition of each of the basic forms of good, a third requirement: of fundamental impartiality among the human subjects who are or may be partakers of those goods.

My own well-being (which, as we shall see, includes a concern for the well-being of others, my friends: VI.4; but ignore this for the moment) is reasonably the first claim on my interest, concern, and effort. Why can I so regard it? Not because it is of more value than the well-being of others, simply because it is mine: intelligence and reasonableness can find no basis in the mere fact that A is A and is not B (that I am I and am

9 Cf. *Theory of Justice*, p. 527.

not you) for evaluating his (our) well-being differentially. No: the only *reason* for me to prefer my well-being is that it is through *my* self-determined and self-realizing participation in the basic goods that I can do what reasonableness suggests and requires, viz. favour and realize the forms of human good indicated in the first principles of practical reason.

There is, therefore, reasonable scope for self-preference. But when all allowance is made for that, this third requirement remains, a pungent critique of selfishness, special pleading, double standards, hypocrisy, indifference to the good of others whom one could easily help ("passing by on the other side"), and all the other manifold forms of egoistic and group bias. So much so that many have sought to found ethics virtually entirely on this principle of impartiality between persons. In the modern philosophical discussion, the principle regularly is expressed as a requirement that one's moral judgments and preferences be *universalizable.*

The classical non-philosophical expression of the requirement is, of course, the so-called Golden Rule formulated not only in the Christian gospel but also in the sacred books of the Jews, and not only in didactic formulae but also in the moral appeal of sacred history and parable. It needed no drawing of the moral, no special traditions of moral education, for King David (and every reader of the story of his confrontation with Nathan the prophet) to feel the rational conclusiveness of Nathan's analogy between the rich man's appropriation of the poor man's ewe and the King's appropriation of Uriah the Hittite's wife, and thus the rational necessity for the King to extend his condemnation of the rich man to himself. "You are the man" (2 Samuel 12:7).

"Do to (or for) others what you would have them do to (or for) you." Put yourself in your neighbour's shoes. Do not condemn others for what you are willing to do yourself. Do not (without special reason) prevent others getting for themselves what you are trying to get for yourself. These are requirements of reason, because to ignore them is to be arbitrary as between individuals.

But what are the bounds of reasonable self-preference, of reasonable discrimination in favour of myself, my family, my group(s)? In the Greek, Roman, and Christian traditions of reflection, this question was approached via the heuristic device of adopting the viewpoint, the standards, the principles of justice, of one who sees the whole arena of human affairs and who has the interests of each participant in those affairs equally at heart and equally in mind—the "ideal observer." Such an impartially benevolent "spectator" would condemn some but not all forms of self-preference, and some but not all forms of competition: VII.3–4, below. The heuristic device helps one to attain impartiality as between the possible subjects of human well-being (persons) and to exclude mere bias in one's practical reasoning. It permits one to be impartial, too, among inexhaustibly many of the life-plans that differing individuals may choose. But, of course, it does not suggest "impartiality" about the basic aspects of human good. It does not authorize one to set aside the second requirement of practical reason by indifference to death and disease, by preferring trash to art, by favouring the comforts of ignorance and illusion, by repressing all play as unworthy of man, by praising the ideal of self-aggrandizement and contemning the ideal of friendship, or by treating the search for the ultimate source and destiny of things as of no account or as an instrument of statecraft or a plaything reserved for leisured folk ...

Therein lies the contrast between the classical heuristic device of the benevolently divine viewpoint and the equivalent modern devices for eliminating mere bias, notably the heuristic concept of the social contract. Consider Rawls's elaboration of the social contract strategy, an elaboration which most readily discloses the purpose of that strategy as a measure and instrument of practical reason's requirement of interpersonal impartiality. Every feature of Rawls's construction is designed to guarantee that if a supposed principle of justice is one that would be unanimously agreed on, behind the "veil of ignorance," in the "Original Position," then it must be a principle that is fair and unbiased as between persons. Rawls's heuristic device is thus of some use to anyone who is concerned for the third requirement of practical reasonableness, and in testing its implications. Unfortunately, Rawls disregards the second requirement of practical reasonableness, viz. that each basic or intrinsic human good be treated as a basic and intrinsic good. The conditions of the Original Position are designed by Rawls to guarantee that no principle of justice will systematically favour any life-plan simply because that life-plan participates more fully in human well-being in any or all of its basic aspects (e.g., by favouring knowledge over ignorance and illusion, art over trash, etc.).

And it simply does not follow, from the fact that a principle chosen in the Original Position would be unbiased and fair as between individuals, that a principle which would *not* be chosen in the Original Position must be unfair or not a proper principle of justice in the real world. For in the real world, as Rawls himself admits, intelligence can discern intrinsic basic values and their contraries.[10] Provided we make the distinctions mentioned in the previous section, between basic practical principles and mere matters of taste, inclination, ability, etc., we are able (and are required in reason) to favour the basic forms of good and to avoid and discourage their contraries. In doing so we are showing no improper favour to individuals as such, no unreasonable "respect of persons," no egoistic or group bias, no partiality opposed to the Golden Rule or to any other aspect of this third requirement of practical reason: see VIII.5–6, below.

V.5 DETACHMENT AND COMMITMENT

The fourth and fifth requirements of practical reasonableness are closely complementary both to each other and to the first requirement of adopting a coherent plan of life, order of priorities, set of basic commitments.

In order to be sufficiently open to all the basic forms of good in all the changing circumstances of a lifetime, and in all one's relations, often unforeseeable, with other persons, and in all one's opportunities of effecting their well-being or relieving hardship, one must have a certain detachment from all the specific and limited projects which one undertakes. There is no good reason to take up an attitude to any of one's particular objectives, such that if one's project failed and one's objective eluded one, one would consider one's life drained of meaning. Such an attitude irrationally devalues and treats as meaningless the basic human good of authentic and reasonable self-determination, a good in which one meaningfully participates simply by trying to do something sensible and worthwhile, whether or not that sensible and worthwhile project comes to nothing. Moreover, there are often straightforward and evil consequences of succumbing to the temptation to give one's particular project the overriding and unconditional significance which only a basic value and a general commitment can claim: they are the evil consequences that we call to mind when we think of fanaticism. So the fourth requirement of practical reasonableness can be called detachment. The fifth requirement establishes the balance between fanaticism and dropping out, apathy, unreasonable failure or refusal to "get involved" with anything. It is simply the requirement that having made one's general commitments one must not abandon

10 *Theory of Justice*, p. 328.

them lightly (for to do so would mean, in the extreme case, that one would fail ever to really participate in any of the basic values). And this requirement of fidelity has a positive aspect. One should be looking creatively for new and better ways of carrying out one's commitments, rather than restricting one's horizon and one's effort to the projects, methods, and routines with which one is familiar. Such creativity and development shows that a person, or a society, is really living on the level of practical *principle*, not merely on the level of conventional rules of conduct, rules of thumb, rules of method, etc., whose real appeal is not to reason (which would show up their inadequacies) but to the sub-rational complacency of habit, mere urge to conformity, etc.

V.6 THE (LIMITED) RELEVANCE OF CONSEQUENCES: EFFICIENCY, WITHIN REASON

The sixth requirement has obvious connections with the fifth, but introduces a new range of problems for practical reason, problems which go to the heart of morality. For this is the requirement that one bring about good in the world (in one's own life and the lives of others) by actions that are efficient for their (reasonable) purpose(s). One must not waste one's opportunities by using inefficient methods. One's actions should be judged by their effectiveness, by their fitness for their purpose, by their utility, their consequences ...

There is a wide range of contexts in which it is possible and only reasonable to calculate, measure, compare, weigh, and assess the consequences of alternative decisions. Where a choice must be made it is reasonable to prefer human good to the good of animals. Where a choice must be made it is reasonable to prefer basic human goods (such as life) to merely instrumental goods (such as property). Where damage is inevitable, it is reasonable to prefer stunning to wounding, wounding to maiming, maiming to death: i.e., lesser rather than greater damage to one-and-the-same basic good in one-and-the-same instantiation. Where one way of participating in a human good includes *both* all the good aspects and effects of its alternative, *and* more, it is reasonable to prefer that way: a remedy that both relieves pain and heals is to be preferred to the one that merely relieves pain. Where a person or a society has created a personal or social hierarchy of practical norms and orientations, through reasonable choice of commitments, one can in many cases reasonably measure the benefits and disadvantages of alternatives. (Consider a man who has decided to become a scholar, or a society that has decided to go to war.) Where one is considering objects or activities in which there is reasonably a market, the market provides a common denominator (currency) and enables a comparison to be made of prices, costs, and profits. Where there are alternative techniques or facilities for achieving definite objectives, cost-benefit analysis will make possible a certain range of reasonable comparisons between techniques or facilities. Over a wide range of preferences and wants, it is reasonable for an individual or society to seek to maximize the satisfaction of those preferences or wants.

But this sixth requirement is only one requirement among a number. The first, second, and third requirements require that in seeking to maximize the satisfaction of preferences one should discount the preferences of, for example, sadists (who follow the impulses of the moment, and/or do not respect the value of life, and/or do not universalize their principles of action with impartiality). The first, third, and (as we shall see) seventh and eighth requirements require that cost-benefit analysis be contained within a framework that excludes any project involving certain intentional killings, frauds, manipulations of personality, etc. And the second requirement requires that one recognize that each of the basic aspects of human well-being is equally basic, that none is objectively more important than any of the others, and thus that none can provide a common denominator or single yardstick for assessing the utility of all projects: they are incommensurable, and any calculus of consequences that pretends to commensurate them is irrational.

...

V.7 RESPECT FOR EVERY BASIC VALUE IN EVERY ACT

The seventh requirement of practical reasonableness can be formulated in several ways. A first formulation is that one should not choose to do any act which *of itself does nothing but* damage or impede a realization or participation of any one or more of the basic forms of human good. For the only "reason" for doing such an act, other than the non-reason of some impelling desire, could be that the good *consequences* of the act *outweigh* the damage done in and through the act itself. But, outside merely technical contexts, consequentialist "weighing" is always and necessarily arbitrary and delusive for the reasons indicated in the preceding section. [*Ed. note*: This argument has been omitted.]

Now an act of the sort we are considering will always be done (if it is done intelligently at all) as a means of promoting or protecting, directly or indirectly, one or more of the basic goods, in one or more of their aspects. For anyone who rises above the level of impulse and acts deliberately must be seeking to promote some form of good (even if only the good of authentically powerful self-expression and self-integration which he seeks through sadistic assaults or through malicious treachery or deception, with "no ulterior motives"). Hence, if consequentialist reasoning were reasonable, acts which themselves do nothing but damage or impede a human good could often be justified as parts of, or steps on the way to carrying out, some project for the promotion or protection of some form(s) of good. For example, if consequentialist reasoning were reasonable, one might sometimes reasonably kill some innocent person to save the lives of some hostages. But consequentialist reasoning is arbitrary and senseless, not just in one respect but in many. So we are left with the fact that such a killing is an act which of itself does nothing but damage the basic value of life. The goods that are expected to be secured in and through the consequential release of the hostages (if it takes place) would be secured not in or as an aspect of the killing of the innocent man but in or as an aspect of a distinct, subsequent act, an act which would be one "consequence" amongst the innumerable multitude of incommensurable consequences of the act of killing. Once we have excluded consequentialist reasoning, with its humanly understandable but in truth naively arbitrary limitation of focus to the purported calculus "one life versus many," the seventh requirement is self-evident.

V.8 THE REQUIREMENTS OF THE COMMON GOOD

Very many, perhaps even most, of our concrete moral responsibilities, obligations, and duties have their basis in the eighth requirement. We can label this the requirement of favouring and fostering the common good of one's communities. The sense and implications of this requirement are complex and manifold: see especially VI.8, VII.2–5, IX.l, XI.2, XII.2–3.

V.9 FOLLOWING ONE'S CONSCIENCE

The ninth requirement might be regarded as a particular aspect of the seventh (that no basic good may be directly attacked in any act), or even as a summary of all the requirements. But it is quite distinctive. It is the requirement that one should not do what one judges or thinks or "feels"-all-in-all should not be done. That is to say one must act "in accordance with one's conscience."

This chapter has been in effect a reflection on the workings of conscience. If one were by inclination generous, open, fair, and steady in one's love of human good, or if one's milieu happened to have settled on reasonable *mores*, then one would be able, without solemnity, rigmarole, abstract reasoning, or casuistry, to make the particular practical judgments (i.e., judgments of conscience) that reason requires. If one is not so fortunate in one's inclinations or upbringing, then one's conscience will mislead one, unless one strives to be reasonable and is blessed with a pertinacious intelligence alert to the forms of human good yet undeflected by the sophistries which intelligence so readily generates to rationalize indulgence, time-serving, and self-love. (The stringency of these conditions is the permanent ground for the possibility of authority in morals, i.e., of authoritative guidance, by one who meets those conditions, acknowledged willingly by persons of conscience.)

The first theorist to formulate this ninth requirement in all its unconditional strictness seems to have been Thomas Aquinas: if one chooses to do what one judges to be in the last analysis unreasonable, or if one chooses not to do what one judges to be in the last analysis required by reason, then one's choice is unreasonable (wrongful), however erroneous one's judgments of conscience may happen to be. (A *logically* necessary feature of such a situation is, of course, that one is ignorant of one's mistake.)

This dignity of even the mistaken conscience is what is expressed in the ninth requirement. It flows from the fact that practical reasonableness is not simply a mechanism for producing correct judgments, but an aspect of personal full-being, to be respected (like all the other aspects) in every act as well as "over-all"—whatever the consequences.

V.10 THE PRODUCT OF THESE REQUIREMENTS: MORALITY

Now we can see why some philosophers have located the essence of "morality" in the reduction of harm, others in the increase of well-being, some in social harmony, some in universalizability of practical judgment, some in the all-round flourishing of the individual, others in the preservation of freedom and personal authenticity. Each of these has a place in rational choice of commitments, projects, and particular actions. Each, moreover, contributes to the sense, significance, and force of terms such as "moral," "[morally] ought," and "right"; not every one of the nine requirements has a direct role in every moral judgment, but some moral judgments do sum up the bearing of each and all of the nine on the questions in hand, and every moral judgment sums up the bearing of one or more of the requirements.

...

XII. Unjust Laws

XII.1 A SUBORDINATE CONCERN OF NATURAL LAW THEORY

The long haul through the preceding chapters will perhaps have convinced the reader that a theory of natural law need not have as its principal concern, either theoretical or pedagogical, the affirmation that "unjust laws are not law." Indeed, I know of no theory of natural law in which that affirmation, or anything like it, is more than a subordinate theorem. The principal concern of a theory of natural law is to explore the requirements of practical reasonableness in relation to the good of human beings who, because they live in community with one another, are confronted with problems of justice and rights, of authority, law, and obligation. And the principal jurisprudential concern of a theory of natural law is thus to identify the principles and limits of the Rule of Law (X.4), and to trace the ways in which sound laws, in all their positivity and mutability, are to be derived (not, usually, deduced: X.7) from unchanging principles—principles that have their force from their reasonableness, not from any originating acts or circumstances. Still, even the reader who has not been brought up to believe that "natural law" can be summed up in the slogan "*lex injusta non est lex*" [*Ed. note*: "unjust laws are not laws"] will wish a little more to be said about that slogan and about the effect of unjust exercises of authority upon our responsibilities as reasonable persons.

The ultimate basis of a ruler's authority is the fact that he has the opportunity, and thus the responsibility, of furthering the common good by stipulating solutions to a community's co-ordination problems: IX.4. Normally, though not necessarily, the immediate source of this opportunity and responsibility is the fact that he is designated by or under some authoritative rule as bearer of authority in respect of certain aspects of those problems: IX.4, X.3. In any event, authority is useless for the common good unless the stipulations of those in authority (or which emerge through the formation of authoritative customary rules) are treated as exclusionary reasons, i.e., as sufficient reason for acting notwithstanding that the subject would not himself have made the same stipulation and indeed considers the actual stipulation to be in some respect(s) unreasonable, not fully appropriate for the common good ...: IX.l, IX.2. The principles set out in the preceding three sentences control our understanding both of the types of injustice in the making and administration of law, and of the consequences of such injustice.

XII.2 TYPES OF INJUSTICE IN LAW

First, since authority is derived solely from the needs of the common good, a ruler's use of authority is radically defective if he exploits his opportunities by making stipulations intended by him not for the common good but for his own or his friends' or party's or faction's advantage, or out of malice against some person or group. In making this judgment, we should not be deflected by the fact that most legal systems do not permit the exercise of "constitutional" powers to be challenged on the ground that that exercise was improperly motivated. These restrictions on judicial review are justified, if at all, either by pragmatic considerations or by a principle of separation of powers. In either case, they have no application to the reasonable man assessing the claims of authority upon him. On the other hand, it is quite possible that an improperly motivated law may happen to be in its contents compatible with justice and even promote the common good.

Secondly, since the location of authority is normally determined by authoritative rules dividing up authority and jurisdiction amongst separate office-holders, an office-holder may wittingly or unwittingly exploit his opportunity to affect people's conduct, by making stipulations which stray beyond his authority. Except in "emergency" situations (X.5) in which the law (even the constitution) should be bypassed and in which the source of authority reverts to its ultimate basis (IX.4), an *ultra vires* act is an abuse of power and an injustice to those treated as subject to it. (The injustice is "distributive" inasmuch as the official improperly assumes to himself an excess of authority, and "commutative" inasmuch as the official improperly seeks to subject others to his own decisions.) Lawyers sometimes are surprised to hear the *ultra vires* actions of an official categorized as abuse of power, since they are accustomed to thinking of such actions as "void and of no effect" in law. But such surprise is misplaced; legal rules about void and voidable acts are "deeming" rules, directing judges to treat actions, which are empirically more or less effective, *as if* they had not occurred (at least, as juridical acts), or *as if* from a certain date they had been overridden by an *intra vires* act of repeal or annulment. Quite reasonably, purported juridical acts of officials are commonly presumed to be lawful, and are treated as such by both fellow officials and laymen, unless and until judicially held otherwise. Hence, *ultra vires* official acts, even those which are not immune-for-procedural-or-pragmatic-reasons from successful challenge, will usually subject persons to effects which cannot afterwards be undone; and the bringing about of (the likelihood of) such effects is an abuse of power and an unjust imposition.

Thirdly, the exercise of authority in conformity with the Rule of Law normally is greatly to the common good (even when it restricts the efficient pursuit of other objectives); it is an important aspect of the commutative justice of treating people as entitled to the dignity of self-direction (X.4), and of the distributive justice of affording all an equal opportunity of understanding and complying with the law. Thus the exercise of legal authority otherwise than in accordance with due requirements of manner and form is an abuse and an injustice, unless those involved consent, or ought to consent, to an accelerated procedure in order to cut out "red tape" which in the circumstances would prejudice substantial justice (cf. VII.7).

Fourthly, what is stipulated may suffer from none of these defects of intention, author, and form, and yet be substantively unjust. It may be distributively unjust, by appropriating some aspect of the common stock, or some benefit of common life or enterprise, to a class not reasonably entitled to it on any of the criteria of distributive justice, while denying it to other persons; or by imposing on some a burden from which others are, on no just criterion, exempt. It may be commutatively unjust, by denying to one, some, or everyone an absolute human right, or a human right the exercise of which is in the circumstances possible, consistent with the reasonable requirements of public order, public health, etc., and compatible with the due exercise both of other human rights and of the same human rights by other persons (VII.4–5, VIII.7).

XII.3 EFFECTS OF INJUSTICE ON OBLIGATION

How does injustice, of any of the foregoing sorts, affect the obligation to obey the law?

It is essential to specify the exact sense of this question. Any sound jurisprudence will recognize that someone uttering the question might conceivably mean by "obligation to obey the law" either (i) empirical liability to be subjected to sanction in event of non-compliance; or (ii) legal obligation in the intra-systemic sense ("legal obligation in the legal sense") in which the practical premiss that conformity to law is socially necessary is a framework principle insulated from the rest of practical reasoning; or (iii) legal obligation in the moral sense (i.e., the moral obligation that presumptively is entailed by legal obligation in the intra-systemic or legal sense); or (iv) moral obligation deriving not from the legality of the stipulation-of-obligation but from some "collateral" source (to be explained shortly). None of these interpretations is absurd, and a sound jurisprudence will show to what extent the answers to each will differ and to what extent they are interrelated.

An unsound jurisprudential method will seek to banish the question, in some of its senses, to "another discipline,"[1] or even declare those senses to be nonsense. Thus John Austin:

> Now, to say that human laws which conflict with the divine law are not binding, that is to say, are not laws, *is to talk stark nonsense.* The most pernicious laws, and therefore those which are most opposed to the will of

1 Cf. Hart, *Concept of Law*, p. 205.

> God, have been and are continually enforced as laws by judicial tribunals. Suppose an act innocuous, or Positively beneficial, be prohibited by the sovereign under the penalty of death; if I commit this act, I shall be tried and condemned, and if I object to the sentence, that it is contrary to the law of God, who has commanded that human lawgivers shall not prohibit acts which have no evil consequences, the Court of Justice will demonstrate the inconclusiveness of my reasoning by hanging me up, in pursuance of the law of which I have impugned the validity.[2]

I need not comment on the tone of this treatment of unjust law and conscientious objection. What concerns us is the methodological obtuseness of the words here italicized, the failure to allow that one and the same verbal formulation may bear differing though not necessarily unrelated meanings and express questions whose interrelations and differences can fruitfully be explored.

The first of the four conceivable senses of the question listed above is the least likely, in practice, to be intended by anyone raising the question. (Nevertheless, it is the only sense which Austin explicitly recognizes.) Someone who asks how injustice affects his obligation to conform to law is not likely to be asking for information on the practically important but theoretically banal point of fact, "Am I or am I not likely to be hanged for non-compliance with this law?"

The second of the four listed senses of the question of obligation might seem, at first glance, to be empty. For what is the point of asking whether there is a legal obligation in the legal sense to conform to a stipulation which is in the legal sense obligatory? This objection is, however, too hasty. In my discussion of the formal features of legal order (X.3), of the Rule of Law (X.4), and of legal obligation (XI.4), I emphasized the way in which the enterprise of exercising authority through law proceeds by positing a system of rules which derive their authority not from the intrinsic appropriateness of their content but from the fact of stipulation in accordance with rules of stipulation. I emphasized the degree to which the resulting system is conceived of, in legal thought, as internally complete ("gapless") and coherent, and thus as sealed off (so to speak) from the unrestricted flow of practical reasoning about what is just and for the common good. I treated these "model" features of legal system and legal thought not as mere items in some "legal logic" (which as a matter of logic could certainly differ widely from that model!), but as practically reasonable responses to the need for security and predictability, a need which is indeed a matter of justice and human right. But all this should not disguise the extent to which legal thought in fact (and reasonably) does allow the system of rules to be permeated by principles of practical reasonableness which derive their authority from their appropriateness (in justice and for the common good) and not, or not merely, from their origin in some past act of stipulation or some settled usage. The legal system, even when conceived strictly as a set of normative meaning-contents (in abstraction from institutions, processes, personnel, and attitudes), is more open than the model suggests—open, that is to say, to the unrestricted flow of practical reasoning, in which a stipulation, valid according to the system's formal criteria of validity ("rules of recognition"), may be judged to be, or to have become, unjust and, therefore, after all, wholly or partially inapplicable.

In some legal systems this openness to unvarnished claims about the injustice of an existing or purported law is particularly evident, as in

2 *Province*, p. 185 (emphasis added).

the United States of America. In others, as in English law, it is less obvious but still is familiar to lawyers, for example from the "golden rule" that statutes are to be interpreted so as to avoid "absurdity" or injustice, and from the debates, quite frequent in the highest courts, about the propriety of amending or abandoning even well-established rules or "doctrines" of common law. Those who doubt or minimize the presence of open-ended principles of justice in professional legal thought will usually be found, on close examination, to be making a constitutional claim, viz. that the judiciary ought to leave change and development of law to the legislature. Conversely, those who stress the pervasiveness of such principles and minimize the coverage of practical problems by black-and-white rules will usually be found to be advancing the contradictory constitutional claim. In other words, what is presented[3] as a dispute about the "legal system" *qua* set of normative meaning-contents is in substance, typically, a dispute about the "legal system" *qua* constitutional order of institutions.

In short, even in well-developed legal orders served by a professional caste of lawyers, there are (and reasonably) quite a few opportunities of raising "intra-systemically," for example before a court of law, the question whether what would otherwise be an indubitable legal obligation is in truth not (*legally*) obligatory because it is unjust. On the other hand, since there is little point in meditating about the legal-obligation-imposing force of normative meaning-contents which are not treated as having legal effect in the principal legal institutions of a community (viz. the courts), it is idle to go on asking the question in this sense (the second of the four listed) after the highest court has ruled that in its judgment the disputed law is not unjust or, if unjust, is none the less law, legally obligatory, and judicially enforceable. It is not conducive to clear thought, or to any good practical purpose, to smudge the positivity of law by denying the legal obligatoriness *in the legal or intra-systematic sense* of a rule recently affirmed as legally valid and obligatory by the highest institution of the "legal system." (Austin's concern to make this point, in the "hanging me up" passage, was quite reasonable. What was unreasonable was his failure to acknowledge (a) the limited relevance of the point, and (b) the existence of questions which may be expressed in the same language but which are not determinately answerable intra-systemically.)

The question in its *third* sense therefore arises in clear-cut form when one is confident that the legal institutions of one's community will not accept that the law in question is affected by the injustice one discerns in it. The question can be stated thus: Given that legal obligation presumptively entails a moral obligation, and that the legal system is by and large just, does a particular unjust law impose upon me any moral obligation to conform to it?

Notoriously, many people (let us call them "positivists") propose that this question should not be tackled in "jurisprudence" but should be left to "another discipline," no doubt "political philosophy" or "ethics." Now it is not a purpose of this book to conduct a polemic against anybody's conception of the limits of jurisprudence. Suffice it to mention some disadvantages of this proposal. Firstly, the proposed division is artificial to the extent that the arguments and counter-arguments which it is proposed to expel from jurisprudence are in fact (as we observed in the preceding paragraphs) to be found on the lips of lawyers in court and of judges giving judgment. Of course, the arguments about justice and obligation that find favor in the courts of a given community at a given time may be arguments that would be rejected by a sound and critical ethics or political philosophy. But they are part of

3 As in Dworkin, *Taking Rights Seriously* (London: 1977), chs. 2–4.

the same realm of discourse. One will not understand either the "logic" or the "sociology" of one's own or anyone else's legal system unless one is aware (not merely in the abstract but in detail) how both the arguments in the courts, and the formulation of norms by "theoretical" jurists, are affected, indeed permeated, by the vocabulary, the syntax, and the principles of the "ethics" and "political philosophy" of that community, or of its elite or professional caste. In turn, one will not well understand the ethics or political philosophy of that community or caste unless one has reflected on the *intrinsic* problems of "ethic" and "political philosophy," i.e., on the basic aspects of human well-being and the methodological requirements of practical reasonableness. Finally, one will not well understand these intrinsic problems and principles unless one is aware of the extent to which the language in which one formulates them for oneself, and the concepts which one "makes one's own" are themselves the symbols and concepts of a particular human civilization, a civilization which has worked itself out, as much as anywhere, in its law courts and law schools. This set of considerations affords the first reason why I would not myself accept the proposal to banish to some "other discipline" the question of the moral obligation of an unjust law.

The second reason, not unconnected with the first, is to be found in the argument, developed in my first chapter and not to be repeated here, that a jurisprudence which aspires to be more than the lexicography of a particular culture cannot solve its theoretical problems of definition or concept-formation unless it draws upon at least some of the considerations of values and principles of practical reasonableness which are the subject-matter of "ethics" (or "political philosophy"). Since there can be no sharp distinction between the "two disciplines" at that basic level, it is not clear why the distinction, if such there be, should be thought so very important at other levels.

The third reason is that (not surprisingly, in view of what I have just said) the programme of separating off from jurisprudence all questions or assumptions about the moral significance of law is not consistently carried through by those who propose it. Their works are replete with more or less undiscussed assumptions such as that the formal features of legal order contribute to the practical reasonableness of making, maintaining, and obeying law; that these formal features have some connection with the concept of justice and that, conversely, lawyers are justified in thinking of certain principles of justice as principles of *legality*;[4] and that the fact that a stipulation is *legally* valid gives some reason, albeit not conclusive, for treating it as *morally* obligatory or *morally* permissible to act in accordance with it.[5] But none of these assumptions can be shown to be warranted, or could even be discussed, without transgressing the proposed boundary between jurisprudence and moral or political philosophy—in the way that I have systematically "transgressed" it in the preceding five chapters. Thus the state of the scholarly literature testifies, so to speak, to what a sound philosophy of practical reason establishes abstractly: the principles of practical reasonableness and their requirements form one unit of inquiry which can be subdivided into "moral," "political," and "jurisprudential" only for a pedagogical or expository convenience which risks falsifying the understanding of all three.

What, then, are we to say in reply to the question whether an unjust law creates a moral obligation *in the way* that just law *of itself* does? The right response begins by recalling that the stipulations of those in authority have presumptive obligatory force (in the eyes of the reasonable person thinking unrestrictedly about what to do)

4 See Hart, *Concept of Law*, pp. 156–57, 202.
5 See ibid., pp. 206–07.

only because of what is needed if the common good is to be secured and realized.

All my analyses of authority and obligation can be summed up in the following theorem: the ruler has, very strictly speaking, no right to be obeyed (XI.7); but he has the authority to give directions and make laws that are morally obligatory and that he has the responsibility of enforcing. He has this authority for the sake of the common good (the needs of which can also, however, make authoritative the opinions—as in custom—or stipulations of men who have no authority). Therefore, if he uses his authority to make stipulations against the common good, or against any of the basic principles of practical reasonableness, those stipulations altogether lack the authority they would otherwise have *by virtue of being his*. More precisely, stipulations made for partisan advantage, or (without emergency justification) in excess of legally defined authority, or imposing inequitable burdens on their subjects, or directing the doing of things that should never be done, simply fail, of themselves, to create any moral obligation whatever.

This conclusion should be read with precision. Firstly, it should not be concluded that an enactment which itself is for the common good and compatible with justice is deprived of its moral authority by the fact that the act of enacting it was rendered unjust by the partisan motives of its author. Just as we should not be deflected from adjudging the act of enactment unjust by the fact that improper motivation is not, in a given system, ground for judicial review, so we should not use the availability of judicial review for that ground, in certain other systems of law, as a sufficient basis for concluding that a private citizen (to whom is not entrusted the duty of disciplining wayward officials or institutions) is entitled to treat the improper motives of the authors of a just law as exempting him from his moral duty of compliance. Secondly, it should not be concluded that the distributive injustice of a law exempts from its moral obligation those who are *not* unjustly burdened by it.

Understood with those precisions, my response to the question in its third sense corresponds to the classical position: viz. that for the purpose of assessing one's legal obligations in the moral sense, one is entitled to discount laws that are "unjust" in any of the ways mentioned. Such laws lack the moral authority that in other cases comes simply from their origin, "pedigree," or formal source. In this way, then, *lex injusta non est lex* and *virtutem obligandi non habet*,[6] whether or not it is "legally valid" and "legally obligatory" in the restricted sense that it (i) emanates from a legally authorized source, (ii) will in fact be enforced by courts and/or other officials, and/or (iii) is commonly spoken of as a law like other laws.

But at the same time I must add that the last-mentioned facts, on which the lawyer *qua* lawyer (normally but, as I have noted, not exclusively) may reasonably concentrate, are not irrelevant to the moralist, the reasonable man with his unrestricted perspective.

At this point there emerges our question in the *fourth* of the senses I listed at the beginning of this section. It may be the case, for example,

6 Aquinas, *S.T.* I–II. q. 96, a. 6c; he is referring back to the discussion in a. 4, which (having quoted Augustine's remark (see XII.4, below) about unjust laws not seeming to be law) concludes: "So such [unjust] laws do not oblige in the forum of conscience (except perhaps where the giving of a corrupting example [*scandalum*] or the occasioning of civil disorder [*turbationem*] are to be avoided—for to avoid these, a man ought to yield his right)." He adds that the last-mentioned "exceptional" source or form of obligation to obey the law does not obtain where the injustice of the law is that it promotes something which ought never to be done (forbidden by divine law). Later he speaks similarly of unjust judgments of courts (for "the sentence of the judge is like a particular law for a particular case": II–II, q. 67, a. 1c): e.g., II–II, q. 69, a. 4c, mentioning again *scandalum* and *turbatio*. See also II–II, q. 70, a. 1 ad 2 (the obligation *de jure naturali* to keep a secret may prevail over human law compelling testimony).

that if I am *seen* by fellow citizens to be disobeying or disregarding this "law," the effectiveness of other laws, and/or the general respect of citizens for the authority of a generally desirable ruler or constitution, will probably be weakened, with probable bad consequences for the common good. Does not this collateral fact create a moral obligation? The obligation is to comply with the law, but it should not be treated as an instance of what I have called "legal obligation in the moral sense." For it is not based on the good of *being* law-abiding, but only on the desirability of not rendering ineffective the just parts of the legal system. Hence it will not require compliance with unjust laws according to their tenor or "legislative intent," but only such degree of compliance as is necessary to avoid bringing "the law" (as a whole) "into contempt." This degree of compliance will vary according to time, place, and circumstance; in some limiting cases (e.g., of judges or other officials administering the law) the morally required degree of compliance may amount to full or virtually full compliance, just *as if* the law in question had been a just enactment.

So, if an unjust stipulation is, in fact, homogeneous with other laws in its formal source, in its reception by courts and officials, and in its common acceptance, the good citizen may (not always) be morally required to conform to that stipulation to the extent necessary to avoid weakening "the law," the legal system (of rules, institutions, and dispositions) as a whole. The ruler still has the responsibility of repealing rather than enforcing his unjust law, and in this sense has no right that it should be conformed to. But the citizen, or official, may meanwhile have the diminished, collateral, and in an important sense extra-legal, obligation to obey it.

The foregoing paragraphs oversimplify the problems created for the conscience of reasonable citizens by unreasonableness in lawmaking. They pass over the problems of identifying inequity in distribution of burdens, or excessive or wrongly motivated exercise of authority. They pass over the dilemmas faced by conscientious officials charged with the administration of unjust laws. They pass over all questions about the point at which it may be for the common good to replace a persistently unjust lawmaker, by means that are prohibited by laws of a type normally justified both in their enactment and in their application. They pass over the question whether, notwithstanding the normal impropriety of bringing just laws into contempt, there may be circumstances in which it is justified to use one's public disobedience, whether to an unjust law itself or to a law itself quite just, as an instrument for effecting reform of unjust laws. And they pass over the question whether, in the aftermath of an unjust regime, the responsibility for declaring its unjust laws unjust and for annulling and undoing their legal and other effects should be undertaken by *courts* (on the basis that a court of justice-according-to-law ought not to be required to attribute legal effect to radically unjust laws), or by retrospective *legislation* (on the basis that the change from one legal regime to the other ought to be explicit).

Much can be said on such questions, but little that is not highly contingent upon social, political, and cultural variables. It is universally true that one has an absolute (liberty-) right not to perform acts which anyone has an absolute (claim-) right that one should not perform (VIII.7). But beyond this, one should not expect generally usable but precise guides for action in circumstances where the normally authoritative sources of precise guidance have partially broken down.

3

M.B.E. Smith*

"Is There a Prima Facie Obligation to Obey the Law?"

It isn't a question of whether it was legal or illegal. That isn't enough. The question is, what is morally wrong. (Richard Nixon, "Checkers Speech," 1952)

Many political philosophers have thought it obvious that there is a prima facie obligation to obey the law; and so, in discussing this obligation, they have thought their task to be more that of explaining its basis than of arguing for its existence. John Rawls has, for example, written:

> I shall assume, as requiring no argument, that there is, at least in a society such as ours, a moral obligation to obey the law, although it may, of course, be overriden in certain cases by other more stringent obligations.[1]

As against this, I suggest that it is not at all obvious that there is such an obligation, that this is something that must be shown, rather than so blithely assumed. Indeed, were he uninfluenced by conventional wisdom, a reflective man might on first considering the question be inclined to deny any such obligation: As H. A. Prichard once remarked, "the mere receipt of an order backed by force seems, if anything, to give rise to the duty of resisting, rather than obeying."[2] I shall argue that, although those subject to a government often have a prima facie obligation to obey particular laws (*e.g.*, when disobedience has seriously untoward consequences or involves an act that is *mala in se*), they have no prima facie obligation to obey all its laws. I do not hope to prove this contention beyond a reasonable doubt: My goal is rather the more modest one of showing that it is a reasonable position to maintain by first criticizing arguments that purport to establish the obligation and then presenting some positive argument against it.

First, however, I must explain how I use the phrase "prima facie obligation." I shall say that a person *S* has a prima facie obligation to do an act *X* if, and only if, there is a moral reason for *S* to do *X* which is such that, unless he has a moral reason not to do *X* at least as strong as his reason to do *X*, *S*'s failure to do *X* is wrong.[3] In this discussion it will also be convenient to distinguish two kinds of prima facie obligation via the difference between the two kinds of statement which ascribe them. A specific statement asserts that some particular person has a prima facie obligation to perform some particular act. In contrast, a generic statement (*e.g.*, "Parents have a prima facie obligation to care for their infant children") asserts that everyone who meets a certain description has a prima facie obligation to perform a certain kind of act whenever he has an

---

* Assistant Professor of Philosophy, Smith College. I wish to thank Judith Jarvis Thomson, Hugo A. Bedau, Gerald Barnes, Murray Kiteley, Robert Ackermann, and Stanley Rothman, for their criticism of earlier drafts of this article.

1 Rawls, *Legal Obligation and the Duty of Fair Play*, in Law and Philosophy 10 (S. Hook ed. 1964).

2 H.A. Prichard, *Green's Principles of Political Obligation*, in Moral Obligation 54 (1949).

3 The distinction between prima facie and absolute obligation was first made by W.D. Ross in *The Right and the Good* ch. 2 (1930). My account of prima facie obligation differs somewhat from Ross'; but I believe it adequately captures current philosophical usage. As for absolute obligation, I shall not often speak of it; but when I do, what I shall mean by "*S* has an absolute obligation to do *X*" is that "*S*'s failure to do *X* is wrong."

opportunity to do so. I shall therefore say that a person *S* has a specific prima facie obligation to do *X* if, and only if, the specific statement "*S* has a prima facie obligation to do *X*" is true; and that he has a generic prima facie obligation to do *X* if, and only if, *S* meets some description *D* and the generic statement "Those who are *D* have a prima facie obligation to do *X*" is true.[4]

Now, the question of whether there is a prima facie obligation to obey the law is clearly about a generic obligation. Everyone, even the anarchist, would agree that in many circumstances individuals have specific prima facie obligations to obey specific laws. Since it is clear that there is in most circumstances a specific prima facie obligation to refrain from murder, rape, or breach of contract, it is plain that in these circumstances each of us has a specific prima facie obligation not to violate laws which prohibit these acts. Again, disobeying the law often has seriously untoward consequences; and, when this is so, virtually everyone would agree that there is a specific prima facie obligation to obey. Therefore, the interesting question about our obligation vis-à-vis the law is not "Do individual citizens ever have specific prima facie obligations to obey particular laws?," but rather "Is the moral relation of any government to its citizens such that they have a prima facie obligation to do certain things merely because they are legally required to do so?" This is, of course, equivalent to asking "Is there a generic prima facie obligation to obey the law?" Hereafter, when I use the phrase "the prima facie obligation to obey the law" I shall be referring to a generic obligation.

One final point in clarification: As used here, the phrase "prima facie" bears a different meaning than it does when used in legal writing. In legal materials, the phrase frequently refers to evidence sufficiently persuasive so as to require rebuttal. Hence, were a lawyer to ask "Is there a prima facie obligation to obey the law?," a reasonable interpretation of his question might be "May a reasonable man take mere illegality to be sufficient evidence that an act is morally wrong, so long as there is no specific evidence tending to show it is right?" Let us call this the "lawyer's question." Now, the question of primary concern in this inquiry is "Is there any society in which mere illegality is a moral reason for an act's being wrong?" The difference between these questions is that, were there a prima facie obligation to obey the law in the lawyer's sense, mere illegality would, in the absence of specific evidence to the contrary, be evidence of wrongdoing, but it would not necessarily be relevant to a determination of whether lawbreaking is wrong where there is reason to think such conduct justified or even absolutely obligatory. In contrast, if there is a prima facie obligation to obey the law in the sense in which I am using the phrase, the mere illegality of an act is always relevant to the determination of its moral character, despite whatever other reasons are present.[5] Hence, there may be a prima facie obligation to

4 My motive for distinguishing generic and specific prima facie obligations is simply convenience, and not because I think it provides a perspicuous way of classifying prima facie obligations. As a classification it is obviously defective: The two kinds of obligation overlap, since in a trivial sense every specific obligation can be construed as a generic one; and there are some prima facie obligations (*e.g.*, the obligation to keep one's promise), that fit neither definition.

5 An example may help to make the point clear. If I promise that I will meet someone at a certain time, I have a prima facie obligation to keep my promise. Now, were this merely a prima facie obligation in the lawyer's sense, without evidence to the contrary the fact that I had promised would be sufficient to hold that a breach of my promise was wrong, yet it would not be evidence of wrongdoing were there reason to believe the breach was justified or even obligatory. But, in fact, this is not what we think of promising. We think that if someone promises to do a thing there is a strong moral reason for him to do it and that, although this reason may sometimes be opposed by stronger reasons to the contrary, its weight does not disappear. In such cases, my promise is yet relevant to what I am absolutely obligated to do, although it is not always determinative. But, even when this reason is outweighed, it still discloses its existence by imposing fresh prima facie obligations (*e.g.*, to tell the person I promised why I broke it). Hence, there is a prima facie obligation to keep one's promise in the sense in which I here use the phrase.

obey the law in the lawyer's sense and yet be no such obligation in the sense of the phrase used here. Near the end of this article I shall return briefly to the lawyer's question; for the present, I raise it only that it may not be confused with the question I wish to examine.

I

The arguments I shall examine fall into three groups: First, those which rest on the benefits each individual receives from government; second, those relying on implicit consent or promise; third, those which appeal to utility or the general good. I shall consider each group in turn.

Of those in the first group, I shall begin with the argument from gratitude. Although they differ greatly in the amount of benefits they provide, virtually all governments do confer substantial benefits on their subjects. Now, it is often claimed that, when a person accepts benefits from another, he thereby incurs a debt of gratitude towards his benefactor. Thus, if it be maintained that obedience to the law is the best way of showing gratitude towards one's government, it may with some plausibility be concluded that each person who has received benefits from his government has a prima facie obligation to obey the law.

On reflection, however, this argument is unconvincing. First, it may reasonably be doubted whether most citizens have an obligation to act gratefully towards their government. Ordinarily, if someone confers benefits on me without any consideration of whether I want them, and if he does this in order to advance some purpose other than promotion of my particular welfare, I have no obligation to be grateful towards him. Yet the most important benefits of government are not accepted by its citizens, but are rather enjoyed regardless of whether they are wanted. Moreover, a government typically confers these benefits, not to advance the interests of particular citizens, but rather as a consequence of advancing some purpose of its own. At times, its motives are wholly admirable, as when it seeks to promote the general welfare; at others, they are less so, as when it seeks to stay in power by catering to the demands of some powerful faction. But, such motives are irrelevant: Whenever government forces benefits on me for reasons other than my particular welfare, I clearly am under no obligation to be grateful to it.

Second, even assuming *arguendo* that each citizen has an obligation to be grateful to his government, the argument still falters. It is perhaps true that cheerful and willing obedience is the best way to show one's gratitude towards government, in that it makes his gratitude unmistakable. But, when a person owes a debt of gratitude towards another, he does not necessarily acquire a prima facie obligation to display his gratitude in the most convincing manner: A person with demanding, domineering parents might best display his gratitude towards them by catering to their every whim, but he surely has no prima facie obligation to do so. Without undertaking a lengthy case-by-case examination, one cannot delimit the prima facie obligation of acting gratefully, for its existence and extent depends on such factors as the nature of the benefits received, the manner in which they are conferred, the motives of the benefactor, and so forth. But, even without such an examination, it is clear that the mere fact that a person has conferred on me even the most momentous benefits does not establish his right to dictate all of my behavior; nor does it establish that I always have an obligation to consider his wishes when I am deciding what I shall do. If, then, we have a prima facie obligation to act gratefully towards government, we undoubtedly have an obligation to promote its interests when this does not involve great sacrifice on our part and to respect some of its wishes concerning that part of our behavior which does not directly affect its interests. But, our having this obligation to be grateful surely does not establish that we have a prima facie obligation to obey the law.

A more interesting argument from the benefits individuals receive from government is the argument from fair play. It differs from the argument from gratitude in contending that the prima facie obligation to obey the law is owed, not to one's government but rather to one's fellow citizens. Versions of this argument have been offered by H. L. A. Hart and John Rawls.

According to Hart, the mere existence of cooperative enterprise gives rise to a certain prima facie obligation. He argues that:

> when a number of persons conduct any joint enterprise according to rules and thus restrict their liberty, those who have submitted to these restrictions when required have a right to a similar submission from those who have benefitted by their submission. The rules may provide that officials should have authority to enforce obedience and make further rules, and this will create a structure of legal rights and duties, but the moral obligation to obey the rules in such circumstances is *due to* the cooperating members of the society, and they have the correlative moral right to obedience.[6]

Rawls' account of this obligation in his essay, *Legal Obligation and the Duty of Fair Play*,[7] is rather more complex. Unlike Hart, he sets certain requirements on the kinds of cooperative enterprises that give rise to the obligation: First, that success of the enterprise depends on near-universal obedience to its rules, but not on universal cooperation; second, that obedience to its rules involves some sacrifice, in that obeying the rules restricts one's liberty; and finally, that the enterprise conform to the principles of justice.[8] Rawls also offers an explanation of the obligation: He argues that, if a person benefits from participating in such an enterprise and if he intends to continue receiving its benefits, he acts unfairly when he refuses to obey its rules. With Hart, however, Rawls claims that this obligation is owed not to the enterprise itself, nor to its officials, but rather to those members whose obedience has made the benefits possible. Hart and Rawls also agree that this obligation of fair play—"fair play" is Rawls' term—is a fundamental obligation, not derived from utility or from mutual promise or consent.[9] Finally, both Hart and Rawls conceive of legal systems, at least those in democratic societies, as complex practices of the kind which give rise to the obligation of fair play; and they conclude that those who benefit from such legal systems have a prima facie obligation to obey their laws.

These arguments deserve great respect. Hart and Rawls appear to have isolated a kind of prima facie obligation overlooked by other philosophers and have thereby made a significant contribution to moral theory. However, the significance of their discovery to jurisprudence is

---

6 Hart, *Are There Any Natural Rights?*, 64 Phil. Rev. 185 (1955). I must note that Hart does not use the phrase "prima facie obligation," maintaining that his argument establishes an obligation sans phrase to comply with the rules of cooperative enterprises. However, since his use of "obligation" seems much the same as my use of "prima facie obligation," I shall ignore his terminological scruples.

7 Rawls, *supra* note 26. The same argument appears, although in less detail, in Rawls, *Justice as Fairness*, 67 Phil. Rev. 164 (1958), and Rawls, *The Justification of Civil Disobedience*, in Civil Disobedience: Theory and Practice (H.A. Bedau ed. 1969).

8 Rawls, *Legal Obligation and the Duty of Fair Play*, in Law and Philosophy 10 (S. Hook ed. 1964). According to Rawls, the principles of justice are

> that everyone have an equal right to the most extensive liberty compatible with a like liberty for all; ... [and] that inequalities are arbitrary unless it is reasonable to expect that they will work out for everyone's advantage and provided that the positions and offices to which they attached or from which they may be gained are open to all.

Id. at 11.

9 *Id.* at 15; Hart, *supra* note 31, at 185.

less clear. Although Hart and Rawls have discovered the obligation of fair play, they do not properly appreciate its limits. Once these limits are understood, it is clear that the prima facie obligation to obey the law cannot be derived from the duty of fair play.

The obligation of fair play seems to arise most clearly within small, voluntary cooperative enterprises. Let us suppose that a number of persons have gone off into the wilderness to carve out a new society, and that they have adopted certain rules to govern their communal life. Their enterprise meets Rawls' requirements on success, sacrifice, and justice. We can now examine the moral situation of the members of that community in a number of circumstances, taking seriously Hart's insistence that cooperating members have a right to the obedience of others and Rawls' explanation of this right and its correlative obligation on grounds of fairness.

Let us take two members of the community, *A* and *B*. *B*, we may suppose, has never disobeyed the rules, and *A* has benefitted from *B*'s previous submission. Has *B* a right to *A*'s obedience? It would seem necessary to know the consequences of *A*'s obedience. If, in obeying the rules, *A* will confer on *B* a benefit roughly equal to those he has received from *B*, it would be plainly unfair for *A* to withhold it from *B*; and so, in this instance, *B*'s right to *A*'s obedience is clear. Similarly, if, in disobeying the rule, *A* will harm the community, *B*'s right to *A*'s obedience is again clear. This is because in harming the community *A* will harm *B* indirectly, by threatening the existence or efficient functioning of an institution on which *B*'s vital interests depend. Since *A* has benefitted from *B*'s previous submission to the rules, it is unfair for *A* to do something which will lessen *B*'s chances of receiving like benefits in the future. However, if *A*'s compliance with some particular rule does not benefit *B* and if his disobedience will not harm the community, it is difficult to see how fairness to *B* could dictate that *A* must comply. Surely, the fact that *A* has benefitted from *B*'s submission does not give *B* the right to insist that *A* obey when *B*'s interests are unaffected. *A* may in this situation have an obligation to obey, perhaps because he has promised or because his disobedience would be unfair to some other member; but, if he does disobey, he has surely not been unfair to *B*.

We may generalize from these examples. Considerations of fairness apparently do show that, when cooperation is perfect and when each member has benefitted from the submission of every other, each member of an enterprise has a prima facie obligation to obey its rules when obedience benefits some other member or when disobedience harms the enterprise. For, if in either circumstance a member disobeys, he is unfair to at least one other member and is perhaps unfair to them all. However, if a member disobeys when his obedience would have benefitted no other member and when his disobedience does no harm, his moral situation is surely different. If his disobedience is then unfair, it must be unfair to the group but not to any particular member. But this, I take it, is impossible: Although the moral properties of a group are not always a simple function of the moral properties of its members, it is evident that one cannot be unfair to a group without being unfair to any of its members. It would seem, then, that even when cooperation is perfect, considerations of fairness do not establish that members of a cooperative enterprise have a simple obligation to obey all of its rules, but have rather the more complex obligation to obey when obedience benefits some other member or when disobedience harms the enterprise. This does not; it is worth noting, reduce the obligation of fair play to a kind of utilitarian obligation, for it may well be that fair play will dictate in certain circumstances that a man obey when disobedience would have better consequences. My point is merely that the obligation of fair play governs a man's actions only when some benefit or harm turns on whether he obeys. Surely, this is as should be, for questions of fairness typically arise from situations in which burdens or benefits are distributed or in which some harm is done.

The obligation of fair play is therefore much more complex than Hart or Rawls seem to have imagined. Indeed, the obligation is even more complex than the above discussion suggests, for the assumption of perfect cooperation is obviously unrealistic. When that assumption is abandoned, the effect of previous disobedience considered, and the inevitable disparity among the various members' sacrifice in obeying the rules taken into account, the scope of the obligation is still further limited; we shall then find that it requires different things of different members, depending on their previous pattern of compliance and the amount of sacrifice they have made.[10] These complications need not detain us, however, for they do not affect the fact that fairness requires obedience only in situations where noncompliance would withhold benefits from someone or harm the enterprise. Now it must be conceded that all of this makes little difference when we confine our attention to small, voluntary, cooperative enterprises. Virtually any disobedience may be expected to harm such enterprises to some extent, by diminishing the confidence of other members in its probable success and therefore reducing their incentive to work diligently towards it. Moreover, since they are typically governed by a relatively small number of rules, none of which ordinarily require behavior that is useless to other members, we may expect that when a member disobeys he will probably withhold a benefit from some other member and that he has in the past benefitted significantly from that member's obedience. We may therefore expect that virtually every time the rules of a small, voluntary enterprise call on a member to obey he will have a specific prima facie obligation to do so because of his obligation of fair play.

In the case of legal systems, however, the complexity of the obligation makes a great deal of difference. Although their success may depend on the "habit of obedience" of a majority of their subjects, all legal systems are designed to cope with a substantial amount of disobedience.[11] Hence, individual acts of disobedience to the law only rarely have an untoward effect on legal systems. What is more, because laws must necessarily be designed to cover large numbers of cases, obedience to the law often benefits no one. Perhaps the best illustration is obedience of the traffic code: Very often I benefit no one when I stop at a red light or observe the speed limit. Finally, virtually every legal system contains a number of pointless or even positively harmful laws, obedience to which either benefits no one or, worse still, causes harm. Laws prohibiting homosexual activity or the dissemination of birth

10 Those intrigued by the mention of these additional factors may be interested to know that, when imperfect cooperation is taken into account, it can be shown that considerations of fairness establish no more than: (1) that a member *A* of a cooperative enterprise has a prima facie obligation to obey when his obedience will benefit some other member *B* from whose submission *A* has previously benefitted and it is not the case that *B* has withheld from *A* more significant benefits than *A* withholds from *B*; and (2) that *A* has a prima facie obligation to obey when his disobedience harms the enterprise and there is some other member *B* from whose submission *A* has previously benefitted and *B* has by his disobedience harmed the enterprise less than the harm which would be done by *A*'s disobedience.

As for the effect of disparity in sacrifice, it was only recently suggested to me that this factor must be taken into account, and I have not yet attempted to determine its effects precisely. A moment's reflection discloses, however, that this additional factor would make the obligation still more complex. Were anyone to attempt a precise specification of the citizen's obligations vis-à-vis the laws of his government, he would have to master these complexities; but my task is not so ambitious.

11 Indeed, it seems strange that Rawls should have attempted to base the prima facie obligation to obey the law on fair play, since he maintains that this latter obligation is incurred within cooperative enterprises that depend on near-universal cooperation. Rawls, *Legal Obligation and the Duty of Fair Play*, in Law and Philosophy 10 (S. Hook ed. 1964).

control information are surely in this category. Hence, even if legal systems are the kind of cooperative enterprise that gives rise to the obligation of fair play, in a great many instances that obligation will not require that we obey specific laws. If, then, there is a generic prima facie obligation to obey the laws of any legal system, it cannot rest on the obligation of fair play. The plausibility of supposing that it does depends on an unwarranted extrapolation from what is largely true of our obligations within small, cooperative enterprises to what must always be true of our obligations within legal systems.

In his recent book, Rawls has abandoned the argument from fair play as proof that the entire citizenry of even just governments has a prima facie obligation to obey the law. He now distinguishes between obligations (*e.g.*, to be fair or to keep promises) and natural duties (*e.g.*, to avoid injury to others). Obligations, according to Rawls, are incurred only by one's voluntary acts, whereas this is not true of natural duties.[12] In his book, he retains the obligation of fair play (now "fairness"); but he now thinks that this obligation applies only to those citizens of just governments who hold office or who have advanced their interests through the government. He excludes the bulk of the citizenry from having a prima facie obligation to obey the law on the ground that, for most persons, receiving benefits from government is nothing they do voluntarily, but is rather something that merely happens to them.[13] He does not, however, take this to imply that most citizens of a reasonably just government are morally free to disobey the law: He maintains that everyone who is treated by such a government with reasonable justice has a natural duty to obey all laws that are not grossly unjust, on the ground that everyone has a natural duty to uphold and to comply with just institutions.[14]

It is tempting to criticize Rawls' present position in much the same way that I criticized his earlier one. One might argue that, while it is true that officeholders and those who have profited by invoking the rules of a just government must in fairness comply with its laws when disobedience will result in harm to that government or when it withholds a benefit from some person who has a right to it, it is simply false that fairness dictates obedience when disobedience does no harm or withholds no benefit. One might further argue that the utility of a just government is such that one has a prima facie duty to obey when disobedience is harmful to it, but that, so long as disobedience does no harm, the government's character is irrelevant to the question of whether one has a prima facie obligation to obey. These criticisms would, I think, show that if we are to base our normative ethics on an appeal to intuitively reasonable principles of duty and obligation, Rawls' present position is no more satisfying than is his earlier one. However, although certainly relevant to an assessment of Rawls' present position, these arguments cannot be regarded as decisive, for in his book Rawls does not rely on a bare appeal to moral intuition. He does not disregard the evidence of intuition, and he is glad to enlist its aid when he can; but, in putting forward particular principles of duty and obligation, he is more concerned with showing that they follow from his general theory of justice. Hence, to refute Rawls' present position, one would have to set out his elaborate theory and then show either that it is mistaken or that the particular claims he makes on its basis do not follow from it. Such a task is beyond the scope of this article; and I shall therefore be content to observe that Rawls' present

12 J. Rawls, *A Theory of Justice* 108 (1971).
13 *Id.* at 336, 344.
14 *Id.* at 334–37, 350–62.

position lacks intuitive support and, hence, that it rests solely on a controversial ethical theory and a complicated argument based upon it, neither of which have as yet emerged unscathed from the fire of critical scrutiny. His view deserves great respect and demands extended discussion, but it is not one which we must now accept, on pain of being unreasonable.

II

The second group of arguments are those from implicit consent or promise. Recognizing that among the clearest cases of prima facie obligation are those in which a person voluntarily assumes the obligation, some philosophers have attempted to found the citizen's obligation to obey the law upon his consent or promise to do so. There is, of course, a substantial difficulty in any such attempt, viz., the brute fact that many persons have never so agreed. To accommodate this fact, some philosophers have invoked the concept of implicit promise or consent. In the *Second Treatise*, Locke argued that mere residence in a country, whether for an hour or a lifetime, constitutes implicit consent to its law.[15] Plato[16] and W. D. Ross[17] made the similar argument that residence in a country and appeal to the protection of its laws constitutes an implicit promise to obey.

Nevertheless, it is clear that residence and use of the protection of the law do not constitute any usual kind of consent to a government nor any usual kind of promise to obey its laws. The phrases "implicit consent" and "implicit promise" are somewhat difficult to understand, for they are not commonly used; nor do Locke, Plato, or Ross define them. Still, a natural way of understanding them is to assume that they refer to acts which differ from explicit consent or promise only in that, in the latter cases, the person has said "I consent ..." or "I promise ...," whereas in the former, he has not uttered such words but has rather performed some act which counts as giving consent or making a promise. Now, as recent investigation in the philosophy of language has shown, certain speech acts are performed only when someone utters certain words (or performs some other conventional act) with the intention that others will take what he did as being an instance of the particular act in question.[18] And it is certain that, in their ordinary usage, "consenting" and "promising" refer to speech acts of this kind. If I say to someone, "I promise to give you fifty dollars," but it is clear from the context that I do not intend that others will take my utterance as a promise, no one would consider me as having promised. Bringing this observation to bear on the present argument, it is perhaps possible that some people reside in a country and appeal to the protection of its laws with the intention that others will take their residence and appeal as consent to the laws or as a promise to obey; but this is surely true only of a very small number, consisting entirely of those enamoured with social contract theory.[19]

It may be argued, however, that my criticism rests on an unduly narrow reading of the words "consent" and "promise." Hence, it may be supposed that, if I am to refute the implicit consent or promise arguments, I must show that there is no other sense of the words "consent" or "promise" in which it is true that citizens, merely by living in a state and going about their usual business, thereby consent or promise to obey the law. This objection is difficult to meet, for I know of

15 J. Locke, *Two Treatises of Government* Bk. II, section 119 (1690).
16 Plato, Dialogues 435 (B. Jowett transl. 1892).
17 Ross, *supra* note 28, at 27.
18 Cf. Strawson, *Intention and Convention in Speech Acts*, 73 Phil. Rev. 439, 448–49, 457–59 (1964).
19 A similar argument could also be made utilizing the analysis of promising in J. Searle, *Speech Acts: An Essay in the Philosophy of Language* 60 (1969).

no way to show that there is no sense of either word that is suitable for contractarian purposes. However, I can show that two recent attempts, by John Plamenatz and Alan Gewirth, to refurbish the implicit consent argument along this line have been unsuccessful.[20] I shall not quarrel with their analyses of "consent," though I am suspicious of them; rather, I shall argue that given their definitions of "consent" the fact that a man consents to government does not establish that he has a prima facie obligation to obey the law.

Plamenatz claims that there are two kinds of consent. The first, which is common-garden variety consent, he terms "direct." He concedes that few citizens directly consent to their government.[21] He suggests, however, that there is another kind of consent, which he calls "indirect," and that, in democratic societies, consent in this sense is widespread and establishes a prima facie obligation to obey the law. Indirect consent occurs whenever a person freely votes or abstains from voting.[22] Voting establishes a prima facie obligation of obedience because:

> Even if you dislike the system and wish to change it, you put yourself by your vote under a [prima facie] obligation to obey whatever government comes legally to power.... For the purpose of an election is to give authority to the people who win it and, if you vote knowing what you are doing and without being compelled to do it, you voluntarily take part in a process which gives authority to these people.[23]

Plamenatz does not explain why abstention results in a prima facie obligation, but perhaps his idea is that, if a person abstains, he in effect acknowledges the authority of whoever happens to win.

The key premise then in the argument is that "the purpose of an election is to give authority to the people who win it," and it is clear that Plamenatz believes that this implies that elections do give authority to their winners. In assessing the truth of these contentions, it is, of course, vital to know what Plamenatz means by "authority." Unfortunately, he does not enlighten us, and we must therefore speculate as to his meaning. To begin, the word "authority," when used without qualification, is often held to mean the same as "legitimate authority." Since prima facie obligation is the weakest kind of obligation, part of what we mean when we ascribe authority to some government is that those subject to it have at least a prima facie obligation to obey. However, if this is what Plamenatz means by "authority," his argument simply begs the question: For, in order to be justified in asserting that the purpose of an election is to confer authority and that elections succeed in doing this, he must first show that everyone subject to an elected government has a prima facie obligation to obey its law, both those eligible to vote and those ineligible.

It is possible, however, that Plamenatz is using "authority" in some weaker sense, one that

20 Another recent tacit consent theory is found in J. Tussman, *Obligation and the Body Politic* (1960). I shall not discuss this theory, however, because it has already received adequate criticism in Pitkin, *Obligation and Consent I*, 59 Am. Pol. Sci. Rev. 990 (1965). Nor shall I discuss Pitkin's own "hypothetical consent" theory that obedience is owed to those governments to which one ought to consent, because in her discussion of how political obligation is justified she does not appeal to the concept of hypothetical consent. She takes the problem of justifying political obligation to be the question "Why am I ever obligated to obey even legitimate authority?" She gives the question short shrift, however, replying that it is simply part of the meaning of the phrase "legitimate authority" that those subject to legitimate authority have a prima facie obligation to obey it. See Pitkin, *Obligation and Consent II*, 60 Am. Pol. Sci. Rev. 39, 45–49 (1966).

21 J. Plamenatz, Man and Society 228, 238–59 (1963).

22 *Id.* at 239–40.

23 *Id.*

does not entail that everyone subject to it has a prima facie obligation to obey. If this is so, his premises will perhaps pass, but he must then show that those who are eligible to take part in conferring authority have a prima facie obligation to obey it. However, it is difficult to see how this can be done. First, as Plamenatz recognizes, voting is not necessarily consenting in the "direct" or usual sense, and merely being eligible to vote is even more clearly not consenting. Hence, the alleged prima facie obligation of obedience incurred by those eligible to vote is not in consequence of their direct consent. Second, Plamenatz cannot appeal to "common moral sentiment" to bolster his argument: This is because if we really believed that those eligible to vote have a prima facie obligation to obey, an obligation not incurred by the ineligible, we should then believe that the eligible have a stronger obligation than those who are ineligible. But, as far as I can tell, we do not ordinarily think that this is true. Finally, Plamenatz cannot rely on a purely conceptual argument to make his point. It is by no means an analytic truth that those subject to elected governments have a prima facie obligation to obey the law.[24] The radical who says, "The present government of the United States was freely elected, but because it exploits people its citizens have no obligation to obey it," has perhaps said something false, but he has not contradicted himself. Plamenatz's argument is therefore either question-begging or inconclusive, depending on what he means by "authority."

Gewirth's argument is similar to Plamenatz's in that he also holds that a person's vote establishes his prima facie obligation of obedience. He argues that men consent to government when "certain institutional arrangements exist in the community as a whole," including "the maintenance of a method which leaves open to every sane, noncriminal adult the opportunity to discuss, criticize, and vote for or against the government."[25] He holds that the existence of such consent "justifies" government and establishes the subject's prima facie obligation to obey because:

> The method of consent combines and safeguards the joint values of freedom and order as no other method does. It provides a choice in the power of government which protects the rights of the electorate more effectively than does any other method. It does more justice to man's potential rationality than does any other method, for it gives all men the opportunity to participate in a reasoned discussion of the problem of society and to make their discussion effective in terms of political control.[26]

---

24 A defender of Plamenatz, John Jenkins, appears to hold that something like this is an analytic truth, maintaining that:

> if a person supposes that he has no obligation to a successful candidate because that candidate happens not to be the person for whom he cast his vote, then there is an excellent case for saying that the man has failed to understand the nature of the electoral process.

Jenkins, *Political Consent*, 20 Phil. Q. 61 (1970).

This seems a silly claim. Many who voted for George McGovern believe themselves to be under no obligation to Richard Nixon. Some are highly educated and close observers of the political scene. Were such a person to explain his belief that he is not obligated to Nixon solely on the ground that he did not vote for him, we might think him mistaken or wish that he had chosen a better reason, but we should have no reason at all to think that he fails to understand "the nature of the electoral process."

25 Earlier in his discussion Gewirth distinguishes three senses of "consent": an "occurrence" sense, a "dispositional" sense, and an "opportunity" sense. *Id.* at 131. It is only the last that will concern us here, since he admits that the prima facie obligation to obey the law cannot be shown by relying on the occurrence or the dispositional senses. Gewirth, *Political Justice*, in Social Justice 138 (R. Brandt ed. 1962).

26 *Id.* at 139.

As it stands, Gewirth's argument is incomplete. He makes certain claims about the benefits of government by consent which are open to reasonable doubt. Some communists, for example, would hold that Gewirth's method of consent has led to exploitation, and that human rights and freedom are better protected by the rule of the party. This aside, Gewirth's argument still needs strengthening. The fact that certain benefits are given only by government with a method of consent establishes only that such a government is better than one which lacks such a method. But, to show that one government is better than another, or even to show that it is the best possible government, does not prove that its subjects have a prima facie obligation to obey its laws: There is a prior question, which remains to be settled, as to whether there can be a prima facie obligation to obey any government. Gewirth does not carry the argument farther in his discussion of "consent," but earlier in his paper he hints as to how he would meet this objection. He argues that "government as such" is justified, or made legitimate, by its being necessary to avoid certain evils.[27] Indeed, although he does not explicitly so state, he seems to think that utilitarian considerations demonstrate that there is a prima facie obligation to obey any government that protects its subjects from these evils, but that there is an additional prima facie obligation to obey a government with a method of consent because of the more extensive benefits it offers. In the next section, I shall discuss whether a direct appeal to utility can establish a prima facie obligation to obey the law.

III

I shall consider three utilitarian arguments: the first appealing to a weak form of act-utilitarianism, the second and third to rule-utilitarian theories. To my knowledge, the first argument has never been explicitly advanced. It is nevertheless worth considering, both because it possesses a certain plausibility and because it has often been hinted at when philosophers, lawyers, and political theorists have attempted to derive an obligation to obey the law from the premise that government is necessary to protect society from great evil. The argument runs as follows:

> There is obviously a prima facie obligation to perform acts which have good consequences. Now, government is absolutely necessary for securing the general good: The alternative is the state of nature in which everyone is miserable, in which life is "solitary, poor, nasty, brutish and short." But, no government can long stand in the face of widespread disobedience, and government can therefore promote the general good only so long as its laws are obeyed. Therefore, obedience to the law supports the continued existence of government and, hence, always has good consequences. From this it follows that there is a prima facie obligation to obey the law.

On even brief scrutiny, however, this argument quickly disintegrates. The first thing to be noticed is that its principle of prima facie obligation is ambiguous. It may be interpreted as postulating either (a) an obligation to perform those acts which have any good consequences, or (b) an obligation to perform optimific acts (i.e., those whose consequences are better than their alternatives). Now, (a) and (b) are in fact very different principles. The former is obviously absurd. It implies, for example, that I have a prima facie obligation to kill whomever I meet, since this would have the good consequence of helping to reduce overpopulation. Thus, the only weak

27 *Id.* at 135.

act-utilitarian principle with any plausibility is (b). But, regardless of whether (b) is acceptable—and some philosophers would not accept it—[28] the conclusion that there is a prima facie obligation to obey the law, cannot be derived from it, inasmuch as there are obvious and familiar cases in which breach of a particular law has better consequences than obedience. The only conclusion to be derived from (b) is that there is a specific prima facie obligation to obey the law whenever obedience is optimific. But no generic prima facie obligation to obey can be derived from weak act-utilitarianism.[29]

The second utilitarian argument appeals not to the untoward consequences of individual disobedience, but rather to those of general disobedience. Perhaps the most common challenge to those who defend certain instances of civil disobedience is "What would happen if everyone disobeyed the law?" One of the arguments implicit in this question is the generalization argument, which may be expanded as follows:

> No one can have a right to do something unless everyone has a right to do it. Similarly, an act cannot be morally indifferent unless it would be morally indifferent if everyone did it. But, everyone's breaking the law is not a matter of moral indifference; for no government can survive in such a circumstance and, as we have already agreed, government is necessary for securing and maintaining the general good. Hence, since the consequences of general disobedience would be disastrous, each person subject to law has a prima facie obligation to obey it.

In assessing this argument, we must first recognize that the generalization argument is a moral criterion to be applied with care, as virtually everyone who has discussed it has recognized.[30] If we simply note that if everyone committed a certain act there would be disastrous consequences and thereupon conclude that there is a prima facie obligation not to commit acts of that kind, we will be saddled with absurdities. We will have to maintain, for example, that there is a prima facie obligation not to eat dinner at five o'clock, for if everyone did so, certain essential services could not be maintained. And, for similar reasons, we will have to maintain that there is a prima facie obligation not to produce food. Now, those who believe that the generalization argument is valid argue that such absurdities arise when the criterion is applied to acts which are either too generally described or described in terms of morally irrelevant features. They would argue that the generalization argument appears to go awry when applied to these examples because the description "producing food" is too general to give the argument purchase and

28 For example, some philosophers would hold that there is a prima facie obligation to refrain from acts which have undesirable consequences, but not that there is an obligation to perform the one act which has the best consequences. See, *e.g.*, M.G. Singer, *Generalization in Ethics*, ch. 7 (1961).

29 For purposes of clarification, I should emphasize that I am here concerned with act utilitarianism as a theory of prima facie, not absolute, obligation. There is no incongruity here. The consequences of acts count as having great moral significance on virtually every moral theory; and so, one need not be a strict act utilitarian in order to maintain the principle that there is a prima facie obligation to act optimifically. Indeed, for a strict act utilitarian such as Bentham, it is pointless to worry about whether there is a prima facie obligation to obey the law: He would hold that there is an absolute obligation to obey the law when, and only when, obedience is optimific, and would there end the discussion. At most, an act utilitarian would hold that the rule "Obey the law" is a useful rule of thumb, to be followed only when the consequences of obedience or disobedience are difficult to discern.

30 Singer, *supra* note 53, at ch. 4.

because the temporal specification in "eating dinner at five o'clock" is morally irrelevant.[31]

However, such a restriction on the generalization argument is fatal to its use in proving a prima facie obligation to obey the law. This is because a person who denies any such obligation is surely entitled to protest that the description "breaking the law" is overly general, on the ground that it refers to acts of radically different moral import.[32] Breaking the law perhaps always has some bad consequences; but sometimes the good done by it balances the bad or even outweighs it. And, once we take these differences in consequences into account, we find that utilitarian generalization, like weak act-utilitarianism, can only establish a specific prima facie obligation to obey the law when obedience is optimific. Were everyone to break the law when obedience is optimific, the consequences would undoubtedly be disastrous; but it is by no means clear that it would be disastrous if everyone broke the law when obedience is not optimific. Since no one knows, with respect to any society, how often obedience is not optimific, no one can be certain as to the consequences of everyone acting in this way. Indeed, for all we know, if everyone broke the law when obedience was not optimific the good done by separate acts of lawbreaking might more than compensate for any public disorder which might result. In sum, even if the generalization argument is regarded as an acceptable principle of prima facie obligation, the most it demonstrates is that there is a specific prima facie obligation to obey the law whenever the consequences of obedience are optimific.

Some readers—especially those unfamiliar with the recent literature on utilitarianism[33]—may suspect that this last argument involves sleight of hand. They may object:

> In your discussion of the generalization argument, you argued that we have no way of knowing the consequences if everyone disobeyed when obedience was not optimific. But, your argument rests on the premise that the act-utilitarian formula can be perfectly applied, whereas this is in fact impossible: The consequences of many acts are difficult or impossible to foretell; and so, were we all to attempt to be act utilitarians, we would either make horrendous mistakes or be paralyzed into inaction. In constructing a rule-utilitarian theory of prima facie obligations, we should therefore concentrate not on the consequences of everyone following certain rules, but rather on the consequences of everyone trying to follow them. And, it seems reasonable to believe that, on such a theory, the rule "Obey the law" would receive utilitarian blessing.

As it stands, this objection is overdrawn. My argument does not presuppose that persons can

31 I have borrowed these cases and this strategy for handling them from Singer. *Id.* at 71–83.

32 According to Singer, a mark of a description's being overly general is that the generalization argument is "invertible" with respect to it, *i.e.*, the consequences of everyone's doing the act (given that description) is disastrous and the consequences of everyone's failing to do it is also disastrous. *Id.* at 76–77. It is relesant to note that the generalization argument is plainly invertible with respect to the description "breaking the law." Sometimes breaking the law is the only way to avoid a great evil; and so, if everyone were always to obey the law, such evils could never be avoided.

33 That the generalization argument and weak act utilitarianism offer the same advice on the topic of obedience to the law should surprise no one familiar with D. Lyons, *Forms and Limits of Utilitarianism* (1965). Lyons there shows that act utilitarianism and the generalization argument are extensionally equivalent. There is, it should be noted, a substantial difference between Lyons' argument for equivalence and the argument I have here offered. Lyons argues for equivalence on a priori grounds, whereas I have relied on the empirical impossibility of determining the consequences of everyone disobeying the law when obedience is not optimific.

generally succeed in applying the act-utilitarian formula: I merely speculated on the consequences of everyone behaving in a certain way; and I made no assumption as to what made them act that way. Moreover, the objection severely overestimates the difficulty in being a confirmed act-utilitarian. Still, the objection makes one substantial point that deserves further attention. Rule-utilitarian theories which focus on the consequences of everyone accepting (although not always following) a certain set of rules do differ markedly from the generalization argument; and so the question remains as to whether such a theory could establish a prima facie obligation to obey the law. I shall therefore discuss whether the most carefully developed such theory, that given by R. B. Brandt,[34] does just this.

In Brandt's theory, one's obligations are (within certain limits) relative to his society and are determined by the set of rules whose acceptance in that society would have better consequences than would acceptance of any other set.[35] According to this theory, then, there can be a generic prima facie obligation to obey the law within a given society if, and only if, general acceptance of the rule "Obey the law," as a rule of prima facie obligation, would have better consequences than were no rule accepted with respect to obeying the law, as well as better consequences than were some alternative rule accepted (*e.g.*, "Obey the law when obedience to the law is optimific," or "Obey the law so long as it is just"). Now, to many it may seem obvious that the ideal set of rules for any society will contain the rule "Obey the law," on the ground that, were its members not generally convinced of at least a prima facie obligation to obey, disobedience would be widespread, resulting in a great many crimes against person and property. But, there are two reasons to doubt such a gloomy forecast. First, we must surely suppose that in this hypothetical society the laws are still backed by sanctions, thereby giving its members a strong incentive to obey its laws. Second, we must also assume that the members of that society accept other moral rules (*e.g.*, "Do not harm others," "Keep promises," "Tell the truth") which will give them a moral incentive to obey the law in most circumstances. It is, in short, a mistake to believe that unless people are convinced that they have a generic prima facie obligation to obey the law, they cannot be convinced that in most circumstances they have a specific prima facie obligation to obey particular laws. We may therefore expect that, even though members of our hypothetical society do not accept a moral rule about obedience to the law per se, they will still feel a prima facie obligation to act in accordance with the law, save when disobedience does no harm. There is, then, no reason to think that an orgy of lawbreaking would ensue were no rule about obedience to the law generally recognized; nor, I think, is there any good reason to believe that acceptance of the rule "Obey the law" would in any society have better consequences than were no such rule recognized. And, if this is so, there is surely no reason

---

34 Brandt, *Toward a Credible Utilitarianism*, in *Morality and the Language of Conduct* 107 (H.N. Costenada & G. Nakhnikian eds. 1963). In the following I shall not be attacking a position Brandt holds, but only an argument that might be offered on the basis of his theory. In fact, in *Utility and the Obligation to Obey the Law*, in Law and Philosophy 43, 47–49 (S. Hook ed. 1964), Brandt expresses doubt as to whether there is such an obligation.

35 According to Brandt's theory, there is an absolute obligation to perform an act if it conforms with that learnable set of rules the recognition of which as morally binding—roughly at the time of the act—by everyone in the society of the agent, except for the retention by individuals of already formed and decided moral convictions, would maximize intrinsic value. Brandt, *Toward a Credible Utilitarianism*, in Morality and the Language of Conduct 107, 139 (H.N. Castenada & G. Nakhnikian eds. 1963). He distinguishes three levels of rules, the first stating prima facie obligations and the latter two dealing with cases in which lower-level rules conflict. At every level, however, those in the favored set of rules are those whose recognition would have the best consequences, i.e., consequences better than were any alternative rule accepted, as well as better than were no such rule accepted. *Id.* at 118–19.

to think that recognition of this rule would have better consequences than recognition of some alternative rule. In sum, Brandt's theory requires that we be able to determine the truth-value of a large number of counterfactual propositions about what would happen were entire societies persuaded of the truth of certain moral rules. But, even if we assume—and it is hardly clear that we should[36]—that we can reliably determine the truth-value of such counter-factuals through "common sense" and our knowledge of human nature, Brandt's form of rule utilitarianism gives no support for the proof of a prima facie obligation to obey the law.

IV

In the foregoing discussion, I have played the skeptic, contending that no argument has as yet succeeded in establishing a prima facie obligation to obey the law. I want now to examine this supposed obligation directly. I shall assume *arguendo* that such an obligation exists in order to inquire as to how it compares in moral weight with other prima facie obligations. As we shall see, this question is relevant to whether we should hold that such an obligation exists.

To discuss this question, I must, of course, first specify some test for determining the weight of a prima facie obligation. It will be recalled that I defined "prima facie obligation" in terms of wrongdoing: To say that a person *S* has a prima facie obligation to do an act *X* is to say that *S* has a moral reason to do *X* which is such that, unless he has a reason not to do *X* that is at least as strong, *S*'s failure to do *X* is wrong. Now, we are accustomed, in our reflective moral practice, to distinguish degrees of wrongdoing. And so, by appealing to this notion, we can formulate two principles that may reasonably be held to govern the weight of prima facie obligations: First, that a prima facie obligation is a serious one if, and only if, an act which violates that obligation and fulfils no other is seriously wrong; and, second, that a prima facie obligation is a serious one if, and only if, violation of it will make considerably worse an act which on other grounds is already wrong.[37] These principles, which constitute tests for determining an obligation's weight, are closely related, and application of either to a given prima facie obligation is a sufficient measure; but I shall apply both to the presumed prima facie obligation to obey the law in order to make my argument more persuasive.

First, however, we should convince ourselves of the reliability of these tests by applying them to some clear cases. I suppose it will be granted that we all have a prima facie obligation not to kill (except perhaps in self-defense), and that this obligation is most weighty. Our first test corroborates this, for, if a person kills another when he is not defending himself and if he has no specific prima facie obligation to kill that person, his act is seriously wrong. By contrast, our prima facie obligation to observe rules of etiquette—if indeed there is any such obligation—is clearly trifling. This is borne out by our test, for if I belch audibly

36 As an illustration of the difficulty, Brandt suggests that the first-level rule "Keep your promises" is neither the one that we accept nor the rule about promising that would maximize utility. *Id.* at 131–32. I think he is right to say that it is not the rule we accept, but how does he know that some more complex rule maximizes utility?

37 The second principle may be thought objectionable on the ground that it trivializes obviously weighty prima facie obligations. It may perhaps be held that, were a man to kill a thousand persons, his act would not have been much worse had he killed but one more. The principle therefore seems to imply that the prima facie obligation not to kill that one person is trivial. The objection is plausible, but misguided. Surely there is a substantial moral difference between killing a thousand persons and killing a thousand-and-one—exactly the difference between killing one person and killing none. To deny this is to imply that the thousand-and-first person's life has little moral significance. At first glance, however, we may be inclined to take the difference to be trivial, because both acts are so monstrous that we should rarely see any point in distinguishing between them. That this objection might be raised against the principle was pointed out to me by Anne Bowen.

in the company of those who think such behavior rude, my wrongdoing is at most trivial. The same results are obtained under our second test. If I attempt to extort money from someone my act is much worse if I kill one of his children and threaten the rest than if I merely threatened them all; and so the obligation not to kill again counts as substantial. Similarly, the prima facie obligation to observe the rules of etiquette is again trivial, for if I am rude during the extortion my act is hardly worse than it would have been had I been polite.

By neither of these tests, however, does the prima facie obligation to obey the law count as substantial. As for the first test, let us assume that while driving home at two o'clock in the morning I run a stop sign. There is no danger, for I can see clearly that there was no one approaching the intersection, nor is there any impressionable youth nearby to be inspired to a life of crime by my flouting of the traffic code. Finally, we may assume that I nevertheless had no specific prima facie obligation to run the stop sign. If, then, my prima facie obligation to obey the law is of substantial moral weight, my action must have been a fairly serious instance of wrongdoing. But clearly it was not. If it was wrong at all—and to me this seems dubious—it was at most a mere peccadillo. As for the second test, we may observe that acts which are otherwise wrong are not made more so—if they are made worse at all—by being illegal.[38] If I defraud someone my act is hardly worse morally by being illegal than it would have been were it protected by some legal loophole. Thus, if there is a prima facie obligation to obey the law, it is at most of trifling weight.

This being so, I suggest that considerations of simplicity indicate that we should ignore the supposed prima facie obligation to obey the law and refuse to count an act wrong merely because it violates some law. There is certainly nothing to be lost by doing this, for we shall not thereby recommend or tolerate any conduct that is seriously wrong, nor shall we fail to recommend any course of action that is seriously obligatory. Yet, there is much to be gained, for in refusing to let trivialities occupy our attention, we shall not be diverted from the important questions to be asked about illegal conduct, *viz.*, "What kind of act was it?," "What were its consequences?," "Did the agent intend its consequences?," and so forth. Morality is, after all, a serious business; and we are surely right not to squander our moral attention and concern on matters of little moral significance.

To illustrate what can be gained, let us consider briefly the issue of civil disobedience. Most philosophers who have written on the subject have argued that, at least in democratic societies, there is always a strong moral reason to obey the law. They have therefore held that civil disobedience is a tactic to be employed only when all legal means of changing an unjust law have failed, and that the person who engages in it must willingly accept punishment as a mark of respect for the law and recognition of the seriousness of lawbreaking. However, once we abandon the notion that civil disobedience is morally significant per se, we shall judge it in the same way we judge most other kinds of acts, that is, on the basis of their character and consequences. Indeed, we can then treat civil disobedience just as we regard many other species of illegal conduct. If breaking the law involves an act which is *mala in se* or if it has untoward consequences, we are ordinarily prepared to condemn it and to think that the malefactor ought to accept punishment.

---

38 I have taken this point from W. Blackstone, *Commentaries* 54:

> Neither do divine or natural *duties* (such as, for instance, the worship of God, the maintenance of children, and the like) receive any stronger sanction from being also declared to be duties by the law of the land. The case is the same as to crimes and misdemeanors, that are forbidden by the superior laws, and therefore styled *mala in se*, such as murder, theft, and perjury; which contract no additional turpitude from being declared unlawful by the inferior legislature.

But if lawbreaking does not involve an act that is *mala in se* and if it has no harmful consequences, we do not ordinarily condemn it, nor do we think that its perpetrator must accept punishment, unless evading punishment itself has untoward consequences. If we adopt this view of civil disobedience, we shall have done much to escape the air of mystery that hovers about most discussions of it.

Of course, this is not to say it will be easy to determine when civil disobedience is justified. Some have maintained that the civil disobedience of the last decade has led to increasing violation of laws which safeguard people and property.[39] If this is true, each instance of disobedience which has contributed to this condition has a share in the evil of the result. Others maintain that such disobedience has had wholly good consequences, that it has helped to remedy existing injustice and to restrain government from fresh injustice.[40] Still others think its consequences are mixed. Which position is correct is difficult to determine. I myself am inclined to believe that, although the consequences have been mixed, the good far outweigh the bad; but I would be hard pressed to prove it. What is clear, however, is that either abandoning or retaining the supposed prima facie obligation to obey the law will not help settle these questions about consequences. But, if we do abandon it, we shall then at least be able to focus on these questions without having to worry about a prima facie obligation of trivial weight that must nevertheless somehow be taken into account. Finally, if we abandon the prima facie obligation to obey the law, we shall perhaps look more closely at the character of acts performed in the course of civil disobedience, and this may, in turn, lead to fruitful moral speculation. For example, we shall be able to distinguish between acts which cannot conceivably violate the obligation of fair play (*e.g.*, burning one's draft card) and acts which may do so (*e.g.*, tax refusal or evasion of military service). This in turn may provide an incentive to reflect further on the obligation of fair play, to ask, for example, whether Rawls is right in his present contention that a person can incur the obligation of fair play only so long as his acceptance of the benefits of a cooperative enterprise is wholly voluntary.

V

It is now time to take stock. I initially suggested that it is by no means obvious that there is any prima facie obligation to obey the law. In the foregoing, I have rejected a number of arguments that purport to establish its existence. The only plausible argument I have not rejected is the one of Rawls that purports to prove that there is a natural duty to obey the laws of reasonably just governments. However, I did note that his position lacks intuitive support and rests on a controversial ethical theory which has not yet withstood the test of critical scrutiny. Finally, I have shown that even if such an obligation is assumed, it is of trivial weight and that there are substantial advantages in ignoring it. I suggest that all of this makes it reasonable to maintain that there is in no society a prima facie obligation to obey the law.

Before I conclude my discussion, however, I want to tie up one loose thread. Near the beginning of my argument I distinguished the question to be discussed from that which I called the lawyer's question, "May a reasonable man take mere illegality to be sufficient evidence that an act is morally wrong, so long as he lacks specific evidence that tends to show that it is right?" Since I have raised the question, I believe that, for the sake of completeness, I should consider it, if only briefly. To begin, it seems very doubtful that there

39 C. Whittaker, *First Lecture*, in Law, Order and Civil Disobedience (1967).
40 *See* H. Zinn, Disobedience and Democracy (1968).

is, in the lawyer's sense, a prima facie obligation to obey the law. It is undoubtedly true that most instances of lawbreaking are wrong, but it is also true that many are not: This is because there are, as Lord Devlin once remarked, "many fussy regulations whose breach it would be pedantic to call immoral,"[41] and because some breaches of even non-fussy regulations are justified. Now, unless—as in a court of law—there is some pressing need to reach a finding, the mere fact that most *A*s are also *B* does not, in the absence of evidence that a particular *A* is not *B*, warrant an inference that the *A* in question is also a *B*: In order for this inference to be reasonable, one must know that virtually all *A*s are *B*s. Since, then, it rarely happens that there is a pressing need to reach a moral finding, and since to know merely that an act is illegal is not to know very much of moral significance about it, it seems clear that, if his only information about an act was that it was illegal, a reasonable man would withhold judgment until he learned more about it. Indeed, this is not only what the fictitious reasonable man would do, it is what we should expect the ordinary person to do. Suppose we were to ask a large number of people: "Jones has broken a law; but I won't tell you whether what he did is a serious crime or merely violation of a parking regulation, nor whether he had good reason for his actions. Would you, merely on the strength of what I have just told you, be willing to say that what he did was morally wrong?" I have conducted only an informal poll; but, on its basis, I would wager that the great majority would answer "I can't yet say—you must tell me more about what Jones did."

More importantly, it appears to make little difference what answer we give to the lawyer's question. While an affirmative answer establishes a rule of inference that an illegal act is wrong in the absence of specific information tending to show it to be right, it is a rule that would in fact virtually never be applied in any reasonable determination of whether an illegal act is wrong. If, on the one hand, we have specific information about an illegal act which tends to show it to be right, then the rule is irrelevant to our determination of the act's moral character. Should we be inclined, in this instance, to hold the act wrong we must have specific information which tends to show this; and it is clear that our conclusions about its moral character must be based on this specific information, and not on the supposed reasonableness of holding illegal conduct wrong in the absence of specific information tending to show it is right. On the other hand, if we have specific information tending to show that an illegal act is wrong and no information tending to show it is right, the rule is applicable but otiose: Since we have ample specific reason to condemn the act, the rule is superfluous to our judgment. It would seem, then, that the rule is relevant only when we have no specific information about the illegal conduct's rightness or wrongness; and this, I suggest, is something that virtually never occurs. When we are prompted to make a moral judgment about an illegal act, we virtually always know something of its character or at least its consequences; and it is these that we consider important in determining the rightness or wrongness of lawbreaking. In short, it seems to make little difference what answer we give to the lawyer's question; I raise it here only that it may hereafter be ignored.

In conclusion, it is, I think, important to recognize that there is nothing startling in what I am recommending, nothing that in any way outrages common sense. Even the most conscientious men at times violate trivial and pointless laws for some slight gain in convenience and, when they do so, they do not feel shame or remorse. Similarly, when they observe other men behaving in a like fashion, they do not think of passing

41 P. Devlin, *The Enforcement of Morals* 27 (1965).

moral censure. For most people, violation of the law becomes a matter for moral concern only when it involves an act which is believed to be wrong on grounds apart from its illegality. Hence, anyone who believes that the purpose of normative ethics is to organize and clarify our reflective moral practice should be skeptical of any argument purporting to show that there is a prima facie obligation to obey the law. It is necessary to state this point with care: I am not contending that reflective and conscientious citizens would, if asked, deny that there is a prima facie obligation to obey the law. Indeed, I am willing to concede that many more would affirm its existence than deny it. But, this is in no way inconsistent with my present point. We often find that reflective people will accept general statements which are belied by their actual linguistic practice. That they also accept moral generalizations that are belied by their actual reflective moral practice should occasion no surprise.

This last point may, however, be challenged on the ground that it implies that there is in our reflective moral practice no distinction between raw power and legitimate authority. As I noted above, the concept of legitimate authority is often analyzed in terms of the right to command, where "right" is used in the strict sense as implying some correlative obligation of obedience. Given this definition, if it is true that the principle "There is a prima facie obligation to obey the law" is not observed in our reflective moral practice, it follows that we do not really distinguish between governments which possess legitimate authority (*e.g.*, that of the United States) and those which do not (*e.g.*, the Nazi occupation government of France). And this, it may justly be held, is absurd. What I take this argument to show, however, is not that the principle is enshrined in our reflective morality, but rather that what we ordinarily mean when we ascribe legitimate authority to some government is not captured by the usual analysis of "legitimate authority." It is a mistake to believe that, unless we employ the concept of authority as it is usually analyzed, we cannot satisfactorily distinguish between the moral relation of the government of the United States vis-à-vis Americans and the moral relation of the Nazi occupation government vis-à-vis Frenchmen. One way of doing this, for example, is to define "legitimate authority" in terms of "the right to command and to enforce obedience," where "right" is used in the sense of "what is morally permissible." Thus, according to this analysis of the notion, the government of the United States counts as having legitimate authority over its subjects because within certain limits there is nothing wrong in its issuing commands to them and enforcing their obedience, whereas the Nazi occupation government lacked such authority because its issuing commands to Frenchmen was morally impermissible. It is not my intention to proffer this as an adequate analysis of the notion of legitimate authority or to suggest that it captures what we ordinarily mean when we ascribe such authority to some government. These are difficult matters, and I do not wish to address myself to them here. My point is rather that the questions "What governments enjoy legitimate authority?" and "Have the citizens of any government a prima facie obligation to obey the law?" both can be, and should be, kept separate.

Study Questions

1. Is practical reason of the type discussed by Aquinas and Finnis relative to particular times, places, or cultures?
2. How persuasive is Finnis's account of situations in which legal obligations are properly rejected and disobeyed? Can Finnis's account be made more precise or thorough?
3. What implications does natural law theory have for tolerance of diverse ways of life?
4. How persuasive is Finnis's argument that descriptive jurisprudence is not useful unless it proceeds with the goals of prescription or reform in mind?
5. Are "basic goods" of the kind discussed by Finnis really universal for all humans, or do these goods reflect a male-centered or other kind of elite view of our lives and needs?
6. Are there resources in natural law theory that could help to answer the challenge Smith identifies, that there is no prima facie obligation to obey the law?

Further Readings

American Journal of Jurisprudence
Aristotle, *Nicomachean Ethics*, trans. T. Irwin. Indianapolis: Hackett, 1985.
Anver Emon, *Islamic Natural Law Theories*. Oxford: Oxford UP, 2010.
John Finnis, ed., *Natural Law*. 2 vols. Aldershot: Ashgate, 1991.
Lon L. Fuller, *The Morality of Law*. New Haven: Yale UP, 1969.
Robert P. George, *In Defense of Natural Law*. Oxford: Clarendon P, 1999.
—, ed., *Natural Law Theory: Contemporary Essays*. Oxford: Oxford UP, 1992.
Mark C. Murphy, *Natural Law in Jurisprudence and Politics*. Cambridge: Cambridge UP, 2006.

SECTION 2

Legal Positivism

Introduction

This section presents the work of writers who defend the idea called legal positivism. Most simply put, legal positivists argue that there is no necessary connection between law and morality. Our readings begin with the work of the Victorian-era lawyer and theorist John Austin (1790–1859). Austin trained and practiced briefly as a lawyer, but found his abilities lay in directions other than practice. Through the efforts of Utilitarian philosopher Jeremy Bentham and other prominent thinkers, Austin was the first person to hold the Chair in Jurisprudence and the Law of Nations at the University of London. There he gave the lectures leading to *The Province of Jurisprudence Determined*, in which he argued that we must distinguish "law as it is from law as it ought to be."[1] This introduction will focus on the English legal philosopher H.L.A. Hart, the best-known modern defender of legal positivism. For many years his work was regarded as "the ruling theory of law," even by his critics.[2] Professor Hart was a successful lawyer before World War II (1939–45), and in 1948 he became Professor of Jurisprudence in Oxford University where he spent the remainder of his long career until his death in 1992. Professor Hart is most famous for his new defense of the central idea of legal positivism in his book *The Concept of Law*. The articles included in this section contain Austin's argument for legal positivism and Hart's proposed modifications. We also include a selection from Hart's most prominent critic, Ronald Dworkin. The debate between Hart and Dworkin over the nature of law and judges' interpretation of it began in earnest following the publication of *The Concept of Law* in 1961, which seemed to offer the best account of law. Dworkin subsequently offered widely accepted arguments against Hart's view, and positivism is no longer clearly the ruling theory of law. As the consequences of the Hart-Dworkin debate have been explored by legal theorists, new positivist theories are being developed by some of the authors listed in the *Further Readings* for this chapter.

1. Why Separate Law and Morality?

It is important to understand the social context of Hart's defense of legal positivism. Hart's appointment at Oxford came in 1948, in a world recovering from the physical destruction of war and the shock of discovering the extent of the Holocaust. At the Nuremberg Trials in Germany beginning in 1946, many Germans accused of horrible crimes against humanity offered the defense that they were only following orders and so could not be held responsible for their actions. Prosecutors, and eventually judges, opposed this argument, and argued that certain orders require such terrible actions that those orders must be rejected and disobeyed. The judges at Nuremberg appeared to accept that there can only be obligation to obey laws which are morally justified. The judges accepted the argument that the so-called laws allowing and sometimes requiring certain

1 John Austin, *The Province of Jurisprudence Determined.*
2 Ronald Dworkin, *Taking Rights Seriously*, Preface, i.

horrible actions were in fact never genuine laws, therefore there never was a genuine obligation to obey. So holding persons responsible for war crimes was not simply imposing the will of the victor on the helpless loser. Rather, war crimes trials were justified because the judges simply applied the real law which existed all along. At the time of the Nuremberg Trials, this seemed to be the best and perhaps the only way to hold war criminals responsible for actions which were legally justified at the time they were committed.

In this context, Hart's defense of legal positivism was shocking and unusual. Why claim that law and morality have no necessary connection when it seems so completely clear that law and morality *must* be connected if justice is to be done? The simplest positivist answer to this question can be summarized in a single word: *clarity*. By recognizing that laws can be used for many different purposes, both good and bad, we gain a clearer picture of the possibilities and limits of law as a tool for guiding behavior. Hart worried that if we deny that laws can be morally bad but still be laws, we ignore the fact that there are important similarities of function among all laws, morally good or bad. Our picture of law as it is may not present an attractive view of humans, but clarity about the nature of law requires that we include in our picture all relevant evidence, attractive or not. Clarity of this sort is valuable for more than its own sake: a clear understanding of the nature of law can be very useful to those who wish to reform law rationally and efficiently.

The importance of Hart's work comes from more than his defense of an unpopular yet important view. Hart's enduring importance lies in his new ideas for analysis of law. At the beginning of *The Concept of Law* Hart uses a phrase which indicates the direction of his analysis, calling *The Concept of Law* an "essay in descriptive sociology."[3] The precise meaning of this phrase has puzzled Hart's admirers and his critics. However, it is possible to explain at least partially what Hart seems to mean by saying that his investigation of law is "descriptive" and in some sense "sociological." Throughout his legal philosophy, Hart supposes that description of a thing *adds* to our understanding of that thing. So when we are concerned with law, we describe laws and law-following as part of our development of a broader picture of law as a social phenomenon. It is important to note also that by using "description" Hart means to exclude assessing the value of a thing at the same time as we describe it. According to Hart, we can reduce unhelpful obscurity and vagueness in our understanding of a thing if we describe it first, and later evaluate it. This sense of description appears to be compatible with an understanding of sociology as a discipline concerned with *observation* of social phenomena. As we shall see in a moment, one of Hart's most important contributions to the philosophy of law is borrowed from a sociological understanding of what can be learned about the idea of law from observation of situations where what is said to be "law" exists.

2. The Idea of Rules

Hart borrows from sociology the idea of a "social rule." We are all familiar with some of the general characteristics of rules. We follow rules every day as we play sports, borrow things from friends, and wait our turn. One of Hart's special insights into law comes with his description of the way what is said to be "law" involves special types of social rules. According to Hart, law, where it is said to exist, is typically found in the form of a system made up of two types of rules. The first type, called "primary rules," make certain conduct non-optional. For example, we might devise a rule which says, "Club members who use club equipment *must* return it to the equipment shed."

3 H.L.A. Hart, *The Concept of Law*, Preface, i.

Here the use of the word "must" shows that the rule is non-optional. Primary rules are made, changed, and eliminated by use of "secondary rules." Let us work through an example. Suppose a new and slightly obnoxious member of our club protests that our rule is hopelessly old-fashioned, so inappropriate to the needs of a modern sports club. If our club's organization includes secondary rules, we may have a clear way of coping with the new member's protest. We point to a secondary rule of our club, which might say, "Any member who wishes to introduce, protest and change, or remove a club rule may do so at any club meeting attended by at least two thirds of the club's members." This secondary rule explains both what can be done to primary rules (introduction, change, elimination), and how to do it.

The idea of primary and secondary rules is at the core of Hart's understanding of law. However, the picture is not yet complete. Suppose the new member of the club hears our explanation of the secondary rules used to change the primary rules and says, "That's all very interesting, but irrelevant, since I've decided that the rule I dislike doesn't apply to me, so my problem is solved." This response to our claim that the new member is bound by some rule raises an interesting problem. How are we to determine with certainty what the law is in some situation, and who is subject to the law? The answer to this question is the idea of a "rule of recognition." The rule of recognition shows the characteristics of valid rules of the system—the rules "recognized" by judges and other officials as the rules of the system. The rule of recognition is sometimes called the "master rule" to mark its special status as the most important of the secondary rules. A rule of recognition can be simple, such as "whatever Parliament has enacted," or complex, consisting of several sources of law carefully ordered. It is best, however, to see the rule of recognition as something *shown* by the officials of the system. By using and applying certain rules to themselves and others, officials such as judges show everyone in the system which rules are regarded as valid by the officials.

Suppose the new member of our club hears all of this and rejects our patient and reasonable explanation of how we know that certain rules of the club apply to the new member. Suppose the new member quickly kicks each of us in the shins and races off with club equipment while we clutch our shins in agony and wonder why they have behaved so oddly. We soon realize that there is a fundamental difference between the new member of the club and the rest of us. We *accept* the rules of the club while they do not. Hart has an interesting and controversial way of explaining this difference. Those who accept the rules have what Hart calls the "internal point of view" to the rules. Those who do not accept the rules take the "external point of view." So how can we know that the new member of our club is properly said to take the external point of view to the club's rules?

Hart supposes that people who accept rules both physically obey those rules and use those rules as a basis for criticism and direction of social pressure against those who disobey the rules. Those with the internal point of view to the rules speak of them in a particular way, sometimes pointing to conduct as wrong without needing to refer explicitly to the rule because the rule is so widely known. Consider, for example, the well-known legal rule that vehicles must stop at red lights. Those who know and accept the rule might criticize its violation by saying, "Stop! The light is red!" Or, "You nitwit! That light was red! You ought to have stopped!" In each case, the rule is not stated because it is so well known, and the speaker refers implicitly to the rule. Yet even if the rule is not known to the person about to break it, if that person generally has the internal point of view to the rules, the mere mention of the rule typically gives the person a reason to act as the rule requires. Consider again the example of the rules of a club. One member might say to another "You can't leave those there—they must be hung up properly, as the rules require." An ordinary response from another club member might be, "Sorry, I didn't realize that was the rule. I'll hang them up." Those who have the internal point of view take the existence of a rule as a good reason for acting in the way the rule requires. Often the specific identity of the rule is not at issue, although a club member might, after a reprimand, find a copy of the club rules to refresh his or her memory.

On the other hand, those with the external point of view typically speak quite differently about the rules. The shin-kicking new member of the club indicates by their actions that they do not accept the club's rules. We might find further evidence of their external point of view if we were to overhear them telling an acquaintance about the club and its rules: "The fools who are members of the club I joined have made a useless rule about the use of club equipment—but why should I care? I've taken what I want, and I'll return it if and when it suits me." The new member of the club shows us, in their speaking of club rules as something *others* hold, that they do not accept the rules of the club as binding on *them*. As members of a club, we do not have many options when we consider what we ought to do about the new member's rule-breaking. We may visit him or write a letter to demand the return of club equipment, or we might change the locks at the club and decide to terminate their membership, or perhaps even dissolve the club as members grow tired of spending their time on conflict resolution. What we may not do, however, is use force to compel the new member to abide by the club's rules. Perhaps the club might have hired a security guard to watch over club equipment, so we have nearby what looks to be something like a club police force. Yet if we try to employ the security guard to physically compel the new member to follow club rules, we are very likely to learn from the security guard that their powers are very limited. When push comes to shove as disagreements rise beyond the merely verbal, the security guard's main function is to alert what news reports often call "the authorities"—in this case likely the official police force of the jurisdiction in question, whether city or province or state or national.

3. Legal Obligation and Coercion

Here the analogy between a club and a legal system breaks down. Both involve rule-following, but only the legal system claims a *monopoly* on legitimate use of force. Hart's most important improvement over Austin comes with Hart's attempt to give a realistic understanding of the relationship between coercion and law. Austin argued that at the core of the idea of law we find orders backed by threats. As you will see in Hart's revised argument for legal positivism, Hart supposes that orders and threats are only *part* of an accurate description of what is said to be law and legal obligation. Legal obligations, according to Hart, are something more complex than "the gunman situation writ large." Hart explains the difference between legal obligation and the gunman situation in terms which may now sound odd to North Americans, and to many in Britain as well. Hart writes that there is a difference between the statement that someone "was obliged to do something and the assertion that he had an obligation to do it."[4] This way of using "obliged" is no longer common, but Hart's meaning is still clear enough. If you choose to comply with the orders of a person issuing orders while holding a gun in a threatening manner, we do not suppose you have made a free choice when you obey the orders. We say, Hart observes, that the gunman has "obliged" you to do as he wishes. Note also that we do not usually hold persons

4 Hart, "Law as the Union of Primary and Secondary Rules," in *The Concept of Law*.

accountable for what they have been coerced to do. We do, however, hold persons accountable for what they have an obligation to do. If you have an obligation, you may choose to act as the obligation requires or you may break that obligation. Either way, we hold you responsible for your actions as freely chosen, and praise or criticize you accordingly. To have an obligation is therefore not simply to follow orders backed by threats, but to be subject to a social situation in which a rule is generally accepted as providing a very strong reason for acting in a certain way. As Hart explains it, "Rules are conceived and spoken of as imposing obligations when the general demand for conformity is insistent and the social pressure brought to bear on those who deviate or threaten to deviate is great."[5]

Hart's new explanation of legal obligation captures the fact that we obey the law and *use* the law as a standard of behavior even when the law poses no threat through giving us a reason to be afraid to disobey. We may each have different reasons for obeying the law, according to Hart, but typically at least some of the time those reasons do not include fear of coercion. Some of the time, we agree to some particular way of doing things as a matter of co-ordination for mutual gain, and no threats are needed to get us to do things that way. For example, a threat of coercion is not needed to convince people to drive on one side of the road rather than the other, since there are obvious mutual gains to be had (predictability and safety in driving) by agreeing to drive on one side. In this instance, a legal obligation to drive on the right (as in North America) is generally accepted for commonsensical reasons exclusive of fear of coercion.

Hart's positivist explanation of legal obligation fits neatly with the remainder of his descriptive, morally neutral account of law. Hart supposes that in the typical place where "law" and "legal obligation" are said to exist, there is an accepted system of primary and secondary rules, and a rule of recognition. Hart admits that many laws aim to achieve morally good purposes, but he insists that it is not *necessary* for laws to have morally good purposes. According to Hart, so long as the goal of the law is *thought* to be important, it does not matter to the law's status as a law whether the goal is morally good, bad, or indifferent. Hart recognizes that various societies in the world use law to promote very different visions of the best way to live.

4. Ronald Dworkin: Law as Rules and Principles

Professor Ronald Dworkin was among the most famous of contemporary legal philosophers in the twentieth and early twenty-first centuries, both in Britain where he was Hart's successor as Professor of Jurisprudence at Oxford University, and in the United States, where he taught at the New York University School of Law. Within legal philosophy, he is famous for his criticism of Hart's positivism and his development of a new theory of law. Outside of legal philosophy, he was known for his vigorous participation in American debates over such troubling issues as abortion and the best interpretation of the American Constitution.

In his 1967 article "The Model of Rules I," included here, Dworkin criticizes several views defended by Hart. Many criticisms are offered, however, one in particular has been widely recognized as especially important, even by Hart himself. Dworkin argues that there is a serious hole in Hart's explanation of what judges do when they apply the law: in his effort to explain how judges in fact interpret legal rules, Hart forgets the role of *principles* in judges' reasoning when they decide cases.

As Dworkin sketches Hart's view, Hart endorses a "pedigree" theory of the validity of legal rules. According to this theory, judges

5 Ibid.

identify and distinguish valid legal rules from other rules (e.g., rules of etiquette or morality, or lawyers' mistaken arguments about legal rules) by looking at where the rules come from. Valid legal rules have the right pedigree—they are derived from accepted sources in statute, custom, case law, and so forth.

In what might be called "easy" cases, judges reach a decision by applying a clearly understood legal rule with an appropriate pedigree to the facts of the case. However, complications can arise which make the process of reaching a decision much more difficult. The law may be written in ambiguous terms, or the most clearly applicable legal rule may not exactly fit the set of facts to which it is to be applied. In cases of this sort, judges cannot simply appeal to the core meaning of a legal rule. Instead they must venture out into the surrounding penumbra of the rule's meaning, and apply a more controversial and less settled understanding of the rule to the facts of the case at hand. In some cases, the judges' task will be even more difficult: the facts of a certain case may extend *beyond* the scope of the legal rule. In such "hard" cases, judges are said by Hart to use *discretion* and *make* law. To the extent that judges make a new legal rule where none previously existed, discretionary decisions appear to step outside the law and thus deserve to be called "extra-legal." But this does not mean that they are simply wild decisions guided by nothing more than judges' personal tastes. Hart explains: "We can say laws are incurably incomplete and we must decide the penumbral cases rationally by reference to social aims."[6] In other words, judges assess the purpose or social aim of a legal rule, and in their decisions they advance the spirit of the law even when the letter of the law does not clearly apply.

This account of hard cases does not go far enough, according to Dworkin. He believes it is possible to be more specific about the factors weighing in judges' reasoning, and in being more specific we uncover a rather different and better picture of law. Dworkin argues that in hard cases judges do not reach outside the law to non- or extra-legal standards in order to arrive at decisions. Rather, where legal rules fail to provide adequate guidance, judges use "legal principles" as a basis for decisions. "Principles" are "considerations of justice or fairness," and, according to Dworkin, these principles may be found throughout the law. Dworkin makes this point in his discussion of two American cases, *Henningsen v. Bloomfield Motors, Inc.* and *Riggs v. Palmer*. In both cases, Dworkin claims, the courts rely on principles found in the law rather than legal rules to reach a decision. For the purposes of this introduction, the identity of the principles at play in these cases is not important. What *is* important is the *difference* between rules and principles, and Dworkin's reasons for thinking that Hart has committed a serious error in failing to note the place of legal principles alongside legal rules.

Rules and principles are both standards which guide judges' reasoning when judges try to reach decisions in cases. Rules and principles differ in the *type* of guidance they offer. Dworkin thinks rules and principles may be logically distinguished by the way in which they operate in judges' reasoning. Rules, according to Dworkin, are standards which apply in an "all or nothing fashion"—either a rule does apply, or it does not. Principles, on the other hand, *contribute* to judges' reasoning toward a decision, but do not require any specific decision. Dworkin draws a series of contrasts to clarify the *logical* difference between rules and principles.

First, rules can have exceptions, while principles do not. If a rule does not quite capture a rule-maker's purpose, the rule-maker may add an exception to the rule, e.g., "Always return club

6 See in this section Hart, "Positivism and the Separation of Law and Morals," § III.

equipment to the storage shed *except* those items which are too large to fit in the shed." Principles are unaffected by exceptions and there is no need to take them into account when phrasing the principle. Dworkin points to the legal principle that no man may profit from his own wrong. Even if it is possible to find in the law certain counter-examples to this principle, these counter-examples do not disprove the claim that the principle exists. Principles embody a more general claim that, for the most part, a certain standard exists, and in matters where the standard is relevant, it ought to weigh in reasoning about those matters.

Second, while rules contain conditions which ordinarily make clear when the rule has or has not been followed, principles do not have any such conditions to be met. Principles simply give a reason to make a decision in a particular way, but do not specify what that decision must be. For example, we might be at our club and find that a member has left a medium-sized piece of quite expensive equipment outside the equipment shed, and in our deliberations over whether we ought to fine the offender for an infraction of club rules, we may be uncertain whether the equipment really counts as "large equipment" within the meaning of the club rule regarding storage of equipment. Our deliberations may be swayed one way or another by a member noting that "it's a principle of our club to behave responsibly with club equipment, and surely leaving our best equipment unsecured is irresponsible." The rule itself is no clearer, but we *are* given a *reason* to decide in one way (in favor of fining the offender) rather than another.

Third, principles have "weight" in judges' reasoning while rules do not. We noted above that Dworkin supposes that rules operate in an on/off fashion: a rule either applies to the facts at hand and requires a particular decision, or it does not. Principles, however, only add weight to the argument in favor of deciding a case in one way rather than another. Returning to the example sketched above, when we consider whether we ought to fine the club member who left a medium-sized piece of equipment outside the equipment shed, we might be swayed in favor of charging a fine by the principle that members ought to behave responsibly, and we might say that we are less concerned with the precise details of what counts as "large equipment" and more concerned to enforce the principle that members ought to behave responsibly with expensive equipment. We might then say that the lack of clarity in the club rule is no excuse. The principle of responsibility is sufficient reason for members to take further steps to ensure the safety of club equipment when unsure about the meaning of the club rule, and this principle gives us sufficient reason to extend the "penumbral" meaning of the rule regarding large equipment to cover medium-sized equipment as well, thus justifying our assessing the offending club member with a fine. In this case, the principle cited has weight in our reasoning, not requiring that we decide to fine the offender, but providing us with a reason to interpret the club rule in one way (to include medium-sized equipment) rather than another (accepting the literal meaning of the rule as excluding the possibility of fining a member for leaving medium-sized equipment outside). It is important to note also that in a given case principles may compete against one another. In our example, we might weigh *against* the principle of responsibility another principle, that no one should be punished arbitrarily for breaking rules which did not clearly exist prior to the time of the alleged offence. Principles compete against one another, and judges must in their deliberations consider which principles have the most weight in a particular case, and rely on those principles accordingly. Judges, according to Dworkin, must use their discretion in a very specific way: to choose among legal principles already at play in the body of the law.

What are we to make of Hart's views in light of this criticism? If Dworkin is right, and Hart has simply missed a large element of judicial reasoning, at the very least Hart must revise his theory to meet these objections. At worst, if Dworkin is correct about the importance of legal principles *and* Hart can find no way to fit these morally charged principles into his view of law, Dworkin has found a serious problem with legal positivism. If judges do in fact rely on moral principles in their deliberations, then Hart cannot be correct in his claim that law can be identified without reference to its moral merit. The separation thesis must then be abandoned, and the other insights of legal positivism into law are also thrown into doubt.

4
John Austin

from *The Province of Jurisprudence Determined*

Lecture I

The matter of jurisprudence is positive law: law, simply and strictly so called: or law set by political superiors to political inferiors. But positive law (or law, simply and strictly so called) is often confounded with objects to which it is related by *resemblance*, and with objects to which it is related in the way of *analogy*: with objects which are *also* signified, *properly* and *improperly*, by the large and vague expression *law*. To obviate the difficulties springing from that confusion, I begin my projected Course with determining the province of jurisprudence, or with distinguishing the matter of jurisprudence from those various related objects: trying to define the subject of which I intend to treat, before I endeavour to analyse its numerous and complicated parts.

A law, in the most general and comprehensive acceptation in which the term, in its literal meaning, is employed, may be said to be a rule laid down for the guidance of an intelligent being by an intelligent being having power over him. Under this definition are included, and without impropriety, several species. It is necessary to define accurately the line of demarcation which separates these species from one another, as much mistiness and intricacy has been infused into the science of jurisprudence by their being confounded or not clearly distinguished. In the comprehensive sense above indicated, or in the largest meaning which it has, without extension by metaphor or analogy, the term *law* embraces the following objects:—Laws set by God to his human creatures, and laws set by men to men.

The whole or a portion of the laws set by God to men is frequently styled the law of nature, or natural law: being, in truth, the only natural law of which it is possible to speak without a metaphor, or without a blending of objects which ought to be distinguished broadly. But, rejecting the appellation Law of Nature as ambiguous and misleading, I name those laws or rules, as considered collectively or in a mass, the *Divine law*, or the *law of God*.

Laws set by men to men are of two leading or principal classes: classes which are often blended, although they differ extremely; and which, for that reason, should be severed precisely, and opposed distinctly and conspicuously.

Of the laws or rules set by men to men, some are established by *political* superiors, sovereign and subject: by persons exercising supreme and subordinate *government*, in independent nations, or independent political societies. The aggregate of the rules thus established, or some aggregate forming a portion of that aggregate, is the appropriate matter of jurisprudence, general or particular. To the aggregate of the rules thus established, or to some aggregate forming a portion of that aggregate, the term *law*, as used simply and strictly, is exclusively applied. But, as contradistinguished to *natural* law, or to the law of *nature* (meaning, by those expressions, the law of God), the aggregate of the rules, established by political superiors, is frequently styled *positive* law, or law existing *by position*. As contradistinguished to the rules which I style *positive morality*, and on which I shall touch immediately, the aggregate of the rules, established by political superiors, may also be marked commodiously with the name of *positive law*. For the sake, then, of getting a name brief and distinctive at once, and agreeably to frequent usage, I style that aggregate of rules, or any portion of that aggregate, *positive law*: though rules, which are *not* established by political superiors, are also *positive*, or exist *by position*, if they be rules or laws, in the proper signification of the term.

Though *some* of the laws or rules, which are set by men to men, are established by political superiors, others are *not* established by political superiors, or are not established by political superiors, in that capacity or character.

Closely analogous to human laws of this second class, are a set of objects frequently but *improperly* termed *laws*, being rules set and enforced by *mere opinion*, that is, by the opinions or sentiments held or felt by an indeterminate body of men in regard to human conduct. Instances of such a use of the term *law* are the expressions—"The law of honour"; "The law set by fashion"; and rules of this species constitute much of what is usually termed "International law."

The aggregate of human laws properly so called belonging to the second of the classes above mentioned, with the aggregate of objects *improperly* but by *close analogy* termed laws, I place together in a common class, and denote them by the term *positive morality*. The name *morality* severs them from *positive law*, while the epithet *positive* disjoins them from the *law of God*. And to the end of obviating confusion, it is necessary or expedient that they *should* be disjoined from the latter by that distinguishing epithet. For the name *morality (or morals)*, when standing unqualified or alone, denotes indifferently either of the following objects: namely, positive morality *as it is*, or without regard to its merits; and positive morality *as it would be*, if it conformed to the law of God, and were, therefore, deserving of *approbation*. Besides the various sorts of rules which are included in the literal acceptation of the term law, and those which are by a close and striking analogy, though improperly, termed laws, there are numerous applications of the term law, which rest upon a slender analogy and are merely metaphorical or figurative. Such is the case when we talk of *laws* observed by the lower animals; of *laws* regulating the growth or decay of vegetables; of *laws* determining the movements of inanimate bodies or masses. For where *intelligence* is not, or where it is too bounded to take the name of *reason*, and, therefore, is too bounded to conceive the purpose of a law, there is not the *will* which law can work on, or which duty can incite or restrain. Yet through these misapplications of a *name*, flagrant as the metaphor is, has the field of jurisprudence and morals been deluged with muddy speculation.

Having suggested the *purpose* of my attempt to determine the province of jurisprudence: to distinguish positive law, the appropriate matter of jurisprudence, from the various objects to which it is related by resemblance, and to which it is related, nearly or remotely, by a strong or slender analogy: I shall now state the essentials of a *law* or *rule* (taken with the largest signification which can be given to the term *properly*).

Every *law* or *rule* (taken with the largest signification which can be given to the term *properly*) is a *command*. Or, rather, laws or rules, properly so called, are a *species* of commands. Now, since the term *command* comprises the term *law*, the first is the simpler as well as the larger of the *two*. But, simple as it is, it admits of explanation. And, since it is the *key* to the sciences of jurisprudence and morals, its meaning should be analysed with precision. Accordingly, I shall endeavour, in the first instance, to analyse the meaning of "*command*": an analysis which, I fear, will task the patience of my hearers, but which they will bear with cheerfulness, or, at least, with resignation, if they consider the difficulty of performing it. The elements of a science are precisely the parts of it which are explained least easily. Terms that are the largest, and, therefore, the simplest of a series, are without equivalent expressions into which we can resolve them *concisely*. And when we endeavour to *define* them, or to translate them into terms which we suppose are better understood, we are forced upon awkward and tedious circumlocutions.

If you express or intimate a wish that I shall do or forbear from some act, and if you will visit me with an evil in case I comply not with your wish, the *expression* or *intimation* of your wish is a *command*. A command is distinguished from other significations of desire, not by the style in which the desire is signified, but by the power and the purpose of the party commanding to inflict an evil or pain in case the desire be disregarded. If you cannot or will not harm me, in case I comply not with your wish, the expression of your wish is not a command, although you utter your wish in imperative phrase. If you are able and willing to harm me in case I comply not with your wish, the expression of your wish amounts to a command, although you are prompted by a spirit of courtesy to utter it in the shape of a request. "*Preces erant, sed quibus contradici non posset.*" [*Ed. note*: "These were only requests, but they could not be denied."] Such is the language of Tacitus, when speaking of a petition by the soldiery to a son and lieutenant of Vespasian.

A command, then, is a signification of desire. But a command is distinguished from other significations of desire by this peculiarity: that the party to whom it is directed is liable to evil from the other in case he comply not with the desire.

Being liable to evil from you if I comply not with a wish which you signify, I am *bound* or *obliged* by your command, or I lie under a *duty* to obey it. If, in spite of that evil in prospect, I comply not with the wish which you signify, I am said to disobey your command, or to violate the duty which it imposes.

Command and duty are, therefore, correlative terms: the meaning denoted by each being implied or supposed by the other. Or (changing the expression) wherever a duty lies, a command has been signified; and whenever a command is signified, a duty is imposed.

Concisely expressed, the meaning of the correlative expressions is this. He who will inflict an evil in case his desire be disregarded, utters a command by expressing or intimating his desire: He who is liable to the evil in case he disregard the desire, is bound or obliged by the command.

The evil which will probably be incurred in case a command be disobeyed or (to use an equivalent expression) in case a duty be broken, is frequently called a *sanction*, or an *enforcement of obedience*. Or (varying the phrase) the command or the duty is said to be *sanctioned* or *enforced* by the chance of incurring the evil.

Considered as thus abstracted from the command and the duty which it enforces, the evil to be incurred by disobedience is frequently styled a *punishment*. But, as punishments, strictly so called, are only a *class* of sanctions, the term is too narrow to express the meaning adequately.

I observe that Dr. Paley, in his analysis of the term *obligation*, lays much stress upon the *violence* of the motive to compliance. In so far as I can gather a meaning from his loose and inconsistent statement, his meaning appears to be this: that unless the motive to compliance be *violent* or *intense*, the expression or intimation of a wish is not a *command*, nor does the party to whom it is directed lie under a *duty* to regard it.

If he means, by a *violent* motive, a motive operating with certainty, his proposition is manifestly false. The greater the evil to be incurred in case the wish be disregarded, and the greater the *chance* of incurring it on that same event, the greater, no doubt, is the chance that the wish will *not* be disregarded. But no conceivable motive will *certainly* determine to compliance, or no conceivable motive will render obedience inevitable. If Paley's proposition be true, in the sense which I have now ascribed to it, commands and duties are simply impossible. Or, reducing his proposition to absurdity by a consequence as manifestly false, commands and duties are possible, but are never disobeyed or broken.

If he means by a *violent* motive, an evil which inspires fear, his meaning is simply this: that the party bound by a command is bound by the prospect of an evil. For that which is not feared is not apprehended as an evil; or (changing the shape of the expression) is not an evil in prospect.

The truth is, that the magnitude of the eventual evil, and the magnitude of the chance of incurring it, are foreign to the matter in question. The greater the eventual evil, and the greater the chance of incurring it, the greater is the efficacy of the command, and the greater is the strength of the obligation: Or (substituting expressions exactly equivalent), the greater is the chance that the command will be obeyed, and that the duty will not be broken. But where there is the smallest *chance* of incurring the smallest evil, the expression of a wish amounts to a command, and, therefore, imposes a duty. The sanction, if you will, is feeble or insufficient; but still there *is* a sanction, and, therefore, a duty and a command.

By some celebrated writers (by Locke, Bentham, and, I think, Paley), the term *sanction*, or *enforcement of obedience*, is applied to conditional good as well as to conditional evil: to reward as well as to punishment. But, with all my habitual veneration for the names of Locke and Bentham, I think that this extension of the term is pregnant with confusion and perplexity.

Rewards are, indisputably, *motives* to comply with the wishes of others. But to talk of commands and duties as *sanctioned* or *enforced* by rewards, or to talk of rewards as *obliging* or *constraining* to obedience, is surely a wide departure from the established meaning of the terms.

If *you* expressed a desire that I should render a service, and if you proffered a reward as the motive or inducement to render it, *you* would scarcely be said to *command* the service, nor should *I*, in ordinary language, be *obliged* to render it. In ordinary language, *you* would *promise* me a reward, on condition of my rendering the service, whilst *I* might be *incited* or *persuaded* to render it by the hope of obtaining the reward.

Again: If a law hold out a *reward*, as an inducement to do some act, an eventual *right* is conferred, and not an *obligation* imposed, upon those who shall act accordingly: The *imperative* part of the law being addressed or directed to the party whom it requires to *render* the reward.

In short, I am determined or inclined to comply with the wish of another, by the fear of disadvantage or evil. I am also determined or inclined to comply with the wish of another, by the hope of advantage or good. But it is only by the chance of incurring evil, that I am *bound* or *obliged* to compliance. It is only by conditional *evil*, that duties are *sanctioned* or *enforced*. It is the power and the purpose of inflicting eventual *evil*, and *not* the power and the purpose of imparting eventual *good*, which gives to the expression of a wish the name of a *command*.

If we put *reward* into the import of the term *sanction*, we must engage in a toilsome struggle with the current of ordinary speech; and shall often slide unconsciously, notwithstanding our efforts to the contrary, into the narrower and customary meaning. It appears, then, from what has been premised, that the ideas or notions comprehended by the term *command* are the following.

1. A wish or desire conceived by a rational being, that another rational being shall do or forbear. 2. An evil to proceed from the former, and to be incurred by the latter, in case the latter comply not with the wish. 3. An expression or intimation of the wish by words or other signs.

It also appears from what has been premised, that *command*, *duty*, and *sanction* are inseparably connected terms: that each embraces the same ideas as the others, though each denotes those ideas in a peculiar order or series.

"A wish conceived by one, and expressed or intimated to another, with an evil to be inflicted and incurred in case the wish be disregarded," are signified directly and indirectly by each of the three expressions. Each is the name of the same complex notion.

But when I am talking *directly* of the expression or intimation of the wish, I employ the term *command*: The expression or intimation of the wish being presented *prominently* to my hearer; whilst the evil to be incurred, with the chance of incurring it, are kept (if I may so express myself) in the background of my picture.

When I am talking *directly* of the chance of incurring the evil, or (changing the expression) of the liability or obnoxiousness to the evil, I employ the term *duty*, or the term *obligation*: The liability or obnoxiousness to the evil being put foremost, and the rest of the complex notion being signified implicitly.

When I am talking *immediately* of the evil itself, I employ the term *sanction*, or a term of the like import: The evil to be incurred being signified directly; whilst the obnoxiousness to that evil, with the expression or intimation of the wish, are indicated indirectly or obliquely.

To those who are familiar with the language of logicians (language unrivalled for brevity, distinctness, and precision), I can express my meaning accurately in a breath.—Each of the three terms *signifies* the same notion; but each *denotes* a different part of that notion, and *connotes* the residue.

Commands are of two species. Some are *laws* or *rules*. The others have not acquired an appropriate name, nor does language afford an expression which will mark them briefly and precisely. I must, therefore, note them as well as I can by the ambiguous and inexpressive name of "*occasional* or *particular* commands."

The term *laws* or *rules* being not unfrequently applied to occasional or particular commands, it is hardly possible to describe a line of separation which shall consist in every respect with established forms of speech. But the distinction between laws and particular commands may, I think, be stated in the following manner.

By every command, the party to whom it is directed is obliged to do or to forbear.

Now where it obliges *generally* to acts or forbearances of a *class*, a command is a law or rule. But where it obliges to a *specific* act or forbearance, or to acts or forbearances which it determines *specifically* or *individually*, a command is occasional or particular.

In other words, a class or description of acts is determined by a law or rule, and acts of that class or description are enjoined or forbidden generally. But where a command is occasional or particular, the act or acts, which the command enjoins or forbids, are assigned or determined by their specific or individual natures as well as by the class or description to which they belong.

The statement which I have given in abstract expressions I will now endeavour to illustrate by apt examples.

If you command your servant to go on a given errand, or *not* to leave your house on a given evening, or to rise at such an hour on such a morning, or to rise at that hour during the next week or month, the command is occasional or particular. For the act or acts enjoined or forbidden are specially determined or assigned.

But if you command him *simply* to rise at that hour, or to rise at that hour *always*, or to rise at that hour *till further orders*, it may be said, with propriety, that you lay down a *rule* for the guidance of your servant's conduct. For no specific act is assigned by the command, but the command obliges him generally to acts of a determined class.

If a regiment be ordered to attack or defend a post, or to quell a riot, or to march from their present quarters, the command is occasional or particular. But an order to exercise daily till further orders shall be given would be called a *general* order, and *might* be called a *rule*.

If Parliament prohibited simply the exportation of corn, either for a given period or indefinitely, it would establish a law or rule: a *kind* or *sort* of acts being determined by the command, and acts of that kind or sort being *generally* forbidden. But an order issued by Parliament to meet an impending scarcity, and stopping the exportation of corn *then shipped and in port*, would not be a law or rule, though issued by the sovereign legislature. The order regarding exclusively a specified quantity of corn, the negative acts or forbearances, enjoined by the command, would be determined specifically or individually by the determinate nature of their subject.

As issued by a sovereign legislature, and as wearing the form of a law, the order which I have now imagined would probably be *called* a law. And hence the difficulty of drawing a distinct boundary between laws and occasional commands.

Again: An act which is not an offence, according to the existing law, moves the sovereign to displeasure: and, though the authors of the act are legally innocent or unoffending, the sovereign commands that they shall be punished. As enjoining a specific punishment in that specific case, and as not enjoining generally acts or forbearances of a class, the order uttered by the sovereign is not a law or rule.

Whether such an order would be *called* a law, seems to depend upon circumstances which are purely immaterial: immaterial, that is, with reference to the present purpose, though material with reference to others. If made by a sovereign assembly deliberately, and with the forms of legislation, it would probably be called a law. If uttered by an absolute monarch, without deliberation or ceremony, it would scarcely be confounded with acts of legislation, and would be styled an arbitrary command. Yet, on either of these suppositions, its nature would be the same. It would not be a law or rule, but an occasional or particular command of the sovereign One or Number.

To conclude with an example which best illustrates the distinction, and which shows the importance of the distinction most conspicuously, *judicial commands* are commonly occasional or particular, although the commands which they are calculated to enforce are commonly laws or rules.

For instance, the lawgiver commands that thieves shall be hanged. A specific theft and a specified thief being given, the judge commands that the thief shall be hanged, agreeably to the command of the lawgiver. Now the lawgiver determines a class or description of acts; prohibits acts of the class generally and indefinitely; and commands, with the like generality, that punishment shall follow transgression. The command of the lawgiver is, therefore, a law or rule. But the command of the judge is occasional or particular.

For he orders a specific punishment, as the consequence of a specific offence.

According to the line of separation which I have now attempted to describe, a law and a particular command are distinguished thus.—Acts or forbearances of a class are enjoined *generally* by the former. Acts *determined specifically*, are enjoined or forbidden by the latter.

A different line of separation has been drawn by Blackstone and others. According to Blackstone and others, a law and a particular command are distinguished in the following manner.—A law obliges *generally* the members of the given community, or a law obliges *generally* persons of a given class. A particular command obliges a *single* person, or persons whom it determines *individually*.

That laws and particular commands are not to be distinguished thus, will appear on a moment's reflection.

For, *first*, commands which oblige generally the members of the given community, or commands which oblige generally persons of given classes, are not always laws or rules. Thus, in the case already supposed; that in which the sovereign commands that all corn actually shipped for exportation be stopped and detained; the command is obligatory upon the whole community, but as it obliges them only to a set of acts individually assigned, it is not a law. Again, suppose the sovereign to issue an order, enforced by penalties, for a general mourning, on occasion of a public calamity. Now, though it is addressed to the community at large, the order is scarcely a rule, in the usual acceptation of the term. For, though it obliges generally the members of the entire community, it obliges to acts which it assigns specifically, instead of obliging generally to acts or forbearances of a class. If the sovereign commanded that *black* should be the dress of his subjects, his command would amount to a law. But if he commanded them to wear it on a specified occasion, his command would be merely particular.

And, *secondly*, a command which obliges exclusively persons individually determined, may amount, notwithstanding, to a law or rule.

For example, A father may set a *rule* to his child or children: a guardian, to his ward: a master, to his slave or servant. And certain of God's *laws* were as binding on the first man, as they are binding at this hour on the millions who have sprung from his loins.

Most, indeed, of the laws which are established by political superiors, or most of the laws which are simply and strictly so called, oblige generally the members of the political community, or oblige generally persons of a class. To frame a system of duties for every individual of the community, were simply impossible: and if it were possible, it were utterly useless. Most of the laws established by political superiors are, therefore, *general* in a twofold manner: as enjoining or forbidding generally acts of kinds or sorts; and as binding the whole community, or, at least, whole classes of its members.

But if we suppose that Parliament creates and grants an office, and that Parliament binds the grantee to services of a given description, we suppose a law established by political superiors, and yet exclusively binding a specified or determinate person.

Laws established by political superiors, and exclusively binding specified or determinate persons, are styled, in the language of the Roman jurists, *privilegia*. Though that, indeed, is a name which will hardly denote them distinctly: for, like most of the leading terms in actual systems of law, it is not the name of a definite class of objects, but of a heap of heterogeneous objects.[1]

It appears, from what has been premised, that a law, properly so called, may be defined in the following manner.

A law is a command which obliges a person or persons.

But, as contradistinguished or opposed to an occasional or particular command, a law is a command which obliges a person or persons, and obliges *generally* to acts or forbearances of a *class*.

In language more popular but less distinct and precise, a law is a command which obliges a person or persons to a *course* of conduct.

Laws and other commands are said to proceed from *superiors*, and to bind or oblige *inferiors*. I will, therefore, analyse the meaning of those correlative expressions; and will try to strip them of a certain mystery, by which that simple meaning appears to be obscured.

Superiority is often synonymous with *precedence* or *excellence*. We talk of superiors in rank; of superiors in wealth; of superiors in virtue: comparing certain persons with certain other persons; and meaning that the former precede or excel the latter in rank, in wealth, or in virtue.

But, taken with the meaning wherein I here understand it, the term *superiority* signifies *might*: the power of affecting others with evil or pain, and of forcing them, through fear of that evil, to fashion their conduct to one's wishes.

For example, God is emphatically the *superior* of Man. For his power of affecting us with pain, and of forcing us to comply with his will, is unbounded and resistless.

To a limited extent, the sovereign One or Number is the superior of the subject or citizen: the master, of the slave or servant: the father, of the child.

In short, whoever can *oblige* another to comply with his wishes, is the *superior* of that other, so far as the ability reaches: The party who is obnoxious to the impending evil, being, to that same extent, the *inferior*.

The might or superiority of God is simple or absolute. But in all or most cases of human superiority, the relation of superior and inferior, and the relation of inferior and superior, are reciprocal. Or (changing the expression) the party who is the superior as viewed from one aspect, is the inferior as viewed from another.

For example, To an indefinite, though limited extent, the monarch is the superior of the governed: his power being commonly sufficient to enforce compliance with his will. But the governed, collectively or in mass, are also the superior of the monarch: who is checked in the abuse of his might by his fear of exciting their anger; and of rousing to active resistance the might which slumbers in the multitude.

A member of a sovereign assembly is the superior of the judge: the judge being bound by the law which proceeds from that sovereign body. But, in his character of citizen or subject, he is the inferior of the judge: the judge being the minister of the law, and armed with the power of enforcing it.

It appears, then, that the term *superiority* (like the terms *duty* and *sanction*) is implied by the term command. For superiority is the power of enforcing compliance with a wish: and the expression or intimation of a wish, with the

1 Where a *privilegium* merely imposes a duty, it exclusively obliges a determinate person or persons. But where a *privilegium* confers a right, and the right conferred *avails against the world at large*, the law is *privilegium* as viewed from a certain aspect, but is also *a general law* as viewed from another aspect. In respect of the right conferred, the law exclusively regards a determinate person, and, therefore, is *privilegium*. In respect of the duty imposed, and corresponding to the right conferred, the law regards generally the members of the entire community.

This I shall explain particularly at a subsequent point of my Course, when I consider the peculiar nature of so-called *privilegia*, or of so-called *private laws*.

power and the purpose of enforcing it, are the constituent elements of a command.

"That *laws* emanate from *superiors*" is, therefore, an identical proposition. For the meaning which it affects to impart is contained in its subject.

If I mark the peculiar source of a given law, or if I mark the peculiar source of laws of a given class, it is possible that I am saying something which may instruct the hearer. But to affirm of laws universally "that they flow from *superiors*," or to affirm of laws universally "that *inferiors* are bound to obey them," is the merest tautology and trifling.

Like most of the leading terms in the science of jurisprudence and morals, the term *laws* is extremely ambiguous. Taken with the largest signification which can be given to the term properly, *laws* are a species of *commands*. But the term is improperly applied to various objects which have nothing of the imperative character: to objects which are *not* commands; and which, therefore, are *not* laws, properly so called.

Accordingly, the proposition "that laws are commands" must be taken with limitations. Or, rather, we must distinguish the various meanings of the term *laws*; and must restrict the proposition to that class of objects which is embraced by the largest signification that can be given to the term properly.

I have already indicated, and shall hereafter more fully describe, the objects improperly termed laws, which are *not* within the province of jurisprudence (being either rules enforced by opinion and closely analogous to laws properly so called, or being laws so called by a metaphorical application of the term merely). There are other objects improperly termed laws (not being commands) which yet may properly be included within the province of jurisprudence. These I shall endeavour to particularise:—

1. Acts on the part of legislatures to *explain* positive law, can scarcely be called laws, in the proper signification of the term. Working no change in the actual duties of the governed, but simply declaring what those duties are, they properly are acts of *interpretation* by legislative authority. Or, to borrow an expression from the writers on the Roman Law, they are acts of *authentic* interpretation.

But, this notwithstanding, they are frequently styled laws; *declaratory* laws, or declaratory statutes. They must, therefore, be noted as forming an exception to the proposition "that laws are a species of commands."

It often, indeed, happens (as I shall show in the proper place), that laws declaratory in name are imperative in effect: Legislative, like judicial interpretation, being frequently deceptive; and establishing new law, under guise of expounding the old.

2. Laws to repeal laws, and to release from existing duties, must also be excepted from the proposition "that laws are a species of commands." In so far as they release from duties imposed by existing laws, they are not commands, but revocations of commands. They authorize or permit the parties, to whom the repeal extends, to do or to forbear from acts which they were commanded to forbear from or to do. And, considered with regard to *this*, their immediate or direct purpose, they are often named *permissive laws*, or, more briefly and more properly, *permissions*. Remotely and indirectly, indeed, permissive laws are often or always imperative. For the parties released from duties are restored to liberties or rights: and duties answering those rights are, therefore, created or revived.

But this is a matter which I shall examine with exactness, when I analyse the expressions "legal right," "permission by the sovereign or state," and "civil or political liberty."

3. Imperfect laws, or laws of imperfect obligation, must also be excepted from the proposition "that laws are a species of commands."

An imperfect law (with the sense wherein the term is used by the Roman jurists) is a law which wants a sanction, and which therefore, is not binding. A law declaring that certain acts are crimes, but annexing no punishment to the commission of acts of the class, is the simplest and most obvious example.

Though the author of an imperfect law signifies a desire, he manifests no purpose of enforcing compliance with the desire. But where there is not a purpose of enforcing compliance with the desire, the expression of a desire is not a command. Consequently, an imperfect law is not so properly a law, as counsel, or exhortation, addressed by a superior to inferiors. Examples of imperfect laws are cited by the Roman jurists. But with us in England, laws professedly imperative are always (I believe) perfect or obligatory. Where the English legislature affects to command, the English tribunals not unreasonably presume that the legislature exacts obedience. And, if no specific sanction be annexed to a given law, a sanction is supplied by the courts of justice, agreeably to a general maxim which obtains in cases of the kind.

The imperfect laws, of which I am now speaking, are laws which are imperfect, in the sense of *the Roman jurists*: that is to say, laws which speak the desires of political superiors, but which their authors (by oversight or design) have not provided with sanctions. Many of the writers on *morals*, and on the so called *law of nature*, have annexed a different meaning to the term *imperfect*. Speaking of imperfect obligations, they commonly mean duties which are *not legal*: duties imposed by commands of God, or duties imposed by positive morality, as contradistinguished to duties imposed by positive law. An *imperfect* obligation, in the sense of the Roman jurists, is exactly equivalent to no obligation at all. For the term *imperfect* denotes simply, that the law wants the sanction appropriate to laws of the kind. An imperfect obligation, in the other meaning of the expression, is a religious or a moral obligation. The term imperfect does not denote that the law imposing the duty wants the appropriate sanction. It denotes that the law imposing the duty is *not* a law established by a political superior: that it wants that *perfect*, or that surer or more cogent sanction, which is imparted by the sovereign or state.

I believe that I have now reviewed all the classes of objects, to which the term laws is improperly applied. The laws (improperly so called) which I have here lastly enumerated, are (I think) the only laws which are not commands, and which yet may be properly included within the province of jurisprudence. But though these, with the so called laws set by opinion and the objects metaphorically termed laws, are the only laws which *really* are not commands, there are certain laws (properly so called) which may *seem* not imperative. Accordingly, I will subjoin a few remarks upon laws of this dubious character.

1. There are laws, it may be said, which *merely* create *rights*: And, seeing that every command imposes a *duty*, laws of this nature are not imperative.

But, as I have intimated already, and shall show completely hereafter, there are no laws *merely* creating *rights*. There are *laws*, it is true, which *merely* create *duties*: duties not correlating with correlating rights, and which, therefore may be styled *absolute*.

But every law, really conferring a right, imposes expressly or tacitly a *relative* duty, or a duty correlating with the right. If it specify the remedy to be given, in case the right shall be infringed, it imposes the relative duty expressly. If the remedy to be given be not specified, it refers tacitly to pre-existing law, and clothes the right which it purports to create with a remedy provided by that law. Every law, really conferring a right, is, therefore, imperative: as imperative, as if its only purpose were the creation of a duty, or as if the relative duty, which it inevitably imposes, were merely absolute.

The meanings of the term *right*, are various and perplexed; taken with its proper meaning, it comprises ideas which are numerous and complicated; and the searching and extensive analysis, which the term, therefore, requires, would occupy more room than could be given to it in the present lecture: It is not, however, necessary, that the analysis should be performed here. I propose, in my earlier lectures, to determine the province of jurisprudence; or to distinguish the laws established by political superiors, from the various laws, proper and improper, with which they are frequently confounded. And this I may accomplish exactly enough, without a nice inquiry into the import of the term *right*.

2. According to an opinion which I must notice *incidentally* here, though the subject to which it relates will be treated *directly* hereafter, *customary laws* must be excepted from the proposition "that laws are a species of commands."

By many of the admirers of customary laws (and, especially, of their German admirers), they are thought to oblige legally (independently of the sovereign or state), *because* the citizens or subjects have observed or kept them. Agreeably to this opinion, they are not the *creatures* of the sovereign or state, although the sovereign or state may abolish them at pleasure. Agreeably to this opinion, they are positive law (or law, strictly so called), inasmuch as they are enforced by the courts of justice: But, that notwithstanding, they exist *as positive law* by the spontaneous adoption of the governed, and not by position or establishment on the part of political superiors. Consequently, customary laws, considered as positive law, are not commands. And, consequently, customary laws, considered as positive law, are not laws or rules properly so called.

An opinion less mysterious, but somewhat allied to this, is not uncommonly held by the adverse party: by the party which is strongly opposed to customary law; and to all law made judicially, or in the way of judicial legislation. According to the latter opinion, all judge-made law, or all judge-made law established by *subject* judges, is purely the creature of the judges by whom it is established immediately. To impute it to the sovereign legislature, or to suppose that it speaks the will of the sovereign legislature, is one of the foolish or knavish *fictions* with which lawyers, in every age and nation, have perplexed and darkened the simplest and clearest truths.

I think it will appear, on a moment's reflection, that each of these opinions is groundless: that customary law is *imperative*, in the proper signification of the term; and that all judge-made law is the creature of the sovereign or state.

At its origin, a custom is a rule of conduct which the governed observe spontaneously, or not in pursuance of a law set by a political superior. The custom is transmuted into positive law, when it is adopted as such by the courts of justice, and when the judicial decisions fashioned upon it are enforced by the power of the state. But before it is adopted by the courts, and clothed with the legal sanction, it is merely a rule of positive morality: a rule generally observed by the citizens or subjects; but deriving the only force, which it can be said to possess, from the general disapprobation falling on those who transgress it.

Now when judges transmute a custom into a legal rule (or make a legal rule not suggested by a custom), the legal rule which they establish is established by the sovereign legislature. A subordinate or subject judge is merely a minister. The portion of the sovereign power which lies at his disposition is merely delegated. The rules which he makes derive their legal force from authority given by the state: an authority which the state may confer expressly, but which it commonly imparts in the way of acquiescence. For, since the state may reverse the rules which he makes, and yet permits him to enforce them by the power of the political community, its sovereign will "that his rules shall obtain as law" is clearly evinced by its conduct, though not by its express declaration.

The admirers of customary law love to trick out their idol with mysterious and imposing attributes. But to those who can see the difference between positive law and morality, there is nothing of mystery about it. Considered as rules of positive morality, customary laws arise from the consent of the governed, and not from the position or establishment of political superiors. But, considered as moral rules turned into positive laws, customary laws are established by the state: established by the state directly, when the customs are promulged in its statutes; established by the state circuitously, when the customs are adopted by its tribunals.

The opinion of the party which abhors judge-made laws, springs from their inadequate conception of the nature of commands.

Like other significations of desire, a command is express or tacit. If the desire be signified by *words* (written or spoken), the command is express. If the desire be signified by conduct (or by any signs of desire which are *not* words), the command is tacit.

Now when customs are turned into legal rules by decisions of subject judges, the legal rules which emerge from the customs are tacit commands of the sovereign legislature. The state, which is able to abolish, permits its ministers to enforce them: and it, therefore, signifies its pleasure, by that its voluntary acquiescence, "that they shall serve as a law to the governed."

My present purpose is merely this: to prove that the positive law styled *customary* (and all positive law made judicially) is established by the state directly or circuitously, and, therefore, is *imperative*. I am far from disputing, that law made judicially (or in the way of improper legislation) and law made by statute (or in the properly legislative manner) are distinguished by weighty differences. I shall inquire, in future lectures, what those differences are; and why subject judges, who are properly ministers of the law, have commonly shared with the sovereign in the business of making it.

I assume, then, that the only laws which are not imperative, and which belong to the subject-matter of jurisprudence, are the following—1. Declaratory laws, or laws explaining the import of existing positive law. 2. Laws abrogating or repealing existing positive law. 3. Imperfect laws, or laws of imperfect obligation (with the sense wherein the expression is used by the Roman jurists).

But the space occupied in the science by these improper laws is comparatively narrow and insignificant. Accordingly, although I shall take them into account so often as I refer to them directly, I shall throw them out of account on other occasions. Or (changing the expression) I shall limit the term law to laws which are imperative, unless I extend it expressly to laws which are not.

...

[*Ed. note*: The following material excerpted from Chapter V of *The Province of Jurisprudence Determined* examines the relationship between law and morality and contains some of Austin's arguments for the conceptual separation of law and legal obligation from morality and moral obligation.]

Lecture V

... The existence of law is one thing; its merit or demerit is another. Whether it be or be not is one enquiry; whether it be or be not conformable to an assumed standard, is a different enquiry. A law, which actually exists, is a law, though we happen to dislike it, or though it vary from the text, by which we regulate our approbation and disapprobation. This truth, when formally announced as an abstract proposition, is so simple and glaring that it seems idle to insist upon it. But simple and glaring as it is, when enunciated in abstract expressions the enumeration of the instances in which it has been forgotten would fill a volume.

Sir William Blackstone, for example, says in his "Commentaries," that the laws of God are superior in obligation to all other laws; that no human laws should be suffered to contradict them; that human laws are of no validity if contrary to them; and that all valid laws derive their force from that Divine original.

Now, he *may* mean that all human laws ought to conform to the Divine laws. If this be his meaning, I assent to it without hesitation. The evils which we are exposed to suffer from the hands of God as a consequence of disobeying His commands are the greatest evils to which we are obnoxious; the obligations which they impose are consequently paramount to those imposed by any other laws, and if human commands conflict with the Divine law, we ought to disobey the command which is enforced by the less powerful sanction; this is implied in the term *ought*: the proposition is identical, and therefore perfectly indisputable—it is our interest to choose the smaller and more uncertain evil, in preference to the greater and surer. If this be Blackstone's meaning, I assent to his proposition, and have only to object to it, that it tells us just nothing.

Perhaps, again, he means that human lawgivers are themselves obliged by the Divine laws to fashion the laws which they impose by that ultimate standard, because if they do not, God will punish them. To this also I entirely assent: for if the index to the law of God be the principle of utility, that law embraces the whole of our voluntary actions in so far as motives applied from without are required to give them a direction conformable to the general happiness.

But the meaning of this passage of Blackstone, if it has a meaning, seems rather to be this: that no human law which conflicts with the Divine law is obligatory or binding; in other words, that no human law which conflicts with the Divine law *is a law*, for a law without an obligation is a contradiction in terms. I suppose this to be his meaning, because when we say of any transaction that it is invalid or void, we mean that it is not binding: as, for example, if it be a contract, we mean that the political law will not lend its sanction to enforce the contract.

Now, to say that human laws which conflict with the Divine law are not binding, that is to say, are not laws, is to talk stark nonsense. The most pernicious laws, and therefore those which are most opposed to the will of God, have been and are continually enforced as laws by judicial tribunals. Suppose an act innocuous, or positively beneficial, be prohibited by the sovereign under the penalty of death; if I commit this act, I shall be tried and condemned, and if I object to the sentence, that it is contrary to the law of God, who has commanded that human lawgivers shall not prohibit acts which have no evil consequences, the Court of Justice will demonstrate the inconclusiveness of my reasoning by hanging me up, in pursuance of the law of which I have impugned the validity. An exception, demurrer, or plea, founded on the law of God was never heard in a Court of Justice, from the creation of the world down to the present moment.

But this abuse of language is not merely puerile, it is mischievous. When it is said that a law ought to be disobeyed, what is meant is that we are urged to disobey it by motives more cogent and compulsory than those by which it is itself sanctioned. If the laws of God are certain, the motives which they hold out to disobey any human command which is at variance with them are paramount to all others. But the laws of God are not always certain. All divines, at least all reasonable divines, admit that no scheme of duties perfectly complete and unambiguous was ever imparted to us by revelation. As an index to the Divine will, utility is obviously insufficient. What appears pernicious to one person may appear beneficial to another. And as for the moral sense, innate practical principles, conscience they are merely convenient cloaks for ignorance or sinister interest: they mean either that I hate the law to which I object and cannot tell why, or that I hate the law, and that the cause of my hatred is one which I find it incommodious to avow. If I say openly, I hate the law, *ergo*, it is not binding and ought to be disobeyed, no one will listen to me; but by calling my hate my conscience or my moral sense, I urge the same argument in another and a more plausible form: I seem to assign a reason for my dislike, when in truth I have only given it a sounding and specious name. In times of civil discord the mischief of this detestable abuse of language is apparent. In quiet times the dictates of utility are fortunately so obvious that the anarchical doctrine sleeps, and men habitually admit the validity of laws which they dislike. To prove by pertinent reasons that a law is pernicious is highly useful, because such process may lead to the abrogation of the pernicious law. To incite the public to resistance by determinate views of *utility* may be useful, for resistance, grounded on clear and definite prospects of good, is sometimes beneficial. But to proclaim generally that all laws which are pernicious or contrary to the will of God are void and not to be tolerated, is to preach anarchy, hostile and perilous as much to wise and benign rule as to stupid and galling tyranny.

In another passage of his "Commentaries," Blackstone enters into an argument to prove that a master cannot have a right to the labour of his slave. Had he contented himself with expressing his *disapprobation*, a very well-grounded one certainly, of the institution of slavery, no objection could have been made to his so expressing himself. But to dispute the existence or the possibility of the right is to talk absurdly. For in every age, and in almost every nation, the right has been given by positive law, whilst that pernicious disposition of positive law has been backed by the positive morality of the free or master classes.

...

[*Ed. note*: The following material excerpted from Chapter VI of *The Province of Jurisprudence Determined* examines the idea of sovereignty.]

Chapter VI

... I shall analyse the expression *sovereignty*, the correlative expression *subjection*, and the inseparably connected expression *independent political society*. With the ends or final causes for which governments *ought* to exist, or with their different degrees of fitness to attain or approach those ends, I have no concern. I examine the notions of *sovereignty* and *independent political society*, in order that I may finish the purpose to which I have adverted above: in order that I may distinguish completely the appropriate province of jurisprudence from the regions which lie upon its confines, and by which it is encircled. It is necessary that I should examine those notions, in order that I may finish that purpose. For the essential difference of a positive law (or the difference that severs it from a law which is not a positive law) may be stated thus. Every positive law, or every law simply and strictly so called, is set by a sovereign person, or a sovereign body of persons, to a member or members of the independent political society wherein that person or body is sovereign or supreme. Or (changing the expression) it is set by a monarch, or sovereign number, to a person or persons in a state of subjection to its author. Even though it sprung directly from another fountain or source, it *is* a positive law, or a law strictly so called, by the institution of that present sovereign in the character of political superior. Or (borrowing the language of Hobbes) "the legislator is he, not by whose authority the law was first made, but by whose authority it continues to be a law."

Having stated the topic or subject appropriate to my present discourse, I proceed to distinguish sovereignty from other superiority or might, and to distinguish society political and independent from society of other descriptions.

The superiority which is styled sovereignty, and the independent political society which sovereignty implies, is distinguished from other superiority, and from other society, by the following marks or characters.—1. The *bulk* of the given society are in a *habit* of obedience or submission to a *determinate* and *common* superior: let that common superior be a certain individual person, or a certain body or aggregate of individual persons. 2. That certain individual or that certain body of individuals, is *not* in a habit of obedience to a determinate human superior. Laws (improperly so called) which opinion sets or imposes, may permanently affect the conduct of that certain individual or body. To express or tacit commands of other determinate parties, that certain individual or body may yield occasional submission. But there is no determinate person, or determinate aggregate of persons, to whose commands, express or tacit, that certain individual or body renders habitual obedience.

Or the notions of sovereignty and independent political society may be expressed concisely thus.— If a *determinate* human superior, *not* in a habit of obedience to a like superior, receive *habitual* obedience from the *bulk* of a given society, that determinate superior is sovereign in that society, and the society (including the superior) is a society political and independent.

To that determinate superior, the other members of the society are *subject*: or on that determinate superior, the other members of the society are *dependent*. The position of its other members towards that determinate superior, is a *state of subjection*, or *a state of dependence*. The mutual relation which subsists between that superior and them, may be styled the *relation of sovereign and subject*, or *the relation of sovereignty and subjection*.

Hence it follows, that it is only through an ellipsis, or an abridged form of expression, that the *society* is styled *independent*. The party truly independent (independent, that is to say, of a determinate human superior), is not the society, but the sovereign portion of the society: that certain member of the society, or that certain body of its members, to whose commands, expressed or intimated, the generality or bulk of its members render habitual obedience. Upon that certain person, or certain body of persons, the other members of the society are *dependent*: or to that certain person, or certain body of persons, the other members of the society are *subject*. By "an independent political society," or "an independent and sovereign nation," we mean a political society consisting of a sovereign and subjects, as opposed to a political society which is merely subordinate: that is to say, which is merely a limb or member of another political society, and which therefore consists entirely of persons in a state of subjection.

In order that a given society may form a society political and independent, the two distinguishing marks which I have mentioned above must unite. The *generality* of the given society must be in the *habit* of obedience to a *determinate* and *common* superior: whilst that determinate person, or determinate body of persons must *not* be habitually obedient to a determinate person or body. It is the union of that positive, with this negative mark, which renders that certain superior sovereign or supreme, and which renders that given society (including that certain superior) a society political and independent.

To show that the union of those marks renders a given society a society political and independent, I call your attention to the following positions and examples.

1. In order that a given society may form a society political, the generality or bulk of its members must be in a *habit* of obedience to a determinate and common superior.

In case the generality of its members obey a determinate superior, but the obedience be rare or transient and not habitual or permanent, the relation of sovereignty and subjection is not created thereby between that certain superior and the members of that given society. In other words, that determinate superior and the members of that given society do not become thereby an independent political society. Whether that given society be political and independent or not, it is not an independent political society whereof that certain superior is the sovereign portion.

For example: In 1815 the allied armies occupied France; and so long as the allied armies occupied France, the commands of the allied sovereigns were obeyed by the French government, and, through the French government, by the French people generally. But since the commands and the obedience were comparatively rare and transient, they were not sufficient to constitute the relation of sovereignty and subjection between the allied sovereigns and the members of the invaded nation. In spite of those commands, and in spite of that obedience, the French government was sovereign or independent. Or in spite of those commands and in spite of that obedience, the French government and its subjects were an independent political society whereof the allied sovereigns were not the sovereign portion.

Now if the French nation, before the obedience to those sovereigns, had been an independent society in a state of nature or anarchy, it would not have been changed by the obedience into a society political. And it would not have been changed by the obedience into a society political, because the obedience was not habitual. For, inasmuch as the obedience was not habitual, it was not changed by the obedience from a society political and independent, into a society political but subordinate.—A given society, therefore, is not a society political, unless the generality of its members be in a *habit* of obedience to a determinate and common superior.

Again: A feeble state holds its independence precariously, or at the will of the powerful states to whose aggressions it is obnoxious. And since it is obnoxious to their aggressions, it and the bulk of its subjects render obedience to commands which they occasionally express or intimate. Such, for instance, is the position of the Saxon government and its subjects in respect of the conspiring sovereigns who form the Holy Alliance. But since the commands and the obedience are comparatively few and rare, they are not sufficient to constitute the relation of sovereignty and subjection between the powerful states and the feeble state with its subjects. In spite of those commands, and in spite of that obedience, the feeble state is sovereign or independent. Or in spite of those commands, and in spite of that obedience, the feeble state and its subjects are an independent political society whereof the powerful states are not the sovereign portion. Although the powerful states are permanently *superior*, and although the feeble state is permanently *inferior*, there is neither a *habit* of command on the part of the former, nor a *habit* of obedience on the part of the latter. Although the latter is unable to defend and maintain its independence, the latter is independent of the former in fact or practice.

From the example now adduced, as from the example adduced before, we may draw the following inference: that a given society is not a society political, unless the generality of its members be in the *habit* of obedience to a determinate and common superior.—By the obedience to the powerful states, the feeble state and its subjects are not changed from an independent, into subordinate political society. And they are not changed by the obedience into subordinate political society, because the obedience is not habitual. Consequently, if they were a natural society (setting that obedience aside), they would not be changed by that obedience into a society political.

2. In order that a given society may form a society political, habitual obedience must be rendered, by the *generality* or *bulk* of its members, to a determinate and *common* superior. In other words, habitual obedience must be rendered, by the *generality* or *bulk* of its members, to *one and*

the same determinate person, or determinate, body of persons.

Unless habitual obedience be rendered by the *bulk* of its members, and be rendered by the bulk of its members to *one and the same* superior, the given society is either in a state of nature, or is split into two or more independent political societies.

For example: In case a given society be torn by intestine war, and in case the conflicting parties be nearly balanced, the given society is in one of the two positions which I have now supposed.—As there is no common superior to which the bulk of its members render habitual obedience, it is not a political society single or undivided.—If the bulk of each of the parties be in a habit of obedience to its head, the given society is broken into two or more societies, which, perhaps, may be styled independent political societies.—If the bulk of each of the parties be not in that habit of obedience, the given society is simply or absolutely in a state of nature or anarchy. It is either resolved or broken into its individual elements, or into numerous societies of an extremely limited size: of a size so extremely limited, that they could hardly be styled societies independent and *political*. For, as I shall show hereafter, a given independent society would hardly be styled *political*, in case it fell short of a *number* which cannot be fixed with precision, but which may be called considerable, or not extremely minute.

3. In order that a given society may form a society political, the generality or bulk of its members must habitually obey a superior *determinate* as well as common.

On this position I shall not insist here. For I have shown sufficiently in my fifth lecture, that no indeterminate party can command expressly or tacitly, or can receive obedience or submission: that no indeterminate body is capable of corporate conduct, or is capable, as a body, of positive or negative deportment.

4. It appears from what has preceded, that, in order that a given society may form a society political, the bulk of its members must be in a habit of obedience to a certain and common superior. But, in order that the given society may form a society political and independent, that certain superior must not be habitually obedient to a determinate human superior.

5

H.L.A. Hart

"Positivism and the Separation of Law and Morals"

In this article I shall discuss and attempt to defend a view which Mr. Justice Holmes, among others, held and for which he and they have been much criticized. But I wish first to say why I think that Holmes, whatever the vicissitudes of his American reputation may be, will always remain for Englishmen a heroic figure in jurisprudence. This will be so because he magically combined two qualities: one of them is imaginative power, which English legal thinking has often lacked; the other is clarity, which English legal thinking usually possesses. The English lawyer who turns to read Holmes is made to see that what he had taken to be settled and stable is really always on the move. To make this discovery with Holmes is to be with a guide whose words may leave you unconvinced, sometimes even repelled, but never mystified. Like our own Austin, with whom Holmes shared many ideals and thoughts, Holmes was sometimes clearly wrong; but again like Austin, when this was so he was always wrong clearly. This surely is a sovereign virtue in jurisprudence. Clarity I know is said not to be enough; this may be true, but there are still questions in jurisprudence where the issues are confused because they are discussed in a style which Holmes would have spurned for its obscurity. Perhaps this is inevitable: jurisprudence trembles so uncertainly on the margin of many subjects that there will always be need for someone, in Bentham's phrase, "to pluck the mask of Mystery" from its face.[1] This is true, to a pre-eminent degree, of the subject of this article. Contemporary voices tell us we must recognize something obscured by the legal "positivists" whose day is now over: that there is a "point of intersection between law and morals,"[2] or that what *is* and what *ought* to be are somehow indissolubly fused or inseparable,[3] though the positivists denied it. What do these phrases mean? Or rather which of the many things that they *could* mean, *do* they mean? Which of them do "positivists" deny and why is it wrong to do so?

I.

I shall present the subject as part of the history of an idea. At the close of the eighteenth century and the beginning of the nineteenth the most earnest thinkers in England about legal and social problems and the architects of great reforms were the great Utilitarians. Two of them, Bentham and Austin, constantly insisted on the need to distinguish, firmly and with the maximum of clarity, law as it is from law as it ought to be. This theme haunts their work, and they condemned the natural-law thinkers precisely because they had blurred this apparently simple but vital distinction. By contrast, at the present time in this country and to a lesser extent in England, this separation between law and morals is held to be superficial and wrong. Some critics have thought that it blinds men to the true nature of law and its roots in social life.[4] Others have thought it not only intellectually misleading but corrupting in practice, at its worst apt to weaken resistance to state tyranny or absolutism,[5] and at its best apt to bring law into disrespect. The nonpejorative name "Legal Positivism," like most terms which are used as missiles in intellectual battles, has come to stand for a baffling multitude of different sins. One of them is the sin, real or alleged, of insisting, as Austin and Bentham did, on the separation of law as it is and law as it ought to be.

How then has this reversal of the wheel come about? What are the theoretical errors in this distinction? Have the practical consequences of stressing the distinction as Bentham and Austin did been bad? Should we now reject it

1 Bentham, *A Fragment on Government*, in I *Works* 221, 235 (Bowring ed. 1859) (preface, 41st para.).

2 D'Entrèves, *Natural Law* 116 (2d ed. 1952).

3 Fuller, *The Law in Quest for Itself* 12 (1940); Brecht, *The Myth of Is and Ought*, 54 *Harv. L. Rev.* 811 (1941); Fuller, "Human Purpose and Natural Law," 53 *J. Philos.* 697 (1953).

4 See Friedmann, *Legal Theory* 154, 294–95 (3d ed. 1953). Friedmann also says of Austin that "by his sharp distinction between the science of legislation and the science of law," he "inaugurated an era of legal positivism and self-sufficiency which enabled the rising national State to assert its authority undisturbed by juristic doubts." *Id.* at 416. Yet, "the existence of a highly organised State which claimed sovereignty and unconditional obedience of the citizen" is said to be "the political condition which makes analytical positivism possible." *Id.* at 163. There is therefore some difficulty in determining which, in this account, is to be hen and which egg (analytical positivism or political condition). Apart from this, there seems to be little evidence that any national State rising in or after 1832 (when the *Province of Jurisprudence Determined* was first published) was enabled to assert its authority by Austin's work or "the era of legal positivism" which he "inaugurated."

5 See Radbruch, *Die Erneuerung des Rechts*, 2 *Die Wandlung* 8 (Germany 1947); Radbruch, *Gesetzliches Unrecht und* Übergesetzliches *Recht*, I *Süddeutsche Juristen-Zeitung* 105 (Germany 1946) (reprinted in Radbruch, *Rechtsphilosophie* 347 [4th ed. 1950]). Radbruch's views are discussed at pp. 617–21 [pp. 129–32] *infra*.

or keep it? In considering these questions we should recall the social philosophy which went along with the Utilitarians' insistence on this distinction. They stood firmly but on their own utilitarian ground for all the principles of liberalism in law and government. No one has ever combined, with such even-minded sanity as the Utilitarians, the passion for reform with respect for law together with a due recognition of the need to control the abuse of power even when power is in the hands of reformers. One by one in Bentham's works you can identify the elements of the *Rechtstaat* and all the principles for the defense of which the terminology of natural law has in our day been revived. Here are liberty of speech, and of press, the right of association,[6] the need that laws should be published and made widely known before they are enforced,[7] the need to control administrative agencies,[8] the insistence that there should be no criminal liability without fault,[9] and the importance of the principle of legality, *nulla poena sine lege*.[10] Some, I know, find the political and moral insight of the Utilitarians a very simple one, but we should not mistake this simplicity for superficiality nor forget how favorably their simplicities compare with the profundities of other thinkers. Take only one example: Bentham on slavery. He says the question at issue is not whether those who are held as slaves can reason, but simply whether they suffer.[11] Does this not compare well with the discussion of the question in terms of whether or not there are some men whom Nature has fitted only to be the living instruments of others? We owe it to Bentham more than anyone else that we have stopped discussing this and similar questions of social policy in that form.

So Bentham and Austin were not dry analysts fiddling with verbal distinctions while cities burned, but were the vanguard of a movement which laboured with passionate intensity and much success to bring about a better society and better laws. Why then did they insist on the separation of law as it is and law as it ought to be? What did they mean? Let us first see what they said. Austin formulated the doctrine:

> The existence of law is one thing; its merit or demerit is another. Whether it be or be not is one enquiry; whether it be or be not conformable to an assumed standard, is a different enquiry. A law, which actually exists, is a law, though we happen to dislike it, or though it vary from the text, by which we regulate our approbation and disapprobation. This truth, when formally announced as an abstract proposition, is so simple and glaring that it seems idle to insist upon it. But simple and glaring as it is, when enunciated in abstract expressions the enumeration of the instances in which it has been forgotten would fill a volume.
>
> Sir William Blackstone, for example, says in his "Commentaries," that the laws of God are superior in

6 Bentham, *A Fragment on Government*, in I *Works* 221, 230 (Bowring ed. 1859) (preface, 16th para.); Bentham, *Principles of Penal Law*, in I *Works* 365, 574–75, 576–78 (Bowring ed. 1859) (pt. III, c. XXI, 8th para., 12th para.).

7 Bentham, *Of Promulgation of the Laws*, in I *Works* 155 (Bowring ed. 1859); Bentham, *Principles of the Civil Code*, in I *Works* 297, 323 (Bowring ed. 1859) (pt. I, c. XVII, 2d para.); Bentham, *A Fragment on Government*, in I *Works* 221, 233 n.[*m*] (Bowring ed. 1859) (preface, 35th para.).

8 Bentham, *Principles of Penal Law*, in I *Works* 365, 576 (Bowring ed. 1859) (pt. III, c. XXI, 10th para., 11th para.).

9 Bentham, *Principles of Morals and Legislation*, in I *Works* I, 84 (Bowring ed. 1859) (c. XIII).

10 Bentham, *Anarchical Fallacies*, in 2 *Works* 489, 511–12 (Bowring ed. 1859) (art. VIII); Bentham, *Principles of Morals and Legislation*, in I *Works* I, 144 (Bowring ed. 1859) (c. XIX, 11th para.).

11 *Id.* at 142 n.§ (c. XIX, 4th para. n.§).

> obligation to all other laws; that no human laws should be suffered to contradict them; that human laws are of no validity if contrary to them; and that all valid laws derive their force from that Divine original.
>
> Now, he *may* mean that all human laws ought to conform to the Divine laws. If this be his meaning, I assent to it without hesitation.... Perhaps, again, he means that human lawgivers are themselves obliged by the Divine laws to fashion the laws which they impose by that ultimate standard, because if they do not, God will punish them. To this also I entirely assent ...
>
> But the meaning of this passage of Blackstone, if it has a meaning, seems rather to be this: that no human law which conflicts with the Divine law is obligatory or binding; in other words, that no human law which conflicts with the Divine law *is a law*....[12]

Austin's protest against blurring the distinction between what law is and what it ought to be is quite general: it is a mistake, whatever our standard of what ought to be, whatever "the text by which we regulate our approbation or disapprobation." His examples, however, are always a confusion between law as it is and law as morality would require it to be. For him, it must be remembered, the fundamental principles of morality were God's commands, to which utility was an "index": besides this there was the actual accepted morality of a social group or "positive" morality.

Bentham insisted on this distinction without characterizing morality by reference to God but only, of course, by reference to the principles of utility. Both thinkers' prime reason for this insistence was to enable men to see steadily the precise issues posed by the existence of morally bad laws, and to understand the specific character of the authority of a legal order. Bentham's general recipe for life under the government of laws was simple: it was "*to obey punctually; to censure freely*."[13] But Bentham was especially aware, as an anxious spectator of the French revolution, that this was not enough: the time might come in any society when the law's commands were so evil that the question of resistance had to be faced, and it was then essential that the issues at stake at this point should neither be oversimplified nor obscured.[14] Yet, this was precisely what the confusion between law and morals had done and Bentham found that the confusion had spread symmetrically in two different directions. On the one hand Bentham had in mind the anarchist who argues thus: "This ought not to be the law, therefore it is not and I am free not merely to censure but to disregard it." On the other hand he thought of the reactionary who argues: "This is the law, therefore it is what it ought to be," and thus stifles criticism at its birth. Both errors, Bentham thought, were to be found in Blackstone: there was his incautious statement

---

12 Austin, *The Province of Jurisprudence Determined* 184–85 (Library of Ideas ed. 1954).

13 Bentham, *A Fragment on Government*, in I Works 221, 230 (Bowring ed. 1859) (preface, fifth para.).

14 See Bentham, *Principles of Legislation*, in *The Theory of Legislation* I, 65 n.* (Ogden ed. 1931) (c. XII, 2d para. n.*). Here we touch upon the most difficult of questions. If the law is not what it ought to be; if it openly combats with the principle of utility; ought we to obey it? Ought we to violate it? Ought we to remain neuter between the law which commands an evil, and morality which forbids it? See also Bentham, *A Fragment on Government*, in I *Works* 221, 287–88 (Bowring ed. 1859) (c. IV, 20th–25th paras.).

that human laws were invalid if contrary to the law of God,[15] and "that spirit of obsequious *quietism* that seems constitutional in our Author" which "will scarce ever let him recognise a difference" between what is and what ought to be.[16] This indeed was for Bentham the occupational disease of lawyers: "[I]n the eyes of lawyers—not to speak of their dupes—that is to say, as yet, the generality of non-lawyers the *is* and *ought to be* ... were one and indivisible."[17] There are therefore two dangers between which insistence on this distinction will help us to steer: the danger that law and its authority may be dissolved in man's conceptions of what law ought to be and the danger that the existing law may supplant morality as a final test of conduct and so escape criticism.

In view of later criticisms it is also important to distinguish several things that the Utilitarians did not mean by insisting on their separation of law and morals. They certainly accepted many of the things that might be called "the intersection of law and morals." First, they never denied that, as a matter of historical fact, the development of legal systems had been powerfully influenced by moral opinion, and, conversely, that moral standards had been profoundly influenced by law, so that the content of many legal rules mirrored moral rules or principles. It is not in fact always easy to trace this historical causal connection, but Bentham was certainly ready to admit its existence; so too Austin spoke of the "frequent coincidence"[18] of positive law and morality and attributed the confusion of what law is with what law ought to be to this very fact.

Secondly, neither Bentham nor his followers denied that by explicit legal provisions moral principles might at different points be brought into a legal system and form part of its rules or that courts might be legally bound to decide in accordance with what they thought just or best. Bentham indeed recognized, as Austin did not, that even the supreme legislative power might be subjected to legal restraints by a constitution[19] and would not have denied that moral principles, like those of the fifth amendment, might form the content of such legal constitutional restraints. Austin differed in thinking that restraints on the supreme legislative power could not have the force of law, but would remain merely political or moral checks;[20] but of course he would have recognized that a statute, for example, might confer a delegated legislative power and restrict the area of its exercise by reference to moral principles.

What both Bentham and Austin were anxious to assert were the following two simple things: first, in the absence of an expressed constitutional or legal provision, it could not follow from the mere fact that a rule violated standards of morality that it was not a rule of law; and conversely, it could not follow from the mere fact that a rule was morally desirable that it was a rule of law.

The history of this simple doctrine in the nineteenth century is too long and too intricate to trace here. Let me summarize it by saying that after it was propounded to the world by Austin it dominated English jurisprudence and constitutes part of the framework of most of those curiously English and perhaps unsatisfactory

15 I Blackstone, *Commentaries* *41. Bentham criticized "this dangerous maxim," saying "the natural tendency of such a doctrine is to impel a man, by the force of conscience, to rise up in arms against any law whatever that he happens not to like." Bentham, *A Fragment on Government*, in I *Works* 221, 287 (Bowring ed. 1859) (c. IV, 19th para.). See also Bentham, *A Comment on the Commentaries* 49 (1928) (c. III). For an expression of a fear lest anarchy result from such a doctrine, combined with a recognition that resistance may be justified on grounds of utility, see Austin, *op. cit. supra* note 12, at 186.

16 Bentham, *A Fragment on Government*, in I *Works* 221, 294 (Bowring ed. 1859) (c. V, 10th para.).

17 Bentham, *A Commentary on Humphrey's Real Property Code*, in 5 *Works* 389 (Bowring ed. 1843).

18 Austin, *op. cit. supra* note 12, at 162.

19 Bentham, *A Fragment on Government*, in I *Works* 221, 289–90 (Bowring ed. 1859) (c. IV, 33d–34th paras.).

20 See Austin, *op. cit. supra* note 12, at 231.

productions—the omnibus surveys of the whole field of jurisprudence. A succession of these were published after a full text of Austin's lectures finally appeared in 1863. In each of them the utilitarian separation of law and morals is treated as something that enables lawyers to attain a new clarity. Austin was said by one of his English successors, Amos, "to have delivered the law from the dead body of morality that still clung to it";[21] and even Maine, who was critical of Austin at many points, did not question this part of his doctrine. In the United States men like N. St. John Green,[22] Gray, and Holmes considered that insistence on this distinction had enabled the understanding of law as a means of social control to get off to a fruitful new start; they welcomed it both as self-evident and as illuminating as a revealing tautology. This distinction is, of course, one of the main themes of Holmes's most famous essay "The Path of the Law,"[23] but the place it had in the estimation of these American writers is best seen in what Gray wrote at the turn of the century in *The Nature and Sources of the Law*. He said:

> The great gain in its fundamental conceptions which Jurisprudence made during the last century was the recognition of the truth that the Law of a State ... is not an ideal, but something which actually exists.... [I]t is not that which ought to be, but that which is. To fix this definitely in the Jurisprudence of the Common Law, is the feat that Austin accomplished.[24]

II.

So much for the doctrine in the heyday of its success. Let us turn now to some of the criticisms. Undoubtedly, when Bentham and Austin insisted on the distinction between law as it is and as it ought to be, they had in mind *particular* laws the meanings of which were clear and so not in dispute, and they were concerned to argue that such laws, even if morally outrageous, were still laws. It is, however, necessary, in considering the criticisms which later developed, to consider more than those criticisms which were directed to this particular point if we are to get at the root of the dissatisfaction felt; we must also take account of the objection that, even if what the Utilitarians said on this particular point were true, their insistence on it, in a terminology suggesting a general cleavage between what is and ought to be law, obscured the fact that at other points there is an essential point of contact between the two. So in what follows I shall consider not only criticisms of the particular point which the Utilitarians had in mind, but also the claim that an essential connection between law and morals emerges if we examine how laws, the meanings of which are in dispute, are interpreted and applied in concrete cases; and that this connection emerges again if we widen our point of view and ask, not whether every particular rule of law must satisfy a moral minimum in order to be a law, but whether a

---

21 Amos, *The Science of Law* 4 (5th ed. 1881). See also Markby, *Elements of Law* 4–5 (5th ed. 1896): Austin, by establishing the distinction between positive law and morals, not only laid the foundation for a science of law, but cleared the conception of law ... of a number of pernicious consequences to which ... it had been supposed to lead. Positive laws, as Austin has shown, must be legally binding, and yet a law may be unjust ... He has admitted that law itself may be immoral, in which case it may be our moral duty to disobey it....
Cf. Holland, *Jurisprudence* 1–20 (1880).

22 See Green, Book Review, 6 *Am. L. Rev.* 57, 61 (1871) (reprinted in Green, *Essays and Notes on the Law of Tort and Crime* 31, 35 [1933]).

23 10 *Harv. L. Rev.* 457 (1897).

24 Gray, *The Nature and Sources of the Law* 94 (1st ed. 1909) (§213).

system of rules which altogether failed to do this could be a legal system.

There is, however, one major initial complexity by which criticism has been much confused. We must remember that the Utilitarians combined with their insistence on the separation of law and morals two other equally famous but distinct doctrines. One was the important truth that a purely analytical study of legal concepts, a study of the meaning of the distinctive vocabulary of the law, was as vital to our understanding of the nature of law as historical or sociological studies, though of course it could not supplant them. The other doctrine was the famous imperative theory of law—that law is essentially a command.

These three doctrines constitute the utilitarian tradition in jurisprudence; yet they are distinct doctrines. It is possible to endorse the separation between law and morals and to value analytical inquiries into the meaning of legal concepts and yet think it wrong to conceive of law as essentially a command. One source of great confusion in the criticism of the separation of law and morals was the belief that the falsity of any one of these three doctrines in the utilitarian tradition showed the other two to be false; what was worse was the failure to see that there were three quite separate doctrines in this tradition. The indiscriminate use of the label "positivism" to designate ambiguously each one of these three separate doctrines (together with some others which the Utilitarians never professed) has perhaps confused the issue more than any other single factor.[25] Some of the early American critics of the Austinian doctrine were, however, admirably clear on just this matter.

Gray, for example, added at the end of the tribute to Austin, which I have already quoted, the words, "He may have been wrong in treating the Law of the State as being the command of the sovereign"[26] and he touched shrewdly on many points where the command theory is defective. But other critics have been less clearheaded and have thought that the inadequacies of the command theory which gradually came to light were sufficient to demonstrate the falsity of the separation of law and morals.

This was a mistake, but a natural one. To see how natural it was we must look a little more closely at the command idea. The famous theory that law is a command was a part of a wider and more ambitious claim. Austin said that the notion of a command was "the *key* to the sciences of jurisprudence and morals,"[27] and contemporary attempts to elucidate moral judgments in terms of "imperative" or "prescriptive" utterances echo this ambitious claim. But the command theory, viewed as an effort to identify even the quintessence of law, let alone the quintessence of morals, seems breathtaking in its simplicity and quite

25 It may help to identify five (there may be more) meanings of "positivism" bandied about in contemporary jurisprudence:

(1) the contention that laws are commands of human beings, see pp. 120–23 *infra*,

(2) the contention that there is no necessary connection between law and morals or law as it is and ought to be, see pp. 115–19 *supra*,

(3) the contention that the analysis (or study of the meaning) of legal concepts is (a) worth pursuing and (b) to be distinguished from historical inquiries into the causes or origins of laws, from sociological inquiries into the relation of law and other social phenomena, and from the criticism or appraisal of law whether in terms of morals, social aims, "functions," or otherwise, see pp. 135–36 *infra*,

(4) the contention that a legal system is a "closed logical system" in which correct legal decisions can be deduced by logical means from predetermined legal rules without reference to social aims, policies, moral standards, see pp. 124–26 *infra*, and

(5) the contention that moral judgments cannot be established or defended, as statements of facts can, by rational argument, evidence, or proof ("noncognitivism" in ethics), see pp. 135–36 *infra*.

Bentham and Austin held the views described in (1), (2), and (3) but not those in (4) and (5). Opinion (4) is often ascribed to analytical jurists, see pages pp. 124–26 *infra*, but I know of no "analyst" who held this view.

26 Gray, *The Nature and Sources of the Law* 94–95 (2d ed. 1921).

27 Austin, *op. cit. supra* note 12, at 13.

inadequate. There is much, even in the simplest legal system, that is distorted if presented as a command. Yet the Utilitarians thought that the essence of a legal system could be conveyed if the notion of a command were supplemented by that of a habit of obedience. The simple scheme was this: What is a command? It is simply an expression by one person of the desire that another person should do or abstain from some action, accompanied by a threat of punishment which is likely to follow disobedience. Commands are laws if two conditions are satisfied: first, they must be general; second, they must be commanded by what (as both Bentham and Austin claimed) exists in every political society whatever its constitutional form, namely, a person or a group of persons who are in receipt of habitual obedience from most of the society but pay no such obedience to others. These persons are its sovereign. Thus law is the command of the uncommanded commanders of society—the creation of the legally untrammelled will of the sovereign who is by definition outside the law.

It is easy to see that this account of a legal system is thread-bare. One can also see why it might seem that its inadequacy is due to the omission of some essential connection with morality. The situation which the simple trilogy of command, sanction, and sovereign avails to describe, if you take these notions at all precisely, is like that of a gunman saying to his victim, "Give me your money or your life." The only difference is that in the case of a legal system the gunman says it to a large number of people who are accustomed to the racket and habitually surrender to it. Law surely is not the gunman situation writ large, and legal order is surely not to be thus simply identified with compulsion.

This scheme, despite the points of obvious analogy between a statute and a command, omits some of the most characteristic elements of law. Let me cite a few. It is wrong to think of a legislature (and a fortiori an electorate) with a changing membership, as a group of persons habitually obeyed: this simple idea is suited only to a monarch sufficiently long-lived for a "habit" to grow up. Even if we waive this point, nothing which legislators do makes law unless they comply with fundamental accepted rules specifying the essential lawmaking procedures. This is true even in a system having a simple unitary constitution like the British. These fundamental accepted rules specifying what the legislature must do to legislate are not commands habitually obeyed, nor can they be expressed as habits of obedience to persons. They lie at the root of a legal system, and what is most missing in the utilitarian scheme is an analysis of what it is for a social group and its officials to accept such rules. This notion, not that of a command as Austin claimed, is the "key to the science of jurisprudence," or at least one of the keys.

Again, Austin, in the case of a democracy, looked past the legislators to the electorate as "the sovereign" (or in England as part of it). He thought that in the United States the mass of the electors to the state and federal legislatures were the sovereign whose commands, given by their "agents" in the legislatures, were law. But on this footing the whole notion of the sovereign outside the law being "habitually obeyed" by the "bulk" of the population must go: for in this case the "bulk" obeys the bulk, that is, it obeys itself. Plainly the general acceptance of the authority of a lawmaking procedure, irrespective of the changing individuals who operate it from time to time, can be only distorted by an analysis in terms of mass habitual obedience to certain persons who are by definition outside the law, just as the cognate but much simpler phenomenon of the general social acceptance of a rule, say of taking off the hat when entering a church, would be distorted if represented as habitual obedience by the mass to specific persons.

Other critics dimly sensed a further and more important defect in the command theory, yet blurred the edge of an important criticism by assuming that the defect was due to the failure to insist upon some important connection between law and morals. This more radical defect is as follows. The picture that the command theory draws of life under law is essentially a simple relationship of the commander to the commanded, of superior to inferior, of top to bottom; the relationship is vertical between the commanders or authors of the law conceived of as essentially outside the law and those who are commanded and subject to the law. In this picture no place, or only an accidental or subordinate place, is afforded for a distinction between types of legal rules which are in fact radically different. Some laws require men to act in certain ways or to abstain from acting whether they wish to or not. The criminal law consists largely of rules of this sort: like commands they are simply "obeyed" or "disobeyed." But other legal rules are presented to society in quite different ways and have quite different functions. They provide facilities more or less elaborate for individuals to create structures of rights and duties for the conduct of life within the coercive framework of the law. Such are the rules enabling individuals to make contracts, wills, and trusts, and generally to mould their legal relations with others. Such rules, unlike the criminal law, are not factors designed to obstruct wishes and choices of an antisocial sort. On the contrary, these rules provide facilities for the realization of wishes and choices. They do not say (like commands) "do this whether you wish it or not," but rather "if you wish to do this, here is the way to do it." Under these rules we exercise powers, make claims, and assert rights. These phrases mark off characteristic features of laws that confer rights and powers; they are laws which are, so to speak, put at the disposition of individuals in a way in which the criminal law is not. Much ingenuity has gone into the task of "reducing" laws of this second sort to some complex variant of laws of the first sort. The effort to show that laws conferring rights are "really" only conditional stipulations of sanctions to be exacted from the person ultimately under a legal duty characterizes much of Kelsen's work.[28] Yet to urge this is really just to exhibit dogmatic determination to suppress one aspect of the legal system in order to maintain the theory that the stipulation of a sanction, like Austin's command, represents the quintessence of law. One might as well urge that the rules of baseball were "really" only complex conditional directions to the scorer and that this showed their real or "essential" nature.

One of the first jurists in England to break with the Austinian tradition, Salmond, complained that the analysis in terms of commands left the notion of a right unprovided with a place.[29] But he confused the point. He argued first, and correctly, that if laws are merely commands it is inexplicable that we should have come to speak of legal rights and powers as conferred or arising under them, but then wrongly concluded that the rules of a legal system must necessarily be connected with moral rules or principles of justice and that only on this footing could the phenomenon of legal rights be explained. Otherwise, Salmond thought, we would have to say that a mere "verbal coincidence" connects the concepts of legal and moral right. Similarly, continental critics of the Utilitarians, always alive to the complexity of the notion of a subjective right, insisted that the command theory gave it no place. Hägerström insisted that if laws were merely commands the notion of an individual's

28 See, e.g., Kelsen, *General Theory of Law and State* 58–61, 143–44 (1945). According to Kelsen, all laws, not only those conferring rights and powers, are reducible to such "primary norms" conditionally stipulating sanctions.

29 Salmond, *The First Principles of Jurisprudence* 97–98 (1893). He protested against "the creed of what is termed the English school of jurisprudence," because it "attempted to deprive the idea of law of that ethical significance which is one of its most essential elements." *Id.* at 9, 10.

right was really inexplicable, for commands are, as he said, something which we either obey or we do not obey; they do not confer rights.[30] But he, too, concluded that moral, or, as he put it, common-sense, notions of justice must therefore be necessarily involved in the analysis of any legal structure elaborate enough to confer rights.[31]

Yet, surely these arguments are confused. Rules that confer rights, though distinct from commands, need not be moral rules or coincide with them. Rights, after all, exist under the rules of ceremonies, games, and in many other spheres regulated by rules which are irrelevant to the question of justice or what the law ought to be. Nor need rules which confer rights be just or morally good rules. The rights of a master over his slaves show us that. "Their merit or demerit," as Austin termed it, depends on how rights are distributed in society and over whom or what they are exercised. These critics indeed revealed the inadequacy of the simple notions of command and habit for the analysis of law; at many points it is apparent that the social acceptance of a rule or standard of authority (even if it is motivated only by fear or superstition or rests on inertia) must be brought into the analysis and cannot itself be reduced to the two simple terms. Yet nothing in this showed the utilitarian insistence on the distinction between the existence of law and its "merits" to be wrong.

III.

I now turn to a distinctively American criticism of the separation of the law that is from the law that ought to be. It emerged from the critical study of the judicial process with which American jurisprudence has been on the whole so beneficially occupied. The most skeptical of these critics—the loosely named "Realists" of the 1930s—perhaps too naïvely accepted the conceptual framework of the natural sciences as adequate for the characterization of law and for the analysis of rule-guided action of which a living system of law at least partly consists. But they opened men's eyes to what actually goes on when courts decide cases, and the contrast they drew between the actual facts of judicial decision and the traditional terminology for describing it as if it were a wholly logical operation was usually illuminating; for in spite of some exaggeration the "Realists" made us acutely conscious of one cardinal feature of human language and human thought, emphasis on which is vital not only for the understanding of law but in areas of philosophy far beyond the confines of jurisprudence. The insight of this school may be presented in the following example. A legal rule forbids you to take a vehicle into the public park. Plainly this forbids an automobile, but what about bicycles, roller skates, toy automobiles? What about airplanes? Are these, as we say, to be called "vehicles" for the purpose of the rule or not? If we are to communicate with each other at all, and if, as in the most elementary form of law, we are to express our intentions that a certain type of behavior be regulated by rules, then the general words we use—like "vehicle" in the case I consider—must have some standard instance in which no doubts are felt about its application. There must be a core of settled meaning, but there will be, as well, a penumbra of debatable cases in which words are neither obviously applicable nor obviously ruled out. These cases will each have some features in common with the standard case; they will lack others or be accompanied by features not present in the standard case. Human invention and natural

30 Hägerström, *Inquiries into the Nature of Law and Morals* 217 (Olivecrona ed. 1953): "[T]he whole theory of the subjective rights of private individuals is incompatible with the imperative theory." See also *id.* at 221: The description of them [claims to legal protection] as rights is wholly derived from the idea that the law which is concerned with them is a true expression of rights and duties in the sense in which the popular notion of justice understands these terms.

31 *Id.* at 218.

processes continually throw up such variants on the familiar, and if we are to say that these ranges of facts do or do not fall under existing rules, then the classifier must make a decision which is not dictated to him, for the facts and phenomena to which we fit our words and apply our rules are as it were *dumb*. The toy automobile cannot speak up and say, "I am a vehicle for the purpose of this legal rule," nor can the roller skates chorus, "We are not a vehicle." Fact situations do not await us neatly labeled, creased, and folded, nor is their legal classification written on them to be simply read off by the judge. Instead, in applying legal rules, someone must take the responsibility of deciding that words do or do not cover some case in hand with all the practical consequences involved in this decision.

We may call the problems which arise outside the hard core of standard instances or settled meaning "problems of the penumbra"; they are always with us whether in relation to such trivial things as the regulation of the use of the public park or in relation to the multidimensional generalities of a constitution. If a penumbra of uncertainty must surround all legal rules, then their application to specific cases in the penumbral area cannot be a matter of logical deduction, and so deductive reasoning, which for generations has been cherished as the very perfection of human reasoning, cannot serve as a model for what judges, or indeed anyone, should do in bringing particular cases under general rules. In this area men cannot live by deduction alone. And it follows that if legal arguments and legal decisions of penumbral questions are to be rational, their rationality must lie in something other than a logical relation to premises. So if it is rational or "sound" to argue and to decide that for the purposes of this rule an airplane is not a vehicle, this argument must be sound or rational without being logically conclusive. What is it then that makes such decisions correct or at least better than alternative decisions? Again, it seems true to say that the criterion which makes a decision sound in such cases is some concept of what the law ought to be; it is easy to slide from that into saying that it must be a moral judgment about what law ought to be. So here we touch upon a point of necessary "intersection between law and morals" which demonstrates the falsity or, at any rate, the misleading character of the Utilitarians' emphatic insistence on the separation of law as it is and ought to be. Surely, Bentham and Austin could only have written as they did because they misunderstood or neglected this aspect of the judicial process, because they ignored the problems of the penumbra.

The misconception of the judicial process which ignores the problems of the penumbra and which views the process as consisting pre-eminently in deductive reasoning is often stigmatized as the error of "formalism" or "literalism." My question now is, how and to what extent does the demonstration of this error show the utilitarian distinction to be wrong or misleading? Here there are many issues which have been confused, but I can only disentangle some. The charge of formalism has been leveled both at the "positivist" legal theorist and at the courts, but of course it must be a very different charge in each case. Leveled at the legal theorist, the charge means that he has made a theoretical mistake about the character of legal decision; he has thought of the reasoning involved as consisting in deduction from premises in which the judges' practical choices or decisions play no part. It would be easy to show that Austin was guiltless of this error: only an entire misconception of what analytical jurisprudence is and why he thought it important has led to the view that he, or any other analyst, believed that the law was a closed logical system in which judges deduced their decisions from premises.[32] On the contrary, he was very much alive to the character of language, to its vagueness or open character;[33] he thought that in the penumbral situation judges must necessarily legislate,[34] and, in accents that sometimes recall those of the late Judge Jerome Frank, he berated the common-law judges for legislating feebly and timidly and for blindly relying on real or fancied analogies with past cases instead of adapting their decisions to the growing needs of society as revealed by the moral standard of utility.[35] The villains of this piece, responsible for the conception of the judge as an automaton, are not the Utilitarian thinkers. The responsibility, if it is to be laid at the door of any theorist, is with thinkers like Blackstone and, at an earlier stage, Montesquieu. The root of this evil is preoccupation with the separation of powers and Blackstone's "childish fiction" (as Austin termed it) that judges only "find," never "make," law.

But we are concerned with "formalism" as a vice not of jurists but of judges. What precisely is it for a judge to commit this error, to be a "formalist," "automatic," a "slot machine"? Curiously enough the literature which is full of the denunciation of these vices never makes this clear in concrete terms; instead we have only descriptions which cannot mean what they appear to say: it is said that in the formalist error courts make an excessive use of logic, take a thing to "a dryly logical extreme,"[36] or make an excessive use of analytical methods. But just how in being a formalist does a judge make an excessive use of logic? It is

32 This misunderstanding of analytical jurisprudence is to be found in, among others, Stone, *The Province and Function of Law* 141 (1950): In short, rejecting the implied assumption that all propositions of all parts of the law must be logically consistent with each other and proceed on a single set of definitions ... he [Cardozo, J.,] denied that the law is actually what the analytical jurist, *for his limited purposes*, assumes it to be.

See also *id.* at 49, 52, 138, 140; Friedmann, *Legal Theory* 209 (3rd ed. 1953). This misunderstanding seems to depend on the unexamined and false belief that analytical studies of the meaning of legal terms would be impossible or absurd if, to reach sound decisions in particular cases, more than a capacity for formal logical reasoning from unambiguous and clear predetermined premises is required.

33 See the discussion of vagueness and uncertainty in law, in Austin, *op. cit. supra* note 12, at 202–05, 207, in which Austin recognized that, in consequence of this vagueness, often only "fallible tests" can be provided for determining whether particular cases fall under general expressions.

34 See Austin, *op. cit. supra* note 12, at 191: "I cannot understand how any person who has considered the subject can suppose that society could possibly have gone on if judges had not legislated...." As a corrective to the belief that the analytical jurist must take a "slot machine" or "mechanical" view of the judicial process it is worth noting the following observations made by Austin:

1) Whenever law has to be applied, the "'competition of opposite analogies'" may arise, for the case "may resemble in some of its points" cases to which the rule has been applied in the past and in other points "cases from which the application of the law has been withheld." 2 Austin, *Lectures on Jurisprudence* 633 (5th ed. 1885).
2) Judges have commonly decided cases and so derived new rules by "building" on a variety of grounds including sometimes (in Austin's opinion too rarely) their views of what law ought to be. Most commonly they have derived law from preexisting law by "consequence founded on analogy," i.e., they have made a new rule "in *consequence* of the existence of a similar rule applying to subjects which are *analogous*...." 2 *id.* at 638–39.
3) "[I]f every rule in a system of law were perfectly definite or precise," these difficulties incident to the application of law would not arise. "But the ideal completeness and correctness I now have imagined is not attainable in fact.... though the system had been built and ordered with matchless solicitude and skill." 2 *id.* at 997–98. Of course he thought that much could and should be done by codification to eliminate uncertainty. See 2 *id.* at 662–81.

35 2 *id.* at 641: Nothing, indeed, can be more natural, than that legislators, direct or judicial (especially if they be narrow-minded, timid and unskillful), should lean as much as they can on the examples set by their predecessors.

See also 2 *id.* at 647: But it is much to be regretted that Judges of capacity, experience and weight, have not seized every opportunity of introducing a new rule (a rule beneficial for the future).... This is the reproach I should be inclined to make against Lord Eldon.... [T]he judges of the Common Law Courts would not do what they ought to have done, namely to model their rules of law and of procedure to the growing exigencies of society, instead of stupidly and sulkily adhering to the old and barbarous usages.

36 *Hynes v. New York Cent. R.R.*, 231 N.Y. 229, 235, 131 N.E. 898, 900 (1921); see Pound, *Interpretations of Legal History* 123 (2d ed. 1930); Stone, *op. cit. supra* note 32, at 140–41.

clear that the essence of his error is to give some general term an interpretation which is blind to social values and consequences (or which is in some other way stupid or perhaps merely disliked by critics). But logic does not prescribe interpretation of terms; it dictates neither the stupid nor intelligent interpretation of any expression. Logic only tells you hypothetically that *if* you give a certain term a certain interpretation then a certain conclusion follows. Logic is silent on how to classify particulars—and this is the heart of a judicial decision. So this reference to logic and to logical extremes is a misnomer for something else, which must be this. A judge has to apply a rule to a concrete case—perhaps the rule that one may not take a stolen "vehicle" across state lines, and in this case an airplane has been taken.[37] He either does not see or pretends not to see that the general terms of this rule are susceptible of different interpretations and that he has a choice left open uncontrolled by linguistic conventions. He ignores, or is blind to, the fact that he is in the area of the penumbra and is not dealing with a standard case. Instead of choosing in the light of social aims, the judge fixes the meaning in a different way. He either takes the meaning that the word most obviously suggests in its ordinary nonlegal context to ordinary men, or one which the word has been given in some other legal context, or, still worse, he thinks of a standard case and then arbitrarily identifies certain features in it—for example, in the case of a vehicle, (1) normally used on land, (2) capable of carrying a human person, (3) capable of being self-propelled—and treats these three as always necessary and always sufficient conditions for the use in all contexts of the word "vehicle," irrespective of the social consequences of giving it this interpretation. This choice, not "logic," would force the judge to include a toy motor car (if electrically propelled) and to exclude bicycles and the airplane. In all this there is possibly great stupidity but no more "logic," and no less, than in cases in which the interpretation given to a general term and the consequent application of some general rule to a particular case is consciously controlled by some identified social aim.

Decisions made in a fashion as blind as this would scarcely deserve the name of decisions; we might as well toss a penny in applying a rule of law. But it is at least doubtful whether any judicial decisions (even in England) have been quite as automatic as this. Rather, either the interpretations stigmatized as automatic have resulted from the conviction that it is fairer in a criminal statute to take a meaning which would jump to the mind of the ordinary man at the cost even of defeating other values, and this itself is a social policy (though possibly a bad one); or much more frequently, what is stigmatized as "mechanical" and "automatic" is a determined choice made indeed in the light of a social aim but of a conservative social aim. Certainly many of the Supreme Court decisions at the turn of the century which have been so stigmatized[38] represent clear choices in the penumbral area to give effect to a policy of a conservative type. This is peculiarly true of Mr. Justice Peckham's opinions defining the spheres of police power and due process.[39]

But how does the wrongness of deciding cases in an automatic and mechanical way and the rightness of deciding cases by reference to social purposes show that the utilitarian insistence on the distinction between what the law is and what it ought to be is wrong? I take it that no one who wished to use these vices of formalism as proof that the distinction between what

37 See *McBoyle v. United States*, 283 U.S. 25 (1931).

38 See, e.g., Pound, "Mechanical Jurisprudence," 8 *Colum. L. Rev.* 605, 615–16 (1908).

39 See, e.g., *Lochner v. New York*, 198 U.S. 45 (1905). Justice Peckham's opinion that there were no reasonable grounds for interfering with the right of free contract by determining the hours of labour in the occupation of a baker may indeed be a wrong-headed piece of conservatism but there is nothing automatic or mechanical about it.

is and what ought to be is mistaken would deny that the decisions stigmatized as automatic are law; nor would he deny that the system in which such automatic decisions are made is a legal system. Surely he would say that they are law, but they are bad law, they ought not to be law. But this would be to use the distinction, not to refute it; and of course both Bentham and Austin used it to attack judges for failing to decide penumbral cases in accordance with the growing needs of society.

Clearly, if the demonstration of the errors of formalism is to show the utilitarian distinction to be wrong, the point must be drastically restated. The point must be not merely that a judicial decision to be rational must be made in the light of some conception of what ought to be, but that the aims, the social policies and purposes to which judges should appeal if their decisions are to be rational, are themselves to be considered as part of the law in some suitably wide sense of "law" which is held to be more illuminating than that used by the Utilitarians. This restatement of the point would have the following consequence: instead of saying that the recurrence of penumbral questions shows us that legal rules are essentially incomplete, and that, when they fail to determine decisions, judges must legislate and so exercise a creative choice between alternatives, we shall say that the social policies which guide the judges' choice are in a sense there for them to discover; the judges are only "drawing out" of the rule what, if it is properly understood, is "latent" within it. To call this judicial legislation is to obscure some essential continuity between the clear cases of the application and the penumbral decisions. I shall question later whether this way of talking is salutory, but I wish at this time to point out something obvious, but likely, if not stated, to tangle the issues. It does not follow that, because the opposite of a decision reached blindly in the formalist or literalist manner is a decision intelligently reached by reference to some conception of what ought to be, we have a junction of law and morals. We must, I think, beware of thinking in a too simple-minded fashion about the word "ought." This is not because there is no distinction to be made between law as it is and ought to be. Far from it. It is because the distinction should be between what is and what from many different points of view ought to be. The word "ought" merely reflects the presence of some standard of criticism; one of these standards is a moral standard but not all standards are moral. We say to our neighbour, "You ought not to lie," and that may certainly be a moral judgment, but we should remember that the baffled poisoner may say, "I ought to have given her a second dose." The point here is that intelligent decisions which we oppose to mechanical or formal decisions are not necessarily identical with decisions defensible on moral grounds. We may say of many a decision: "Yes, that is right; that is as it ought to be," and we may mean only that some accepted purpose or policy has been thereby advanced; we may not mean to endorse the moral propriety of the policy or the decision. So the contrast between the mechanical decision and the intelligent one can be reproduced inside a system dedicated to the pursuit of the most evil aims. It does not exist as a contrast to be found only in legal systems which, like our own, widely recognize principles of justice and moral claims of individuals.

An example may make this point plainer. With us the task of sentencing in criminal cases is the one that seems most obviously to demand from the judge the exercise of moral judgment. Here the factors to be weighed seem clearly to be moral factors: society must not be exposed to wanton attack; too much misery must not be inflicted on either the victim or his dependents; efforts must be made to enable him to lead a better life and regain a position in the society whose laws he has violated. To a judge striking the balance among these claims, with all the discretion and perplexities involved, his task seems as plain an example of the exercise of moral judgment as could be; and it seems to be the polar opposite of some mechanical application of a tariff of penalties fixing a sentence careless of the moral claims which in our system have to be weighed. So here intelligent and rational decision is guided however uncertainly by moral aims. But we have only to vary the example to see that this need not necessarily be so and surely, if it need not necessarily be so, the Utilitarian point remains unshaken. Under the Nazi regime men were sentenced by courts for criticism of the regime. Here the choice of sentence might be guided exclusively by consideration of what was needed to maintain the state's tyranny effectively. What sentence would both terrorize the public at large and keep the friends and family of the prisoner in suspense so that both hope and fear would cooperate as factors making for subservience? The prisoner of such a system would be regarded simply as an object to be used in pursuit of these aims. Yet, in contrast with a mechanical decision, decision on these grounds would be intelligent and purposive, and from one point of view the decision would be as it ought to be. Of course, I am not unaware that a whole philosophical tradition has sought to demonstrate the fact that we cannot correctly call decisions or behavior truly rational unless they are in conformity with moral aims and principles. But the example I have used seems to me to serve at least as a warning that we cannot use the errors of formalism as something which per se demonstrates the falsity of the Utilitarian insistence on the distinction between law as it is and law as *morally* it ought to be.

We can now return to the main point. If it is true that the intelligent decision of penumbral questions is one made not mechanically but in the light of aims, purposes, and policies, though not necessarily in the light of anything we would call moral principles, is it wise to express this important fact by saying that the firm utilitarian distinction between what the law is and what it ought to be should be dropped? Perhaps the claim that it is wise cannot be theoretically refuted for it is, in effect, an *invitation* to revise our conception of what a legal rule is. We are invited to include in the "rule" the various aims and policies in the light of which its penumbral cases are decided on the ground that these aims have, because of their importance, as much right to be called law as the core of legal rules whose meaning is settled. But though an invitation cannot be refuted, it may be refused and I would proffer two reasons for refusing this invitation. First, everything we have learned about the judicial process can be expressed in other less mysterious ways. We can say laws are incurably incomplete and we must decide the penumbral cases rationally by reference to social aims. I think Holmes, who had such a vivid appreciation of the fact that "general propositions do not decide concrete cases," would have put it that way. Second, to insist on the Utilitarian distinction is to emphasize that the hard core of settled meaning is law in some centrally important sense and that even if there are borderlines, there must first be lines. If this were not so the notion of rules controlling courts' decisions would be senseless as some of the "Realists"—in their most extreme moods, and, I think, on bad grounds—claimed.[40]

---

40 One recantation of this extreme position is worth mention in the present context. In the first edition of *The Bramble Bush*, Professor Llewellyn committed himself wholeheartedly to the view that "what these officials do about disputes is, to my mind, the law itself" and that "*rules* ... are important so far as they help you ... predict what judges will do.... That is all their importance, except as pretty playthings." Llewellyn, *The Bramble Bush* 3, 5 (1st ed. 1930). In the second edition he said that these were "unhappy words when not more fully developed, and they are plainly at best a very partial statement of the whole truth.... [O]ne office of law is to control officials in some part, and to guide them even ... where no thoroughgoing control is possible, or is desired.... [T]he words fail to take proper account ... of the office of the institution of law as an instrument of conscious shaping...." Llewellyn, *The Bramble Bush* 9 (2d ed. 1951).

By contrast, to soften the distinction, to assert mysteriously that there is some fused identity between law as it is and as it ought to be, is to suggest that all legal questions are fundamentally like those of the penumbra. It is to assert that there is no central element of actual law to be seen in the core of central meaning which rules have, that there is nothing in the nature of a legal rule inconsistent with *all* questions being open to reconsideration in the light of social policy. Of course, it is good to be occupied with the penumbra. Its problems are rightly the daily diet of the law schools. But to be occupied with the penumbra is one thing, to be preoccupied with it another. And preoccupation with the penumbra is, if I may say so, as rich a source of confusion in the American legal tradition as formalism in the English. Of course we might abandon the notion that rules have authority; we might cease to attach force or even meaning to an argument that a case falls clearly within a rule and the scope of a precedent. We might call all such reasoning "automatic" or "mechanical," which is already the routine invective of the courts. But until we decide that this *is* what we want, we should not encourage it by obliterating the Utilitarian distinction.

IV.

The third criticism of the separation of law and morals is of a very different character; it certainly is less an intellectual argument against the Utilitarian distinction than a passionate appeal supported not by detailed reasoning but by reminders of a terrible experience. For it consists of the testimony of those who have descended into Hell, and, like Ulysses or Dante, brought back a message for human beings. Only in this case the Hell was not beneath or beyond earth, but on it; it was a Hell created on earth by men for other men.

This appeal comes from those German thinkers who lived through the Nazi regime and reflected upon its evil manifestations in the legal system. One of these thinkers, Gustav Radbruch, had himself shared the "positivist" doctrine until the Nazi tyranny, but he was converted by this experience and so his appeal to other men to discard the doctrine of the separation of law and morals has the special poignancy of a recantation. What is important about this criticism is that it really does confront the particular point which Bentham and Austin had in mind in urging the separation of law as it is and as it ought to be. These German thinkers put their insistence on the need to join together what the Utilitarians separated just where this separation was of most importance in the eyes of the Utilitarians; for they were concerned with the problem posed by the existence of morally evil laws.

Before his conversion Radbruch held that resistance to law was a matter for the personal conscience, to be thought out by the individual as a moral problem, and the validity of a law could not be disproved by showing that its requirements were morally evil or even by showing that the effect of compliance with the law would be more evil than the effect of disobedience. Austin, it may be recalled, was emphatic in condemning those who said that if human laws conflicted with the fundamental principles of morality then they cease to be laws, as talking "stark nonsense."

> The most pernicious laws, and therefore those which are most opposed to the will of God, have been and are continually enforced as laws by judicial tribunals. Suppose an act innocuous, or positively beneficial, be prohibited by the sovereign under the penalty of death; if I commit this act, I shall be tried and condemned, and if I object to the sentence, that it is contrary to the law of God ... the court of justice will demonstrate the inconclusiveness of my reasoning by hanging me up, in

> pursuance of the law of which I have impugned the validity. An exception, demurrer, or plea, founded on the law of God was never heard in a Court of Justice, from the creation of the world down to the present moment.[41]

These are strong, indeed brutal words, but we must remember that they went along—in the case of Austin and, of course, Bentham—with the conviction that if laws reached a certain degree of iniquity then there would be a plain moral obligation to resist them and to withhold obedience. We shall see, when we consider the alternatives, that this simple presentation of the human dilemma which may arise has much to be said for it.

Radbruch, however, had concluded from the ease with which the Nazi regime had exploited subservience to mere law—or expressed, as he thought, in the "positivist" slogan "law as law" (*Gesetz als Gesetz*)—and from the failure of the German legal profession to protest against the enormities which they were required to perpetrate in the name of law, that "positivism" (meaning here the insistence on the separation of law as it is from law as it ought to be) had powerfully contributed to the horrors. His considered reflections led him to the doctrine that the fundamental principles of humanitarian morality were part of the very concept of *Recht* or Legality and that no positive enactment or statute, however clearly it was expressed and however clearly it conformed with the formal criteria of validity of a given legal system, could be valid if it contravened basic principles of morality. This doctrine can be appreciated fully only if the nuances imported by the German word *Recht* are grasped. But it is clear that the doctrine meant that every lawyer and judge should denounce statutes that transgressed the fundamental principles not as merely immoral or wrong but as having no legal character, and enactments which on this ground lack the quality of law should not be taken into account in working out the legal position of any given individual in particular circumstances. The striking recantation of his previous doctrine is unfortunately omitted from the translation of his works, but it should be read by all who wish to think afresh on the question of the interconnection of law and morals.[42]

It is impossible to read without sympathy Radbruch's passionate demand that the German legal conscience should be open to the demands of morality and his complaint that this has been too little the case in the German tradition. On the other hand there is an extraordinary naïveté in the view that insensitiveness to the demands of morality and subservience to state power in a people like the Germans should have arisen from the belief that law might be law though it failed to conform with the minimum requirements of morality. Rather this terrible history prompts inquiry into why emphasis on the slogan "law is law," and the distinction between law and morals, acquired a sinister character in Germany, but elsewhere, as with the Utilitarians themselves, went along with the most enlightened liberal attitudes. But something more disturbing than naïveté is latent in Radbruch's whole presentation of the issues to which the existence of morally iniquitous laws give rise. It is not, I think, uncharitable to say that we can see in his argument that he has only half digested the spiritual message of liberalism which he is seeking to convey to the legal profession. For everything that he says is really dependent upon an enormous

41 Austin, *The Province of Jurisprudence Determined* 185 (Library of Ideas ed. 1954).

42 See Radbruch, *Gesetzliches Unrecht und* Übergesetzliches *Recht*, I *Süddeutsche Juristen-Zeitung* 105 (Germany 1946) (reprinted in Radbruch, *Rechtsphilosophie* 347 [4th ed. 1950]). I have used the translation of part of this essay and of Radbruch, *Die Erneurung des Rechts*, 2. *Die Wandlung* 8 (Germany 1947), prepared by Professor Lon Fuller of the Harvard Law School as a mimeographed supplement to the readings in jurisprudence used in his course at Harvard.

overvaluation of the importance of the bare fact that a rule may be said to be a valid rule of law, as if this, once declared, was conclusive of the final moral question: "Ought this rule of law to be obeyed?" Surely the truly liberal answer to any sinister use of the slogan "law is law" or of the distinction between law and morals is, "Very well, but that does not conclude the question. Law is not morality; do not let it supplant morality."

However, we are not left to a mere academic discussion in order to evaluate the plea which Radbruch made for the revision of the distinction between law and morals. After the war Radbruch's conception of law as containing in itself the essential moral principle of humanitarianism was applied in practice by German courts in certain cases in which local war criminals, spies, and informers under the Nazi regime were punished. The special importance of these cases is that the persons accused of these crimes claimed that what they had done was not illegal under the laws of the regime in force at the time these actions were performed. This plea was met with the reply that the laws upon which they relied were invalid as contravening the fundamental principles of morality. Let me cite briefly one of these cases.[43]

In 1944 a woman, wishing to be rid of her husband, denounced him to the authorities for insulting remarks he had made about Hitler while home on leave from the German army. The wife was under no legal duty to report his acts, though what he had said was apparently in violation of statutes making it illegal to make statements detrimental to the government of the Third Reich or to impair by any means the military defense of the German people. The husband was arrested and sentenced to death, apparently pursuant to these statutes, though he was not executed but was sent to the front. In 1949 the wife was prosecuted in a West German court for an offense which we would describe as illegally depriving a person of his freedom (*rechtswidrige Freiheitsberaubung*). This was punishable as a crime under the German Criminal Code of 1871 which had remained in force continuously since its enactment. The wife pleaded that her husband's imprisonment was pursuant to the Nazi statutes and hence that she had committed no crime. The court of appeal to which the case ultimately came held that the wife was guilty of procuring the deprivation of her husband's liberty by denouncing him to the German courts, even though he had been sentenced by a court for having violated a statute, since, to quote the words of the court, the statute "was contrary to the sound conscience and sense of justice of all decent human beings." This reasoning was followed in many cases which have been hailed as a triumph of the doctrines of natural law and as signaling the overthrow of positivism. The unqualified satisfaction with this result seems to me to be hysteria. Many of us might applaud the objective—that of punishing a woman for an outrageously immoral act—but this was secured only by declaring a statute established since 1934 not to have the force of law, and at least the wisdom of this course must be doubted. There were, of course, two other choices. One was to let the woman go unpunished; one can sympathize with and endorse the view that this might have been a bad thing to do. The other was to face the fact that if the woman were to be punished it must be pursuant to the introduction of a frankly retrospective law and with a full consciousness of what was sacrificed in securing her punishment in this way. Odious as retrospective criminal legislation and punishment may be, to have pursued it openly in this case would at least have had the merits of candour. It would have made plain that in punishing the woman a choice had to be made

43 Judgment of July 27, 1949, Oberlandesgericht, Bamberg, 5 *Süddeutsche Juristen-Zeitung* 207 (Germany 1950), 64 *Harv. L. Rev.* 1005 (1951); see Friedmann, *Legal Theory* 457 (3rd ed. 1953).

between two evils, that of leaving her unpunished and that of sacrificing a very precious principle of morality endorsed by most legal systems. Surely if we have learned anything from the history of morals it is that the thing to do with a moral quandary is not to hide it. Like nettles, the occasions when life forces us to choose between the lesser of two evils must be grasped with the consciousness that they are what they are. The vice of this use of the principle that, at certain limiting points, what is utterly immoral cannot be law or lawful is that it will serve to cloak the true nature of the problems with which we are faced and will encourage the romantic optimism that all the values we cherish ultimately will fit into a single system, that no one of them has to be sacrificed or compromised to accommodate another.

> "All Discord Harmony not understood,
> All Partial Evil Universal Good"

This is surely untrue and there is an insincerity in any formulation of our problem which allows us to describe the treatment of the dilemma as if it were the disposition of the ordinary case.

It may seem perhaps to make too much of forms, even perhaps of words, to emphasize one way of disposing of this difficult case as compared with another which might have led, so far as the woman was concerned, to exactly the same result. Why should we dramatize the difference between them? We might punish the woman under a new retrospective law and declare overtly that we were doing something inconsistent with our principles as the lesser of two evils; or we might allow the case to pass as one in which we do not point out precisely where we sacrifice such a principle. But candour is not just one among many minor virtues of the administration of law, just as it is not merely a minor virtue of morality. For if we adopt Radbruch's view, and with him and the German courts make our protest against evil law in the form of an assertion that certain rules cannot be law because of their moral iniquity, we confuse one of the most powerful, because it is the simplest, forms of moral criticism. If with the Utilitarians we speak plainly, we say that laws may be law but too evil to be obeyed. This is a moral condemnation which everyone can understand and it makes an immediate and obvious claim to moral attention. If, on the other hand, we formulate our objection as an assertion that these evil things are not law, here is an assertion which many people do not believe, and if they are disposed to consider it at all, it would seem to raise a whole host of philosophical issues before it can be accepted. So perhaps the most important single lesson to be learned from this form of the denial of the Utilitarian distinction is the one that the Utilitarians were most concerned to teach: when we have the ample resources of plain speech we must not present the moral criticism of institutions as propositions of a disputable philosophy.

V.

I have endeavored to show that, in spite of all that has been learned and experienced since the Utilitarians wrote, and in spite of the defects of other parts of their doctrine, their protest against the confusion of what is and what ought to be law has a moral as well as an intellectual value. Yet it may well be said that, though this distinction is valid and important if applied to any particular law of a system, it is at least misleading if we attempt to apply it to "law," that is, to the notion of a legal system, and that if we insist, as I have, on the narrower truth (or truism), we obscure a wider (or deeper) truth. After all, it may be urged, we have learned that there are many things which are untrue of laws taken separately, but which are true and important in a legal system considered as a whole. For example, the connection between law and sanctions and between the existence of law and its "efficacy" must be understood in this more general way. It is surely not arguable (without some desperate extension of the word "sanction" or artificial narrowing of the word "law") that every law in a municipal legal system must have a sanction, yet it is at least plausible to argue that a legal system must, to be a legal system, provide sanctions for certain of its rules. So too, a rule of law may be said to exist though enforced or obeyed in only a minority of cases, but this could not be said of a legal system as a whole. Perhaps the differences with respect to laws taken separately and a legal system as a whole are also true of the connection between moral (or some other) conceptions of what law ought to be and law in this wider sense.

This line of argument, found (at least in embryo form) in Austin, where he draws attention to the fact that every developed legal system contains certain fundamental notions which are "necessary" and "bottomed in the common nature of man,"[44] is worth pursuing—up to a point—and I shall say briefly why and how far this is so.

We must avoid, if we can, the arid wastes of inappropriate definition, for, in relation to a concept as many-sided and vague as that of a legal system, disputes about the "essential" character, or necessity to the whole, of any single element soon begin to look like disputes about whether chess could be "chess" if played without pawns. There is a wish, which may be understandable, to cut straight through the question whether a legal system, to be a legal system, must measure up to some moral or other standard with simple statements of fact: for example, that no system which utterly failed in this respect has ever existed or could endure; that the normally fulfilled assumption that a legal system aims at some form of justice colours the whole way in which we interpret specific rules in particular cases, and if this normally fulfilled assumption were not fulfilled no one would have any reason to obey except fear (and probably not that) and still less, of course, any moral obligation to obey. The connection between law and moral standards and principles of justice is therefore as little arbitrary and as "necessary" as the connection between law and sanctions, and the pursuit of the question whether this necessity is logical (part of the "meaning" of law) or merely factual or causal can safely be left as an innocent pastime for philosophers.

Yet in two respects I should wish to go further (even though this involves the use of a philosophical fantasy) and show what could intelligibly be meant by the claim that certain provisions in a legal system are "necessary." The world in which we live, and we who live in it, may one day change in many different ways; and if this change were radical enough not only would certain statements of fact now true be false and vice versa, but whole ways of thinking and talking which constitute our present conceptual apparatus, through which we see the world and each other, would lapse. We have only to consider how the whole of our social, moral, and legal life, as we understand it now, depends on the contingent fact that though our bodies do change in shape, size, and other physical properties they do not do this so drastically nor with such quicksilver rapidity and irregularity that we cannot identify each other as the same persistent individual over considerable spans of time. Though this is but a contingent fact which may one day be different, on it at present rest huge structures of our thought and principles of action and social life. Similarly, consider the following possibility (not because it is more than a possibility but because it reveals why we think certain things necessary in a legal system and what we mean by this): suppose that men were to become invulnerable to attack by each other, were clad perhaps like giant land crabs with an impenetrable carapace, and could extract the food they needed from the

44 Austin, *Uses of the Study of Jurisprudence*, in *The Province of Jurisprudence Determined* 365, 373, 367–69 (Library of Ideas ed. 1954).

air by some internal chemical process. In such circumstances (the details of which can be left to science fiction) rules forbidding the free use of violence and rules constituting the minimum form of property—with its rights and duties sufficient to enable food to grow and be retained until eaten—would not have the necessary nonarbitrary status which they have for us, constituted as we are in a world like ours. At present, and until such radical changes supervene, such rules are so fundamental that if a legal system did not have them there would be no point in having any other rules at all. Such rules overlap with basic moral principles vetoing murder, violence, and theft; and so we can add to the factual statement that all legal systems in fact coincide with morality at such vital points, the statement that this is, in this sense, necessarily so. And why not call it a "natural" necessity?

Of course even this much depends on the fact that in asking what content a legal system must have we take this question to be worth asking only if we who consider it cherish the humble aim of survival in close proximity to our fellows. Natural-law theory, however, in all its protean guises, attempts to push the argument much further and to assert that human beings are equally devoted to and united in their conception of aims (the pursuit of knowledge, justice to their fellow men) other than that of survival, and these dictate a further necessary content to a legal system (over and above my humble minimum) without which it would be pointless. Of course we must be careful not to exaggerate the differences among human beings, but it seems to me that above this minimum the purposes men have for living in society are too conflicting and varying to make possible much extension of the argument that some fuller overlap of legal rules and moral standards is "necessary" in this sense.

Another aspect of the matter deserves attention. If we attach to a legal system the minimum meaning that it must consist of general rules—general both in the sense that they refer to courses of action, not single actions, and to multiplicities of men, not single individuals—this meaning connotes the principle of treating like cases alike, though the criteria of when cases are alike will be, so far, only the general elements specified in the rules. It is, however, true that *one* essential element of the concept of justice is the principle of treating like cases alike. This is justice in the administration of the law, not justice of the law. So there is, in the very notion of law consisting of general rules, something which prevents us from treating it as if morally it is utterly neutral, without any necessary contact with moral principles. Natural procedural justice consists therefore of those principles of objectivity and impartiality in the administration of the law which implement just this aspect of law and which are designed to ensure that rules are applied only to what are genuinely cases of the rule or at least to minimize the risks of inequalities in this sense.

These two reasons (or excuses) for talking of a certain overlap between legal and moral standards as necessary and natural, of course, should not satisfy anyone who is really disturbed by the Utilitarian or "positivist" insistence that law and morality are distinct. This is so because a legal system that satisfied these minimum requirements might apply, with the most pedantic impartiality as between the persons affected, laws which were hideously oppressive, and might deny to a vast rightless slave population the minimum benefits of protection from violence and theft. The stink of such societies is, after all, still in our nostrils and to argue that they have (or had) no legal system would only involve the repetition of the argument. Only if the rules failed to provide these essential benefits and protection for anyone—even for a slave-owning group—would the minimum be unsatisfied and the system sink to the status of a set of meaningless taboos. Of course no one denied those benefits would have any reason to obey except fear and would have every moral reason to revolt.

VI.

I should be less than candid if I did not, in conclusion, consider something which, I suspect, most troubles those who react strongly against "legal positivism." Emphasis on the distinction between law as it is and law as it ought to be may be taken to depend upon and to entail what are called "subjectivist" and "relativist" or "noncognitive" theories concerning the very nature of moral judgments, moral distinctions, or "values." Of course the Utilitarians themselves (as distinct from later positivists like Kelsen) did not countenance any such theories: however unsatisfactory their moral philosophy may appear to us now. Austin thought ultimate moral principles were the command of God, known to us by revelation or through the "index" of utility, and Bentham thought they were verifiable propositions about utility. Nonetheless I think (though I cannot prove) that insistence upon the distinction between law as it is and ought to be has been, under the general head of "positivism," confused with a moral theory according to which statements of what is the case ("statements of fact") belong to a category or type radically different from statements of what ought to be ("value statements"). It may therefore be well to dispel this source of confusion.

There are many contemporary variants of this type of moral theory: according to some, judgments of what ought to be, or ought to be done, either are or include as essential elements expressions of "feeling," "emotion," or "attitudes" or "subjective preferences"; in others such judgments both express feelings or emotions or attitudes and enjoin others to share them. In other variants such judgments indicate that a particular case falls under a general principle or policy of action which the speaker has "chosen" or to which he is "committed" and which is itself not a recognition of what is the case but analogous to a general "imperative" or command addressed to all including the speaker himself. Common to all these variants is the insistence that judgments of what ought to be done, because they contain such "non-cognitive" elements, cannot be argued for or established by rational methods as statements of fact can be, and cannot be shown to follow from any statement of fact but only from other judgments of what ought to be done in conjunction with some statement of fact. We cannot, on such a theory, demonstrate, e.g., that an action was wrong, ought not to have been done, merely by showing that it consisted of the deliberate infliction of pain solely for the gratification of the agent. We only show it to be wrong if we add to those verifiable "cognitive" statements of fact a general principle not itself verifiable or "cognitive" that the infliction of pain in such circumstances is wrong, ought not to be done. Together with this general distinction between statements of what is and what ought to be go sharp parallel distinctions between statements about means and statements of moral ends. We can rationally discover and debate what are appropriate means to given ends, but ends are not rationally discoverable or debatable; they are "fiats of the will," expressions of "emotions," "preferences," or "attitudes."

Against all such views (which are of course far subtler than this crude survey can convey) others urge that all these sharp distinctions between is and ought, fact and value, means and ends, cognitive and noncognitive, are wrong. In acknowledging ultimate ends or moral values we are recognizing something as much imposed upon us by the character of the world in which we live, as little a matter of choice, attitude, feeling, emotion as the truth of factual judgments about what is the case. The characteristic moral argument is not one in which the parties are reduced to expressing or kindling feelings or emotions or issuing exhortations or commands to each other but one by which parties come to acknowledge after closer examination and reflection that an initially disputed case falls within the ambit of a vaguely apprehended principle (itself no more "subjective," no more a "fiat of our will" than any other principle of classification) and this has as much title to be called "cognitive" or "rational" as any other initially disputed classification of particulars.

Let us now suppose that we accept this rejection of "non-cognitive" theories of morality and this denial of the drastic distinction in type between statements of what is and what ought to be, and that moral judgments are as rationally defensible as any other kind of judgments. What would follow from this as to the nature of the connection between law as it is and law as it ought to be? Surely, from this alone, nothing. Laws, however morally iniquitous, would still (so far as this point is concerned) be laws. The only difference which the acceptance of this view of the nature of moral judgments would make would be that the moral iniquity of such laws would be something that could be demonstrated; it would surely follow merely from a statement of what the rule required to be done that the rule was morally wrong and so ought not to be law or conversely that it was morally desirable and ought to be law. But the demonstration of this would not show the rule not to be (or to be) law. Proof that the principles by which we evaluate or condemn laws are rationally discoverable, and not mere "fiats of the will," leaves untouched the fact that there are laws which may have any degree of iniquity or stupidity and still be laws. And conversely there are rules that have every moral qualification to be laws and yet are not laws.

Surely something further or more specific must be said if disproof of "noncognitivism" or kindred theories in ethics is to be relevant to the distinction between law as it is and law as it ought to be, and to lead to the abandonment at some point or some softening of this distinction. No one has done more than Professor Lon Fuller of the Harvard Law School in his various writings to make clear such a line of argument and I will end by criticising what I take to be its central point. It is a point which again emerges when we consider not those legal rules or parts of legal rules the meanings of which are clear and excite no debate but the interpretation of rules in concrete cases where doubts are initially felt and argument develops about their meaning. In no legal system is the scope of legal rules restricted to the range of concrete instances which were present or are believed to have been present in the minds of legislators; this indeed is one of the important differences between a legal rule and a command. Yet, when rules are recognized as applying to instances beyond any that legislators did or could have considered, their extension to such new cases often presents itself not as a deliberate choice or fiat on the part of those who so interpret the rule. It appears neither as a decision to give the rule a new or extended meaning nor as a guess as to what legislators, dead perhaps in the eighteenth century, would have said had they been alive in the twentieth century. Rather, the inclusion of the new case under the rule takes its place as a natural elaboration of the rule, as something implementing a "purpose" which it seems natural to attribute (in some sense) to the rule itself rather than to any particular person dead or alive. The Utilitarian description of such interpretative extension of old rules to new cases as judicial legislation fails to do justice to this phenomenon; it gives no hint of the differences between a deliberate fiat or decision to treat the new case in the same way as past cases and a recognition (in which there is little that is deliberate or even voluntary) that inclusion of the new case under the rule will implement or articulate a continuing and identical purpose, hitherto less specifically apprehended.

Perhaps many lawyers and judges will see in this language something that precisely fits their experience; others may think it a romantic gloss on facts better stated in the Utilitarian language of judicial "legislation" or in the modern American terminology of "creative choice."

To make the point clear Professor Fuller uses a nonlegal example from the philosopher Wittgenstein which is, I think, illuminating.

> Someone says to me: "Show the children a game." I teach them gaming with dice and the other says "I did not mean that sort of game." Must the exclusion of the game with dice have come before his mind when he gave me the order?[45]

Something important does seem to me to be touched on in this example. Perhaps there are the following (distinguishable) points. First, we normally do interpret not only what people are trying to do but what they say in the light of assumed common human objectives so that unless the contrary were expressly indicated we would not interpret an instruction to show a young child a game as a mandate to introduce him to gambling even though in other contexts the word "game" would be naturally so interpreted. Second, very often, the speaker whose words are thus interpreted might say: "Yes, that's what I mean [or 'that's what I meant all along'] though I never thought of it until you put this particular case to me." Third, when we thus recognize, perhaps after argument or consultation with others, a particular case not specifically envisaged beforehand as falling within the ambit of some vaguely expressed instruction, we may find this experience falsified by description of it as a mere decision on our part so to treat the particular case, and that we can only describe this faithfully as coming to realize and to articulate what we "really" want or our "true purpose"—phrases which Professor Fuller uses later in the same article.[46]

I am sure that many philosophical discussions of the character of moral argument would benefit from attention to cases of the sort instanced by Professor Fuller. Such attention would help to provide a corrective to the view that there is a sharp separation between "ends" and "means" and that in debating "ends" we can only work on each other nonrationally, and that rational argument is reserved for discussion of "means." But I think the relevance of his point to the issue whether it is correct or wise to insist on the distinction between law as it is and law as it ought to be is very small indeed. Its net effect is that in interpreting legal rules there are some cases which we find after reflection to be so natural an elaboration or articulation of the rule that to think of and refer to this as "legislation," "making law," or a "fiat" on our part would be misleading. So, the argument must be, it would be misleading to distinguish in such cases between what the rule is and what it ought to be—at least in some sense of ought. We think it ought to include the new case and come to see after reflection that it really does. But even if this way of presenting a recognizable experience as an example of a fusion between is and ought to be is admitted, two caveats must be borne in mind. The first is that "ought" in this case need have nothing to do with morals for the reasons explained already in section III: there may be just the same sense that a new case will implement and articulate the purpose of a rule in interpreting the rules of a game or some hideously immoral code of oppression whose immorality is appreciated by those called in to interpret it. They too can see what the "spirit" of the game they are playing requires in previously unenvisaged cases. More important is this: after all is said and done we must remember how rare in the law is the phenomenon held to justify this way of talking, how exceptional is this feeling that one way of deciding a case is imposed upon us as the only natural or rational elaboration of some rule. Surely it cannot be doubted that, for most cases of interpretation, the language of choice

45 Fuller, "Human Purpose and Natural Law," 53 *J. Philos.* 697, 700 (1956).
46 *Id.* at 701, 702.

between alternatives, "judicial legislation" or even "fiat" (though not arbitrary fiat), better conveys the realities of the situation.

Within the framework of relatively well-settled law there jostle too many alternatives too nearly equal in attraction between which judge and lawyer must uncertainly pick their way to make appropriate here language which may well describe those experiences which we have in interpreting our own or others' principles of conduct, intention, or wishes, when we are not conscious of exercising a deliberate choice, but rather of recognising something awaiting recognition. To use in the description of the interpretation of laws the suggested terminology of a fusion or inability to separate what is law and ought to be will serve (like earlier stories that judges only find, never make, law) only to conceal the facts, that here if anywhere we live among uncertainties between which we have to choose, and that the existing law imposes only limits on our choice and not the choice itself.

6

H.L.A. Hart

from *The Concept of Law**

A Fresh Start

In the last three chapters [of *The Concept of Law*] we have seen that, at various crucial points, the simple model of law as the sovereign's coercive orders failed to reproduce some of the salient features of a legal system. To demonstrate this, we did not find it necessary to invoke (as earlier critics have done) international law or primitive law which some may regard as disputable or borderline examples of law; instead we pointed to certain familiar features of municipal law in a modern state, and showed that these were either distorted or altogether unrepresented in this over-simple theory.

The main ways in which the theory failed are instructive enough to merit a second summary. First, it became clear that though of all the varieties of law, a criminal statute, forbidding or enjoining certain actions under penalty, most resembles orders backed by threats given by one person to others, such a statute none the less differs from such orders in the important respect that it commonly applies to those who enact it and not merely to others. Secondly, there are other varieties of law, notably those conferring legal powers to adjudicate or legislate (public powers) or to create or vary legal relations (private powers) which cannot, without absurdity, be construed as orders backed by threats. Thirdly, there are legal rules which differ from orders in their mode of origin, because they are not brought into being by anything analogous to explicit prescription. Finally, the analysis of law in terms of the sovereign, habitually obeyed

* Hart, H.L.A. From Chapter V: "Law as the Union of Primary and Secondary Rules" (pp. 79–96); and Chapter VI: "The Foundations of a Legal System" (pp. 97–114); of *The Concept of Law*, Oxford University Press, 1961.

and necessarily exempt from all legal limitation, failed to account for the continuity of legislative authority characteristic of a modern legal system, and the sovereign person or persons could not be identified with either the electorate or the legislature of a modern state.

It will be recalled that in thus criticizing the conception of law as the sovereign's coercive orders we considered also a number of ancillary devices which were brought in at the cost of corrupting the primitive simplicity of the theory to rescue it from its difficulties. But these too failed. One device, the notion of a *tacit* order, seemed to have no application to the complex actualities of a modern legal system, but only to very much simpler situations like that of a general who deliberately refrains from interfering with orders given by his subordinates. Other devices, such as that of treating power-conferring rules as mere fragments of rules imposing duties, or treating all rules as directed only to officials, distort the ways in which these are spoken of, thought of, and actually used in social life. This had no better claim to our assent than the theory that all the rules of a game are "really" directions to the umpire and the scorer. The device, designed to reconcile the self-binding character of legislation with the theory that a statute is an order given to *others*, was to distinguish the legislators acting in their official capacity, as *one* person ordering *others* who include themselves in their private capacities. This device, impeccable in itself, involved supplementing the theory with something it does not contain: this is the notion of a rule defining what must be done to legislate; for it is only in conforming with such a rule that legislators have an official capacity and a separate personality to be contrasted with themselves as private individuals.

The last three chapters are therefore the record of a failure and there is plainly need for a fresh start. Yet the failure is an instructive one, worth the detailed consideration we have given it, because at each point where the theory failed to fit the facts it was possible to see at least in outline why it was bound to fail and what is required for a better account. The root cause of failure is that the elements out of which the theory was constructed, viz. the ideas of orders, obedience, habits, and threats, do not include, and cannot by their combination yield, the idea of a rule, without which we cannot hope to elucidate even the most elementary forms of law. It is true that the idea of a rule is by no means a simple one: we have already seen in Chapter III the need, if we are to do justice to the complexity of a legal system, to discriminate between two different though related types. Under rules of the one type, which may well be considered the basic or primary type, human beings are required to do or abstain from certain actions, whether they wish to or not. Rules of the other type are in a sense parasitic upon or secondary to the first; for they provide that human beings may by doing or saying certain things introduce new rules of the primary type, extinguish or modify old ones, or in various ways determine their incidence or control their operations. Rules of the first type impose duties; rules of the second type confer powers, public or private. Rules of the first type concern actions involving physical movement or changes; rules of the second type provide for operations which lead not merely to physical movement or change, but to the creation or variation of duties or obligations.

We have already given some preliminary analysis of what is involved in the assertion that rules of these two types exist among a given social group, and in this chapter we shall not only carry this analysis a little farther but we shall make the general claim that in the combination of these two types of rule there lies what Austin wrongly claimed to have found in the notion of coercive orders, namely, "the key to the science of jurisprudence." We shall not indeed claim that wherever the word "law" is "properly" used this combination of primary and secondary rules is to be found; for it is clear that the diverse range of cases of which the word "law" is used are not linked by any such simple uniformity, but by less direct relations—often of analogy of either form or content—to a central case. What we shall attempt to show, in this and the succeeding chapters, is that most of the features of law which have proved most perplexing and have both provoked and eluded the search for definition can best be rendered clear, if these two types of rule and the interplay between them are understood. We accord this union of elements a central place because of their explanatory power in elucidating the concepts that constitute the framework of legal thought. The justification for the use of the word "law" for a range of apparently heterogeneous cases is a secondary matter which can be undertaken when the central elements have been grasped.

The Idea of Obligation

It will be recalled that the theory of law as coercive orders, notwithstanding its errors, started from the perfectly correct appreciation of the fact that where there is law, there human conduct is made in some sense non-optional or obligatory. In choosing this starting-point the theory was well inspired, and in building up a new account of law in terms of the interplay of primary and secondary rules we too shall start from the same idea. It is, however, here, at this crucial first step, that we have perhaps most to learn from the theory's errors.

Let us recall the gunman situation. A orders B to hand over his money and threatens to shoot him if he does not comply. According to the theory of coercive orders this situation illustrates the notion of obligation or duty in general. Legal obligation is to be found in this situation writ large; A must be the sovereign habitually obeyed and the orders must be general, prescribing courses of conduct, not single actions. The plausibility of the claim that the gunman situation displays the meaning of obligation lies in the fact that it is certainly one in which we would say that B, if he obeyed, was "obliged" to hand over his money. It is, however, equally certain that we should misdescribe the situation if we said, on these facts, that B "had an obligation" or a "duty" to hand over the money. So from the start it is clear that we need something else for an understanding of the idea of obligation. There is a difference, yet to be explained, between the assertion that someone *was obliged* to do something and the assertion that he *had an obligation* to do it. The first is often a statement about the beliefs and motives with which an action is done: B was obliged to hand over his money may simply mean, as it does in the gunman case, that he believed that some harm or other unpleasant consequences would befall him if he did not hand it over and he handed it over to avoid those consequences. In such cases the prospect of what would happen to the agent if he disobeyed has rendered something he would otherwise have preferred to have done (keep the money) less eligible.

Two further elements slightly complicate the elucidation of the notion of being obliged to do something. It seems clear that we should not think of B as obliged to hand over the money if the threatened harm was, according to common judgments, trivial in comparison with the disadvantage or serious consequences, either for B or for others, of complying with the orders, as it would be, for example, if A merely threatened to pinch B. Nor perhaps should we say that B was obliged, if there were no reasonable grounds for thinking that A could or would probably implement his threat of relatively serious harm. Yet, though such references to common judgments of comparative harm and reasonable estimates of likelihood, are implicit in this notion, the statement that a person was obliged to obey someone is, in the main, a psychological one referring to the beliefs and motives with which an action was done. But the statement that someone *had an obligation* to do something is of a very different type and there are many signs of this difference. Thus not only is it the case that the facts about B's action and his beliefs and motives in the gunman case, though sufficient to warrant the statement that B was obliged to hand over his purse, are *not sufficient* to warrant the statement that he had an obligation to do this; it is also the case that facts of this sort, i.e., facts about beliefs and motives, are *not necessary* for the truth of a statement that a person had an obligation to do something. Thus the statement that a person had an obligation, e.g., to tell the truth or report for military service, remains true even if he believed (reasonably or unreasonably) that he would never be found out and had nothing to fear from disobedience. Moreover, whereas the statement that he had this obligation is quite independent of the question whether or not he in fact reported for service, the statement that someone was obliged to do something, normally carries the implication that he actually did it.

Some theorists, Austin among them, seeing perhaps the general irrelevance of the person's beliefs, fears, and motives to the question whether he had an obligation to do something, have defined this notion not in terms of these subjective facts, but in terms of the *chance* or *likelihood* that the person having the obligation will suffer a punishment or "evil" at the hands of others in the event of disobedience. This, in effect, treats statements of obligation not as psychological statements but as predictions or assessments of chances of incurring punishment or "evil." To many later theorists this has appeared as a revelation, bringing down to earth an elusive notion and restating it in the same clear, hard, empirical terms as are used in science. It has, indeed, been accepted sometimes as the only alternative to metaphysical conceptions of obligation or duty as invisible objects mysteriously existing "above" or "behind" the world of ordinary, observable facts. But there are many reasons for rejecting this interpretation of statements of obligation as predictions, and it is not, in fact, the only alternative to obscure metaphysics.

The fundamental objection is that the predictive interpretation obscures the fact that, where rules exist, deviations from them are not merely grounds for a prediction that hostile reactions will follow or that a court will apply sanctions to those who break them, but are also a reason or justification for such reaction and for applying the sanctions. We have already drawn attention in Chapter IV to this neglect of the internal aspect of rules and we shall elaborate it later in this chapter.

There is, however, a second, simpler, objection to the predictive interpretation of obligation. If it were true that the statement that a person had an obligation meant that *he* was likely to suffer in the event of disobedience, it would be a contradiction to say that he had an obligation, e.g., to report for military service but that, owing to the fact that he had escaped from the jurisdiction, or had successfully bribed the police or the court, there was not the slightest chance of his being caught or made to suffer. In fact, there is no contradiction in saying this, and such statements are often made and understood.

It is, of course, true that in a normal legal system, where sanctions are exacted for a high proportion of offences, an offender usually runs a risk of punishment; so, usually the statement that a person has an obligation and the statement that he is likely to suffer for disobedience will both be true together. Indeed, the connection between these two statements is somewhat stronger than this: at least in a municipal system it may well be true that, unless *in general* sanctions were likely to be exacted from offenders, there would be little or no point in making particular statements about a person's obligations. In this sense, such statements may be said to presuppose belief in the continued normal operation of the system of sanctions much as the statement "he is out" in cricket presupposes, though it does not assert, that players, umpire, and scorer will probably take the usual steps. None the less, it is crucial for the understanding of the idea of obligation to see that in individual cases the statement that a person has an obligation under some rule and the prediction that he is likely to suffer for disobedience may diverge.

It is clear that obligation is not to be found in the gunman situation, though the simpler notion of being obliged to do something may well be defined in the elements present there. To understand the general idea of obligation as a necessary preliminary to understanding it in its legal form, we must turn to a different social situation which, unlike the gunman situation, includes the existence of social rules; for this situation contributes to the meaning of the statement that a person has an obligation in two ways. First, the existence of such rules, making certain types of behaviour a standard, is the normal, though unstated, background or proper context for such a statement; and, secondly, the distinctive function of such a statement is to apply such a general rule to a particular person by calling attention to the fact that his case falls under it. We have already seen in Chapter IV that there is involved in the existence of any social rules a combination of regular conduct with a distinctive attitude to that conduct as a standard. We have also seen the main ways in which these differ from mere social habits, and how the varied normative vocabulary ("ought," "must," "should") is used to draw attention to the standard and to deviations from it, and to formulate the demands, criticisms, or acknowledgements which may be based on it. Of this class of normative words the words "obligation" and "duty" form an important sub-class, carrying with them certain implications not usually present in the others. Hence, though a grasp of the elements generally differentiating social rules from mere habits is certainly indispensable for understanding the notion of obligation or duty, it is not sufficient by itself.

The statement that someone has or is under an obligation does indeed imply the existence of a rule; yet it is not always the case that where rules exist the standard of behaviour required by them is conceived of in terms of obligation. "He ought to have" and "He had an obligation to" are not always interchangeable expressions, even though they are alike in carrying an implicit reference to existing standards of conduct or are used in drawing conclusions in particular cases from a general rule. Rules of etiquette or correct speech are certainly rules: they are more than convergent habits or regularities of behaviour; they are taught and efforts are made to maintain them; they are used in criticizing our own and other people's behaviour in the characteristic normative vocabulary. "You ought to take your hat off," "It is wrong to say 'you was.'" But to use in connection with rules of this kind the words "obligation" or "duty" would be misleading and not merely stylistically odd. It would misdescribe a social situation; for though the line separating rules of obligation from others is at points a vague one, yet the main rationale of the distinction is fairly clear.

Rules are conceived and spoken of as imposing obligations when the general demand for conformity is insistent and the social pressure brought to bear upon those who deviate or threaten to deviate is great. Such rules may be wholly customary in origin: there may be no centrally organized system of punishments for breach of the rules; the social pressure may take only the form of a general diffused hostile or critical reaction which may stop short of physical sanctions. It may be limited to verbal manifestations of disapproval or of appeals to the individuals' respect for the rule violated; it may depend heavily on the operation of feelings of shame, remorse, and guilt. When the pressure is of this last-mentioned kind we may be inclined to classify the rules as part of the morality of the social group and the obligation under the rules as moral obligation. Conversely, when physical sanctions are prominent or usual among the forms of pressure, even though these are neither closely defined nor administered by officials but are left to the community at large, we shall be inclined to classify the rules as a primitive or rudimentary form of law. We may, of course, find both these types of serious social pressure behind what is, in an obvious sense, the same rule of conduct; sometimes this may occur with no indication that one of them is peculiarly appropriate as primary and the other secondary, and then the question whether we are confronted with a rule of morality or rudimentary law may not be susceptible of an answer. But for the moment the possibility of drawing the line between law and morals need not detain us. What is important is that the insistence on importance or *seriousness* of social pressure behind the rules is the primary factor determining whether they are thought of as giving rise to obligations.

Two other characteristics of obligation go naturally together with this primary one. The rules supported by this serious pressure are thought important because they are believed to be necessary to the maintenance of social life or some highly prized feature of it. Characteristically, rules so obviously essential as those which restrict the free use of violence are thought of in terms of obligation. So too rules which require honesty or truth or require the keeping of promises, or specify what is to be done by one who performs a distinctive role or function in the social group are thought of in terms of either "obligation" or perhaps more often "duty." Secondly, it is generally recognized that the conduct required by these rules may, while benefiting others, conflict with what the person who owes the duty may wish to do. Hence obligations and duties are thought of as characteristically involving sacrifice or renunciation, and the standing possibility of conflict between obligation or duty and interest is, in all societies, among the truisms of both the lawyer and the moralist.

The figure of a *bond* binding the person obligated, which is buried in the word "obligation," and the similar notion of a debt latent in the word "duty" are explicable in terms of these three factors, which distinguish rules of obligation or duty from other rules. In this figure, which haunts much legal thought, the social pressure appears as a chain binding those who have obligations so that they are not free to do what they want. The other end of the chain is sometimes held by the group or their official representatives, who insist on performance or exact the penalty: sometimes it is entrusted by the group to a private individual who may choose whether or not to insist on performance or its equivalent in value to him. The first situation typifies the duties or obligations of criminal law and the second those of civil law where we think of private individuals having rights correlative to the obligations.

Natural and perhaps illuminating though these figures or metaphors are, we must not allow them to trap us into a misleading conception of obligation as essentially consisting in some feeling of pressure or compulsion experienced by those who have obligations. The fact that rules of obligation are generally supported by serious social pressure does not entail that to have an obligation under the rules is to experience feelings of compulsion or pressure. Hence there is no contradiction in saying of some hardened swindler, and it may often be true, that he had an obligation to pay the rent but felt no pressure to pay when he made off without doing so. To *feel* obliged and to have an obligation are different though frequently concomitant things. To identify them would be one way of misinterpreting, in terms of psychological feelings, the important internal aspect of rules to which we drew attention in Chapter III.

Indeed, the internal aspect of rules is something to which we must again refer before we can dispose finally of the claims of the predictive theory. For an advocate of that theory may well ask why, if social pressure is so important a feature of rules of obligation, we are yet so concerned to stress the inadequacies of the predictive theory; for it gives this very feature a central place by defining obligation in terms of the likelihood that threatened punishment or hostile reaction will follow deviation from certain lines of conduct. The difference may seem slight between the analysis of a statement of obligation as a prediction, or assessment of the chances, of hostile reaction to deviation, and our own contention that though this statement presupposes a background in which deviations from rules are generally met by hostile reactions, yet its characteristic use is not to predict this but to say that a person's case falls under such a rule. In fact, however, this difference is not a slight one. Indeed, until its importance is grasped, we cannot properly understand the whole distinctive style of human thought, speech, and action which is involved in the existence of rules and which constitutes the normative structure of society.

The following contrast again in terms of the "internal" and "external" aspect of rules may serve to mark what gives this distinction its great importance for the understanding not only of law but of the structure of any society. When a social group has certain rules of conduct, this fact affords an opportunity for many closely related yet different kinds of assertion; for it is possible to be concerned with the rules, either merely as an observer who does not himself accept them, or as a member of the group which accepts and uses them as guides to conduct. We may call these respectively the "external" and the "internal" points of view. Statements made from the external point of view may themselves be of different kinds. For the observer may, without accepting the rules himself, assert that the group accepts the rules, and thus may from outside refer to the way in which *they* are concerned with them from the internal point of view. But whatever the rules are, whether they are those of games, like chess or cricket, or moral or legal rules, we can if we choose occupy the position of an observer who does not even refer in this way to the internal point of view of the group. Such an observer is content merely to record the regularities of observable behaviour in which conformity with the rules partly consists and those further regularities, in the form of the hostile reaction, reproofs, or punishments, with which deviations from the rules are met. After a time the external observer may, on the basis of the regularities observed, correlate deviation with hostile reaction, and be able to predict with a fair measure of success, and to assess the chances that a deviation from the group's normal behaviour will meet with hostile reaction or punishment. Such knowledge may not only reveal much about the group, but might enable him to live among them without unpleasant consequences which would attend one who attempted to do so without such knowledge.

If, however, the observer really keeps austerely to this extreme external point of view and does not give any account of the manner in which members of the group who accept the rules view their own regular behaviour, his description of their life cannot be in terms of rules at all, and so not in the terms of the rule-dependent notions of obligation or duty. Instead, it will be in terms of observable regularities of conduct, predictions, probabilities, and signs. For such an observer, deviations by a member of the group from normal conduct will be a sign that hostile reaction is likely to follow, and nothing more. His view will be like the view of one who, having observed the working of a traffic signal in a busy street for some time, limits himself to saying that when the light turns red there is a high probability that the traffic will stop. He treats the light merely as a natural *sign that* people will behave in certain ways, as clouds are a *sign that* rain will come. In so doing he will miss out a whole dimension of the social life of those whom he is watching, since for them the red light is not merely a sign that others will stop: they look upon it as a *signal for* them to stop, and so a reason for stopping in conformity to rules which make stopping when the light is red a standard of behaviour and an obligation. To mention this is to bring into the account the way in which the group regards its own behaviour. It is to refer to the internal aspect of rules seen from their internal point of view.

The external point of view may very nearly reproduce the way in which the rules function in the lives of certain members of the group, namely those who reject its rules and are only concerned with them when and because they judge that unpleasant consequences are likely to follow violation. Their point of view will need for its expression, "I was obliged to do it," "I am likely to suffer for it if ...," "You will probably suffer for it if ...," "They will do that to you if...." But they will not need forms of expression like "I had an obligation" or "You have an obligation" for these are required only by those who see their own and other persons' conduct from the internal point of view. What the external point of view, which limits itself to the observable regularities of behaviour, cannot reproduce is the way in which the rules function as rules in the lives of those who normally are the majority of society. These are the officials, lawyers, or private persons who use them, in one situation after another, as guides to the conduct of social life, as the basis for claims, demands, admissions, criticism, or punishment, viz., in all the familiar transactions of life according to rules. For them the violation of a rule is not merely a basis for the prediction that a hostile reaction will follow but a *reason* for hostility.

At any given moment the life of any society which lives by rules, legal or not, is likely to consist in a tension between those who, on the one hand, accept and voluntarily co-operate in maintaining the rules, and so see their own and other persons' behaviour in terms of the rules, and those who, on the other hand, reject the rules and attend to them only from the external point of view as a sign of possible punishment. One of the difficulties facing any legal theory anxious to do justice to the complexity of the facts is to remember the presence of both these points of view and not to define one of them out of existence. Perhaps all our criticisms of the predictive theory of obligation may be best summarized as the accusation that this is what it does to the internal aspect of obligatory rules.

The Elements of Law

It is, of course, possible to imagine a society without a legislature, courts, or officials of any kind. Indeed, there are many studies of primitive communities which not only claim that this possibility is realized but depict in detail the life of a society where the only means of social control is that general attitude of the group towards its own standard modes of behaviour in terms of which we have characterized rules of obligation. A social structure of this kind is often referred to as one of "custom"; but we shall not use this term, because it often implies that the customary rules are very old and supported with less social pressure than other rules. To avoid these implications we shall refer to such a social structure as one of primary rules of obligation. If a society is to live by such primary rules alone, there are certain conditions which, granted a few of the most obvious truisms about human nature and the world we live in, must clearly be satisfied. The first of these conditions is that the rules must contain in some form restrictions on the free use of violence, theft, and deception to which human beings are tempted but which they must, in general, repress, if they are to coexist in close proximity to each other. Such rules are in fact always found in the primitive societies of which we have knowledge, together with a variety of others imposing on individuals various positive duties to perform services or make contributions to the common life. Secondly, though such a society may exhibit the tension, already described, between those who accept the rules and those who reject the rules except where fear of social pressure induces them to conform, it is plain that the latter cannot be more than a minority, if so loosely organized a society of persons, approximately equal in physical strength, is to endure: for otherwise those who reject the rules would have too little social pressure to fear. This too is confirmed by what we know of primitive communities where, though there are dissidents and malefactors, the majority live by the rules seen from the internal point of view.

More important for our present purpose is the following consideration. It is plain that only a small community closely knit by ties of kinship, common sentiment, and belief, and placed in a stable environment, could live successfully by such a regime of unofficial rules. In any other conditions such a simple form of social control must prove defective and will require supplementation in different ways. In the first place, the rules by which the group lives will not form a system, but will simply be a set of separate standards, without any identifying or common mark, except of course that they are the rules which a particular group of human beings accepts. They will in this respect resemble our own rules of etiquette. Hence if doubts arise as to what the rules are or as to the precise scope of some given rule, there will be no procedure for settling this doubt, either by reference to an authoritative text or to an official whose declarations on this point are authoritative. For, plainly, such a procedure and the acknowledgement of either authoritative text or persons involve the existence of rules of a type different from the rules of obligation or duty which *ex hypothesi* are all that the group has. This defect in the simple social structure of primary rules we may call its *uncertainty*.

A second defect is the *static* character of the rules. The only mode of change in the rules known to such a society will be the slow process of growth, whereby courses of conduct once thought optional become first habitual or usual, and then obligatory, and the converse process of decay, when deviations, once severely dealt with, are first tolerated and then pass unnoticed. There will be no means, in such a society, of deliberately adapting the rules to changing circumstances, either by eliminating old rules or introducing new ones: for, again, the possibility of doing this presupposes the existence of rules of a different type from the primary rules of obligation by which alone the society lives. In an extreme case the rules may be static in a more drastic sense. This, though never perhaps fully realized in any actual community, is worth considering because the remedy for it is something very characteristic of law. In this extreme case, not only would there be no way of deliberately changing the general rules, but the obligations which arise under the rules in particular cases could not be varied or modified by the deliberate choice of any individual. Each individual would simply have fixed obligations or duties to do or abstain from doing certain things. It might indeed very often be the case that others would benefit from the performance of these obligations; yet if there are only primary rules of obligation they would have no power to release those bound from performance or to transfer to others the benefits which would accrue from performance. For such operations of release or transfer create changes in the initial positions of individuals under the primary rules of obligation, and for these operations to be possible there must be rules of a sort different from the primary rules.

The third defect of this simple form of social life is the *inefficiency* of the diffuse social pressure by which the rules are maintained. Disputes as to whether an admitted rule has or has not been violated will always occur and will, in any but the smallest societies, continue interminably, if there is no agency specially empowered to ascertain finally, and authoritatively, the fact of violation. Lack of such final and authoritative determinations is to be distinguished from another weakness associated with it. This is the fact that punishments for violations of the rules, and other forms of social pressure involving physical effort or the use of force, are not administered by a special agency but are left to the individuals affected or to the group at large. It is obvious that the waste of time involved in the group's unorganized efforts to catch and punish offenders, and the smouldering vendettas which may result from self-help in the absence of an official monopoly of "sanctions," may be serious. The history of law does, however, strongly suggest that the lack of official agencies to determine authoritatively the fact of violation of the rules is a much more serious defect; for many societies have remedies for this defect long before the other.

The remedy for each of these three main defects in this simplest form of social structure consists in supplementing the *primary* rules of obligation with *secondary* rules which are rules of a different kind. The introduction of the remedy for each defect might, in itself, be considered a step from the prelegal into the legal world; since each remedy brings with it many elements that permeate law: certainly all three remedies together are enough to convert the regime of primary rules into what is indisputably a legal system. We shall consider in turn each of these remedies and show why law may most illuminatingly be characterized as a union of primary rules of obligation with such secondary rules. Before we do this, however, the following general points should be noted. Though the remedies consist in the introduction of rules which are certainly different from each other; as well as from the primary rules of obligation which they supplement, they have important features in common and are connected in various ways. Thus they may all be said to be on a different level from the primary rules, for they are all *about* such rules; in the sense that while primary rules are concerned with the actions that individuals must or must not do, these secondary rules are all concerned with the primary rules themselves. They specify the ways in which the primary rules may be conclusively ascertained, introduced, eliminated, varied, and the fact of their violation conclusively determined.

The simplest form of remedy for the *uncertainty* of the regime of primary rules is the introduction of what we shall call a "rule of recognition." This will specify some feature or features possession of which by a suggested rule is taken as a conclusive affirmative indication that it is a rule of the group to be supported by the social pressure it exerts. The existence of such a rule of recognition may take any of a huge variety of forms, simple or complex. It may, as in the early law of many societies, be no more than that an authoritative list or text of the rules is to be found in a written document or carved on some public monument. No doubt as a matter of history this step from the pre-legal to the legal may be accomplished in distinguishable stages, of which the first is the mere reduction to writing of hitherto unwritten rules. This is not itself the crucial step, though it is a very important one: what is crucial is the acknowledgement of reference to the writing or inscription as *authoritative*, i.e., as the *proper* way of disposing of doubts as to the existence of the rule. Where there is such an acknowledgement there is a very simple form of secondary rule: a rule for conclusive identification of the primary rules of obligation.

In a developed legal system the rules of recognition are of course more complex; instead of identifying rules exclusively by reference to a text or list they do so by reference to some general characteristic possessed by the primary rules. This may be the fact of their having been enacted by a specific body, or their long customary practice, or their relation to judicial decisions. Moreover, where more than one of such general characteristics are treated as identifying criteria, provision may be made for their possible conflict by their arrangement in an order of superiority, as by the common subordination of custom or precedent to statute, the latter being a superior source of law. Such complexity may make the rules of recognition in a modern legal system seem very different from the simple acceptance of an authoritative text: yet even in this simplest form, such a rule brings with it many elements distinctive of law. By providing an authoritative mark it introduces, although in embryonic form, the idea of a legal system: for the rules are now not just a discrete unconnected set but are, in a simple way, unified. Further, in the simple operation of identifying a given rule as possessing the required feature of being an item on an authoritative list of rules we have the germ of the idea of legal validity.

The remedy for the *static* quality of the regime of primary rules consists in the introduction of what we shall call "rules of change." The simplest form of such a rule is that which empowers an individual or body of persons to introduce new primary rules for the conduct of the life of the group, or of some class within it, and to eliminate old rules. As we have already argued in Chapter IV it is in terms of such a rule, and not in terms of orders backed by threats, that the ideas of legislative enactment and repeal are to be understood. Such rules of change may be very simple or very complex: the powers conferred may be unrestricted or limited in various ways: and the rules may, besides specifying the persons who are to legislate, define in more or less rigid terms the procedure to be followed in legislation. Plainly, there will be a very close connection between the rules of change and the rules of recognition: for where the former exists the latter will necessarily incorporate a reference to legislation as an identifying feature of the rules, though it need not refer to all the details of procedure involved in legislation. Usually some official certificate or official copy will, under the rules of recognition, be taken as a sufficient proof of due enactment. Of course if there is a social structure so simple that the only "source of law" is legislation, the rule of recognition will simply specify enactment as the unique identifying mark or criterion of validity of the rules. This will be the case for example in the imaginary kingdom of Rex I depicted in Chapter IV: there the rule of recognition would simply be that whatever Rex I enacts is law.

We have already described in some detail the rules which confer on individuals power to vary their initial positions under the primary rules. Without such private power-conferring rules society would lack some of the chief amenities which law confers upon it. For the operations which these rules make possible are the making of wills, contracts, transfers of property, and many other voluntarily created structures of rights and duties which typify life under law, though of course an elementary form of power-conferring rule also underlies the moral institution of a promise. The kinship of these rules with the rules of change involved in the notion of legislation is clear, and as recent theory such as Kelsen's has shown, many of the features which puzzle us in the institutions of contract or property are clarified by thinking of the operations of making a contract or transferring property as the exercise of limited legislative powers by individuals.

The third supplement to the simple regime of primary rules, intended to remedy the *inefficiency* of its diffused social pressure, consists of secondary rules empowering individuals to make authoritative determinations of the question whether, on a particular occasion, a primary rule has been broken. The minimal form of adjudication consists in such determinations, and we shall call the secondary rules which confer the power to make them "rules of adjudication." Besides identifying the individuals who are to adjudicate, such rules will also define the procedure to be followed. Like the other secondary rules these are on a different level from the primary rules: though they may be reinforced by further rules imposing duties on judges to adjudicate, they do not impose duties but confer judicial powers and a special status on judicial declarations about the breach of obligations. Again these rules, like the other secondary rules, define a group of important legal concepts: in this case the concepts of judge or court, jurisdiction and judgment. Besides these resemblances to the other secondary rules, rules of adjudication have intimate connections with them. Indeed, a system which has rules of adjudication is necessarily also committed to a rule of recognition of an elementary and imperfect sort. This is so because, if courts are empowered to make authoritative determinations of the fact that a rule has been broken, these cannot avoid being taken as authoritative determinations of what the rules are. So the rule which confers jurisdiction will also be a rule of recognition, identifying the primary rules through the judgments of the courts and these judgments will become a "source" of law. It is true that this form of rule of recognition, inseparable from the minimum form of jurisdiction, will be very imperfect. Unlike an authoritative text or a statute book, judgments may not be couched in general terms and their use as authoritative guides to the rules depends on a somewhat shaky inference from particular decisions, and the reliability of this must fluctuate both with the skill of the interpreter and the consistency of the judges.

It need hardly be said that in few legal systems are judicial powers confined to authoritative determinations of the fact of violation of the primary rules. Most systems have, after some delay, seen the advantages of further centralization of social pressure, and have partially prohibited the use of physical punishments or violent self help by private individuals. Instead they have supplemented the primary rules of obligation by further secondary rules, specifying or at least limiting the penalties for violation, and have conferred upon judges, where they have ascertained the fact of violation, the exclusive power to direct the application of penalties by other officials. These secondary rules provide the centralized official "sanctions" of the system.

If we stand back and consider the structure which has resulted from the combination of primary rules of obligation with the secondary rules of recognition, change and adjudication, it is plain that we have here not only the heart of a legal system, but a most powerful tool for the analysis of much that has puzzled both the jurist and the political theorist.

Not only are the specifically legal concepts with which the lawyer is professionally concerned, such as those of obligation and rights, validity and source of law, legislation and jurisdiction, and sanction, best elucidated in terms of this combination of elements. The concepts (which bestride both law and political theory) of the state, of authority, and of an official require a similar analysis if the obscurity which still lingers about them is to be dissipated. The reason why an analysis in these terms of primary and secondary rules has this explanatory power is not far to seek. Most of the obscurities and distortions surrounding legal and political concepts arise from the fact that these essentially involve reference to what we have called the internal point of view: the view of those who do not merely record and predict behaviour conforming to rules, but *use* the rules as standards for the appraisal of their own and others' behaviour. This requires more detailed attention in the analysis of legal and political concepts than it has usually received. Under the simple regime of primary rules the internal point of view is manifested in its simplest form, in the use of those rules as the basis of criticism, and as the justification of demands for conformity, social pressure, and punishment. Reference to this most elementary manifestation of the internal point of view is required for the analysis of the basic concepts of obligation and duty. With the addition to the system of secondary rules, the range of what is said and done from the internal point of view is much extended and diversified. With this extension comes a whole set of new concepts and they demand a reference to the internal point of view for their analysis. These include the notions of legislation, jurisdiction, validity, and, generally, of legal powers, private and public. There is a constant pull towards an analysis of these in the terms of ordinary or "scientific," fact-stating or predictive discourse. But this can only reproduce their external aspect: to do justice to their distinctive, internal aspect we need to see the different ways in which the law-making operations of the legislator, the adjudication of a court, the exercise of private or official powers, and other "acts-in-the-law" are related to secondary rules.

In the next chapter we shall show how the ideas of the validity of law and sources of law, and the truths latent among the errors of the doctrines of sovereignty may be rephrased and clarified in terms of rules of recognition. But we shall conclude this chapter with a warning: though the combination of primary and secondary rules merits, because it explains many aspects of law, the central place assigned to it, this cannot by itself illuminate every problem. The union of primary and secondary rules is at the centre of a legal system; but it is not the whole, and as we move away from the centre we shall have to accommodate, in ways indicated in later chapters, elements of a different character....

Rule of Recognition and Legal Validity

According to the theory criticized in Chapter IV the foundations of a legal system consist of the situations in which the majority of a social group habitually obey the orders backed by threats of the sovereign person or persons, who themselves habitually obey no one. This social situation is, for this theory, both a necessary and a sufficient condition for the existence of law. We have already exhibited in some detail the incapacity of this theory to account for some of the salient features of a modern municipal legal system: yet nonetheless, as its hold over the minds of many thinkers suggests, it does contain, though in a blurred and misleading form, certain truths about certain important aspects of law. These truths can, however, only be clearly presented, and their importance rightly assessed, in terms of the more complex social situation where a secondary rule of recognition is accepted and used for the identification of primary rules of obligation. It is this situation which deserves, if anything does, to be called the foundations of a legal system. In this chapter we shall discuss various elements of this situation which have received only partial or misleading expression in the theory of sovereignty and elsewhere.

Wherever such a rule of recognition is accepted, both private persons and officials are provided with authoritative criteria for identifying primary rules of obligation. The criteria so provided may, as we have seen, take any one or more of a variety of forms: these include reference to an authoritative text; to legislative enactment; to customary practice; to general declarations of specified persons, or to past judicial decisions in particular cases. In a very simple system like the world of Rex I depicted in Chapter IV, where only what he enacts is law and no legal limitations upon his legislative power are imposed by customary rule or constitutional document, the sole criterion for identifying the law will be a simple reference to the fact of enactment by Rex I. The existence of this simple form of rule of recognition will be manifest in the general practice, on the part of officials or private persons, of identifying the rules by this criterion. In a modern legal system where there are a variety of "sources" of law, the rule of recognition is correspondingly more complex: the criteria for identifying the law are multiple and commonly include a written constitution, enactment by a legislature, and judicial precedents. In most cases, provision is made for possible conflict by ranking these criteria in an order of relative subordination and primacy. It is in this way that in our system "common law" is subordinate to "statute."

It is important to distinguish this relative *subordination* of one criterion to another from *derivation*, since some spurious support for the view that all law is essentially or "really" (even if only "tacitly") the product of legislation, has been gained from confusion of these two ideas. In our own system, custom and precedent are subordinate to legislation since customary and common law rules may be deprived of their status as law by statute. Yet they owe their status of law, precarious as this may be, not to a "tacit" exercise of legislative power but to the acceptance of a rule of recognition which accords them this independent though subordinate place. Again, as in the simple case, the existence of such a complex rule of recognition with this hierarchical ordering of distinct criteria is manifested in the general practice of identifying the rules by such criteria.

In the day-to-day life of a legal system its rule of recognition is very seldom expressly formulated as a rule; though occasionally, courts in England may announce in general terms the relative place of one criterion of law in relation to another, as when they assert the supremacy of Acts of Parliament over other sources or suggested sources of law. For the most part the rule of recognition is not stated, but its existence is *shown* in the way in which particular rules are identified, either by courts or other officials or private persons or their advisers. There is, of course, a difference in the use made by courts of the criteria provided by the rule and the use of them by others: for when courts reach a particular conclusion on the footing that a particular rule has been correctly identified as law, what they say has a special authoritative status conferred on it by other rules. In this respect, as in many others, the rule of recognition of a legal system is like the scoring rule of a game. In the course of the game the general rule defining the activities which constitute scoring (runs, goals, &c.) is seldom formulated; instead it is *used* by officials and players in identifying the particular phases which count towards winning. Here too, the declarations of officials (umpire or scorer) have a special authoritative status attributed to them by other rules. Further, in both cases there is the possibility of a conflict between these authoritative applications of the rule and the general understanding of what the rule plainly requires according to its terms. This, as we shall see later, is a complication which must be catered for in any account of what it is for a system of rules of this sort to exist.

The use of unstated rules of recognition, by courts and others, in identifying particular rules of the system is characteristic of the internal point of view. Those who use them in this way thereby manifest their own acceptance of them as guiding rules and with this attitude there goes a characteristic vocabulary different from the natural expressions of the external point of view. Perhaps the simplest of these is the expression, "It is the law that ...," which we may find on the lips not only of judges, but of ordinary men living under a legal system, when they identify a given rule of the system. This, like the expression "Out" or "Goal," is the language of one assessing a situation by reference to rules which he in common with others acknowledges as appropriate for this purpose. This attitude of shared acceptance of rules is to be contrasted with that of an observer who records *ab extra* the fact that a social group accepts such rules but does not himself accept them. The natural expression of this external point of view is not "It is the law that ..." but "In England they recognize as law ... whatever the Queen in Parliament enacts...." The first of these forms of expression we shall call an *internal statement* because it manifests the internal point of view and is naturally used by one who, accepting the rule of recognition and without stating the fact that it is accepted, applies the rule in recognizing some particular rule of the system as valid. The second form of expression we shall call an *external statement* because it is the natural language of an external observer of the system who, without himself accepting its rule of recognition, states the fact that others accept it.

If this use of an accepted rule of recognition in making internal statements is understood and carefully distinguished from an external statement of fact that the rule is accepted, many obscurities concerning the notion of legal "validity" disappear. For the word "valid" is most frequently, though not always, used, in just such internal statements, applying to a particular rule of a legal system, an unstated but accepted rule of recognition. To say that a given rule is valid is to recognize it as passing all the tests provided by the rule of recognition and so as a rule of the system. We can indeed simply say that the statement that a particular rule is valid means that it satisfies all the criteria provided by the rule of recognition. This is incorrect only to the extent that it might obscure the internal character of such statements; for, like the cricketers' "Out," these statements of validity normally apply to a particular case a rule of recognition accepted by the speaker and others, rather than expressly state that the rule is satisfied.

Some of the puzzles connected with the idea of legal validity are said to concern the relation between the validity and the "efficacy" of law. If by "efficacy" is meant that the fact that a rule of law which requires certain behaviour is obeyed more often than not, it is plain that there is no necessary connection between the validity of any particular rule and *its* efficacy, unless the rule of recognition of the system includes among its criteria, as some do, the provision (sometimes referred to as a rule of obsolescence) that no rule is to count as a rule of the system if it has long ceased to be efficacious.

From the inefficacy of a particular rule, which may or may not count against its validity, we must distinguish a general disregard of the rules of the system. This may be so complete in character and so protracted that we should say, in the case of a new system, that it had never established itself as the legal system of a given group, or, in the case of a once-established system, that it had ceased to be the legal system of the group. In either case, the normal context or background for making any internal statement in terms of the rules of the system is absent. In such cases it would be generally *pointless* either to assess the rights and duties of particular persons by reference to the primary rules of a system or to assess the validity of any of its rules by reference to its rules of recognition. To insist on applying a system of rules which had either never actually been effective or had been discarded would, except in special circumstances mentioned below, be as futile as to assess the progress of a game by reference to a scoring rule which had never been accepted or had been discarded.

One who makes an internal statement concerning the validity of a particular rule of a system may be said to *presuppose* the truth of the external statement of fact that the system is generally efficacious. For the normal use of internal statements is in such a context of general efficacy. It would however be wrong to say that statements of validity mean that the system is generally efficacious. For though it is normally pointless or idle to talk of the validity of a rule of a system which has never established itself or has been discarded, none the less it is not meaningless nor is it always pointless. One vivid way of teaching Roman Law is to speak *as if* the system were efficacious still and to discuss the validity of particular rules and solve problems in their terms; and one way of nursing hopes for the restoration of an old social order destroyed by revolution, and rejecting the new, is to cling to the criteria of legal validity of the old regime. This is implicitly done by the White Russian who still claims property under some rule of descent which was a valid rule of Tsarist Russia.

A grasp of the normal contextual connection between the internal statement that a given rule of a system is valid and the external statement of fact that the system is generally efficacious, will help us see in its proper perspective the common theory that to assert the validity of a rule is to predict that it will be enforced by courts or some other official action taken. In many ways this theory is similar to the predictive analysis of obligation which we considered and rejected in the last chapter. In both cases alike the motive for advancing this predictive theory is the conviction that only thus can metaphysical interpretations be avoided: that either a statement that a rule is valid must ascribe some mysterious property which cannot be detected by empirical means or it must be a prediction of future behaviour of officials. In both cases also the plausibility of the theory is due to the same important fact: that the truth of the external statement of fact, which an observer might record, that the system is generally efficacious and likely to continue so, is normally presupposed by anyone who accepts the rules and makes an internal statement of obligation or validity. The two are certainly very closely associated. Finally, in both cases alike the mistake of the theory is the same: it consists in neglecting the special character of the internal statement and treating it as an external statement about official action.

This mistake becomes immediately apparent when we consider how the judge's own statement that a particular rule is valid functions in judicial decision; for, though here too, in making such a statement, the judge presupposes but does not state the general efficacy of the system, he plainly is not concerned to predict his own or others' official action. His statement that a rule is valid is an internal statement recognizing that the rule satisfies the tests for identifying what is to count as law in his court, and constitutes not a prophecy of but part of the *reason* for his decision. There is indeed a more plausible case for saying that a statement that a rule is valid is a prediction when such a statement is made by a private person; for in the case of conflict between unofficial statements of validity or invalidity and that of a court in deciding a case, there is often good sense in saying that the former must then be withdrawn. Yet even here, as we shall see when we come in Chapter VII to investigate the significance of such conflicts between official declarations and the plain requirements of the rules, it may be dogmatic to assume that it is withdrawn as a statement now shown to be *wrong*, because it has falsely *predicted* what a court would say. For there are more reasons for withdrawing statements than the fact that they are wrong, and also more ways of being wrong than this allows.

The rule of recognition providing the criteria by which the validity of other rules of the system is assessed is in an important sense, which we shall try to clarify, an *ultimate* rule: and where, as is usual, there are several criteria ranked in order of relative subordination and primacy, one of them is *supreme*. These ideas of the ultimacy of the rule of recognition and the supremacy of one of its criteria merit some attention. It is important to disentangle them from the theory, which we have rejected, that somewhere in every legal system, even though it lurks behind legal forms, there must be a sovereign legislative power which is legally unlimited.

Of these two ideas, supreme criterion and ultimate rule, the first is the easiest to define. We may say that a criterion of legal validity or source of law is supreme if rules identified by reference to it are still recognized as rules of the system, even if they conflict with rules identified by reference to the other criteria, whereas rules identified by reference to the latter are not so recognized if they conflict with the rules identified by reference to the supreme criterion. A similar explanation in comparative terms can be given of the notions of "superior" and "subordinate" criteria which we have already used. It is plain that the notions of a superior and a supreme criterion merely refer to a *relative* place on a scale and do not import any notion of legally *unlimited* legislative power.

Yet "supreme" and "unlimited" are easy to confuse—at least in legal theory. One reason for this is that in the simpler forms of legal system the ideas of ultimate rule of recognition, supreme criterion, and legally unlimited legislature seem to converge. For where there is a legislature subject to no constitutional limitations and competent by its enactment to deprive all other rules of law emanating from other sources of their status as law, it is part of the rule of recognition in such a system that enactment by that legislature is the supreme criterion of validity. This is, according to constitutional theory, the position in the United Kingdom. But even systems like that of the United States in which there is no such legally unlimited legislature may perfectly well contain an ultimate rule of recognition which provides a set of criteria of validity, one of which is supreme. This will be so, where the legislative competence of the ordinary legislature is limited by a constitution which contains no amending power, or places some clauses outside the scope of that power. Here there is no legally unlimited legislature, even in the widest interpretation of "legislature"; but the system of course contains an ultimate rule of recognition and, in the clauses of its constitution, a supreme criterion of validity.

The sense in which the rule of recognition is the *ultimate* rule of a system is best understood if we pursue a very familiar chain of legal reasoning. If the question is raised whether some suggested rule is legally valid, we must, in order to answer the question, use a criterion of validity provided by some other rule. Is this purported by-law of the Oxfordshire County Council valid? Yes: because it was made in exercise of the powers conferred, and in accordance with the procedure specified, by a statutory order made by the Minister of Health. At this first stage the statutory order provides the criteria in terms of which the validity of the by-law is assessed. There may be no practical need to go farther; but there is a standing possibility of doing so. We may query the validity of the statutory order and assess its validity in terms of the statute empowering the minister to make such orders. Finally, when the validity of the statute has been queried and assessed by reference to the rule that what the Queen in Parliament enacts is law, we are brought to a stop in inquiries concerning validity: for we have reached a rule which, like the intermediate statutory order and statute, provides criteria for the assessment of the validity of other rules; but it is also unlike them in that there is no rule providing criteria for the assessment of its own legal validity.

There are, indeed, many questions which we can raise about this ultimate rule. We can ask whether it is the practice of courts, legislatures, officials, or private citizens in England actually to use this rule as an ultimate rule of recognition. Or has our process of legal reasoning been an idle game with the criteria of validity of a system now discarded? We can ask whether it is a satisfactory form of legal system which has such a rule at its root. Does it produce more good than evil? Are there prudential reasons for supporting it? Is there a moral obligation to do so? These are plainly very important questions; but, equally plainly, when we ask them about the rule of recognition, we are no longer attempting to answer the same kind of question about it as those which we answered about other rules with its aid. When we move from saying that a particular enactment is valid, because it satisfies the rule that what the Queen in Parliament enacts is law, to saying that in England this last rule is used by courts, officials, and private persons as the ultimate rule of recognition, we have moved from an internal statement of law asserting the validity of a rule of the system to an external statement of fact which an observer of the system might make even if he did not accept it. So too when we move from the statement that a particular enactment is valid, to the statement that the rule of recognition of the system is an excellent one and the system based on it is one worthy of support, we have moved from a statement of legal validity to a statement of value.

Some writers, who have emphasized the legal ultimacy of the rule of recognition, have expressed this by saying that, whereas the legal validity of other rules of the system can be demonstrated by reference to it, its own validity cannot be demonstrated but is "assumed" or "postulated" or is a "hypothesis." This may, however, be seriously misleading. Statements of legal validity made about particular rules in the day-to-day life of a legal system whether by judges, lawyers, or ordinary citizens do indeed carry with them certain presuppositions. They are internal statements of law expressing the point of view of those who accept the rule of recognition of the system and, as such, leave unstated much that could be stated in external statements of fact about the system. What is thus left unstated forms the normal background or context of statements of legal validity and is thus said to be "presupposed" by them. But it is important to see precisely what these presupposed matters are, and not to obscure their character. They consist of two things. First, a person who seriously asserts the validity of some given rule of law, say a particular statute, himself makes use of a rule of recognition which he accepts as appropriate for identifying the law. Secondly, it is the case that this rule of recognition, in terms of which he assesses the validity of a particular statute, is not only accepted by him but is the rule of recognition actually accepted and employed in the general operation of the system. If the truth of this presupposition were doubted, it could be established by reference to actual practice: to the way in which courts identify what is to count as law, and to the general acceptance of or acquiescence in these identifications.

Neither of these two presuppositions are well described as "assumptions" of a "validity" which cannot be demonstrated. We only need the word "validity," and commonly only use it, to answer questions which arise *within* a system of rules where the status of a rule as a member of the system depends on its satisfying certain criteria provided by the rule of recognition. No such question can arise as to the validity of the very rule of recognition which provides the criteria; it can neither be valid nor invalid but is simply accepted as appropriate for use in this way. To express this simple fact by saying darkly that its validity is "assumed but cannot be demonstrated," is like saying that we assume, but can never demonstrate, that the standard metre bar in Paris which is the ultimate test of the correctness of all measurement in metres, is itself correct.

A more serious objection is that talk of the "assumption" that the ultimate rule of recognition is valid conceals the essentially factual character of the second presupposition which lies behind the lawyers' statement of validity. No doubt the practice of judges, officials, and others, in which the actual existence of a rule of recognition consists, is a complex matter. As we shall see later, there are certainly situations in which questions as to the precise content and scope of this kind of rule, and even as to its existence, may not admit of a clear or determinate answer. None the less it is important to distinguish "assuming the validity" from "presupposing the existence" of such a rule; if only because failure to do this obscures what is meant by the assertion that such a rule *exists*.

In the simple system of primary rules of obligation sketched in the last chapter, the assertion that a given rule existed could only be an external statement of fact such as an observer who did not accept the rules might make and verify by ascertaining whether or not, as a matter of fact, a given mode of behaviour was generally accepted as a standard and was accompanied by those features which, as we have seen, distinguish a social rule from mere convergent habits. It is in this way also that we should now interpret and verify the assertion that in England a rule—though not a legal one—exists that we must bare the head on entering a church. If such rules as these are found to exist in the actual practice of a social group, there is no separate question of their validity to be discussed, though of course their value or desirability is open to question. Once their existence has been established as a fact we should only confuse matters by affirming or denying that they were valid or by saying that "we assumed" but could not show their validity. Where, on the other hand, as in a mature legal system, we have a system of rules which includes a rule of recognition so that the status of a rule as a member of the system now depends on whether it satisfies certain criteria provided by the rule of recognition, this brings with it a new application of the word "exist." The statement that a rule exists may now no longer be what it was in the simple case of customary rules—an external statement of the *fact* that a certain mode of behaviour was generally accepted as a standard in practice. It may now be an internal statement applying an accepted but unstated rule of recognition and meaning (roughly) no more than "valid given the system's criteria of validity." In this respect, however, as in others a rule of recognition is unlike other rules of the system. The assertion that it exists can only be an external statement of fact. For whereas a subordinate rule of a system may be valid and in that sense "exist" even if it is generally disregarded, the rule of recognition exists only as a complex, but normally concordant, practice of the courts, officials, and private persons in identifying the law by reference to certain criteria. Its existence is a matter of fact.

New Questions

Once we abandon the view that the foundations of a legal system consist in a habit of obedience to a legally unlimited sovereign and substitute for this the conception of an ultimate rule of recognition which provides a system of rules with its criteria of validity, a range of fascinating and important questions confronts us. They are relatively new questions; for they were veiled so long as jurisprudence and political theory were committed to the older ways of thought. They are also difficult questions, requiring for a full answer, on the one hand a grasp of some fundamental issues of constitutional law and on the other an appreciation of the characteristic manner in which legal forms may silently shift and change. We shall therefore investigate these questions only so far as they bear upon the wisdom or unwisdom of insisting, as we have done, that a central place should be assigned to the union of primary and secondary rules in the elucidation of the concept of law.

The first difficulty is that of classification; for the rule which, in the last resort, is used to identify the law escapes the conventional categories used for describing a legal system, though these are often taken to be exhaustive. Thus, English constitutional writers since Dicey have usually repeated the statement that the constitutional arrangements of the United Kingdom consist partly of laws strictly so called (statutes, orders in council, and rules embodied in precedents) and partly of conventions which are mere usages, understandings, or customs. The latter include important rules such as that the Queen may not refuse her consent to a bill duly passed by Peers and Commons; there is, however, no legal duty on the Queen to give her consent and such rules are called conventions because the courts do not recognize them as imposing a legal duty. Plainly the rule that what the Queen in Parliament enacts is law does not fall into either of these categories. It is not a convention, since the courts are most intimately concerned with it and they use it in identifying the law; and it is not a rule on the same level as the "laws strictly so called" which it is used to identify. Even if it were enacted by statute, this would not reduce it to the level of a statute; for the legal status of such an enactment necessarily would depend on the fact that the rule existed antecedently to and independently of the enactment. Moreover, as we have shown in the last section, its existence, unlike that of a statute, must consist in an actual practice.

This aspect of things extracts from some a cry of despair: how can we show that the fundamental provisions of a constitution which are surely law are really law? Others reply with the insistence that at the base of legal systems there is something which is "not law," which is "pre-legal," "metalegal," or is just "political fact." This uneasiness is a sure sign that the categories used for the description of this most important feature in any system of law are too crude. The case for calling the rule of recognition "law" is that the rule providing criteria for the identification of other rules of the system may well be thought a defining feature of a legal system, and so itself worth calling "law"; the case for calling it "fact" is that to assert that such a rule exists is indeed to make an external statement of an actual fact concerning the manner in which the rules of an "efficacious" system are identified. Both these aspects claim attention but we cannot do justice to them both by choosing one of the labels "law" or "fact." Instead, we need to remember that the ultimate rule of recognition may be regarded from two points of view: one is expressed in the external statement of fact that the rule exists in the actual practice of the system; the other is expressed in the internal statements of validity made by those who use it in identifying the law.

A second set of questions arises out of the hidden complexity and vagueness of the assertion that a legal system *exists* in a given country or among a given social group. When we make this assertion we in fact refer in compressed, portmanteau form to a number of heterogeneous social facts, usually concomitant. The standard terminology of legal and political thought, developed in the shadow of a misleading theory, is apt to oversimplify and obscure the facts. Yet when we take off the spectacles constituted by this terminology and look at the facts, it becomes apparent that a legal system, like a human being, may at one stage be unborn, at a second not yet wholly independent of its mother, then enjoy a healthy independent existence, later decay and finally die. These halfway stages between birth and normal, independent existence and, again, between that and death, put out of joint our familiar ways of describing legal phenomena. They are worth our study because, baffling as they are, they throw into relief the full complexity of what we take for granted when, in the normal case, we make the confident and true assertion that in a given country a legal system exists.

One way of realizing this complexity is to see just where the simple, Austinian formula of a general habit of obedience to orders fails to reproduce or distorts the complex facts which constitute the minimum conditions which a society must satisfy if it is to have a legal system. We may allow that this formula does designate one necessary condition: namely, that where the laws impose obligations or duties these should be generally obeyed or at any rate not generally disobeyed. But though essential, this only caters for what we may term the "end product" of the legal system, where it makes its impact on the private citizen; whereas its day-to-day existence consists also in the official creation, the official identification, and the official use and application of law. The relationship with law involved here can be called "obedience" only if that word is extended so far beyond its normal use as to cease to characterize informatively these operations. In no ordinary sense of "obey" are legislators obeying rules when, in enacting laws, they conform to the rules conferring their legislative powers, except of course when the rules conferring such powers are reinforced by rules imposing a duty to follow them. Nor, in failing to conform with these rules do they "disobey" a law, though they may fail to make one. Nor does the word "obey" describe well what judges do when they apply the system's rule of recognition and recognize a statute as valid law and use it in the determination of disputes. We can of course, if we wish, preserve the simple terminology of "obedience" in face of the facts by many devices. One is to express, e.g., the use made by judges of general criteria of validity in recognizing a statute, as a case of obedience to orders given by the "Founders of the Constitution," or (where there are no "Founders") as obedience to a "depsychologized command," i.e., a command without a commander. But this last should perhaps have no more serious claims on our attention than the notion of a nephew without an uncle. Alternatively we can push out of sight the whole official side to law and forgo the description of the use of rules made in legislation and adjudication, and instead, think of the whole official world as one person (the "sovereign") issuing orders, through various agents or mouthpieces, which are habitually obeyed by the citizen. But this is either no more than a convenient shorthand for complex facts which still await description, or a disastrously confusing piece of mythology.

It is natural to react from the failure of attempts to give an account of what it is for a legal system to exist, in the agreeably simple terms of the habitual obedience which is indeed characteristic of (though it does not always exhaustively describe) the relationship of the ordinary citizen to law, by making the opposite error. This consists in taking what is characteristic (though again not exhaustive) of the official activities, especially the judicial attitude or relationship to law, and treating this as an adequate account of what must exist in a social group which has a legal system. This amounts to replacing the simple conception that the bulk of society habitually obey the law with the conception that they must generally share, accept, or regard as binding the ultimate rule of recognition specifying the criteria in terms of which the validity of laws are ultimately assessed. Of course we can imagine, as we have done in Chapter III, a simple society where knowledge and understanding of the sources of law are widely diffused. There the "constitution" was so simple that no fiction would be involved in attributing knowledge and acceptance of it to the ordinary citizen as well as to the officials and lawyers. In the simple world of Rex I we might well say that there was more than mere habitual obedience by the bulk of the population to his word. There it might well be the case that both they and the officials of the system "accepted," in the same explicit, conscious way, a rule of recognition specifying Rex's word as the criterion of valid law for the whole society, though subjects and officials would have different roles to play and different relationships to the rules of law identified by this criterion. To insist that this state of affairs, imaginable in a simple society, always or usually exists in a complex modern state would be to insist on a fiction. Here surely the reality of the situation is that a great proportion of ordinary citizens—perhaps a majority—have no general conception of the legal structure or of its criteria of validity. The law which he obeys is something which he knows of only as "the law." He may obey it for a variety of different reasons and among them may often, though not always, be the knowledge that it will be best for him to do so. He will be aware of the general likely consequences of disobedience: that there are officials who may arrest him and others who will try him and send him to prison for breaking the law. So long as the laws which are valid by the system's tests of validity are obeyed by the bulk of the population this surely is all the evidence we need in order to establish that a given legal system exists.

But just because a legal system is a complex union of primary and secondary rules, this evidence is not all that is needed to describe the relationships to law involved in the existence of a legal system. It must be supplemented by a description of the relevant relationship of the officials of the system to the secondary rules which concern them as officials. Here what is crucial is that there should be a unified or shared official acceptance of the rule of recognition containing the system's criteria of validity. But it is just here that the simple notion of general obedience, which was adequate to characterize the indispensable minimum in the case of ordinary citizens, is inadequate. The point is not, or not merely, the "linguistic" one that "obedience" is not naturally used to refer to the way in which these secondary rules are respected as rules by courts and other officials. We could find, if necessary, some wider expression like "follow," "comply," or "conform to" which would characterize both what ordinary citizens do in relation to law when they report for military service and what judges do when they identify a particular statute as law in their courts, on the footing that what the Queen in Parliament enacts is law. But these blanket terms would merely mask vital differences which must be grasped if the minimum conditions involved in the existence of the complex social phenomenon which we call a legal system is to be understood.

What makes "obedience" misleading as a description of what legislators do in conforming to the rules conferring their powers, and of what courts do in applying an accepted ultimate rule of recognition, is that obeying a rule (or an order) *need* involve no thought on the part of the person obeying that what he does is the right thing both for himself and for others to do: he need have no view of what he does as a fulfilment of a standard of behaviour for others of the social group. He need not think of his conforming behaviour as "right," "correct," or "obligatory." His attitude, in other words, need not have any of that critical character which is involved whenever social rules are accepted and types of conduct are treated as general standards. He need not, though he may, share the internal point of view accepting the rules as standards for all to whom they apply. Instead, he may think of the rule only as something demanding action from *him* under threat of penalty; he may obey it out of fear of the consequences, or from inertia, without thinking of himself or others as having an obligation to do so and without being disposed to criticize either himself or others for deviations. But this merely personal concern with the rules, which is all the ordinary citizen *may* have in obeying them, cannot characterize the attitude of the courts to the rules with which they operate as courts. This is most patently the case with the ultimate rule of recognition in terms of which the validity of other rules is assessed. This, if it is to exist at all, must be regarded from the internal point of view as a public, common standard of correct judicial decision, and not as something which each judge merely obeys for his part only. Individual courts of the system though they may, on occasion, deviate from these rules must, in general, be critically concerned with such deviations as lapses from standards, which are essentially common or public. This is not merely a matter of the efficiency or health of the legal system, but is logically a necessary condition of our ability to speak of the existence of a single legal system. If only some judges acted "for their part only" on the footing that what the Queen in Parliament enacts is law, and made no criticisms of those who did not respect this rule of recognition, the characteristic unity and continuity of a legal system would have disappeared. For this depends on the acceptance, at this crucial point, of common standards of legal validity. In the interval between these vagaries of judicial behaviour and the chaos which would ultimately ensue when the ordinary man was faced with contrary judicial orders, we would be at a loss to describe the situation. We would be in the presence of a *lusus naturae* worth thinking about only because it sharpens our awareness of what is often too obvious to be noticed.

There are therefore two minimum conditions necessary and sufficient for the existence of a legal system. On the one hand, those rules of behaviour which are valid according to the system's ultimate criteria of validity must be generally obeyed, and, on the other hand, its rules of recognition specifying the criteria of legal validity and its rules of change and adjudication must be effectively accepted as common public standards of official behaviour by its officials. The first condition is the only one which private citizens *need* satisfy: they may obey each "for his part only" and from any motive whatever; though in a healthy society they will in fact often accept these rules as common standards of behaviour and acknowledge obligation to obey them, or even trace this obligation to a more general obligation to respect the constitution. The second condition must also be satisfied by the officials of the system. They must regard these as common standards of official behaviour and appraise critically their own and each other's deviations as lapses. Of course it is also true that besides these there will be many primary rules which apply to officials in their merely personal capacity which they need only obey.

The assertion that a legal system exists is therefore a Janus-faced statement looking both towards obedience by ordinary citizens and to the acceptance by officials of secondary rules as critical common standards of official behaviour. We need not be surprised at this duality. It is merely the reflection of the composite character of a legal system as compared with a simpler decentralized pre-legal form of social structure which consists only of primary rules. In the simpler structure, since there are no officials, the rules must be widely accepted as setting critical standards for the behaviour of the group. If, there, the internal point of view is not widely disseminated there could not logically be any rules. But where there is a union of primary and secondary rules, which is, as we have argued, the most fruitful way of regarding a legal system, the acceptance of the rules as common standards for the group may be split off from the relatively passive matter of the ordinary individual acquiescing in the rules by obeying them for his part alone. In an extreme case the internal point of view with its characteristic normative use of legal language ("This is a valid rule") might be confined to the official world. In this more complex system, only officials might accept and use the system's criteria of legal validity. The society in which this was so might be deplorably sheeplike; the sheep might end in the slaughter-house. But there is little reason for thinking that it could not exist or for denying it the title of a legal system....

7
Ronald Dworkin
"The Model of Rules I"

1. Embarrassing Questions

Lawyers lean heavily on the connected concepts of legal right and legal obligation. We say that someone has a legal right or duty, and we take that statement as a sound basis for making claims and demands, and for criticizing the acts of public officials. But our understanding of these concepts is remarkably fragile, and we fall into trouble when we try to say what legal rights and obligations are. We say glibly that whether someone has a legal obligation is determined by applying "the law" to the particular facts of his case, but this is not a helpful answer, because we have the same difficulties with the concept of law.

We are used to summing up our troubles in the classic questions of jurisprudence: What is "the law"? When two sides disagree, as often happens, about a proposition "of law," what are they disagreeing about, and how shall we decide which side is right? Why do we call what "the law" says a matter of legal "obligation"? Is "obligation" here just a term of art, meaning only what the law says? Or does legal obligation have something to do with moral obligation? Can we say that we have, in principle at least, the same reasons for meeting our legal obligations that we have for meeting our moral obligations?

These are not puzzles for the cupboard, to be taken down on rainy days for fun. They are sources of continuing embarrassment, and they nag at our attention. They embarrass us in dealing with particular problems that we must solve, one way or another. Suppose a novel right-of-privacy case comes to court, and there is no statute or precedent claimed by the plaintiff. What role in the court's decision should be played by the fact that most people in the community think that private individuals are "morally" entitled to that particular privacy? Supposing the Supreme Court orders some prisoner freed because the police used procedures that the Court now says are constitutionally forbidden, although the Court's earlier decisions upheld these procedures. Must the Court, to be consistent, free all other prisoners previously convicted through these same procedures?[1] Conceptual puzzles about "the law" and "legal obligation" become acute when a court is confronted with a problem like this.

These eruptions signal a chronic disease. Day in and day out we send people to jail, or take money away from them, or make them do things they do not want to do, under coercion of force, and we justify all of this by speaking of such persons as having broken the law or having failed to meet their legal obligations, or having interfered with other people's legal rights. Even in clear cases (a bank robber or a wilful breach of contract), when we are confident that someone had a legal obligation and broke it, we are not able to give a satisfactory account of what that means, or why that entitles the state to punish or coerce him. We may feel confident that what we are doing is proper, but until we can identify the principles we are following we cannot be sure that they are sufficient, or whether we are applying them consistently. In less clear cases, when the issue of whether an obligation has been broken is for some reason controversial, the pitch of these nagging questions rises, and our responsibility to find answers deepens.

Certain lawyers (we may call them "nominalists") urge that we solve these problems by ignoring them. In their view the concepts of "legal obligation" and "the law" are myths, invented and sustained by lawyers for a dismal mix of conscious and subconscious motives. The puzzles we find in these concepts are merely symptoms that they are myths. They are unsolvable because unreal, and our concern with them is just one feature of our enslavement. We would do better to flush away the puzzles and the concepts altogether, and pursue our important social objectives without this excess baggage.

This is a tempting suggestion, but it has fatal drawbacks. Before we can decide that our concepts of law and of legal obligation are myths, we must decide what they are. We must be able to state, at least roughly, what it is we all believe that is wrong. But the nerve of our problem is that we have great difficulty in doing just that. Indeed, when we ask what law is and what legal obligations are, we are asking for a theory of how we use those concepts and of the conceptual commitments our use entails. We cannot conclude, before we have such a general theory, that our practices are stupid or superstitious.

1 See *Linkletter v. Walker*, 381 U.S. 618 (1965).

Of course, the nominalists think they know how the rest of us use these concepts. They think that when we speak of "the law" we mean a set of timeless rules stocked in some conceptual warehouse awaiting discovery by judges, and that when we speak of legal obligation we mean the invisible chains these mysterious rules somehow drape around us. The theory that there are such rules and chains they call "mechanical jurisprudence," and they are right in ridiculing its practitioners. Their difficulty, however, lies in finding practitioners to ridicule. So far they have had little luck in caging and exhibiting mechanical jurisprudents (all specimens captured—even Blackstone and Joseph Beale—have had to be released after careful reading of their texts).

In any event, it is clear that most lawyers have nothing like this in mind when they speak of the law and of legal obligation. A superficial examination of our practices is enough to show this for we speak of laws changing and evolving, and of legal obligation sometimes being problematical. In these and other ways we show that we are not addicted to mechanical jurisprudence.

Nevertheless, we do use the concepts of law and legal obligation, and we do suppose that society's warrant to punish and coerce is written in that currency. It may be that when the details of this practice are laid bare, the concepts we do use will be shown to be as silly and as thick with illusion as those the nominalists invented. If so, then we shall have to find other ways to describe what we do, and either provide other justifications or change our practices. But until we have discovered this and made these adjustments, we cannot accept the nominalists' premature invitation to turn our backs on the problems our present concepts provide.

Of course the suggestion that we stop talking about "the law" and "legal obligation" is mostly bluff. These concepts are too deeply cemented into the structure of our political practices—they cannot be given up like cigarettes or hats. Some of the nominalists have half-admitted this and said that the myths they condemn should be thought of as Platonic myths and retained to seduce the masses into order. This is perhaps not so cynical a suggestion as it seems; perhaps it is a covert hedging of a dubious bet.

If we boil away the bluff, the nominalist attack reduces to an attack on mechanical jurisprudence. Through the lines of the attack, and in spite of the heroic calls for the death of law, the nominalists themselves have offered an analysis of how the terms "law" and "legal obligation" should be used which is not very different from that of more classical philosophers. Nominalists present their analysis as a model of how legal institutions (particularly courts) "really operate." But their model differs mainly in emphasis from the theory first made popular by the nineteenth century philosopher John Austin, and now accepted in one form or another by most working and academic lawyers who hold views on jurisprudence. I shall call this theory, with some historical looseness, "legal positivism." I want to examine the soundness of legal positivism, particularly in the powerful form that Professor H.L.A. Hart has given to it. I choose to focus on his position, not only because of its clarity and elegance, but because here, as almost everywhere else in legal philosophy, constructive thought must start with a consideration of his views.

2. Positivism

Positivism has a few central and organizing propositions as its skeleton, and though not every philosopher who is called a positivist would subscribe to these in the way I present them, they do define the general position I want to examine. These key tenets may be stated as follows:

(a) The law of a community is a set of special rules used by the community directly or indirectly for the purpose of determining which behavior will be punished or coerced by the public power. These special rules can be identified and distinguished by specific criteria, by tests having to do not with their content but with their *pedigree* or the manner in which they were adopted or developed. These tests of pedigree can be used to distinguish valid legal rules from spurious legal rules (rules which lawyers and litigants wrongly argue are rules of law) and also from other sorts of social rules (generally lumped together as "moral rules") that the community follows but does not enforce through public power.

(b) The set of these valid legal rules is exhaustive of "the law," so that if someone's case is not clearly covered by such a rule (because there is none that seems appropriate, or those that seem appropriate are vague, or for some other reason) then that case cannot be decided by "applying the law." It must be decided by some official, like a judge, "exercising his discretion," which means reaching beyond the law for some other sort of standard to guide him in manufacturing a fresh legal rule or supplementing an old one.

(c) To say that someone has a "legal obligation" is to say that his case falls under a valid legal rule that requires him to do or to forbear from doing something. (To say he has a legal right, or has a legal power of some sort, or a legal privilege or immunity, is to assert, in a shorthand way, that others have actual or hypothetical legal obligations to act or not to act in certain ways touching him.) In the absence of such a valid legal rule there is no legal obligation; it follows that when the judge decides an issue by exercising his discretion, he is not enforcing a legal right as to that issue.

This is only the skeleton of positivism. The flesh is arranged differently by different positivists, and some even tinker with the bones. Different versions differ chiefly in their description of the fundamental test of pedigree a rule must meet to count as a rule of law.

Austin, for example, framed his version of the fundamental test as a series of interlocking definitions and distinctions.[2] He defined having an obligation as lying under a rule, a rule as a general command, and a command as an expression of desire that others behave in a particular way, backed by the power and will to enforce that expression in the event of disobedience. He distinguished classes of rules (legal, moral or religious) according to which person or group is the author of the general command the rule represents. In each political community, he thought, one will find a sovereign—a person or a determinate group whom the rest obey habitually, but who is not in the habit of obeying anyone else. The legal rules of a community are the general commands its sovereign has deployed. Austin's definition of legal obligation followed from this definition of law. One has a legal obligation, he thought, if one is among the addressees of some general order of the sovereign, and is in danger of suffering a sanction unless he obeys that order.

Of course, the sovereign cannot provide for all contingencies through any scheme of orders, and some of his orders will inevitably be vague or have furry edges. Therefore (according to Austin) the sovereign grants those who enforce the law (judges) discretion to make fresh orders when novel or troublesome cases are presented. The judges then make new rules or adapt old rules, and the sovereign either overturns their creations or tacitly confirms them by failing to do so.

Austin's model is quite beautiful in its simplicity. It asserts the first tenet of positivism, that the law is a set of rules specially selected to govern public order, and offers a simple factual test—what has the sovereign commanded?—as the sole criterion for identifying those special rules. In time, however, those who studied and tried to apply Austin's model found it too simple. Many objections were raised, among which were two that seemed fundamental. First, Austin's key assumption that in each community

2 J. Austin, *The Province of Jurisprudence Determined* (1832).

a determinate group or institution can be found, which is in ultimate control of all other groups, seemed not to hold in a complex society. Political control in a modern nation is pluralistic and shifting, a matter of more or less, of compromise and cooperation and alliance, so that it is often impossible to say that any person or group has that dramatic control necessary to qualify as an Austinian sovereign. One wants to say, in the United States for example, that the "people" are sovereign. But this means almost nothing, and in itself provides no test for determining what the "people" have commanded, or distinguishing their legal from their social or moral commands.

Second, critics began to realize that Austin's analysis fails entirely to account for, even to recognize, certain striking facts about the attitudes we take toward "the law." We make an important distinction between law and even the general orders of a gangster. We feel that the law's strictures—and its sanctions—are different in that they are obligatory in a way that the outlaw's commands are not. Austin's analysis has no place for any such distinction, because it defines an obligation as subjection to the threat of force, and so founds the authority of law entirely on the sovereign's ability and will to harm those who disobey. Perhaps the distinction we make is illusory—perhaps our feelings of some special authority attaching to the law is based on religious hangover or another sort of mass self-deception. But Austin does not demonstrate this, and we are entitled to insist that an analysis of our concept of law either acknowledge and explain our attitudes, or show why they are mistaken.

H.L.A. Hart's version of positivism is more complex than Austin's, in two ways. First, he recognizes, as Austin did not, that rules are of different logical kinds. (Hart distinguishes two kinds, which he calls "primary" and "secondary" rules.) Second, he rejects Austin's theory that a rule is a kind of command, and substitutes a more elaborate general analysis of what rules are. We must pause over each of these points, and then note how they merge in Hart's concept of law.

Hart's distinction between primary and secondary rules is of great importance.[3] Primary rules are those that grant rights or impose obligations upon members of the community. The rules of the criminal law that forbid us to rob, murder or drive too fast are good examples of primary rules. Secondary rules are those that stipulate how, and by whom, such primary rules may be formed, recognized, modified or extinguished. The rules that stipulate how Congress is composed, and how it enacts legislation, are examples of secondary rules. Rules about forming contracts and executing wills are also secondary rules because they stipulate how very particular rules governing particular legal obligations (i.e., the terms of a contract or the provisions of a will) come into existence and are changed.

His general analysis of rules is also of great importance.[4] Austin had said that every rule is a general command, and that a person is obligated under a rule if he is liable to be hurt should he disobey it. Hart points out that this obliterates the distinction between being *obliged* to do some thing and being *obligated* to do it. If one is bound by a rule he is obligated, not merely obliged, to do what it provides, and therefore being bound by a rule must be different from being subject to an injury if one disobeys an order. A rule differs from an order, among other ways, by being *normative*, by setting a standard of behavior that has a call on its subject beyond the threat that may enforce it. A rule can never be binding just because some person with physical power wants it to be so. He must have authority to issue the rule or it is no rule, and such *authority* can only come from

3 See H.L.A. Hart, *The Concept of Law*, 89–96 (1961).
4 *Id.* at 79–88.

another rule which is already binding on those to whom he speaks. That is the difference between a valid law and the orders of a gunman.

So Hart offers a general theory of rules that does not make their authority depend upon the physical power of their authors. If we examine the way different rules come into being, he tells us, and attend to the distinction between primary and secondary rules, we see that there are two possible sources of a rule's authority:[5]

(a) A rule may become binding upon a group of people because that group through its practices *accepts* the rule as a standard for its conduct. It is not enough that the group simply conforms to a pattern of behavior: even though most Englishmen may go to the movies on Saturday evening, they have not accepted a rule requiring that they do so. A practice constitutes the acceptance of a rule only when those who follow the practice regard the rule as binding, and recognize the rule as a reason or justification for their own behavior and as a reason for criticizing the behavior of others who do not obey it.

(b) A rule may also become binding in quite a different way, namely by being enacted in conformity with some *secondary* rule that stipulates that rules so enacted shall be binding. If the constitution of a club stipulates, for example, that by-laws may be adopted by a majority of the members, then particular by-laws so voted are binding upon all the members, not because of any practice of acceptance of these particular by-laws, but because the constitution says so. We use the concept of *validity* in this connection: rules binding because they have been created in a manner stipulated by some secondary rule are called "valid" rules.

Thus we can record Hart's fundamental distinction this way: a rule may be binding (a) because it is accepted or (b) because it is valid.

Hart's concept of law is a construction of these various distinctions.[6] Primitive communities have only primary rules, and these are binding entirely because of practices of acceptance. Such communities cannot be said to have "law," because there is no way to distinguish a set of legal rules from amongst other social rules, as the first tenet of positivism requires. But when a particular community has developed a fundamental secondary rule that stipulates how legal rules are to be identified, the idea of a distinct set of legal rules, and thus of law, is born.

Hart calls such a fundamental secondary rule a "rule of recognition." The rule of recognition of a given community may be relatively simple ("What the king enacts is law") or it may be very complex (the United States Constitution, with all its difficulties of interpretation, may be considered a single rule of recognition). The demonstration that a particular rule is valid may therefore require tracing a complicated chain of validity back from that particular rule ultimately to the fundamental rule. Thus a parking ordinance of the city of New Haven is valid because it is adopted by a city council, pursuant to the procedures and within the competence specified by the municipal law adopted by the state of Connecticut, in conformity with the procedures and within the competence specified by the constitution of the state of Connecticut, which was in turn adopted consistently with the requirements of the United States Constitution.

Of course, a rule of recognition cannot itself be valid, because by hypothesis it is ultimate, and so cannot meet tests stipulated by a more fundamental rule. The rule of recognition is the sole rule in a legal system whose binding force depends upon its acceptance. If we wish to know what rule of recognition a particular community has adopted or follows, we must observe how

5 *Id.* at 97–107.
6 *Id. passim*, particularly ch. 6.

its citizens, and particularly its officials, behave. We must observe what ultimate arguments they accept as showing the validity of a particular rule, and what ultimate arguments they use to criticize other officials or institutions. We can apply no mechanical test, but there is no danger of our confusing the rule of recognition of a community with its rules of morality. The rule of recognition is identified by the fact that its province is the operation of the governmental apparatus of legislatures, courts, agencies, policemen, and the rest.

In this way Hart rescues the fundamentals of positivism from Austin's mistakes. Hart agrees with Austin that valid rules of law may be created through the acts of officials and public institutions. But Austin thought that the authority of these institutions lay only in their monopoly of power. Hart finds their authority in the background of constitutional standards against which they act, constitutional standards that have been accepted, in the form of a fundamental rule of recognition, by the community which they govern. This background legitimates the decisions of government and gives them the cast and call of obligation that the naked commands of Austin's sovereign lacked. Hart's theory differs from Austin's also, in recognizing that different communities use different ultimate tests of law, and that some allow other means of creating law than the deliberate act of a legislative institution. Hart mentions "long customary practice" and "the relation [of a rule] to judicial decisions" as other criteria that are often used, though generally along with and subordinate to the test of legislation.

So Hart's version of positivism is more complex than Austin's, and his test for valid rules of law is more sophisticated. In one respect, however, the two models are very similar. Hart, like Austin, recognizes that legal rules have furry edges (he speaks of them as having "open texture") and, again like Austin, he accounts for troublesome cases by saying that judges have and exercise discretion to decide these cases by fresh legislation.[7] (I shall later try to show why one who thinks of law as a special set of rules is almost inevitably drawn to account for difficult cases in terms of someone's exercise of discretion.)

3. Rules, Principles, and Policies

I want to make a general attack on positivism, and I shall use H.L.A. Hart's version as a target, when a particular target is needed. My strategy will be organized around the fact that when lawyers reason or dispute about legal rights and obligations, particularly in those hard cases when our problems with these concepts seem most acute, they make use of standards that do not function as rules, but operate differently as principles, policies, and other sorts of standards. Positivism, I shall argue, is a model of and for a system of rules, and its central notion of a single fundamental test for law forces us to miss the important roles of these standards that are not rules.

I just spoke of "principles, policies, and other sorts of standards." Most often I shall use the term "principle" generically, to refer to the whole set of these standards other than rules; occasionally, however, I shall be more precise, and distinguish between principles and policies. Although nothing in the present argument will turn on the distinction, I should state how I draw it. I call a "policy" that kind of standard that sets out a goal to be reached, generally an improvement in some economic, political, or social feature of the community (though some goals are negative, in that they stipulate that some present feature is to be protected from adverse change). I call a "principle" a standard that is to be observed, not because it will advance or secure an economic, political, or social situation deemed desirable, but because it is a requirement of justice or fairness or some

7 *Id.* ch. 7.

other dimension of morality. Thus the standard that automobile accidents are to be decreased is a policy, and the standard that no man may profit by his own wrong a principle. The distinction can be collapsed by construing a principle as stating a social goal (i.e., the goal of a society in which no man profits by his own wrong), or by construing a policy as stating a principle (i.e., the principle that the goal the policy embraces is a worthy one) or by adopting the utilitarian thesis that principles of justice are disguised statements of goals (securing the greatest happiness of the greatest number). In some contexts the distinction has uses which are lost if it is thus collapsed.[8]

My immediate purpose, however, is to distinguish principles in the generic sense from rules, and I shall start by collecting some examples of the former. The examples I offer are chosen haphazardly; almost any case in a law school casebook would provide examples that would serve as well. In 1889 a New York court, in the famous case of *Riggs v. Palmer*[9] had to decide whether an heir named in the will of his grandfather could inherit under that will, even though he had murdered his grandfather to do so. The court began its reasoning with this admission: "It is quite true that statutes regulating the making, proof and effect of wills, and the devolution of property, if literally construed, and if their force and effect can in no way and under no circumstances be controlled or modified, give this property to the murderer."[10] But the court continued to note that "all laws as well as all contracts may be controlled in their operation and effect by general, fundamental maxims of the common law. No one shall be permitted to profit by his own fraud, or to take advantage of his own wrong, or to found any claim upon his own iniquity, or to acquire property by his own crime."[11] The murderer did not receive his inheritance.

In 1960, a New Jersey court was faced, in *Henningsen v. Bloomfield Motors, Inc.*[12] with the important question of whether (or how much) an automobile manufacturer may limit his liability in case the automobile is defective. Henningsen had bought a car, and signed a contract which said that the manufacturer's liability for defects was limited to "making good" defective parts—"this warranty being expressly in lieu of all other warranties, obligations or liabilities." Henningsen argued that, at least in the circumstances of his case, the manufacturer ought not to be protected by this limitation, and ought to be liable for the medical and other expenses of persons injured in a crash. He was not able to point to any statute, or to any established rule of law, that prevented the manufacturer from standing on the contract. The court nevertheless agreed with Henningsen. At various points in the court's argument the following appeals to standards are made: (a) "[We] must keep in mind the general principle that, in the absence of fraud, one who does not choose to read a contract before signing it cannot later relieve himself of its burdens."[13] (b) "In applying that principle, the basic tenet of freedom of competent parties to contract is a factor of importance."[14] (c) "Freedom of contract is not such an immutable doctrine as to admit of no qualification in the area in which we are concerned."[15] (d) "In a society such as ours, where the automobile

8 See Chapter 4. See also Dworkin, "Wasserstrom: The Judicial Decision," 75 *Ethics* 47 (1964), reprinted as "Does Law Have a Function?" 74 *Yale Law Journal* 640 (1965).
9 115 N.Y. 506, 22 N.E. 188 (1889).
10 *Id.* at 509, 22 N.E. at 189.
11 *Id.* at 511, 22 N.E. at 190.
12 32 N.J. 358, 161 A.2d 69 (1960).
13 *Id.* at 386, 161 A.2d at 84.
14 *Id.*
15 *Id.* at 388, 161 A.2d at 86.

is a common and necessary adjunct of daily life, and where its use is so fraught with danger to the driver, passengers and the public, the manufacturer is under a special obligation in connection with the construction, promotion and sale of his cars. Consequently, the courts must examine purchase agreements closely to see if consumer and public interests are treated fairly."[16] (e) "'[I]s there any principle which is more familiar or more firmly embedded in the history of Anglo-American law than the basic doctrine that the courts will not permit themselves to be used as instruments of inequity and injustice?'"[17] (f) "'More specifically the courts generally refuse to lend themselves to the enforcement of a "bargain" in which one party has unjustly taken advantage of the economic necessities of other....'"[18]

The standards set out in these quotations are not the sort we think of as legal rules. They seem very different from propositions like "The maximum legal speed on the turnpike is sixty miles an hour" or "A will is invalid unless signed by three witnesses." They are different because they are legal principles rather than legal rules.

The difference between legal principles and legal rules is a logical distinction. Both sets of standards point to particular decisions about legal obligation in particular circumstances, but they differ in the character of the direction they give. Rules are applicable in an all-or-nothing fashion. If the facts a rule stipulates are given, then either the rule is valid, in which case the answer it supplies must be accepted, or it is not, in which case it contributes nothing to the decision.

This all-or-nothing approach is seen most plainly if we look at the way rules operate, not in law, but in some enterprise they dominate—a game, for example. In baseball a rule provides that if the batter has had three strikes, he is out. An official cannot consistently acknowledge that this is an accurate statement of a baseball rule, and decide that a batter who has had three strikes is not out. Of course, a rule may have exceptions (the batter who has taken three strikes is not out if the catcher drops the third strike). However, an accurate statement of the rule would take this exception into account, and any that did not would be incomplete. If the list of exceptions is very large, it would be too clumsy to repeat them each time the rule is cited; there is, however, no reason in theory why they could not all be added on, and the more that are, the more accurate is the statement of the rule.

If we take baseball rules as a model, we find that rules of law, like the rule that a will is invalid unless signed by three witnesses, fit the model well. If the requirement of three witnesses is a valid legal rule, then it cannot be that a will has been signed by only two witnesses and is valid. The rule might have exceptions, but if it does then it is inaccurate and incomplete to state the rule so simply, without enumerating the exceptions. In theory, at least, the exceptions could all be listed, and the more of them that are, the more complete is the statement of the rule.

But this is not the way the sample principles in the quotations operate. Even those which look most like rules do not set out legal consequences that follow automatically when the conditions provided are met. We say that our law respects the principle that no man may profit from his own wrong, but we do not mean that the law never permits a man to profit from wrongs he commits. In fact, people often profit, perfectly legally, from their legal wrongs. The most notorious case is adverse possession—if I trespass on your land long enough, some day I will gain a

16 *Id.* at 387, 161 A.2d at 85.
17 *Id.* at 389, 161 A.2d at 86 (quoting Frankfurter, J., in *United States v. Bethlehem Steel*, 315 U.S. 289, 326 [1942]).
18 *Id.*

right to cross your land whenever I please. There are many less dramatic examples. If a man leaves one job, breaking a contract, to take a much higher paying job, he may have to pay damages to his first employer, but he is usually entitled to keep his new salary. If a man jumps bail and crosses state lines to make a brilliant investment in another state, he may be sent back to jail, but he will keep his profits.

We do not treat these—and countless other counter-instances that can easily be imagined—as showing that the principle about profiting from one's wrongs is not a principle of our legal system, or that it is incomplete and needs qualifying exceptions. We do not treat counter-instances as exceptions (at least not exceptions in the way in which a catcher's dropping the third strike is an exception) because we could not hope to capture these counter-instances simply by a more extended statement of the principle. They are not, even in theory, subject to enumeration, because we would have to include not only these cases (like adverse possession) in which some institution has already provided that profit can be gained through a wrong, but also those numberless imaginary cases in which we know in advance that the principle would not hold. Listing some of these might sharpen our sense of the principle's weight (I shall mention that dimension in a moment), but it would not make for a more accurate or complete statement of the principle.

A principle like "No man may profit from his own wrong" does not even purport to set out conditions that make its application necessary. Rather, it states a reason that argues in one direction, but does not necessitate a particular decision. If a man has or is about to receive something, as a direct result of something illegal he did to get it, then that is a reason which the law will take into account in deciding whether he should keep it. There may be other principles or policies arguing in the other direction—a policy of securing title, for example, or a principle limiting punishment to what the legislature has stipulated. If so, our principle may not prevail, but that does not mean that it is not a principle of our legal system, because in the next case, when these contravening considerations are absent or less weighty, the principle may be decisive. All that is meant, when we say that a particular principle is a principle of our law, is that the principle is one which officials must take into account, if it is relevant, as a consideration inclining in one direction or another.

The logical distinction between rules and principles appears more clearly when we consider principles that do not even look like rules. Consider the proposition, set out under "(d)" in the excerpts from the *Henningsen* opinion, that "the manufacturer is under a special obligation in connection with the construction, promotion and sale of his cars." This does not even purport to define the specific duties such a special obligation entails, or to tell us what rights automobile consumers acquire as a result. It merely states—and this is an essential link in the *Henningsen* argument—that automobile manufacturers must be held to higher standards than other manufacturers, and are less entitled to rely on the competing principle of freedom of contract. It does not mean that they may never rely on that principle, or that courts may rewrite automobile purchase contracts at will; it means only that if a particular clause seems unfair or burdensome, courts have less reason to enforce the clause than if it were for the purchase of neckties. The "special obligation" counts in favor, but does not in itself necessitate, a decision refusing to enforce the terms of an automobile purchase contract.

This first difference between rules and principles entails another. Principles have a dimension that rules do not—the dimension of weight or importance. When principles intersect (the policy of protecting automobile consumers intersecting with principles of freedom of contract, for example), one who must resolve the conflict has to take into account the relative weight of each. This cannot be, of course, an exact measurement, and the judgment that a particular principle or policy is more important than another will often be a controversial one. Nevertheless, it is an integral part of the concept of a principle that it has this dimension, that it makes sense to ask how important or how weighty it is.

Rules do not have this dimension. We can speak of rules as being *functionally* important or unimportant (the baseball rule that three strikes are out is more important than the rule that runners may advance on a balk, because the game would be much more changed with the first rule altered than the second). In this sense, one legal rule may be more important than another because it has a greater or more important role in regulating behavior. But we cannot say that one rule is more important than another within the system of rules, so that when two rules conflict one supersedes the other by virtue of its greater weight.

If two rules conflict, one of them cannot be a valid rule. The decision as to which is valid, and which must be abandoned or recast, must be made by appealing to considerations beyond the rules themselves. A legal system might regulate such conflicts by other rules, which prefer the rule enacted by the higher authority, or the rule enacted later, or the more specific rule, or something of that sort. A legal system may also prefer the rule supported by the more important principles. (Our own legal system uses both of these techniques.)

It is not always clear from the form of a standard whether it is a rule or a principle. "A will is invalid unless signed by three witnesses" is not very different in form from "A man may not profit from his own wrong," but one who knows something of American law knows that he must take the first as stating a rule and the second as stating a principle. In many cases the distinction is difficult to make—it may not have been settled how the standard should operate, and this issue may itself be a focus of controversy. The first amendment to the United States Constitution contains the provision that Congress shall not abridge freedom of speech. Is this a rule, so that if a particular law does abridge freedom of speech, it follows that it is unconstitutional? Those who claim that the first amendment is "an absolute" say that it must be taken in this way, that is, as a rule. Or does it merely state a principle, so that when an abridgement of speech is discovered, it is unconstitutional unless the context presents some other policy or principle which in the circumstances is weighty enough to permit the abridgement? That is the position of those who argue for what is called the "clear and present danger" test or some other form of "balancing."

Sometimes a rule and a principle can play much the same role, and the difference between them is almost a matter of form alone. The first section of the Sherman Act states that every contract in restraint of trade shall be void. The Supreme Court had to make the decision whether this provision should be treated as a rule in its own terms (striking down every contract "which restrains trade," which almost any contract does) or as a principle, providing a reason for striking down a contract in the absence of effective contrary policies. The Court construed the provision as a rule, but treated that rule as containing the word "unreasonable," and as prohibiting only "unreasonable" restraints of trade.[19] This allowed the provision to function logically as a rule (whenever a court finds that the restraint is "unreasonable" it is bound to hold the contract invalid) and substantially as a principle (a court must take into account a variety of other principles and policies in determining whether

19 *Standard Oil v. United States*, 221 U.S. *1*, 60 (1911); *United States v. American Tobacco Co.*, 221 U.S. 106, 180 (1911).

a particular restraint in particular economic circumstances is "unreasonable").

Words like "reasonable," "negligent," "unjust," and "significant" often perform just this function. Each of these terms makes the application of the rule which contains it depend to some extent upon principles or policies lying beyond the rule, and in this way makes that rule itself more like a principle. But they do not quite turn the rule into a principle, because even the least confining of these terms restricts the *kind* of other principles and policies on which the rule depends. If we are bound by a rule that says that "unreasonable" contracts are void, or that grossly "unfair" contracts will not be enforced, much more judgment is required than if the quoted terms were omitted. But suppose a case in which some consideration of policy or principle suggests that a contract should be enforced even though its restraint is not reasonable, or even though it is grossly unfair. Enforcing these contracts would be forbidden by our rules, and thus permitted only if these rules were abandoned or modified. If we were dealing, however, not with a rule but with a policy against enforcing unreasonable contracts, or a principle that unfair contracts ought not to be enforced, the contracts could be enforced without alteration of the law.

4. Principles and the Concept of Law

Once we identify legal principles as separate sorts of standards, different from legal rules, we are suddenly aware of them all around us. Law teachers teach them, lawbooks cite them, legal historians celebrate them. But they seem most energetically at work, carrying most weight, in difficult lawsuits like *Riggs* and *Henningsen*. In cases like these, principles play an essential part in arguments supporting judgments about particular legal rights and obligations. After the case is decided, we may say that the case stands for a particular rule (e.g., the rule that one who murders is not eligible to take under the will of his victim). But the rule does not exist before the case is decided; the court cites principles as its justification for adopting and applying a new rule. In *Riggs*, the court cited the principle that no man may profit from his own wrong as a background standard against which to read the statute of wills and in this way justified a new interpretation of that statute. In *Henningsen*, the court cited a variety of intersecting principles and policies as authority for a new rule respecting manufacturers' liability for automobile defects.

An analysis of the concept of legal obligation must therefore account for the important role of principles in reaching particular decisions of law. There are two very different tacks we might take:

(a) We might treat legal principles the way we treat legal rules and say that some principles are binding as law and must be taken into account by judges and lawyers who make decisions of legal obligation. If we took this tack, we should say that in the United States, at least, the "law" includes principles as well as rules.

(b) We might, on the other hand, deny that principles can be binding the way some rules are. We would say, instead, that in cases like *Riggs* or *Henningsen* the judge reaches beyond the rules that he is bound to apply (reaches, that is, beyond the "law") for extra-legal principles he is free to follow if he wishes.

One might think that there is not much difference between these two lines of attack, that it is only a verbal question of how one wants to use the word "law." But that is a mistake, because the choice between these two accounts has the greatest consequences for an analysis of legal obligation. It is a choice between two *concepts* of a legal principle, a choice we can clarify by comparing it to a choice we might make between two concepts of a legal rule. We sometimes say of someone that he "makes it a rule" to do something, when we mean that he has chosen to follow a certain practice. We might say that someone has made it a rule, for example, to run a mile before breakfast because he wants to be healthy and believes in a regimen. We do not mean, when we say this, that he is *bound* by the rule that he must run a mile before breakfast, or even that he regards it as binding upon him. Accepting a rule as binding is something different from making it a rule to do something. If we use Hart's example again, there is a difference between saying that Englishmen make it a rule to see a movie once a week, and saying that the English have a rule that one must see a movie once a week. The second implies that if an Englishman does not follow the rule, he is subject to criticism or censure, but the first does not. The first does not exclude the possibility of a *sort* of criticism—we can say that one who does not see movies is neglecting his education—but we do not suggest that he is doing something wrong *just* in not following the rule.[20]

If we think of the judges of a community as a group, we could describe the rules of law they follow in these two different ways. We could say, for instance, that in a certain state the judges make it a rule not to enforce wills unless there are three witnesses. This would not imply that the rare judge who enforces such a will is doing anything wrong just for that reason. On the other hand we can say that in that state a rule of law requires judges not to enforce such wills; this does imply that a judge who enforces them is doing something wrong. Hart, Austin and other positivists, of course, would insist on this latter account of legal rules; they would not at all be satisfied with the "make it a rule" account. It is not a verbal question of which account is right. It is a question of which describes the social situation more accurately. Other important issues turn on which description we accept. If judges simply "make it a rule" not to enforce certain contracts, for example, then we cannot say, before the decision, that anyone is "entitled" to that result, and that proposition cannot enter into any justification we might offer for the decision.

The two lines of attack on principles parallel these two accounts of rules. The first tack treats principles as binding upon judges, so that they are wrong not to apply the principles when they are pertinent. The second tack treats principles as summaries of what most judges "make it a principle" to do when forced to go beyond the standards that bind them. The choice between these approaches will affect, perhaps even determine, the answer we can give to the question whether the judge in a hard case like *Riggs* or *Henningsen* is attempting to enforce pre-existing legal rights and obligations. If we take the first tack, we are still free to argue that because such judges are applying binding legal standards they are enforcing legal rights and obligations. But if we take the second, we are out of court on that issue, and we must acknowledge that the murderer's family in *Riggs* and the manufacturer in *Henningsen* were deprived of their property by an act of judicial discretion applied *ex post facto*. This may not shock many readers—the notion of judicial discretion has percolated through the legal community—but it does illustrate one of the most nettlesome of the puzzles that drive philosophers to worry about legal obligation. If taking property away in cases like these cannot be justified by appealing to an established obligation, another justification must be found, and nothing satisfactory has yet been supplied.

In my skeleton diagram of positivism, previously set out, I listed the doctrine of judicial discretion as the second tenet. Positivists hold that when a case is not covered by a clear rule, a judge must exercise his discretion to decide that case by what amounts to a fresh piece of legislation. There may be an important connection between this doctrine and the question of which of the two approaches to legal principles we must

20 The distinction is in substance the same as that made by Rawls, "Two Concepts of Rules," 64 *Philosophical Review* 3 (1955).

take. We shall therefore want to ask whether the doctrine is correct, and whether it implies the second approach, as it seems on its face to do. En route to these issues, however, we shall have to polish our understanding of the concept of discretion. I shall try to show how certain confusions about that concept and in particular a failure to discriminate different senses in which it is used, account for the popularity of the doctrine of discretion. I shall argue that in the sense in which the doctrine does have a bearing on our treatment of principles, it is entirely unsupported by the arguments the positivists use to defend it.

5. Discretion

The concept of discretion was lifted by the positivists from ordinary language, and to understand it we must put it back in *habitat* for a moment. What does it mean, in ordinary life, to say that someone "has discretion"? The first thing to notice is that the concept is out of place in all but very special contexts. For example, you would not say that I either do or do not have discretion to choose a house for my family. It is not true that I have "no discretion" in making that choice, and yet it would be almost equally misleading to say that I do have discretion. The concept of discretion is at home in only one sort of context; when someone is in general charged with making decisions subject to standards set by a particular authority. It makes sense to speak of the discretion of a sergeant who is subject to orders of superiors, or the discretion of a sports official or contest judge who is governed by a rule book or the terms of the contest. Discretion, like the hole in a doughnut, does not exist except as an area left open by a surrounding belt of restriction. It is therefore a relative concept. It always makes sense to ask, "Discretion under which standards?" or "Discretion as to which authority?" Generally the context will make the answer to this plain, but in some cases the official may have discretion from one standpoint though not from another.

Like almost all terms, the precise meaning of "discretion" is affected by features of the context. The term is always colored by the background of understood information against which it is used. Although the shadings are many, it will be helpful for us to recognize some gross distinctions.

Sometimes we use "discretion" in a weak sense, simply to say that for some reason the standards an official must apply cannot be applied mechanically but demand the use of judgment. We use this weak sense when the context does not already make that clear, when the background our audience assumes does not contain that piece of information. Thus we might say, "The sergeant's orders left him a great deal of discretion," to those who do not know what the sergeant's orders were or who do not know something that made those orders vague or hard to carry out. It would make perfect sense to add, by way of amplification, that the lieutenant had ordered the sergeant to take his five most experienced men on patrol but that it was hard to determine which were the most experienced.

Sometimes we use the term in a different weak sense, to say only that some official has final authority to make a decision and cannot be reviewed and reversed by any other official. We speak this way when the official is part of a hierarchy of officials structured so that some have higher authority but in which the patterns of authority are different for different classes of decision. Thus we might say that in baseball certain decisions, like the decision whether the ball or the runner reached second base first, are left to the discretion of the second base umpire, if we mean that on this issue the head umpire has no power to substitute his own judgment if he disagrees.

I call both of these senses weak to distinguish them from a stronger sense. We use "discretion" sometimes not merely to say that an official must use judgment in applying the standards set him by authority, or that no one will review that exercise of judgment, but to say that on some issue he is simply not bound by standards set by the authority in question. In this sense we say that a sergeant has discretion who has been told to pick any five men for patrol he chooses or that a judge in a dog show has discretion to judge airedales before boxers if the rules do not stipulate an order of events. We use this sense not to comment on the vagueness or difficulty of the standards, or on who has the final word in applying them, but on their range and the decisions they purport to control. If the sergeant is told to take the five most experienced men, he does not have discretion in this strong sense because that order purports to govern his decision. The boxing referee who must decide which fighter has been the more aggressive does not have discretion, in the strong sense, for the same reason.[21]

If anyone said that the sergeant or the referee had discretion in these cases, we should have to understand him, if the context permitted, as using the term in one of the weak senses. Suppose, for example, the lieutenant ordered the sergeant to select the five men he deemed most experienced, and then added that the sergeant had discretion to choose them. Or the rules provided that the referee should award the round to the more aggressive fighter, with discretion in selecting him. We should have to understand these statements in the second weak sense, as speaking to the question of review of the decision. The first weak sense—that the decisions take judgment—would be otiose, and the third, strong sense is excluded by the statements themselves.

We must avoid one tempting confusion. The strong sense of discretion is not tantamount to license, and does not exclude criticism. Almost any situation in which a person acts (including those in which there is no question of decision under special authority, and so no question of discretion) makes relevant certain standards of rationality, fairness, and effectiveness. We criticize each other's acts in terms of these standards, and there is no reason not to do so when the acts are within the center rather than beyond the perimeter of the doughnut of special authority. So we can say that the sergeant who was given discretion (in the strong sense) to pick a patrol did so stupidly or maliciously or carelessly, or that the judge who had discretion in the order of viewing dogs made a mistake because he took boxers first although there were only three airedales and many more boxers. An official's discretion means not that he is free to decide without recourse to standards of sense and fairness, but only that his decision is not controlled by a standard furnished by the particular authority we have in mind when we raise the question of discretion. Of course this latter sort of freedom is important; that is why we have the strong sense of discretion. Someone who has discretion in this third sense can be criticized, but not for being disobedient, as in the case of the soldier. He can be said to have made a mistake, but not to have deprived a participant of a decision to which he was entitled, as in the case of a sports official or contest judge.

We may now return, with these observations in hand, to the positivists' doctrine of judicial discretion. That doctrine argues that if a case is not controlled by an established rule, the judge must decide it by exercising discretion. We want to examine this doctrine and to test its bearing on our treatment of principles; but first we must ask in which sense of discretion we are to understand it.

Some nominalists argue that judges always have discretion, even when a clear rule is in point, because judges are ultimately the final arbiters of the law. This doctrine of discretion uses the

21 I have not spoken of that jurisprudential favorite, "limited" discretion, because that concept presents no special difficulties if we remember the relativity of discretion. Suppose the sergeant is told to choose from "amongst" experienced men, or to "take experience into account." We might say either that he has (limited) discretion in picking his patrol, or (full) discretion to either pick amongst experienced men or decide what else to take into account.

second weak sense of that term, because it makes the point that no higher authority reviews the decisions of the highest court. It therefore has no bearing on the issue of how we account for principles, any more than it bears on how we account for rules.

The positivists do not mean their doctrine this way, because they say that a judge has no discretion when a clear and established rule is available. If we attend to the positivists' arguments for the doctrine we may suspect that they use discretion in the first weak sense to mean only that judges must sometimes exercise judgment in applying legal standards. Their arguments call attention to the fact that some rules of law are vague (Professor Hart, for example, says that all rules of law have "open texture"), and that some cases arise (like *Henningsen*) in which no established rule seems to be suitable. They emphasize that judges must sometimes agonize over points of law, and that two equally trained and intelligent judges will often disagree.

These points are easily made; they are commonplace to anyone who has any familiarity with law. Indeed, that is the difficulty with assuming that positivists mean to use "discretion" in this weak sense. The proposition that when no clear rule is available discretion in the sense of judgment must be used is a tautology. It has no bearing, moreover, on the problem of how to account for legal principles. It is perfectly consistent to say that the judge in *Riggs*, for example, had to use judgment, and that he was bound to follow the principle that no man may profit from his own wrong. The positivists speak as if their doctrine of judicial discretion is an insight rather than a tautology, and as if it does have a bearing on the treatment of principles. Hart, for example, says that when the judge's discretion is in play, we can no longer speak of his being bound by standards, but must speak rather of what standards he "characteristically uses."[22] Hart thinks that when judges have discretion, the principles they cite must be treated on our second approach, as what courts "make it a principle" to do.

It therefore seems that positivists, at least sometimes, take their doctrine in the third, strong sense of discretion. In that sense it does bear on the treatment of principles; indeed, in that sense it is nothing less than a restatement of our second approach. It is the same thing to say that when a judge runs out of rules he has discretion, in the sense that he is not bound by any standards from the authority of law, as to say that the legal standards judges cite other than rules are not binding on them.

So we must examine the doctrine of judicial discretion in the strong sense. (I shall henceforth use the term "discretion" in that sense.) Do the principles judges cited in cases like *Riggs* or *Henningsen* control their decisions, as the sergeant's orders to take the most experienced men or the referee's duty to choose the more aggressive fighter control the decisions of these officials? What arguments could a positivist supply to show that they do not?

(1) A positivist might argue that principles cannot be binding or obligatory. That would be a mistake. It is always a question, of course, whether any particular principle is *in fact* binding upon some legal official. But there is nothing in the logical character of a principle that renders it incapable of binding him. Suppose that the judge in *Henningsen* had failed to take any account of the principle that automobile manufacturers have a special obligation to their consumers, or the principle that the courts seek to protect those whose bargaining position is weak, but had simply decided for the defendant by citing the principle of freedom of contract without more. His critics would not have been content to point out that he had not taken account of considerations

22 H.L.A. Hart, *The Concept of Law*, 144 (1961).

that other judges have been attending to for some time. Most would have said that it was his duty to take the measure of these principles and that the plaintiff was entitled to have him do so. We mean no more, when we say that a *rule* is binding upon a judge, than that he must follow it if it applies, and that if he does not he will on that account have made a mistake.

It will not do to say that in a case like *Henningsen* the court is only obligated to take particular principles into account, or that it is "institutionally" obligated, or obligated as a matter of judicial "craft," or something of that sort. The question will still remain why this type of obligation (whatever we call it) is different from the obligation that rules impose upon judges, and why it entitles us to say that principles and policies are not part of the law but are merely extra-legal standards "courts characteristically use."

(2) A positivist might argue that even though some principles are binding, in the sense that the judge must take them into account, they cannot determine a particular result. This is a harder argument to assess because it is not clear what it means for a standard to "determine" a result. Perhaps it means that the standard *dictates* the result whenever it applies so that nothing else counts. If so, then it is certainly true that the individual principles do not determine results, but that is only another way of saying that principles are not rules. Only rules dictate results, come what may. When a contrary result has been reached, the rule has been abandoned or changed. Principles do not work that way; they incline a decision one way, though not conclusively, and they survive intact when they do not prevail. This seems no reason for concluding that judges who must reckon with principles have discretion because a set of principles *can* dictate a result. If a judge believes that principles he is bound to recognize point in one direction and that principles pointing in the other direction, if any, are not of equal weight, then he must decide accordingly, just as he must follow what he believes to be a binding rule. He may, of course, be wrong in his assessment of the principles, but he may also be wrong in his judgment that the rule is binding. The sergeant and the referee, we might add, are often in the same boat. No one factor dictates which soldiers are the most experienced or which fighter the more aggressive. These officials must make judgments of the relative weights of these various factors; they do not on that account have discretion.

(3) A positivist might argue that principles cannot count as law because their authority, and even more so their weight, are congenitally *controversial.* It is true that generally we cannot *demonstrate* the authority or weight of a particular principle as we can sometimes demonstrate the validity of a rule by locating it in an act of Congress or in the opinion of an authoritative court. Instead, we make a case for a principle, and for its weight, by appealing to an amalgam of practice and other principles in which the implications of legislative and judicial history figure along with appeals to community practices and understandings. There is no litmus paper for testing the soundness of such a case—it is a matter of judgment, and reasonable men may disagree. But again this does not distinguish the judge from other officials who do not have discretion. The sergeant has no litmus paper for experience, the referee none for aggressiveness. Neither of these has discretion, because he is bound to reach an understanding, controversial or not, of what his orders or the rules require, and to act on that understanding. That is the judge's duty as well.

Of course, if the positivists are right in another of their doctrines—the theory that in each legal system there is an ultimate *test* for binding law like Professor Hart's rule of recognition—it follows that principles are not binding law. But the incompatibility of principles with the positivists' theory can hardly be taken as an argument that principles must be treated any particular way.

That begs the question; we are interested in the status of principles because we want to evaluate the positivists' model. The positivist cannot defend his theory of a rule of recognition by fiat; if principles are not amenable to a test he must show some other reason why they cannot count as law. Since principles seem to play a role in arguments about legal obligation (witness, again, *Riggs* and *Henningsen*), a model that provides for that role has some initial advantage over one that excludes it, and the latter cannot properly be inveighed in its own support.

These are the most obvious of the arguments a positivist might use for the doctrine of discretion in the strong sense, and for the second approach to principles. I shall mention one strong counterargument against that doctrine and in favor of the first approach. Unless at least some principles are acknowledged to be binding upon judges, requiring them as a set to reach particular decisions, then no rules, or very few rules, can be said to be binding upon them either.

In most American jurisdictions, and now in England also, the higher courts not infrequently reject established rules. Common law rules—those developed by earlier court decisions—are sometimes overruled directly, and sometimes radically altered by further development. Statutory rules are subjected to interpretation and reinterpretation, sometimes even when the result is not to carry out what is called the "legislative intent."[23] If courts had discretion to change established rules, then these rules would of course not be binding upon them, and so would not be law on the positivists' model. The positivist must therefore argue that there are standards, themselves binding upon judges, that determine when a judge may overrule or alter an established rule, and when he may not.

When, then, is a judge permitted to change an existing rule of law? Principles figure in the answer in two ways. First, it is necessary, though not sufficient, that the judge find that the change would advance some principle, which principle thus justifies the change. In *Riggs* the change (a new interpretation of the statute of wills) was justified by the principle that no man should profit from his own wrong; in *Henningsen* the previously recognized rules about automobile manufacturers' liability were altered on the basis of the principles I quoted from the opinion of the court.

But not any principle will do to justify a change, or no rule would ever be safe. There must be some principles that count and others that do not, and there must be some principles that count for more than others. It could not depend on the judge's own preferences amongst a sea of respectable extra-legal standards, any one in principle eligible, because if that were the case we could not say that any rules were binding. We could always imagine a judge whose preferences amongst extra-legal standards were such as would justify a shift or radical reinterpretation of even the most entrenched rule.

Second, any judge who proposes to change existing doctrine must take account of some important standards that argue against departures from established doctrine, and these standards are also for the most part principles. They include the doctrine of "legislative supremacy," a set of principles that require the courts to pay a qualified deference to the acts of the legislature. They also include the doctrine of precedent, another set of principles reflecting the equities and efficiencies of consistency. The doctrines of legislative supremacy and precedent incline toward the *status quo*, each within its sphere, but they do not command it. Judges are not free, however, to pick and choose amongst the principles and policies that make up these doctrines—if they were, again, no rule could be said to be binding.

23 See Wellington and Albert, "Statutory Interpretation and the Political Process: A Comment on *Sinclair v. Atkinson*," 72 *Yale L. J.* 1547 (1963).

Consider, therefore, what someone implies who says that a particular rule is binding. He may imply that the rule is affirmatively supported by principles the court is not free to disregard, and which are collectively more weighty than other principles that argue for a change. If not, he implies that any change would be condemned by a combination of conservative principles of legislative supremacy and precedent that the court is not free to ignore. Very often, he will imply both, for the conservative principles, being principles and not rules, are usually not powerful enough to save a common law rule or an aging statute that is entirely unsupported by substantive principles the court is bound to respect. Either of these implications, of course, treats a body of principles and policies as law in the sense that rules are; it treats them as standards binding upon the officials of a community, controlling their decisions of legal right and obligation.

We are left with this issue. If the positivists' theory of judicial discretion is either trivial because it uses "discretion" in a weak sense, or unsupported because the various arguments we can supply in its defense fall short, why have so many careful and intelligent lawyers embraced it? We can have no confidence in our treatment of that theory unless we can deal with that question. It is not enough to note (although perhaps it contributes to the explanation) that "discretion" has different senses that may be confused. We do not confuse these senses when we are not thinking about law.

Part of the explanation, at least, lies in a lawyer's natural tendency to associate laws and rules, and to think of "the law" as a collection or system of rules. Roscoe Pound, who diagnosed this tendency long ago, thought that English speaking lawyers were tricked into it by the fact that English uses the same word, changing only the article, for "a law" and "the law."[24] (Other languages, on the contrary, use two words: "loi" and "droit," for example, and "Gesetz" and "Recht.") This may have had its effect, with the English speaking positivists, because the expression "a law" certainly does suggest a rule. But the principal reason for associating law with rules runs deeper, and lies, I think, in the fact that legal education has for a long time consisted of teaching and examining those established rules that form the cutting edge of law.

In any event, if a lawyer thinks of law as a system of rules, and yet recognizes, as he must, that judges change old rules and introduce new ones, he will come naturally to the theory of judicial discretion in the strong sense. In those other systems of rules with which he has experience (like games), the rules are the only special authority that govern official decisions, so that if an umpire could change a rule, he would have discretion as to the subject matter of that rule. Any principles umpires might mention when changing the rules would represent only their "characteristic" preferences. Positivists treat law like baseball revised in this way.

There is another, more subtle consequence of this initial assumption that law is a system of rules. When the positivists do attend to principles and policies, they treat them as rules *manquées*. They assume that *if* they are standards of law they must be rules, and so they read them as standards that are trying to be rules. When a positivist hears someone argue that legal principles are part of the law, he understands this to be an argument for what he calls the "higher law" theory, that these principles are the rules of a law about the law.[25] He refutes this theory by pointing out that these "rules" are sometimes followed and sometimes not, that for every "rule" like "no man shall profit from his own wrong" there is another

24 R. Pound, *An Introduction to the Philosophy of Law* 56 (rev. ed. 1954).
25 See, e.g., Dickinson, "The Law Behind Law (pts. 1 & 2)," 29, *Columbia Law Review* 112, 254 (1929).

competing "rule" like "the law favors security of title," and that there is no way to test the validity of "rules" like these. He concludes that these principles and policies are not valid rules of a law above the law, which is true, because they are not rules at all. He also concludes that they are extra-legal standards which each judge selects according to his own lights in the exercise of his discretion, which is false. It is as if a zoologist had proved that fish are not mammals, and then concluded that they are really only plants.

6. The Rule of Recognition

This discussion was provoked by our two competing accounts of legal principles. We have been exploring the second account, which the positivists seem to adopt through their doctrine of judicial discretion, and we have discovered grave difficulties. It is time to return to the fork in the road. What if we adopt the first approach? What would the consequences of this be for the skeletal structure of positivism? Of course we should have to drop the second tenet, the doctrine of judicial discretion (or, in the alternative, to make plain that the doctrine is to be read merely to say that judges must often exercise judgment). Would we also have to abandon or modify the first tenet, the proposition that law is distinguished by tests of the sort that can be set out in a master rule like Professor Hart's rule of recognition? If principles of the *Riggs* and *Henningsen* sort are to count as law, and we are nevertheless to preserve the notion of a master rule for law, then we must be able to deploy some test that all (and only) the principles that do count as law meet. Let us begin with the test Hart suggests for identifying valid *rules* of law, to see whether these can be made to work for principles as well.

Most rules of law, according to Hart, are valid because some competent institution enacted them. Some were created by a legislature, in the form of statutory enactments. Others were created by judges who formulated them to decide particular cases, and thus established them as precedents for the future. But this test of pedigree will not work for the *Riggs* and *Henningsen* principles. The origin of these as legal principles lies not in a particular decision of some legislature or court, but in a sense of appropriateness developed in the profession and the public over time. Their continued power depends upon this sense of appropriateness being sustained. If it no longer seemed unfair to allow people to profit by their wrongs, or fair to place special burdens upon oligopolies that manufacture potentially dangerous machines, these principles would no longer play much of a role in new cases, even if they had never been overruled or repealed. (Indeed, it hardly makes sense to speak of principles like these as being "overruled" or "repealed." When they decline they are eroded, not torpedoed.)

True, if we were challenged to back up our claim that some principle is a principle of law, we would mention any prior cases in which that principle was cited, or figured in the argument. We would also mention any statute that seemed to exemplify that principle (even better if the principle was cited in the preamble of the statute, or in the committee reports or other legislative documents that accompanied it). Unless we could find some such institutional support, we would probably fail to make out our case, and the more support we found, the more weight we could claim for the principle.

Yet we could not devise any formula for testing how much and what kind of institutional support is necessary to make a principle a legal principle, still less to fix its weight at a particular order of magnitude. We argue for a particular principle by grappling with a whole set of shifting, developing and interacting standards (themselves principles rather than rules) about institutional responsibility, statutory interpretation, the persuasive force of various sorts of precedent, the relation of all these to contemporary moral practices, and hosts of other such standards. We could not bolt all of these together into a single "rule," even a complex one, and if we could the result would bear little relation to Hart's picture of a rule of recognition, which is the picture of a fairly stable master rule specifying "some feature or features possession of which by a suggested rule is taken as a conclusive affirmative indication that it is a rule ..."[26]

Moreover, the techniques we apply in arguing for another principle do not stand (as Hart's rule of recognition is designed to) on an entirely different level from the principles they support. Hart's sharp distinction between acceptance and validity does not hold. If we are arguing for the principle that a man should not profit from his own wrong, we could cite the acts of courts and legislatures that exemplify it, but this speaks as much to the principle's acceptance as its validity. (It seems odd to speak of a principle as being valid at all, perhaps because validity is an all-or-nothing concept, appropriate for rules, but inconsistent with a principle's dimension of weight.) If we are asked (as we might well be) to defend the particular doctrine of precedent, or the particular technique of statutory interpretation, that we used in this argument, we should certainly cite the practice of others in using that doctrine or technique. But we should also cite other general principles that we believe support that practice, and this introduces a note of validity into the chord of acceptance. We might argue, for example, that the use we make of earlier cases and statutes is supported by a particular analysis of the point of the practice of legislation or the doctrine of precedent, or by the principles of democratic theory, or by a particular position on the proper division of authority between national and local institutions, or something else of that sort. Nor is this path of support a one-way street leading to some ultimate principle resting on acceptance alone. Our principles of legislation, precedent, democracy, or federalism might be challenged too; and if they were we should argue for them, not only in terms of practice, but in terms of each other and in terms of the implications of trends of judicial and legislative decisions, even though this last would involve appealing to those same doctrines of interpretation we justified through the principles we are now trying to support. At this level of abstraction, in other words, principles rather hang together than link together.

So even though principles draw support from the official acts of legal institutions, they do not have a simple or direct enough connection with these acts to frame that connection in terms of criteria specified by some ultimate master rule of recognition. Is there any other route by which principles might be brought under such a rule?

Hart does say that a master rule might designate as law not only rules enacted by particular legal institutions, but rules established by *custom* as well. He has in mind a problem that bothered other positivists, including Austin. Many of our most ancient legal rules were never explicitly created by a legislature or a court. When they made their first appearance in legal opinions and texts, they were treated as already being part of the law because they represented the customary practice of the community, or some specialized part of it, like the business community. (The examples ordinarily given are rules of mercantile practice, like the rules governing what rights arise under a standard form of commercial paper.)[27] Since Austin thought that all law was the command of a determinate sovereign, he held that these customary practices were not law until the courts (as agents of the sovereign) recognized them,

26 H.L.A. Hart, *The Concept of Law* 92 (1961).

27 See Note, "Custom and Trade Usage: Its Application to Commercial Dealings and the Common Law," 55 *Columbia Law Review* 1192 (1955), and materials cited therein at 1193 n. 1. As that note makes plain, the actual practices of courts in recognizing trade customs follow the pattern of applying a set of general principles and policies rather than a test that could be captured as part of a rule of recognition.

and that the courts were indulging in a fiction in pretending otherwise. But that seemed arbitrary. If everyone thought custom might in itself be law, the fact that Austin's theory said otherwise was not persuasive.

Hart reversed Austin on this point. The master rule, he says, might stipulate that some custom counts as law even before the courts recognize it. But he does not face the difficulty this raises for his general theory because he does not attempt to set out the criteria a master rule might use for this purpose. It cannot use, as its only criterion, the provision that the community regard the practice as *morally* binding, for this would not distinguish legal customary rules from moral customary rules, and of course not all of the community's long-standing customary moral obligations are enforced at law. If, on the other hand, the test is whether the community regards the customary practice as *legally* binding, the whole point of the master rule is undercut, at least for this class of legal rules. The master rule, says Hart, marks the transformation from a primitive society to one with law, because it provides a test for determining social rules of law other than by measuring their acceptance. But if the master rule says merely that whatever other rules the community accepts as legally binding are legally binding, then it provides no such test at all, beyond the test we should use were there no master rule. The master rule becomes (for these cases) a non-rule of recognition; we might as well say that every primitive society has a secondary rule of recognition, namely the rule that whatever is accepted as binding is binding. Hart himself, in discussing international law, ridicules the idea that such a rule could be a rule of recognition, by describing the proposed rule as "an empty repetition of the mere fact that the society concerned ... observes certain standards of conduct as obligatory rules."[28]

Hart's treatment of custom amounts, indeed, to a confession that there are at least some rules of law that are not binding because they are valid under standards laid down by a master rule but are binding—like the master rule—because they are accepted as binding by the community. This chips at the neat pyramidal architecture we admired in Hart's theory: we can no longer say that only the master rule is binding because of its acceptance, all other rules being valid under its terms.

This is perhaps only a chip, because the customary rules Hart has in mind are no longer a very significant part of the law. But it does suggest that Hart would be reluctant to widen the damage by bringing under the head of "custom" all those crucial principles and policies we have been discussing. If he were to call these part of the law and yet admit that the only test of their force lies in the degree to which they are accepted as law by the community or some part thereof, he would very sharply reduce that area of the law over which his master rule held any dominion. It is not just that all the principles and policies would escape its sway, though that would be bad enough. Once these principles and policies are accepted as law, and thus as standards judges must follow in determining legal obligations, it would follow that *rules* like those announced for the first time in *Riggs* and *Henningsen* owe their force at least in part to the authority of principles

28 H.L.A. Hart, *The Concept of Law* 230 (1961). A master rule might specify some particular feature of a custom that is independent of the community's attitude; it might provide, for example, that all customs of very great age, or all customs having to do with negotiable instruments count as law. I can think of no such features that in fact distinguish the customs that have been recognized as law in England or America, however. Some customs that are not legally enforceable are older than some that are, some practices relating to commercial paper are enforced and others not, and so forth. In any event, even if a distinguishing feature were found that identified all rules of law established by custom, it would remain unlikely that such a feature could be found for principles which vary widely in their subject matter and pedigree and some of which are of very recent origin.

and policies, and so not entirely to the master rule of recognition.

So we cannot adapt Hart's version of positivism by modifying his rule of recognition to embrace principles. No tests of pedigree, relating principles to acts of legislation, can be formulated, nor can his concept of customary law, itself an exception to the first tenet of positivism, be made to serve without abandoning that tenet altogether. One more possibility must be considered, however. If no rule of recognition can provide a test for identifying principles, why not say that principles are ultimate, and *form* the rule of recognition of our law? The answer to the general question "What is valid law in an American jurisdiction?" would then require us to state all the principles (as well as ultimate constitutional rules) in force in that jurisdiction at the time, together with appropriate assignments of weight. A positivist might then regard the complete set of these standards as the rule of recognition of the jurisdiction. This solution has the attraction of paradox, but of course it is an unconditional surrender. If we simply designate our rule of recognition by the phrase "the complete set of principles in force," we achieve only the tautology that law is law. If, instead, we tried actually to list all the principles in force we would fail. They are controversial, their weight is all important, they are numberless, and they shift and change so fast that the start of our list would be obsolete before we reached the middle. Even if we succeeded, we would not have a key for law because there would be nothing left for our key to unlock.

I conclude that if we treat principles as law we must reject the positivists' first tenet, that the law of a community is distinguished from other social standards by some test in the form of a master rule. We have already decided that we must then abandon the second tenet—the doctrine of judicial discretion—or clarify it into triviality. What of the third tenet, the positivists' theory of legal obligation?

This theory holds that a legal obligation exists when (and only when) an established rule of law imposes such an obligation. It follows from this that in a hard case—when no such established rule can be found—there is no legal obligation until the judge creates a new rule for the future. The judge may apply that new rule to the parties in the case, but this is *ex post facto* legislation, not the enforcement of an existing obligation.

The positivists' doctrine of discretion (in the strong sense) required this view of legal obligation, because if a judge has discretion there can be no legal right or obligation—no entitlement—that he must enforce. Once we abandon that doctrine, however, and treat principles as law, we raise the possibility that a legal obligation might be imposed by a constellation of principles as well as by an established rule. We might want to say that a legal obligation exists whenever the case supporting such an obligation, in terms of binding legal principles of different sorts, is stronger than the case against it.

Of course, many questions would have to be answered before we could accept that view of legal obligation. If there is no rule of recognition, no test for law in that sense, how do we decide which principles are to count, and how much, in making such a case? How do we decide whether one case is better than another? If legal obligation rests on an undemonstrable judgment of that sort, how can it provide a justification for a judicial decision that one party had a legal obligation? Does this view of obligation square with the way lawyers, judges and laymen speak, and is it consistent with our attitudes about moral obligation? Does this analysis help us to deal with the classical jurisprudential puzzles about the nature of law?

These questions must be faced, but even the questions promise more than positivism provides. Positivism, on its own thesis, stops short of just those puzzling, hard cases that send us to look for theories of law. When we read these cases, the positivist remits us to a doctrine of discretion that leads nowhere and tells nothing. His picture of law as a system of rules has exercised a tenacious hold on our imagination, perhaps through its very simplicity. If we shake ourselves loose from this model of rules, we may be able to build a model truer to the complexity and sophistication of our own practices.

Study Questions

1. Does Hart offer persuasive criticisms of Austin's "command theory" of legal obligation?
2. How is Hart's explanation of the "minimum natural law content" of a legal system compatible with his thesis that there is no necessary connection between law and morality?
3. Does Hart's characterization of legal standards as a special type of rule capture adequately all types of legal standard?
4. How persuasive are Hart's criticisms of Austin's idea of the "sovereign"? Can Austin's idea be modified to save it from Hart's criticism?
5. What is the rule of recognition for your country? What difficulties will any investigator encounter when trying to specify a rule of recognition for any given social situation?
6. Are Dworkin's criticisms of Hart's idea of "social rules" persuasive?
7. Does Dworkin's account of judicial discretion explain successfully how judges need not venture outside the law in making decisions in unclear areas of law?

Further Readings

Michael Bayles, *Hart's Legal Philosophy: An Examination*. Dordrecht: Kluwer, 1992.
Tom Campbell, *Prescriptive Legal Positivism: Law, Rights and Democracy*. London: UCL P, 2004.
Marshall Cohen, ed., *Ronald Dworkin and Contemporary Jurisprudence*. Totowa, NJ: Rowman and Allanheld, 1983.
Jules Coleman, *The Practice of Principle*. Oxford: Clarendon P, 2001.
—, ed., *Hart's Postscript: Essays on the Postscript to The Concept of Law*. Oxford: Oxford UP, 2001.
Julie Dickson, *Evaluation and Legal Theory*. Portland, OR: Hart, 2001.
Ruth Gavison, ed., *Issues in Contemporary Legal Philosophy: The Influence of H.L.A. Hart*. Oxford: Clarendon P, 1987.
Robert P. George, ed., *The Autonomy of Law: Essays in Legal Positivism*. Oxford: Clarendon P, 1996.
Nicola Lacey, *H.L.A. Hart; A Life*. Oxford: Oxford UP, 2004.
W.L. Morison, *John Austin*. Stanford: Stanford UP, 1982.
Joseph Raz, *The Authority of Law: Essays on Law and Morality*. 2nd ed. Oxford: Oxford UP, 2009.
Brian Tamanaha, *A General Jurisprudence of Law and Society*. Oxford: Oxford UP, 2001.
Wilfrid Waluchow, *Inclusive Legal Positivism*. Oxford: Clarendon P, 1994.

SECTION 3

Legal Realism and Legal Reasoning

Introduction

"Legal Realism" is the name given to the views of a group of American jurists whose writing dominated American legal thought in the early to mid-twentieth century.[1] Legal Realists, as they are called, are best known for their opposition to the "classical" or "formalist" view that law consists of a body of definite, logically related rules applied in a logical and impersonal fashion by impartial judges. According to Legal Realists, the actual facts about the nature of law and legal systems are a great deal more complex than this simple, optimistic picture allows. Much of what is called "Legal Realism" is devoted to showing the classical view to be composed largely of what the Legal Realist writer Jerome Frank called "myths." The Legal Realists were not, however, entirely agreed in their assessments of precisely why the classical theory of law ought to be abandoned, so they ought not to be thought of as a "school" of thinkers devoted as a group to supporting certain views. Their association was much more loose. Nonetheless, as we shall see, it is still possible to identify some general views shared by Legal Realists.

The classical view that the Legal Realists opposed was developed in the late nineteenth and early twentieth centuries by judges and lawyers who tried to demonstrate that law could be a "science," complete with methods allowing a knowledgeable practitioner to answer with scientific certainty the question "What is the law in this instance?" According to the classical approach, this question always has a definite, certain answer, and that answer can always be found with nothing more than knowledge of the customs, conventions, court decisions, and legislation which constitute the law. There need never be any appeal to any standards or information found outside the law.

On the classical theory of law, the determination of what the law is in a given case is never a matter of individual judgment or interpretation. Rather, it is simply a matter of discovering or clarifying what the law already says, and applying it to the facts of the case at hand. Judges who discover and apply the law in this way are properly said to be impartial: they are simply applying mechanically and logically the principles and rules of interpretation of law to determine the correct result in individual cases. There is no danger that two persons who commit the same act yet appear before different judges will be treated any differently, because the judges never have any opportunity to inject their own personal beliefs regarding, for example, morality or economics into the judgment. Justice is in this sense "blind," because judges simply determine the facts in a given case and apply pre-existing rules which exist whether judges like those rules or not.

There can be no doubt that this picture of the courts and the law has attractive aspects. It captures the common hope that judges impose the law and not simply their own personal convictions; and it expresses the hope that laws are

1 "Legal Realism" is sometimes used to refer also to Scandinavian Legal Realism, advanced in the writings of, e.g., Karl Olivecrona, Alf Ross, and others. Here we are concerned with American Legal Realism only.

standards with a definite range of meanings which do not change from moment to moment. Yet according to the Legal Realists, this picture of law is fundamentally flawed, and a new understanding of law is needed. Here we explore three of the Legal Realists' major criticisms of orthodox legal theory, and examine their attempts to introduce reforms to resolve the problems they saw. We also introduce the view of a prominent critic of Legal Realism, Ronald Dworkin, whose theory of "constructive interpretation" is in many ways a direct answer to the challenge which Legal Realists raise about the limits of judicial reasoning.

1. Skepticism about the Objectivity of Judges' Reasoning

One hallmark of Legal Realists is their concern with the courts' role in shaping the law. The Legal Realists claimed that judges are *not* impartial discoverers of pre-existing rules. Such rules, say the Legal Realists, far from being discovered and applied in a logical fashion, are flexible and open to interpretation, and that interpretation frequently depends on judges' personal and political biases or philosophies of law and interpretation. The realist writer Oliver Wendell Holmes expresses succinctly the Legal Realists' concern that courts do not operate in a neutral, impartial way:

> The life of the law has not been logic: it has been experience. The felt necessities of the time, the prevalent moral and political theories, intuitions of public policy, avowed or unconscious, even the prejudices which judges share with their fellow-men, have had a good deal more to do than the syllogism in determining the rules by which men should be governed. The law embodies the story of a nation's development through many centuries, and it cannot be dealt with as if it contained only the axioms and corollaries of a book of mathematics....[2]

Holmes provides here a useful list of some of the influences which play a role in judges' reasoning. First, judges may in their decisions reflect contemporary public values. The law may be ambiguous and judges may choose to read it in a way which advances community standards or other values already broadly accepted in a particular society. Second, judges may interpret the law in light of what judges believe to be the best moral theories available. Judges may, for example, attempt to apportion civil damages in a way which seems to be morally justified according to a currently accepted moral theory, even when no part of the law instructs that judges must impose morally justified judgments. Third, judges may knowingly or subconsciously interpret the law in a way which advances what judges believe is the public interest. (Judges' understanding of the public interest may, of course, be at odds with what the public interest actually is, or what a legislature or other law-making body conceives to be the public interest.) Fourth, judges, as any other persons, are prone to prejudices which may sway them away from what the text of the law requires. With this observation we see most clearly the truth contained in Holmes's assertion that the life of law has been experience rather than logic. Judges are humans formed by their experience of the world, and it seems that judges are not always able to detach themselves from their experiences in order to reason in a purely logical way.

2. Skepticism Regarding Logical Reasoning about the Law

The Legal Realists were quick to realize the implications of their observations of the variability of

2 Oliver Wendell Holmes, *The Common Law* (Boston: Little, Brown, 1881), p. 1.

judges' reasoning. If judges are not impartial interpreters who rely on logic alone as they find what the law is, it is not plausible to claim that there are certain, definite answers to the question "What is the law in this instance?" The answer to that question may be determined in part by examining the relevant statutes, cases, and so forth; but the character and leanings of the judge must always be taken into account also. It is perhaps reasonable to claim that legal rules do have a definite *range* of meanings, but the limits of that range are determined as much by psychological facts as by logic.

At the same time as the Legal Realists recorded these shrewd observations of the actual operations of courts, the new discipline of psychology and the established discipline of philosophy made discoveries which seemed to confirm the Legal Realists' views. At the turn of the century and throughout the period when Legal Realists were most active, psychology appeared to be on the verge of explaining nearly all human attitudes and behavior. The Legal Realists were particularly interested in the idea that persons' actions and views might be more the product of their environment than of their own reasoning, and the idea that there could be a "sub-conscious" which influences conscious persons' reasoning without their knowledge. Various Legal Realists attempted to show that judges' reasoning reflected not a mechanical application of logic to the rules of law, but rather the views of a particular social and economic class, or judges' personal peculiarities. Developments in philosophy provided further evidence that judges were likely not operating as the classical view supposed they were. Many philosophers of logic and philosophers of language came to believe that the language of law is much more flexible or "open-textured" than previously believed. There are terms and phrases in ordinary language (and the language used in the law) which have not a single, set meaning, but rather a range of meanings, and so legal rules using those terms might reasonably be interpreted in different ways in different situations, all without going plainly against the ordinary meaning of the language of the legal rules.

3. Skepticism about Law as Consisting of "Preexisting" or "Settled" Rules

It is unsurprising, given the emergence of evidence casting doubt on the classical view of judges' determination of legal rules, that Legal Realists thought that the meaning of the text of the law is in principle uncertain. This uncertainty raises (at least) two problems. First, if the law is uncertain, can ordinary citizens be justifiably confident that the law will protect them? Will a contract made today mean the same thing tomorrow? Second, if the law is in principle unsettled and may be interpreted in various ways by different judges, can ordinary citizens rest assured that they will be held to reasonable standards and treated fairly in any court, regardless of the identity of the judge? To the first question the Legal Realists answered that legal certainty of the sort desired by the classical legal theorists is a myth. Instead, many Legal Realists claimed, the law cannot be known prior to its interpretation by the courts. To say what the law is in a given case, according to the Legal Realists, is nothing more and nothing less than to make a prediction of what the courts will do. This is the nearest approximation of certainty in determining what the law is in a given case. In considering the Legal Realists' solution to the second problem, we turn from their skepticism regarding the classical theory of law to their attempts to fix the problems they found in the classical theory.

4. Legal Realists' Program of Reform

The Legal Realists' solution to the second problem was typical of their attempts to reform the law: they tried to turn the apparent weaknesses of law and judges into virtues. According to the Legal Realists, if the law is phrased in terms whose meaning appears different in different contexts, then judges ought in those different contexts to try honestly and without pretense to advance the public interest. And if it is impossible for judges to apply the law impartially and mechanically, the Legal Realists thought, then the next best thing is to rely on the wisdom of judges and require explicitly that they use their understanding of the changing needs and values of society to apply the law in a way which best serves those needs and promotes those values. Here one of the main problems with Legal Realism appears. Although the Legal Realists were anxious to reveal law and its operations for what they were, the Legal Realists' attempts to reform the law were not so well argued as their criticisms of the law. In particular, there seems to be a tension between their advocacy of an active role for judges in using the law as a tool to promote the public interest, and their contrasting belief that law exists and can be identified as law even if it does not serve the public interest or is plainly immoral.

Most Legal Realists accepted, with Legal Positivists, that the existence of law is independent of its justification. Even poorly phrased, badly devised, or clearly immoral laws may still be laws which courts have a duty to uphold. The Legal Realists had both social scientific and political reasons to accept this view. First, the Legal Realists accepted the insight of sociology that laws change to meet changing values in the societies they govern, and so were committed to what H.L.A. Hart later called the "separation thesis" of legal positivism. Second, the Legal Realists were Americans working within the accepted framework of American constitutional democracy, and so were committed to accepting that the law is made by authority of the majority of the people, and judges have a duty to apply the law as the expression of the will of the people. This may require judges to apply laws which they personally think unjustified, but in a democracy, it is necessary that judges defer to the wishes of the people. The problem emerging here is not difficult to see. On the one hand, Legal Realists wanted judges to turn the uncertainty of legal rules into an asset, by requiring judges to interpret legal rules in the way which best advanced the public interest. Yet on the other hand, the Legal Realists recognized and accepted that in a democracy the voters and not the judges ought to determine what is in the public interest. Many critics of Legal Realism think that the Legal Realists did not provide solutions to the problems they saw in the classical view of law, and instead only drew renewed attention to the difficulty of writing legal rules sufficiently clearly to ensure that in applying those laws judges advance the wishes of the public as understood not by judges but by the voting public.

These tensions in the Legal Realists' position should not be taken as detracting from the value of the assault on classical jurisprudence. We have as a lasting legacy of the Legal Realists the sense among lawyers, judges, legislators, and some portion of the public in common law systems, that the law is not a set, unchangeable tool. Rather, as the Legal Realists' criticisms have shown, the law is a flexible instrument which can be changed and used to advance the public interest. Much of the effect Legal Realists have had on contemporary thinking about the law is a result of their tremendous influence on legal education in the United States of America in the interwar years, roughly 1920–40. During this time Legal Realists held conferences for discussion of reform of law and changed the way law was taught in law schools by bringing sociologists, economists, and others into the law schools. Some Legal Realists reached prominent positions as judges and government administrators.

5. Oliver Wendell Holmes and Brian Leiter

The authors included here are two of the foremost representatives of Legal Realism, one classic and one contemporary. Oliver Wendell Holmes predates the main period of Legal Realism, yet it is in his writing that some of the clearest exposition of the central themes of Legal Realism may be found. Holmes was famous in his day as a justice in the state of Massachusetts, and later as a United States Supreme Court Justice. His essay "The Path of the Law," excerpted here, was originally given as a speech at the dedication of a new law school hall at Boston University. In it may be found several of the themes discussed above, expressed in a way designed to convince the law students, lawyers, and judges who sat in the audience. Legal Realists, such as Holmes, were deeply committed to reform of a system in which they all felt they had a personal stake, as judges, scholars, lawyers, and private citizens, and this commitment is reflected in the urgency of their prose.

The second selection in this section is written by a prominent contemporary defender of American Legal Realism, Professor Brian Leiter, who holds appointments in both the Department of Philosophy and Faculty of Law at the University of Chicago. Drawing on his experience as a practicing lawyer, Professor Leiter has been instrumental in reviving Legal Realism and demonstrating its distinctive contribution in mainstream legal theory. His article, focused on a representative sample of US Supreme Court judicial decisions, illustrates several of the Legal Realist themes identified above. He observes how the indeterminacy of sources of law, the freedom judges have to read past cases loosely or strictly, and the ability of judges to make plainly mistaken findings of law, all combine in various ways to support the thesis that judges rely on much more than just settled law to arrive at their conclusions. Judges, Leiter contends, rely at key junctures on their moral and political views. This fact leads him to his central conclusion: judges, especially appellate level judges such as those on the Supreme Court, are significantly engaged in law-making, especially at the constitutional level, and are not merely applying the law. A more accurate view, Leiter argues, understands the Supreme Court as a "super-legislature."

6. Ronald Dworkin

Ronald Dworkin is familiar to us from the last section, where we introduced his influential criticisms of legal positivism. Here we include a selection from Dworkin's *Law's Empire*, in which he advances his view of "law as integrity." "Law as integrity" is presented as an alternative to what Dworkin calls "conventionalism" (a set of views very near legal positivism) and "pragmatism" (a set of views very near legal realism). According to law as integrity, judges neither find nor make law. Instead, they *interpret* law. Dworkin employs a carefully explained, technical sense of "interpretation" as an attitude or approach to the thing being interpreted, and not just a series of techniques to be mechanically applied to law by judges. This explanation of interpretation as part of law as integrity appears to be part description and part prescription, saying that judges do act this way and that their doing so in the right way is good so deserves acceptance on the part of persons subject to so governed by law.

Interpretation, on Dworkin's view, involves explaining something with the aim of understanding its purpose, and trying to understand that purpose in its best light. Dworkin sometimes calls this "constructive interpretation." (This sense of interpretation is familiar to lawyers and judges, who use what are called "rules of construction" to guide interpretation of law.) When interpreting law to make it the best that it can be, judges are not simply left to their own devices, according to Dworkin. Rather, judicial interpretation has two dimensions: fit and justification. Judges try to interpret laws in a way which is consistent with and fits with past decisions and the body of laws as a whole. The dimension of "fit" is thus backward-looking as judges interpret laws in a way which integrates them into past decisions (usually in a fairly narrow area of law). Judges also try to interpret laws in a way which best justifies them and the entire body of laws according to the best available standards of political morality. The dimension of justification is thus forward-looking as judges interpret laws in a way which leaves the body of laws *as a whole* best justified according to the best available principles of political morality. Judges interpret the law in this way, according to Dworkin, because they aim to live in a "community of principle"—a community striving for justice.

Dworkin adds two further explanations of the actions of judges committed to law as integrity. The first is the chain novel analogy. Dworkin compares judges' interpretation of law to a novel written by many authors. The law, Dworkin suggests, is very much like a novel or perhaps a soap-opera screenplay when written by many writers. Even if different writers have different personal views as to the best way to develop the plot and theme of the novel or soap-opera, they are constrained by the plot and theme established by previous writers, and must from time to time compromise their own personal views in order to write in a way which leaves the novel most coherent and internally consistent. The law is like this insofar as many different judges over several hundred years have given decisions which have added to the case law contributing to the identity of the law and the principles in it, and judges have recognized the principles of political morality as justified constraints on their interpretation of law.

The second constraint Dworkin explains might be called the "single author" constraint. The law, viewed as something like a chain novel written to be the best it can be, is also similar to the chain novel insofar as the multiple authors of the chain novel try to write as though they were one. Judges attempt to decide cases in a way which makes the law coherent and integrated in the way it might be if a single author had decided all cases ever brought before the courts.

Law as integrity does not promise that adjudication of this sort will always be easy. On the contrary, because reasonable persons may disagree about the best way to interpret law with respect to fit *and* justification there may frequently be considerable dispute over the best interpretation of the law in a particular instance. There may be further dispute over the best course for law to take as it develops in response to new social situations. Which principles ought to be advanced in which areas of law? Which reading of the law best preserves the consistency of the preceding body of law? In their decisions in specific cases, individual judges each advance a specific conception of law, each interpreting the law with special emphasis on a particular understanding of legal principles which the individual judge thinks leaves the body of laws best justified as a whole. The law may appear to develop in contradictory directions, as judges at varying levels of the court system issue contradictory judgments, and the identity of that area of the law becomes clear only over time as judgments are overruled by higher courts or replaced by legislation. Judges committed to law as integrity do not automatically produce a coherent, consistent, and perfectly justified body of law, according to Dworkin; but this is a minor point compared to the more important point that these judges *try* to produce such a body of law.

After having read the selections by Holmes, Leiter, and Dworkin, you may find it difficult to decide who has the better account of judicial reasoning. It may be helpful to your deliberations to consider whether there is a sense in which each may be motivated by a different set of concerns and ask different questions about the same subject matter. To what extent, then, do the Legal Realists and Dworkin disagree? And to what extent is the appearance of disagreement in fact better understood as differences in investigative goals and questions asked to build understanding reaching those goals?

8
Oliver Wendell Holmes

"The Path of the Law,"[1] from *The Common Law*

When we study law we are not studying a mystery but a well-known profession. We are studying what we shall want in order to appear before judges, or to advise people in such a way as to keep them out of court. The reason why it is a profession, why people will pay lawyers to argue for them or to advise them, is that in societies like ours the command of the public force is intrusted to the judges in certain cases, and the whole power of the state will be put forth, if necessary, to carry out their judgments and decrees. People want to know under what circumstances and how far they will run the risk of coming against what is so much stronger than themselves, and hence it becomes a business to find out when this danger is to be feared. The object of our study, then, is prediction, the prediction of the incidence of the public force through the instrumentality of the court.

The means of the study are a body of reports, of treatises, and of statutes, in this country and in England, extending back for six hundred years, and now increasing annually by hundreds. In these sibylline leaves are gathered the scattered prophecies of the past upon the cases in which the axe will fall. These are what properly have been called the oracles of the law. Far the most important and pretty nearly the whole meaning of every new effort of legal thought is to make these prophecies more precise, and to generalize them into a thoroughly connected system. The process is one, from a lawyer's statement of a case, eliminating as it does all the dramatic elements with which his client's story has clothed it, and retaining only the facts of legal import, up to the final analyses and abstract universals of theoretic jurisprudence. The reason why a lawyer does not mention that his client wore a white hat when he made a contract, while Mrs. Quickly would be sure to dwell upon it along with the parcel gilt goblet and the sea-coal fire, is that he forsees that the public force will act in the same way whatever his client had upon his head. It is to make the prophecies easier to be remembered and to be understood that the teachings of the decisions of the past are put into general propositions and gathered into textbooks, or that statutes are passed in a general form. The primary rights and duties with which jurisprudence busies itself again are nothing but prophecies. One of the many evil effects of the confusion between legal and moral ideas, about which I shall have something to say in a moment, is that theory is apt to get the cart before the horse, and to consider the right or the duty as something existing apart from and independent of the consequences of its breach, to which certain sanctions are added afterward. [But, as I shall try to show, a legal duty so called is nothing but a prediction that if a man does or omits certain things he will be made to suffer in this or that way by judgment of the court;—and so of a legal right.]

...

The first thing for a businesslike understanding of the matter is to understand its limits, and therefore I think it desirable at once to point out

1 An Address delivered by Mr. Justice Holmes, of the Supreme Judicial Court of Massachusetts, at the dedication of the new hall of the Boston University School of Law, on January 8, 1897, copyrighted by O.W. Holmes, 1897.

and dispel a confusion between morality and law, which sometimes rises to the height of conscious theory, and more often and indeed constantly is making trouble in detail without reaching the point of consciousness. You can see very plainly that a bad man has as much reason as a good one for wishing to avoid an encounter with the public force, and therefore you can see the practical importance of the distinction between morality and law. A man who cares nothing for an ethical rule which is believed and practised by his neighbors is likely nevertheless to care a good deal to avoid being made to pay money, and will want to keep out of jail if he can.

I take it for granted that no hearer of mine will misinterpret what I have to say as the language of cynicism. The law is the witness and external deposit of our moral life. Its history is the history of the moral development of the race. The practice of it, in spite of popular jests, tends to make good citizens and good men. When I emphasize the difference between law and morals I do so with reference to a single end, that of learning and understanding the law. For that purpose you must definitely master its specific marks, and it is for that that I ask you for the moment to imagine yourselves indifferent to other and greater things.

I do not say that there is not a wider point of view from which the distinction between law and morals becomes of secondary or no importance, as all mathematical distinctions vanish in presence of the infinite. But I do say that that distinction is of the first importance for the object which we are here to consider,—a right study and mastery of the law as a business with well understood limits, a body of dogma enclosed within definite lines. I have just shown the practical reason for saying so. If you want to know the law and nothing else, you must look at it as a bad man, who cares only for the material consequences which such knowledge enables him to predict, not as a good one, who finds his reasons for conduct, whether inside the law or outside of it, in the vaguer sanctions of conscience. The theoretical importance of the distinction is no less, if you would reason on your subject aright. The law is full of phraseology drawn from morals, and by the mere force of language continually invites us to pass from one domain to the other without perceiving it, as we are sure to do unless we have the boundary constantly before our minds. The law talks about rights, and duties, and malice, and intent, and negligence, and so forth, and nothing is easier, or, I may say, more common in legal reasoning, than to take these words in their moral sense, at some stage of the argument, and so to drop into fallacy. For instance, when we speak of the rights of man in a moral sense, we mean to mark the limits of interference with individual freedom which we think are prescribed by conscience, or by our ideal, however reached. Yet it is certain that many laws have been enforced in the past, and it is likely that some are enforced now, which are condemned by the most enlightened opinion of the time, or which at all events pass the limit of interference as many consciences would draw it. Manifestly, therefore, nothing but confusion of thought can result from assuming that the rights of man in a moral sense are equally rights in the sense of the Constitution and the law. No doubt simple and extreme cases can be put of imaginable laws which the statute-making power would not dare to enact, even in the absence of written constitutional prohibitions, because the community would rise in rebellion and fight; and this gives some plausibility to the proposition that the law, if not a part of morality, is limited by it. But this limit of power is not coextensive with any system of morals. For the most part it falls far within the lines of any such system; and in some cases may extend beyond them, for reasons drawn from the habits of a particular people at a particular time. I once heard the late Professor Agassiz say that a German population would rise if you added two cents to the price of a glass of beer. A statute in such a case would be empty words, not because it was wrong, but because it could not be enforced. No one will deny that wrong statutes can be and are enforced, and we should not all agree as to which were the wrong ones.

The confusion with which I am dealing besets confessedly legal conceptions. Take the fundamental question, What constitutes the law? You will find some text writers telling you that it is something different from what is decided by the courts of Massachusetts or England, that it is a system of reason, that it is a deduction from principles of ethics or admitted axioms or what not, which may or may not coincide with the decisions. But if we take the view of our friend the bad man we shall find that he does not care two straws for the axioms or deductions, but that he does want to know what the Massachusetts or English courts are likely to do in fact. I am much of his mind. The prophecies of what the courts will do in fact, and nothing more pretentious, are what I mean by the law.

Take again a notion which as popularly understood is the widest conception which the law contains;—the notion of legal duty, to which already I have referred. We fill the word with all the content which we draw from morals. But what does it mean to a bad man? Mainly, and in the first place, a prophecy that if he does certain things he will be subjected to disagreeable consequences by way of imprisonment or compensatory payment of money.

...

I mentioned, as other examples of the use by the law of words drawn from morals, malice, intent, and negligence. It is enough to take malice as it is used in the law of civil liability for wrongs—what we lawyers call the law of torts—to show you that it means something different in law from what it means in morals, and also to show how the difference has been obscured by giving to principles which have little or nothing to do with each other the same name. Three hundred years ago a parson preached a sermon and told a story out of Fox's Book of Martyrs of a man who had assisted at the torture of one of the saints, and afterward died, suffering compensatory inward torment. It happened that Fox was wrong. The man was alive and chanced to hear the sermon, and thereupon he sued the parson. Chief Justice Wray instructed the jury that the defendant was not liable, because the story was told innocently, without malice. He took malice in the moral sense, as importing a malevolent motive. But nowadays no one doubts that a man may be liable, without any malevolent motive at all, for false statements manifestly calculated to inflict temporal damage. In stating the case in pleading, we still should call the defendant's conduct malicious; but, in my opinion at least, the word means nothing about motives, or even about the defendant's attitude toward the future, but only signifies that the tendency of his conduct under the known circumstances was very mainly to cause the plaintiff temporal harm.[2]

...

So much for the limits of the law. The next thing which I wish to consider is what are the forces which determine its content and its growth. You may assume, with Hobbes and Bentham and Austin, that all law emanates from the sovereign, even when the first human beings to enunciate it are the judges, or you may think that law is the voice of the Zeitgeist, or what you like. It is all one to my present purpose. Even if every decision required the sanction of an emperor with despotic power and a whimsical turn of mind, we should be interested none the less, still with

2 See *Hanson v. Globe Newspaper Co.*, 159 Mass. 293, 302.

a view to prediction, in discovering some order, some rational explanation, and some principle of growth for the rules which he laid down. In every system there are such explanations and principles to be found. It is with regard to them that a second fallacy comes in, which I think it important to expose.

The fallacy to which I refer is the notion that the only force at work in the development of the law is logical. In the broadest sense, indeed, that notion would be true. The postulate on which we think about the universe is that there is a fixed quantitative relation between every phenomenon and its antecedents and consequents. If there is such a thing as a phenomenon without these fixed quantitative relations, it is a miracle. It is outside the law of cause and effect, and as such transcends our power of thought, or at least is something to or from which we cannot reason. The condition of our thinking about the universe is that it is capable of being thought about rationally, or, in other words, that every part of it is effect and cause in the same sense in which those parts are with which we are most familiar. So in the broadest sense it is true that the law is a logical development, like everything else. The danger of which I speak is not the admission that the principles governing other phenomena also govern the law, but the notion that a given system, ours, for instance, can be worked out like mathematics from some general axioms of conduct. This is the natural error of the schools, but it is not confined to them. I once heard a very eminent judge say that he never let a decision go until he was absolutely sure that it was right. So judicial dissent often is blamed, as if it meant simply that one side or the other were not doing their sums right, and, if they would take more trouble, agreement inevitably would come.

This mode of thinking is entirely natural. The training of lawyers is a training in logic. The processes of analogy, discrimination, and deduction are those in which they are most at home. The language of judicial decision is mainly the language of logic. And the logical method and form flatter that longing for certainty and for repose which is in every human mind. But certainty generally is illusion, and repose is not the destiny of man. Behind the logical form lies a judgment as to the relative worth and importance of competing legislative grounds, often an inarticulate and unconscious judgment, it is true, and yet the very root and nerve of the whole proceeding. You can give any conclusion a logical form. You always can imply a condition in a contract. But why do you imply it? It is because of some belief as to the practice of the community or of a class, or because of some opinion as to policy, or, in short, because of some attitude of yours upon a matter not capable of exact quantitative measurement, and therefore not capable of founding exact logical conclusions. Such matters really are battle grounds where the means do not exist for determinations that shall be good for all time, and where the decision can do no more than embody the preference of a given body in a given time and place. We do not realize how large a part of our law is open to reconsideration upon a slight change in the habit of the public mind. No concrete proposition is self-evident, no matter how ready we may be to accept it, not even Mr. Herbert Spencer's. Every man has a right to do what he wills, provided he interferes not with a like right on the part of his neighbors.

Why is a false and injurious statement privileged, if it is made honestly in giving information about a servant? It is because it has been thought more important that information should be given freely, than that a man should be protected from what under other circumstances would be an actionable wrong. Why is a man at liberty to set up a business which he knows will ruin his neighbor? It is because the public good is supposed to be best subserved by free competition. Obviously such judgments of relative importance may vary in different times and places. Why does a judge instruct a jury that an employer is not liable to an employee for an injury received in the course of his employment unless he is negligent, and why do the jury generally find for the plaintiff if the case is allowed to go to them? It is because the traditional policy of our law is to confine liability to cases where a prudent man might have foreseen the injury, or at least the danger, while the inclination of a very large part of the community is to make certain classes of persons insure the safety of those with whom they deal. Since the last words were written, I have seen the requirement of such insurance put forth as part of the programme of one of the best known labor organizations. There is a concealed, half conscious battle on the question of legislative policy, and if any one thinks that it can be settled deductively, or once for all, I only can say that I think he is theoretically wrong, and that I am certain that his conclusion will not be accepted in practice *semper ubique et ab omnibus*.

...

At present, in very many cases, if we want to know why a rule of law has taken its particular shape, and more or less if we want to know why it exists at all, we go to tradition. We follow it into the Year Books, and perhaps beyond them to the customs of the Salian Franks, and somewhere in the past, in the German forests, in the needs of Norman kings, in the assumptions of a dominant class, in the absence of generalized ideas, we find out the practical motive for what now best is justified by the mere fact of its acceptance and that men are accustomed to it. The rational study of law is still to a large extent the study of history. History must be a part of the study, because without it we cannot know the precise scope of rules which it is our business to know. It is a part of the rational study, because it is the first step toward an enlightened scepticism, that is, toward a deliberate reconsideration of the worth of those rules. When you get the dragon out of his cave on to the plain and in the daylight, you can count his teeth and claws, and see just what is his strength. But to get him out is only the first step. The next is either to kill him, or to tame him and make him a useful animal. For the rational study of the law the black-letter man may be the man of the present, but the man of the future is the man of statistics and the master of economics. It is revolting to have no better reason for a rule of law than that so it was laid down in the time of Henry IV. It is still more revolting if the grounds upon which it was laid down have vanished long since, and the rule simply persists from blind imitation of the past ...

...

I trust that no one will understand me to be speaking with disrespect of the law, because I criticise it so freely. I venerate the law, and especially our system of law, as one of the vastest products of the human mind. No one knows better than I do the countless number of great intellects that have spent themselves in making some addition or improvement, the greatest of which is trifling when compared with the mighty whole. It has the final title to respect that it exists, that it is not a Hegelian dream, but a part of the lives of men. But one may criticise even what one reveres. Law is the business to which my life is devoted, and I should show less than devotion if I did not do what in me lies to improve it, and, when I perceive what seems to me the ideal of its future, if I hesitated to point it out and to press toward it with all my heart.

9

Brian Leiter*

"Constitutional Law, Moral Judgment, and the Supreme Court as Super-Legislature"

I propose to defend and explore three claims in this Essay. First, there is very little actual "law" in federal constitutional law in the United States, especially with respect to cases that end up at the Supreme Court. There, the Court operates as a kind of super-legislature, albeit one with limited jurisdiction. The jurisdiction is limited in two important ways: first, the Court can only pass on issues that are brought before it; and second, the Court is constrained, to some extent, by its past decisions and by constitutional and legislative texts. The problem, however, is that those constraints *underdetermine* the Court's decisions in most cases, so the Court essentially makes its final choice among the legally viable options based on the moral and political values of the Justices, and not simply on the basis of legally binding standards. The latter claim is, in part, a jurisprudential thesis about what constitutes "legally binding standards." I shall defend the first claim by reference to the most plausible account of the nature of law—the legal positivist theory developed by H.L.A. Hart and Joseph Raz.

Second, the absence of law in so many parts of federal constitutional law means that the quality of moral and political judgment exercised by judges is of decisive importance in how they fulfill their role. Thus, it should be the overriding factor in the appointment of federal appellate judges, especially Supreme Court Justices. That brings me to my third claim, namely, that all political actors know that the Supreme Court often operates as a super-legislature, and thus that the moral and political views of the Justices are decisive criteria for their appointment. This almost banal truth is, however, rarely discussed in the public confirmation process, but is common knowledge among political and legal insiders. To be sure, there is always media speculation about the political predilections of the nominees, but their actual moral and political views are treated as off limits in the real confirmation process. This antidemocratic secrecy is, in my view, deeply wrong and must be replaced with a realistic acknowledgment of the role of the Supreme Court as a political actor of limited jurisdiction. I will illustrate these claims by discussing a number of important public law cases, recent and not-so-recent.

What does it mean to say there is very little "law" in American constitutional law? That requires us to have some view about what it means to say law exists, and so I must begin with some discussion of basic jurisprudential questions. To that end, I will follow the most promising theory about the nature of law: the

* Karl N. Llewellyn Professor of Jurisprudence and Director of the Center for Law, Philosophy, & Human Values, University of Chicago. An earlier version of this lecture was presented as the 24th Mathew O. Tobriner Memorial Lecture in Constitutional Law at University of California Hastings College of the Law in San Francisco on January 12, 2015. I am grateful to Aziz Huq and Nicholas Stephanopoulos for very helpful and detailed comments on an earlier draft; to Will Baude for additional feedback on that draft; to Mike Seidman for shrewd and illuminating advice on the penultimate draft; and to Phil Smoke, University of Chicago Law School Class of 2015, for excellent research assistance. Finally, my thanks to the audience at the Tobriner Lecture, and especially to Judge Joseph Grodin for a helpful correspondence afterwards.

legal positivism of H.L.A. Hart and his student Joseph Raz.[1] Let us start with some terminology. Human societies are awash in norms, by which I mean demands of the form, "You ought to do X," or "You ought not do Y."[2] Some norms are merely norms of etiquette: for example, "You ought not talk on your cell phone during the lecture" or "You ought not talk with your mouth full at the table." Others are norms of prudence or self-interest: "You ought to attend class, lest you fail the exam!" Some are moral norms: "You ought to consider how your actions will affect the well-being of others." And some are *norms of the legal system*, for example, "You ought not go faster than fifty-five miles per hour on the highway." The categories are not mutually exclusive: sometimes moral norms such as, "You ought not murder innocents," are also legal norms, and sometimes norms of prudence are too, as in, "You must wear a seatbelt while driving." Norms of etiquette are rarely legal norms, many moral norms are not legal ones, and many legal norms are not ones we think of as representing moral or ethical obligations. For instance, we do not think the English are immoral for driving on the left of the road rather than the right, but we recognize they have a legal obligation to do so. The jurisprudential question is: how do we mark the difference? And the legal positivist answer is: norms are *legally valid*—that is, norms of the legal system—in virtue of satisfying criteria in that system's "rule of recognition" as Hart called it.[3] A rule of recognition specifies the criteria in virtue of which particular norms are taken to be norms of the legal system. Such criteria can include legislative enactment, executive orders, judicial decisions, and so on.

Rules of recognition in modern legal systems are, admittedly, complex. Consider: a norm is a valid norm of the California legal system if it has been enacted by the California legislature and signed by the Governor, and has not been deemed unconstitutional as a matter of state or federal law by a state or federal court and has not been preempted by a constitutional federal law; a norm can also be a valid norm in the California system if it has been enacted by Congress and signed by the President, and has not been deemed unconstitutional by the Court of Appeals for the Ninth Circuit or by the Supreme Court; a norm can also be a legally valid norm in the California legal system if it figures in the holding of a California court that has not been reversed by a higher California or federal court; and so on. This omits executive orders and administrative rulings, also subject to various kinds of judicial review.

A good part of legal education is education in the rule of recognition of one's legal system, although it is rarely denominated as such in the law school classroom. But what makes it the case that California's rule of recognition is what it is? Hart's great insight was that, at bottom, legal systems rest upon nothing more than a conventional practice of officials, notably judges. The California Constitution is a binding norm of the California legal system *only because* judges in California treat it as binding on their decisions; so too with the Federal Constitution, and so too with legislative enactments, administrative decisions, and the like. That a rule of recognition exists, and that it has the particular content it does, depends entirely on officials converging on certain criteria of legal validity and on their treating such criteria as obligatory or binding—accepting them from an "internal point of view" as Hart famously said.[4]

1 See Brian Leiter, "The Case for Legal Positivism as an Account of the Artefact Law," in *Law as an Artifact* (L. Burazin & K. Himma eds.) (forthcoming 2016), for a discussion on legal positivism.

2 There are many other kinds of norms, including permissions such as "You may do X." I use deontic norms as the central case.

3 See H.L.A. Hart, *The Concept of Law* 100-10 (3d ed. 2012).

4 See *id.* at 90-92.

That the officials converge on certain criteria is an empirical question, manifest in their decisions and sometimes the reasons given for them; that they treat such criteria as obligatory is manifest in their language and their behavior: for example, in their willingness to criticize other judges who depart from those criteria, and in the language they use to justify their own conduct.

A wonderful example of Hart's point comes from the case of Chief Justice Roy Moore of the Alabama Supreme Court, who, in 2003, refused to abide by a decision of the Court of Appeals for the Eleventh Circuit holding that the presence of a statue of the Ten Commandments in the Alabama Supreme Court building violated the Establishment Clause of the Constitution.[5] There was no doubt that under the applicable rule of recognition, the Eleventh Circuit had authority over Chief Justice Moore with regard to the constitutionality of the placement of that statue. And when Chief Justice Moore defied the Eleventh Circuit's decision, the officials of the Alabama legal system made manifest their acceptance of this aspect of the rule of recognition from an internal point of view. They not only criticized Chief Justice Moore's refusal to comply with the order, but they convened the necessary procedures to remove him from office.[6]

We may imagine a more fanciful example to illustrate Hart's view that where a rule of recognition exists, officials of the system accept that rule from an internal point of view—that is, they treat it as obligatory. Suppose Chief Justice Roberts comes to UC Hastings, and a student asks, "Justice Roberts, why are you and the other Justices always worried about whether laws are constitutional? I mean, who cares? Why not just make a sensible decision?" Once he gets past being surprised, the Chief Justice, we can be sure, would *not* give the following answer: "I'll tell you why we're always talking about the Constitution: being Chief Justice is a great job, it's got prestige, lifetime tenure, a great pension too. If I didn't treat the Constitution as a constraint on what we do, I'm worried I'd get impeached and have to give up this wonderful sinecure I have." Instead of averting to crass self-interested reasons like these for taking the Constitution seriously, the Chief Justice is far more likely to appeal to the professional oath of office he took as a Justice to uphold the Constitution, as well as to the moral and political virtues of our constitutional system as he understands them. I want to be clear: I am quite sure those are the actual reasons the Chief Justice, like other justices and judges, take the constitutionality of statutes seriously. Where legal systems exist, officials of the system, including the judges, really do accept the criteria of legal validity, such as constitutionality, from an internal point of view.

But this now brings us back to the problem with which we started. Constitutionality is only a criterion of legal validity in the rule of recognition of the American legal system if judges generally treat it as such and accept it from an internal point of view. The difficulty is that, while all judges treat the constitutional document as legally binding, they differ wildly on how to ascertain the meaning of its provisions. Justice Scalia, for example, thinks the original public meaning of the provisions of the Constitution determines its requirements; Justice Thomas sometimes agrees with him, but no one else does.[7] As a matter of the rule

5 *Glassroth v. Moore*, 335 F.3d 1282, 1282 (11th Cir. 2003).

6 Jeffrey Gettleman, "Court Orders Alabama's Chief Justice Removed from Bench," *N.Y. Times*, (Nov. 13, 2003), http://www.nytimes.com/2003/11/13/national/13CND-JUDG.html. Chief Justice Moore was subsequently reelected, which, alas, says more about the Alabama electorate than about the officials of the legal system, who acted appropriately. *See* Brianne Britzius, "Roy Moore Elected New Alabama Chief Justice," *WSFA12* (Nov. 13, 2012), http://www.wsfa.com/story/20025004/roy-moore-elected-new-alabama-chief-justice.

7 Other Justices will avert to originalist considerations but do not regard them as decisive the way Justice Scalia purports to do.

of recognition of American constitutional law, it is obviously false that the original public meaning of the Constitution is what is legally binding on the courts.[8] Some judges treat the plain meaning as binding, some appeal to the structure of the Constitution, and almost all defer to past judicial interpretations of constitutional provisions (whether based on original meaning or not) as binding—an example of what my colleague David Strauss calls our "constitutional common law."[9] Since federal judges do not converge on a single way of fixing constitutional meaning, it follows, on the positivist view, that in large parts of so-called "constitutional law" there really is no law because there are no criteria of legal validity generally accepted and applied by judges.[10]

Not all areas of what we call constitutional law are so unsettled—unanimous decisions by the Supreme Court on many constitutional issues are rather good evidence in support of that point. But even divided decisions can turn out to be widely accepted as settled. Let us recall the 1989 case *Texas v. Johnson*,[11] in which the Supreme Court decided that a law prohibiting desecration of the flag violated the First Amendment, a decision in which Justices Scalia and Kennedy joined the majority opinion by Justice Brennan. Twenty-five years later, the case stands as good law: the government cannot, constitutionally, punish burning the American flag. Lower court judges understand that a Supreme Court decision like *Johnson* binds them to invalidate any blanket ban on flag burning, and thus the issue has hardly arisen since.

Then, however, we have an issue like whether the Second Amendment protects an individual right to own guns. For most of the twentieth century, it was settled law that it does not. After all, the Amendment reads: "A well regulated Militia, being necessary to the security of a free State, the right of the people to keep and bear Arms, shall not be infringed."[12] One natural reading, one that dominated for most of our constitutional history, was that this protected the right of states to arm their militias. That the Amendment really protects an individual right to bear arms was famously deemed a "fraud on the American public" by the late Chief Justice Warren Burger, a Republican appointee.[13] That "fraud" is now the law of the land, thanks to a 2008 decision by the super-legislature in *District of Columbia v. Heller*,[14] which bypassed precedent and received the original public meaning as read by Justice Scalia in the majority and disputed at length by Justice Stevens in the dissent. The historical evidence is obviously mixed, and my colleague Judge Richard Posner's verdict on the decision, in a well-known *New Republic* article at the time, still seems apt:

> Lawyers are advocates for their clients, and judges are advocates for whichever side of the case they have decided to vote for. The judge sends his law clerks scurrying to the library and to the Web for bits and pieces of historical documentation. When the clerks are the numerous and able clerks of

8 Richard H. Fallon, Jr., "Constitutional Precedent Viewed Through the Lens of Hartian Positivist Jurisprudence," 86 *N.C. L. Rev.* 1107 (2008).

9 See David A. Strauss, "Common Law Constitutional Interpretation," 63 *U. Chi. L. Rev.* 877, 929 (1996). In the lower federal courts, something like the "common law constitutionalism" approach dominates due to convergence among officials on the binding force of Supreme Court decisions. But even then, there remains plenty of room for the exercise of quasi-legislative powers.

10 See Brian Leiter, "Explaining Theoretical Disagreement," 76 *U. Chi. L. Rev.* 1215, 1224-32 (2009), for a discussion of how this extends beyond constitutional law in some measure in the United States.

11 491 U.S. 397 (1989).

12 U.S. Const. amend. II.

13 *The MacNeil/Lehrer NewsHour: First Freedoms* (PBS television broadcast Dec. 16, 1991).

14 554 U.S. 570 (2008).

Supreme Court justices, enjoying the assistance of the capable staffs of the Supreme Court library and the Library of Congress, and when dozens and sometimes hundreds of amicus curiae briefs have been filed, many bulked out with the fruits of their authors' own law-office historiography, it is a simple matter, especially for a skillful rhetorician such as Scalia, to write a plausible historical defense of his position.

But it was not so simple in *Heller*, and Scalia and his staff labored mightily to produce a long opinion (the majority opinion is almost 25,000 words long) that would convince, or perhaps just overwhelm, the doubters. The range of historical references in the majority opinion is breathtaking, but it is not evidence of disinterested historical inquiry. It is evidence of the ability of well-staffed courts to produce snow jobs ...

For more than two centuries, the "right" to private possession of guns, supposedly created by the Second Amendment, had lain dormant. Constitutional rights often lie dormant, spectral subjects of theoretical speculation, until some change in the social environment creates a demand for their vivification and enforcement. But nothing has changed in the social environment to justify giving the Second Amendment a new life discontinuous with its old one: a new wine in a decidedly old wineskin. There is no greater urgency about allowing people to possess guns for self-defense or defense of property today than there was thirty years ago, when the prevalence of violent crime was greater, or for that matter one hundred years ago. Only the membership of the Supreme Court has changed.

If constitutional decisions are to be determined by the balance between liberals and conservatives on the Supreme Court, the fig-leafing that we find in *Heller*—the historicizing glaze on personal values and policy preferences—will continue to be irresistibly tempting to the justices, with their large and tireless staffs and their commitment to a mystique of "objective" interpretation. There is no way to purge political principles from constitutional decision-making, but they do not have to be liberal or conservative principles. A preference for judicial modesty—for less interference by the Supreme Court with the other branches of government—cannot be derived by some logical process from constitutional text or history. It would have to be imposed. It would be a discretionary choice by the justices. But judging from *Heller*, it would be a wise choice. It would go some distance toward de-politicizing the Supreme Court. It would lower the temperature of judicial confirmation hearings, widen the field of selection of justices, and enable the Supreme Court to attend to the many important non-constitutional issues that it is inclined to neglect.[15]

---

15 Richard A. Posner, "In Defense of Looseness," *New Republic*, Aug. 27, 2008, at 35.

A preference for judicial modesty is, however, also a political choice,[16] as Judge Posner recognizes, one that will serve to immunize from judicial review whatever the prevailing ideology of the other branches of the government is at that time. So the real question is why, when we confirm Justices to the super-legislature, do we not have a public discussion of their political principles? That is the question Judge Posner's apt critique raises.

The Supreme Court's role as super-legislature emerges in the recent voting rights case, *Shelby County v. Holder*.[17] Here, a bare majority of the super-legislature invalidated section 4 of the Voting Rights Act that the actual legislature, that is, Congress, had evaluated and extended in 2006.[18] The *Shelby County* decision did so based on the finding of five members of the super-legislature that section 4—which specified the formula for determining which states with a history of voting discrimination required federal preapproval for election law changes—is no longer necessary, contrary to the view, apparently, of the actual legislature seven years earlier.[19] In an opinion by Chief Justice Roberts, the five super-legislators explained that while "Congress compiled thousands of pages of evidence before reauthorizing the Voting Rights Act," these did not justify the original 1965 formula for preclearance.[20] Why not? According to Chief Justice Roberts, there was "no logical relation" to the section 4 requirements, that these requirements were "irrational" given the record, indeed, "played no role" in the preclearance formulas.[21] This is all just rhetorical flourish, of course, for a different legislative judgment: it is obviously not irrational to rectify a wrong with a possibly over inclusive measure when the wrong is sufficiently serious that one wants to secure its elimination. As Justice Ginsburg, for the dissenters, observed:

> Congress determined, based on a voluminous record, that the scourge of discrimination was not yet extirpated. The question this case presents is who decides whether, as currently operative, [pre-clearance in accordance with the section 4 formula] remains justifiable, this Court, or a Congress charged with the obligation to enforce the post-Civil War Amendments "by appropriate legislation." With overwhelming support in both Houses, Congress concluded that, for two prime reasons, [the preclearance formula] should continue in force, unabated. First, continuance would facilitate completion of the impressive gains thus far made; and second, continuance would guard against backsliding. Those assessments were well within Congress' province to make and should elicit this Court's unstinting approbation.[22]

Alas, a majority of the super-legislature did not offer approbation to the actual legislature's assessment, instead substituting its judgment on

16 There is ambiguity in the notion of a "political" choice, though the basic idea is that it is a choice motivated by adherence to a norm that has no legal status but instead reflects commitments for how the polity as a whole should be organized—such norms may run the gamut from partisanship for the narrow agenda of a particular party to a vision of the just society.

17 133 S. Ct. 2612 (2013).

18 Note that the fundamental question in *Shelby County* was a constitutional, not statutory, one; namely, was section 4 a constitutional (that is, rational) exercise of Congressional power to enforce the Reconstruction Amendments (including, the Fourteenth and Fifteenth Amendments) to the Constitution?

19 *Shelby County*, 133 S. Ct. at 2629.

20 *Id.*

21 *Id.* at 2629-31.

22 *Id.* at 2632-33.

the policy merits for Congress's. If *Shelby County* were anomalous, this might not be notable, but the point is that it is fairly typical of what happens in the public law domain.

The problem is exacerbated, of course, because the Supreme Court *selects* its docket—it picks the cases it wants to hear, and unsurprisingly it picks the cases where the federal circuits conflict or where the law is up for grabs, up for grabs in precisely the sense that the rule of recognition does not clearly settle what should be done. Of course, the Supreme Court, having claimed for itself—without any basis in the constitutional text—final authority to adjudicate constitutional questions two centuries ago in *Marbury v. Madison*[23] (one of the more successful revisions of the American rule of recognition in our history), sometimes takes cases that might appear settled, a clear indication that the Court intends to exercise its super-legislative authority. Recall *New York v. United States*[24] from 1992, one of the early cases[25] that signaled the intent of some members of the super-legislature to redraw the boundaries of federal power after an earlier super-legislature appointed by President Franklin Roosevelt redrew them in the late 1930s and early 1940s to make the New Deal possible. *New York* concerned the Low-Level Radioactive Waste Policy Amendments Act of 1985, which the State of New York challenged as betraying federalism values by violating state autonomy. Under what one might have thought the controlling precedent, *Garcia v. San Antonio Metropolitan Transit Authority*,[26] just seven years earlier, *New York* should have been an "easy" case, that is, one in which the law clearly dictated that New York would lose. *Garcia*, which concerned federal regulations about wages and working hours, held (or so it seemed at the time!) that the only protection for federalism values, like state autonomy, came from the political process itself, that is from the fact that the states were all represented in Congress; and only if there was a breakdown in the political process, so the *Garcia* court suggested, would the Supreme Court intervene. *New York* was a clear case from the standpoint of *Garcia*: the Federal Radioactive Waste Management Act had been enacted by Congress *after being drafted by the various states*. The states, in effect, wanted Congress to bind them to the agreement they had reached among themselves. This would seem to be a paradigmatic case of federalism values in action: autonomous states strike a bargain about how to dispose of their radioactive waste, and then ask Congress to enforce the bargain.

Once the super-legislature known as the Supreme Court granted certiorari in the matter everyone was on notice, of course, that the super-legislature planned to act. And act it did: in its majority opinion, Justice O'Connor took a page from the great American Legal Realist Karl Llewellyn's explanation of the malleability of precedent from his 1930 book *The Bramble Bush*.[27] In Llewellyn's famous rendering, appellate courts approach precedents in one of two ways: they read "unwelcome" precedent strictly; that is, they characterize their holding in a way that is highly specific to the facts of the earlier case in order to distinguish it from the case currently before the court.[28] In Llewellyn's obviously facetious example, a strict reading of an earlier court's holding might be, "This rule holds only

23 5 U.S. 137 (1803).
24 505 U.S. 144 (1992).
25 See *Gregory v. Ashcroft*, 501 U.S. 452, 461 (1991).
26 469 U.S. 528 (1985).
27 Karl N. Llewellyn, *The Bramble Bush* 68-71 (11th prtg. 2008).
28 See *id.*

of redheaded Walpoles in pale magenta Buick cars."[29] By contrast, a "loose" reading of a precedent abstracts away from the particular facts of the case in favor of a generic rule of law that the court would like to treat as binding in the present instance. Not every "strict" or "loose" reading is going to be plausible, but Llewellyn, as the smart and experienced lawyer he was, is plainly correct that the doctrine of precedent affords courts enough latitude in construing the holdings of earlier cases to make precedent a feeble constraint on present decision in many cases. And that is precisely what happened in *New York*.

Justice O'Connor, in the majority opinion, faced an obvious problem as I mentioned: under *Garcia*, the Federal Radioactive Waste Act looked like a clear case of the political process operating to protect the interests of the states. After all, the states had drafted the Act in negotiations with each other, and then asked Congress to enact it. Presumably O'Connor lacked the votes to overrule *Garcia*—a move that would have been unseemly, in any case, given that *Garcia* had overruled another case, *National League of Cities v. Usery*,[30] less than a decade before! So, taking a page from Llewellyn's book, she set out to *distinguish Garcia* by reading it strictly. According to Justice O'Connor's majority opinion,[31] the rule in *Garcia*—the rule that the only protection for federalism values comes from the political process itself—applies *only* in cases where the federal regulation applies to *both* public and private entities, as was true of the wage and hour regulations at issue in *Garcia*. In fact, Garcia itself did not make an issue out of this, but now, seven years later in *New York*, Justice O'Connor did: for the Federal Radioactive Waste Management Act applied only to public entities, namely states, and so according to Justice O'Connor presented a different issue than in *Garcia*. With *Garcia* distinguished, Justice O'Connor proceeded into an historical analysis and ultimately invalidated a portion of the Act.[32] Those details do not matter for our purposes.

The dissenting opinion by Justice White[33] also took a page from Llewellyn: he effectively accused the majority of distinguishing *Garcia* on the basis of factual differences that did not make a difference—in effect, Justice White complained, the majority opinion said the rule in *Garcia* applies only to "redheaded Walpoles in pale magenta Buick cars."[34] From Justice White's perspective, the difference between a federal regulation that reached public and private entities as opposed to only public ones was irrelevant, *New York* was an easy case, and *Garcia* should have controlled the result.[35]

I want to be clear that I do not think either majority or dissent was right "as a matter of law" in this case. To be sure, Justice O'Connor did a poor job of explaining why the factual difference between *Garcia* and *New York* actually mattered, but an explanation is not hard to come by: surely it is not crazy to think state autonomy might be more at risk when a federal regulation *only applies to the states*, as opposed to regulating public and private actors equally. At the same time, Justice White's view was equally plausible as a matter of law: the *Garcia* rule emphasized the importance of the political process as a safeguard for state autonomy, and the underlying facts in *New York* seemed to indicate a political process functioning well, and indeed, driven by

29 *Id.* at 68.
30 426 U.S. 833 (1976).
31 See *New York v. United States*, 505 U.S. 144, 149-88 (1992).
32 *Id.* at 155.
33 *Id.* at 188-211.
34 See Llewellyn, *supra* note 32, at 68.
35 See *New York*, 505 U.S. at 188-211.

the states themselves, until the state of New York had some buyer's remorse.

If the preceding is correct, then we should ask what really happened in *New York*. The case, as students of federalism know, was near the beginning of a series of Supreme Court cases in which, for the first time since the triumph of the New Deal, the Court began placing some limits on the exercise of federal power. President Reagan, who appointed Justice O'Connor a decade earlier, ran partly on this issue, the issue of state autonomy from federal overreach. And so, for Justice O'Connor, a new-fangled conservative in the Reagan mold, New York presented an opportunity to state loud and clear that there really are limits on federal power. By contrast, for Justice White, an old-fangled conservative, appointed by President Kennedy in the early 1960s, the New Deal revolution had settled all the questions about the scope of federal power. Justice White was a law-and-order conservative, skeptical of the expanding rights of criminal defendants, as well as of abortion rights, but he was fully accepting of the transformation of the constitutional system created by the New Deal. The federal legislature voted to bind the states to a proposal for disposing radioactive waste that they themselves had drafted; in *New York*, the super-legislature known as the Supreme Court voted to overturn part of that plan. In doing so, they did not act as the law requires: only a naïf could believe that. Instead, they exercised moral and political judgment, and acted accordingly.

Let us now fast forward to the present, last term's decision in *Burwell v. Hobby Lobby*.[36] In *Hobby Lobby*, the Supreme Court upheld a challenge by closely held corporations to a requirement of the Affordable Care Act—more precisely, the mandate imposed by the Department of Health and Human Services under that Act—that employers (of a certain size) pay for employee health insurance that covers, among other things, four kinds of (allegedly) post-conception contraceptive drugs and devices. The challenge was based on the Religious Freedom Restoration Act ("RFRA"), a 1993 law that attempted to restore the constitutional protections for "free exercise" of religion that had existed prior to Justice Scalia's majority opinion in *Employment Division v. Smith*.[37] That 1990 decision held that the state need not grant religious exemptions for neutral laws of general applicability—neutral in the sense that their purpose was not (facially or otherwise) to substantially burden a particular religious faith.[38] Thus, under *Smith*, the federal government did not need to find a less burdensome alternative to a law that imposed incidental but substantial burdens on free exercise of religion.

The *Hobby Lobby* decision found, plausibly, that the owners of the closely held corporations challenging the mandate genuinely believed that life begins at conception, so that they genuinely believed that postconception contraception was akin to murder.[39] I want to emphasize that three aspects of the *Hobby Lobby* decision seem to me fairly banal, given the existence of RFRA: First, that the free exercise of religion of a closely held corporation is not meaningfully distinguishable from the free exercise of religion by the individuals who closely own the corporation (in other words, closely held corporations are "persons" for purposes of RFRA). Second, that since the federal government had already provided an opt-out provision from the mandate for nonprofit entities with religious objections (like the University of Notre Dame), one that did not shift costs to the

36 134 S. Ct. 2751 (2014).
37 494 U.S. 872, 874-90 (1990). Congress, and many states, reacted against this decision, and Congress subsequently passed RFRA, which now prohibits the federal government from substantially burdening religion when alternatives are available.
38 *Id.* at 882.
39 *Hobby Lobby*, 134 S. Ct. at 2764-66, 2775.

employees seeking contraceptive coverage, then it was clear that there were regulatory alternatives available to the federal government to insure that contraception was available to female employees that did not impose a substantial burden on religious belief. And third, that under our constitutional regime of religious liberty, courts must take seriously someone's religious belief that life begins at conception. I, myself, disagree with this latter aspect of our constitutional system, just as I also think RFRA is a bad law,[40] but that is not at issue in my doubts about *Hobby Lobby*. My doubts lie elsewhere.

The crucial legal question presented in *Hobby Lobby*, granting the points I have just conceded, is whether requiring a closely held corporation to pay for health insurance that an employee might use to access medical services of which her employer disapproves constitutes a "substantial burden" on the free exercise of the employer's religion in a society which is not a theocracy, that is, in a society in which, for example, employees need not subscribe to the religion of their employers. The idea that it would constitute a substantial burden ought to have seemed preposterous on its face. Yet in the majority opinion of the super-legislature by Justice Alito, we are told that the belief of the owners of the closely held corporations of paying for insurance which their employees could use to secure contraceptive services that the employers disapproved of "implicates a difficult and important question of religion and moral philosophy, namely, the circumstances under which it is wrong for a person to perform an act that is innocent in itself but that has the effect of enabling or facilitating the commission of an immoral act by another."[41] It is not for the courts, Justice Alito asserts, to tell "the plaintiffs that their beliefs are flawed."[42] The job of the courts is only to determine whether the beliefs are sincere religious beliefs, which everyone, including me, grants that they are.

This sounds reasonable until one considers a scenario in which the religious plaintiffs profess the following putatively religious belief: "This law substantially burdens our free exercise of religion." That looks rather like a legal conclusion masquerading as a religious belief, but now we need to ask how such a scenario is any different from the position of the challengers in *Hobby Lobby*? If you believe that paying for medical insurance that can be used by your employees to access medical procedures of which you disapprove violates your free exercise rights, that is a legal question for the courts. The courts can grant that *you really believe this*, indeed, that you hold a particular philosophical or religious view about "the circumstances under which it is wrong for a person to perform an act that is innocent in itself but that has the effect of enabling or facilitating the commission of an immoral act by another."[43] But calling it a "philosophical" or religious view does not change the fact that it states a legal conclusion, specifically, that the law requiring you to pay for the medical insurance substantially burdens your religion.

In short, we can agree with Justice Alito that the Supreme Court has long held that it will not adjudicate whether religious beliefs are sensible, only whether they are *religious* and *sincerely held*. But that does not mean that the courts must defer to the religious person's beliefs about whether the law substantially burdens their religion: that has to be a legal question for the courts, or the courts are out of business. The super-legislature should have acted like an actual

40 See Brian Leiter, *Why Tolerate Religion?* (2013) (criticizing the singling out of religious liberty for special legal protections).
41 *Hobby Lobby*, 134 S. Ct. at 2778.
42 *Id.*
43 See *id.*

court and found there was no "substantial burden" on *Hobby Lobby*.[44]

It is important to notice that the mistake in Justice Alito's reasoning was, in fact, a *legal* mistake, not in the sense that he failed to recognize the relevant sources of law but in the sense that he failed to understand the conceptual or logical entailments from those sources. More precisely, Justice Alito failed to correctly distinguish the *legal* question whether a particular law actually imposes a "substantial burden" on religious exercise from the non-legal question that courts are not supposed to adjudicate, namely, whether claimant's religious beliefs are reasonable. If it were really the case that courts must defer to the claimant's allegedly *religious beliefs about substantial burdens—that is, about whether their legal rights are violated*—then there is nothing for the courts to do. Since that is absurd, Justice Alito obviously made a serious mistake in his legal reasoning.

Even if the super-legislature's mistake in *Hobby Lobby* was a *legal* mistake, it still calls attention again to the importance of moral and political judgment by the members of this super-legislature, since their moral and political values may explain their propensity to make certain kinds of mistakes. Remember that the Supreme Court, two hundred years ago in *Marbury v. Madison*, successfully claimed for itself the power to settle *constitutional* questions, meaning that the actual legislature cannot easily undo the mistakes that are motivated by the moral and political beliefs of the Justices—in this case, the desire of the conservative majority of the super-legislature to signal their fundamental sympathy with religious conservatives. To be sure, *Hobby Lobby* concerns RFRA, not the First Amendment, though RFRA was, at a minimum, purporting to re-establish an earlier constitutional regime. But it is a reasonable prediction that Congress will not revisit RFRA to undo the *Hobby Lobby* decision. Thus, even the plain legal mistakes of the super-legislature give us further reason to want to know the moral and political views of the Justices before they are appointed, since those views will illuminate precisely the domains in which they are likely to make errors.

Alas, the only people who are led to believe that Supreme Court Justices are appointed based simply on their legal skill and knowledge are the American people, meaning the electorate.[45] Every American president, from at least Roosevelt to Reagan to the present, understands that the Supreme Court often acts as a super-legislature, and therefore one had better try to appoint legislators, that is, Justices, who share the moral and political views of the appointing president. Let me share an amusing, but revealing, story my colleague, Judge Posner, told me—and which he has shared with many others so I am not betraying any secrets here. Judge Posner was appointed to the Court of Appeals for the Seventh Circuit in 1981 when, as he said to my jurisprudence class one year, people didn't realize President Reagan was "stacking" the courts with "right-wingers like me." Those are Judge Posner's words, though as all lawyers know, he has proven to be far less of a right-winger than the current Republican Party might have hoped. In any case, Judge Posner's point was that the media did not pay much attention to Senate confirmation hearings then. Judge

44 Justice Ginsburg makes this point in dissent. *Id.* at 2798.

45 The public is not wholly ignorant, to be sure. A CBS News poll in 2012 found that three-quarters of Americans believe that Supreme Court Justices "sometimes let their own personal or political views influence their decisions." See *Supreme Court/ Judiciary*, PollingReport.com, http://www.pollingreport.com/court.htm (last visited Aug. 5, 2015). The Public Religion Institute in 2013 found that fifty-five percent of those surveyed thought Supreme Court Justices were influenced by their own political views "a lot," while thirty-two percent thought they were influenced only "a little," and eight percent "not at all." *Id.* Despite these suspicions, when Supreme Court Justices are confirmed by the Senate, inquiry into their personal or political views is treated as off-limits. (Thanks to Mike Seidman for help on this topic.)

Posner's hearing was presided over by Senator Strom Thurmond of South Carolina, even then, in the early 1980s, a nearly octogenarian segregationist trying to pass as a member of the modern world. Senator Thurmond, reading from his prepared script, asked, "Do you agree that judges should just apply the law; they shouldn't make the law?"[46] Judge Posner, being a smart lawyer and scholar, explained that the choice was a false one: appellate courts are repeatedly asked to decide cases in which the law is not settled—that is one reason the cases are litigated through the stage of appellate review, after all—and in those cases, the courts must provide authoritative resolution, essential to a civilized society. So, of course, appellate judges must sometimes make new law, since no legislature—as Hart observed a half-century ago—could possibly anticipate all the problems that will arise. In other words, appellate judges must exercise moral and political judgment, an unavoidable part of their job. Senator Thurmond, already well into his dotage, did not respond to the actual answer, but moved on to the next question in his script. Now we come to the punch line of this curious story: when Judge Posner received the transcript of his confirmation hearing several weeks later, Senator Thurmond's initial question was correctly recorded, namely, "Do you agree that judges should just apply the law; they shouldn't make the law?"[47] But instead of Judge Posner's actual answer, the transcript read that Judge Posner simply replied, "Yes."[48]

Now this is America in 1981, not Stalinist Russia. Yet a federal judicial nominee's *actual* answer to a silly question by a political hack was *erased* from the historical record in order to comport with the political agenda of a President—Ronald Reagan—who liked to claim that he only wanted to appoint judges who apply the law, rather than make the law. But President Reagan and his advisors knew this was nonsense, just like Judge Posner. They knew that appellate judges must inevitably exercise moral and political judgment beyond the issues settled by the law in order to resolve the actual disputes that come before the appellate courts. How, in a democratic society, can such secrecy be justified?

In my view, it cannot. We should tell the truth to the electorate: lawmakers cannot anticipate all problems that will arise, but in a civilized society, we need courts to provide authoritative resolutions of disputes that are left unsettled by the existing sources of law. Courts play that role, and the "higher" the court, the more likely it is that court will be asked to exercise circumscribed moral and political judgment, akin to what we expect from honest legislators, assuming that term is not an oxymoron in America these days. Therefore, when such judges are to be appointed, the nominal representatives of the people should evaluate the quality of moral and political judgment the nominee would exercise. Will the nominee reflexively side with markets against state regulation, with majorities against minorities, with the religious against the non-religious, with color-blindness against sensitivity to the pernicious role of race in society, with the police against criminal defendants, with the current ideological fixations of the Republican Party against the current ideological fixations of the Democratic Party? Is the nominee sensitive to injustice, to the powerless, to the losers in the political process, or does she side reflexively with those in power, with the status quo? These questions should be central to the confirmation process of members of the super-legislature—or rather, they should be central *in public* to that process, since they are obviously central to the actual nominators. They are also, to be sure, the subject

46 See Christopher Shea, "The Last Honest Judicial Hearing?" *Wall St. J.* (Sept. 21, 2011, 12:19 PM), http://blogs.wsj.com/ideas-market/2011/09/21/the-last-honest-judicial-hearing/.

47 *Id.*

48 See *id.*

of speculation, rumors, and gossip, but that is not the same as making them central to the actual proceedings in which the Senate confirms a nominee. There are, certainly, many issues in which legal expertise is essential, but there is no shortage of candidates with the requisite expertise to parse technical points of law and it is rare indeed that a president puts forward a candidate for the super-legislature lacking that competence. What is not rare, unfortunately, is for presidents to put forward candidates for the super-legislature whom they choose based on their moral and political views, but then fail to acknowledge that fact to the rest of the polity, and indeed, to object when the Senate even asks about those views.

There is, one must acknowledge, a genuine worry about encouraging candor on these matters. The worry, simply put, is that it will embolden judges to overreach the legal limits *even more* than they already do. Perhaps so, but the status quo is that elected officials appoint super-legislators because of their moral and political views, but no one is permitted to discuss that fact in public. If, in fact, we had a public discussion of what all the insiders know—namely, that appellate judges at the highest levels *must* exercise moral and political judgment—then perhaps those judges who actually survive the process will be those whose moral and political judgments comport more closely with those of the polity at large.[49] A polity that might welcome a liberal one decade might not welcome her a decade later, and so that is yet another reason to abolish lifetime tenure for federal judges in favor of fixed term appointments, as other scholars have proposed.[50] But even before that happens, I do not see how, in a democratic society where transparency in the exercise of public power (outside a select realm of areas, such as national security) is a fundamental value, we can continue to tolerate the current charade of nominating lawyers to the Supreme Court without vetting, fully and in public, their moral and political views. Those crucial views will determine their decisions in a range of momentous constitutional matters, and sometimes not only there.

10
Ronald Dworkin
"Integrity in Law," from *Law's Empire*

A Large View

In this chapter we construct the third conception of law I introduced in Chapter 3. Law as integrity denies that statements of law are either the backward-looking factual reports of conventionalism or the forward-looking instrumental programs of legal pragmatism. It insists that legal claims are interpretive judgments and therefore combine

49 I assume for the sake of argument that majority approval suffices to "legitimate" the moral and political views of the judges. For independent reasons, this strikes me as dubious, but that would require a separate argument.

50 See, e.g., *Reforming the Court: Term Limits for Supreme Court Justices* (Roger C. Cramton & Paul D. Carrington eds., 2006); Letter from Paul Carrington, Professor, Duke University School of Law, et al. to Joseph Biden, Vice President, et al. (Feb. 2009), available at http://www.scotusblog.com/2009/02/groups-proposals-for-supreme-court-reform.

backward- and forward-looking elements; they interpret contemporary legal practice seen as an unfolding political narrative. So law as integrity rejects as unhelpful the ancient question whether judges find or invent law; we understand legal reasoning, it suggests, only by seeing the sense in which they do both and neither.

INTEGRITY AND INTERPRETATION

The adjudicative principle of integrity instructs judges to identify legal rights and duties, so far as possible, on the assumption that they were all created by a single author—the community personified—expressing a coherent conception of justice and fairness. We form our third conception of law, our third view of what rights and duties flow from past political decisions, by restating this instruction as a thesis about the grounds of law. According to law as integrity, propositions of law are true if they figure in or follow from the principles of justice, fairness, and procedural due process that provide the best constructive interpretation of the community's legal practice. Deciding whether the law grants Mrs. McLoughlin* compensation for her injury, for example, means deciding whether legal practice is seen in a better light if we assume the community has accepted the principle that people in her position are entitled to compensation.

Law as integrity is therefore more relentlessly interpretive than either conventionalism or pragmatism. These latter theories offer themselves *as* interpretations. They are conceptions of law that claim to show our legal practices in the best light these can bear, and they recommend, in their post-interpretive conclusions, distinct styles or programs for adjudication. But the programs they recommend are not themselves programs *of* interpretation: they do not ask judges deciding hard cases to carry out any further, essentially interpretive study of legal doctrine. Conventionalism requires judges to study law reports and parliamentary records to discover what decisions have been made by institutions conventionally recognized to have legislative power. No doubt interpretive issues will arise in that process: for example, it may be necessary to interpret a text to decide what statutes our legal conventions construct from it. But once a judge has accepted conventionalism as his guide, he has no further occasion for interpreting the legal record as a whole in deciding particular cases. Pragmatism requires judges to think instrumentally about the best rules for the future. That exercise may require interpretation of something beyond legal material: a utilitarian pragmatist may need to worry about the best way to understand the idea of community welfare, for example. But once again, a judge who accepts pragmatism is then done with interpreting legal practice as a whole.

Law as integrity is different: it is both the product of and the inspiration for comprehensive

---

* *Ed. note*: Here Dworkin refers to an English case he discusses in Chapter I of *Law's Empire*, *McLoughlin v. O'Brian* [1983] 1 A.C. 410, reversing [1981] Q.B. 599. Dworkin's sketch of the case (at p. 24) is as follows:

Mrs. McLoughlin's husband and four children were injured in an automobile accident in England at about 4 p.m. on October 19, 1973. She heard about the accident at home from a neighbor at about 6 p.m. and went immediately to the hospital, where she learned that her daughter was dead and saw the serious condition of her husband and other children. She suffered nervous shock and later sued the defendant driver, whose negligence had caused the accident, as well as other parties who were in different ways involved, for compensation for her emotional injuries. Her lawyer pointed to several earlier decisions of English courts awarding compensation to people who had suffered emotional injury on seeing serious injury to a close relative. But in all these cases the plaintiff had either been at the scene of the accident or had arrived within minutes. In a 1972 case, for example, a wife recovered—won compensation—for emotional injury; she had come upon the body of her husband immediately after his fatal accident [*Marshall v. Lionel Enterprises Inc.* (1972) O.R. 177]. In 1967 a man who was not related to any of the victims of a train crash worked for hours trying to rescue victims and suffered nervous shock from the experience. He was allowed to recover [*Chadwick v. British Transport* (1967) 1 W.L.R. 912]. Mrs. McLoughlin's lawyer relied on these cases as precedents, decisions which had made it part of the law that people in her position are entitled to compensation.

interpretation of legal practice. The program it holds out to judges deciding hard cases is essentially, not just contingently, interpretive; law as integrity asks them to continue interpreting the same material that it claims to have successfully interpreted itself. It offers itself as continuous with—the initial part of—the more detailed interpretations it recommends. We must therefore now return to the general study of interpretation we began in Chapter 2. We must continue the account given there of what interpretation is and when it is done well, but in more detail and directed more to the special interpretive challenge put to judges and others who must say what the law is.

INTEGRITY AND HISTORY

History matters in law as integrity: very much but only in a certain way. Integrity does not require consistency in principle over all historical stages of a community's law; it does not require that judges try to understand the law they enforce as continuous in principle with the abandoned law of a previous century or even a previous generation. It commands a horizontal rather than vertical consistency of principle across the range of the legal standards the community now enforces. It insists that the law—the rights and duties that flow from past collective decisions and for that reason license or require coercion—contains not only the narrow explicit content of these decisions but also, more broadly, the scheme of principles necessary to justify them. History matters because that scheme of principle must justify the standing as well as the content of these past decisions. Our justification for treating the Endangered Species Act as law, unless and until it is repealed, crucially includes the fact that Congress enacted it, and any justification we supply for treating that fact as crucial must itself accommodate the way we treat other events in our political past.

Law as integrity, then, begins in the present and pursues the past only so far as and in the way its contemporary focus dictates. It does not aim to recapture, even for present law, the ideals or practical purposes of the politicians who first created it. It aims rather to justify what they did (sometimes including, as we shall see, what they said) in an overall story worth telling now, a story with a complex claim: that present practice can be organized by and justified in principles sufficiently attractive to provide an honorable future. Law as integrity deplores the mechanism of the older "law is law" view as well as the cynicism of the newer "realism." It sees both views as rooted in the same false dichotomy of finding and inventing law. When a judge declares that a particular principle is instinct in law, he reports not a simple-minded claim about the motives of past statesmen, a claim a wise cynic can easily refute, but an interpretive proposal: that the principle both fits and justifies some complex part of legal practice, that it provides an attractive way to see, in the structure of that practice, the consistency of principle integrity requires. Law's optimism is in that way conceptual; claims of law are endemically constructive, just in virtue of the kind of claims they are. This optimism may be misplaced: legal practice may in the end yield to nothing but a deeply skeptical interpretation. But that is not inevitable just because a community's history is one of great change and conflict. An imaginative interpretation can be constructed on morally complicated, even ambiguous terrain.

The Chain of Law

THE CHAIN NOVEL

I argued in Chapter 2 that creative interpretation takes its formal structure from the idea of intention, not (at least not necessarily) because it aims to discover the purposes of any particular historical person or group but because it aims to impose purpose over the text or data or tradition being interpreted. Since all creative interpretation shares this feature, and therefore has a normative aspect or component, we profit from comparing law with other forms or occasions of interpretation. We can usefully compare the judge deciding what the law is on some issue not only with the citizens of courtesy deciding what that tradition requires, but with the literary critic teasing out the various dimensions of value in a complex play or poem.

Judges, however, are authors as well as critics. A judge deciding *McLoughlin* or *Brown** adds to the tradition he interprets; future judges confront a new tradition that includes what he has done. Of course literary criticism contributes to the traditions of art in which authors work; the character and importance of that contribution are themselves issues in critical theory. But the contribution of judges is more direct, and the distinction between author and interpreter more a matter of different aspects of the same process. We can find an even more fruitful comparison between literature and law, therefore, by constructing an artificial genre of literature that we might call the chain novel.

In this enterprise a group of novelists writes a novel *seriatim*; each novelist in the chain interprets the chapters he has been given in order to write a new chapter, which is then added to what the next novelist receives, and so on. Each has the job of writing his chapter so as to make the novel being constructed the best it can be, and the complexity of this task models the complexity of deciding a hard case under law as integrity. The imaginary literary enterprise is fantastic but not unrecognizable. Some novels have actually

* *Ed. note*: Here Dworkin refers to a famous American case he discusses in Chapter I of *Law's Empire*, *Brown v. Board of Education* 347 U.S. 483 (1954). Dworkin's sketch of the case (at pp. 29–30) is as follows:

After the American Civil War the victorious North amended the Constitution to end slavery and many of its incidents and consequences. One of these amendments, the Fourteenth, declared that no state might deny any person the "equal protection of the laws." After Reconstruction the southern states, once more in control of their own politics, segregated many public facilities by race. Blacks had to ride in the back of the bus and were allowed to attend only segregated schools with other blacks. In the famous case of *Plessy v. Ferguson* [163 U.S. 537 (1896)] the defendant argued, ultimately before the Supreme Court, that these practices of segregation automatically violated the equal protection clause. The Court rejected their claim; it said that the demands of that clause were satisfied if the states provide separate but equal facilities and that the fact of segregation alone did not make facilities automatically unequal.

In 1954 a group of black schoolchildren in Topeka, Kansas, raised the question again. A great deal had happened to the United States in the meantime—a great many blacks had died for that country in a recent war, for example—and segregation seemed more deeply wrong to more people than it had when *Plessy* was decided. Nevertheless, the states that practiced segregation resisted integration fiercely, particularly in the schools. Their lawyers argued that since *Plessy* was a decision by the Supreme Court, that precedent had to be respected. This time the Supreme Court decided for the black plaintiffs. Its decision was unexpectedly unanimous, though the unanimity was purchased by an opinion, written by Chief Justice Earl Warren, that was in many ways a compromise. He did not reject the "separate but equal" formula outright; instead he relied on controversial sociological evidence to show that racially segregated schools could not be equal, for that reason alone. Nor did he say flatly that *if* the present decision was inconsistent with *Plessy*, then that earlier decision was being overruled. The most important compromise, for practical purposes, was in the design of the remedy the opinion awarded the plaintiffs. It did not order the schools of the southern states to be desegregated immediately, but only, in a phrase that became an emblem of hypocrisy and delay, "with all deliberate speed."

The decision was very controversial, the process of integration that followed was slow, and significant progress required many more legal, political, and even physical battles. Critics said that segregation, however deplorable as a matter of political morality, is not unconstitutional. They pointed out that the phrase "equal protection" does not in itself decide whether segregation is forbidden or not, that the particular congressmen and state officials who drafted, enacted, and ratified the Fourteenth Amendment were well aware of segregated education and apparently thought their amendment left it perfectly legal, and that the Court's decision in *Plessy* was an important precedent of almost ancient lineage and ought not lightly be overturned. These were arguments about the proper grounds of constitutional law, not arguments of morality or repair: many who made them agreed that segregation was immoral and that the Constitution would be a better document if it had forbidden it. Nor were the arguments of those who agreed with the Court arguments of morality or repair. If the Constitution did not as a matter of law prohibit official racial segregation, then the decision in *Brown* was an illicit constitutional amendment, and few who supported the decision thought they were supporting that. This case, like our other sample cases, was fought over the question of law. Or so it seems from the opinion, and so it seemed to those who fought it.

been written in this way, though mainly for a debunking purpose, and certain parlor games for rainy weekends in English country houses have something of the same structure. Television soap operas span decades with the same characters and some minimal continuity of personality and plot, though they are written by different teams of authors even in different weeks. In our example, however, the novelists are expected to take their responsibilities of continuity more seriously; they aim jointly to create, so far as they can, a single unified novel that is the best it can be.[1]

Each novelist aims to make a single novel of the material he has been given, what he adds to it, and (so far as he can control this) what his successors will want or be able to add. He must try to make this the best novel it can be construed as the work of a single author rather than, as is the fact, the product of many different hands. That calls for an overall judgment on his part, or a series of overall judgments as he writes and rewrites. He must take up some view about the novel in progress, some working theory about its characters, plot, genre, theme, and point, in order to decide what counts as continuing it and not as beginning anew. If he is a good critic, his view of these matters will be complicated and multifaceted, because the value of a decent novel cannot be captured from a single perspective. He will aim to find layers and currents of meaning rather than a single, exhaustive theme. We can, however, in our now familiar way give some structure to any interpretation he adopts, by distinguishing two dimensions on which it must be tested. The first is what we have been calling the dimension of fit. He cannot adopt any interpretation, however complex, if he believes that no single author who set out to write a novel with the various readings of character, plot, theme, and point that interpretation describes could have written substantially the text he has been given. That does not mean his interpretation must fit every bit of the text. It is not disqualified simply because he claims that some lines or tropes are accidental, or even that some events of plot are mistakes because they work against the literary ambitions the interpretation states. But the interpretation he takes up must nevertheless flow throughout the text; it must have general explanatory power, and it is flawed if it leaves unexplained some major structural aspect of the text, a subplot treated as having great dramatic importance or a dominant and repeated metaphor. If no interpretation can be found that is not flawed in that way, then the chain novelist will not be able fully to meet his assignment; he will have to settle for an interpretation that captures most of the text, conceding that it is not wholly successful. Perhaps even that partial success is unavailable; perhaps every interpretation he considers is inconsistent with the bulk of the material supplied to him. In that case he must abandon the enterprise, for the consequence of taking the interpretive attitude toward the text in question is then a piece of internal skepticism: that nothing can count as continuing the novel rather than beginning anew.

He may find, not that no single interpretation fits the bulk of the text, but that more than one does. The second dimension of interpretation then requires him to judge which of these eligible readings makes the work in progress best, all things considered. At this point his more substantive aesthetic judgments, about the importance or insight or realism or beauty of different

1 Perhaps this is an impossible assignment; perhaps the project is doomed to produce not just an impossibly bad novel but no novel at all, because the best theory of art requires a single creator or, if more than one, that each must have some control over the whole. (But what about legends and jokes? What about the Old Testament, or, on some theories, the *Iliad*?) I need not push that question further, because I am interested only in the fact that the assignment makes sense, that each of the novelists in the chain can have some grasp of what he is asked to do, whatever misgivings he might have about the value or character of what will then be produced.

ideas the novel might be taken to express, come into play. But the formal and structural considerations that dominate on the first dimension figure on the second as well, for even when neither of two interpretations is disqualified out of hand as explaining too little, one may show the text in a better light because it fits more of the text or provides a more interesting integration of style and content. So the distinction between the two dimensions is less crucial or profound than it might seem. It is a useful analytical device that helps us give structure to any interpreter's working theory or style. He will form a sense of when an interpretation fits so poorly that it is unnecessary to consider its substantive appeal, because he knows that this cannot outweigh its embarrassments of fit in deciding whether it makes the novel better, everything taken into account, than its rivals. This sense will define the first dimension for him. But he need not reduce his intuitive sense to any precise formula; he would rarely need to decide whether some interpretation barely survives or barely fails, because a bare survivor, no matter how ambitious or interesting it claimed the text to be, would almost certainly fail in the overall comparison with other interpretations whose fit was evident.

We can now appreciate the range of different kinds of judgments that are blended in this overall comparison. Judgments about textual coherence and integrity, reflecting different formal literary values, are interwoven with more substantive aesthetic judgments that themselves assume different literary aims. Yet these various kinds of judgments, of each general kind, remain distinct enough to check one another in an overall assessment, and it is that possibility of contest, particularly between textual and substantive judgments, that distinguishes a chain novelist's assignment from more independent creative writing. Nor can we draw any flat distinction between the stage at which a chain novelist interprets the text he has been given and the stage at which he adds his own chapter, guided by the interpretation he has settled on. When he begins to write he might discover in what he has written a different, perhaps radically different, interpretation. Or he might find it impossible to write in the tone or theme he first took up, and that will lead him to reconsider other interpretations he first rejected. In either case he returns to the text to reconsider the lines it makes eligible.

SCROOGE

We can expand this abstract description of the chain novelist's judgment through an example. Suppose you are a novelist well down the chain. Suppose Dickens never wrote *A Christmas Carol*, and the text you are furnished, though written by several people, happens to be the first part of that short novel. You consider these two interpretations of the central character: Scrooge is inherently and irredeemably evil, an embodiment of the untarnished wickedness of human nature freed from the disguises of convention he rejects; or Scrooge is inherently good but progressively corrupted by the false values and perverse demands of high capitalist society. Obviously it will make an enormous difference to the way you continue the story which of these interpretations you adopt. If you have been given almost all of *A Christmas Carol* with only the very end to be written—Scrooge has already had his dreams, repented, and sent his turkey—it is too late for you to make him irredeemably wicked, assuming you think, as most interpreters would, that the text will not bear that interpretation without too much strain. I do not mean that no interpreter could possibly think Scrooge inherently evil after his supposed redemption. Someone might take that putative redemption to be a final act of hypocrisy, though only at the cost of taking much else in the text not at face value. This would be a poor interpretation, not because no one could think it a good one, but because it is in fact, on all the criteria so far described, a poor one.[2]

But now suppose you have been given only the first few sections of *A Christmas Carol*. You find that neither of the two interpretations you are considering is decisively ruled out by anything in the text so far; perhaps one would better explain some minor incidents of plot that must be left unconnected on the other, but each interpretation can be seen generally to flow through the abbreviated text as a whole. A competent novelist who set out to write a novel along either of the lines suggested could well have written what you find on the pages. In that case you have a further decision to make. Your assignment is to make of the text the best it can be, and you will therefore choose the interpretation you believe makes the work more significant or otherwise better. That decision will probably (though not inevitably) depend on whether you think that real people somewhat like Scrooge are born bad or are corrupted by capitalism. But it will depend on much else as well, because your aesthetic convictions are not so simple as to make only this aspect of a novel relevant to its overall success. Suppose you think that one interpretation integrates not only plot but image and setting as well; the social interpretation accounts, for example, for the sharp contrast between the individualistic fittings and partitions of Scrooge's countinghouse and the communitarian formlessness of Bob Cratchit's household. Now your aesthetic judgment—about which reading makes the continuing novel better as a novel—is itself more complex because it must identify and trade off different dimensions of value in a novel. Suppose you believe that the original sin reading is much the more accurate depiction of human nature, but that the sociorealist reading provides a deeper and more interesting formal structure for the novel. You must then ask yourself which interpretation makes the work of art better on the whole. You may never have reflected on that sort of question before—perhaps the tradition of criticism in which you have been trained takes it for granted that one or the other of these dimensions is the more important—but that is no reason why you may not do so now. Once you make up your mind you will believe that the correct interpretation of Scrooge's character is the interpretation that makes the novel better on the whole, so judged.

This contrived example is complex enough to provoke the following apparently important question. Is your judgment about the best way to interpret and continue the sections you have been given of *A Christmas Carol* a free or a constrained judgment? Are you free to give effect to your own assumptions and attitudes about what novels should be like? Or are you bound to ignore these because you are enslaved by a text you cannot alter? The answer is plain enough: neither of these two crude descriptions—of total creative freedom or mechanical textual constraint—captures your situation, because each must in some way be qualified by the other. You will sense creative freedom when you compare your task with some relatively more mechanical one, like direct translation of a text into a foreign language. But you will sense constraint when you compare it with some relatively less guided one, like beginning a new novel of your own.

It is important not only to notice this contrast between elements of artistic freedom and textual constraint but also not to misunderstand its character. It is *not* a contrast between those aspects of interpretation that are dependent on and those that are independent of the interpreter's aesthetic convictions. And it is not a contrast between those aspects that may be and those that cannot be controversial. For the constraints that you sense as limits to your freedom to read *A Christmas Carol* so as to make Scrooge

2 See the debate cited in Chapter 2, n. 16.

irredeemably evil are as much matters of judgment and conviction, about which different chain novelists might disagree, as the convictions and attitudes you call on in deciding whether the novel would have been better if he had been irredeemably evil. If the latter convictions are "subjective" (I use the language of external skepticism, reluctantly, because some readers will find it helpful here) then so are the former. Both major types of convictions any interpreter has—about which readings fit the text better or worse and about which of two readings makes the novel substantively better—are internal to his overall scheme of beliefs and attitudes; neither type is independent of that scheme in some way that the other is not.

That observation invites the following objection. "If an interpreter must in the end rely on what seems right to him, as much in deciding whether some interpretation fits as in deciding whether it makes the novel more attractive, then he is actually subject to no genuine constraint at all, because no one's judgment can be constrained except by external, hard facts that everyone must agree about." The objection is misconceived because it rests on a piece of dogmatism. It is a familiar part of our cognitive experience that some of our beliefs and convictions operate as checks in deciding how far we can or should accept or give effect to others, and the check is effective even when the constraining beliefs and attitudes are controversial. If one scientist accepts stricter standards for research procedure than another, he will believe less of what he would like to believe. If one politician has scruples that another politician in good faith rejects, the first will be constrained when the second is not. There is no harm, once again, in using the language of subjectivity the external skeptic favors. We might say that in these examples the constraint is "internal" or "subjective." It is nevertheless phenomenologically genuine, and that is what is important here. We are trying to see what interpretation is like from the point of view of the interpreter, and from that point of view the constraint he feels is as genuine as if it were uncontroversial, as if everyone else felt it as powerfully as he does. Suppose someone then insists that from an "objective" point of view there is no real constraint at all, that the constraint is *merely* subjective. If we treat this further charge as the external skeptic's regular complaint, then it is pointless and misleading in the way we noticed in Chapter 2. It gives a chain novelist no reason to doubt or abandon the conclusions he reaches, about which interpretations fit the text well enough to count, for example, or so poorly that they must be rejected if other interpretations, otherwise less attractive, are available.

The skeptical objection can be made more interesting, however, if we weaken it in the following way. It now insists that a felt constraint may sometimes be illusory not for the external skeptic's dogmatic reason, that a genuine constraint must be uncontroversial and independent of other beliefs and attitudes, but because it may not be sufficiently disjoint, within the system of the interpreter's more substantive artistic convictions, ever actually to check or impede these, even from his point of view.[3] That is a lively possibility, and we must be on guard against it when we criticize our own or other people's interpretive arguments. I made certain assumptions about the structure of your aesthetic opinions when I imagined your likely overall judgment about *A Christmas Carol.* I assumed that the different types of discrete judgments you combine in your overall opinion are sufficiently independent of one another, within the system of your ideas, to allow some to constrain others. You reject reading Scrooge's supposed redemption as hypocritical for "formal" reasons about coherence

3 See *A Matter of Principle*, chap. 7.

and integration of plot and diction and figure. A decent novel (you think) would not make a hypocritical redemption the upshot of so dramatic and shattering an event as Scrooge's horrifying night. These formal convictions are independent of your more substantive opinions about the competing value of different literary aims: even if you think a novel of original sin would be more exciting, that does not transform your formal conviction into one more amenable to the original sin interpretation. But suppose I am wrong in these assumptions about your mental life. Suppose we discover in the process of argument that your formal convictions are actually soldered to and driven by more substantive ones. Whenever you prefer a reading of some text on substantive grounds, your formal convictions automatically adjust to endorse it as a decent reading of that text. You might, of course, only be pretending that this is so, in which case you are acting in bad faith. But the adjustment may be unconscious, in which case you think you are constrained but, in the sense that matters, you actually are not. Whether any interpreter's convictions actually check one another, as they must if he is genuinely interpreting at all, depends on the complexity and structure of his pertinent opinions as a whole.

Our chain-novel example has so far been distorted by the unrealistic assumption that the text you were furnished miraculously had the unity of something written by a single author. Even if each of the previous novelists in the chain took his responsibilities very seriously indeed, the text you were given would show the marks of its history, and you would have to tailor your style of interpretation to that circumstance. You might not find any interpretation that flows through the text, that fits everything the material you have been given treats as important. You must lower your sights (as conscientious writers who join the team of an interminable soap opera might do) by trying to construct an interpretation that fits the bulk of what you take to be artistically most fundamental in the text. More than one interpretation may survive this more relaxed test. To choose among these, you must turn to your background aesthetic convictions, including those you will regard as formal. Possibly no interpretation will survive even the relaxed test. That is the skeptical possibility I mentioned earlier: you will then end by abandoning the project, rejecting your assignment as impossible. But you cannot know in advance that you will reach that skeptical result. You must try first. The chain-novel fantasy will be useful in the later argument in various ways, but that is the most important lesson it teaches. The wise-sounding judgment that no one interpretation could be best must be earned and defended like any other interpretive claim.

A MISLEADING OBJECTION

A chain novelist, then, has many difficult decisions to make, and different chain novelists can be expected to make these differently. But his decisions do not include, nor are they properly summarized as, the decision whether and how far he should depart from the novel-in-progress he has been furnished. For he has nothing he *can* depart from or cleave to until he has constructed a novel-in-process from the text, and the various decisions we have canvassed are all decisions he must make just to do this. Suppose you have decided that a sociorealist interpretation of the opening sections of *A Christmas Carol* makes that text, on balance, the best novel-so-far it can be, and so you continue the novel as an exploration of the uniformly degrading master-servant relation under capitalism rather than as a study of original sin. Now suppose someone accuses you of rewriting the "real" novel to produce a different one that you like better. If he means that the "real" novel can be discovered in some way other than by a process of interpretation of the sort you conducted, then he has misunderstood not only the chain-novel enterprise but the nature of literature and criticism. Of course, he may mean only that he disagrees with the particular interpretive and aesthetic convictions on which you relied. In that case your disagreement is not that he thinks you should respect the text, while you think you are free to ignore it. Your disagreement is more interesting: you disagree about what respecting this text means.

Law: The Question of Emotional Damages

Law as integrity asks a judge deciding a common-law case like *McLoughlin* to think of himself as an author in the chain of common law. He knows that other judges have decided cases that, although not exactly like his case, deal with related problems; he must think of their decisions as part of a long story he must interpret and then continue, according to his own judgment of how to make the developing story as good as it can be. (Of course the best story for him means best from the standpoint of political morality, not aesthetics.) We can make a rough distinction once again between two main dimensions of this interpretive judgment. The judge's decision—his postinterpretive conclusions—must be drawn from an interpretation that both fits and justifies what has gone before, so far as that is possible. But in law as in literature the interplay between fit and justification is complex. Just as interpretation within a chain novel is for each interpreter a delicate balance among different types of literary and artistic attitudes, so in law it is a delicate balance among political convictions of different sorts; in law as in literature these must be sufficiently related yet disjoint to allow an overall judgment that trades off an interpretation's success on one type of standard against its failure on another. I must try to exhibit that complex structure of legal interpretation, and I shall use for that purpose an imaginary judge of superhuman intellectual power and patience who accepts law as integrity.

Call him Hercules.[4] In this and the next several chapters we follow his career by noticing the types of judgments he must make and tensions he must resolve in deciding a variety of cases. But I offer this caution in advance. We must not suppose that his answers to the various questions he encounters *define* law as integrity as a general conception of law. They are the answers I now think best. But law as integrity consists in an approach, in questions rather than answers, and other lawyers and judges who accept it would give different answers from his to the questions it asks. You might think other answers would be better. (So might I, after further thought.) You might, for example, reject Hercules' views about how far people's legal rights depend on the reasons past judges offered for their decisions enforcing these rights, or you might not share his respect for what I shall call "local priority" in common-law decisions. If you reject these discrete views because you think them poor constructive interpretations of legal practice, however, you have not rejected law as integrity but rather have joined its enterprise.

SIX INTERPRETATIONS

Hercules must decide *McLoughlin*. Both sides in that case cited precedents; each argued that a decision in its favor would count as going on as before, as continuing the story begun by the judges who decided those precedent cases. Hercules must form his own view about that issue. Just as a chain novelist must find, if he can, some coherent view of character and theme such that a hypothetical single author with that view could have written at least the bulk of the novel so far, Hercules must find, if he can, some coherent theory about legal rights to compensation for emotional injury such that a single political official with that theory could have reached most of the results the precedents report.

4 Hercules played an important part in *Taking Rights Seriously*, chap. 4.

He is a careful judge, a judge of method. He begins by setting out various candidates for the best interpretation of the precedent cases even before he reads them. Suppose he makes the following short list: (1) No one has a moral right to compensation except for physical injury. (2) People have a moral right to compensation for emotional injury suffered at the scene of an accident against anyone whose carelessness caused the accident but have no right to compensation for emotional injury suffered later. (3) People should recover compensation for emotional injury when a practice of requiring compensation in their circumstances would diminish the overall costs of accidents or otherwise make the community richer in the long run. (4) People have a moral right to compensation for any injury, emotional or physical, that is the direct consequence of careless conduct, no matter how unlikely or unforeseeable it is that that conduct would result in that injury. (5) People have a moral right to compensation for emotional or physical injury that is the consequence of careless conduct, but only if that injury was reasonably foreseeable by the person who acted carelessly. (6) People have a moral right to compensation for reasonably foreseeable injury but not in circumstances when recognizing such a right would impose massive and destructive financial burdens on people who have been careless out of proportion to their moral fault.

These are all relatively concrete statements about rights and, allowing for a complexity in (3) we explore just below, they contradict one another. No more than one can figure in a single interpretation of the emotional injury cases. (I postpone the more complex case in which Hercules constructs an interpretation from competitive rather than contradictory principles, that is, from principles that can live together in an overall moral or political theory though they sometimes pull in different directions.)[5] Even so, this is only a partial list of the contradictory interpretations someone might wish to consider; Hercules chooses it as his initial short list because he knows that the principles captured in these interpretations have actually been discussed in the legal literature. It will obviously make a great difference which of these principles he believes provides the best interpretation of the precedents and so the nerve of his postinterpretive judgment. If he settles on (1) or (2), he must decide for Mr. O'Brian; if on (4), for Mrs. McLoughlin. Each of the others requires further thought, but the line of reasoning each suggests is different. (3) invites an economic calculation. Would it reduce the cost of accidents to extend liability to emotional injury away from the scene? Or is there some reason to think that the most efficient line is drawn just between emotional injuries at and those away from the scene? (5) requires a judgment about foreseeability of injury, which seems to be very different, and (6) a judgment both about foreseeability and the cumulative risk of financial responsibility if certain injuries away from the scene are included.

Hercules begins testing each interpretation on his short list by asking whether a single political official could have given the verdicts of the precedent cases if that official were consciously and coherently enforcing the principles that form the interpretation. He will therefore dismiss interpretation (1) at once. No one who believed that people never have rights to compensation for emotional injury could have reached the results of those past decisions cited in *McLoughlin* that allowed compensation. Hercules will also dismiss interpretation (2), though for a different reason. Unlike (1), (2) fits the past decisions; someone who accepted (2) as a standard would have reached these decisions, because they all allowed recovery for emotional injury at the scene and

5 See the discussion of critical legal studies later in this chapter.

none allowed recovery for injury away from it. But (2) fails as an interpretation of the required kind because it does not state a principle of justice at all. It draws a line that it leaves arbitrary and unconnected to any more general moral or political consideration.

What about (3)? It might fit the past decisions, but only in the following way. Hercules might discover through economic analysis that someone who accepted the economic theory expressed by (3) and who wished to reduce the community's accident costs would have made just those decisions. But it is far from obvious that (3) states any principle of justice or fairness. Remember the distinction between principles and policies we discussed toward the end of the last chapter. (3) supposes that it is desirable to reduce accident costs overall. Why? Two explanations are possible. The first insists that people have a right to compensation whenever a rule awarding compensation would produce more wealth for the community overall than a rule denying it. This has the form, at least, of a principle because it describes a general right everyone is supposed to have. I shall not ask Hercules to consider (3) understood in that way now, because he will study it very carefully in Chapter 8. The second, quite different, explanation suggests that it is sometimes or even always in the community's general interest to promote overall wealth in this way, but it does not suppose that anyone has any right that social wealth always be increased. It therefore sets out a policy that government might or might not decide to pursue in particular circumstances. It does not state a principle of justice, and so it cannot figure in an interpretation of the sort Hercules now seeks.[6]

Law as integrity asks judges to assume, so far as this is possible, that the law is structured by a coherent set of principles about justice and fairness and procedural due process, and it asks them to enforce these in the fresh cases that come before them, so that each person's situation is fair and just according to the same standards. That style of adjudication respects the ambition integrity assumes, the ambition to be a community of principle. But as we saw at the end of Chapter 6, integrity does not recommend what would be perverse, that we should all be governed by the same goals and strategies of policy on every occasion. It does not insist that a legislature that enacts one set of rules about compensation today, in order to make the community richer on the whole, is in any way committed to serve that same goal of policy tomorrow. For it might then have other goals to seek, not necessarily in place of wealth but beside it, and integrity does not frown on this diversity. Our account of interpretation, and our consequent elimination of interpretation (3) read as a naked appeal to policy, reflects a discrimination already latent in the ideal of integrity itself.

We reach the same conclusion in the context of *McLoughlin* through a different route, by further reflection on what we have learned about interpretation. An interpretation aims to show what is interpreted in the best light possible, and an interpretation of any part of our law must therefore attend not only to the substance of the decisions made by earlier officials but also to how—by which officials in which circumstances—these decisions were made. A legislature does not need reasons of principle to justify the rules it enacts about driving, including rules about compensation for accidents, even though these rules will create rights and duties for the future that will then be enforced by coercive threat. A legislature may justify its decision to create new rights

6 The disagreement between Lords Edmund Davies and Scarman in *McLoughlin*, described in Chapter 1, was perhaps over just this claim. Edmund Davies's suggestions, about the arguments that might justify a distinction between compensable and non-compensable emotional injury, seemed to appeal to arguments of policy Scarman refused to acknowledge as appropriate.

for the future by showing how these will contribute, as a matter of sound policy, to the overall good of the community as a whole. There are limits to this kind of justification, as we noticed in Chapter 6. The general good may not be used to justify the death penalty for careless driving. But the legislature need not show that citizens already have a moral right to compensation for injury under particular circumstances in order to justify a statute awarding damages in those circumstances.

Law as integrity assumes, however, that judges are in a very different position from legislators. It does not fit the character of a community of principle that a judge should have authority to hold people liable in damages for acting in a way he concedes they had no legal duty not to act. So when judges construct rules of liability not recognized before, they are not free in the way I just said legislators are. Judges must make their common-law decisions on grounds of principle, not policy: they must deploy arguments why the parties actually had the "novel" legal rights and duties they enforce at the time the parties acted or at some other pertinent time in the past.[7] A legal pragmatist would reject that claim. But Hercules rejects pragmatism. He follows law as integrity and therefore wants an interpretation of what judges did in the earlier emotional damage cases that shows them acting in the way he approves, not in the way he thinks judges must decline to act. It does not follow that he must dismiss interpretation (3) read in the first way I described, as supposing that past judges acted to protect a general legal right to compensation when this would make the community richer. For if people actually have such a right, others have a corresponding duty, and judges do not act unjustly in ordering the police to enforce it. The argument disqualifies interpretation (3) only when this is read to deny any such general duty and to rest on grounds of policy alone.

EXPANDING THE RANGE

Interpretations (4), (5), and (6) do, however, seem to pass these initial tests. The principles of each fit the past emotional injury decisions, at least on first glance, if only because none of these precedents presented facts that would discriminate among them. Hercules must now ask, as the next stage of his investigation, whether any one of the three must be ruled out because it is incompatible with the bulk of legal practice more generally. He must test each interpretation against other past judicial decisions, beyond those involving emotional injury, that might be thought to engage them. Suppose he discovers, for example, that past decisions provide compensation for physical injury caused by careless driving only if the injury was reasonably foreseeable. That would rule out interpretation (4) unless he can find some principled distinction between physical and emotional injury that explains why the conditions for compensation should be more restrictive for the former than the latter, which seems extremely unlikely.

Law as integrity, then, requires a judge to test his interpretation of any part of the great network of political structures and decisions of his community by asking whether it could form part of a coherent theory justifying the network as a whole. No actual judge could compose anything approaching a full interpretation of all of his community's law at once. That is why we are imagining a Herculean judge of superhuman talents and endless time. But an actual judge can imitate Hercules in a limited way. He can allow the scope of his interpretation to fan out from the cases immediately in point to cases in the same general area or department of law, and then still farther, so far as this seems promising. In practice

7 See *Taking Rights Seriously*, chap. 4.

even this limited process will be largely unconscious: an experienced judge will have a sufficient sense of the terrain surrounding his immediate problem to know instinctively which interpretation of a small set of cases would survive if the range it must fit were expanded. But sometimes the expansion will be deliberate and controversial. Lawyers celebrate dozens of decisions of that character, including several on which the modern law of negligence was built.[8] Scholarship offers other important examples.[9]

Suppose a modest expansion of Hercules' range of inquiry does show that plaintiffs are denied compensation if their physical injury was not reasonably foreseeable at the time the careless defendant acted, thus ruling out interpretation (4). But this does not eliminate either (5) or (6). He must expand his survey further. He must look also to cases involving economic rather than physical or emotional injury, where damages are potentially very great: for example, he must look to cases in which professional advisers like surveyors or accountants are sued for losses others suffer through their negligence. Interpretation (5) suggests that such liability might be unlimited in amount, no matter how ruinous in total, provided that the damage is foreseeable, and (6) suggests, on the contrary, that liability is limited just because of the frightening sums it might otherwise reach. If one interpretation is uniformly contradicted by cases of that sort and finds no support in any other area of doctrine Hercules might later inspect, and the other is confirmed by the expansion, he will regard the former as ineligible, and the latter alone will have survived. But suppose he finds, when he expands his study in this way, a mixed pattern. Past decisions permit extended liability for members of some professions but not for those of others, and this mixed pattern holds for other areas of doctrine that Hercules, in the exercise of his imaginative skill, finds pertinent.

The contradiction he has discovered, though genuine, is not in itself so deep or pervasive as to justify a skeptical interpretation of legal practice as a whole, for the problem of unlimited damages, while important, is not so fundamental that contradiction within it destroys the integrity of the larger system. So Hercules turns to the second main dimension, but here, as in the chain-novel example, questions of fit surface again, because an interpretation is *pro tanto* more satisfactory if it shows less damage to integrity than its rival. He will therefore consider whether interpretation (5) fits the expanded legal record better than (6). But this cannot be a merely mechanical decision; he cannot simply count the number of past decisions that must be conceded to be "mistakes" on each interpretation. For these numbers may reflect only accidents like the number of cases that happen to have come to court and not been settled before verdict. He must take into account not only the numbers of decisions counting for each interpretation, but whether the decisions expressing one principle seem more important or fundamental or wide-ranging than the decisions expressing the other. Suppose interpretation (6) fits only those past judicial decisions involving charges of negligence against one particular profession—say, lawyers—and interpretation (5) justifies all other cases, involving all other professions, and also fits other kinds of economic damage cases as well. Interpretation (5) then fits the legal record better on the whole, even if the number of cases involving lawyers is for some reason numerically greater, unless the argument shifts again, as it well might, when the field of study expands even more.

Now suppose a different possibility: that though liability has in many and varied cases

8 See *Thomas v. Winchester*, 6 N.Y. 397, and *MacPherson v. Buick Motor Co.*, 217 N.Y. 382, 111 N.E. 1050.

9 C. Haar and D. Fessler, *The Wrong Side of the Tracks* (New York, 1986), is a recent example of integrity working on a large canvas.

actually been limited to an amount less than interpretation (5) would allow, the opinions attached to these cases made no mention of the principle of interpretation (6), which has in fact never before been recognized in official judicial rhetoric. Does that show that interpretation (5) fits the legal record much better, or that interpretation (6) is ineligible after all? Judges in fact divide about this issue of fit. Some would not seriously consider interpretation (6) if no past judicial opinion or legislative statement had ever explicitly mentioned its principle. Others reject this constraint and accept that the best interpretation of some line of cases may lie in a principle that has never been recognized explicitly but that nevertheless offers a brilliant account of the actual decisions, showing them in a better light than ever before.[10] Hercules will confront this issue as a special question of political morality. The political history of the community is *pro tanto* a better history, he thinks, if it shows judges making plain to their public, through their opinions, the path that later judges guided by integrity will follow and if it shows judges making decisions that give voice as well as effect to convictions about morality that are widespread through the community. Judicial opinions formally announced in law reports, moreover, are themselves acts of the community personified that, particularly if recent, must be taken into the embrace of integrity.[11] These are among his reasons for somewhat preferring an interpretation that is not too novel, not too far divorced from what past judges and other officials said as well as did. But he must set these reasons against his more substantive political convictions about the relative moral value of the two interpretations, and if he believes that interpretation (6) is much superior from that perspective, he will think he makes the legal record better overall by selecting it even at the cost of the more procedural values. Fitting what judges did is more important than fitting what they said.

Now suppose an even more unpatterned record. Hercules finds that unlimited liability has been enforced against a number of professions but has not been enforced against a roughly equal number of others, that no principle can explain the distinction, that judicial rhetoric is as split as the actual decisions, and that this split extends into other kinds of actions for economic damage. He might expand his field of survey still further, and the picture might change if he does. But let us suppose he is satisfied that it will not. He will then decide that the question of fit can play no more useful role in his deliberations even on the second dimension. He must now emphasize the more plainly substantive aspects of that dimension: he must decide which interpretation shows the legal record to be the best it can be from the standpoint of substantive political morality. He will compose and compare two stories. The first supposes that the community personified has adopted and is enforcing the principle of foreseeability as its test of moral responsibility for damage caused by negligence, that the various decisions it has reached are intended to give effect to that principle, though it has often lapsed and reached decisions that foreseeability would condemn. The second supposes, instead, that the community has adopted and is enforcing the principle of foreseeability limited by some overall ceiling on liability, though it has often lapsed from that principle. Which story shows the community in a better light, all things considered, from the standpoint of political morality?

Hercules' answer will depend on his convictions about the two constituent virtues of political morality we have considered: justice and

10 See, for example, Benjamin Cardozo's decision in *Hynes v. New York Central R.R. Co.*, 231 N.Y. 229.

11 These various arguments why a successful interpretation must achieve some fit with past judicial opinions as well as with the decisions themselves are discussed in Chapter 9 in the context of past legislative statements.

fairness.[12] It will depend, that is, not only on his beliefs about which of these principles is superior as a matter of abstract justice but also about which should be followed, as a matter of political fairness, in a community whose members have the moral convictions his fellow citizens have. In some cases the two kinds of judgment—the judgment of justice and that of fairness—will come together. If Hercules and the public at large share the view that people are entitled to be compensated fully whenever they are injured by others' carelessness, without regard to how harsh this requirement might turn out to be, then he will think that interpretation (5) is plainly the better of the two in play. But the two judgments will sometimes pull in different directions. He may think that interpretation (6) is better on grounds of abstract justice, but know that this is a radical view not shared by any substantial portion of the public and unknown in the political and moral rhetoric of the times. He might then decide that the story in which the state insists on the view he thinks right, but against the wishes of the people as a whole, is a poorer story, on balance. He would be preferring fairness to justice in these circumstances, and that preference would reflect a higher-order level of his own political convictions, namely his convictions about how a decent government committed to both fairness and justice should adjudicate between the two in this sort of case.

Judges will have different ideas of fairness, about the role each citizen's opinion should ideally play in the state's decision about which principles of justice to enforce through its central police power. They will have different higher-level opinions about the best resolution of conflicts between these two political ideals. No judge is likely to hold the simplistic theory that fairness is automatically to be preferred to justice or vice versa. Most judges will think that the balance between the opinions of the community and the demands of abstract justice must be struck differently in different kinds of cases. Perhaps in ordinary commercial or private law cases, like *McLoughlin*, an interpretation supported in popular morality will be deemed superior to one that is not, provided it is not thought very much inferior as a matter of abstract justice. But many judges will think the interpretive force of popular morality very much weaker in constitutional cases like *Brown*, because they will think the point of the Constitution is in part to protect individuals from what the majority thinks right.[13]

...

A Provisional Summary

... Judges who accept the interpretive ideal of integrity decide hard cases by trying to find, in some coherent set of principles about people's rights and duties, the best constructive interpretation of the political structure and legal doctrine of their community. They try to make that complex structure and record the best these can be. It is analytically useful to distinguish different dimensions or aspects of any working theory. It will include convictions about both fit and justification. Convictions about fit will provide a rough threshold requirement that an interpretation of some part of the law must meet if it is to be eligible at all. Any plausible working theory would disqualify an interpretation of our own law that denied legislative competence or supremacy outright or that claimed a general principle of private law requiring the rich to share their wealth with the poor. That threshold will eliminate interpretations that some judges would otherwise prefer, so the brute facts of legal history will in this way limit the role any judge's personal

12 I have in mind the distinction and the special sense of fairness described in Chapter 6.

13 But see the discussion of "passivism" as a theory of constitutional adjudication in Chapter 10.

convictions of justice can play in his decisions. Different judges will set this threshold differently. But anyone who accepts law as integrity must accept that the actual political history of his community will sometimes check his other political convictions in his overall interpretive judgment. If he does not—if his threshold of fit is wholly derivative from and adjustable to his convictions of justice, so that the latter automatically provide an eligible interpretation—then he cannot claim in good faith to be interpreting his legal practice at all. Like the chain novelist whose judgments of fit automatically adjusted to his substantive literary opinions, he is acting from bad faith or self-deception.

Hard cases arise, for any judge, when his threshold test does not discriminate between two or more interpretations of some statute or line of cases. Then he must choose between eligible interpretations by asking which shows the community's structure of institutions and decisions—its public standards as a whole—in a better light from the standpoint of political morality. His own moral and political convictions are now directly engaged. But the political judgment he must make is itself complex and will sometimes set one department of his political morality against another: his decision will reflect not only his opinions about justice and fairness but his higher-order convictions about how these ideals should be compromised when they compete. Questions of fit arise at this stage of interpretation as well, because even when an interpretation survives the threshold requirement, any infelicities of fit will count against it, in the ways we noticed, in the general balance of political virtues. Different judges will disagree about each of these issues and will accordingly take different views of what the law of their community, properly understood, really is.

Any judge will develop, in the course of his training and experience, a fairly individualized working conception of law on which he will rely, perhaps unthinkingly, in making these various judgments and decisions, and the judgments will then be, for him, a matter of feel or instinct rather than analysis. Even so, we as critics can impose structure on his working theory by teasing out its rules of thumb about fit—about the relative importance of consistency with past rhetoric and popular opinion, for example—and its more substantive opinions or leanings about justice and fairness. Most judges will be like other people in their community, and fairness and justice will therefore not often compete for them. But judges whose political opinions are more eccentric or radical will find that the two ideals conflict in particular cases, and they will have to decide which resolution of that conflict would show the community's record in the best light. Their working conceptions will accordingly include higher-order principles that have proved necessary to that further decision. A particular judge may think or assume, for example, that political decisions should mainly respect majority opinion, and yet believe that this requirement relaxes and even disappears when serious constitutional rights are in question.

We should now recall two general observations we made in constructing the chain-novel model, because they apply here as well. First, the different aspects or dimensions of a judge's working approach—the dimensions of fit and substance, and of different aspects of substance—are in the last analysis all responsive to his political judgment. His convictions about fit, as these appear either in his working threshold requirement or analytically later in competition with substance, are political not mechanical. They express his commitment to integrity: he believes that an interpretation that falls below his threshold of fit shows the record of the community in an irredeemably bad light, because proposing that interpretation suggests that the community has characteristically dishonored its own principles. When an interpretation meets the threshold, remaining defects of fit may be compensated, in his overall judgment, if the principles of that interpretation are particularly attractive, because then he sets off the community's infrequent lapses in respecting these principles against its virtue in generally observing them. The constraint fit imposes on substance, in any working theory, is therefore the constraint of one type of political conviction on another in the overall judgment which interpretation makes a political record the best it can be overall, everything taken into account. Second, the mode of this constraint is the mode we identified in the chain novel. It is not the constraint of external hard fact or of interpersonal consensus. But rather the structural constraint of different kinds of principle within a system of principle, and it is none the less genuine for that.

No mortal judge can or should try to articulate his instinctive working theory so far, or make that theory so concrete and detailed, that no further thought will be necessary case by case. He must treat any general principles or rules of thumb he has followed in the past as provisional and stand ready to abandon these in favor of more sophisticated and searching analysis when the occasion demands. These will be moments of special difficulty for any judge, calling for fresh political judgments that may be hard to make. It would be absurd to suppose that he will always have at hand the necessary background convictions of political morality for such occasions. Very hard cases will force him to develop his conception of law and his political morality together in a mutually supporting way. But it is nevertheless possible for any judge to confront fresh and challenging issues as a matter of principle, and this is what law as integrity demands of him. He must accept that in finally choosing one interpretation over another of a much contested line of precedents, perhaps after demanding thought and shifting conviction, he is developing his working conception of law in one rather than another direction. This must seem to him the right direction as a matter of political principle, not just appealing for the moment because it recommends an attractive decision in the immediate case. There is, in this counsel, much room for deception, including self-deception. But on most occasions it will be possible for judges to recognize when they have submitted an issue to the discipline it describes. And also to recognize when some other judge has not.

Study Questions

1. Why does Holmes suppose the view of the "bad man" provides an answer to the question "What is law?"?
2. To what extent does legal realism still require a concept of law?
3. What, if anything, is wrongly omitted from a realist picture of law which focuses on the operations of courts, as Holmes and Leiter do?
4. How successful are Dworkin's two central metaphors in his argument for law as integrity? Can these metaphors apply to any legal system?
5. Can an approach of constructive interpretation guard against the kind of biases and dispositions the legal realists think are characteristic of judicial decision-making?

Further Readings

Benjamin N. Cardozo, *The Nature of the Judicial Process*. New Haven: Yale UP, 1921.
Neil Duxbury, *Patterns of American Jurisprudence*. Oxford: Clarendon P, 1995.
Ronald Dworkin, *Justice in Robes*. Cambridge, MA: Harvard UP, 2006.
William W. Fisher, Morton J. Horwitz, and Thomas A. Reed, eds., *American Legal Realism*. Oxford: Oxford UP, 1993.
John Chipman Gray, *The Nature and Sources of the Law*. New York: Columbia UP, 1909.
Stephen Guest, *Ronald Dworkin*. Edinburgh: Edinburgh UP, 1997.
Scott Hershovitz, ed., *Exploring Law's Empire: The Jurisprudence of Ronald Dworkin*. Oxford: Oxford UP, 2006.
Brian Leiter, *Naturalized Jurisprudence: Essays on American Legal Realism and Naturalism in Legal Philosophy*. Oxford: Oxford UP, 2007.
Karl Llewellyn, *Bramble Bush: On Our Law and Its Study*. Oxford: Oceana Publications, 1960.
Stefan Sciaraffa and Wil Waluchow, eds., *The Legacy of Ronald Dworkin*. Oxford: Oxford UP, 2016.

SECTION 4

Feminist Jurisprudence and Critical Race Theory

Introduction

This section contains work from the feminist jurisprudence movement and the Critical Race Theory movement. These movements share certain features, so while we discuss each movement independently, it may be helpful to begin with a short list of similarities.

First, both movements are relatively new. Feminist jurisprudence is rooted in the second wave feminist movement of the 1960s. Critical Race Theory or "CRT" gained its name in 1989, drawing inspiration from the Critical Legal Studies or "CLS" movement which emerged from a conference held in Madison, Wisconsin in the summer of 1977. The conference brought together a group of lawyers, law professors, sociologists and anthropologists who shared general socialist leanings and great dissatisfaction with prevailing views of law and legal practice—particularly views which apparently ignore the extent to which law is an embodiment of the interests of the most powerful persons in a given society.

Second, both feminist jurisprudence and CRT are composed largely of "outsiders on the inside" of law schools and universities, united in their concern to understand the gap between the ideals taught in law schools, and the actual consequences and character of life under law. These movements began from the "outsider" observation that important aspects of lived experience are sometimes ignored by academic treatment of law, and insist that actual experience of law in the world must be better accounted for by law and legal theory.

Third, both movements are skeptical of "conceptual" jurisprudence of the sort done by positivists and natural lawyers. Taking a position reminiscent of the American Legal Realists, many feminists and CRT scholars are skeptical of the possibility of "objective" or "neutral" analysis of legal concepts such as legal system, legal norms, legal duties, legal rights, property, and harm. According to feminists, the law and legal concepts reflect a distinctively male or "patriarchal" view of the world. According to Critical Legal Studies scholars the law and legal concepts reflect a certain narrow group of political values—an insight they derive from Marxist thought. Critical Race Theory accepts this insight, then turns it on its head, asking us to examine not just the way class or group interests influence law, but the way law affects the specific lived experience of individual members of a particular group, such as racialized persons. We then find, CRT scholars argue, that apparently neutral legal concepts are often interpreted and applied in ways which reinforce the interests of elites. Some CRT writers go so far as to argue that key legal concepts are indeterminate, lacking fixed edges to their meaning and application. They point to various examples of indeterminate legal concepts whose application in practice shows little about any possible determinate "core" meaning of the term, and much more about the interests of those with power to apply the concept in practice. The idea of legal equality, for example, is sometimes interpreted in a "color-blind" or "difference-blind" fashion as though that will ensure that racialized persons are not singled out for discrimination. Yet this "blindness" is in fact discriminatory in its own way, as it ignores the fact that, for example,

African American women differ from African American men in their needs, experiences, and opportunities, and the needs and experience of African Americans may differ from the needs and experience of Hispanic-Americans. Legal concepts such as equality must be interpreted and applied much differently if they are to be more than tools of elite interests.

Fourth, feminist jurisprudence and CRT writers agree that gender and race have been mistakenly viewed as topics at the edge of jurisprudence, worth considering only once core tasks in conceptual jurisprudence are complete. Feminist and CRT writers hold the opposite view: gender and race should be at the center of jurisprudence, since gender and race are at the center of the assumptions of the elites who control the structure and practice of law in ways which distort and undervalue the experience and needs of women and racialized persons. This insight is the key to another, closely associated insight. The centrality of gender and race to elite conceptions of law means that male-serving and racist legal structures and practices are not occasional missteps in the life of legal systems. Instead, feminists and CRT writers argue, male-centered and racist social structures and law are the norm—a state of affairs which needs to change, but until that time of change, stands as the ordinary, normal social situation.

Fifth, each movement holds that the political and legal spheres of public life are inseparable. The orthodox view holds that politics ends once legislation is enacted. After that point, the will of the legislative body is captured in a legal rule with determinate content and meaning, applied by politically neutral judges who merely enforce the will of the legislative body. Yet according to feminist jurisprudence and CRT scholars, the making of law and the application of law are never distinct. In fact, judges' application of law frequently reflects the fact that judges come from the same social class or gender or race as legislators and share legislators' views about the values which ought to be supported by the courts. Feminist jurisprudence shares with American Legal Realism the conviction that more attention must be paid to the people and institutions which apply laws, and more attention must be paid to the impossibility of achieving politically neutral interpretation and application of legal norms.

Sixth, both feminists and CRT scholars look to history and social science for evidence that law, legal concepts, and legal institutions contain biases against certain groups or interests. Evidence from disciplines such as sociology and criminology show that gender, class, and ethnic differences between rulers and ruled are large, even in common law societies whose laws and democratic systems promote equality of opportunity and do not explicitly give any one group privileges not equally available to any other group.

Seventh, and linked to the sixth similarity, feminists and CRT writers are concerned with the *substantive* effect of law more than its *formal* appearance. This is a crucial shared concern. Where orthodox legal theory often proceeds on the assumption that the institutions and language of the law are very closely related to what in fact happens in the world, feminists and CRT scholars argue that there is often a great difference between the formal language and apparatus of the law and the actual practical, or substantive, effect of law. Both feminism and CRT point to equality rights to illustrate this point: despite the introduction of equality rights in common law systems, women and minorities have not in fact achieved effective, substantive equality with white men in daily life. At best, only partial progress has been made toward the state of equality required by law. Reflection on the reasons behind the failure of "color-blind" and "gender-blind" attempts to achieve equality may even cause us to doubt the value of the ideal of equality as the best means to justice for all. Perhaps we need something quite different, possibly a kind of *pluralism* recognizing the diversity of experiences and human situations governed by law, adjusted to meet their diverse characteristics and needs. Whatever we do, feminists and CRT scholars, in particular, are agreed that reform is needed. Precisely what ought to be done, and how, remains a matter of controversy.

1. Feminist Jurisprudence

Feminist jurisprudence spans a large spectrum of views about the differences between characteristically male and female reasoning and experience of the world, and political views about what changes ought to be made in law to reflect those differences. Feminist jurisprudence is likely best characterized in terms of two central features agreed upon by nearly all feminists. Feminists agree that male-dominated institutions and ways of thinking must be rejected, and nearly all feminists advocate rapid, effective reform promoted through changes in present laws and in the ways lawmakers think about making laws. Considerable debate surrounds both aspects of feminist jurisprudence. To what *extent* are male-dominated perspectives flawed and in need of repair? What *sort* of repair is appropriate? Is law as traditionally conceived *worth repairing* and revising to meet women's needs? Feminist thought is so diverse that it is impossible to isolate "the feminist position" on one of these issues without unfairly ignoring another plausible and clearly feminist position. The article by Professor Patricia Smith included here treats the diversity of feminist thought in closer detail, so we leave this topic to her.

What remains to be said in an introduction is that feminist advocacy for legal reform has achieved what many of its supporters regard as success in specific matters of importance to women. Areas of laws including criminal law treating sexual violence, family law, and employment law all bear the influence of feminist jurisprudence. Yet few supporters of feminist jurisprudence suppose its arguments have had the effect they are due when their real merit is fully understood. So unlike the Critical Legal Studies movement's gradual loss of a sense of a need for its existence, the feminist jurisprudence movement sees its work as far from being done. At present, the remaining work appears to be associated with both historic feminist concerns regarding the patriarchy, and newer concerns expressed by theorists and practitioners reflecting on male-dominated institutions from the perspective of persons whose identities and interests are not those of the male-dominated institutions, yet are not the same as those expressed by historic feminist critics.

In the first quarter of the twenty-first century discussion of personal identity has raised a set of challenges to dominant legal understandings of personhood and to common law systems' commitment to the equality of all persons before the law. Attention to the distinction between sex as a matter of biology and gender as a matter of role or identity has driven debate regarding a number of matters once regarded as largely settled, from questions regarding the nature of marriage to questions regarding the nature of a family, with important implications for the way persons conduct their life plans as individuals and as families. At the intersection between social morality and law, the interplay between the two sometimes engages questions far beyond the historic focus of legal theory. Yet history reminds us that legal theory cannot easily isolate its questions from nearby areas of social inquiry. Today all legal systems in the common law tradition recognize that women are persons, fundamentally equal to men before the law. That status is, however, relatively recent. In the case of Canada, for example, in what is known as the "Persons Case," the judges deciding *Edwards v. Canada (Attorney General)* positively recognized women as persons in the sense required to be "qualified persons" eligible for appointment to Canada's Senate—and prior to that decision, women were not regarded as "persons" so could not be senators. The decision has had profound effects in Canada as several generations of Canadian women have been born and lived as "persons" without any question as to their status. We will see in the decades to come how new discussions of the nature of gender identity may provide a basis for new criticism and reform of law related to personal identity, and how in some matters settled law may remain settled and evidence created or found to support natural law theories contending that law can and must correspond to the knowable natural order of things.

1.1 CRITICISM OF LAWS ADVANCING PATRIARCHAL VIEWS

The roots of feminist thought, in the western world and beyond, lie in dissatisfaction with *patriarchy*—literally, "father-rule." Early feminist writers lived in a social environment controlled by men and directed largely to serving the interests of men. Consciously or not, male holders of power tended to exclude women from power, and when making laws these power-holders usually excluded female perspectives and experience. It is unsurprising, then, that much early feminist writing about law focused on the law's treatment of women as less than equal, and argued that such treatment was based on an arbitrary, ill-considered distinction between men and women. Many feminist writers came to believe that patriarchal domination of society is much more deeply entrenched than initially expected, and a great effort has been made to understand the *extent* to which male-dominated modes of thinking have been embedded so deeply in social practices that they are taken as the "obvious" or "natural" perspective. While conducting this investigation into male nature and male bias in law and other social practices, many feminists have tried to develop a contrasting view of female nature and typically female characteristics, to better understand which aspects of law are most dominated by masculine modes of thought. This has revealed a huge number of problems, as women vary in religion, culture, level of education, and so forth. So even when feminist writers are convinced that some aspect of social life is dominated by patriarchy, it is often very difficult to uncover the identity of any distinctively and essentially female perspective, both because it is obscured by so many generations of patriarchal domination and because women's perspectives are so diverse. Debate continues regarding the possibility of feminist "essentialism," the view that some parts of female experience are universal and so form the essential or necessary core of a feminist account of some topic. Some of the most successful attempts to determine the existence of a distinctly female perspective on law and social norms have come in work on areas of law relevant to all women: rape, pornography, abortion and reproductive rights, marriage, and traditionally unpaid domestic labor. Historically women have had the least control over these aspects of their lives, and the law in these areas has typically been designed by men without consultation with women. Feminist writers working in these areas have contributed a great deal to the legal literature and to reform of law.

1.2 CRITICISM OF THE PATRIARCHAL MODE OF THINKING

From what has been said above, it may seem that feminist jurisprudence has been more critical than constructive and directed only toward reform of law in ways directly relevant to women. Seen in this light, feminist jurisprudence appears to fall short of being a theory of law or of forming a basis for a larger theory of law in the future. Yet this would be a serious misunderstanding of the possibilities opened by feminist jurisprudence. Feminists' attempts to reform laws which harm women are motivated in part by the obvious need to stop the harmful effects of bad law sooner rather than later; but many feminists are also motivated by the need to show plain, indisputable examples of the way patriarchy and patriarchal thinking have become embedded in law. Such examples are evidence for feminists' larger concern that typically male ways of thinking about law must be replaced.

In an article included in this volume, University of Michigan law professor Catharine MacKinnon suggests that it is difficult to even conceive of what a feminist jurisprudence might look like. Why is this so difficult? According to feminist thought, patriarchal modes of thinking dominate the way we evaluate claims to knowledge and claims about the existence of certain features of social life (e.g., the existence of oppression). MacKinnon and many other feminist writers believe that it is difficult to uncover female perspectives and female ideas for reform of law because women are so completely immersed in a male-dominated and frequently hostile society. An analogy will help to clarify the situation: it is as if feminists find themselves in a society which assumes that everyone is right-handed, yet feminists are left-handed and are forced to use the available right-handed tools until something better can be devised. And of course, in a situation where a right-handed tool has accomplished the task in an apparently adequate manner for a long time, there would be a great deal of debate about the design of the new tool for left-handers. Should it be an exact copy of the right-handed tool but converted to the left-handed way of doing things, or should it be a different tool altogether? Many feminists claim that the law should be revised entirely, to escape what they perceive to be the negative consequences of patriarchal *epistemology* (theory of knowledge) and *ontology* (theory of what it is for something to exist). A new jurisprudence must reflect women's experience and women's perceptions of social relations, acknowledge the existence of unfair and oppressive social norms which must be eliminated, and acknowledge the value of women's knowledge gained from their position as the oppressed. So, although there can be no doubting the importance of feminist criticism of laws relating specifically to women, the more far-reaching feminist challenge is epistemological and ontological—a challenge to re-examine and revise the foundations of legal thought.

2. Critical Race Theory

Critical Race Theory includes a wide range of views, so this introduction necessarily offers only a sketch of themes and points of departure shared by CRT writers. As you explore Critical Race Theory, it is also worth remembering that it is always dangerous to try to identify central themes of movements which are new and still finding their identity. This danger may be especially evident in thinking about Critical Race Theory, a movement which emphasizes experiences of race which might not be fully understood by writers who have not had those experiences themselves. It is up to you to consider this possibility, and to use these introductory remarks on CRT themes as just that: an introduction to be supplemented with your own reading and thinking.

The article provided here was written by one of the founders of the Critical Race Theory movement, Professor Richard Delgado of the University of Alabama. Delgado's article expresses what this introduction identifies as some defining themes of Critical Race Theory, and shows us what those themes do to advance our understanding of race and law in both American society and others. Some of the conclusions of Delgado's argument may also be very useful, for example, to the understanding of societies such as South Africa in which race has long played a central role in conceptions of society, law, and justice.

2.1 NARRATIVES

Critical Race Theory writers have often tried to break out of usual or expected ways of expressing experiences relevant to understanding the actual effects of law on minorities of color. One especially controversial approach is the use of narratives, dramatic representations of particular situations. Professor Richard Delgado is famous for his *Rodrigo Chronicles*, which use a narrative approach. Something of the flavor of that style can be found in the article by Professor Delgado included here. He begins his discussion with a dialogue between a lawyer and St. Peter as the lawyer asks to be let into heaven. Some critics of this approach say that it loses the message in the mechanism of the dramatic dialogue, or worse, that the narrative approach is just not capable of providing the sort of careful, rigorous marshalling of evidence and argument needed to support CRT's insights. Others respond that dramatic characterizations of ideas have long been known to be effective as ways of putting a certain kind of argument forward. Plato, for example, conducted dialogues in which a particular approach to questioning ideas is shown in action as well as discussed in more formal terms.

Critical Race Theorists have used narrative approaches in various ways, all united in expressing specific experiences that resist easy classification under an essentialist account of what it is like to be a member of a racialized group. Some narratives are used to provide a context for an account of an experience which might otherwise be easily misinterpreted. Other narratives try to express vividly and forcefully an experience whose nature and importance might not be completely captured by ordinary methods of description. Still other narratives show how events might be viewed differently by someone with a different set of assumptions and priorities. In the article provided here, Delgado's lawyer is quite surprised that his having followed the rules might not be enough to get him into heaven. His point of view led him to assume that following the rules was the same thing as doing justice and being the kind of person worthy of admission to heaven. This narrative approach offers a striking and memorable way to raise the question of the limits of a particular point of view to life under law, leaving the reader ready to hear more about what might be missing from particular ways of understanding law.

2.2 SPECIFIC EXPERIENCES UNDER SPECIFIC LAWS

At the core of the Critical Legal Studies movement there is wide agreement that law and legal systems very often fall short of delivering justice. Instead, law and legal systems tend to be the tools of elites who intentionally or unthinkingly use law to support their own elite interests. As we saw in discussion of the similarities between the feminist jurisprudence movement and Critical Race Theory, CRT writers have often agreed with the general claim that law is a tool used by elites to manipulate others. Where CLS does not go far enough, according to many CRT writers, is in its understanding of the specific and diverse ways in which minorities of color can experience the way elites use law to support their interests.

Professor Delgado's article is an excellent example of the way many CRT writers have used close analysis of a specific situation to simultaneously draw attention to the issues in that particular situation, and to make a larger point. Professor Delgado uses the interaction between the apparently compatible civil liberty of freedom of speech[1]

1 This is the civil right protected in the United States Constitution's first amendment, which reads, "Congress shall make no law respecting an establishment of religion, or prohibiting the free exercise thereof; or abridging the freedom of speech, or of the press; or the right of the people peaceably to assemble, and to petition the Government for a redress of grievances."

and the civil right to equality[2] to show that they are in tension or competition in various ways. Racialized persons have suffered the consequences of some of these tensions, particularly when free speech rights serve to protect hate speech that aims to undermine equality. At the same time he develops the more general argument that this particular conflict between a civil right and a civil liberty is just one instance of the way conflicts between civil rights and civil liberties are more generally resolved so that the dominance of elites over racialized persons is reinforced.

Immediately following his narrative regarding the lawyer and St. Peter, Delgado's article asks a question which builds from the narrative's contrast of rule-following with actual justice, asking us to now consider in greater detail the actual effects and interactions of ideals and laws. He asks: "What is the relationship between the group of largely formal rules known as civil liberties and the set of substantive values known as racial justice or civil rights?" Professor Delgado begins his answer to the question by examining the way freedom of speech (a civil liberty) really does sometimes support civil rights (such as equality), together with an explanation of the justifications often given when exercise of freedom of speech seems to endanger justice, often by conflicting with civil rights. Analysis of the value of freedom of speech does not, however, stop there.

In what might be regarded as the core of his argument, Delgado explains the elements of a Critical Race Theory analysis of freedom of speech. Tracing a chain of court decisions as well as arguments from Critical Race Theory writers, Delgado shows how legal theorists and practitioners have come to recognize that the practice of free speech is more complicated than its supporters let on. Professor Delgado identifies three aspects of the complex interaction between free speech (a positive "freedom to" speak) and the social and legal context in which speech is made, a context including a civil right to equality (a negative "freedom from" certain forms of discrimination).

The first interaction is the "conceptual" or theoretical conflict between speech and equality, closely related to what Delgado views as a conflict between the capitalist or free market economic model, and the needs of democracy. The civil liberty of free speech is typically exercised by individuals, yet its effects can be felt by both individuals and groups. In an extreme instance of legally protected speech, hate speech by an individual can damage an entire group and its attempts to assert its members' civil right to a quality of citizenship equal to that enjoyed by other citizens. Similarly, a system of property-holding which serves free-market goals tends to be a system in which a few persons control a great deal of private property and the majority have relatively little. Hate speech can make a powerful contribution to this imbalance, as the denial of equality can limit access to employment and property, leaving poorer citizens focusing on survival rather than democratic participation. If liberties can routinely be interpreted in ways which impair equality rights, originally designed to carry force equal to that of the liberties, what is the real value of the equality rights? This conceptual tension shows that further attention is needed, Delgado suggests, to the way we understand the balance between the important interests expressed in both civil liberties and civil rights.

The second interaction is "historical," drawing attention to the way the balance between specific

2 This is the civil right protected in the United States Constitution's fourteenth amendment, which reads in part, "All persons born or naturalized in the United States, and subject to the jurisdiction thereof, are citizens of the United States and of the State wherein they reside. No State shall make or enforce any law which shall abridge the privileges or immunities of citizens of the United States; nor shall any State deprive any person of life, liberty, or property, without due process of law; nor deny to any person within its jurisdiction the equal protection of the laws."

civil liberties and specific civil rights has varied over time. When the United States has focused on its core ideals as it has sought to define itself in the face of international competition and opposition, civil rights have been strongly emphasized. Yet when the United States has suffered a sense of insecurity, civil rights have sometimes been curbed as part of efforts to regain a sense of security. Civil rights, then, are perhaps not the bedrock of American society, always guaranteeing a basic minimum kind of citizenship for all.

Identification of an "ideological and constitutional" tension between free speech and justice completes Delgado's discussion. Professor Delgado argues that it is a mistake to think that America's great successes as a society can be attributed to its support of civil liberties such as free speech rights. While there are great American successes in terms of national wealth and power, freedom of speech has received too much credit for its contribution. Freedom of speech is also closely tied to the less happy results of America's constitution and political ideals. Professor Delgado points to the way free speech rights have protected media stereotypes which leave real people bearing the weight of false claims about the threat or burden posed by persons fitting within a stereotype. The continued strength of American democracy and justice requires a different approach to interpreting the proper balance between civil liberties and civil rights, perhaps permitting slightly weaker civil liberties in some circumstances, to allow civil rights their proper effect and to foster a just American society and legal system. It may be helpful to a thorough understanding of Delgado's argument on this topic to spend some time investigating the recent history of hate speech in the United States, Canada, the United Kingdom, and elsewhere. You might, for example, look at Alabama of the early 1960s, where Governor George Wallace famously said in his 1963 inaugural speech that he would support "segregation today, segregation tomorrow, segregation forever."

2.3 A PRAGMATIC ATTITUDE TOWARD RIGHTS

Many CRT writers have been quite forceful in their insistence that the problems with existing legal orders can only be fixed by quite radical reforms. Professor Delgado's arguments are one instance of the much more pragmatic tendencies of many Critical Race Theorists. As Delgado's article makes clear, there is no shortage of evidence that civil liberties have sometimes been harmful or of little use to minorities of color, yet civil liberties have also been of undeniable benefit to minorities of color. Professor Delgado's conclusion faces the double-edged nature of civil liberties and their relation to civil rights. He suggests that there is an ongoing tension between two "equally valid" views of the world driving the sometimes opposed positions of those who emphasize the individual-focused aspects of civil liberties, and those who support the group- or community-focused aspects of civil rights. Both emphases are part of a viable overall system of justice under law, Delgado seems to suggest. Changes are certainly needed, according to his form of Critical Race Theory, but these changes can be identified while using some of the tools available in the system undergoing change.

It is up to you to consider the value of the pragmatic approach of many Critical Race Theorists, and to evaluate the CRT contribution to the understanding of law, legal concepts, and the relation between legal practice and legal ideals. As you consider the strengths and weaknesses of Delgado's argument, you can find more resources for your thinking in the references listed in the *Further Readings* for this chapter.

3. Intersectionality of Sex and Race

It might be easily thought that while there are many sources of inequality, such as gender-based and race-based inequality, as described above, there is no further or special value in considering whether their interaction and combination might offer us new insight. In the work by Professor Kimberlé Crenshaw included here, Crenshaw argues for the importance of the insight gained by analyzing sexual discrimination and racial discrimination together, and not as discrete forms of discrimination. Professor Crenshaw, who is also a prominent American civil rights advocate, examines several cases to illustrate how American anti-discrimination law fails to see Black women as a distinct group, subject to a special form of compounded discrimination rooted in the intersection of sex and race.

Consider the following hypothetical example. Suppose that a group of Black women challenge a company's hiring practices, claiming that Black women have been and continue to be seriously disadvantaged and overlooked. As anti-discrimination law works in many jurisdictions, the group must show that they have been discriminated against on the basis on both—taken individually—their sex and their race. But as they attempt to do so, they run into problems. They cannot demonstrate that they have been discriminated against on the basis of their sex, for the company can show that it has hired and continues to hire female employees. They also cannot demonstrate that they have been discriminated against on the basis of their race, for the company can show that it has hired and continues to hire Black employees. The problem, however, is that all the female employees are white, and all the Black employees are male. As long as the law does not recognize the intersection of grounds of discrimination, Black women as a distinct group, with distinct claims of discrimination, will never be recognized.

Professor Crenshaw surveys several areas of law and policy to show the tensions and conflicts which arise for Black women, who often must choose, to the exclusion of the other, which ground of discrimination is to matter most, their sex or their race. She also shows how such a choice, which dominant forms of law and policy force upon them, in turn can create further tensions, conflicts, and divisions within feminist and Black communities, since pursuit of one goal can often come at the cost of another. As Professor Crenshaw explains, the solution to intersectional discrimination must be responsive to the diagnosis:

> These problems of exclusion cannot be solved simply by including Black women within an already established analytical structure. Because the intersectional experience is greater than the sum of racism and sexism, any analysis that does not take intersectionality into account cannot sufficiently address the particular manner in which Black women are subordinated. Thus, for feminist theory and antiracist policy discourse to embrace the experiences and concerns of Black women, the entire framework that has been used as a basis for translating "women's experience" or "the Black experience" into concrete policy demands must be rethought and recast.

Professor Crenshaw's work has inspired both new work on the intersection of sex and race, and investigation of other forms of intersectionality involving combinations of other prominent grounds of discrimination, including disability, class, LGBTQ+, and ethnicity. "Intersectional theory" is now a well-established approach in the US and elsewhere to assessing the character and impact of anti-discrimination laws and policies. As you think about the various laws and policies affecting you and others around you, you may wish to consider how these laws and policies attempt to generalize across all experiences in a "neutral" or "objective" fashion, and doing so may fail to be attentive to the various ways in which they do not properly particularize the experiences of diverse individuals and groups. Agreement that all persons should be equal before the law may offer an incomplete foundation for legal systems seeking to implement the principle of the agreement in practice, as experience captured by legal scholars and others has shown that being proclaimed to be equal before the law and actually being so are often quite different for reasons closely connected to particular experiences of particular persons.

11

Patricia Smith

"Feminist Jurisprudence and the Nature of Law," from *Feminist Jurisprudence**

What is feminist jurisprudence? One prominent feminist scholar, Catharine MacKinnon, explained that feminist jurisprudence is the analysis of law from the perspective of all women. This provides us with a good point of departure, as it captures the central focus of feminism, which is to attempt to represent women's side of things. Feminist theory recognizes that throughout history and even today, public discourse has been almost exclusively conducted by men from (quite naturally) the perspective of men. That is, the nature of women has been formulated by men, and the interests of women have been determined by men. Historically, women have never been allowed to represent themselves. They have always been represented by men, but this representation has hardly been accurate or fair. Even though it claims to represent all human beings, the fact is that public discourse has left out, silenced, misrepresented, disadvantaged, and subordinated women throughout all of history, relegating them to a single role and reserving the rest of life for men. MacKinnon's explanation underscores this point.

Using her explanation as a definition, however, might create the impression that there is a single perspective of all women, which is certainly false. Not even all feminists hold a single perspective, and not all women, of course, are feminists. But all feminism does begin with one presumption, namely, that a patriarchal world is not good for women. Virtually everyone agrees that the world is, in fact, patriarchal; that is, human societies have always been organized in a hierarchical structure that subordinates women to men. This is simply the observation of a social fact. Until recently it was virtually impossible to imagine the world any other way, and even now a great many men and women think that patriarchy is good, natural, or inevitable. Feminists think that patriarchy (the subjugation of women) is not good, not ordained by nature, and not inevitable.

The rejection of patriarchy is the one point on which all feminists agree. It is also apparently a distinguishing feature of feminism as a school of thought, as no other school of thought focuses on the critique of institutions and attitudes as patriarchal. Only feminism analyzes the patriarchal

* Smith, Patricia. From Introduction (pp. 3–12), *Feminist Jurisprudence*, ed. Patricia Smith, Oxford University Press.

origin, nature, and effects of human attitudes, concepts, relations, and institutions and criticizes them on that ground. So we might take as a reasonable working definition that feminist jurisprudence is the analysis and critique of law as a patriarchal institution.

This analysis and critique manifests itself in a variety of ways, owing partly to the range of issues it covers and partly to divergence among feminists on virtually all points other than the rejection of patriarchy. Feminists tend to concentrate on issues of particular concern to women, such as equal protection law; discrimination in education, hiring, promotion, and pay; protection of reproductive freedom and other freedoms; protection from rape, sexual harassment, and spouse abuse; regulation of sexual and reproductive services such as surrogate mother contracts, prostitution, and pornography; and patriarchal bias in law and adjudication. But feminist analysis is appropriate to any area, concepts, relations, and institutions of law, and many legal theorists offer feminist critiques of standard legal categories such as contracts, property, and tort law. Clearly, the issues covered by feminist jurisprudence are as wide ranging as the areas covered by law. To appreciate the diversity of feminist jurisprudence, consider the differences among feminist theories.

Feminist Theories

The earliest explicit feminist writing is associated with the liberal tradition, as exemplified by Mary Wollstonecraft's eighteenth-century book *A Vindication of the Rights of Woman*, by John Stuart Mill's nineteenth-century *Subjection of Women*, and by Betty Friedan's twentieth-century *Feminine Mystique*. The general view is that the subordination of women is caused by the legal and social barriers that block or preclude their access to the public sphere of economic and political life. Liberal feminists demand that liberals follow their own principles of universal human rights. If all human beings are moral equals, as liberals have claimed since at least the seventeenth century, then men and women should be treated equally, which means that no one should be excluded from participating in political, educational, or economic life. Because they followed the classical liberal tradition, the early liberal feminists tended to be very individualistic, arguing for equal rights and equal freedom. They felt that the law should be gender blind, that there should be no special restrictions or special assistance on the basis of sex. Most of the gains made for women's equal rights and freedom in the 1960s and 1970s were made using liberal feminist arguments. The solution to the oppression of women, in this view, is to remove all formal barriers to their equal participation in social, political, and economic life, thus providing equal opportunity for all.

In the 1970s and 1980s some liberal feminists (including Friedan) began to rethink their position, as simply removing formal or legal restrictions did not seem to provide equal opportunity after all. Women still faced a great deal of informal discrimination and an uphill battle against old stereotypes that portrayed them as emotional, incompetent, and passive. Furthermore, even women who did manage to break into the male world of politics, economics, or academic life found themselves faced with a choice of eliminating any personal life whatsoever or working a double day, a choice that men did not have to face. Women found themselves responsible for home and family whether or not they also had a career, and this meant that most women could not compete on an equal footing with men who did not have this responsibility, precisely because it had been delegated to women. In response to this situation, many liberal feminists began to focus more on the socialization of children, the removal of stereotypes, the reorganization of family life, and the restructuring of state institutions to be more supportive of family needs. This change in focus mirrors the difference between classical liberal and modern welfare liberal views, but it is not a real change of position. The view of liberal feminists, whether classical or modern, is still that the solution to the oppression of women is to provide equal opportunity for all. The difference between the two views is in what constitutes equal opportunity.

Radical feminists believe that neither the classical nor the modern liberal view adequately explains women's oppression or provides effective solutions to it. Changing economic structures, eliminating political and educational barriers, and even socializing children will not abolish the subjugation of women so long as society is organized in a patriarchal system. Patriarchy is so pervasive that it structures our thoughts and attitudes, our assumptions and basic institutions, including the family and church. The only way to change the position of women is to change the way we think about gender itself, to reexamine our assumptions about our nature and relations to others. Although radical feminist views vary widely, most do focus on some aspect of the effect that biology has on women's psychology, their lives and their status, to recognize good effects as valuable and to overcome negative ones.

Some radical feminists (such as Adrienne Rich or Mary O'Brien) have concentrated on the significance of women as mothers (as child bearers and rearers), arguing either that women must be relieved of having the sole responsibility for these things or that because women are responsible for them, they must also be in control of them. Others (such as Shulamith Firestone or Kate Millett) look at the ways that gender and sexuality oppress women, for example, through sexual harassment, spouse abuse, rape, pornography, and the use of women as sex objects. Most radical feminists insist that male power or male dominance is the basis of the construction of gender and that this construction pervades all other institutions and ensures the perpetuation of patriarchy and thus the subordination of women. Some have suggested the promotion of androgeny (the appropriation of the full range of traits to both men and women) as a solution to the problem of patriarchy. Others contend that androgeny is not liberating for women and that the goal is, rather, to revalue those characteristics associated with the feminine role, such as nurturing and gentleness. Still others believe that because the feminine role and character have been constructed by patriarchy, women must reconstruct them for themselves—must find their true nature. Overall, in the most general terms, the focus of radical feminism is on the domination of women by men through the social construction of gender within patriarchy. For them the solution to the oppression of women is to reverse the institutional structures of domination and to reconstruct gender, thereby eliminating patriarchy.

Marxist and socialist feminists, however, believe that the construction of gender is not the primary issue. They think that equality for women is not possible in a class-based society established on the basic principles of private property and exploitation of the powerless. According to the Marxists, the oppression of women originated, or at least solidified, when the introduction of capitalism and private property sharply divided the world into private and public spheres of life, relegated women to the noneconomic private sphere, and devalued that sphere, that is, made it worthless in market terms. To relieve the oppression of women, the capitalist system must be replaced with a socialist system in which no class will be economically dependent or exploited by any other. The solution to the oppression of women is to change the economic system so that women will not be economically dependent, marginal, and exploited.

Many modern socialist feminists have nonetheless become dissatisfied with the traditional Marxist approach, as it fails to account adequately for the oppression of women as women rather than as workers, fails to explain the domination of women in the private as well as the public sphere, and fails to provide an analysis of gender and patriarchy. Some feminists have tried to combine economic (Marxist or socialist) theories with radical theories or psychoanalytical theories that attempt to deal with gender and patriarchy as such. In fact, many modern feminists think that no single theory can account for all aspects of the domination and oppression of women.

Furthermore, some feminists deny altogether the usefulness of general theories in their traditional form. This skepticism or denial of the utility of theory, at least "Grand Theory," is commonly associated with a loose collection of views often called *postmodern or French feminism*. The term *French feminism* originated from the fact that most of the early contributors were French (e.g., Hélène Cixous and Luce Irigaray) and that most follow the work of French thinkers associated with the postmodern movement, such as Jacques Derrida, Jacques Lacan, and Jean-François Lyotard. In law and jurisprudence, this approach is associated with a movement called *critical legal studies*, with which many post-modern feminists are closely associated. Like most postmodern thinkers, these feminists deny that categorical, abstract theories derived through reason and assumptions about the essence of human nature can serve as the foundation of knowledge. They call such ambitious theorizing *phallologocentric*, meaning that it is centered on an absolute word (*logos*) that reflects a male perspective (*phallus*). They claim that it is a male approach to believe that a single answer or a single truth can be found that will organize all issues and lead to a single reformative strategy. Above all, postmodern feminism is critical. Often following Derrida, many postmodern feminists use techniques of *deconstruction* to expose the internal contradictions of apparently coherent systems of thought. This has been a useful method of debunking patriarchal structures of thought and social organization, including law. Other postmodern feminists, following Lacan, are interested in reinterpreting traditional Freudian psychoanalysis, with all its implications for biological determinism and the subordination of women.

In addition, many postmodern feminists display attachments to existentialism in terms of their focus on the "Other." Existentialists have always portrayed the Other as a negative status. To be the Other is to be objectified, determined, and marginalized. Simone de Beauvoir considered the fundamental question of feminism to be "why is woman the Other?" She considered the oppression of women to be an expression of their status as the Other, as the sex objectified by men. Postmodern feminists, however, celebrate Otherness. Because they are criticizing the mainstream of thought and society, the "Law of the Fathers" or the "Symbolic Order," there is a positive side to Otherness, as it disassociates itself from the mainstream accepted structures of reality, knowledge, and society: To be Other to patriarchy is not necessarily a bad thing.

In general, postmodern feminists do not offer a single solution to the oppression of women, first, because they do not think that there can be single solutions to anything. Second, to propose a single solution to *the* oppression of women suggests that all women's experiences are alike, that women's oppression is a unitary thing. But real human problems cannot be solved by abstract rules and generalizations. Rather, attacking the oppression of women requires contextual judgments that recognize and accommodate the particularity of human experience. As Deborah Rhode put it, "Such an approach demands that feminists shift self-consciously among needs to acknowledge both distinctiveness and commonality between sexes and unity and diversity among their members." For postmodern feminists there is no single solution and no single oppression of women, but only solutions tailored to the concrete experience of actual people.

One problem with postmodern views, particularly those associated with deconstruction, is that they tend to be better at destroying theories than at building them, which may generate a debilitating skepticism that is not useful to the feminist cause in the long run. One response to this skepticism has been a revitalization of pragmatism within feminism. Pragmatism also subscribes to a postmodern antiessentialist theory of human nature and knowledge. In law it is associated with legal realist theory, which views law as a dynamic process of conflict resolution and focuses on the function of courts to analyze law and legal reasoning. Feminists are drawn to the practical, personal, contextual approach of pragmatism, which coincides with feminist rejection of traditional abstract categories, dichotomies, and the conceptual pretensions of the logical analysis of law.

Finally, a trend sometimes called *relational feminism* in some ways reverses the focus of some earlier theories, especially liberal theories that call for equal rights for women on the ground that men and women are fundamentally similar. Many recent relational feminist writers have been greatly influenced by the work of Harvard-educational psychologist Carol Gilligan. In her book *In a Different Voice*, Gilligan hypothesizes that men and women are not fundamentally similar; rather, men and women typically undergo a different moral development. The predominant moral attitude of men she calls the *ethic of justice*, which concentrates on abstract rules, principles, and rights. The predominant moral attitude of women Gilligan calls the *ethic of care*, which focuses on concrete relationships, concern for others, and responsibility. The important thing for Gilligan is to recognize the value of both, and especially not to devalue the ethic of care.

Following Gilligan, many relational feminists have argued that the important task for feminists today is not to fit women into a man's world, not to assimilate women into patriarchy, and not to prove that women can function like men and meet male norms, but to change institutions to reflect and accommodate the value that should properly be accorded to characteristics and virtues traditionally associated with women, nurturing virtues such as love, sympathy, patience, and concern. It is not that women should change to meet existing institutions but that institutions should be changed to accommodate women (or at least the best virtues associated with women). Of course, when put in these terms, most feminists would agree. No feminist thinks that women should be turned into clones of men, and there is increasing concern over what might be lost in the unthinking assimilation of women into male institutions.

The difference between liberal feminists on the one hand and relational feminists on the other represents a split among feminists and others as to whether men and women are fundamentally similar or fundamentally different, particularly in psychological and/or moral terms. This split is actually an old one that was prominent in the early twentieth century in debates about women's rights. The question is whether women, being basically similar to men, require equal treatment or, being significantly different from men, require special treatment. This question is reflected in many jurisprudential and legal debates today, and each side has its hazards. The deficiency of the liberal view is that treating men and women as exactly alike ignores genuine physical and social differences that tend to disadvantage the vast majority of women. But the deficiency of the relational view is that it can easily be transformed into the old, traditional stereotype of women as biologically domestic and dependent, which perpetuate bias, discrimination, and domination instead of counteracting it. Many feminists now think that this old debate needs to be ended or transcended, but exactly how to do this is not clear. It is clear, however, that the sameness/difference debate is a snag that has often divided feminists and hindered social progress.

There are (at least) three points that provide some ground for optimism that the old sameness/difference debate may, this time, be overcome. First, for postmodern theorists, the sameness/difference problem is a nonstarter in the first place, because dichotomies like sameness and difference are illusions caused by the flawed structural frameworks that generate them. That is, they rely on a faulty essentialist view of human nature. Insofar as post-modern thinking dominates intellectual life (which it may, at least among feminists, as the antiessentialist view is shared by pragmatists, existentialists, and many Marxists, socialists, and liberals), the sameness/difference problem has already been resolved by an overall critical view that does not recognize an essential human nature.

Second, unlike feminist theories of an earlier era, virtually every feminist theory today challenges male norms. This, for example, is the intended objective of relational feminism, even though it is highly susceptible to abuse or misinterpretation. So the following question has been raised: Even if men and women are different, why should the standard of measure be male? The simple (and accurate) answer, that historically it has always been male, is one explanation, but it is obviously not a justification. Because historical standards relied on historical discrimination, some ground other than history must be found for retaining them. But no other supportable ground has been forthcoming.

Finally, the fact that many feminists see the sameness/difference debate as a misformulation of the problem provides more possibilities for progress beyond it. To see how easy it is to fall into the patriarchal trap, look back to the statement that the question is whether women, being basically similar to men, require equal treatment, or being significantly different from men, require special treatment. What may not be obvious is that this essentially means, Heads I win, tails you lose. That is, it assumes the outcome in advance, for to agree that if women are "different" (i.e., different from men) they will require "special treatment" is to assume a male or patriarchal standard of what normal treatment is. Feminists today reject such a formulation of the problem, and so this question is no longer viewed as the crucial question that must be answered before further steps can be taken. In fact, many feminists now think that it is not even an answerable, or perhaps even a meaningful, question, and some have proposed alternative views. For example, some feminists suggest that it is not difference but disadvantage that should be the goal of legal and social reform; some argue that the focus should be directly on eliminating domination; and some seek common standards of human flourishing and/or pragmatic approaches that can contextualize the problem instead of presuming abstract or essentialist models of human nature or the structure of gender.

We do not need a final unified vision of society and gender, however, to argue against oppression, disadvantage, domination, and discrimination. We do not need to know beforehand the nature of the good society or the ideal person so long as we know what prevents a society from being minimally good or prevents an individual from realizing the basic potentials of personhood. We do not need an ultimate vision when we have not yet met threshold conditions for a minimally just society. Many visions are possible, and many theories are useful. The commitment to foster open dialogue that allows the expression of diverse views and gives particular attention to eliciting views not usually heard is a unifying thread among feminists that attempts to represent the commonality of fundamental values without misrepresenting the plurality of experience.

Some Basic Objections

The acceptance of diversity within feminism has led some critics (and even some feminists) to contend that there is therefore no common feminist perspective. There is no point of view of all women. Feminism can be reduced to those theories that inform its many facets. Liberal feminism is reducible to liberalism; postmodern feminism is reducible to post-modernism; and so on. Thus, it is claimed, feminism provides no new idea, no new theory. It is simply the application of old theories to the particular problem of women's oppression.

This objection is mistaken, however, for several reasons. First, even if it were true of some views (such as liberal feminism or Marxist feminism), it cannot be true of radical feminism, because the centerpiece of radical feminism is the structure of gender or sexual identity itself. Radical feminism starts with the idea of sexism as gender, the idea that gender is socially constructed within a hierarchy that embodies male domination and female subordination. Everything else flows from that. One may agree or disagree with this idea, but it cannot be reduced to another theory.

Furthermore, this core insight now informs all other feminist theories, whose differences are largely differences of emphasis. Nearly all feminists are too eclectic to fit neatly into any one category, and so it is misleading to set up categories or theories as though they worked in that limiting sort of way for feminists. Creating distinct or rigid categories within which to fit particular accounts or limit dialogue is a decidedly antifeminist way of proceeding, as feminists generally oppose this sort of abstract conceptualization without attention to context and detail. Instead, the way to use the general descriptions of the various feminist theories, such as those in the previous section, is simply to note and trace their influences, interactions, and manifestations in the particular views that people offer on specific issues. The function of general descriptions of theories in feminism is clarification and simplification, not limitation or reduction.

Finally, the one thing that unites all feminist theories and distinguishes them from all other theories is that their primary goal is the rejection of patriarchy. No matter what differences there are among these divergent views, and there certainly are many, this one point of reference is always shared. It is an irreducible point, and it distinguishes feminism from all the other ones.

Nonetheless, one can argue that if the entire project of feminist jurisprudence is to show that law is patriarchal, it is not intellectually very interesting. How can an entire jurisprudence be supported by the single ground of rejecting patriarchy? But this is a political position, one may contend, not a philosophical one.

The problem with this objection is that it assumes that the recognition and rejection of patriarchy is a small point, when in fact it is a revolutionary one. Likewise, noting that the world is not flat but round is a small point in the sense that it can be stated in a brief and simple sentence, and it is not philosophical in the sense that it is the observation of an empirical fact. But in another sense, it changes everything. Its implications are profound, and exploring some of those implications is of great philosophical interest, and so it is with the rejection of patriarchy.

Thus, the one new thing about feminism (or feminist jurisprudence) is the very fact that it is feminism, that it constitutes a critique of patriarchal institutions from the perspective of women. To put it more generally, it constitutes, at least potentially, a genuine critique of patriarchal institutions, structures, and assumptions from the perspective of a group that is outside those patriarchal structures, institutions, and assumptions, at least in the sense (among other things) that it did not participate in their formulation. This is the first time in the history of civilization that anything like that has been possible at a level that can be taken seriously.

Intellectually, this provides a new basis for an external critique of social structures. In *The Structure of Scientific Revolutions*, Thomas Kuhn explains such external critiques as paradigm shifts that represent revolutionary changes in thinking. Internal critique refines thinking within a framework. External critique rejects the old framework altogether and proposes a new paradigm in its place. External critique is not everything, but it can be extremely useful, especially for spotting assumptions that otherwise go unexamined because they are unnoticed. Internal critique tends to develop and refine details and spot inconsistencies within a structure or framework. External critique can challenge the entire framework, and thus external critique is also the most threatening and the hardest to understand or accept. It is like Martin Luther saying to the pope, "Why, as a Christian, do I need to be Catholic at all?" Luther's critique is external to Catholicism but still internal to Christianity and, of course, to religion. When Nietzsche declared that "God is dead," his critique was external to the idea of religion. Needless to say, both critiques were viewed with hostility and disbelief by those who were defending the status quo. Similarly, feminist jurisprudence challenges basic legal categories and concepts rather than analyzing them as given. Feminist jurisprudence asks what is implied in traditional categories, distinctions, or concepts and rejects them if they imply the subordination of women. In this sense, feminist jurisprudence is normative and claims that traditional jurisprudence and law are implicitly normative as well.

Because of this, feminist jurisprudence has the potential to offer some of the most intellectually stimulating critiques of legal structures today, and this would be much more readily recognized if it were not so politically and socially frightening. That is the problem with revolutionary critique: It is revolutionary. This means, first, that it is hard to understand or else to take seriously. Revolutionary external critique may sound strange, heretical, irrational, or silly because it starts from a different set of basic assumptions. The most difficult thing in the world for two people (let alone a group of people) to discuss reasonably are differing basic assumptions. They need some common ground to begin the discussion. So the first problem is just to understand the critique or to be able to take it seriously. The elimination of patriarchy would constitute a cultural revolution at least as profound as the Copernican revolution, the Protestant revolution, or the Industrial Revolution. Could anyone living before these revolutions imagine what life or human thought would be like after them? The first response to early feminism was ridicule. People could not imagine the status or role of women being different from what it always had been.

Second, if the critique is understood and taken seriously, it often scares people to death. Why? Why was the pope upset with Luther? Revolutionary critiques are frightening just because they are revolutionary. If they succeed, life will never be the same again. The end of patriarchy will be the end of social life as we know it. And so the critique of patriarchy tends to generate hostility, misunderstanding, ridicule, and fear almost as soon as it is mentioned. Like religion, it is one of the most difficult topics to discuss with, for example, nonbelievers. Accordingly, most feminists discuss the critique of patriarchy primarily with one another, and for good reason. Anyone who speaks of it too much "in public" is considered an extremist (and generally tiresome and ill-tempered as well). For these reasons (and some others) many women disassociate themselves from feminism, and most men do not want to hear about it. It is dubbed a women's issue and ignored. And when some feminist takes the critique directly to the patriarchs, so to speak, it tends to be hostilely delivered or hostilely received, or both.

Feminists tend, therefore, to concentrate on more specific issues rather than on the general critique, and there are many good reasons for doing that, in addition to the difficulty of the more general topic. Nevertheless, the critique of patriarchy is the general rationale behind feminism itself and behind all those discussions of more specific topics, such as pregnancy leave, rape, pornography, or child care. That means that all those issues also proceed from different basic assumptions, which in turn can lead to the same problems just mentioned: hostility, ridicule, disregard, and resistance. And this also expresses the progress of so-called women's issues.

All that is understandable, but it is not excusable, nor is it wise. Hostility is misplaced when directed against cultural revolutions, which is what we are talking about here. Cultural revolutions are profound but not violent. Cultural revolution is the discovery (usually after the fact) that everyone or almost everyone has joined a new order (usually without realizing it). It is internally developed rather than externally imposed. When women and men no longer think of women first and foremost as mothers, and secondarily as anything else, then the world will have changed. When women are thought of and think of themselves as primarily self-supporting and not as dependent, the world will have changed. In sum, when women and men actually think of themselves as equals, the world will have changed. In a cultural revolution, what changes is what people think, their basic assumptions about what is normal. So, cultural revolutions are inevitable because they follow from a change of worldview.

Thus, cultural revolutions should not be confused with political revolutions, which are not necessarily internal and not inevitable. Hostility to political revolutions makes sense. Hostility to cultural revolutions is understandable but relatively useless. To return to my analogy, it really did not do the Catholic church any good at all to reject Martin Luther when the rest of the world was ready for him. At a certain point in time, certain ideas become part of history, and they cannot be reversed. They can be affected, sometimes revised or modestly changed, possibly guided or directed, but not reversed or erased.

This is now the status of the women's movement and feminist thought. It cannot be reversed or erased. The bridges have been burned. This can easily be seen by comparing the lives of women today with those of one hundred years ago. Some of the biggest steps in the revolution have already been taken, as is illustrated by the legal changes in the status of women, which recognize them as independent individuals and equal citizens. Whether the legal system fashions the future from cooperative endeavor or hammers it out of the adversarial system, it will respond to the requirements of social change. To think, therefore, that the rejection of patriarchy is philosophically or intellectually uninteresting is to underestimate the extent or profundity of the change entailed in rejecting it. For philosophers and social analysts to ignore the feminist revolution today, thinking their work is outside it, is like philosophers and social analysts some centuries ago who ignored the Industrial Revolution, thinking that their work was outside it. Basic revolutions such as this touch everything and change assumptions about human nature and human life. Nothing could be more philosophically interesting.

The Pervasiveness of Patriarchy

Obviously, some thinkers reject the idea that the feminist critique is as fundamental or as revolutionary as I am suggesting. Accordingly, the following chapters [of *Feminist Jurisprudence*] are intended to represent the breadth of feminist jurisprudence, which in turn illustrates the pervasiveness of patriarchy and the enormity of the change that follows from its rejection. Several important areas are, however, not represented, owing to limitations of space. Of particular note here is the feminist work on reproductive rights, the nature of self-defense, child custody and family law, divorce and property settlement, and the nature and function of rights.

This book is intended to illuminate the extent and subtlety of patriarchy, particularly in regard to an interesting recent phenomenon. Historically, the challenge was to prove that women were entitled to be treated equally with men. That battle is still not completely over, but many people today are convinced that women are entitled to equal treatment. The interesting twist is that although many people do believe that men and women are entitled to equal treatment, they also believe that this goal has already been accomplished in law. Because formal barriers (at least the most obvious ones) have, for the most part, been removed—women can vote, hold office, attend college, participate in business, own property, execute contracts, and so forth—many people think that legal equality has been achieved. So, discrepancies in accomplishments—the wage gap, for example—must be explained by differences in abilities or by social factors that are beyond the purview of law. But the chapters in this volume show that this view is premature. Law is affected by patriarchy in many subtle ways that have not yet been eradicated by the simple change of some obvious sexist barriers like the prohibition of women from voting or owning property. Patriarchy is an all-encompassing worldview, and as an institution of patriarchy, law reflects that worldview as well. But because of its distinctive features as law—its reliance on precedent, which perpetuates the status quo—law is not like an ordinary mirror that instantly reflects the reality before it. Rather, it is like a magic mirror that always reflects a vision that is slightly in the past; that is, it can reflect reality only if reality moves slowly. Transient changes are therefore not reflected. Big changes or fast changes are reflected only after a period of transition. Because law is a somewhat selective, delayed-action mirror, feminist jurisprudence is concerned with correcting the current lag.

12

Catharine A. MacKinnon

"Toward Feminist Jurisprudence," from *Toward a Feminist Theory of the State*

> Happy above all Countries is our Country where that equality is found, without destroying the necessary subordination.
> —Thomas Lee Shippen (1788)

> If I fight, some day some woman will win.
> —Michelle Vinson (1987)

A jurisprudence is a theory of the relation between life and law. In life, "woman" and "man" are widely experienced as features of being, not constructs of perception, cultural interventions, or forced identities. Gender, in other words, is lived as ontology, not as epistemology. Law actively participates in this transformation of perspective into being. In liberal regimes, law is a particularly potent source and badge of legitimacy, and site and cloak of force. The force underpins the legitimacy as the legitimacy conceals the force. When life becomes law in such a system, the transformation is both formal and substantive. It reenters life marked by power.

In male supremacist societies, the male standpoint dominates civil society in the form of the objective standard—that standpoint which, because it dominates in the world, does not appear to function as a standpoint at all. Under its aegis, men dominate women and children, three-quarters of the world. Family and kinship rules and sexual mores guarantee reproductive ownership and sexual access and control to men as a group. Hierarchies among men are ordered on the basis of race and class, stratifying women as well. The state incorporates these facts of social power in and as law. Two things happen: Law becomes legitimate, and social dominance becomes invisible. Liberal legalism is thus a medium for making male dominance both invisible and legitimate by adopting the male point of view in law at the same time as it enforces that view on society. Through legal mediation, male dominance is made to seem a feature of life, not a one-sided construct imposed by force for the advantage of a dominant group. To the degree it succeeds ontologically, male dominance does not look epistemological: Control over being produces control over consciousness, fusing material conditions with consciousness in a way that is inextricable short of social change. Dominance reified becomes difference. Coercion legitimated becomes consent. Reality objectified becomes ideas; ideas objectified become reality. Politics neutralized and naturalized becomes morality. Discrimination in society becomes nondiscrimination in law. Law is a real moment in the social construction of these mirror-imaged inversions as truth. Law, in societies ruled and penetrated by the liberal form, turns angle of vision and construct of social meaning into dominant institution. In the liberal state, the rule of law—neutral, abstract, elevated, pervasive—both institutionalizes the power of men over women and institutionalizes power in its male form.

From a feminist perspective, male supremacist jurisprudence erects qualities valued from the male point of view as standards for the proper and actual relation between life and law. Examples include standards for scope of judicial review, norms of judicial restraint, reliance on precedent, separation of powers, and the division between public and private law. Substantive doctrines like standing, justiciability, and state action adopt the same stance. Those with power in civil society, not women, design its norms and institutions, which become the status quo. Those with power, not usually women, write constitutions, which become law's highest standards. Those with power in political systems that women did not design and from which women have been excluded write legislation, which sets ruling values. Then, jurisprudentially, judicial review is said to go beyond its proper scope—to delegitimate courts and the rule of law itself—when legal questions are not confined to assessing the formal correspondence between legislation and the constitution, or legislation and social reality, but scrutinize the underlying substance. Lines of precedent fully developed before women were permitted to vote, continued while women were not allowed to learn to read and write, sustained under a reign of sexual terror and abasement and silence and misrepresentation continuing to the present day are considered valid bases for defeating "unprecedented" interpretations or initiatives from women's point of view. Doctrines of standing suggest that because women's deepest injuries are shared in some way by most or all women, no individual woman is differentially injured enough to be able to sue for women's deepest injuries.

Structurally, only when the state has acted can constitutional equality guarantees be invoked.[1] But no law gives men the right to rape women. This has not been necessary, since no rape law has ever seriously undermined the terms of men's entitlement to sexual access to women. No government is, yet, in the pornography business. This has not been necessary, since no man who wants pornography encounters serious trouble getting it, regardless of obscenity laws. No law gives fathers

1 In the United States, the "state action" requirement restricts review under the Fourteenth Amendment. See Lawrence Tribe, *American Constitutional Law* (Mineola, NY: Foundation P, 1978), pp. 1688–1720, for summary. In Canada, under the Canadian Charter of Rights and Freedoms, Section 32 restricts charter review to acts of government.

the right to abuse their daughters sexually. This has not been necessary, since no state has ever systematically intervened in their social possession of and access to them. No law gives husbands the right to batter their wives. This has not been necessary, since there is nothing to stop them. No law silences women. This has not been necessary, for women are previously silenced in society—by sexual abuse, by not being heard, by not being believed, by poverty, by illiteracy, by a language that provides only unspeakable vocabulary for their most formative traumas, by a publishing industry that virtually guarantees that if they ever find a voice it leaves no trace in the world. No law takes away women's privacy. Most women do not have any to take, and no law gives them what they do not already have. No law guarantees that women will forever remain the social unequals of men. This is not necessary, because the law guaranteeing sex equality requires, in an unequal society, that before one can be equal legally, one must be equal socially. So long as power enforced by law reflects and corresponds—in form and in substance—to power enforced by men over women in society, law is objective, appears principled, becomes just the way things are. So long as men dominate women effectively enough in society without the support of positive law, nothing constitutional can be done about it.

Law from the male point of view combines coercion with authority, policing society where its edges are exposed: at points of social resistance, conflict, and breakdown. Since there is no place outside this system from a feminist standpoint, if its solipsistic lock could be broken, such moments could provide points of confrontation, perhaps even openings for change. The point of view of a total system emerges as particular only when confronted, in a way it cannot ignore, by a demand from another point of view. This is why epistemology must be controlled for ontological dominance to succeed and why consciousness raising is subversive. It is also why, when law sides with the powerless, as it occasionally has,[2] it is said to engage in something other than law—politics or policy or personal opinion—and to delegitimate itself.[3] When seemingly ontological conditions are challenged from the collective standpoint of a dissident reality, they become visible as epistemological. Dominance suddenly appears no longer inevitable. When it loses its ground, it loosens its grip.

Thus when the Supreme Court held that racial segregation did not violate equality rights, it said that those who felt that to be segregated on the basis of race implied inferiority merely chose to place that construction upon it. The harm of forced separation was a matter of point of view.[4] When the Supreme Court later held that racial segregation violated equality rights, it said that segregation generated a feeling of inferiority in the hearts and minds of black children which was unlikely ever to be undone. Both Courts observed the same reality: the feelings of inferiority generated by apartheid. *Plessy* saw it from the standpoint of white supremacy; *Brown* saw it from the standpoint of the black challenge to white supremacy, envisioning a social equality that did not yet exist. Inequality is difficult to see when everything tells the unequal that the status quo is equality—for them. To the Supreme Court, the way black people saw their own condition went from being sneered at as a point of view within their own control, a self-inflicted epistemological harm, to being a constitutional measure of the harm a real social condition imposed upon them. Consciousness raising shifts the episteme in a similar way, exposing the political behind the personal, the dominance

2 *Brown v. Board of Education*, 347 U.S. 483 (1954); *Swann v. Charlotte-Mecklenburg Board of Education*, 402 U.S. 2 (1971); *Griggs v. Duke Power*, 401 U.S. 424 (1971).

3 Herbert Wechsler, "Toward Neutral Principles of Constitutional Law," 73 *Harvard Law Review* 1 (1959).

4 *Plessy v. Ferguson*, 163 U.S. 537, 551(1896); Wechsler, "Toward Neutral Principles," p. 33.

behind the submission, participating in altering the balance of power subtly but totally. The question is, What can extend this method to the level of the state for women?

To begin with, Why law? Marx saw the modern state as "the official expression of antagonism in civil society."[5] Because political power in such a state could emancipate the individual only within the framework of the existing social order, law could emancipate women to be equal only within "the slavery of civil society."[6] By analogy, women would not be freed from forced sex, but freed to engage in it and initiate it. They would not be freed from reproductive tyranny and exploitation, but freed to exercise it. They would not be liberated from the dialectic of economic and sexual dominance and submission, but freed to dominate. Depending upon the substantive analysis of civil dominance, either women would dominate men, or some women (with all or some men) would dominate other women. In other words, the liberal vision of sex equality would be achieved. Feminism unmodified, methodologically post-Marxist feminism, aspires to better.

From the feminist point of view, the question of women's collective reality and how to change it merges with the question of women's point of view and how to know it. What do women live, hence know, that can confront male dominance? What female ontology can confront male epistemology; that is, what female epistemology can confront male ontology? What point of view can question the code of civil society? The answer is simple, concrete, specific, and real: women's social inequality with men on the basis of sex, hence the point of view of women's subordination to men. Women are not permitted fully to know what sex equality would look like, because they have never lived it. It is idealist, hence elitist, to hold that they do. But they do not need to. They know inequality because they have lived it, so they know what removing barriers to equality would be. Many of these barriers are legal; many of them are social; most of them exist at an interface between law and society.

Inequality on the basis of sex, women share. It is women's collective condition. The first task of a movement for social change is to face one's situation and name it. The failure to face and criticize the reality of women's condition, a failure of idealism and denial, is a failure of feminism in its liberal forms. The failure to move beyond criticism, a failure of determinism and radical paralysis, is a failure of feminism in its left forms. Feminism on its own terms has begun to give voice to and describe the collective condition of women as such, so largely composed as it is of all women's particularities. It has begun to uncover the laws of motion of a system that keeps women in a condition of imposed inferiority. It has located the dynamic of the social definition of gender in the sexuality of dominance and subordination, the sexuality of inequality: sex as inequality and inequality as sex. As sexual inequality is gendered as man and women, gender inequality is sexualized as dominance and subordination. The social power of men over women extends through laws that purport to protect women as part of the community, like the rape law; laws that ignore women's survival stake in the issue, like the obscenity law, or obscure it, like the abortion law; and laws that announce their intent to remedy that inequality but do not, like the sex equality law. This law derives its authority from reproducing women's social inequality to men in legal inequality, in a seamless web of life and law.

Feminist method adopts the point of view of women's inequality to men. Grasping women's

5 Karl Marx, *The Poverty of Philosophy* (New York: International Publishers, 1963), p. 174.

6 Karl Marx and Friedrich Engels, *The Holy Family*, trans. R. Dixon (Moscow: Progress, 1956), p. 157. See generally M. Cain and A. Hunt, *Marx and Engels on Law* (London: Academic P, 1979).

reality from the inside, developing its specificities, facing the intractability and pervasiveness of male power, relentlessly criticizing women's condition as it identifies with all women, it has created strategies for change, beginning with consciousness raising. On the level of the state, legal guarantees of equality in liberal regimes provide an opening. Sex inequality is the true name for women's social condition. It is also, in words anyway, illegal sometimes. In some liberal states, the belief that women already essentially have sex equality extends to the level of law. From a perspective that understands that women do not have sex equality, this law means that once equality is meaningfully defined, the law cannot be applied without changing society. To make sex equality meaningful in law requires identifying the real issues, and establishing that sex inequality, once established, matters.

Sex equality in law has not been meaningfully defined for women but has been defined and limited from the male point of view to correspond to the existing social reality of sex inequality. An alternative approach to this mainstream view threads through existing law. It is the reason sex equality law exists at all. In this approach, inequality is a matter not of sameness and difference, but of dominance and subordination. Inequality is about power, its definition, and its maldistribution. Inequality at root is grasped as a question of hierarchy, which—as power succeeds in constructing social perception and social reality—derivatively becomes categorical distinctions, differences. Where mainstream equality law is abstract, this approach is concrete; where mainstream equality law is falsely universal, this approach remains specific.[7] The goal is not to make legal categories that trace and trap the status quo, but to confront by law the inequalities in women's condition in order to change them.

This alternative approach centers on the most sex-differential abuses of women as a gender, abuses that sex equality law in its sameness/difference obsession cannot confront. It is based on the reality that feminism, beginning with consciousness raising, has most distinctively uncovered, a reality about which little systematic was known before 1970: the reality of sexual abuse. It combines women's sex-based destitution and enforced dependency and permanent relegation to disrespected and starvation-level work—the lived meaning of class for women—with the massive amount of sexual abuse of girls apparently endemic to the patriarchal family, the pervasive rape and attempted rape about which nothing is done, the systematic battery of women in homes, and prostitution—the fundamental condition of women—of which the pornography industry is an arm. Keeping the reality of gender in view makes it impossible to see gender as a difference, unless this subordinated condition of women is that difference. This reality has called for a new conception of the problem of sex inequality, hence a new legal conception of it, both doctrinally and jurisprudentially.

Experiences of sexual abuse have been virtually excluded from the mainstream doctrine of sex equality because they happen almost exclusively to women and because they are experienced as sex. Sexual abuse has not been seen to raise sex equality issues because these events happen specifically and almost exclusively to women as women. Sexuality is socially organized to require sex inequality for excitement and satisfaction. The least extreme expression of gender inequality, and the prerequisite for all of it, is

7 Examples are *Loving v. Virginia*, 388 U.S. 1 (1967); *Brown v. Board of Education*, 347 U.S. 483 (1954); some examples of the law against sexual harassment (e.g., *Barnes v. Costle*, 561 F.2d 983 [D.C. Cir. 1977]; *Vinson v. Taylor*, 753 F.2d 141 [D.C. Cir. 1985], aff'd. 477 U.S. 57 [1986]; *Priest v. Rotary*, 98 F.R.D. 755 [D.Cal. 1983]), some athletics cases (e.g., *Clark v. Arizona Interscholastic Assn.*, 695 F.2d 1126 [9th Cir. 1986]), some affirmative action cases (e.g., *Johnson v. Transportation Agency, Santa Clara County*, 480 U.S. 616 [1987]), and *California Federal Savings and Loan Association v. Guerra*, 492 U.S. 272 (1987).

dehumanization and objectification. The most extreme is violence. Because sexual objectification and sexual violence are almost uniquely done to women, they have been systematically treated as the sex difference when they represent the socially situated subjection of women to men. The whole point of women's social relegation to inferiority as a gender is that this is not generally done to men. The systematic relegation of an entire people to a condition of inferiority is attributed to them, made a feature of theirs, and read out of equality demands and equality law when it is termed a *difference*. This condition is ignored entirely, with all the women who are determined by it, when only features women share with the privileged group are allowed to substantiate equality claims.

It follows that seeing sex equality questions as matters of reasonable or unreasonable classification of relevant social characteristics expresses male dominance in law. If the shift in perspective from gender as difference to gender as dominance is followed, gender changes from a distinction that is ontological and presumptively valid to a detriment that is epistemological and presumptively suspect. The given becomes the contingent. In this light, liberalism, purporting to discover gender, has discovered male and female in the mirror of nature; the left has discovered masculine and feminine in the mirror of society. The approach from the standpoint of the subordination of women to men, by contrast, criticizes and claims the specific situation of women's enforced inferiority and devaluation, pointing a way out of the infinity of reflections in law-and-society's hall of mirrors where sex equality law remains otherwise trapped.

Equality understood substantively rather than abstractly, defined on women's own terms and in terms of women's concrete experience, is what women in society most need and most do not have. Equality is also what society holds that women have already and therefore guarantees women by positive law. The law of equality, statutory and constitutional, therefore provides a peculiar jurisprudential opportunity, a crack in the wall between law and society. Law does not usually guarantee rights to things that do not exist. This may be why equality issues have occasioned so many jurisprudential disputes about what law is and what it can and should do. Every demand from women's point of view looks substantive, just as every demand from women's point of view requires change. Can women, demanding actual equality through law, be part of changing the state's relation to women and women's relation to men?

The first step is to claim women's concrete reality. Women's inequality occurs in a context of unequal pay, allocation to disrespected work, demeaned physical characteristics, targeting for rape, domestic battery, sexual abuse as children, and systematic sexual harassment. Women are daily dehumanized, used in denigrating entertainment, denied reproductive control, and forced by the conditions of their lives into prostitution. These abuses occur in a legal context historically characterized by disenfranchisement, preclusion from property ownership, exclusion from public life, and lack of recognition of sex-specific injuries.[8] Sex inequality is thus a social and political institution.

The next step is to recognize that male forms of power over women are affirmatively embodied as individual rights in law. When men lose power, they feel they lose rights. Often they are not wrong. Examples include the defense of mistaken belief in consent in the rape law, which legally determines whether or not a rape occurred from

8 This context was argued as the appropriate approach to equality in an intervention by the Women's Legal Education and Action Fund (LEAF) in *Law Society of British Columbia v. Andrews* (May 22, 1987) before the Supreme Court of Canada. This approach to equality in general, giving priority to concrete disadvantage and rejecting the "similarly situated" test, was adopted by the Supreme Court of Canada in that case (1989)—D.L.R. (3d)—.

the rapist's perspective; freedom of speech, which gives pimps rights to torture, exploit, use, and sell women to men through pictures and words and gives consumers rights to buy them; the law of privacy, which defines the home and sex as presumptively consensual and protects the use of pornography in the home; the law of child custody, which purports gender neutrality while applying a standard of adequacy of parenting based on male-controlled resources and male-defined norms, sometimes taking children away from women but more generally controlling women through the threat and fear of loss of their children. Real sex equality under law would qualify or eliminate these powers of men, hence men's current "rights" to use, access, possess, and traffic women and children.

In this context, many issues appear as sex equality issues for the first time—sexual assault, for example. Rape is a sex-specific violation. Not only are the victims of rape overwhelmingly women, perpetrators overwhelmingly men, but also the rape of women by men is integral to the way inequality between the sexes occurs in life. Intimate violation with impunity is an ultimate index of social power. Rape both evidences and practices women's low status relative to men. Rape equates female with violable and female sexuality with forcible intrusion in a way that defines and stigmatizes the female sex as a gender. Threat of sexual assault is threat of punishment for being female. The state has laws against sexual assault, but it does not enforce them. Like lynching at one time, rape is socially permitted, though formally illegal. Victims of sex crimes, mostly women and girls, are thus disadvantaged relative to perpetrators of sex crimes, largely men.

A systemic inequality between the sexes therefore exists in the social practice of sexual violence, subjection to which defines women's status, and victims of which are largely women, and in the operation of the state, which *de jure* outlaws sexual violence but de facto permits men to engage in it on a wide scale. Making sexual assault laws gender neutral does nothing to address this, nothing to alter the social equation of female with rapeable, and may obscure the sex specificity of the problem. Rape should be defined as sex by compulsion, of which physical force is one form. Lack of consent is redundant and should not be a separate element of the crime.[9] Expanding this analysis would support as sex equality initiatives laws keeping women's sexual histories out of rape trials[10] and publication bans on victims' names and identities.[11] The defense of mistaken belief in consent—which measures whether a rape occurred from the standpoint of the (male) perpetrator—would violate women's sex equality rights by law because it takes the male point of view on sexual violence against women.[12] Similarly, the systematic failure of the state to enforce the rape law effectively or at all excludes women from equal access to justice, permitting women to be savaged on a mass scale, depriving them of equal protection and equal benefit of the laws.

Reproductive control, formerly an issue of privacy, liberty, or personal security, would also become a sex equality issue. The frame for

9 See Ill. Rev. Stat. 1985, ch. 38, par. 12–14; *People v. Haywood*, 515 N.E.2d 45 (Ill. App. 1987) (prosecution not required to prove nonconsent, since sexual penetration by force implicitly shows nonconsent); but cf. *People v. Coleman*, 520 N.E.2d 55 (III. App. 1987) (state must prove victim's lack of consent beyond reasonable doubt).

10 This is argued by LEAF in its intervention application with several groups in *Seaboyer v. The Queen* (July 12, 1988) and *Gayme v. The Queen* (November 18, 1988), both on appeal before the Supreme Court of Canada. The rulings below are *The Queen v. Seaboyer and Gayme* (1986) 50 C.R. (3d) 395 (Ont. C.A.).

11 LEAF and a coalition of rape crisis centers, groups opposing sexual assault of women and children, and feminist media made this argument in an intervention in *The Queen v. Canadian Newspapers Co., Ltd.* The Canadian statute was upheld by a unanimous court. (1988)—D.L.R. (3d)—.

12 This is argued by LEAF intervening in *The Queen v. Gayme*.

analyzing reproductive issues would expand from focus on the individual at the moment of the abortion decision to women as a group at all reproductive moments. The social context of gender inequality denies women control over the reproductive uses of their bodies and places that control in the hands of men. In a context of inadequate and unsafe contraceptive technology, women are socially disadvantaged in controlling sexual access to their bodies through social learning, lack of information, social pressure, custom, poverty and enforced economic dependence, sexual force, and ineffective enforcement of laws against sexual assault. As a result, they often do not control the conditions under which they become pregnant. If intercourse cannot be presumed to be controlled by women, neither can pregnancy. Women have also been allocated primary responsibility for intimate care of children yet do not control the conditions under which they rear them, hence the impact of these conditions on their own lives.

In this context, access to abortion is necessary for women to survive unequal social circumstances. It provides a form of relief, however punishing, in a life otherwise led in conditions that preclude choice in ways most women have not been permitted to control. This approach also recognizes that whatever is done to the fetus is done to a woman. Whoever controls the destiny of a fetus controls the destiny of a woman. Whatever the conditions of conception, if reproductive control of a fetus is exercised by anyone but the woman, reproductive control is taken only from women, as women. Preventing a woman from exercising the only choice an unequal society leaves her is an enforcement of sex inequality. Giving women control over sexual access to their bodies and adequate support of pregnancies and care of children extends sex equality. In other words, forced maternity is a practice of sex inequality.[13] Because motherhood without choice is a sex equality issue, legal abortion should be a sex equality right. Reproductive technology, sterilization abuse, and surrogate motherhood, as well as abortion funding, would be transformed if seen in this light.

Pornography, the technologically sophisticated traffic in women that expropriates, exploits, uses, and abuses women, also becomes a sex equality issue. The mass production of pornography universalizes the violation of the women in it, spreading it to all women, who are then exploited, used, abused, and reduced as a result of men's consumption of it. In societies pervaded by pornography, all women are defined by it: This is what a woman wants; this is what a woman is. Pornography sets the public standard for the treatment of women in private and the limits of tolerance for what can be permitted in public, such as in rape trials. It sexualizes the definition of male as dominant and female as subordinate. It equates violence against women with sex and provides an experience of that fusion. It engenders rape, sexual abuse of children, battery, forced prostitution, and sexual murder.

In liberal legalism, pornography is said to be a form of freedom of speech. It seems that women's inequality is something pornographers want to say, and saying it is protected even if it requires doing it. Being the medium for men's speech supersedes any rights women have. Women become men's speech in this system. Women's speech is silenced by pornography and the abuse that is integral to it. From women's point of view, obscenity law's misrepresentation of the problem as moral and ideational is replaced with the understanding that the problem of pornography is political and practical. Obscenity law is based on the point of view of male dominance. Once this is exposed, the urgent issue of freedom of speech for women is not primarily the avoidance of state intervention

13 This argument was advanced by LEAF in an intervention in *Borowski v. Attorney General of Canada* (October 7, 1987).

as such, but getting equal access to speech for those to whom it has been denied. First the abuse must be stopped.[14] The endless moral debates between good and evil, conservative and liberal, artists and philistines, the forces of darkness and repression and suppression and the forces of light and liberation and tolerance would be superseded by the political debate, the abolitionist debate: Are women human beings or not? Apparently, the answer provided by legal mandates of sex equality requires repeating.

The changes that a sex equality perspective provides as an interpretive lens include the law of sex equality itself. The intent requirement would be eliminated. The state action requirement would weaken. No distinction would be made between nondiscrimination and affirmative action. Burdens of proof would presuppose inequality rather than equality as a factual backdrop and would be more substantively sensitive to the particularities of sex inequality. Comparable worth would be required. Statistical proofs of disparity would be conclusive. The main question would be, Does a practice participate in the subordination of women to men, or is it no part of it? Whether statutes are sex specific or gender neutral would not be as important as whether they work to end or reinforce male supremacy, whether they are concretely grounded in women's experience of subordination or not. Discrimination law would not be confined to employment, education, and accommodation. Civil remedies in women's hands would be emphasized. Gay and lesbian rights would be recognized as sex equality rights. Since sexuality largely defines gender, discrimination based on sexuality is discrimination based on gender. Other forms of social discrimination and exploitation by men against women, such as prostitution and surrogate motherhood, would become actionable.

The relation between life and law would also change. Law, in liberal jurisprudence, objectifies social life. The legal process reflects itself in its own image, makes be there what it puts there, while presenting itself as passive and neutral in the process. To undo this, it will be necessary to grasp the dignity of women without blinking at the indignity of women's condition, to envision the possibility of equality without minimizing the grip of inequality, to reject the fear that has become so much of women's sexuality and the corresponding denial that has become so much of women's politics, and to demand civil parity without pretending that the demand is neutral or that civil equality already exists. In this attempt, the idealism of liberalism and the materialism of the left have come to much the same for women. Liberal jurisprudence that the law should reflect nature or society and left jurisprudence that all law does or can do is reflect existing social relations are two guises of objectivist epistemology. If objectivity is the epistemological stance of which women's sexual objectification is the social process, its imposition the paradigm of power in the male form, then the state appears most relentless in imposing the male point of view when it comes closest to achieving its highest formal criterion of distanced aperspectivity. When it is most ruthlessly neutral, it is most male; when it is most sex blind, it is most blind to the sex of the standard being applied. When it most closely conforms to precedent, to "facts," to legislative intent, it most closely enforces socially male norms and most thoroughly precludes questioning their content as having a point of view at all.

Abstract rights authoritize the male experience of the world. Substantive rights for women would not. Their authority would be the currently unthinkable: nondominant authority, the authority of excluded truth, the voice of silence. It would

14 The Anti-Pornography Civil Rights Ordinance aims to do this. See Andrea Dworkin and Catharine A. MacKinnon, *Pornography and Civil Rights: A New Day for Women's Equality* (Minneapolis: Organizing Against Pornography, 1988).

stand against both the liberal and left views of law. The liberal view that law is society's text, its rational mind, expresses the male view in the normative mode; the traditional left view that the state, and with it the law, is superstructural or epiphenomenal expresses it in the empirical mode. A feminist jurisprudence, stigmatized as particularized and protectionist in male eyes of both traditions, is accountable to women's concrete conditions and to changing them. Both the liberal and the left views rationalize male power by presuming that it does not exist, that equality between the sexes (room for marginal corrections conceded) is society's basic norm and fundamental description. Only feminist jurisprudence sees that male power does exist and sex equality does not, because only feminism grasps the extent to which antifeminism is misogyny and both are as normative as they are empirical. Masculinity then appears as a specific position, not just the way things are, its judgments and partialities revealed in process and procedure, adjudication and legislation.

Equality will require change, not reflection—a new jurisprudence, a new relation between life and law. Law that does not dominate life is as difficult to envision as a society in which men do not dominate women, and for the same reasons. To the extent feminist law embodies women's point of view, it will be said that its law is not neutral. But existing law is not neutral. It will be said that it undermines the legitimacy of the legal system. But the legitimacy of existing law is based on force at women's expense. Women have never consented to its rule—suggesting that the system's legitimacy needs repair that women are in a position to provide. It will be said that feminist law is special pleading for a particular group and one cannot start that or where will it end. But existing law is already special pleading for a particular group, where it has ended. The question is not where it will stop but whether it will start for any group but the dominant one. It will be said that feminist law cannot win and will not work. But this is premature. Its possibilities cannot be assessed in the abstract but must engage the world. A feminist theory of the state has barely been imagined; systematically, it has never been tried.

13

Richard Delgado

"About Your Masthead: A Preliminary Inquiry into the Compatibility of Civil Rights and Civil Liberties"

Introduction: Formal Rules and Substantive Justice

One day, a lawyer dies and goes to Heaven, where he is met by St. Peter outside the Pearly Gates.

"What do we have here?" St. Peter asks.

"A lawyer," he replies.

"Another one. We've sure been getting a lot of those lately. Well, what do you have to say for yourself?"

"I followed all the rules," the lawyer replies, modestly, but with quiet pride.

> *"I never broke any of the canons of professional responsibility, and I got all my briefs in on time. Except one, when my wife had a baby. But the judge gave me an extension."*
>
> *"Not bad. Did you represent plaintiffs or defendants?"*
>
> *"Both, in equal numbers. And I was respectful to everyone—my adversary, witnesses, and, of course, the judge."*
>
> *"Let's see," says St. Peter, picking up a thick book marked LEGALITY. After thumbing through a few pages, he says "Here you are. Right there on page three. Not bad. It seems you colored between the lines at all times. You cited case law accurately, so far as we can tell, given the indeterminacy thesis.*[1] *And you never coached a witness or engaged in a conflict of interest."*
>
> *"So, do I get in?" the lawyer asks, eagerly.*
>
> *"There's just one more thing," St. Peter replies, picking up a second book labeled JUSTICE. "Hmmm. I don't see you on page three in this one." He leafs through several more pages, then looks up. "We'll have to look into this a little further. Please take a seat over there for a minute." Clapping his hands: "Research assistant!"*[2]

The point of this story, of course, is that formal rules do not necessarily guarantee justice; indeed some of history's most ignoble chapters—slavery, Indian relocation, World War II internment, the Holocaust, Operation Wetback—seem to have been completely legal at the time.[3] This quandary suggests a second one that is the subject of this Essay: What is the relationship between the group of largely formal rules known as civil liberties and the set of substantive values known as racial justice or civil rights?

The editors of *CR-CL* [*Harvard Civil Rights-Civil Liberties Law Review*] have invited me to offer my thoughts on the relationship between civil rights and civil liberties. Both are emblazoned on their masthead. A few years ago, one of my favorite authors, historian Robin Kelley, wrote a prize-winning book about white media, black culture, and the huge gulf between them, entitled *Yo' Mama's Disfunktional*.[4] Does a similar gap exist between civil rights and civil liberties? Is the masthead dysfunctional, committing *CR-CL* by its terms to an inherently self-contradictory agenda, like a law review that billed itself as "The Global Development and Environmental Protection Journal" or "The Review of Religion and Atheism"?

---

1 On the indeterminacy thesis, see Robert L. Hayman, Jr., Nancy Levit, and Richard Delgado, *Jurisprudence Classical and Contemporary: From Natural Law to Postmodernism* 402–09, 431 (2002).

2 This story occurred to me when I learned that a liberal legal advocacy organization declined to send a speaker to a Harvard Law School program on the ground that civil rights and civil liberties are exactly the same and cannot conflict. Telephone conversation with Joi Chaney, Editor, *CR-CL* (Apr. 2, 2003).

3 See, e.g., *Dred Scott v. Sandford*, 60 U.S. (19 How.) 393 (1856) (declaring that slaves and their descendants are not US citizens entitled to the privileges and immunities of citizenship); *Korematsu v. United States*, 323 U.S. 214 (1944) (upholding internment of Japanese Americans). See also Juan Perea et al., *Race and Races: Cases and Resources for a Diverse America* 190, 317, 320 (2000) (discussing Indian relocation and Operation Wetback, a Congressionally approved program in which at least 1.3 million Latinos, many of them US citizens, were deported in 1954).

4 Robin D.G. Kelley, *Yo' Mama's Disfunktional: Fighting the Culture Wars in Urban America* (1997) (showing how establishment writers and social scientists depict black "ghetto" society according to frames of reference radically different from those of the residents of inner-city neighborhoods).

Are civil liberties and civil rights in tension, pulling in different directions? Is it possible for a society to have both, in full measure and without limitation? If not, should *CR-CL* split up into two separate journals? Part I of this Essay examines a few instances in which civil rights and civil liberties may be entirely compatible. Then, Part II shows how our system of civil rights and civil liberties can exhibit tensions and strains, as exemplified in the area of hate speech. Part III explains the source of these tensions, while Part IV offers some thoughts on how to live with them. I hope that what follows will prove helpful not just in this one area but will also enable us to understand better the relations between civil rights and civil liberties in general. As you may recall, the poor lawyer who spent his life maximizing one variable is still sitting anxiously on that chair outside the Pearly Gates, waiting for the overall verdict on whether his life served justice in the law.

I. Some Initial Instances in Which Civil Rights and Civil Liberties May Be Compatible

In one sense, civil liberties and civil rights are certainly compatible in that they are both aspects of the good life. One would not want to live in a society that scrupulously protected the interests of minority groups and did not tolerate violations of their civil rights but denied its citizens the rights of free speech, privacy, worship and assembly. By the same token, one would not want to live in a society that safeguarded those rights but treated minorities harshly outside those spheres.

This, however, is not to say very much about their fundamental compatibility. Civil rights and civil liberties may both be desirable, though not simultaneously. When one legal interest is realized, it may interfere with another.[5] One might occupy a higher place in our echelon of values, so that we hesitate to advance the other at its expense.[6] Civil rights and civil liberties might not always be coextensive, so that one could maximize one value in certain settings without interfering with the other. In other settings, the two might conflict.[7] They may be only trivially compatible because of an unimportant element they have in common[8] or by means of a bogus monetization.[9]

One can insist that another person's favorite interest, *properly understood*, is really an aspect of one's own,[10] or imagine civil rights and civil liberties only during good times, when society is faced with little scarcity and people are on their best behavior.[11] One can also frame the issue as pitting a grand, systemic value against an individualized, particularized one held unreasonably

5 For example, national security may conflict with the right of privacy.

6 One might argue that environmental protection trumps the right to drive a large, gas-guzzling car.

7 National security (again) may or may not affect the right to travel—by car to the grocery store versus by private plane above a military base or to a theater of conflict.

8 For example, the Iraqi and US scrap metal associations might both agree that the war in Iraq was a bonanza.

9 Recall how the Bush administration, in March 2003, called for a study to explore assigning monetary values to each of our civil liberties. The idea is that, in times of war, the Executive branch would like to feel free to engage in surveillance of private citizens, read their mail and credit card records, and see what books and videos they check out from libraries. To prevent its doing so too cavalierly, the Office of Management and Budget proposed to find out how much value citizens assign these rights; the government would then weigh that against the value it placed on national security objectives. According to press accounts, the ACLU thought this was a good idea. See Edmund L. Andrews, "Threats and Responses: Liberty and Security," *N.Y. Times*, Mar. 11, 2003, at A13.

10 For example, some pro-development forces insist that environmental interests, properly understood, are really part of national energy policy.

11 In an idyllic society, in which few speakers use hate speech to threaten equality and human dignity, why would one need hate speech controls? Racist speech would carry little sting, while protection against the rare case could chill legitimate expression.

by the other side.[12] For example, adherents of free speech absolutism sometimes assert the worth of the generalized value society derives from our system of freedom of expression in light of the momentary annoyance of a Latino or black who is the target of a single, isolated racial epithet. How can the temporary offense of mere wounded feelings stack up against the tremendous gains, including inventions, libraries, presidential debates, and PBS, that spring from our system of free expression?[13]

These efforts at reconciliation are unsuccessful because they dodge hard cases, minimize conflicts that are real, or define the area of disagreement in a manner that allows only one answer.[14] Using the example of hate speech, I will demonstrate that the alleged tension between civil liberties and civil rights is real, and examine what drives it and how we should think about and learn to live with it.

II. Hate Speech and the Debate Surrounding Civil Rights and Civil Liberties

Free speech absolutists and critical race theorists have taken opposing positions regarding hate speech. Absolutists, including the ACLU [*Ed. note*: American Civil Liberties Union], maintain that a certain amount of vigorous criticism, even hate speech, is inherent in a democracy such as ours. A vital liberty and a cornerstone of democracy, speech must never be suppressed. In contrast, the Critical Race Theory position holds that hate speech silences its victims, contributes to a climate of disrespect for women and minorities, and undermines the very democracy that free speech is said to undergird. Each side marshals case law and policy justifications in support of its position.

A. THE ABSOLUTIST POSITION

The national organization of the ACLU represents the absolutist position, that all speech should receive blanket protection under the First Amendment.[15] Except for speech used in the furtherance of crime, few restraints on its exercise are acceptable. If campus authorities wish to confront a tide of racist slurs, graffiti, and e-mails disparaging students of color, a speech code is not an appropriate remedy. Instead, it is argued that minority students should learn to speak back or ignore the offenders.[16] Authorities can condemn

12 In the free-speech-versus-hate-speech setting, see Samuel Walker, *Hate Speech: The History of an American Controversy* 20–21, 165- 67 (1994); Nadine Strossen, "Regulating Racist Speech on Campus," in *Speaking of Race, Speaking of Sex: Hate Speech, Civil Rights and Civil Liberties* 212 (Henry Louis Gates et al. eds., 1994) [hereinafter, Strossen, "Regulating Racist Speech"]; Nadine Strossen, "A Feminist Critique of 'The' Feminist Critique of Pornography," 79 *Va. L. Rev.* 1099, 1170–71 (1993) [hereinafter, Strossen, "A Feminist Critique"].

13 Of course, advocates for minority causes are sometimes guilty of asking the same sort of loaded question. They may ask how anyone could sacrifice *their* favorite value—equality—for the mere momentary relief some Nazi or skinhead derives from hurling invective or burning a cross in the front yard of an African American family. See Richard Delgado, "Campus Antiracism Rules: Constitutional Narratives in Collision," 85 *Nw. U. L. Rev.* 343 (1991) [hereinafter Delgado, "Narratives in Collision"] (calling attention to this and similar strategies on the part of the minority Left). Both approaches juxtapose an emaciated, individualized, slice-of-life version of the competing interest against a robust, grand picture of their own; guess which one prevails? See Richard Delgado and Jean Stefancic, *Understanding Words that Wound* (forthcoming 2004) [hereinafter Delgado and Stefancic, *Understanding Words that Wound*] (discussing this strategy).

14 For instance, one might argue that equality is a matter of giving everyone enough rights, and so civil rights collapses into—and is "nothing more than"—civil liberties distributed widely and impartially. See Peter Weston, "The Empty Idea of Equality," 95 *Harv. L. Rev.* 537 (1982) (making a version of this argument). If this were the case, however, the problem with which this essay is concerned would emerge in another form, since one very large component of rights (free speech) would be at odds with another (freedom from hate speech). Similarly, the counterposing of a large, generalized value dressed up in dramatic language against the opponent's value depicted in emaciated, unattractive terms is a transparent debater's device—the way one asks the question implies that only one answer is possible. See *supra* note 13.

15 See, e.g., Nat Hentoff, *Free Speech for Me—But Not for Thee* (1992); Aryeh Neier, *Defending My Enemy* (1979); Walker, *supra* note 12; Strossen, "Regulating Racist Speech," supra note 12.

16 See, e.g., Hentoff, *supra* note 15, at 100–02, 111, 159, 167 (forcefully advocating the talk-back solution).

racist remarks, declaring them tawdry and in poor taste.[17] Moreover, if hate speech is delivered in a way that inspires fear, authorities can charge assault; if the speech defaces university property, they can charge trespass or similar offenses.[18] Civil rights and minority interests are thus worthy of protection but only insofar as they do not limit speech.

The absolutist scholars believe that both constitutional bedrock and current case law support their position. Doctrines such as the prohibition of content and viewpoint discrimination,[19] Supreme Court decisions such as *R.A.V. v. St. Paul*,[20] *Texas v. Johnson*,[21] and *New York Times v. Sullivan*,[22] and a trio of lower court cases invalidating university speech codes at Wisconsin,[23] Michigan,[24] and Stanford,[25] all suggest that campus hate speech rules are unlikely to withstand judicial scrutiny.[26]

Still, a few cases can be read to uphold speech codes,[27] and the belated development of First Amendment legal realism[28] has been engendering doubt in some of the faithful absolutist scholars. In response, they have sought to fortify their position with policy arguments. One, the "best friend" argument, holds that free speech is minorities' most reliable ally. If those clamoring for hate speech regulation knew the history of minorities in this country, the argument goes, they would realize the vital part that speech, marching, and protests have played in the struggle for civil rights; consequently, they would hesitate to impose limitations on such a precious instrument.[29] A second, "pressure valve" argument holds that permitting racists to unburden themselves of vituperative language allows them to discharge anger that might otherwise explode in more damaging forms, such as physical attacks. If outsider groups realized this, they would stop demanding hate speech rules that only place them in greater jeopardy.[30] A third argument asserts that hate speech rules will end up hurting minorities because authorities will inevitably apply the new rules against them when they speak out against their oppressors. Lastly, another absolutist argument holds that more speech is always the preferred response to bad speech. Hate speech rules preempt private responses, so that minorities never learn how to defend themselves. Talking back to the aggressor is empowering, while

17 See Charles Calleros, "Paternalism, Counterspeech, and Campus Hate Speech," 27 *Ariz. St. L.J.* 1249 (1995); Nadine Strossen, "Regulating Hate Speech on Campus: A Modest Proposal?," 1990 *Duke L.J.* 484, 562 (1990) [hereinafter Strossen, "Hate Speech on Campus"].

18 Nadine Strossen made this comment during a debate with this author at Cornell University in the fall of 1995.

19 See Laurence Tribe, *American Constitutional Law* 790 (2nd ed. 1988).

20 505 U.S. 377 (1992) (striking down an ordinance prohibiting hate speech and conduct).

21 491 U.S. 397 (1989) (striking down a flag-burning statute).

22 376 U.S. 254 (1964) (increasing protection for disfavored libelous speech).

23 *UWM Post, Inc. v. Bd. of Regents of Univ. of Wis. Sys.*, 774 F. Supp. 1163 (E.D. Wis. 1991).

24 *Doe v. Univ. of Mich.*, 721 F. Supp. 852 (E.D. Mich. 1989).

25 *Corry v. Stanford Univ.*, No. 1-94-CV-740309 (Cal. Super. Ct. Feb. 27, 1995).

26 For a review of the ACLU position, see Strossen, "Hate Speech on Campus," *supra* note 17. See also Marjorie Heins, "Banning Words: A Comment on Words that Wound," 18 *Harv. C.R.-C.L. L. Rev.* 585 (1983) (reviewing these First Amendment doctrines).

27 See, e.g., *Beauharnais v. Illinois*, 343 U.S. 250 (1952) (upholding criminal libel statute in face of First Amendment challenge).

28 See J.M. Balkin, "Some Realism about Pluralism: Legal Realist Approaches to the First Amendment," 1990 *Duke L.J.* 375 (1990); Richard Delgado, "First Amendment Formalism is Giving Way to First Amendment Legal Realism," 29 *Harv. C.R.-C.L. L. Rev.* 169 (1994) [hereinafter Delgado, "Giving Way"]; Stanley Ingber, "The Marketplace of Ideas: A Legitimizing Myth," 1984 *Duke L.J.* 1 (1984).

29 See Richard Delgado and David Yun, "Pressure Valves and Bloodied Chickens: An Analysis of Paternalistic Objections to Hate-Speech Regulation," 82 *Cal. L. Rev.* 871, 881–82 (1994) [hereinafter Delgado and Yun, "Bloodied Chickens"].

30 *Id.* at 876–80.

running to the authorities whenever one hears a hurtful word increases one's sense of helplessness and victimization.[31] Free speech absolutists deploy such policy arguments to reason that even if free speech law were to some extent malleable, decision makers should exercise discretion in favor of the cherished freedom of expression.

B. THE CRITICAL RACE THEORY POSITION

Twenty years ago, *CR-CL* published the first piece of legal scholarship specifically addressing hate speech. Entitled "Words that Wound: A Tort Action for Racial Insults, Epithets, and Name-Calling,"[32] the article reviewed a number of harms associated with hate speech and name-calling. Urging recognition of a new, freestanding tort, I pointed out that courts were already affording relief under such rubrics as defamation, intentional infliction of emotional distress, assault, and statutory discrimination. A number of United States courts and a landmark Canadian Supreme Court decision followed suit.[33]

A few years later, critical race theorist Mari Matsuda, in a much-cited article, urged that protection against hate speech should be expanded to include public law remedies, such as criminal prosecutions.[34] Then, in the course of a colloquy with ACLU president and law professor Nadine Strossen, Charles Lawrence argued that *Brown v. Board of Education* was a hate speech case, specifically addressing the problem of campus antiracism rules. When the Court reversed long-standing precedent and held that separate schooling sent a socially pernicious message to black schoolchildren, Lawrence argued that it was tacitly holding that certain messages of hate and inferiority should not be spoken. *Brown*, then, would stand as a precedent justifying campus rules aimed at curtailing racist hate speech.[35]

These three articles, and a book growing out of them,[36] could be said to constitute the first wave of hate speech writing and activism. The next major development saw diverging lines of case authority and the advent of a legal theory aimed at interpreting them. In the early 1990s, two federal courts endorsed the absolutist position in striking down campus hate speech rules at leading universities,[37] while the Canadian Supreme Court, citing American critical race theorists, weighed in with a free speech case asserting more or less the direct opposite.[38] At the same time, federal and state courts were affirming causes of action for minority and female plaintiffs targeted by hate speech in other settings, such as K–12 schools and at work.[39]

Many people then questioned what was happening in the civil rights and civil liberties arena. A second article in the pages of *CR-CL* posited that the judiciary was belatedly beginning to apply the lessons of legal realism to the First Amendment.[40] Rejecting mechanistic tests, shopworn maxims, and per se rules, courts were beginning to consider a host of factors, including setting, power disparities, history, communication theory, and social science, on the way to a decision.[41] Scholars addressed each of the paternalistic objections to

31 *Id.* at 883–85.
32 Richard Delgado, "Words that Wound: A Tort Action for Racial Insults, Epithets, and Name-Calling," 17 Harv. *C.R.-C.L. L. Rev.* 133 (1982) [hereinafter Delgado, "Words that Wound: A Tort Action"].
33 See Delgado and Stefancic, *Understanding Words that Wound, supra* note 13 (discussing this subsequent history).
34 Mari J. Matsuda, "Public Response to Racist Speech: Considering the Victim's Story," 87 *Mich. L. Rev.* 2320 (1989).
35 See Charles R. Lawrence III, "If He Hollers Let Him Go: Regulating Racist Speech on Campus," 1990 *Duke L.J.* 431 (1990).
36 Richard Delgado et al., *Words that Wound: Critical Race Theory, Assaultive Speech, and the First Amendment* (1993).
37 UWM Post, 774 F. Supp. 1163; *Doe v. Univ. of Mich.*, 721 F. Supp. 852.
38 *The Queen v. Keegstra*, [1990] 3 S.C.R. 697.
39 See Delgado and Stefancic, *Understanding Words that Wound, supra* note 13.
40 Delgado, "Giving Way," *supra* note 28.
41 *Id.* at 174.

hate speech regulation put forth by liberals[42] and another "toughlove" set favored by the neoconservative right.[43] These authors also examined First Amendment romanticism and the idea that only by protecting "the speech we hate" can we safeguard the speech we love.[44]

Further scholarship built upon narrative theory and cognitive psychology to address why more speech—an accurate, countervailing message—cannot always counter the evil of hate speech and why judges find it so difficult to balance free speech and extrinsic interests.[45] Authors examined the experience of other Western democracies that prize freedom of expression, but that nevertheless punish hate speech;[46] they demonstrated that a climate of hate propaganda often precedes and accompanies atrocities like Indian extermination or the Holocaust.[47] The debate over hate speech, then, has become more nuanced, while showing no sign of diminished intensity.

III. The Source of the Tension

If the hate speech debate highlights a tension between civil liberties and civil rights generally, what is the source of that tension conceptually, historically, and ideologically?

A. CONCEPTUALLY

Speech and equality are, as mentioned earlier, aspects of the good life. But they correspond to somewhat different facets. Like most civil liberties, speech exhibits an individual dimension; it is an element of self-expression. Unlike equality and civil rights, which are inherently social in nature, liberty interests are ones we are capable of exercising by ourselves. "Leave me alone; I've got my rights." "Stay off that property; it's mine." "I'll say what I please, this is a free country." As our Critical Legal Studies forebears pointed out, rights of this type correspond to our individual natures. They separate us, emphasizing our individualistic, rights-guarding, solitary tendencies.[48]

Although that characterization might seem needlessly dire, with hate speech at least it may contain a grain of truth. Race may be a social construction, requiring a tacit agreement to endow certain minor human differences with great significance. But how do racial categories receive their content, if not from a system of images, messages, media roles and coverage, narratives, scripts, jokes, and code words such as "those people," "inner city resident," and "unassimilable hordes"—in short, hate speech?[49]

---

42 See Delgado and Yun, "Bloodied Chickens," *supra* note 29.

43 See Richard Delgado and David Yun, "The Neoconservative Case Against Hate-Speech Regulation—Lively, D'Souza, Gates, Carter, and the Toughlove Crowd," 47 *Vand. L. Rev.* 1807 (1994).

44 Richard Delgado and David Yun, "'The Speech We Hate': First Amendment Totalism, the ACLU, and the Principle of Dialogic Politics," 27 *Ariz. St. L.J.* 1281 (1995).

45 Richard Delgado and Jean Stefancic, "Images of the Outsider in American Law and Culture: Can Free Expression Remedy Systemic Social Ills?," 77 *Cornell L. Rev.* 1258 (1992); Richard Delgado and Jean Stefancic, "Norms and Narratives: Can Judges Avoid Serious Moral Error?," 69 *Tex. L. Rev.* 1929 (1991). See also Richard Delgado and Jean Stefancic, "Hateful Speech, Loving Communities: Why Our Notion of 'A Just Balance' Changes So Slowly," 82 *Cal. L. Rev.* 851 (1994) [hereinafter Delgado and Stefancic, "Hateful Speech"].

46 See, e.g., Kevin Boyle, "Hate Speech—The United States Versus the Rest of the World," 53 *Me. L. Rev.* 487, 489 (2001). See also Lee Bollinger, *The Tolerant Society* 38 (1986).

47 See generally Alexander Tsesis, *Destructive Messages: How Hate Speech Paves the Way for Harmful Social Movements* (2002).

48 See, e.g., Richard Delgado, "Critical Legal Studies and the Realities of Race—Does the Fundamental Contradiction Have a Corollary?," 23 *Harv. C.R.-C.L. L. Rev.* 407 (1988) (considering the Critical Legal Studies view of rights in relation to minorities' situation); Richard Delgado, "The Ethereal Scholar: Does Critical Legal Studies Have What Minorities Want?," 22 *Harv. C.R.-C.L. L. Rev.* 301 (1987); Peter Gabel, "The Phenomenology of Rights-Consciousness and the Pact of the Withdrawn Selves," 62 *Tex. L. Rev.* 1563 (1984). Civil liberties may hold special appeal to those whose experience has taught them that solo activity is the road to happiness and success; civil rights and broad social justice may attract those whose lives have taught them the need for cooperation and community.

49 See Delgado and Stefancic, "Images of the Outsider," *supra* note 45.

Defenders of hate speech emphasize its liberty aspect; detractors focus on its impact on social values and justice. The tension arises from what each group chooses to highlight in its own and then minimize in the other's position.

A second dichotomy, between capitalism and democratic ideals, built into our system of law and politics takes on special force in connection with hate speech.[50] Our public law, as everyone knows, is committed to radical democracy. All men and women are equal; one person, one vote, and so on. By the same token, our system of tripartite government features a system of checks and balances, with each branch of government playing its own role and limiting the discretion of the others.[51] Our private law, however, is based on libertarian principles and, in the marketplace, capitalism.[52]

This disjunction between a public law full of lofty democratic precepts and aspirations, and a system of moneymaking essentially governed by the acquisitive impulse and protection of settled interests, rarely attracts notice, at least when the two spheres are operating smoothly.[53] Hate speech is a civil liberty that, much like most manifestations of racial discrimination, distorts the marketplace so that private preferences operate irrationally and are impervious to change. It also disserves the dominant values of the public sphere, endangering democratic decision-making and full inclusion.[54] Regardless of the public or private terms with which one seeks to justify hate speech, one finds little to commend in it. A strange form of liberty, it wars with other liberties at the same time that it erodes the system of mutual respect on which our society aspires to build a just state.

B. HISTORICALLY

If civil rights and civil liberties correspond to different impulses and conceptions of national life, they also contract and expand in response to different forces. Many free speech advocates seem to assume a romantic dynamic in which both civil rights and civil liberties expand in response to advancing morality. They believe that when we are good, virtuous, generous, and mindful of our better natures, we expand both our freedoms and the inclusiveness of our institutions.

Derrick Bell and other historians have shown that the interaction of civil rights and civil liberties is more complicated than this idealistic view.[55] Civil rights expand most during wartime or periods of international competition, such as the Cold War, when African Americans registered impressive gains.[56] Those times, of course, are when civil liberties are most in danger of contraction.[57] Conversely, during times of *internal* competition and scarcity, for example when jobs are scarce, the nation experiences an upsurge in racism and a decrease in generosity towards the perceived outcast.[58] But domestic socioeconomic competition seems to have little effect on our regime of civil liberties. Thus, the material forces that drive civil rights and civil liberties differ. One could, of course, still maintain that the two

50 See Richard Delgado, "Where Is My Body? Stanley Fish's Long Goodbye to Law," 99 *Mich. L. Rev.* 1370, 1384–89 (2001).
51 *Id.* at 1380–89.
52 *Id.* at 1385–89.
53 *Id.* at 1386.
54 See Richard Delgado, "Rodrigo's Second Chronicle: The Economics and Politics of Race," 91 *Mich. L. Rev.* 1183, 1189–98 (1993).
55 See, e.g., Derrick Bell, "*Brown v. Board of Education* and the Interest-Convergence Dilemma," 93 *Harv. L. Rev.* 518 (1980).
56 See Mary Dudziak, *Cold War Civil Rights: Race and the Image of American Democracy* 79–114, 249–54 (2000). See also Richard Delgado, "Explaining the Rise and Fall of African American Fortunes—Interest Convergence and Civil Rights Gains," 37 *Harv. C.R.-C.L. L. Rev.* 369 (2002) (book review) (discussing Cold War tensions as contributing to *Brown v. Board of Education* and the Civil Rights Act of 1964).
57 See Richard Delgado, *Justice at War: Civil Liberties and Civil Rights During Times of Crisis* 56–91 (2003).
58 This socioeconomic competition theory of racism and discrimination was probably first explained by Gordon Allport. See generally Gordon W. Allport, *The Nature of Prejudice* (1979).

are aspects of the same broader system of social goods or ideal governance. But one would need to concede, I think, that they flourish and contract at different times, in response to different forces.

C. IDEOLOGICALLY AND CONSTITUTIONALLY

The original Constitution protected the property and political interests of white males, while providing for the continuation of the institution of slavery in no fewer than six clauses.[59] When the Bill of Rights added protection of speech, the Framers almost certainly had in mind the speech, music, literature, arts, and scientific discourse of elite, educated white males, rather than that of women writers, poets, anarchists, immigrants, or black slaves.[60] The document was, in short, stronger on liberty than equality. The protection of the latter came much later, after a bloody civil war and three constitutional amendments.

One could argue that the Fourteenth Amendment gives the First Amendment an equality-protecting gloss, since a common legal maxim holds that a later writing supersedes a previous one on the same subject.[61] But courts and the ACLU have not endorsed this argument. In the meantime, the two sets of constitutional values—protecting equality and safeguarding liberty—operate side by side. They enable us to say, at times of crisis, "We may be sacrificing X—temporarily and slightly—but we are still the Y-est country in the world." Embracing contradictory values enhances legitimacy; when the need arises, one can limit one value and point out how the other remains in full force.

Occasionally, one hears that it is the First Amendment that makes America the most prosperous, freest, most generous country in the world, with the highest standard of living and the greatest degree of personal freedom. However, it may be that the exceptions to the system of free expression, rather than the system itself, make America the country it is. The United States today stands unquestionably atop the world in two dominant respects—military might and economic power.[62] But if our system of free speech plays any part in those achievements, it is because of the protection we afford official and commercial secrets, inventions and creative works.[63] And, of course, everyone knows that the speech of soldiers and government workers is much less free than that of the citizenry at large.

Apart from economic and military power, the United States does not stand at the top of the world.[64] A great income gap separates the richest and poorest sectors, and the country also exhibits high rates of misery in minority communities, including suicide, alcoholism, divorce, incarceration, and early death.[65] Hate speech and media stereotypes, which undoubtedly contribute to the discrimination that engenders this misery, are free under current law. Free speech law, then, may contribute to the flaws of the United States, while the exceptions are responsible for much of its military-industrial prowess. Our reigning free speech ideology pays scant attention to this, just as it screens from view the compromises between liberty and equality reflected in the original Constitution. Thus, many people would wrongly conclude that speech is equally good for everyone and responsible for much of this country's wealth and well-being, when matters are

59 See Derrick Bell, *Race, Racism, and American Law* 45–48 (3rd ed. 2000).
60 See Delgado and Stefancic, "Hateful Speech," *supra* note 45, at 862.
61 See Richard Delgado, "Toward a Legal Realist View of the First Amendment," 113 *Harv. L. Rev.* 778, 800 (2000).
62 *Id.* at 794–95.
63 *Id.*
64 *Id.*
65 *Id.*

more complicated than that and close to being the other way around.

IV. Is Your Masthead Dysfunctional? How to Live with Competing Paradigms While on the Law Review or Anywhere Else

We want and need both liberty and equality. Yet those two values often are at odds. Hate speech may bring this conflict into bold relief, but I suspect that examining other areas would reveal similar strains and tensions between what we consider civil rights and civil liberties.

In part because we bring different histories to such controversies, we tend to act as though one half of the problem is insignificant or should be solved by the other side's coming around to our position. For instance, when some people learn that a university is considering a hate speech code, they will frame the issue as a First Amendment problem. This position then shifts the burden to the adversary to show that the interest in protecting members of the minority community from insults and name-calling is compelling enough to overcome the usual presumption that speech should be free.[66] Moreover, the university must show that no less restrictive means are available to advance its objective of protecting outsider groups from disparagement. It must also contend with a host of legal rules, such as the prohibition on content or viewpoint regulation,[67] and maxims such as "the best cure for bad speech is more speech."[68] Furthermore, what of the decision maker who will adjudicate claims under the new rules? Might he or she not turn into an overbearing tyrant, imposing his or her own notions of political correctness on an environment that flourishes best when speech is free? For the one whose sympathies run to free speech, certain slopes will look slippery and hard to draw. Couldn't practically everything be considered hate speech, even *Hamlet*?

Others, however, will frame the problem in terms of a different value, equality.[69] Hate speech targets vulnerable minority groups by silencing, marginalizing, and causing some to underperform or drop out. It teaches all who hear or learn about it that equality and civil rights are of no great value, and demoralizes those who would wish to live in a more respectful society. This group will see nothing problematic with granting campuses the power to enact reasonable rules protecting vulnerable members of their communities in order to safeguard core values and institutional concerns emanating from the Thirteenth and Fourteenth amendments.[70]

If one characterizes the issue in this light, a similar set of doctrines and discursive strategies comes into play, but from a different direction. The side championing the right of the hate speaker now needs to show that protecting that form of speech is compelling enough to overcome the legal system's usual presumption in favor of equality and civil rights. It will need to show that the interest of the supremacist in hurling abuse is discharged in the way least damaging to equality. This group, too, will harbor concerns about the adjudicator of such controversies, but from the opposite standpoint. Will he or she have a sufficient background in minority history, code words, and vulnerabilities to know what to look for? A

66 Delgado, "Narratives in Collision," *supra* note 13, at 345–46.

67 See *supra* text accompanying note 19. See also Rodney A. Smolla, "Information as Contraband: The First Amendment and Liability for Trafficking in Speech," 96 *Nw. U. L. Rev.* 1099, 1122 (2002).

68 See *supra* text accompanying note 16. See also Felicity Barringer, "Campus Battle Pits Freedom of Speech against Racial Slurs," *N.Y. Times*, Apr. 25, 1989, at A1; Garry Wills, "In Praise of Censure," *Time*, July 31, 1989, at 71.

69 See Delgado, "Narratives in Collision," *supra* note 13, at 345–46 (commenting on how the adversaries' slopes always look slipperier than one's own).

70 *Id.* at 346.

different set of slopes will look slippery, different lines hard to draw.[71]

It is not just that the two sides begin with different constitutional paradigms. Each hears and is attuned to different stories. One side will see the issue as an extension of society's struggle against superstition and ignorance.[72] Its heroes will be Hollywood figures who stood up to the House Un-American Activities Committee, martyrs like Socrates, Galileo, and Peter Zenger, and theorists like Hobbes, Voltaire, and Hume who defended the value of free expression. They will evoke struggles against state-sponsored censorship, Hollywood blacklists, official religion, and book burning.[73] Juxtaposed with stories like these, the interest of a minority group in guarding against an occasional wounded feeling will not loom large.

The other side, however, will tell a story of its own.[74] That story includes World War II resistance fighters who stood up for Jews and members of the underground railroad who risked their lives to help slaves reach freedom. It includes Martin Luther King, college students who put their lives on the line during the Civil Rights movement, and Mexican farmworkers who picketed California grape producers to protest inhumane working conditions. Compared to that stirring, centuries-long struggle for equality and human decency, the interest of an ignoramus or white supremacist in cussing out a fellow student of color will look pretty attenuated.[75]

My view, and here is where your masthead comes in, is that both views are equally valid but not because they are complementary or coexist easily side by side. They are no more compatible than a private system of competitive free market economics that coexists with a public law system based on radical democracy and equal participation.[76]

Nor can judges easily and comfortably balance the two sets of values. Any new proposal (such as hate speech rules) runs counter to a host of entrenched narratives. The judge, a member of an interpretive community, will be asked to strike the balance in a way that changes the contours of that community,[77] treating groups who are currently outsiders with greater respect than that which they now receive. Judges are not simply balancing two discrete interests, like one neighbor's desire to have a fence and another's wish to receive unblocked sunlight in her living room. Rather they are deciding between two versions of speech/equality, two interpretive communities in which we might live.[78] It is easy to overlook that a vigorous system of free speech requires a respectful audience, while equality, at least in an instrumental sense, requires speech, remonstrance, the right to petition and protest unfair conditions. Thus, speech and equality both presuppose and endanger each other by mechanisms so subtle and linked that shifting the balance in either direction from that to which we are accustomed is a formidable task.[79] The group asking for change can easily be seen as impossible, petty, humorless, or dangerous fanatics prepared to sacrifice precious rights and liberties.

---

71 *Id.* at 345–46.
72 *Id.*
73 *Id.* at 347 (citing Zechariah Chafee, *Free Speech in the United States* 497–501 [1941]).
74 *Id.*
75 *Id.*
76 See *supra* text accompanying notes 50–54.
77 Delgado and Stefancic, "Hateful Speech," *supra* note 45, at 854–59.
78 *Id.* This, in turn, would seem to require a pre-political normative reckoning—perhaps because relatively few cases call for this sort of analysis.
79 *Id.* at 854–59, 868–69.

Still, one can reason around the edges. For example, concerted speech, as hate speech is apt to be since it often targets the same victim time and again, stands on a different footing from the isolated kind. Equality means something more when a black undergraduate is told to go back to Africa than it does when a shopper knocks some groceries off a shelf and is reproved for being a clumsy oaf.[80] We can expand analysis, as the legal realists urge, to include considerations of power, communication science and social theory in examining speech in different settings. We can, occasionally, move each other marginally in a different direction, by force of argument or an apt example.

Changing the way we look at core values, especially in relation to others with which they hold a close association, is a challenging, sometimes uncomfortable task. Recall the lawyer we left nervously waiting to find out his standing in that second book, the one that evaluated him from the unfamiliar reference point of justice. I do not believe such predicaments are forms of cultural schizophrenia. Instead, I think the willingness to confront social reality in all its guises is an indication of courage and good health. *CR-CL*, in my opinion, should keep its masthead exactly the same—but continue to consider, struggle, and reckon with the tension it bespeaks.

14
Kimberlé Crenshaw*

"Demarginalizing the Intersection of Race and Sex: A Black Feminist Critique of Antidiscrimination Doctrine, Feminist Theory and Antiracist Politics"

One of the very few Black women's studies books is entitled *All the Women Are White; All the Blacks Are Men, But Some of Us are Brave.*[1] I have chosen this title as a point of departure in my efforts to develop a Black feminist criticism[2] because it sets forth a problematic consequence of the tendency to treat race and gender as mutually exclusive categories of experience and analysis.[3] In this talk, I want to examine how this tendency is perpetuated by a single-axis framework that is

80 See Delgado, "Words that Wound: A Tort Action," *supra* note 32, at 136 (arguing that racist slurs are more damaging than most other kinds).

* Acting Professor of Law, University of California, Los Angeles Law School.

1 Gloria T. Hull, et al., eds. (The Feminist Press, 1982).

2 For other work setting forth a Black feminist perspective on law, see Judy Scales-Trent, *Black Women and the Constitution: Finding Our Place, Asserting Our Rights* (*Voices of Experience: New Responses to Gender Discourse*), 24 Harv CR-CL L Rev 9 (1989); Regina Austin, *Sapphire-Bound!*, forthcoming in Wisc Women's L J (1989); Angela Harris, *Race and Essentialism in Feminist Legal Theory* (unpublished manuscript on file with author); and Paulette M. Caldwell, *A Hair Piece* (unpublished manuscript on file with author).

3 The most common linguistic manifestation of this analytical dilemma is represented in the conventional usage of the term "Blacks and women." Although it may be true that some people mean to include Black women in either "Blacks" or "women," the context in which the term is used actually suggests that often Black women are not considered. See, for example, Elizabeth Spelman, *The Inessential Woman* 114–15 (Beacon Press, 1988) (discussing an article on Blacks and women in the military where "the racial identity of those identified as 'women' does not become explicit until reference is made to Black women, at which point it also becomes clear that the category of women excludes Black women"). It seems that if Black women were explicitly included, the preferred term would be either "Blacks and white women" or "Black men and all women."

dominant in antidiscrimination law and that is also reflected in feminist theory and antiracist politics.

I will center Black women in this analysis in order to contrast the multidimensionality of Black women's experience with the single-axis analysis that distorts these experiences. Not only will this juxtaposition reveal how Black women are theoretically erased, it will also illustrate how this framework imports its own theoretical limitations that undermine efforts to broaden feminist and antiracist analyses. With Black women as the starting point, it becomes more apparent how dominant conceptions of discrimination condition us to think about subordination as disadvantage occurring along a single categorical axis. I want to suggest further that this single-axis framework erases Black women in the conceptualization, identification and remediation of race and sex discrimination by limiting inquiry to the experiences of otherwise-privileged members of the group. In other words, in race discrimination cases, discrimination tends to be viewed in terms of sex- or class-privileged Blacks; in sex discrimination cases, the focus is on race- and class-privileged women.

This focus on the most privileged group members marginalizes those who are multiply-burdened and obscures claims that cannot be understood as resulting from discrete sources of discrimination. I suggest further that this focus on otherwise-privileged group members creates a distorted analysis of racism and sexism because the operative conceptions of race and sex become grounded in experiences that actually represent only a subset of a much more complex phenomenon.

After examining the doctrinal manifestations of this single-axis framework, I will discuss how it contributes to the marginalization of Black women in feminist theory and in antiracist politics. I argue that Black women are sometimes excluded from feminist theory and antiracist policy discourse because both are predicated on a discrete set of experiences that often does not accurately reflect the interaction of race and gender. These problems of exclusion cannot be solved simply by including Black women within an already established analytical structure. Because the intersectional experience is greater than the sum of racism and sexism, any analysis that does not take intersectionality into account cannot sufficiently address the particular manner in which Black women are subordinated. Thus, for feminist theory and antiracist policy discourse to embrace the experiences and concerns of Black women, the entire framework that has been used as a basis for translating "women's experience" or "the Black experience" into concrete policy demands must be rethought and recast.

As examples of theoretical and political developments that miss the mark with respect to Black women because of their failure to consider intersectionality, I will briefly discuss the feminist critique of rape and separate spheres ideology, and the public policy debates concerning female-headed households within the Black community.

I. The Antidiscrimination Framework

A. THE EXPERIENCE OF INTERSECTIONALITY AND THE DOCTRINAL RESPONSE

One way to approach the problem of intersectionality is to examine how courts frame and interpret the stories of Black women plaintiffs. While I cannot claim to know the circumstances underlying the cases that I will discuss, I nevertheless believe that the way courts interpret claims made by Black women is itself part of Black women's experience and, consequently, a cursory review of cases involving Black female plaintiffs is quite revealing. To illustrate the difficulties inherent in judicial treatment of intersectionality, I will consider three Title VII[4] cases: *DeGraffenreid v General Motors*,[5] *Moore v Hughes Helicopter*[6] and *Payne v Travenol*.[7]

1. *DeGraffenreid v General Motors*.

In *DeGraffenreid*, five Black women brought suit against General Motors, alleging that the employer's seniority system perpetuated the effects of past discrimination against Black women. Evidence adduced at trial revealed that General Motors simply did not hire Black women prior to 1964 and that all of the Black women hired after 1970 lost their jobs in a seniority-based layoff during a subsequent recession. The district court granted summary judgment for the defendant, rejecting the plaintiffs' attempt to bring a suit not on behalf of Blacks or women, but specifically on behalf of Black women. The court stated:

> [P]laintiffs have failed to cite any decisions which have stated that Black women are a special class to be protected from discrimination. The Court's own research has failed to disclose such a decision. The plaintiffs are clearly entitled to a remedy if they have been discriminated against. However, they should not be allowed to combine statutory remedies to create a new 'super-remedy' which would give them relief beyond what the drafters of the relevant statutes intended. Thus, this lawsuit must be examined to see if it states a cause of action for race discrimination, sex discrimination, or alternatively either, but not a combination of both.[8]

Although General Motors did not hire Black women prior to 1964, the court noted that "General Motors has hired ... female employees for a number of years prior to the enactment of the Civil Rights Act of 1964."[9] Because General Motors did hire women—albeit *white women*—during the period that no Black women were hired, there was, in the court's view, no sex discrimination that the seniority system could conceivably have perpetuated.

After refusing to consider the plaintiffs' sex discrimination claim, the court dismissed the race discrimination complaint and recommended its consolidation with another case alleging race discrimination against the same employer.[10] The plaintiffs responded that such consolidation would defeat the purpose of their suit since theirs was not purely a race claim, but an action brought specifically on behalf of Black women alleging race *and* sex discrimination. The court, however, reasoned:

> The legislative history surrounding Title VII does not indicate that the goal of the statute was to create a new classification of 'black women' who would have greater standing than, for example, a black male. The prospect of the creation of new classes of protected minorities, governed only by the mathematical

4 Civil Rights Act of 1964, 42 USC § 2000e, et seq as amended (1982).
5 413 F Supp 142 (E D Mo 1976).
6 708 F2d 475 (9th Cir 1983).
7 673 F2d 798 (5th Cir 1982).
8 *DeGraffenreid*, 413 F Supp at 143.
9 Id at 144.
10 Id at 145. In *Mosley v General Motors*, 497 F Supp 583 (E D Mo 1980), plaintiffs, alleging broad-based racial discrimination at General Motors' St. Louis facility, prevailed in a portion of their Title VII claim. The seniority system challenged in *DeGraffenreid*, however, was not considered in *Mosley*.

> principles of permutation and combination, clearly raises the prospect of opening the hackneyed Pandora's box.[11]

Thus, the court apparently concluded that Congress either did not contemplate that Black women could be discriminated against as "Black women" or did not intend to protect them when such discrimination occurred.[12] The court's refusal in *DeGraffenreid* to acknowledge that Black women encounter combined race and sex discrimination implies that the boundaries of sex and race discrimination doctrine are defined respectively by white women's and Black men's experiences. Under this view, Black women are protected only to the extent that their experiences coincide with those of either of the two groups.[13] Where their experiences are distinct, Black women can expect little protection as long as approaches, such as that in *DeGraffenreid*, which completely obscure problems of intersectionality prevail.

2. *Moore v Hughes Helicopter, Inc.*

Moore v Hughes Helicopters, Inc.[14] presents a different way in which courts fail to understand or recognize Black women's claims. *Moore* is typical of a number of cases in which courts refused to certify Black females as class representatives in race and sex discrimination actions.[15] In *Moore*, the plaintiff alleged that the employer, Hughes Helicopter, practiced race and sex discrimination in promotions to upper-level craft positions and to supervisory jobs. Moore introduced statistical evidence establishing a significant disparity between men and women, and somewhat less of a disparity between Black and white men in supervisory jobs.[16]

---

11 Id at 145.

12 Interestingly, no case has been discovered in which a court denied a white male's attempt to bring a reverse discrimination claim on similar grounds—that is, that sex and race claims cannot be combined because Congress did not intend to protect compound classes. White males in a typical reverse discrimination case are in no better position than the frustrated plaintiffs in *DeGraffenreid*: If they are required to make their claims separately, white males cannot prove race discrimination because white women are not discriminated against, and they cannot prove sex discrimination because Black males are not discriminated against. Yet it seems that courts do not acknowledge the compound nature of most reverse discrimination cases. That Black women's claims automatically raise the question of compound discrimination and white males' "reverse discrimination" cases do not suggest that the notion of compoundedness is somehow contingent upon an implicit norm that is not neutral but is white male. Thus, Black women are perceived as a compound class because they are two steps removed from a white male norm, while white males are apparently not perceived to be a compound class because they somehow represent the norm.

13 I do not mean to imply that all courts that have grappled with this problem have adopted the *DeGraffenreid* approach. Indeed, other courts have concluded that Black women are protected by Title VII. See, for example, *Jefferies v Harris Community Action Ass'n.*, 615 F2d 1025 (5th Cir 1980). I do mean to suggest that the very fact that the Black women's claims are seen as aberrant suggests that sex discrimination doctrine is centered in the experiences of white women. Even those courts that have held that Black women are protected seem to accept that Black women's claims raise issues that the "standard" sex discrimination claims do not. See Elaine W. Shoben, *Compound Discrimination: The Interaction of Race and Sex in Employment Discrimination*, 55 NYU L Rev 793, 803–04 (1980) (criticizing the *Jefferies* use of a sex-plus analysis to create a subclass of Black women).

14 708 F2d 475.

15 See also *Moore v National Association of Securities Dealers*, 27 EPD (CCH) 32,238 (D DC 1981); but see *Edmondson v Simon*, 86 FRD 375 (N D III 1980) (where the court was unwilling to hold as a matter of law that no Black female could represent without conflict the interests of both Blacks and females).

16 708 F2d at 479. Between January 1976 and June 1979, the three years in which Moore claimed that she was passed over for promotion, the percentage of white males occupying first-level supervisory positions ranged from 70.3 to 76.8%; Black males from 8.9 to 10.9%; white women from 1.8 to 3.3%; and Black females from 0 to 2.2%. The overall male/female ratio in the top five labor grades ranged from 100/0% in 1976 to 98/1.8% in 1979. The white/Black ratio was 85/3.3% in 1976 and 79.6/8% in 1979. The overall ratio of men to women in supervisory positions was 98.2 to 1.8% in 1976 to 93.4 to 6.6% in 1979; the Black to white ratio during the same time period was 78.6 to 8.9% and 73.6 to 13.1%

For promotions to the top five labor grades, the percentages were worse. Between 1976 and 1979, the percentage of white males in these positions ranged from 85.3 to 77.9%; Black males 3.3 to 8%; white females from 0 to 1.4%, and Black females from 0 to 0%. Overall, in 1979, 98.2% of the highest level employees were male; 1.8% were female.

Affirming the district court's refusal to certify Moore as the class representative in the sex discrimination complaint on behalf of all women at Hughes, the Ninth Circuit noted approvingly:

> ... Moore had never claimed before the EEOC that she was discriminated against as a female, *but only* as a Black female.... [T]his raised serious doubts as to Moore's ability to adequately represent white female employees.[17]

The curious logic in *Moore* reveals not only the narrow scope of antidiscrimination doctrine and its failure to embrace intersectionality, but also the centrality of white female experiences in the conceptualization of gender discrimination. One inference that could be drawn from the court's statement that Moore's complaint did not entail a claim of discrimination "against females" is that discrimination against Black females is something less than discrimination against females. More than likely, however, the court meant to imply that Moore did not claim that *all* females were discriminated against *but only* Black females. But even thus recast, the court's rationale is problematic for Black women. The court rejected Moore's bid to represent all females apparently because her attempt to specify her race was seen as being at odds with the standard allegation that the employer simply discriminated "against females."

The court failed to see that the absence of a racial referent does not necessarily mean that the claim being made is a more inclusive one. A white woman claiming discrimination against females may be in no better position to represent all women than a Black woman who claims discrimination as a Black female and wants to represent all females. The court's preferred articulation of "against females" is not necessarily more inclusive—it just appears to be so because the racial contours of the claim are not specified.

The court's preference for "against females" rather than "against Black females" reveals the implicit grounding of white female experiences in the doctrinal conceptualization of sex discrimination. For white women, claiming sex discrimination is simply a statement that but for gender, they would not have been disadvantaged. For them there is no need to specify discrimination as *white* females because their race does not contribute to the disadvantage for which they seek redress. The view of discrimination that is derived from this grounding takes race privilege as a given.

Discrimination against a white female is thus the standard sex discrimination claim; claims that diverge from this standard appear to present some sort of hybrid claim. More significantly, because Black females' claims are seen as hybrid, they sometimes cannot represent those who may have "pure" claims of sex discrimination. The effect of this approach is that even though a challenged policy or practice may clearly discriminate against all females, the fact that it has particularly harsh consequences for Black females places Black female plaintiffs at odds with white females.

Moore illustrates one of the limitations of antidiscrimination law's remedial scope and normative vision. The refusal to allow a multiply-disadvantaged class to represent others who may be singularly-disadvantaged defeats efforts to restructure the distribution of opportunity and limits remedial relief to minor adjustments within an established hierarchy. Consequently, "bottom-up" approaches, those which combine all discriminatees in order to challenge an entire employment system, are foreclosed by the limited view of the wrong and the narrow scope of the available remedy. If such "bottom-up" intersectional representation were routinely permitted,

17 708 F2d at 480 (emphasis added).

employees might accept the possibility that there is more to gain by collectively challenging the hierarchy rather than by each discriminatee individually seeking to protect her source of privilege within the hierarchy. But as long as antidiscrimination doctrine proceeds from the premise that employment systems need only minor adjustments, opportunities for advancement by disadvantaged employees will be limited. Relatively privileged employees probably are better off guarding their advantage while jockeying against others to gain more. As a result, Black women—the class of employees which, because of its intersectionality, is best able to challenge all forms of discrimination—are essentially isolated and often required to fend for themselves.

In *Moore*, the court's denial of the plaintiff's bid to represent all Blacks and females left Moore with the task of supporting her race and sex discrimination claims with statistical evidence of discrimination against Black females alone.[18] Because she was unable to represent white women or Black men, she could not use overall statistics on sex disparity at Hughes, nor could she use statistics on race. Proving her claim using statistics on Black women alone was no small task, due to the fact that she was bringing the suit under a disparate impact theory of discrimination.[19]

The court further limited the relevant statistical pool to include only Black women who it determined were qualified to fill the openings in upper-level labor jobs and in supervisory positions.[20] According to the court, Moore had not demonstrated that there were any qualified Black women within her bargaining unit or the general labor pool for either category of jobs.[21] Finally, the court stated that even if it accepted Moore's contention that the percentage of Black females in supervisory positions should equal the percentage of Black females in the employee pool, it still would not find discriminatory impact.[22] Because the promotion of only two Black women into supervisory positions would have achieved the expected mean distribution of Black women within that job category, the court was "unwilling to agree that a prima facie case of disparate impact ha[d] been proven."[23]

The court's rulings on Moore's sex and race claim left her with such a small statistical sample that even if she had proved that there were qualified Black women, she could not have shown discrimination under a disparate impact theory. *Moore* illustrates yet another way that antidiscrimination doctrine essentially erases Black women's distinct experiences and, as a result, deems their discrimination complaints groundless.

3. *Payne v Travenol.*

Black female plaintiffs have also encountered difficulty in their efforts to win certification as class representatives in some race discrimination actions. This problem typically arises in

18 Id at 484–86.

19 Under the disparate impact theory that prevailed at the time, the plaintiff had to introduce statistics suggesting that a policy or procedure disparately affects the members of a protected group. The employer could rebut that evidence by showing that there was a business necessity supporting the rule. The plaintiff then countered the rebuttal by showing that there was a less discriminatory alternative. See, for example, *Griggs v Duke Power*, 401 US 424 (1971); *Connecticut v Teal*, 457 US 440 (1982).

A central issue in a disparate impact case is whether the impact proved is statistically significant. A related issue is how the protected group is defined. In many cases a Black female plaintiff would prefer to use statistics which include white women and/or Black men to indicate that the policy in question does in fact disparately affect the protected class. If, as in *Moore*, the plaintiff may use only statistics involving Black women, there may not be enough Black women employees to create a statistically significant sample.

20 Id at 484.

21 The court buttressed its finding with respect to the upper-level labor jobs with statistics for the Los Angeles Metropolitan Area which indicated that there were only 0.2% Black women within comparable job categories. Id at 485 n 119.

22 Id at 486.

23 Id.

cases where statistics suggest significant disparities between Black and white workers and further disparities between Black men and Black women. Courts in some cases[24] have denied certification based on logic that mirrors the rationale in *Moore*: The sex disparities between Black men and Black women created such conflicting interests that Black women could not possibly represent Black men adequately. In one such case, *Payne v Travenol*,[25] two Black female plaintiffs alleging race discrimination brought a class action suit on behalf of all Black employees at a pharmaceutical plant.[26] The court refused, however, to allow the plaintiffs to represent Black males and granted the defendant's request to narrow the class to Black women only. Ultimately, the district court found that there had been extensive racial discrimination at the plant and awarded back pay and constructive seniority to the class of Black female employees. But, despite its finding of general race discrimination, the court refused to extend the remedy to Black men for fear that their conflicting interests would not be adequately addressed;[27] the Fifth Circuit affirmed.[28]

Notably, the plaintiffs in *Travenol* fared better than the similarly-situated plaintiff in *Moore*: They were not denied use of meaningful statistics showing an overall pattern of race discrimination simply because there were no men in their class. The plaintiffs' bid to represent all Black employees, however, like Moore's attempt to represent all women employees, failed as a consequence of the court's narrow view of class interest.

Even though *Travenol* was a partial victory for Black women, the case specifically illustrates how antidiscrimination doctrine generally creates a dilemma for Black women. It forces them to choose between specifically articulating the intersectional aspects of their subordination, thereby risking their ability to represent Black men, or ignoring intersectionality in order to state a claim that would not lead to the exclusion of Black men. When one considers the political consequences of this dilemma, there is little wonder that many people within the Black community view the specific articulation of Black women's interests as dangerously divisive.

In sum, several courts have proved unable to deal with intersectionality, although for contrasting reasons. In *DeGraffenreid*, the court refused to recognize the possibility of compound discrimination against Black women and analyzed their claim using the employment of white women as the historical base. As a consequence, the employment experiences of white women obscured the distinct discrimination that Black women experienced.

Conversely, in *Moore*, the court held that a Black woman could not use statistics reflecting the overall sex disparity in supervisory and upper-level labor jobs because she had not claimed discrimination as a woman, but "only" as a Black woman. The court would not entertain the notion that

24 See *Strong v Arkansas Blue Cross & Blue Shield, Inc.*, 87 FRD 496 (E D Ark 1980); *Hammons v Folger Coffee Co.*, 87 FRD 600 (W D Mo 1980); *Edmondson v Simon*, 86 FRD 375 (N D Ill 1980); *Vuyanich v Republic National Bank of Dallas*, 82 FRD 420 (N D Tex 1979); *Colston v Maryland Cup Corp.*, 26 Fed Rules Serv 940 (D Md 1978).

25 416 F Supp 248 (N D Miss 1976).

26 The suit commenced on March 2, 1972, with the filing of a complaint by three employees seeking to represent a class of persons allegedly subjected to racial discrimination at the hands of the defendants. Subsequently, the plaintiffs amended the complaint to add an allegation of sex discrimination. Of the original named plaintiffs, one was a Black male and two were Black females. In the course of the three-year period between the filing of the complaint and the trial, the only named male plaintiff received permission of the court to withdraw for religious reasons. Id at 250.

27 As the dissent in *Travenol* pointed out, there was no reason to exclude Black males from the scope of the remedy after counsel had presented sufficient evidence to support a finding of discrimination against Black men. If the rationale for excluding Black males was the potential conflict between Black males and Black females, then "[i]n this case, to paraphrase an old adage, the proof of plaintiffs' ability to represent the interests of Black males was in the representation thereof." 673 F2d at 837–38.

28 673 F2d 798 (5th Cir 1982).

discrimination experienced by Black women is indeed sex discrimination-provable through disparate impact statistics on women.

Finally, courts, such as the one in *Travenol*, have held that Black women cannot represent an entire class of Blacks due to presumed class conflicts in cases where sex additionally disadvantaged Black women. As a result, in the few cases where Black women are allowed to use overall statistics indicating racially disparate treatment, Black men may not be able to share in the remedy.

Perhaps it appears to some that I have offered inconsistent criticisms of how Black women are treated in antidiscrimination law: I seem to be saying that in one case, Black women's claims were rejected and their experiences obscured because the court refused to acknowledge that the employment experience of Black women can be distinct from that of white women, while in other cases, the interests of Black women were harmed because Black women's claims were viewed as so distinct from the claims of either white women or Black men that the court denied to Black females representation of the larger class. It seems that I have to say that Black women are the same and harmed by being treated differently, or that they are different and harmed by being treated the same. But I cannot say both.

This apparent contradiction is but another manifestation of the conceptual limitations of the single-issue analyses that intersectionality challenges. The point is that Black women can experience discrimination in any number of ways and that the contradiction arises from our assumptions that their claims of exclusion must be unidirectional. Consider an analogy to traffic in an intersection, coming and going in all four directions. Discrimination, like traffic through an intersection, may flow in one direction, and it may flow in another. If an accident happens in an intersection, it can be caused by cars traveling from any number of directions and, sometimes, from all of them. Similarly, if a Black woman is harmed because she is in the intersection, her injury could result from sex discrimination or race discrimination.

Judicial decisions which premise intersectional relief on a showing that Black women are specifically recognized as a class are analogous to a doctor's decision at the scene of an accident to treat an accident victim only if the injury is recognized by medical insurance. Similarly, providing legal relief only when Black women show that their claims are based on race or on sex is analogous to calling an ambulance for the victim only after the driver responsible for the injuries is identified. But it is not always easy to reconstruct an accident: Sometimes the skid marks and the injuries simply indicate that they occurred simultaneously, frustrating efforts to determine which driver caused the harm. In these cases the tendency seems to be that no driver is held responsible, no treatment is administered, and the involved parties simply get back in their cars and zoom away.

To bring this back to a non-metaphorical level, I am suggesting that Black women can experience discrimination in ways that are both similar to and different from those experienced by white women and Black men. Black women sometimes experience discrimination in ways similar to white women's experiences; sometimes they share very similar experiences with Black men. Yet often they experience double-discrimination—the combined effects of practices which discriminate on the basis of race, and on the basis of sex. And sometimes, they experience discrimination as Black women—not the sum of race and sex discrimination, but as Black women.

Black women's experiences are much broader than the general categories that discrimination discourse provides. Yet the continued insistence that Black women's demands and needs be filtered through categorical analyses that completely obscure their experiences guarantees that their needs will seldom be addressed.

B. THE SIGNIFICANCE OF DOCTRINAL TREATMENT OF INTERSECTIONALITY

DeGraffenreid, *Moore* and *Travenol* are doctrinal manifestations of a common political and theoretical approach to discrimination which operates to marginalize Black women. Unable to grasp the importance of Black women's intersectional experiences, not only courts, but feminist and civil rights thinkers as well have treated Black women in ways that deny both the unique compoundedness of their situation and the centrality of their experiences to the larger classes of women and Blacks. Black women are regarded either as too much like women or Blacks and the compounded nature of their experience is absorbed into the collective experiences of either group or as too different, in which case Black women's Blackness or femaleness sometimes has placed their needs and perspectives at the margin of the feminist and Black liberationist agendas.

While it could be argued that this failure represents an absence of political will to include Black women, I believe that it reflects an uncritical and disturbing acceptance of dominant ways of thinking about discrimination. Consider first the definition of discrimination that seems to be operative in antidiscrimination law: Discrimination which is wrongful proceeds from the identification of a specific class or category; either a discriminator intentionally identifies this category, or a process is adopted which somehow disadvantages all members of this category.[29] According to the dominant view, a discriminator treats all people within a race or sex category similarly. Any significant experiential or statistical variation within this group suggests either that the group is not being discriminated against or that conflicting interests exist which defeat any attempts to bring a common claim.[30] Consequently, one generally cannot combine these categories. Race and sex, moreover, become significant only when they operate to explicitly *disadvantage* the victims; because the *privileging* of whiteness or maleness is implicit, it is generally not perceived at all.

Underlying this conception of discrimination is a view that the wrong which antidiscrimination law addresses is the use of race or gender factors to interfere with decisions that would otherwise be fair or neutral. This process-based definition is not grounded in a bottom-up commitment to improve the substantive conditions for those who are victimized by the interplay of numerous factors. Instead, the dominant message of antidiscrimination law is that it will regulate only the limited extent to which race or sex interferes with the process of determining outcomes. This narrow objective is facilitated by the top-down strategy of using a singular "but for" analysis to ascertain the effects of race or sex. Because the scope of antidiscrimination law is so limited, sex and race discrimination have come to be defined in terms of the experiences of those who are privileged *but for* their racial or sexual characteristics. Put differently, the paradigm of sex discrimination tends to be based on the experiences of white women; the model of race discrimination tends to be based on the experiences of the most privileged Blacks. Notions of what constitutes race and sex discrimination are, as a result, narrowly

---

29 In much of antidiscrimination doctrine, the presence of intent to discriminate distinguishes unlawful from lawful discrimination. See *Washington v Davis*, 426 US 229, 239–45 (1976) (proof of discriminatory purpose required to substantiate Equal Protection violation). Under Title VII, however, the Court has held that statistical data showing a disproportionate impact can suffice to support a finding of discrimination. See *Griggs*, 401 US at 432. Whether the distinction between the two analyses will survive is an open question. See *Wards Cove Packing Co., Inc. v Atonio*, 109 S Ct 2115, 2122–23 (1989) (plaintiffs must show more than mere disparity to support a prima facie case of disparate impact). For a discussion of the competing normative visions that underlie the intent and effects analyses, see Alan David Freeman, *Legitimizing Racial Discrimination Through Antidiscrimination Law: A Critical Review of Supreme Court Doctrine*, 62 Minn L Rev 1049 (1978).

30 See, for example, *Moore*, 708 F2d at 479.

tailored to embrace only a small set of circumstances, none of which include discrimination against Black women.

To the extent that this general description is accurate, the following analogy can be useful in describing how Black women are marginalized in the interface between antidiscrimination law and race and gender hierarchies: Imagine a basement which contains all people who are disadvantaged on the basis of race, sex, class, sexual preference, age and/or physical ability. These people are stacked—feet standing on shoulders—with those on the bottom being disadvantaged by the full array of factors, up to the very top, where the heads of all those disadvantaged by a singular factor brush up against the ceiling. Their ceiling is actually the floor above which only those who are not disadvantaged in any way reside. In efforts to correct some aspects of domination, those above the ceiling admit from the basement only those who can say that "but for" the ceiling, they too would be in the upper room. A hatch is developed through which those placed immediately below can crawl. Yet this hatch is generally available only to those who—due to the singularity of their burden and their otherwise privileged position relative to those below—are in the position to crawl through. Those who are multiply-burdened are generally left below unless they can somehow pull themselves into the groups that are permitted to squeeze through the hatch.

As this analogy translates for Black women, the problem is that they can receive protection only to the extent that their experiences are recognizably similar to those whose experiences tend to be reflected in antidiscrimination doctrine. If Black women cannot conclusively say that "but for" their race or "but for" their gender they would be treated differently, they are not invited to climb through the hatch but told to wait in the unprotected margin until they can be absorbed into the broader, protected categories of race and sex.

Despite the narrow scope of this dominant conception of discrimination and its tendency to marginalize those whose experiences cannot be described within its tightly-drawn parameters, this approach has been regarded as the appropriate framework for addressing a range of problems. In much of feminist theory and, to some extent, in antiracist politics, this framework is reflected in the belief that sexism or racism can be meaningfully discussed without paying attention to the lives of those other than the race-, gender- or class-privileged. As a result, both feminist theory and antiracist politics have been organized, in part, around the equation of racism with what happens to the Black middle-class or to Black men, and the equation of sexism with what happens to white women.

Looking at historical and contemporary issues in both the feminist and the civil rights communities, one can find ample evidence of how both communities' acceptance of the dominant framework of discrimination has hindered the development of an adequate theory and praxis to address problems of intersectionality. This adoption of a single-issue framework for discrimination not only marginalizes Black women within the very movements that claim them as part of their constituency but it also makes the illusive goal of ending racism and patriarchy even more difficult to attain.

II. Feminism and Black Women: "Ain't We Women?"

Oddly, despite the relative inability of feminist politics and theory to address Black women substantively, feminist theory and tradition borrow considerably from Black women's history. For example, "Ain't I a Woman" has come to represent a standard refrain in feminist discourse.[31] Yet the lesson of this powerful oratory is not fully appreciated because the context of the delivery is seldom examined. I would like to tell part of the story because it establishes some themes that have characterized feminist treatment of race and illustrates the importance of including Black women's experiences as a rich source for the critique of patriarchy.

In 1851, Sojourner Truth declared "Ain't I a Woman?" and challenged the sexist imagery used by male critics, to justify the disenfranchisement of women.[32] The scene was a Women's Rights Conference in Akron, Ohio; white male hecklers, invoking stereotypical images of "womanhood," argued that women were too frail and delicate to take on the responsibilities of political activity. When Sojourner Truth rose to speak, many white women urged that she be silenced, fearing that she would divert attention from women's suffrage to emancipation. Truth, once permitted to speak, recounted the horrors of slavery, and its particular impact on Black women:

> Look at my arm! I have ploughed and planted and gathered into barns, and no man could head me—and ain't I a woman? I could work as much and eat as much as a man—when I could get it—and bear the lash as well! And ain't I a woman? I have born thirteen children, and seen most of 'em sold into slavery, and when I cried out with my mother's grief, none but Jesus heard me—and ain't I a woman?[33]

By using her own life to reveal the contradiction between the ideological myths of womanhood and the reality of Black women's experience, Truth's oratory provided a powerful rebuttal to the claim that women were categorically weaker than men. Yet Truth's personal challenge to the coherence of the cult of true womanhood was useful only to the extent that white women were willing to reject the racist attempts to rationalize the contradiction—that because Black women were something less than real women, their experiences had no bearing on true womanhood. Thus, this 19th-century Black feminist challenged not only patriarchy, but she also challenged white feminists wishing to embrace Black women's history to relinquish their vestedness in whiteness.

Contemporary white feminists inherit not the legacy of Truth's challenge to patriarchy but, instead, Truth's challenge to their forbearers. Even today, the difficulty that white women have traditionally experienced in sacrificing racial privilege to strengthen feminism renders them susceptible to Truth's critical question. When feminist theory and politics that claim to reflect *women's* experience and *women's* aspirations do not include or speak to Black women, Black women must ask: "Ain't We Women?" If this is so, how can the claims that "women are," "women believe" and "women need" be made when such claims are inapplicable or unresponsive to the needs, interests and experiences of Black women?

The value of feminist theory to Black women is diminished because it evolves from a white racial context that is seldom acknowledged. Not only are women of color in fact overlooked, but their exclusion is reinforced when *white* women speak for

31 See Phyliss Palmer, *The Racial Feminization of Poverty: Women of Color as Portents of the Future for All Women*, Women's Studies Quarterly 11:3–4 (Fall 1983) (posing the question of why "white women in the women's movement had not created more effective and continuous alliances with Black women" when "simultaneously ... Black women [have] become heroines for the women's movement, a position symbolized by the consistent use of Sojourner Truth and her famous words, "Ain't I a Woman?"").

32 See Paula Giddings, *When and Where I Enter: The Impact of Black Women on Race and Sex in America* 54 (William Morrow and Co, Inc, 1st ed 1984).

33 Eleanor Flexner, *Century of Struggle: The Women's Rights Movement in the United States* 91 (Belknap Press of Harvard University Press, 1975). See also Bell Hooks, *Ain't I a Woman* 159–60 (South End Press, 1981).

and as *women*. The authoritative universal voice—usually white male subjectivity masquerading as non-racial, non-gendered objectivity[34]—is merely transferred to those who, but for gender, share many of the same cultural, economic and social characteristics. When feminist theory attempts to describe women's experiences through analyzing patriarchy, sexuality, or separate spheres ideology, it often overlooks the role of race. Feminists thus ignore how their own race functions to mitigate some aspects of sexism and, moreover, how it often privileges them over and contributes to the domination of other women.[35] Consequently, feminist theory remains *white*, and its potential to broaden and deepen its analysis by addressing non-privileged women remains unrealized.

An example of how some feminist theories are narrowly constructed around white women's experiences is found in the separate spheres literature. The critique of how separate spheres ideology shapes and limits women's roles in the home and in public life is a central theme in feminist legal thought.[36] Feminists have attempted to expose and dismantle separate spheres ideology by identifying and criticizing the stereotypes that traditionally have justified the disparate societal roles assigned to men and women.[37] Yet this attempt to debunk ideological justifications for *women's* subordination offers little insight into the domination of Black women. Because the experiential base upon which many feminist insights are grounded is white, theoretical statements drawn from them are overgeneralized at best, and often wrong.[38] Statements such as "men and women are taught to see men as independent, capable, powerful; men and women are taught to see women as dependent, limited in abilities, and passive,"[39] are common within this literature. But this "observation" overlooks the anomalies created by crosscurrents of racism and sexism. Black men and women live in a society that creates sex-based norms and expectations which racism operates simultaneously to deny; Black men are not viewed as powerful, nor are Black women seen as passive. An effort to develop an ideological explanation of gender domination in the Black community should proceed from an understanding of how crosscutting forces establish gender norms and how the conditions

34 "'Objectivity' is itself an example of the reification of white male thought." Hull et al, eds, *But Some of Us Are Brave* at XXV (cited in note 1).

35 For example, many white females were able to gain entry into previously all white male enclaves not through bringing about a fundamental reordering of male versus female work, but in large part by shifting their "female" responsibilities to poor and minority women.

36 Feminists often discuss how gender-based stereotypes and norms reinforce the subordination of women by justifying their exclusion from public life and glorifying their roles within the private sphere. Law has historically played a role in maintaining this subordination by enforcing the exclusion of women from public life and by limiting its reach into the private sphere. See, for example, Deborah L. Rhode, *Association and Assimilation*, 81 Nw U L Rev 106 (1986); Frances Olsen, *From False Paternalism to False Equality: Judicial Assaults on Feminist Community, Illinois 1869–95*, 84 Mich L Rev 1518 (1986); Martha Minow, *Foreword: Justice Engendered*, 101 Harv L Rev 10 (1987); Nadine Taub and Elizabeth M. Schneider, *Perspectives on Women's Subordination and the Role of Law*, in David Kairys, ed, *The Politics of Law* 117–39 (Pantheon Books, 1982).

37 See works cited in note 36.

38 This criticism is a discrete illustration of a more general claim that feminism has been premised on white middle-class women's experience. For example, early feminist texts such as Betty Friedan's *The Feminine Mystique* (W.W. Norton, 1963), placed white middle-class problems at the center of feminism and thus contributed to its rejection within the Black community. See Hooks, *Ain't I a Woman* at 185–96 (cited in note 33) (noting that feminism was eschewed by Black women because its white middle-class agenda ignored Black women's concerns).

39 Richard A. Wasserstrom, *Racism, Sexism and Preferential Treatment: An Approach to the Topics*, 24 UCLA L Rev 581, 588 (1977). I chose this phrase not because it is typical of most feminist statements of separate spheres; indeed, most discussions are not as simplistic as the bold statement presented here. See, for example, Taub and Schneider, *Perspectives on Women's Subordination and the Role of Law* at 117–39 (cited in note 36).

of Black subordination wholly frustrate access to these norms. Given this understanding, perhaps we can begin to see why Black women have been dogged by the stereotype of the pathological matriarch[40] or why there have been those in the Black liberation movement who aspire to create institutions and to build traditions that are intentionally patriarchal.[41]

Because ideological and descriptive definitions of patriarchy are usually premised upon white female experiences, feminists and others informed by feminist literature may make the mistake of assuming that since the role of Black women in the family and in other Black institutions does not always resemble the familiar manifestations of patriarchy in the white community, Black women are somehow exempt from patriarchal norms. For example, Black women have traditionally worked outside the home in numbers far exceeding the labor participation rate of white women.[42] An analysis of patriarchy that highlights the history of white women's exclusion from the workplace might permit the inference that Black women have not been burdened by this particular gender-based expectation. Yet the very fact that Black women must work conflicts with norms that women should not, often creating personal, emotional and relationship problems in Black women's lives. Thus, Black women are burdened not only because they often have to take on responsibilities that are not traditionally feminine but, moreover, their assumption of these roles is sometimes interpreted within the Black community as either Black women's failure to live up to such norms or as another manifestation of racism's scourge upon the Black community.[43] This is one of the many aspects of intersectionality that cannot be understood through an analysis of patriarchy rooted in white experience.

Another example of how theory emanating from a white context obscures the multidimensionality of Black women's lives is found in feminist discourse on rape. A central political issue on the feminist agenda has been the pervasive problem of rape. Part of the intellectual and political effort to mobilize around this issue has involved the development of a historical critique of the role that law has played in establishing the bounds of normative sexuality and in regulating female sexual behavior.[44] Early carnal knowledge statutes and rape laws are understood within this discourse to illustrate that the objective of rape statutes traditionally has not been to protect women from coercive intimacy but to protect and maintain a property-like interest in female chastity.[45] Although feminists quite rightly criticize these objectives, to characterize rape law as reflecting male control over female sexuality is for Black women an oversimplified account and an ultimately inadequate account.

---

40 For example, Black families have sometimes been cast as pathological largely because Black women's divergence from the white middle-class female norm. The most infamous rendition of this view is found in the Moynihan report which blamed many of the Black community's ills on a supposed pathological family structure. For a discussion of the report and its contemporary reincarnation, see [pp. 284–85].

41 See Hooks, *Ain't I a Woman* at 94–99 (cited in note 33) (discussing the elevation of sexist imagery in the Black liberation movement during the 1960s).

42 See generally Jacqueline Jones, *Labor of Love, Labor of Sorrow; Black Women, Work, and the Family from Slavery to the Present* (Basic Books, 1985); Angela Davis, *Women, Race and Class* (Random House, 1981).

43 As Elizabeth Higginbotham noted, "women, who often fail to conform to 'appropriate' sex roles, have been pictured as, and made to feel, inadequate—even though as women, they possess traits recognized as positive when held by men in the wider society. Such women are stigmatized because their lack of adherence to expected gender roles is seen as a threat to the value system." Elizabeth Higginbotham, *Two Representative Issues in Contemporary Sociological Work on Black Women*, in Hull, et al, eds, *But Some of Us Are Brave* at 95 (cited in note 1).

44 See generally Susan Brownmiller, *Against Our Will* (Simon and Schuster, 1975); Susan Estrich, *Real Rape* (Harvard University Press, 1987).

45 See Brownmiller, *Against Our Will* at 17; see generally Estrich, *Real Rape*.

Rape statutes generally do not reflect *male* control over *female* sexuality, but *white* male regulation of *white* female sexuality.[46] Historically, there has been absolutely no institutional effort to regulate Black female chastity.[47] Courts in some states had gone so far as to instruct juries that, unlike white women, Black women were not presumed to be chaste.[48] Also, while it was true that the attempt to regulate the sexuality of white women placed unchaste women outside the law's protection, racism restored a fallen white woman's chastity where the alleged assailant was a Black man.[49] No such restoration was available to Black women.

The singular focus on rape as a manifestation of male power over female sexuality tends to eclipse the use of rape as a weapon of racial terror.[50] When Black women were raped by white

46 One of the central theoretical dilemmas of feminism that is largely obscured by universalizing the white female experience is that experiences that are described as a manifestation of male control over females can be instead a manifestation of dominant group control over all subordinates. The significance is that other nondominant men may not share in, participate in or connect with the behavior, beliefs or actions at issue, and may be victimized themselves by "male" power. In other contexts, however, "male authority" might include nonwhite men, particularly in private sphere contexts. Efforts to think more clearly about when Black women are dominated as *women* and when they are dominated as *Black women* are directly related to the question of when power is *male* and when it is *white male*.

47 See Note, *Rape, Racism and the Law*, 6 Harv Women's L J 103, 117–23 (1983) (discussing the historical and contemporary evidence suggesting that Black women are generally not thought to be chaste). See also Hooks, *Ain't I a Woman* at 54 (cited in note 33) (stating that stereotypical images of Black womanhood during slavery were based on the myth that "all black women were immoral and sexually loose"); Beverly Smith, *Black Women's Health: Notes for a Course*, in Hull et al, eds, *But Some of Us Are Brave* at 110 (cited in note 1) (noting that "... white men for centuries have justified their sexual abuse of Black women by claiming that we are licentious, always 'ready' for any sexual encounter").

48 The following statement is probably unusual only in its candor: "What has been said by some of our courts about an unchaste female being a comparatively rare exception is no doubt true where the population is composed largely of the Caucasian race, but we would blind ourselves to actual conditions if we adopted this rule where another race that is largely immoral constitutes an appreciable part of the population." *Dallas v State*, 76 Fla 358, 79 So 690 (1918), quoted in Note, 6 Harv Women's L J at 121 (cited in note 47).

Espousing precisely this view, one commentator stated in 1902: "I sometimes hear of a virtuous Negro woman but the idea is so absolutely inconceivable to me ... I cannot imagine such a creature as a virtuous Negro woman." Id at 82. Such images persist in popular culture. See Paul Grein, *Taking Stock of the Latest Pop Record Surprises*, LA Times § 6 at 1 (July 7, 1988) (recalling the controversy in the late 70s over a Rolling Stones recording which included the line "Black girls just wanna get fucked all night").

Opposition to such negative stereotypes has sometimes taken the form of sexual conservatism. "A desperate reaction to this slanderous myth is the attempt ... to conform to the strictest versions of patriarchal morality." Smith, *Black Women's Health*, in Hull et al, eds, *But Some of Us Are Brave* at 111 (cited in note 1). Part of this reaction is reflected in the attitudes and policies of Black schools which have been notoriously strict in regulating the behavior of female students. See Gail Elizabeth Wyatt, *The Sexual Experience of Afro-American Women*, in Martha Kirkpatrick, ed, *Women's Sexual Experience: Exploration of the Dark Continent* at 24 (Plenum, 1982) (noting "the differences between the predominantly Afro-American universities, where there was far more supervision regarding sexual behavior, and the majority of white colleges, where there were fewer curfews and restrictions placed on the resident"). Any attempt to understand and critique the emphasis on Black virtue without focusing on the racist ideology that places virtue beyond the reach of Black women would be incomplete and probably incorrect.

49 Because of the way the legal system viewed chastity, Black women could not be victims of forcible rape. One commentator has noted that "[a]ccording to governing sterotypes [sic], chastity could not be possessed by Black women. Thus, Black women's rape charges were automatically discounted, and the issue of chastity was contested only in cases where the rape complainant was a white woman." Note, 6 Harv Women's L J at 126 (cited in note 47). Black women's claims of rape were not taken seriously regardless of the offender's race. A judge in 1912 said: "This court will never take the word of a nigger against the word of a white man [concerning rape]." Id at 120. On the other hand, lynching was considered an effective remedy for a Black man's rape of a white woman. Since rape of a white woman by a Black man was "a crime more horrible than death," the only way to assuage society's rage and to make the woman whole again was to brutally murder the Black man. Id at 125.

50 See *The Rape of Black Women as a Weapon of Terror*, in Gerda Lerner, ed, *Black Women in White America* 172–93 (Pantheon Books, 1972). See also Brownmiller, *Against Our Will* (cited in note 44). Even where Brownmiller acknowledges the use of rape as racial terrorism, she resists making a "special case" for Black women by offering evidence that white women were raped by the Klan as well. Id at 139. Whether or not one considers the racist rape of Black women a "special case," such experiences are probably different. In any case, Brownmiller's treatment of the issue raises serious questions about the ability to sustain an analysis of patriarchy without understanding its multiple intersections with racism.

males, they were being raped not as women generally, but as Black women specifically: Their femaleness made them sexually vulnerable to racist domination, while their Blackness effectively denied them any protection.[51] This white male power was reinforced by a judicial system in which the successful conviction of a white man for raping a Black woman was virtually unthinkable.[52]

In sum, sexist expectations of chastity and racist assumptions of sexual promiscuity combined to create a distinct set of issues confronting Black women.[53] These issues have seldom been explored in feminist literature nor are they prominent in antiracist politics. The lynching of Black males, the institutional practice that was legitimized by the regulation of white women's sexuality, has historically and contemporaneously occupied the Black agenda on sexuality and violence. Consequently, Black women are caught between a Black community that, perhaps understandably, views with suspicion attempts to litigate questions of sexual violence, and a feminist community that reinforces those suspicions by focusing on white female sexuality.[54] The suspicion is compounded by the historical fact that the protection of white female sexuality was often the pretext for terrorizing the Black community. Even today some fear that antirape agendas may undermine antiracist objectives. This is the paradigmatic political and theoretical dilemma created by the intersection of race and gender: Black women are caught between ideological and political currents that combine first to create and then to bury Black women's experiences.

---

51 Lerner, *Black Women in White America* at 173.

52 See generally, Note, 6 Harv Women's L J at 103 (cited in note 47).

53 Paula Giddings notes the combined effect of sexual and racial stereotypes: "Black women were seen having all of the inferior qualities of white women without any of their virtues." Giddings, *When and Where I Enter* at 82 (cited in note 32).

54 Susan Brownmiller's treatment of the Emmett Till case illustrates why antirape politicization makes some African Americans uncomfortable. Despite Brownmiller's quite laudable efforts to discuss elsewhere the rape of Black women and the racism involved in much of the hysteria over the Black male threat, her analysis of the Till case places the sexuality of white women, rather than racial terrorism, at center stage. Brownmiller states: "Rarely has one single case exposed so clearly as Till's the underlying group—male antagonisms over access to women, for what began in Bryant's store should not be misconstrued as an innocent flirtation.... In concrete terms, the accessibility of all white women was on review." Brownmiller, *Against Our Will* at 272 (cited in note 44).

Later, Brownmiller argues:

> And what of the wolf whistle, Till's 'gesture of adolescent bravado'? We are rightly aghast that a whistle could be cause for murder but we must also accept that Emmett Till and J. W. Millam shared something in common. They both understood that the whistle was no small tweet of hubba-hubba or melodious approval for a well-turned ankle. Given the deteriorated situation ... it was a deliberate insult just short of physical assault, a last reminder to Carolyn Bryant that this black boy, Till, had a mind to possess her.

Id at 273.

While Brownmiller seems to categorize the case as one that evidences a conflict over possession, it is regarded in African American history as a tragic dramatization of the South's pathological hatred and fear of African Americans. Till's body, mutilated beyond recognition, was viewed by thousands so that, in the words of Till's mother, "the world could see what they did to my boy." Juan Williams, *Standing for Justice*, in *Eyes on the Prize* 44 (Viking, 1987). The Till tragedy is also regarded as one of the historical events that bore directly on the emergence of the Civil Rights movement. "[W]ithout question it moved black America in a way the Supreme Court ruling on school desegregation could not match." Id. As Williams later observed, "the murder of Emmitt Till had a powerful impact on a generation of blacks. It was this generation, those who were adolescents when Till was killed, that would soon demand justice and freedom in a way unknown in America before." Id at 57. Thus, while Brownmiller looks at the Till case and sees the vicious struggle over the possession of a white woman, African Americans see the case as a symbol of the insane degree to which whites were willing to suppress the Black race. While patriarchal attitudes toward women's sexuality played a supporting role, to place white women center stage in this tragedy is to manifest such confusion over racism as to make it difficult to imagine that the white antirape movement could be sensitive to more subtle racial tensions regarding Black women's participation in it.

III. When and Where I Enter: Integrating an Analysis of Sexism into Black Liberation Politics

Anna Julia Cooper, a 19th-century Black feminist, coined a phrase that has been useful in evaluating the need to incorporate an explicit analysis of patriarchy in any effort to address racial domination.[55] Cooper often criticized Black leaders and spokespersons for claiming to speak for the race, but failing to speak for Black women. Referring to one of Martin Delaney's public claims that where he was allowed to enter, the race entered with him, Cooper countered: "Only the Black Woman can say, when and where I enter ... then and there the whole Negro race enters with me."[56]

Cooper's words bring to mind a personal experience involving two Black men with whom I had formed a study group during our first year of law school. One of our group members, a graduate from Harvard College, often told us stories about a prestigious and exclusive men's club that boasted memberships of several past United States presidents and other influential white males. He was one of its very few Black members. To celebrate completing our first-year exams, our friend invited us to join him at the club for drinks. Anxious to see this fabled place, we approached the large door and grasped the brass door ring to announce our arrival. But our grand entrance was cut short when our friend sheepishly slipped from behind the door and whispered that he had forgotten a very important detail. My companion and I bristled, our training as Black people having taught us to expect yet another barrier to our inclusion; even an informal one-Black-person quota at the establishment was not unimaginable. The tension broke, however, when we learned that *we* would not be excluded because of our race, but that *I* would have to go around to the back door because I was a female. I entertained the idea of making a scene to dramatize the fact that my humiliation as a female was no less painful and my exclusion no more excusable than had we all been sent to the back door because we were Black. But, sensing no general assent to this proposition, and also being of the mind that due to our race a scene would in some way jeopardize all of us, I failed to stand my ground. After all, the Club was about to entertain its first Black guests—even though one would have to enter through the back door.[57]

Perhaps this story is not the best example of the Black community's failure to address problems related to Black women's intersectionality seriously. The story would be more apt if Black women, and only Black women, had to go around to the back door of the club and if the restriction came from within, and not from the outside of the Black community. Still this story does reflect a markedly decreased political and emotional vigilance toward barriers to Black women's enjoyment of privileges that have been won on the basis of race but continue to be denied on the basis of sex.[58]

The story also illustrates the ambivalence among Black women about the degree of political and social capital that ought to be expended toward challenging gender barriers, particularly when the challenges might conflict with the antiracism agenda. While there are a number of reasons—including antifeminist ones—why gender has not figured directly in analyses of the subordination of Black Americans, a central reason is that race is still seen by many as the primary

55 See Anna Julia Cooper, *A Voice from the South* (Negro Universities Press, 1969 reprint of the Aldine Printing House, Ohio, 1892).

56 Id at 31.

57 In all fairness, I must acknowledge that my companion accompanied me to the back door. I remain uncertain, however, as to whether the gesture was an expression of solidarity or an effort to quiet my anger.

58 To this one could easily add class.

oppositional force in Black lives.[59] If one accepts that the social experience of race creates both a primary group identity as well as a shared sense of being under collective assault, some of the reasons that Black feminist theory and politics have not figured prominently in the Black political agenda may be better understood.[60]

The point is not that African Americans are simply involved in a more important struggle. Although some efforts to oppose Black feminism are based on this assumption, a fuller appreciation of the problems of the Black community will reveal that gender subordination does contribute significantly to the destitute conditions of so many African Americans and that it must therefore be addressed. Moreover, the foregoing critique of the single-issue framework renders problematic the claim that the struggle against racism is distinguishable from, much less prioritized over, the struggle against sexism. Yet it is also true that the politics of racial otherness that Black women experience along with Black men prevent Black feminist consciousness from patterning the development of white feminism. For white women, the creation of a consciousness that was distinct from and in opposition to that of white men figured prominently in the development of white feminist politics. Black women, like Black men, live in a community that has been defined and subordinated by color and culture.[61] Although patriarchy clearly operates within the Black community, presenting yet another source of domination to which Black women are vulnerable, the racial context in which Black women find themselves makes the creation of a political consciousness that is oppositional to Black men difficult.

Yet while it is true that the distinct experience of racial otherness militates against the development of an oppositional feminist consciousness, the assertion of racial community sometimes supports defensive priorities that marginalize Black women. Black women's particular interests are thus relegated to the periphery in public policy discussions about the presumed needs of the Black community. The controversy over the movie *The Color Purple* is illustrative. The animating fear behind much of the publicized protest was that by portraying domestic abuse in a Black family, the movie confirmed the negative stereotypes of Black men.[62] The debate over the propriety of presenting such an image on the screen overshadowed the issue of sexism and patriarchy in the Black community. Even though it was sometimes acknowledged that the Black community was not immune from domestic violence and other manifestations of gender

59 An anecdote illustrates this point. A group of female law professors gathered to discuss "Isms in the Classroom." One exercise led by Pat Cain involved each participant listing the three primary factors that described herself. Almost without exception, white women in the room listed their gender either primarily or secondarily; none listed their race. All of the women of color listed their race first, and then their gender. This seems to suggest that identity descriptions seem to begin with the primary source of opposition with whatever the dominant norm is. See Pat Cain, *Feminist Jurisprudence: Grounding the Theories* 19–20 (unpublished manuscript on file with author) (explaining the exercise and noting that "no white woman ever mentions race, whereas every woman of color does" and that, similarly, "straight women do not include 'heterosexual' ... whereas lesbians who are open always include 'lesbian'").

60 For a comparative discussion of Third World feminism paralleling this observation, see Kumari Jayawardena, *Feminism and Nationalism in the Third World* 1–24 (Zed Books Ltd, 1986). Jayawardena states that feminism in the Third World has been "accepted" only within the central struggle against international domination. Women's social and political status has improved most when advancement is necessary to the broader struggle against imperialism.

61 For a discussion of how racial ideology creates a polarizing dynamic which subordinates Blacks and privileges whites, see Kimberlé Crenshaw, *Race, Reform and Retrenchment: Transformation and Legitimation in Antidiscrimination Law,* 101 Harv L Rev 1331, 1371–76 (1988).

62 Jack Matthews, *Three Color Purple Actresses Talk About Its Impact,* LA Times § 6 at 1 (Jan 31, 1986); Jack Matthews, *Some Blacks Critical of Spielberg's Purple,* LA Times § 6 at 1 (Dec 20, 1985). But see Gene Siskel, *Does 'Purple' Hate Men?,* Chicago Tribune § 13 at 16 (Jan 5, 1986); Clarence Page, *Toward a New Black Cinema,* Chicago Tribune § 5 at 3 (Jan 12, 1986).

subordination, some nevertheless felt that in the absence of positive Black male images in the media, portraying such images merely reinforced racial stereotypes.[63] The struggle against racism seemed to compel the subordination of certain aspects of the Black female experience in order to ensure the security of the larger Black community.

The nature of this debate should sound familiar to anyone who recalls Daniel Moynihan's diagnosis of the ills of Black America.[64] Moynihan's report depicted a deteriorating Black family, foretold the destruction of the Black male householder and lamented the creation of the Black matriarch. His conclusions prompted a massive critique from liberal sociologists[65] and from civil rights leaders.[66] Surprisingly, while many critics characterized the report as racist for its blind use of white cultural norms as the standard for evaluating Black families, few pointed out the sexism apparent in Moynihan's labeling Black women as pathological for their "failure" to live up to a white female standard of motherhood.[67]

The latest versions of a Moynihanesque analysis can be found in the Moyers televised special, *The Vanishing Black Family*,[68] and, to a lesser extent, in William Julius Wilson's *The Truly Disadvantaged*.[69] In *The Vanishing Black Family*, Moyers presented the problem of female-headed households as a problem of irresponsible sexuality, induced in part by government policies that encouraged family breakdown.[70] The theme of the report was that the welfare state reinforced the deterioration of the Black family by rendering the Black male's role obsolete. As the argument goes, because Black men know that someone will take care of their families, they are free to make babies and leave them. A corollary to the Moyers view is that welfare is also dysfunctional because it allows poor women to leave men upon whom they would otherwise be dependent.

Most commentators criticizing the program failed to pose challenges that might have revealed the patriarchal assumptions underlying much of the Moyers report. They instead focused on

63 A consistent problem with any negative portrayal of African Americans is that they are seldom balanced by positive images. On the other hand, most critics overlooked the positive transformation of the primary male character in *The Color Purple*.

64 Daniel P. Moynihan, *The Negro Family: The Case for National Action* (Office of Policy Planning and Research, United States Department of Labor, 1965).

65 See Lee Rainwater and William L. Yancey, *The Moynihan Report and the Politics of Controversy* 427–29 (MIT Press, 1967) (containing criticisms of the Moynihan Report by, among others, Charles E. Silberman, Christopher Jencks, William Ryan, Laura Carper, Frank Riessman and Herbert Gans).

66 Id at 395–97 (critics included Martin Luther King, Jr., Benjamin Payton, James Farmer, Whitney Young, Jr. and Bayard Rustin).

67 One of the notable exceptions is Jacquelyne Johnson Jackson, *Black Women in a Racist Society*, in *Racism and Mental Health* 185–86 (University of Pittsburgh Press, 1973).

68 *The Vanishing Black Family* (PBS Television Broadcast, January 1986).

69 William Julius Wilson, *The Truly Disadvantaged: The Inner City, The Underclass and Public Policy* (The University of Chicago Press, 1987).

70 Columnist Mary McGrory, applauding the show, reported that Moyers found that sex was as common in the Black ghetto as a cup of coffee. McGrory, *Moynihan was Right 21 Years Ago*, The Washington Post B1 and B4 (Jan 26, 1986). George Will argued that oversexed Black men were more of a menace than Bull Conner, the Birmingham Police Chief who in 1968 achieved international notoriety by turning fire hoses on protesting school children. George Will, *Voting Rights Won't Fix It*, The Washington Post A23 (Jan 23, 1986). My guess is that the program has influenced the debate about the so-called underclass by providing graphic support to pre-existing tendencies to attribute poverty to individual immorality. During a recent and memorable discussion on the public policy implications of poverty in the Black community, one student remarked that nothing can be done about Black poverty until Black men stop acting like "roving penises," Black women stop having babies "at the drop of a hat," and they all learn middle-class morality. The student cited the Moyers report as her source.

the dimension of the problem that was clearly recognizable as racist.[71] White feminists were equally culpable. There was little, if any, published response to the Moyers report from the white feminist community. Perhaps feminists were under the mistaken assumption that since the report focused on the Black community, the problems highlighted were racial, not gender based. Whatever the reason, the result was that the ensuing debates over the future direction of welfare and family policy proceeded without significant feminist input. The absence of a strong feminist critique of the Moynihan/Moyers model not only impeded the interests of Black women, but it also compromised the interests of growing numbers of white women heads of household who find it difficult to make ends meet.[72]

William Julius Wilson's *The Truly Disadvantaged* modified much of the moralistic tone of this debate by reframing the issue in terms of a lack of marriageable Black men.[73] According to Wilson, the decline in Black marriages is not attributable to poor motivation, bad work habits or irresponsibility but instead is caused by structural economics which have forced Black unskilled labor out of the work force. Wilson's approach represents a significant move away from that of Moynihan/Moyers in that he rejects their attempt to center the analysis on the morals of the Black community. Yet, he too considers the proliferation of female-headed households as dysfunctional *per se* and fails to explain fully why such households are so much in peril. Because he incorporates no analysis of the way the structure of the economy and the workforce subordinates the interests of women, especially childbearing Black women, Wilson's suggested reform begins with finding ways to put Black men back in the family.[74] In Wilson's view, we must change the economic structure with an eye toward providing more Black jobs for Black men. Because he offers no critique of sexism, Wilson fails to consider economic or social reorganization that directly empowers and supports these single Black mothers.[75]

My criticism is not that providing Black men with jobs is undesirable; indeed, this is necessary not only for the Black men themselves, but for an entire community, depressed and subject to a host of sociological and economic ills that accompany massive rates of unemployment. But as long as we assume that the massive social reorganization Wilson calls for is possible, why not think about it in ways that maximize the choices

71 Although the nearly exclusive focus on the racist aspects of the program poses both theoretical and political problems, it was entirely understandable given the racial nature of the subsequent comments that were sympathetic to the Moyers view. As is typical in discussions involving race, the dialogue regarding the Moyers program covered more than just the issue of Black families; some commentators took the opportunity to indict not only the Black underclass, but the Black civil rights leadership, the war on poverty, affirmative action and other race-based remedies. See, for example, Will, *Voting Rights Won't Fix It* at A23 (cited in note 70).

72 Their difficulties can also be linked to the prevalence of an economic system and family policy that treat the nuclear family as the norm and other family units as aberrant and unworthy of societal accommodation.

73 Wilson, *The Truly Disadvantaged* at 96 (cited in note 69).

74 Id at 154 (suggestions include macroeconomic policies which promote balanced economic growth, a nationally-oriented labor market strategy, a child support assurance program, a child care strategy, and a family allowances program which would be both means tested and race specific).

75 Nor does Wilson include an analysis of the impact of gender on changes in family patterns. Consequently, little attention is paid to the conflict that may result when gender-based expectations are frustrated by economic and demographic factors. This focus on demographic and structural explanations represents an effort to regain the high ground from the Moyers/Moynihan approach, which is more psycho-social. Perhaps because psycho-social explanations have come dangerously close to victim-blaming, their prevalence is thought to threaten efforts to win policy directives that might effectively address deteriorating conditions within the working class and poor Black communities. See Kimberlé Crenshaw, *A Comment on Gender, Difference, and Victim Ideology in the Study of the Black Family*, in *The Decline of Marriage Among African Americans: Causes, Consequences and Policy Implications* (forthcoming 1989).

of Black women?[76] A more complete theoretical and political agenda for the Black underclass must take into account the specific and particular concerns of Black women; their families occupy the bottom rung of the economic ladder, and it is only through placing them at the center of the analysis that their needs and the needs of their families will be directly addressed.[77]

IV. Expanding Feminist Theory and Antiracist Politics by Embracing the Intersection

If any real efforts are to be made to free Black people of the constraints and conditions that characterize racial subordination, then theories and strategies purporting to reflect the Black community's needs must include an analysis of sexism and patriarchy. Similarly, feminism must include an analysis of race if it hopes to express the aspirations of non-white women. Neither Black liberationist politics nor feminist theory can ignore the intersectional experiences of those whom the movements claim as their respective constituents. In order to include Black women, both movements must distance themselves from earlier approaches in which experiences are relevant only when they are related to certain clearly identifiable causes (for example, the oppression of Blacks is significant when based on race, of women when based on gender). The praxis of both should be centered on the life chances and life situations of people who should be cared about without regard to the source of their difficulties.

I have stated earlier that the failure to embrace the complexities of compoundedness is not simply a matter of political will, but is also due to the influence of a way of thinking about discrimination which structures politics so that struggles are categorized as singular issues. Moreover, this structure imports a descriptive and normative view of society that reinforces the status quo.

It is somewhat ironic that those concerned with alleviating the ills of racism and sexism should adopt such a top-down approach to discrimination. If their efforts instead began with addressing the needs and problems of those who are most disadvantaged and with restructuring and remaking the world where necessary, then others who are singularly disadvantaged would also benefit. In addition, it seems that placing those who currently are marginalized in the center is the most effective way to resist efforts to compartmentalize experiences and undermine potential collective action.

It is not necessary to believe that a political consensus to focus on the lives of the most disadvantaged will happen tomorrow in order to recenter discrimination discourse at the intersection. It is enough, for now, that such an effort would encourage us to look beneath the prevailing conceptions of discrimination and to challenge the complacency that accompanies belief in the effectiveness of this framework. By so doing, we may develop language which is critical of the dominant view and which provides some basis for unifying activity. The goal of this activity should be to facilitate the inclusion of marginalized groups for whom it can be said: "When they enter, we all enter."

76 For instance, Wilson only mentions in passing the need for day care and job training for single mothers. Wilson at 153 (cited in note 69). No mention at all is made of other practices and policies that are racist and sexist, and that contribute to the poor conditions under which nearly half of all Black women must live.

77 Pauli Murray observes that the operation of sexism is at least the partial cause of social problems affecting Black women. See Murray, *The Liberation of Black Women*, in Jo Freeman, ed, *Women: A Feminist Perspective* 351–62 (Mayfield Publishing Co, 1975).

Study Questions

1. Can feminist criticisms of law be met by ensuring that women are treated as moral equals under the law?
2. What problems does Professor MacKinnon find with male-centered conceptions of sex equality?
3. What, according to CRT theorists such as Professor Delgado, is wrong with seeking justice for all by treating all citizens in exactly the same way?
4. Does a "Critical Race Theory of Law" emerge from the combination of a narrative approach, focus on particular experiences of law, and a pragmatic attitude to civil rights and liberties? Does justice for minorities of color need such an independent theory?
5. How should we rethink disadvantage, once the problem of intersectionality is properly investigated? Must our concepts of equality and anti-discrimination undergo substantive changes?

Further Readings

Carol A. Aylward, *Canadian Critical Race Theory: Racism and the Law*. Black Point, NS: Fernwood Publishing, 1999.

Judith A. Baer, *Our Lives before the Law: Constructing a Feminist Jurisprudence*. Princeton: Princeton UP, 1999.

Derrick A. Bell, *Race, Racism and American Law*, 4th ed. Boston: Little Brown, 2000.

Brown v. Board of Education of Topeka, 347 U.S. 483 (1954).

Kimberlé Crenshaw, N. Gotanda, G. Peller, and K. Thomas, eds., *Critical Race Theory: The Key Writings that Formed the Movement*. New York: The New P, 1995.

Richard Delgado and Jean Stefancic, *Critical Race Theory: An Introduction*. New York: New York UP, 2001.

Mark Kelman, *A Guide to Critical Legal Studies*. Cambridge, MA: Harvard UP, 1987.

Nicola Lacey, *Unspeakable Subjects*. Oxford: Hart Publications, 1998.

Catharine MacKinnon, *Women's Lives, Men's Laws*. Cambridge, MA: Harvard UP, 2005.

Mari J. Matsuda, *Words that Wound: Critical Race Theory, Assaultive Speech, and the First Amendment: New Perspectives on Law, Culture, and Society*. Boulder, CO: Westview P, 1993.

R v. Butler, [1992] 1 S. C. R. 452.

Patricia Williams, *The Alchemy of Race and Rights*. Cambridge, MA: Harvard UP, 1991.

SECTION 5

Legal Pluralism and Indigenous Law

Introduction

This section explores legal pluralism, an idea referring to the co-existence of more than one legal order or form of law in the same social situation. Legal pluralism is found in contexts such as the resurgence of Indigenous law alongside state legal systems claiming jurisdiction over the same people, activities, and place. We begin with an introduction to legal pluralism, exploring its historical beginnings as a field of academic study before examining some of its core commitments. We then turn to two contexts, one Canadian and one American, where the authors whose work we present see significant steps toward legal pluralism in the way modern sovereign states are relating in new ways to Indigenous legal traditions.

1. Legal Pluralism (Tamanaha)

The idea and term 'legal pluralism' first emerged in the 1970s and 1980s in the work of anthropologists investigating law in colonial and post-colonial contexts. These inquiries aimed to better understand the dynamics and tensions between local or customary norms, and norms imposed by colonial powers. From this origin, 'legal pluralism' has come to refer to a set of views influencing several academic disciplines concerned with understanding diverse forms of legal order around the world, found at various scales from small groups such as tribes, to regional, national, and global communities. While the ideas and interests of legal pluralists are many, all agree that theories or concepts of law which focus entirely on the law of sovereign states—what might be usefully called state-centered theories or concepts of law—miss and distort much of what is important about the social reality of law. Legal pluralists are also united in their view that non-state legal orders, which sometimes complement and sometimes conflict with state law, are not simply exceptions or additions needing accommodation in a comprehensive understanding of law. Rather, understanding of the role of non-state legal orders in relation to state legal orders is equally if not more important to understanding the ways in which societies are governed and function. Many legal pluralists suppose that interactions between state and non-state legal orders show that state-based ways of thinking about fundamental legal concepts are at very least incomplete, if not simply flawed, demanding further investigation and revision of dominant ideas about the nature of law.

This section's readings begin with a selection from work by American socio-legal theorist and law professor Brian Tamanaha. Prior to his academic career, Professor Tamanaha was a practicing lawyer. In the late 1980s he worked in the office of the Attorney General in Yap, one of four states of the Federated States of Micronesia, a federation composed of several islands distributed over a large area in the Western Pacific Ocean. Micronesia presents a fascinating example of a context where foreign norms have been layered on top of local, customary norms. Micronesia's long history includes periods of occupation by successive foreign states, culminating in United States control for most of the second half of the twentieth century. Micronesia has since won a significant degree of political independence, but not without a continuing United States influence, whose effects include application of American law at the same time as local, customary legal norms remain in practice. As Professor Tamanaha explains, all of the national law of the Federated States of Micronesia was transplanted from the United States. That body of law includes the United States Bill of Rights, the law of contract and property, criminal law, and judicial precedents. At the same time, under the Constitution of the Federated States of Micronesia, where local customary Micronesian norms exist, they must always be considered alongside the formal and institutional national laws of Micronesia transplanted from the United States. In evaluating just how significant this transplant is for the law of Micronesia, it is helpful to know that the majority of judges and lawyers in Micronesia are expatriate American lawyers. Lawyers of Micronesian origin are in the minority, and have to date received their training at American law schools. In this meeting of two quite different legal orders, the interaction and sometimes conflict between American law and the local, customary norms of the Micronesian states helps to show ways in which common views of law may depend on assumptions which do not hold across all law-governed societies. Once the limitations of such assumptions are recognized, there is an opportunity to re-think commonly held views.

In the excerpt reproduced in this section, Professor Tamanaha surveys the wide and widening range of meanings and approaches to legal pluralism, then draws on his experience of working as a lawyer in Micronesia to show legal pluralism in action. Reminiscent of debates between natural law theorists and legal positivists, he distinguishes between descriptive and normative versions of legal pluralism. Descriptive versions challenge what can be summarized as 'monistic state law' conceptions or images following the philosophical idea of a 'monad' as a basic unit of being. These views see law as exclusively and entirely a product of sovereign states, with their characteristic claims of comprehensiveness and supremacy over all other normative orders in society. Legal pluralists have identified several instances of non-state law, within and across states, which show the monistic state law image to be more fiction than reality. Normative versions of legal pluralism challenge the value or desirability of having a single, unified, comprehensive, monopolistic and supreme law in all places and times. Normative legal pluralists argue for the positive desirability of diverse and overlapping legal orders which respect the diversity and range of norms of particular communities, from local to global manifestations of law, and other forms of legality along this spectrum.

Tamanaha also draws a useful distinction between 'abstract' legal pluralism and 'folk' legal pluralism. Abstract legal pluralism aims to develop a theoretical concept of law, capable of capturing the many kinds and types of law which legal pluralists investigate. Folk legal pluralism rejects such abstraction, and instead focuses on what particular communities recognize and understand as law. Tamanaha opts for a folk legal pluralist perspective, noting that abstract legal pluralism, much like legal philosophy aimed at discovering the one true and universal concept of law, has so far failed to achieve success, and in his view, is bound to continue to fail. We leave it to you to decide whether Tamanaha's skepticism is justified, or whether, by contrast, a natural law or positivist or other view provides better answers to the question of the nature of law.

Putting Tamanaha's skepticism to one side, let us take up for our use some additional distinctions Tamanaha offers as tools for thinking about the social situations where law is found. First, according to Tamanaha, there is community law, which refers the norms and rules governing day-to-day interactions between persons on matters relating to property, marriage, the use of violence, debts, and similar matters of everyday life as a citizen. Second, there is regime law, which refers to the rules surrounding institutions of governance, the responsibilities of public officials, and taxation, creating the conditions under which day-to-day community law operates. Third and finally, there is cross-polity law, which refers to the rules and procedures dealing with interactions between legal orders, such as may be seen in international law. These categories are all there is to law, according to Tamanaha. There are diverse ways in which these three categories of law occur in particular social situations and diverse community understandings, but there is no further or more basic or more universal nature of law. A final possible virtue of legal pluralism is evident in this body of distinctions. In saying that these distinctions capture all there is to say about the nature of law, legal pluralism offers simplicity of explanation. This simplicity contrasts sharply with complex explanations offered by other theories whose commitment to the centrality of states leaves them adding and subtracting from those theories as they try to extend to explanation of what they characterize in various ways as special cases or exceptions. Simplicity is just one possible virtue of a good theory of law, so we leave it to you to decide whether legal pluralism does all that needs to be done to explain law, or instead offers an oversimplification so work remains to be done.

Two important claimed insights of legal pluralism are especially well illustrated by Professor Tamanaha's work and the evidence he draws from specific uses of law. First, from a legal pluralist perspective, inquiry into what the law is in some situation requires looking to the claims of state or national law, and the claims of other legal orders, with additional attention to what actually happens in daily practice, beyond the mere language of claims and actions sometimes carrying little more than symbolic weight. Second, Tamanaha's version of legal pluralism exhibits a deeper assertion about the nature of law. He aims to show the incompleteness of an understanding of the nature of law that stops at characterizing law as a set of abstract institutional rules, as if those rules determine their own operation and force. A better approach, according to Tamanaha, includes recognizing that law is always partly constituted by social acceptance by the relevant actors within some community. We leave it to you to think about the implications of Tamanaha's argument, if viewed as justified, for matters such as commitment to the ideal of the rule of law. Does the fact that law is always a rule and its practice understood as two dimensions of the same thing mean we are pursuing an impossibility when trying to enact the ideal of the rule of law, understood as a certain kind of regularity and protection independent of the desires of the powerful and those we charge with application of laws? Or do legal pluralist insights simply help us to better understand the practical limits of our hopes for what pursuing the ideal of the rule of law might bring our societies and the individuals within them?

2. Indigenous Legal Traditions in Canada

The next chapter in this section presents some of the work of constitutional law scholar Professor John Borrows, who is Anishinaabe/Ojibway and a member of the Chippewas of the Nawash First Nation in Ontario, Canada. Over the course of several decades Professor Borrows has sought to show that Canada's constitution is misunderstood if viewed as resting exclusively on foundations in English and French law. Borrows argues that Indigenous legal traditions are also part of the historic and current foundations of Canada's constitution, notwithstanding the various ways Indigenous law has been ignored or actively suppressed by successive state governments at both provincial and federal levels. In the selection provided here, Professor Borrows aims to dispel several misconceptions about Indigenous law, and in particular the view that Indigenous law is simply customary law, understood as longstanding norms frozen in time that just happen to have solidified in the practices of Indigenous peoples centuries or millennia ago. Professor Borrows aims to show instead that Indigenous legal traditions are sophisticated and complex, and responsive to contemporary challenges and needs in ways that customary law is not.

Professor Borrows identifies five types of law common to most Indigenous peoples in Canada. First, there is sacred law, the highest form of law, often found in creation stories and revered teachings. Second, there is natural law, consisting in those values and principles which can be learned from careful observation and thought about the natural world, its balance, cyclical character, and function. Third, deliberative law refers to the processes and procedures for reaching collective decisions and agreements, both within particular Indigenous communities and in relation to other communities, both Indigenous and non-Indigenous. Fourth, positive law refers to particular binding decisions and agreements that have been reached, setting out specific rules and directives. Fifth, and finally, there is customary law, which Professor Borrows defines as "those practices developed through repetitive patterns of social interaction that are accepted as binding on those who participate in them."[1]

According to Professor Borrows, there are several reasons to map and explain these different types of law in this way. Demonstration of differences and characterization of relations between types of Indigenous law enables observers to see that Indigenous communities are highly advanced in their regulation of social order in purposive ways, demonstrating adaptive problem-solving capabilities far beyond what can be achieved in application of a simple set of relatively fixed customary norms. Indigenous laws are hierarchically ranked, containing superior laws—sacred laws and natural laws—which provide the foundation for other types of law and guide their use and operation. Deliberative laws in particular show that Indigenous laws are not stagnant. As Indigenous communities face new circumstances, Indigenous law is adapted and developed in ways Borrows shows to be visible in interpretation and application of sacred and natural laws, and interpretation of positive laws and customary laws.

Mapping the types of Indigenous law is both helpful to understanding Indigenous law in its own right, and to understanding how it differs from non-Indigenous and broadly Western ideas of law. There are some similarities to Western ideas. Sacred law, for example, is similar to what Aquinas portrayed as Divine law. Indigenous communities also distinguish natural law from positive law in a way familiar to Western legal theory, regarding the force of positive law as conditional on its conforming with the requirements of sacred law and natural law. Once we have identified points of similarity, some important remaining differences are easily seen. One especially important difference concerns the relation between humans and nature. For example, in the version of natural law theory expressed in the Christian tradition in Western legal theory, the attention given to the nature of the good or objective value tends to be focused on what is good for humans, presumed to be separate from nature, as Finnis does when writing of "basic human goods." In the various Indigenous natural law theories, a different common thread is evident, understanding humans as part of nature, and just one part at that. From this perspective all beings, including human and non-human animals, and rivers and trees and more have their own value as they exist alongside humans.

Attention to deliberative laws in Indigenous law shows another important difference between the underlying commitments of Indigenous law and the contrasting commitments of English and French legal traditions undergirding much Canadian law. Indigenous deliberative laws often

1 John Borrows, *Canada's Indigenous Constitution* (Toronto: University of Toronto Press, 2010), p. 51.

depict procedures in larger processes which identify and emphasize relations. As Professor Borrows shows, deliberative laws are often used in the context of celebrations or feasts, where food is shared and gifts are exchanged. This approach contrasts starkly with the ways formal legislatures such as Canada's Parliament use carefully specified procedural rules to permit typically opposed arguments to be expressed with a view to voting to identify a winning argument. Cultural preferences explain part of this difference, but there may be more to it. Use of deliberative rules in a setting involving the exchange of gifts and sharing of food is relationship-focused, whereas deliberative rules enabling decision-making based on majority votes is much less relationship-focused, with possible consequences for the meaningfulness and practical usefulness of decisions and agreements issuing from each approach to the use of deliberative rules.

Borrows offers a potentially important final reason to map the different types of law found in Indigenous legal traditions. Better understanding of what Indigenous law is and how it complements or contrasts with English and French legal traditions may be key to revitalizing Indigenous law in Canada, in ways bringing greater and better legal and social cohesion among all Canadians. As Borrows argues, "When nation states can learn from and embrace the best traditions of its peoples, they can be strengthened and become more unified. If this process occurs in a fair, orderly, transparent, non-discriminatory yet authoritative way the rule of law is reinforced in the process."[2] Professor Borrows acknowledges there is much work to be done to properly recognize Indigenous legal traditions, and to respect the space in which they are to operate on their own terms and according to their own values. This is nonetheless an objective he believes Canada—and other colonial and post-colonial states—must pursue, not just to remedy past wrongs, but to build a better collective future.

3. Navajo Law

The Navajo Nation is a group of Indigenous peoples in the southwestern part of the United States. Their history of interaction with European colonizers is similar to that of other Indigenous peoples in the Americas. Initial contact with Europeans in the fifteenth and sixteenth centuries was followed by relative peace until disruptive conflicts arose at the beginning of the eighteenth century. In the 1860s the United States defeated the Navajo in battle, and forced the Navajo from their ancestral lands. When it proved expensive to provide ongoing support to the Navajo as they struggled to farm and develop unsuitable land, the United States proposed further re-location beyond the Navajo's ancestral lands. The Navajo refused re-location, insisting instead on return to their ancestral lands. In 1868 a treaty between the United States and the Navajo Nation resulted in the Navajo returning to a part of their original lands, acknowledged by treaty as Navajo land from which they could not be removed. The Navajo consider the 1868 treaty to be sacred law.

The relation of the Navajo Nation to the United States is further defined by a 1959 landmark decision of the United States Supreme Court. In *Williams v. Lee*,[3] the court held that the Navajo Nation court system, and not the court system of the state of Arizona, held authority to resolve a dispute regarding a contract agreed on Navajo Nation land by a member of the Navajo Nation and a non-Navajo merchant. This decision inspired succeeding generations of Navajo Nation courts, and the community more broadly, to revive and express Navajo cultural values and norms in

2 Borrows, *Canada's Indigenous Constitution*, p. 23.
3 358 U.S. 217 (1959).

developing and strengthening Navajo law. Today's Navajo Nation government is visibly equal in sophistication to any other government, operating legislative, executive, and judicial branches that create, use, interpret, and apply Navajo law. The multi-level Navajo Nation court system is of particular interest to scholars of jurisprudence. Its operation of the Navajo Nation Code weaves together and applies Navajo common law and American law, and publishes the results in its own court reporter, the *Navajo Reporter*.

The nature and development of Navajo law is explained by Professor Raymond Austin in his book *Navajo Courts and Navajo Common Law*, from which we have selected an excerpt for you to explore. Professor Austin is a member of the Navajo Nation, a long-serving justice of the Navajo Nation Supreme Court, and now Professor of Applied Indigenous Studies at Northern Arizona University. Professor Austin contends that the way Navajo law is combined with American law is a key part of the Navajo Nation's rebuilding and entrenching its sovereignty in the context of its relation to the United States.

It will help you understand the interaction between United States law and Navajo law to know that Navajo law comprises different kinds of hierarchically ordered law. The first kind consists of three foundational 'Diné' principles deriving their name from the word 'Diné,' meaning 'The People,' and used interchangeably with the word 'Navajo' by the members of the Navajo Nation to refer to themselves. The principles are *hózhǫ́*, *k´é*, and *k´éí*. *Hózhǫ́* broadly, means peace, harmony and balance, and represents a prescriptive or positive commitment to the guiding importance of the Navajo metaphysical belief that everything in the universe is interrelated, so we must be mindful at all times of our interrelations. *K´é* refers specifically to all the relationships among all beings, human, animal, natural, and spiritual, and can be understood as a kind of kinship through positive values. Its more concrete values, as Prof. Austin writes, include "respect, kindness, cooperation, friendliness, reciprocal relations, and love."[4] At a political level, *k´é* is expressed in notions of equality and individual and community rights.[5] Finally, *K´éí* is closely related to *k´é*, and can be understood as a basic principle of descent, clanship, and kinship, applying directly to obligations and responsibilities to clan relatives (as opposed to *k´é*, which applies broadly to all relatives).

'Diné' principles are found in and guide interpretation and application of four different types of law: Traditional Law (laws of the Great Spirit); Customary Law (laws of the Holy Beings); Natural Law (laws of Mother Earth and Father Heaven); and Common Law (laws of the Navajo).[6] 'Diné' principles are very important to the way the Common Law is developed in the hands of Navajo courts and other branches of government, as by the Navajo people, as they continue to develop their contemporary practices and governance in accordance with ancestral values.

The excerpt included here also illustrates, through focus on the *k´é* principle of descent, clanship and kinship, some of the ways in which the Navajo courts have applied Navajo law to modern disputes and forms of governance, incorporating both United States law and Navajo traditional values to reach and develop a distinctive Navajo common law. Professor Austin explains how values of respect, cooperation, kindness, unity, peace and balance underlie Navajo conceptions of equality and egalitarianism, which in turn support practices and commitments of participatory democracy. He provides an especially

4 Austin, *Navajo Courts and Navajo Common Law*, p. 84.
5 Ibid., p. 83.
6 Ibid., p. 42.

helpful example of this fusion in the instance of legal protection of free speech, showing both its place in Navajo values and law, and how traditional Navajo values place limits on its exercise.

As you read you will see that Professor Austin highlights similarities and important differences between Navajo values and Western or non-Indigenous values in law. You will see differences in forms of authority, both vertical (non-Indigenous) and horizontal (Navajo), and differences in dispute resolution styles, including adversarial (non-Indigenous) and peacemaking (Navajo) forms, together with different conceptions of the limits on free speech, with some focused on individualism (non-Indigenous) and others on communal responsibility (Navajo). You may also see similarities and differences not directly addressed by Professor Austin. Consider, for example, similarities and differences between the natural law theory of St. Thomas Aquinas and Navajo natural law. What similarities or differences might be found in the Navajo regard for the importance of positive law—i.e., the decisions reached by authorities, by the Navajo people—and the importance of positive law as seen from the perspective of legal positivists such as John Austin and H.L.A. Hart? How much does the process by which legal decisions are reached matter according to these different perspectives? And finally, just how well can we expect a blending of forms of law to work, understanding, to give just one example, the way American federal and state law are blended by the Navajo with the law of the Navajo Nation? Does the Navajo court and common law offer an example of the way legal pluralism can be employed in strategies of active decolonization creating social good, as Professors Tamanaha and Borrows suggest it can? Or are there remaining irresolvable conflicts and tensions? We leave these questions for you to answer.

15
Brian Tamanaha
"Introduction: Three Themes," from *Legal Pluralism Explained**

[*Ed. note*: Tamanaha refers to other chapters of the book from which this excerpt is taken; these are not included here, but the references have been retained for interested readers.]

Legal pluralism is everywhere. In every social arena one examines, a seeming multiplicity of legal orders exists. There are village, municipal, and county laws of various types; there are state, district, or regional laws of various types; there are national, transnational, and international laws of various types. In many societies there are additional forms of law, like indigenous law, customary law, religious law, and the law of distinct ethnic or cultural communities. The contemporary period has witnessed a vast increase in public and private regulatory regimes on various matters at all levels. Coexisting forms of law may be similar in orientation, coordinated with one another, and mutually supportive or complementary; they

* Tamanaha, Brian. "Introduction: Three Themes," (pp. 1–18) from *Legal Pluralism Explained*, Oxford University Press.

may make competing claims of authority, impose conflicting norms, and operate through contrasting processes; they may exist wholly apart or thoroughly intertwined. Legal pluralism creates uncertainty because people may not know which legal regime will apply to their situation, and it also creates opportunities for people to opportunistically select from among legal regimes, or to pit one form of law against another in pursuit of their goals. Legal officials in situations of legal pluralism face potential rivals, compete for power and resources, and can be mutually cooperative or antagonistic.

Legal pluralism is everywhere in another sense. First mentioned in the 1960s, references to legal pluralism exploded in ensuing decades as the notion propagated across academic fields from anthropology to sociology, legal history, comparative law, international law, transnational law, and jurisprudence.[1] Two decades after its initial introduction in legal anthropology, in a 1988 overview that significantly boosted its visibility, Sally Engle Merry declared: "Legal pluralism is a central theme in the reconceptualization of the law/society relation."[2] More recently, "legal pluralism has become a standard fare in international and comparative law circles."[3] A collection on "pluralist jurisprudence" declared that legal theorists must move beyond their state-centered focus to take account of coexisting forms of law.[4]

Interest in legal pluralism extends beyond academia. Governments and development agencies have spent several billion dollars to develop state legal systems across the Global South with disappointing results.[5] Law and development theory and practice emphasize the importance of the rule of law and economic development. Customary and religious systems of law were seen as parochial, backwards, regressive, and antithetical to women's rights and human rights. World Bank development experts observed, "Development theorists and practitioners have tended to either blindly ignore the ubiquitous phenomena of legal pluralism or regard it as a constraint on development, a defective condition that must be overcome in the name of modernizing, state building, and enhancing 'the rule of law.'"[6] Recently, however, development practitioners "have begun to reexamine some of the underlying assumptions about legal pluralism and to explore the opportunities that might exist in contexts where legal pluralism is a pervasive reality."[7] An international relations theorist focusing on post-conflict situations observed that "Understanding legal pluralism is important for

1 A search in Heinonline reveals very few uses of the phrase "legal pluralism" prior to the 1970s, followed by a rapid increase in the 1980s, 1990s, and thereafter. A Google Ngram of "Legal Pluralism" likewise exhibits a sharp increase in references to legal pluralism in books commencing in the mid-1970s in both relative and absolute numbers. https://books.google.com/ngrams/graph?content=%22legal+pluralism%22&year_start=1800&year_end=2008&corpus=15&smoothing=3&share=&direct_url=t1%3B%2C%22%20legal%20pluralism%20%22%3B%2Cc0#t1%3B%2C%22%20legal%20 pluralism%20 %22%3B%2Cc0.

2 Sally Engle Merry, "Legal Pluralism," 22 Law & Society Review 869 (1988).

3 C. Valcke, "Three Perils of Legal Pluralism," in S.P. Donlan and L. Heckendorn Urscheler, eds., *Concepts of Law: Comparative, Jurisprudential, and Social Scientific Perspectives* (Farnham: Ashgate, 2015) 123.

4 Andrew Halpin and Nicole Roughan, eds., *In Pursuit of Pluralist Jurisprudence* (Cambridge: Cambridge University Press 2017).

5 See Stephen Humphreys, *Theatre of the Rule of Law: Transnational Legal Intervention in Theory and Practice* (Cambridge: Cambridge University Press 2010) 128–32. Brian Z. Tamanaha, "The Primacy of Society and Failures of Law and Development," 44 Cornell International Law Journal 209 (2011).

6 Caroline Sage and Michael Woolcock, "Introduction: Legal Pluralism and Development Policy: Scholars and Practitioners in Dialogue," in Brian Z. Tamanaha, Caroline Sage, and Michael Woolcock, eds., *Legal Pluralism and Development: Scholars and Practitioners in Dialogue* (New York: Cambridge University Press 2012) 1.

7 *Id.* at 2.

any legal or policy intervention, including but by no means limited to state building."[8]

Even as it has secured the attention of growing numbers of scholars and development practitioners, however, the notion of legal pluralism remains mired in complexity, confusion, and disagreement. After reviewing two decades of proliferating literature on legal pluralism jurisprudent William Twining remarked, "I have come away feeling that it is little better than a morass."[9] A factor contributing to the confusion is that scholars from multiple disciplines have invoked the notion of legal pluralism. Each discipline is internally divided into various schools of thought, and academic disciplines differ from one another in their bodies of knowledge, concepts, and objectives. While on the surface it might appear that a single notion of legal pluralism is applied across fields, an impression perpetuated by shared references to the same cluster of theorists (John Griffiths, Eugen Ehrlich, Sally Falk Moore, etc.), different meanings of legal pluralism are being utilized, often unrecognized as such.

Adding to the confusion is the thin meaning and capaciousness of the term *pluralism*. Pluralism simply means more than one, which can be applied to anything and framed at various levels of specificity and generality. The label legal pluralism has been used to refer to a plurality of interpretations of a single set of laws; to subsystems of law within a single system; to the same tribunals applying distinct bodies of law and separate tribunals applying different bodies of law within a system; to hybrid legal systems that grew out of the interaction between distinct bodies of law; to the coexistence of separate forms of law within a single society; to the coexistence of different subject matter regimes within international law; to the coexistence of multiple legal systems between and across states; and other variations. Each of these examples has been discussed in the literature on legal pluralism, though they are very different.

Complexities and disagreement about the meaning of "law" is another source of confusion. A core proposition across most versions of legal pluralism is that state law is not the only form of law. This assertion requires a definition or concept of law or some way to identify what counts as law as well as to distinguish law from non-law. Legal pluralists have grappled with these threshold issues for five decades now, with multiple concepts of law proposed in the literature, and no end in sight. This struggle is understandable. "What is law?" has never been resolved despite a multitude of attempts by theorists going back centuries. Since each version of legal pluralism is shaped by how law is conceived, there are multiple versions of legal pluralism, each built around a different view of law. The consequence is "a pluralism of legal pluralisms."[10] Legal pluralism is a conceptual mess.

This book explains legal pluralism in two senses. First, drawing from history and theory, I explain why and how legal pluralism is a common phenomenon across societies past and present, and I show its consequences. Second, I explain what is involved in theoretical disputes surrounding legal pluralism, and I articulate a way to frame legal pluralism that works for development practitioners, scholars, and theorists. This undertaking poses a formidable challenge. The topic crosses over multiple disciplines and audiences with different interests and concerns,

8 Geoffrey Swenson, "Legal Pluralism in Theory and Practice," 20 International Studies Review 438, 458 (2018).

9 William Twining, "Normative and Legal Pluralism: A Global Perspective," 20 Duke Journal of Comparative and International Law 473, 487 (2010).

10 See Emmanuel Melissaris and Mariano Croce, "A Pluralism of Legal Pluralisms," Oxford Handbooks Online, April 2017, https://www.oxfordhandbooks.com/view/10.1093/oxfordhb/9780199935352.001.0001/oxfordhb-9780199935352-e-22; Margaret Davies, "Plural Pluralities of Law," Halpin and Roughan, *supra* note 4, at 239.

and the literature addressing legal pluralism is enormous and expanding too rapidly to stay abreast of. This book is not a comprehensive review of every situation of legal pluralism and everything written about it in every field, which would fill a never-completed set of volumes. Because legal pluralism is literally everywhere, it is impossible to cover comprehensively. Instead, using illustrative examples, I present legal pluralism in broad strokes that convey the most salient empirical, theoretical, and normative issues and consequences involved, in clear prose aimed at a general audience.

To set up this exploration, in this Introduction I first identify what legal pluralism is framed in opposition to: the image of monistic state law. Next I set forth two streams of legal pluralism: abstract legal pluralism constructed by theorists versus folk legal pluralism understood in social-historical terms. Then I outline three categories of law that appear throughout the book: community law, regime law, and cross-polity law. These are preliminary clarifications of major themes that arise time and again in discussions of legal pluralism, filled out in the course of the book. I close with a brief illustration of legal pluralism.

Monistic State Law

Pluralism can be applied to anything involving more than one. In academic settings it is usually applied by way of contrast to a unity of some sort. "The conceptual logic of pluralism thus pits it dialectically against 'monism,' whatever field of human investigation we care to consider."[11] Legal pluralism stands in opposition to the widely held image of monistic state law. "What Is Legal Pluralism?" (1986) by John Griffiths, which significantly shaped academic understandings of the topic, identifies this target (though he substitutes the typical label "monism" with "centralism"):

> According to what I shall call the ideology of legal centralism, law is and should be the law of the state, uniform for all persons, exclusive of all other law, and administered by a single set of state institutions.... In the legal centralist conception, law is an exclusive, systematic and unified hierarchical ordering of normative propositions, which can be looked at either from the top downwards as depending from a sovereign command (Bodin, Hobbes, Austin) or from the bottom upwards as deriving their validity from ever more general layers of norms until one reaches some ultimate norm(s) (Kelsen, Hart).[12]

"Legal centralism is a myth, an ideal, a claim, an illusion."[13] "A central objective of a descriptive concept of legal pluralism," Griffiths declared, "is therefore destructive: to break the stranglehold of the idea that what law is, is a single, unified and exclusive hierarchical normative ordering depending from the power of the state, and of the illusion that the legal world actually looks the way such a conception requires it to look."[14]

The origins of the monist view of law trace back to two main theorists. Jean Bodin articulated an account of absolutist sovereignty in 1576 that claimed the exclusive power to make law: "It is only sovereign princes who can make law for all subjects without exception, both collectively

11 Gregor McLennan, *Pluralism* (Minneapolis: University of Minnesota Press 1995) 25.

12 J. Griffiths, "What Is Legal Pluralism?," 24 Journal of Legal Pluralism 1, 3 (1986). I have omitted his citations to the theorists listed.

13 *Id.* at 4.

14 *Id.* at 4.

and individually."[15] Thomas Hobbes's famous *Leviathan*,[16] published in the mid-seventeenth century, likewise articulates a supreme, indivisible, lawgiving sovereign located in the abstract state. Both accounts were theoretical abstractions and political advocacy, not consistent with actual arrangements at the time. Multiple sources of law existed in their day and the notion of the state was still in early stages of crystallization.[17]

As the state system solidified in ensuing centuries, what originally was an abstract vision of the state monopoly over law became an implicitly held understanding shared by many theorists and the public in advanced capitalist societies. Max Weber's ideal type of the modern bureaucratic state, which he formulated in the early twentieth century, captures this understanding, as encapsulated in this passage by William Novak:

> (1) A rationalized and generalized legal and administrative order amenable to legislative change; (2) a bureaucratic apparatus of officers conducting official business with reference to an impersonal order of administrative regulations; (3) the power to bind—to rule and regulate—all persons (national citizens) and all actions within the state's official jurisdiction via its laws; and (4) the legitimate authority to use force, violence, and coercion within the prescribed territory as prescribed by the duly constituted government. Unification, centralization, rationalization, organization, administration, and bureaucratization have become the hallmarks of fully developed, essentially modern states.[18]

State law is unified, hierarchically organized, comprehensive, monopolistic, and supreme over all other orders within society. This is the monistic law state.

Prominent twentieth-century legal philosophers have identified these traits as essential features of law. "Since all legal systems claim to be supreme with respect to their subject-community," Joseph Raz asserts, "none can acknowledge any claim to supremacy over the same community which may be made by another legal system."[19] Echoing Bodin, Raz posits supremacy as a criterion for the existence of a legal system: "We would regard an institutionalized system as a legal system only if it is necessarily in some respect the most important institutionalized system which can exist in that society."[20] "In a nutshell," Raz asserts, a legal system is "a system of guidance and adjudication claiming supreme authority within a certain society and therefore, where efficacious, also enjoying such effective authority."[21]

Dissenting voices over the centuries have challenged this vision of the supreme, unified, monopolistic law state on three main grounds: it is inconsistent with many historical and contemporary manifestations of law, multiple forms of law exist besides state law, and it is normatively problematic. Seventeenth-century efforts at achieving greater state uniformity provoked backlash from local communities. "If God, they argued, had created provinces that were naturally

15 Quoting Bodin, in Jens Bartelson, "On the Indivisibility of Sovereignty," 2 Republic of Letters: A Journal for the Study of Knowledge, Politics, and the Arts 85, 87–88 (2011).

16 Thomas Hobbes, *Leviathan* (Oxford: Oxford University Press 1996).

17 Quentin Skinner, "The State," in Terence Ball, James Farr, and Russell L. Hanson, eds., *Political Innovation and Conceptual Change* (Cambridge: Cambridge University Press 1989) 120.

18 William J. Novak, "The Myth of the 'Weak' American State," 113 American Historical Review 752, 761 (2008).

19 Joseph Raz, *The Authority of Law*, 2nd ed. (Oxford: Oxford University Press 2009) 119.

20 *Id.* at 116.

21 *Id.* at 43.

different from each other, it was important that the laws by which they were governed should conform to their distinctive character."[22] Jeremy Bentham criticized Blackstone's account of the supreme sovereign: "The people may be disposed to obey the command of one man against the world in relation to one sort of act, those of another man in relation to another sort of act, else what are we to think of the constitutional laws of the Germanic body."[23] Otto von Gierke in the late nineteenth century argued that law also exists in social associations, a position influentially reiterated by Eugen Ehrlich a generation later.[24] In the early twentieth century, political theorist Harold Laski observed, "We have to admit, so your monist philosopher tells us, that all parts of the State are woven together to make one harmonious whole ... The unity is logically necessary.... Pluralism, in an ultimate sense, is therefore impossible."[25] The monist theory of the state has an affinity with absolutism, Laski warned: "Therefore all order consists in the subordination of the Plurality to Unity, and never and nowhere can a purpose that is common to many be effectual unless the One rules over the Many and directs the Many to the goal."[26] Pragmatist philosopher John Dewey criticized the monist theory of the state as an abstraction that fails to account for myriad variations within and among states.[27] Against this vision, he asserted that "temporal and local diversification is a prime mark of political organization,"[28] and he advocated "a pluralist conception of the state."[29]

Jurists have invoked the monist law state image in conjunction with sovereignty to justify a multitude of dubious assertions and actions. In the past, ideas about sovereignty and monist law provided key justifications for Western colonization, seizing land, and disregarding indigenous law in settler countries. Today the monist law state is an implicit standard widely held by jurists for what a properly constructed system of law consists of, deeming anything that departs from this image inherently flawed and in need of rectification.

One objective of this book is to dislodge the image of the monistic law state. In setting after setting throughout history and today, I show, the monistic view of the law state is descriptively inaccurate and theoretically unsound, and has been applied in normatively problematic ways. Chapter One discusses empires over the last two millennia that secured imperial rule while leaving community laws in place; the decentralized multiplicity of law in medieval Europe; the *millet* system in the Ottoman Empire under which people utilized their own religious law and institutions; extraterritorial courts that European powers created in faraway lands well into the twentieth century; and the British East India Company, which administered separate systems of laws and courts for expatriates, Hindus, and Muslims. Chapter Two examines European colonization, which created transplanted state legal systems alongside pre-existing bodies of customary and religious law, and brought workers from outside in large numbers for plantations and mining, creating a

22 J.H. Elliot, "A Europe of Composite Monarchies," 137 Past and Present 48, 65 (1992).
23 Jeremy Bentham, quoted in H.L.A. Hart, "Bentham on Sovereignty," 2 Irish Jurist 327, 333 (1967).
24 See Otto Gierke, "Basic Concepts of State Law and the Most Recent State Law Theories," 25 University of Wisconsin Studies in the Social Sciences and History 158, 182 (1935); George Heiman, *Otto Gierke, Associations and Law: The Classical and Early Christian Stages* (Toronto: University of Toronto Press 1977).
25 Harold Laski, "The Sovereignty of the State," 13 Journal of Philosophy 85, 87–88 (1915).
26 *Id.* at 87.
27 See John Dewey, *The Public and Its Problems* (Athens, GA: Swallow Press 1954 [1927]) Chapter 2.
28 *Id.* at 47.
29 *Id.* at 73.

wave of legal pluralism across the Global South that remains entrenched today. These two chapters demonstrate that the monist law state is a recent invention inconsistent with many manifestations of law.

Legal theorists are wont to dismiss counter-examples like these as exceptions, deviations, or corruptions that do not challenge their image of the monist law state, which they take for granted as the central case of law. "It is part of the very idea of a central case that there still might be cases (even statistically preponderant cases) that do not exhibit all the features that make the central case the central case," wrote legal philosopher John Gardner.[30] Similarly, Dennis Galligan observed, "Theorists ought to direct their minds to corrupt, defective, exceptional, or marginal legal systems, but having done so, are likely to conclude ... that they make no difference to the concept."[31] Historical instances of legal pluralism and law in the Global South are exotic and interesting, a legal theorist might conclude, but can be adjudged defective or corrupt, not sufficient grounds to question the image of the monist law state. What legal theorists project, however, is a highly idealized image of law that does not comport with reality.

Bringing the examination closer to home, making it harder to dismiss, Chapters Three and Four shift to Western legal systems to expose a variety of legally pluralistic contexts contrary to the monist law state. Chapter Three describes legal institutions of Romani (Gypsy) communities across Europe; indigenous law in New Zealand, Canada, Australia, and the United States; and Rabbinical Courts and Sharia Tribunals in the United States and United Kingdom. Chapter Four examines state law within the United States legal system(s), showing that law is not fully unified and hierarchically organized, a condition that also exists within highly developed national legal systems across Europe. European Union law, applied in the Court of Justice of the European Union as well as in national courts, exists alongside the laws and constitution of each nation, applied by national constitutional and high courts, and added to the pluralistic mix is the European Convention on Human Rights applied by the European Court of Human Rights. Thereafter, I convey the contemporary proliferation of transnational law and regulation in public, private, and hybrid forms, many of which are neither wholly national law nor international law.

These various legal arrangements, I show again and again, are incompatible with the monist law state image in two fundamental respects: state law does not have a monopoly over law within society and state law is not organized as unified hierarchical wholes. My positive account of law replaces the monist image in both respects: showing that state law coexists with other forms of collectively recognized law, and offering a descriptive account of state legal regimes as complexes of innumerable distributed legal institutions throughout society that work in the aggregate, with various interconnections, though not as unified wholes.

These examples and varieties of legal pluralism—external to, internal to, and intermingled with state law—are presented to persuade jurists, theorists, and law and development practitioners to set aside the vision of the monist law state and be open to new ways of conceiving of law that recognizes the pervasiveness of legal pluralism and the variety of ways law exists within, across, and outside of state systems. Legal institutions of various types exhibit varying extents of coordination, cohesion, competition, and conflict.

30 John Gardner, *Law as a Leap of Faith* (Oxford: Oxford University Press 2012) 152.
31 Denis J. Galligan, "Concepts in the Currency of Social Understanding of Law: A Review Essay on the Later Work of William Twining," 35 Oxford Journal of Legal Studies 373, 392 (2015).

Discarding the monistic image of law is important not just for theoretical purposes, and to improve our understanding of law as a social phenomenon, but it also has policy implications. Jurists engaged in law and development activities have long assumed that law across the Global South will, and should, one day evolve toward unified state legal systems. This study offers abundant reasons to believe the imagined evolution toward state law monism will not occur for many generations, if at all. To grasp these situations, law must be conceived of in more variable and pluralistic terms that exist for endemic underlying reasons, not as temporary aberrations.

Abstract Legal Pluralism versus Folk Legal Pluralism

Scholarly discussions of legal pluralism commonly use a distinction first articulated by Griffiths between "weak" and "strong" legal pluralism (relabeled "classic" and "new" by Merry[32]). When Griffiths published his programmatic essay, the term legal pluralism had been used for two decades to refer to postcolonial societies that recognized customary and religious forms of law. He argued that this "weak" legal pluralism is actually a manifestation of legal centralism because it is a product of state recognition. "'Legal pluralism' in the weak sense has little to do with the concept of legal pluralism which is the subject of this article,"[33] he declared, sharply distancing his concept from studies of postcolonial law. His essay centers on "strong" legal pluralism based on a sociological concept of law independent of the state—"an empirical state of affairs, namely the coexistence within a social group of legal orders which do not belong to a single system." As Merry noted, these two contexts of legal pluralism "make odd companions" in that they have different targets and "they come out of different scholarly traditions."[34]

The strong-weak distinction is frequently invoked by scholars, along with Griffiths's argument that only strong is genuine legal pluralism, whereas weak is not. Theorist Ralf Michaels remarked, "Griffiths's emphasis that the character of law should not depend on recognition by the state has been hugely influential within the literature on legal pluralism."[35] Despite its success, the strong-weak distinction is flawed and distorting. Many situations of legal pluralism covered in this text do not map onto his dichotomy between state recognition (weak) versus independent law (strong). Customary and religious forms of law often exist independently through ongoing cultural processes *and* the state recognizes them for various reasons, and often they are intertwined unofficially and officially. The coherence of his strong-weak distinction, furthermore, depends on his scientific conception of law, which does not work, as Griffiths himself came to acknowledge when he later repudiated legal pluralism (for reasons explained in Chapter Five).[36]

A more illuminating distinction can be drawn between what I call "abstract legal pluralism" and "folk legal pluralism," which I elaborate in Chapter Five. Abstract legal pluralism is the product of social scientists and legal theorists whose aim is to provide a scientific or philosophical theory of law;[37] folk legal pluralism understood in social-historical terms focuses on forms

32 Merry, *supra* note 2, at 872–74.

33 Griffiths, *supra* note 12, at 8.

34 Merry, *supra* note 2, at 874.

35 Ralf Michaels, "Law and Recognition—Towards a Relational Concept of Law," in Nicole Roughan and Andrew Halpin, eds., *In Pursuit of Pluralist Jurisprudence* (Cambridge: Cambridge University Press 2017) 99.

36 John Griffiths, "The Idea of Sociology of Law and its Relation to Law and to Sociology," in Michael Freeman, ed., *Law and Sociology* (Oxford: Oxford University Press 2006) 63–64.

37 John Griffiths, "The Division of Labor in Social Control," in Donald Black, ed., *Toward A General Theory of Social Control*, vol. 1 (New York: Academic Press 1984) 39.

of law collectively recognized by people in society, which vary and change over time. Scientific and theoretical concepts of law and legal pluralism are plagued by irresolvable problems, which I detail. This book articulates and applies social-historical folk legal pluralism.

There are numerous versions of abstract legal pluralism, but they share several basic similarities. First, every theory formulates or identifies a concept or definition of law. These concepts of law can be grouped in one of two broad categories: law as normative ordering within social groups, and law as institutionalized norm enforcement. Another common trait of abstract legal pluralism is that the plurality they center on is a *multiplicity of a single form of law* theoretically defined, not a *multiplicity of different kinds of law*. Another trait is that each theory takes a ubiquitous social phenomenon (normative orders, institutionalized rule systems) and relabels it as "law," now theoretically understood. This move leads to another common trait: all versions of abstract legal pluralism suffer from over-inclusiveness by including social phenomena that do not appear to be law. Merry raised this troubling issue in her review of legal pluralism: "Where do we stop speaking of law and find ourselves simply describing social life?"[38] For reasons I explain in Chapter Five, legal pluralism is still plagued by this problem today, three decades after she flagged it.

Folk legal pluralism proceeds in a different fashion and produces a wholly different account of legal pluralism. It does not formulate a scientific or philosophical concept of law. Law is ultimately a folk concept. Folk legal pluralism identifies law by asking what people in a given social arena collectively recognize and treat through their social practices as law (*recht, droit, lex, ius, diritto, prawo*, etc.). Sharia and Halakhah are *law* because Muslims and Jews, respectively, recognize that as law. In contrast to abstract legal pluralism, which centers on a multiplicity of a single phenomenon defined as law, folk legal pluralism is about a multiplicity of different forms of law collectively recognized by people within society (state law, customary law, religious law, etc.), as well as a multiplicity of the same kind of law. This approach does not relabel social phenomena, but instead accepts the collective identification of law by people within the community, and consequently it is not plagued by over-inclusiveness.

Another crucial set of differences arises from these contrasting presuppositions, methods, and orientations. Abstract legal pluralism abstracts from a paradigm of law to produce *a singular concept or definition with a fixed set of defining features* that purportedly provides a standard for what qualifies as law in all contexts. The social-historical theoretical perspective I apply to folk legal pluralism, in contrast, does not formulate an abstract concept of law with a single set of defining features, but instead accepts that collectively recognized manifestations of law vary widely and change over time in connection with surrounding social, cultural, economic, political, technological, and ecological circumstances.[39] Sharia takes a different form in an Islamic theocracy than it does in liberal democracies. Contrary to the abstract monist theory of the law state, John Dewey observed, this perspective entails "a consistently empirical or *historical* treatment of the changes in political forms and arrangements, free from any overriding conceptual domination such as is inevitable when a 'true' state is postulated."[40]

One of the objectives of this book is to expose the irresolvable problems thrown up by abstract

38 Merry, *supra* note 2, at 878.

39 For an account of this view of law, see Brian Z. Tamanaha, *A Realistic Theory of Law* (New York: Cambridge University Press 2017).

40 Dewey, *supra* note 27, at 46.

legal pluralism and to demonstrate the soundness of folk legal pluralism understood in social-historical terms. Illustrating its usefulness, the first four chapters utilize folk legal pluralism without stumbling over theoretical difficulties. The conceptual issues revolving around abstract legal pluralism and folk legal pluralism will be elaborated in detail in Chapter Five. Suffice it to say here that much of the morass surrounding legal pluralism is created by abstract legal pluralism.

Community Law, Regime Law, Cross-Polity Law

Three categories are useful in tracking law across the many different situations addressed in the course of this book: (1) basic laws and institutions of social intercourse within communities addressing property, personal injuries, marriage, divorce, sexual restrictions, inheritance, debts and obligations, and others; the body of rules people utilize in their daily social interaction; (2) regime laws that constitute, support, and enforce the power of the governing regime, including taxation and customs fees, forced labor and military service, laws against sedition, border controls, and much more, with governing regimes frequently nested within or encompassing in whole or part other sub-regimes; (3) laws that deal with matters between and across organized polities, including national law, international law, and transnational law. These categories are based on rough distinctions that emerge from the observation of folk law phenomena across contexts and over time. For ease of reference, I descriptively label these categories, respectively, *community law*, *regime law*, and *cross-polity law*.

Many manifestations of legal pluralism past and present involve juxtapositions among and between manifestations of these three categories of law. The consolidation of the state system across Europe that began to accelerate in the sixteenth century involved a concerted push by state legal officials to encompass community, regime, and cross-polity laws within the unified territorial state. Ruling regimes over homogeneous societies find it easier to enact comprehensive, uniform bodies of administrative, criminal, and civil law applicable to everyone. Ruling regimes over heterogeneous societies with significant populations of different cultural and religious communities must somehow accommodate, officially or unofficially, legal differences across these communities.

An especially fecund source of legal pluralism, which appears time and again in this text, is the resilience of the basic laws and institutions of social intercourse within the community that exist alongside regime law. Empires throughout history have enforced laws that furthered the objectives of the ruling regime while not interfering with community law. Versions of this occurred with European colonization of Africa, the Middle East, Asia, and the Pacific. This legacy still exists today, as described in a report issued by the World Bank legal department:

> In many developing countries, customary systems operating outside of the state regime are often the dominant form of regulation and dispute resolution, covering up to 90% of the population in parts of Africa. In Sierra Leone, for example, approximately 85% of the population falls under the jurisdiction of customary law, defined under the Constitution as "the rules which, by custom, are applicable to particular communities in Sierra Leone." Customary tenure covers 75% of land in most African countries, affecting 90% of land transactions in countries like Mozambique and Ghana.... In many of these countries, systems of justice seem to operate

> almost completely independently of the official state system.[41]

These situations are pluralistic in two senses: multiple communities exist side by side within the territory of a state each following their own customary or religious (community) laws; and state (regime) law enacts its own set of laws on the same matters, from which customary and religious law often diverges.

Recognizing that manifestations of law can vary in connection with surrounding factors makes it possible to observe continuities in bodies of law even as they undergo changes. Consider that customary law in small-scale hunter-gatherer societies often did not involve institutionalized enforcement; in more populous organized societies, like chiefdoms and early states, community laws were enforced by institutions established by the ruling regime. The former situation is community law with no regime law; the latter is regime law that encompasses community law. Cross-polity law has changed over time as well: what began several millennia ago as specific covenants between two polities on matters like treatment of emissaries and foreign merchants, today involves a profusion of regulatory activities between and across polities. Continuity and change also occur in particular bodies of law in relation to surrounding circumstances. For over two millennia, Jewish community law—Halakhah enforced by rabbinical courts—has been subjected to a range of treatment by the governing polity: from repression to ignored to recognition and enforcement. Across these divergent treatments and institutional arrangements, whether underground or with official regime support, many Jewish communities have continued to live in accordance with Halakhah.

Forms of community law, regime law, and cross-polity law are rooted in traditions, manifested in ongoing institutions, and continuously change subject to surrounding influences. Folk legal pluralism takes each form of law on its own terms, follows their historical development, and examines their interconnections (or disjunctions) with surrounding cultural, social, economic, ecological, technological, and political aspects of society as well as their interaction with other forms of law within the same social arena. This lens enables a rich understanding of legal pluralism.

A Snapshot of Legal Pluralism

This brief snapshot helps set the stage for the exploration of legal pluralism that follows. Thirty-five years ago I moved to Yap in the Federated States of Micronesia to assume an Assistant Attorney General position in a newly independent country carved out of the former Trust Territories of the Pacific Islands administered by the United States. The state laws and legal system were transplanted from the United States, including nearly all of the lawyers and high court judges working within the system, who were occupied mainly with government matters and commercial activities, as well as occasional major crimes. In daily social intercourse in the villages people largely followed customary law administered by chiefs, including matters of property, marriage and divorce, and personal injuries, often on terms not reflected in state law. The populace had little knowledge about state law, which was written in American legalese they did not understand, and on the outer islands the state legal system had virtually no presence. The state and national constitutions officially recognized custom and tradition, but had limited interaction with it. A de facto bifurcation (albeit

41 Leila Chirayath, Caroline Sage, and Michael Woolcock, Customary Law and Policy Reform: Engaging with the Plurality of Justice Systems (World Bank Legal Department Paper 2005) 3.

not sharp or fixed) existed between customary law followed within the community and a state legal system mainly occupied with government affairs and major commercial transactions. The arrangement worked cohesively for the most part, each dealing with its own matters, though occasions arose when the two systems came into direct clash.

In two separate incidents a month apart a teenage boy raped a girl. Thereafter, the community of each of the victims met in a customary gathering to discuss what should be done in response. The traditional leaders at these gatherings decided that the boys must be punished—whereupon the victim's relatives and others in the community severely beat the boys.[42] One boy had a bloodied face and broken arm; the other was beaten unconscious and hospitalized for five days (the latter received a more severe punishment because his victim was from a higher caste, which magnifies the offense). A traditional reconciliation ceremony held thereafter resolved the matter within the community.

Following these events, a national prosecutor brought rape charges against the two boys. They admitted their guilt and proceeded to sentencing. State legal officials ordinarily did not file criminal charges when customary punishments were administered because that resolved the matter within the community, but charges were brought in this instance because it was a serious crime under the criminal code that required prosecution. The family of the victims took the side of the defendants in the state proceedings, asserting that the boys had already been appropriately punished. The attorney for a defendant argued that "as a matter of customary law, the beating may have restored [him] fully to the community."[43] Judge Richard Benson (an American expatriate) sentenced the boys to two years in jail. He refused to consider the customary punishment because he did not want to send the message that people could "take the law into their own hands."[44] This language suggests they were acting as vigilantes, not people carrying out legitimate customary punishment on behalf of the community.

On appeal, the Supreme Court ruled that owing to the constitutional clause recognizing custom and tradition, the customary punishment should be considered as a mitigating factor to reduce the punishment. More telling than the outcome is how Judge Edward King (an American expatriate) construed events. Judge King skeptically and disapprovingly described the conduct of the villagers: "Both defendants suffered substantial, even brutal, beatings perpetrated by people who saw themselves as somehow representing the victims and their communities."[45] He asserted the monist view that state law is supreme and exclusive:

> In adopting the Declaration of Rights as part of the Constitution of the Federated States of Micronesia and therefore the supreme law of the land, the people of Micronesia subscribed to various principles which place upon the judiciary the obligation, among others, to assure that arrests are based upon probable cause, the determinations are arrived at fairly, and that punishments for wrongdoing are

---

42 An account of this case is provided in Brian Z. Tamanaha, "A Battle Between Law and Society in Micronesia: An Example of Originalism Gone Awry," 21 Pacific Rim Law & Policy Journal 295 (2012). These events are described in the consolidated reported case Tammed v. FSM, Tamangrow v. FSM, App. No. Y1-1988 (July 17, 1990), 4 Intrm. 266 (App. 1990).

43 *Id.* at 5.

44 *Id.* at 5–6.

45 *Id.* at 6.

> proportionate to the crime and meet prescribed standards.[46]

Judge King condemned the policy of state legal officials of not bringing charges after customary punishment and reconciliation had taken place:

> This practice of course amounts to a substitution of the customary punishment in place of the judicial proceedings and punishment contemplated by the Constitution and state statutes. Under the policy of the Yap attorney general's office, beating is no longer just a customary punishment, but also serves as the entire official state trial and punishment for that specific offense. The traditional leaders who authorized the punishment, and the village members who carried it out, may well be transformed through this ratification into government agents or officials.[47]

State law is the only form of law in Micronesia (in his mind), so therefore, Judge King reasoned, if state legal officials recognize customary punishments by the community, in effect this constitutes *the state's* legal actions. The judge issued a thinly veiled warning that the state could be sued for civil rights violations if they continued to defer to customary punishments.[48]

From the perspective of the community, including the victims and defendants, the punishment was an appropriate customary law response that directly resolved the situation independent of the state legal system. Yapese customary law did not owe its existence to the fact that a clause was included in the written constitution recognizing custom and tradition (drafted by a staff of American lawyers), but rather because as far back as they could remember they carried out their daily social intercourse through this law. It was *their* law literally, which they collectively created through their understandings and actions—unlike the transplanted state legal system that administered laws they did not live by run by officials from another society using technical legal language and procedures they did not understand.

Legal pluralism is complicated and messy and challenges basic assumptions about law perpetuated by the widely held monist law state image. Jurists and judges frequently hold and express monist assumptions about law, while members of the community may collectively recognize other legitimate forms of law functioning alongside state law. Just because state legal officials declare their monopoly over law, this does not make it necessarily so. Jurists sometimes have difficulty seeing beyond their own image and construction of law. Readers must be open to the unfamiliar to appreciate the extraordinary range of manifestations of coexisting forms of law and their implications presented in the course of this book.

46 *Id.* at 24–25.

47 *Id.* at 39.

48 In an article addressing this case he wrote after retiring, King acknowledged that his purpose was to threaten state officials with liability to pressure them to stop their practice of deferring to customary punishments. Edward C. King, "Custom and Constitutionalism in the Federated States of Micronesia," 3 Asian-Pacific Law & Policy Journal 249, 278 (2002).

16

John Borrows

"Sources and Scope of Indigenous Legal Traditions," from *Canada's Indigenous Constitution*

When nation states can learn from and embrace the best traditions of its peoples, they can be strengthened and become more unified. If this process occurs in a fair, orderly, transparent, non-discriminatory yet authoritative way the rule of law is reinforced in the process. The blending and/or coexistence of legal traditions is possible. Many countries successfully incorporate diverse legal traditions that respect different ethnic, cultural, and national groupings.[1] Some of these countries are bijuridical and include both civil law and common law systems.[2] Others are multi-juridical and include customary law regimes alongside civil or common law.[3] Canada should be counted among these multi-juridical countries: it embraces common law, civil law, and Indigenous legal traditions. Canada could be characterized as a juridically pluralistic state because it draws on many sources of law to sustain order.[4] While civil and common law traditions are generally recognized across the country, this is not always the case with Indigenous legal traditions. Yet Indigenous legal traditions can have great force in people's lives despite their lack of prominence in broader circles.[5] Indigenous legal traditions are a reality in Canada and should be more effectively recognized.

There are many negative stereotypes in circulation regarding Indigenous law. Recognition can be enhanced if Indigenous laws are understood in greater detail, free from misleading characterizations. For example, Indigenous peoples are diverse and their laws flow from many

1 Vernon Palmer, ed., *Mixed Jurisdictions Worldwide* (Cambridge: Cambridge University Press, 2001); J.E. Du Plessis, 'Comparative Law and the Study of Mixed Legal Systems,' in Mathias Reimann and Reinhard Zimmermann, eds., *Oxford Handbook of Comparative Law* (Oxford: Oxford University Press, 2006); R. Evans-Jones, 'Receptions of Law, Mixed Legal Systems and the Myth of the Genius of Scots Private Law' (1998) 114 *Law Quarterly Review* 228; E. Örücü et al., eds., *Studies in Legal Systems: Mixed and Mixing* (The Hague: Kluwer, 1996).

2 Some common law/civil law bijuridical countries include Botswana, Burkina-Faso, Burundi, Buthan, Chad, Chile, China, Congo, Cyprus, Japan, Lesotho, Malta, Mauritius, Namibia, Philippines, Puerto Rico, Saint Lucia, Saudi Arabia, Scotland, Seychelles, South Africa, Thailand, Vanuatu, and Yemen.

3 Some countries that combine customary law and other legal traditions are Cameroon, Côte D'Ivoire, Guinea, Eritrea, Ethiopia, Gabon, Gambia, Hong Kong, Indian, Indonesia, Israel, Jordan, Kenya, Korea (North and South), Lesotho, Liberia, Madagascar, Malawi, Malaysia, Mali, Micronesia, Myanmar, Nepal, Niger, Nigeria, Rwanda, Senegal, Sierra Leone, Solomon Islands, Sri Lanka, Swaziland, Taiwan, Tanzania, Uganda, Vanuatu, Western Samoa, Zambia, and Zimbabwe. For an interesting study of Indigenous law's interactions with European law, see Joan Church, 'The Place of Indigenous Law in a Mixed Legal System and a Society in Transformation: A South African Experience' (2005) *ANZLHS E-Journal* 94; D. Visser, 'Cultural Forces in the Making of Mixed Legal Systems' (2003) 78 *Tulane Law Review* 41.

4 For a discussion of legal pluralism, see Sally Engle Merry, 'Legal Pluralism' (1988) *Law and Society Review* 2 at 869.

5 James Tully, *Strange Multiplicity: Constitutionalism in an Age of Diversity* (Cambridge: Cambridge University Press, 1995).

sources.[6] Understanding their communities' legal foundations can lead to a better appreciation of their contemporary potential, including how they might be recognized, interpreted, enforced, and implemented. The underpinnings of Indigenous law are entwined with the social, historical, political, biological, economic, and spiritual circumstances of each group.[7] They are based on many sources, including sacred teachings, naturalistic observations, positivistic proclamations, deliberative practices, and local and national customs. Note that I am specifically making the point that not all Indigenous laws are customary at their root or in their expression, as people often assume.

There are many sources of law within Indigenous communities. Indigenous peoples hold many different views about the character and practice of law, as is the case in Western legal theory. Indigenous peoples hold diverse theories about what gives law its binding force. Disagreement can be an important part of the law, as long as there are sufficient convergences to produce continuous interim settlements.[8] The civil and common law traditions are not disregarded because of deep philosophical disagreements about their nature and sources. Differences of opinion are a part of the vibrancy and strength of Western law because they provide for shifting appeals to legitimacy through time, or even within a single case.[9] When working with Indigenous legal traditions one must take care not to oversimplify their character. Indigenous legal traditions can be just as varied and diverse as Canada's other legal traditions, although they are often expressed in their own unique ways. This chapter will explore Indigenous legal traditions by focusing on their varied sources. It is hoped that by categorizing Indigenous laws in this way readers will be better able to grasp their complexity and understand the choices available to Indigenous peoples when they exercise their laws. It is also hoped that this approach will allow other people to see the choices they have in relation to Indigenous law in Canada.

A. Sacred Law

As in other legal traditions, some Indigenous laws have sacred sources. Laws can be regarded as sacred if they stem from the Creator, creation stories or revered ancient teachings that have withstood the test of time. When laws exist within these categories they are often given the highest respect. Legal traditions based on spiritual

---

6 The earliest practitioners of law in North America were its Indigenous inhabitants. These peoples are known as the 'Aboriginal' or 'Native' peoples of the continent. 'Aboriginal' in Canadian law includes Indian, Inuit, and Métis people: see s. 35(2) of the *Constitution Act, 1982* (Canada), enacted as Schedule B to the *Canada Act, 1982* (U.K.) 1982, c. 11. They include, among others, the ancient and contemporary nations of the Innu, Mi'kmaq, Maliseet, Cree, Anishinabek, Haudenosaunee, Dakota, Lakota, Nakoda, Assinaboine, Saulteaux, Siksika, Secwepemec, Nlha7kapmx, Salish, Nuu-Chah-Nulth, Kwakwaka'wakw, Haida, Carrier, Tsimshian, Nisga'a, Gitksan, Tahltan, Tlingit, Gwichin, Dene, Inuit, and Métis. In relation to this diversity, I wrote in *Recovering Canada: The Resurgence of Indigenous Law* (Toronto: University of Toronto Press, 2002), 3–4:

> The traditions of these Indigenous peoples can be as historically different from one another as other nations and cultures in the world. For example, Canadian Indigenous peoples speak over 50 different Aboriginal languages from 12 distinct language families that have as wide a variation as those of Europe and Asia. The linguistic, genealogical, political, and legal descent of these nations can be traced back through millennia to different regions or territories in northern North America. This explains the wide variety of laws found in Indigenous groups.

7 Gerald Postema, 'On the Moral Presence of Our Past' (1991) 36 *McGill Law Journal* 1153.

8 Jeremy Webber, 'Legal Pluralism and Human Agency' (2006) 44 *Osgoode Hall Law Review* 167.

9 Philip Bobbitt, 'Constitutional Law and Interpretation,' in *A Companion to Philosophy of Law and Legal Theory*, ed. D. Patterson (Oxford: Blackwell, 1996); Philip Bobbitt, *Constitutional Interpretation* (New York: Blackwell, 1991).

principles form an important part of most every culture's legal inheritance.[10] While Canada's legal traditions are becoming increasingly secularized, one cannot deny the role of the metaphysical in our law's formation.[11] For example, the civil law and the common law have been significantly influenced by ideas about religion.[12] The receipt of evidence and the test for truth often rests on appeals to the divine.[13] Our Constitution's preamble states that Canada is 'founded on principles that recognize the supremacy of God.'[14]

Within Indigenous legal traditions, creation stories are often one source of sacred law. These accounts contain rules and norms that give guidance about how to live with the world and overcome conflict. Their reach can be quite expansive because they contain instructions about how all beings should relate to specific territories. They are often meant to apply over an entire region, and in some cases are universal in their range. Due to their broad reach and revered nature, laws that have sacred aspects at their source may be less flexible than laws flowing from other sources. Similarly, their recognition, enforcement, and implementation can often be regarded as foundational to the operation of other laws. Sometimes creation stories involve the formation of the world; at other times they reference the founding of other significant habitations. One notable 'creation story' for some Indigenous people describes how parts of Canada were formed through the application of Indigenous legal traditions. This is particularly apparent in those areas where First Nations used their own laws in negotiating treaties.

I encountered this view when working with Elders in Saskatchewan. They spoke of their treaties as being sacred because they brought Canada into existence within their territories. I encountered this viewpoint when I was asked to prepare a report on the meaning of the 'peace and order' clauses in the numbered treaties in the Canadian West.[15] This work was done through the Office of the Treaty Commissioner, and examined the nature of law within Cree, Anishinabek, and Dene

---

10 Michael Hadley, *The Spiritual Roots of Restorative Justice* (Albany: SUNY Press, 2001); R.H. Helmholz, *The Spirit of the Classical Canon Law* (Athens, Georgia: University of Georgia Press, 1996); Wael B. Hallaq, *The Origins and Evolution of Islamic Law* (Cambridge: Cambridge University Press, 2005); Neil S. Hecht, *An Introduction to the History and Sources of Jewish Law* (New York: Oxford University Press, 1996); Wener F Menski, *Hindu Law: Beyond Tradition and Modernity* (New Delhi: Oxford University Press, 2003); Rebecca French, *The Golden Yoke: The Legal Cosmology of Buddhist Tibet* (Ithaca, NY: Cornell University Press, 1995); Y. Liu, *Origins of Chinese Law: Penal and Administrative Law in its Early Development* (New York: Oxford University Press, 1998).

11 Immanuel Kant, *The Metaphysics of Morals*, trans. Mary J. Gregor (Cambridge: Cambridge University Press, 1996).

12 Harold J. Berman, *The Interaction of Law and Religion* (New York: Abingdon Press, 1974); Peter Radan, Denise Meyerson, and Rosalind Frances Croucher, eds., *Law and Religion: God, the State and the Common Law* (New York: Routledge, 2005); Brian Young, *The Politics of Codification: The Lower Canadian Civil Code of 1866* (Montreal: McGill-Queen's University Press, 1994), 113–20.

13 For further information, see M.H. Ogilvie, *Religious Institutions and the Law in Canada*, 2nd ed. (Toronto: Irwin Law, 2003), chap. 7.

14 Jonathon Penney and Robert Jacob Dannay, 'The Embarassing Preamble? Understanding the Supremacy of God and the Charter' (2006) 39 *UBC Law Review* 287; George Egerton, 'Trudeau, God, and the Canadian Constitution: Religion, Human Rights, and Government Authority in the Making of the 1982 Constitution,' in *Rethinking Church, State, and Modernity: Canada Between Europe and America*, ed. David Lyon and Marguerite Van Die (Toronto: University of Toronto Press, 2000), 90–112.

15 See John Borrows, 'Peace and Order: Describing and Implementing Treaty Justice in Saskatchewan' (paper prepared for the Office of the Treaty Commission, Saskatoon, 2003).

societies.[16] The report also examined the peace and order promises within the treaties which spoke of the need to respect and apply Indigenous law throughout the territories covered by these agreements. From a government perspective, the clauses said the Indians would 'maintain peace and order between each other and also between themselves and other tribes of Indians or whites.'[17] They also said the Indians would 'aid and assist the officers of Her Majesty in bringing to justice and punishment any Indian offending against the stipulations of this treaty or infringing the laws in force in the country so ceded.'

In listening to the Elders speak about the meaning of these legally binding promises, it was clear that they regarded the treaty as flowing from a sacred source. They did not rely on the written text of the treaty to arrive at this conclusion. Because First Nations followed their own legal traditions in creating treaties, their interpretation was that treaties were made with the Creator as well as with the Crown. First Nations felt encouraged in their view by the presence of Christian missionaries during the negotiations, and the Crown's invocation of God throughout their meetings.[18] Elder Norman Sunchild of Treaty 6 said: 'When [Treaty 6 First Nations] finally agreed to the treaty, the Commissioner took the promises in his hand and raised them to the skies, placed the treaties in the hands of

16 In 2001 I was approached by the Office of the Treaty Commissioner to produce a 'Blue Sky' Report about justice in the Saskatchewan Indian treaties. In undertaking this task I was encouraged to be innovative in my research and to speculate in my findings about what justice jurisdiction and delivery might require under the treaty relationship. As such, I was directed to 'look outside the box,' in keeping with the exploratory nature of the parties' Treaty Table process. I was asked to see if relationships of justice could be different in the province if the treaties formed a central part of the parties' relationships. My terms of reference were to 'lead discussions on the present justice system, identify key issues and options based on a review of existing justice system studies, inquiries, and recommendations, and to focus on justice delivery in the future based on the treaty relationship.' I was also to provide an overview of the Crown's views on justice issues at the time of the treaty, and to give an overview of First Nations' views on law and traditional justice concepts discussed at the time of the treaty. To accomplish this work I facilitated two symposia over a two-year period, involving many people representing various interests in the treaty process. I wrote three draft reports before completing a Final Report in 2005 which was approved by the Elders, but remains unpublished because of concerns about the Crown's treatment of oral history in the courts.

17 Treaties 4, 5, and 6 reads as follows:

> The undersigned chiefs, on their behalf and on behalf of all other Indians inhabiting the tract within ceded do hereby solemnly promise and engage to strictly observe this treaty and also to conduct and behave themselves as good and loyal subjects of Her Majesty The Queen. They promise and engage that *they will in all respects obey and abide by the law; that they will maintain peace and order between each other, and also between themselves and other tribes of Indians or whites*, now inhabiting or hereafter to inhabit any part of the said tract, or that they will not molest a person or property of any inhabitants of such ceded tract or the property of Her Majesty The Queen, or interfere with or trouble any person passing or travelling through the said tract or any part thereof, and that *they will aid and assist the officers of Her Majesty in bringing to justice and punishment any Aboriginal offending against the stipulations of this treaty or infringing the laws in force in the country so ceded.* (Emphasis mine.)

The text of Treaties 8 and 10 is only slightly different:

> And the undersigned Cree, Beaver, Chipewyan and other Indian Chiefs and Headmen, on their own behalf and on behalf of all the Indians whom they represent, DO HEREBY SOLEMNLY PROMISE and engage to strictly observe this Treaty, and also to conduct and behave themselves as good and loyal subjects of Her Majesty the Queen.
>
> THEY PROMISE AND ENGAGE that they will, in all respects, obey and abide by the law; that they will maintain peace between each other, and between themselves and other tribes of Indians, and between themselves and others of Her Majesty's subjects, whether Indians, half-breeds or whites, this year inhabiting and hereafter to inhabit any part of the said ceded territory; and that they will not molest the person or property of any inhabitant of such ceded tract, or of any other district or country, or interfere with or trouble any person passing or travelling through the said tract or any part thereof, and that they will assist the officers of Her Majesty in bringing to justice and punishment any Indian offending against the stipulations of this Treaty or infringing the law in force in the country so ceded.

18 Alexander Morris, *The Treaties of Canada with the Indians of Manitoba and the North West Territories Including the Negotiations on Which they were Based* (Toronto: Belfords and Clark and Co., 1880).

the Great Spirit.'[19] Elder Jacob Bill also of Treaty 6 commented: 'It was the will of the Creator that the White man would come to live with us, among us, to share our lives together with him, and also both of us collectively to benefit from the bounty of Mother Earth for all time to come.' He further said: 'Just like the treaty, that's what that is, one law was given, Indian and white, we both gave something special, something to keep, something to reverence, just like the treaty, both Indian and white beneficiaries, we were given a gift from the Creator. The Creator owns us, he is still the boss, nothing is hidden ... just like that little flicker [of fire], that little flame's going out, that's the way the treaty looks, but now that we are sitting here it seems like we need a big flame so we can revive our lives and our relationship, just like we're trying to revive this life so that our young people will have a good life for a long time, for many generations to come. That's why we are here, that's what the Elders seen a long time ago, if the white man listens he too will benefit, a long life for his children and his future generations because he, too, won't sin [pastahowin], he will not feel the brunt of that whip that the Creator has. Nothing will be hurt if both sides start talking to each other as beneficiaries of the treaty.'[20] Some Indigenous laws have sacred sources and the numbered treaties are an example of this type of law.

The laws surrounding Canada's formation in many treaty territories are profound because they are meant to encourage the spiritual, moral and legal capacities of all the people who would come to live here. The sacred nature of the treaties is one reason why many First Nations would not consider abandoning them despite generations of government neglect. It would be a violation of the Creator's law, sacred law, to turn away from their promises to him and others in maintaining peace and order throughout the lands on which they lived.

This view of Canada's creation potentially challenges the approach of some critics who may regard Canada's existence in treaty areas as a transgression of rather than an application of Indigenous law. However, the fact that treaties helped to bring Canada into existence within certain areas should not for that reason alone be regarded as contrary to Indigenous law. Many things, including treaties, can be considered sacred even if they are not given the respect they deserve. However, to appropriately clarify this issue it should be acknowledged that there are some people who regard Canada's creation as profane and understand their history very differently from that taught by some Elders in Saskatchewan. For example, many Haudenosaunee of the eastern Great Lakes do not regard themselves as participating in the creation of Canada. Instead, they regard their treaties as bringing their Confederacy into an alliance with the Crown.[21] As such, many Haudenosaunee people would resist being labelled as Canadian citizens because of their distinct status. For this reason they would not likely regard Canada's creation as a sacred event. Another prominent exception to Canada's creation being regarded as sacred is found within British Columbia—where historic treaties were rare. First Nations in this region would have a hard time accepting claims that Canada was formed through promises to the Creator by reference to their laws. In their case, other people moved into their territories and

19 Harold Cardinal and Walter Hildebrandt, *Treaty Elders of Saskatchewan: Our Dream Is that Our Peoples Will One Day Be Clearly Recognized as Nations* (Calgary: University of Calgary Press, 2000), 6–7.

20 Elder Jacob Bill, cited in John Borrows, 'Peace and Order: Describing and Implementing Treaty Justice in Saskatchewan' (paper prepared for the Office of the Treaty Commissioner, Saskatchewan, 2003), 105–06. Paper on file with the author.

21 Robert S. Allen, *His Majesty's Indian Allies: British Indian Policy in the Defense of Canada, 1774–1815* (Toronto: Dundurn Press, 1992); Carl Benn, *The Iroquois in the War of 1812* (Toronto: University of Toronto Press, 1998).

established governments without their formalized participation and legal consent. In this light, the harsh injustice of British Columbia's resettlement can hardly be[22] regarded as a sacred event. There are other places in Canada where First Nations have suffered a similar fate and thus would look skeptically upon claims that Canada's creation flows from a sacred source. Finally, a sacred view of the treaties might also be somewhat problematic from a certain government perspective, as demonstrated by arguments often made by government lawyers who give treaties the narrowest possible technical interpretation in order to increase the Crown's authority relative to the Indians. Some might even view treaties as filled with fraud, duress, and manipulation—or as expedient temporary bargains, designed by the Crown to separate Indians from their lands and resources for the lowest possible price. However, despite these very real challenges there are large areas of the country where treaties between Indigenous peoples and the Crown referenced Indigenous traditions. The fact that Canada's creation is not universally regarded as flowing from a sacred source does not undermine the laws of those First Nations who see things differently. For people in these spaces, treaties can be regarded as sacred creation stories about Canada's formation if placed in their best light.

Professor Noel Lyon, who taught for thirty years at Queen's Law School, summed up his interpretation of the sacred nature of Saskatchewan's First Nations' Elders views on Canada's law in the following fashion: 'As I've listened to the Elders, I have begun to understand that what I've learned about Aboriginal peoples and their situation in Canada has largely come from written sources, from books, and there are a lot of things that were embedded in me in my legal education that I haven't overcome. The most important one, I think, is that law school indoctrinated me with the belief that the Crown is all-powerful, and I think that's a real problem, because I think legal education, it may not be that bad today, but I think there is a tendency to regard the Crown almost in the way that the First Nations people regard the Creator, as being the source of all things. And from that flows the proposition that the treaties are seen by the non-Aboriginal community as just another body of laws that define the status and rights of Aboriginal peoples, rather than seeing the treaties as a nation-to-nation partnership, inter-societal law ... It had never occurred to me until Elder Crowe said this yesterday or the day before: that the right of the white people to be on this land is founded in the treaty.'[23] From this explanation one can see how treaties can be regarded as a sacred creation story. As such, they join other Indigenous laws that flow from sources that are revered or most highly respected.

B. Natural Law

Aside from sacred sources, Indigenous peoples also find and develop law from observations of the physical world around them.[24] When considering laws from this source, it is often necessary to understand how the earth maintains

22 For more information about the resettlement of British Columbia by non-Aboriginal peoples, see Cole Harris, *The Resettlement of British Columbia: Essays on Colonialism and Geographical Change* (Vancouver: UBC Press, 1997); Cole Harris, *Making Native Space: Colonialism, Resistance and Change in British Columbia* (Vancouver: UBC Press, 2002).

23 Noel Lyon and Elder Jacob Bill, cited in John Borrows, 'Peace and Order: Describing and Implementing Treaty Justice in Saskatchewan' (paper prepared for the Office of the Treaty Commissioner, Saskatchewan, 2003), 105–06. Paper on file with the author.

24 An interesting example of how natural law might develop and be operative within Indigenous communities is found in the writings of Professor Julie Cruickshank. See Julie Cruickshank, *Do Glaciers Listen? Local Knowledge, Colonial Encounters and Social Imagination* (Vancouver: UBC Press, 2005).

functions that benefit us and all other beings.[25] This approach to legal interpretation attempts to develop rules for regulation and conflict resolution from a study of the world's behaviour. Law in this vein can be seen to flow from the consequences of creation or the 'natural' world or environment. Indigenous peoples who practise this form of law might watch how a plant interacts with an insect, and draw legal principles from that experience. Others may study how an insect interrelates with a bird, and take legal guidance from that encounter. Some might examine how a certain bird relates to an animal or another bird and see standards for judgment in this relationship. There might also be analogies drawn from the behaviours of watersheds, rivers, mountains, valleys, meadows or shorelines to guide legal actions. As such, these laws may be regarded as literally being written on the earth.[26]

Note how Indigenous definitions of natural law may at times have a somewhat different emphasis than what is found in many leading natural law theories within Western jurisprudence. The separation of man from nature may not be as stark as in Aristotle's philosophy, where man 'alone has any sense of good and evil, of just and unjust, and the like.'[27] There may also be less emphasis on 'right reason' as universal, and the measure of law's commands and prohibitions, as in the Roman jurist Cicero's works.[28] Furthermore, while Indigenous legal theories about natural law can be diverse and certainly overlap with Western legal theory, there may be less of a belief that living within nature is impossible for human beings without some profound human political intervention, a belief reflected in the works of Thomas Hobbes, Jean-Jacques Rousseau, or John Locke.[29] In contrast with many Western theorists many Indigenous societies do not act in the same way to restrain nature, because they find more to embrace within it. Finally, perhaps many Indigenous peoples might de-emphasize particular Western natural law theories (if they were conscious of them) because these theories so often provided the justification for Indigenous peoples' dispossession.[30] For many Indigenous people, the casebook for learning natural law requires an intimate knowledge of how to read the world;[31] understanding natural law from this point of view does not require an intimate knowledge of how to read legal philosophy.

I have experienced this form of legal reasoning in my own life. My mother is an Elder on our reserve and possesses a sound knowledge of the world immediately surrounding her. She is a person who studies and interprets nature's laws for her family's benefit. Not all legal traditions within Indigenous societies are immediately state-focused. Authority can be based upon kinship and family networks. My mother does not have an

25 Cree Elder Wayne Roan speaks about nature's laws from a Cree perspective on the website Nature's Laws, retrieved 19 September 2008 from www.abheritage.ca/natureslaws/index2.html.

26 Nancy J. Turner, *The Earth's Blanket: Traditional Teachings for Sustainable Living* (Vancouver: Douglas and McIntyre, 2005), 11–40.

27 Aristotle, *Politics*, ed. Trevor Saunders, trans. T.A. Sinclair (New York: Penguin, 1962), Book I, chap. 2.

28 Andrew Dyck, *A Commentary on Cicero, De Legibus* (Ann Arbor: University of Michigan Press, 2004), Book I, chap. 13; Cicero, *The Republic*, trans. Clinton W. Keyes (Cambridge, MA: Harvard University Press, 1928), Book III, chap. 22.

29 Thomas Hobbes, *Leviathan* (London: G. Routledge and Sons, 1887); Jean-Jacques Rousseau, *The Social Contract* (London: Dent, 1973); John Locke, *Two Treatises on Government* (New York: New American Library, 1965).

30 For a critique of Western ideas of natural law, see Myres S. McDougal et al., *Human Rights and World Public Order* (New Haven, CT: Yale University Press, 1980). For an excellent discussion of European conceptions of natural law and its application to Indigenous peoples, see James Anaya, *Indigenous Peoples in International Law*, 2nd ed. (Oxford: Oxford University Press, 2004), 16–19. See also James Tully, *A Discourse on Property: John Locke and his Adversaries* (Cambridge: Cambridge University Press, 1980); James Tully, *Strange Multiplicity: Constitutionalism in an Age of Diversity* (Cambridge: Cambridge University Press, 1995), particularly part 3.

31 *Delgamuukw v. A.G.B.C.* (1991), 79 D.L.R. (4th) 185; [1991] 3 W.W.R. 97; [1991] 5 C.N.L.R. 5 (B.C.S.C.).

education beyond grade eight because she ran away from home at an early age due to family challenges and the threat of removal to a residential school. Despite this lack of formal education, perhaps even because of it, she is one of the wisest people I know. She has an unquenchable thirst for learning. Her knowledge of the earth around her is profound. She frequently talks of her experiences on the land and relates how her perceptions could guide our actions as a family. When we do not follow her judgments we find that we are often in breach of important environmental laws.

For example, in the summer my mother watches for the return of the monarch butterflies and notes how they seem to be scarce when the milkweed plants are fewer in number. Of course she understands that their decline may be attributed to other factors; she is very respectful of scientific explanations and understands the profound complexity of natural forces. However, if no other explanations are forthcoming, and if there are fewer milkweeds on hand, she will inevitably urge us to protect and increase the number of milkweeds around our house. If we do not, she says we will see fewer monarch butterflies. We will also be less likely to enjoy the beauty and variety of other plants that the existence of these butterflies will eventually help to flourish. For her, recognizing and protecting the relationship between butterflies and milkweeds is a principle of natural law. She is our family's prime jurist in such matters because she helps us understand the specific obligations we have in the territories surrounding our home on the reserve. She talks about many other plants besides the milkweeds and will tell us stories about what they teach us.[32] Then she usually takes the principle up one notch and observes that if we have a smaller plant population this usually means we will have fewer bees and other insects in the area. Their absence might affect the availability of fruits and berries in the fall and thus negatively diminish the variety in our diet during that season. My mother also says that fewer insects can lead to fewer birds, and thus we would find less harmony and song in the trees around us. She believes that, for our family, their diminishment affects our emotional outlook in a negative way. She says that we need to hear the birds to know more about ourselves and our environment. When she has been gravely ill, and barely able to leave her home, the songs of the birds have been a source of healing for her. It is thus no surprise that she believes that birdsong is vital to her family's well-being, and thus she watches to ensure we do not do things that will weaken the so-called weeds in the fields and roadsides surrounding our home on the reserve. She has always lamented the use of pesticides and the creation of monocultures in our territories because she feels they negatively affect the plants, insects, birds, and humans on their own terms, and in their relationships with one another. This form of environmentally based family law can be a significant source of legal regulation.

I have heard and read similar teachings and stories from other people around my reserve at Cape Croker. I can remember the time when I more fully realized that the environmental stories I had been hearing for most of my life were one of the sources of law at home. I was just about to begin teaching at Osgoode Hall Law School when I was invited to a discussion about Anishinabek constitutional and environmental law after our annual late summer pow-wow on the reserve. It was a hot August weekend and we had assembled in the Maadookii Senior's Centre to discuss how we might regulate our fisheries and overcome conflict with our peninsula neighbours, who were suspicious or angry about how we would practise conservation. About twenty people were in

32 One such story, related to butterflies, is found in John Borrows, 'Creating an Indigenous Legal Community: 5th Annual John Tait Memorial Lecture' (2005) 50 *McGill Law Journal* 3.

attendance, including Elders, band councillors, schoolteachers, fishermen, and some youth who were home from university for the season. We had recently won a significant case that recognized our treaty right to fish for commercial purposes around the Bruce Peninsula in Georgian Bay.[33] While this was an important victory for our people, non-native fishers were concerned that we would deplete the stocks and disregard provincial conservation laws. We even experienced some violent backlash from a small number of them in the surrounding towns and communities, as our boats were burned and our fishermen were publicly threatened. Everyone assembled wanted to find ways to regulate our own people's use of the resource and assure the broader public that we would not be overfishing because we had laws that penalized this kind of abuse.

As the meeting began, Elder Basil Johnston took the floor for most of the morning and spoke of the world's creation in our territory. He spoke of how the sun, moon, and earth came into being. He related how the first plants, animals, and humans lived peacefully together on the earth. Each being that came to life had a story attached to its genesis, and these stories taught about how each was to be respected and how we were to best relate to them. As I listened to him, I understood he was speaking about the natural sources of our laws and how they could teach us about what was required of us to regulate our behaviour. After some time, he came to the matter at hand: the right to fish. He spoke about how whitefish had been central to our society for generations. He referred to these fish by their Anishinabek name, *adigmeg*, which translated means 'caribou of the sea.' He then told us a story about them. He said the fish would roam where they wanted, and would fail to live in the adjoining waters if they were offended by our overuse or if we desecrated their underwater homes. At this point a fisherman joined the conversation and said that he had witnessed just such an offence when lake trout had been crossed with brook trout and introduced as 'splake' into the waters of Lake Huron at the behest of so-called sports fishermen. The splake did not have the same strong natural enemies and thus they more successfully competed for the same resources as the whitefish, with the result that most whitefish left the area for a time.

At that point, someone else entered the conversation to indicate a way in which our own fishers might offend the fish. There was some concern that certain of our own First Nations citizens would abuse the whitefish. An Elder, Winona Ariaga, told of her remembrance of how her grandparents only took fish from the waters in selected seasons, and at limited times. She said that she was told that if we troubled *adigmeg* by taking them all year long, it would lead to their disappearance. She said this was one reason the old people diversified their economic pursuits and engaged in sugar maple extraction in the spring, hunting in the fall, farming in the summer, and fishing in the remaining intervals. She said no one should take fish all the time, during every season. Her observations were rooted in the long experience of our community's interactions with the natural world, from which she drew principles to guide our discussion. Her teachings were also intermingled with personal observations of the lake, land, fish, and people.

After all these viewpoints had been expressed, it was suggested that the band council should approach the provincial government to determine whether they would be willing to enter into an agreement that respected our laws but also satisfied the provincial authorities that we would not overfish the lake. Many Elders and fishermen put forward their views about what would

33 *R. v. Jones and Nadjiwon*, [1993] 3 C.N.L.R. 182 (Ont. Prov. Div.).

best protect the fish and still ensure a prosperous livelihood for members of the community. The band also insisted on hiring their own professionally trained ichthyologist to ensure that the latest science would be incorporated into their laws. In 1999, an agreement was concluded that allowed some space for our laws in the regulation of our traditional territories' fisheries.[34] While I am not completely sure if or how our August meeting had an effect on these subsequent developments, I do feel that the broader issues we canvassed reinforced the determination to act in accordance with the laws as we interpreted them from the world around us. The legal traditions we reviewed certainly helped to regulate the behaviour of the fishermen I knew.

Perhaps a more public example of law being derived from the environment can be found in the trial of the *Delgamuukw v. Attorney General (British Columbia)* which took place in British Columbia in the early 1990s.[35] In this case, Justice McEachern of the British Columbia Supreme Court heard evidence about the Gitksan peoples' historic use of land in the upper Skeena River area, around Seeley Lake. Over one hundred years prior to the *Delgamuukw* case, Gitksan Chiefs from Gitwangak described their relationship to the land in natural law terms. They said: 'We would liken this district to an animal, and our village, which is situated on it, to its heart. Lorne Creek, which is almost at the end of it, may be likened to one of the animal's feet. We feel that the whiteman by occupying the creek, are, as it were, cutting off a foot. We know that an animal may live without one foot, even without both feet; but we also know that every such loss renders him more helpless.'[36] This statement reveals how the Gitksan drew upon environmental observations to form legal principles to guide their relationships. Their concern about the implications of a fragmented approach to watershed management led them to predict its crippling effects upon the land and people. The analogy of territories to animals and the lessons that are drawn from their use acts as a guide to legally regulate behaviour and minimize disputes.

One hundred years later, during the *Delgamuukw* case, the Gitksan followed a similar pattern, referring to animals' and peoples' activities relative to land to provide criteria for judgment. Elders gave evidence of their laws through their *adaawk*, which are verbal records of their group's origins and experiences with others and the land.[37] For example, Elder Mary Johnson related an *adaawk* about an ancient grizzly bear, a landslide, and the people's transgression of natural law.[38] Her account contains principles about how people should appropriately relate to the fish and contains an interpretation of what would happen to them if they did not respect these beings. Her testimony was recorded by the court as follows:

> After all the fishing is finished and all
> the hunting for—for mountain goats
> and groundhogs and the mountain and
> all the berry picking is finished, then
> they got nothing to do, so the maidens

34 For further context, see Edwin Koenig, *Culture and Ecologies: A Native Fishing Conflict on the Saugeen-Bruce Peninsula* (Toronto: University of Toronto Press, 2005).

35 Gisday Wa and Delgam Uukw, 'Delgam Uukw Speaks,' in *The Spirit in the Land* (Gabriola Island, BC: Reflections, 1992), 7–9. For general commentary about the *Delgamuukw* case, see Dara Culhane, *The Pleasure of the Crown: Anthropology, Law and First Nations* (Vancouver: Talon Books, 1998).

36 Don Monet and Skanu'u, *Colonialism on Trial: Indigenous Land Rights and the Gitksan and Wet'suwet'en Sovereignty Case* (Gabriola Island, BC: New Society Publishers, 1992), 1.

37 Ibid., 26.

38 For another account of this event, see William Robinson as told by Walter Wright, *Men of Medeek*, 2nd ed. (Kitimat, BC: Northern Sentinel Press, 1962).

would go and make the camp at the lake, at the foot of Stekyooden, and they caught some grouse ... [A]fter they were caught many trouts, they cut out the back bone of the skin, and tails are still on the back bone. And as they was staying there, they learned the dances of the people and all the songs, and the way they were—they move when they were dancing. So one time, one young lady cut one of these back bone and put it on her head as a decoration while dancing. And she would happen to be near the—near the lake, and she look at herself at the edge of the lake, and she saw it was the bone looks really, really beautiful and why she dances gracefully. So she ran and told the others what she have found, and show them. Then they all got back bones and decorated their heads with it and some of the people used to come over and watch them and they didn't put a stop to it, and they smiled at what's going on. So after they all went home when it's time to go home, the people of T'am Lax amit heard a terrible noise, and they [...] left the lake and the people watched where the noise comes from, and they've seen some great big trees were throwing about the top of the rest of the tall trees, and they just stood there wondering what happened, until it comes—there is a little stream that runs from the lake and goes into the Skeena River, and that's—and this thing followed the little stream, tramping down the trees. And finally they see this great huge bear, grizzly bear that they have never seen before. And the chiefs sent messengers through the village to—after warriors, to have the warriors ready, which they did. And not long after the messenger went out, all the warriors came out with their spears and arrows and bow and arrow, and hammers that are made with stone, all those from weapons that strong young men use, they all come out bravely to meet this great grizzly bear. And he gets to the water and swam across and—and they went in front, they all went in front of him, but he is—he is a supernatural grizzly bear, they call him Mediik, and whenever they are shot him with an arrow, the arrow flies way up high instead and fall back down again and it hit the warriors, and they were wounded. And this grizzly bear tramped them until they were crushed to the ground, and goes through the village and kills a lot of people. And after that he—he came—he turned and go into the water again, follow the stream where he came from the first place. So the brave warriors went to—to see where he went, and it goes into the lake, disappeared into the lake. That's why the wise elders told the young people not to play around with fish or meat or anything, because the—because the Sun God gave them food to eat and those who—just they should just take enough to eat and not to play with it, that's why this tragedy happens to them.

Q. Did any of the people go back up the trail that this grizzly bear followed down the mountain afterwards?

A. Yeah. They went—they went to follow the trail and that's when they see that he disappeared, his track disappeared into the lake. So they believed

> that it's the revenge of those trouts, because they played around with their bones.
>
> Q. And is that lake—do you know what that lake is known to the nonIndian today, the name of that lake?
>
> A. They call it see Seeley Lake.[39]

Mary Johnson's *adaawk* reveals how Gitksan Elders might use their laws to communicate important principles about how fish should be treated when they are harvested. Past environmental events can be interpreted to provide future guidance to regulate people's conduct. For the Gitksan, as with many Indigenous peoples, the law is read from the land. In Gitksan territory this occurs when one encounters Seely Lake and sees the landslide created by the Giant Grizzly Bear who rushed down the mountain to punish people for their wrongful behaviour with the fish. Standards for judgment are recorded on the earth. While Justice McEachern did not rely upon these accounts to formulate his opinion in the *Delgamuukw* case,[40] the Gitksan continue to reference their *adaawk* and their other legal traditions to regulate and guide their relationships.[41]

C. Deliberative Law

An especially broad source of Indigenous legal tradition is formed through processes of persuasion, deliberation, council, and discussion. While sacred and natural law might sometimes form the backdrop against which debate occurs, the proximate source of most Indigenous law is developed through people talking with one another. The human dimension of these laws means that recognition, enforcement, and implementation make them subject to re-examination and revision through the generations. Indigenous law is not static and can move with the times. The deliberative nature of many Indigenous laws means they can be continuously updated and remain relevant in the contemporary world. When Indigenous people have to persuade one another within their traditions, they must also do so by reference to the entire body of knowledge to which they have access, which includes ancient and modern understandings of human rights, due process, gender equality, and economic considerations. While contemporary concepts will modify and be modified by very old principles and processes, they will also remain distinct by virtue of their particular cultural-legal contexts. Thus, since deliberative Indigenous laws draw upon historical and current legal ideas, they can also more explicitly take account of (and even incorporate where appropriate) legal standards from other legal systems. They can be harmonized with or distinguished from the laws around them based on what counts as persuasive to the group involved in the debate. Since no Indigenous person or community is completely detached from the world, many influences will be brought to bear on Indigenous legal developments. Deliberation aimed at making Indigenous law can occur in formal and informal meetings and gatherings; in these settings laws can be constructed through highly structured or ad hoc means.

The deliberative nature of the Indigenous legal tradition is also a key to resisting fundamentalist and dogmatic legal practices and ideas. When I have discussed Indigenous legal traditions, some people unfamiliar with them have raised concerns about available safeguards and

---

39 *Delgamuukw v. A.G.B.C.*, [1991] 5 C.N.L.R. 5 at 52–53 (B.C.S.C.).

40 Ibid., 49. See Val Napoleon, '*Delgamuukw*: A Legal Straight-Jacket for Oral Histories?' (2005) 20 *Canadian Journal of Law and Society* 2.

41 Richard Daly, *Our Box Was Full: An Ethnography for the Delgamuukw Plaintiffs* (Vancouver: UBC Press, 2004); Frank Cassidy, ed., *Aboriginal Title in British Columbia: Delgamuukw v. the Queen* (Lantzville, BC: Oolichan Press, 1991), 4, 51, 53, 58, 62, 199.

protections for those who are most vulnerable within Indigenous societies. Often these concerns are based on how 'backwards' some Indigenous communities appear in their social relationships,[42] particularly given colonialism's crushing weight.[43] It must be admitted that Indigenous communities experience many pathologies flowing from the dysfunctions of substance abuse, sexual abuse, residential schools, economic dislocation, and non-Aboriginal political interference.[44] Indigenous individuals can also make poor life decisions, like people from any other group. These negative choices are often compounded and made more destructive because of substandard government infrastructure and support within their communities. Such challenges can make it difficult for certain communities to administer their legal traditions in healthy ways. The remedy for this problem lies in helping these communities to heal themselves so that they are in a better position to develop and follow constructive and dynamic laws.[45] Persuasion is most effective when people have confidence in one another's personal and social integrity; thus, healthier relationships can create stronger legal systems because of the increased social capital upon which they can rely.[46] Social capital is the resource generated in group relationships;[47] it can provide important nourishment for Indigenous law because it can foster trust and goodwill, and can engender mutual obligations necessary for effective group action.[48] Thus, as is the case with all societies, Indigenous peoples need to attend to their socio-economic health to strengthen the effectiveness of deliberation within their communities. Healthy participatory legal processes are an important bulwark against oppressive leadership and overbearingly inflexible laws.

At the same time, while it is important to acknowledge the significant struggles some Indigenous communities face in revitalizing their legal traditions, we must also inoculate ourselves against drawing inaccurate and stereotypical conclusions about how Indigenous people will apply their laws in a contemporary context. Indigenous peoples are not 'backwards.'[49] Sometimes, when people say they are concerned about Indigenous legal traditions, their worry is not as much with the community's social state but with the ancient nature and connection Indigenous peoples have to their laws. I have been asked: 'Won't the application of Indigenous law lead to injustice?' When pressed further as to what they mean, people often think Indigenous law will inevitably demean women, deny due process, and be

---

42 Frances Widdowson and Howard Adams, *Disrobing the Aboriginal Industry: The Deception behind Indigenous Cultural Preservation* (Montreal: McGill-Queen's University Press, 2008).

43 Thomas Flanagan, *First Nations, Second Thoughts* (Montreal: McGill-Queen's University Press, 2000).

44 A.C. Hamilton and C.M. Sinclair, 'Aboriginal Women,' in *The Justice System and Aboriginal People: Report of the Aboriginal Justice Inquiry of Manitoba*, ed. A.C. Hamilton and C.M. Sinclair, vol. 1 (Winnipeg: Queen's Printer, 1991), 475–87; Amnesty International, *Stolen Sisters: Discrimination and Violence against Indigenous Women in Canada, A Summary of Amnesty International's Concerns* (London: Amnesty International Secretariat, October 2004); First Nations Child, and Family Caring Society of Canada, *Wen'de: We Are Coming to the Light of Day* (Ottawa: First Nations Child and Family Caring Society of Canada, 2005), 14–15; Suzanne Fournier and Ernie Crey, *Stolen from Our Embrace* (Vancouver: Douglas and McIntyre, 1997).

45 John Borrows, *Seven Generations, Seven Teachings* (Vancouver: National Centre for First Nations Governance, 2007).

46 J. White and P. Maxim, 'Social Capital, Social Cohesion, and Population Outcomes in Canada's First Nations Communities,' in *Aboriginal Conditions: Research as a Foundation for Public Policy*, ed. J. White, P. Maxim, and D. Beavon (Vancouver: UBC Press, 2003), 18.

47 See Robert Putnam, *Bowling Alone: The Collapse and Revival of American Community* (Toronto: Simon and Schuster, 2000).

48 S. Callahan, 'The Capital that Counts' (1996) 123(20) *Commonweal* 123 (November 22, 1996), 7 at 7; J. Coleman, 'Social Capital in the Creation of Human Capital' (1988) 94 *American Journal of Sociology* 98.

49 Robert Odawi Porter, *Sovereignty, Colonialism and Indigenous Nations: A Reader* (Durham, NC: Carolina Academic Press, 2005), especially 503–675.

inconsistent with democracy and cherished ideas about the rule of law.

While it is true that the application of Indigenous law may violate individual rights, all legal systems face potential challenges in this regard. Nevertheless, we must guard against stereotypes which might cause us to see such problems as inevitable within Indigenous societies.[50] Of course, as with any system, Indigenous legal traditions must be attentive to foundational questions of human dignity to have any chance of continued growth and acceptance. Fortunately, Indigenous peoples are very aware of foundational principles of civil, political, social and economic rights and responsibilities upon which legal systems rest. In fact, they call on these ideas all the time in their fight against colonial state domination. The development and application of Indigenous law is unlikely to thrive unless Indigenous peoples themselves also express these core precepts within their own distinctive systems. In fact, a large number of Indigenous people would likely not accept the double standard of expecting colonial governments to respect international human rights while their own governments failed to recognize similar principles. I know I would not accept this result in my own First Nation.

For Indigenous peoples to be persuasive in declaring and developing law they must incorporate human rights principles in some form within their legal systems. These systems of human rights protection may be found in their own historic laws and experience, as well as in current human rights documents and declarations. The problem with the *Indian Act* for many years has been its failure to incorporate human rights standards.[51] While the application of the Canadian *Human Rights Act* may help to partially remedy this deficiency, a fuller solution would allow Indigenous peoples to develop their own legal traditions consistent with international human rights standards.[52] While obligations vary according to the international instrument in question, Indigenous incorporation of these laws would include providing remedies for breaches of human rights, along with educative initiatives, independent monitoring and complaints procedures. The self-governing adoption of international human rights instruments would likely be more persuasive and generate greater loyalty within Indigenous communities than the forced application of another parliamentary enactment which further props up a discredited *Indian Act*. It is just not acceptable to have a racist and sexist document such as the *Indian Act* control peoples' lives. The Canadian *Human Rights Act* does not contain the level of detail necessary to overturn the *Indian Act*'s central assimilatory premises.

Indigenous legal traditions will more likely facilitate dignity and freedom if people inside

---

50 In his *Ending Denial: Understanding Aboriginal Issues* (Toronto: University of Toronto Press, 2008), 4, and citing Sally Engel Merry, 'Human Rights and the Demonization of Culture' (February 2003) *Anthropological News*, anthropologist Wayne Warry has written:

> [T]he idea of cultural relativism is often seen as an anathema to human rights activists, because they work with an out of date notion of culture. For those who see culture as a 'coherent, static and unchanging set of values' culture is a problem. Cruel and inhuman behaviors—for example, female genital mutilation, or female circumcision, or 'honour killings' sanctioned by tribal elders as punishment for having an affair—are immoral by any standard and need not be reformed. But only those who assume a model of culture as static would suggest that these practices be protected in the name of culture or tradition. As Merry notes, this antiquated view of culture 'is increasingly understood as a barrier to the realization of human rights.'

51 *Indian Act*, R.S.C. 1985, c. I-5. For further critique about the human rights limitations of the *Indian Act*, see Menno Boldt, *Surviving as Indians: The Challenge of Self-Government* (Toronto: University of Toronto Press, 1993).

52 Sonia Harris Short, 'The Road to Hell: Indigenous Child Welfare in International Context' (unpublished paper on file with the author).

and outside of our communities drop stereotypes about the timeless, past-tense nature of First Nations life and laws. Of course, many time-revered practices thankfully remain and will positively affect how our laws continue to develop. There is room for ancient precedent in most legal cultures, including those based on Indigenous traditions. At the same time, Indigenous peoples are situated within and increasingly participate in a global context, and many of our laws reflect these diverse influences. Some traditions will eventually be dropped if they are not widely accepted within a contemporary Indigenous community. Indigenous traditions are syncretic, and fused with ideas and practices from many sources. They adapt to changing circumstances in accordance with the needs and priorities of their members and in response to external pressures. Tradition is not abandoned as new ways are introduced. In fact, it is renewed as it combines with vibrant healthy influences from other worthy sources. Indigenous law must continue to engage in conversations with other legal traditions to stand any chance of continually being embraced by a sufficient number of people within our communities.

Fortunately, the fact that many Indigenous laws are based on deliberative processes means that non-aligned or dissenting viewpoints can be taken into account in the law's formulation. When any society identifies, proclaims, and enforces its laws, there is bound to be disagreement. Most legal systems that respect individual freedoms and dignity must find peaceful ways to deal with opposition in their midst. This requires that conflicting viewpoints be processed in a manner that is conducive to orderly and respectful listening, discussion, and resolution. In this spirit, Indigenous peoples often use circles to invite participation in developing legal standards. Circles are considered sacred and represent the bringing together of people in an atmosphere of equality, as they do not raise one person above another.[53] In a circle discussion, everyone is permitted to speak, although only one person speaks at a time. Each must listen and wait his or her turn to respond to others, in an orderly fashion from right to left. Circles are meant to remind people of Mother Earth and their journey through life: from the earth, to infant, to child, through adulthood to old age and back to the earth. As such, circles incorporate environmental patterns in human terms in many ways. Of course, circles can also be conducted in a coercive manner if they become dominated by an unhealthy group or individual, who may unduly pressure participants to give deference to the viewpoints of the dominators. Relationships of power and hierarchy do not necessarily disappear when people make decisions using a circle format. Those who make decisions in a circle setting must be attuned to their potential for duress

53 There can also be sacred elements to the way circles are conducted. Cree Elder Jacob Bill from Saskatchewan has observed:

> At our time when our Elder used to speak to us he used to make us sit in a circle, used to take the pipe first and he used to pray to the Creator first so that we would understand, us young people, anything that he was going to relate, that the Creator would place the words that were going to be passed on to the young people. I guess that's the way, that's the way we received the knowledge that we carry, since that is where it comes from. Life comes from the Creator. We could understand that language what our grandpa had told us. We can see that today what is happening today. Our Elders used to foresee a long ways because the Creator used to help them, the Creator used to show them a future; that is what I see today. The Elders used to say you are not to fight with the white man, tell him, tell him, remind him to remember the treaty. You don't have to give him hard words, just tell him in good words, soft words, understandable words. If you talk to somebody using a low tone of voice they will understand that, but if you get mad nobody will understand. But get along with him; tell him what you want to tell him in a good way what you need. Eventually, a little bit further down the road he will start to listen to you.

Elder Jacob Bill in John Borrows, 'Peace and Order: Describing and Implementing Treaty Justice in Saskatchewan' (paper prepared for the Office of the Treaty Commission, Saskatoon, 2003), 102.

and must implement proper procedures for their conduct.[54] Nevertheless, much deliberative Indigenous law development can be conducted through circles—such as talking circles, healing circles, and reconciliation circles—if protective procedures are present. Band council deliberations and Peacemaker Tribal Courts can also use circles to create rules and regulations or to process disputes.

I have participated in circles in which important legal decisions were made and later enforced. Some of these circles have occurred in the criminal law context and demonstrate how Indigenous legal traditions can become a part of and influence the law's development in broader Canadian society. Perhaps the most prominent example of Indigenous legal traditions being used in an urban context is found in the experiences of Aboriginal Legal Services of Toronto (ALST).[55] ALST was established on 21 February 1990, following years of deliberation, debate, and discussion within Toronto's Indigenous communities. A number of exceptionally knowledgeable and supportive non-Aboriginal people such as Jonathon Rudin also contributed to the development of ALST. The Native Canadian Centre of Toronto compiled the results of community consultations in the mid-1980s through a Needs Assessment Report. Later in the process, prominent yet humble Indigenous Elders gave ALST's founders an important set of traditional teachings and principles to guide their work.[56] As a result, ALST was established to strengthen the capacity of the Aboriginal Sources and Scope of Indigenous Legal Traditions 39 communities and their citizens to deal with justice issues and provide Aboriginal-controlled and culturally-based justice alternatives.[57] It is instructive to note that ALST's existence flows from an inspiring combination of Indigenous and Western legal concerns and knowledge that developed through persuasion, counselling together, and consensus-building.

The deliberative aspects of ALST are also present in the program's daily operation. For example, ALST runs a Community Council Program which draws heavily on dialogical sources of Indigenous law.[58] The Community Council

54 Institute for the Advancement of Aboriginal Women, *Can you Hear Me? How to Get Your Voice Heard for Aboriginal Women*, retrieved 30 March 2005 from Institute for the Advancement of Aboriginal Women website, www.iaaw.ca/Pubs/Can%20you%20Hear%20Me.pdf; Sarah Deer, Bonnie Clairmont, Carrie A. Martell, and Maureen White Eagle, eds., *Sharing Our Stories of Survival: Native Women Surviving Violence* (Lanham, MD: Altamira Press, 2007); Wendy Stewart, Audrey Huntley, and Fay Blaney, *The Implications of Restorative Justice for Aboriginal Women and Children Survivors of Violence: A Comparative Overview of Five Communities In British Columbia* (Ottawa: Law Commission of Canada, 2001).

55 For further information about Aboriginal Legal Services of Toronto, see Craig Proulx, *Reclaiming Aboriginal Justice, Identity and Community* (Saskatoon: Purich Publishing, 2003).

56 Ibid., 47–52.

57 The ALST vision statement reads as follows:

- We seek a community which deals with justice issues in an assertive, constructive and respectful way.
- A community which provides support and guidance to its citizens when they need to interact with the justice system.
- A community involved in developing and implementing justice initiatives and alternatives which are culturally based and community controlled.
- A community where our youth have the opportunities and abilities to deal with justice issues affecting them.
- A community where its citizens have minimum exposure to the existing legal system and are less vulnerable to acts of aggression, of racism and ignorance of who we are.
- A community which resolves its conflicts internally with minimal need for outside involvement.
- A community which promotes a positive environment related to justice issues—an environment based on mutual understandings with non-aboriginal groups/services such as schools, police, and other enforcement agencies.
- A community where its agencies work together to ensure justice and related services and issues are provided in a holistic and integrated way.
- A community where its citizens have the confidence and self-esteem to deal with issues in a constructive way.

58 Craig Proulx, *Reclaiming Aboriginal Justice, Identity and Community* (Saskatoon: Purich Publishing, 2003), 41–52.

is a criminal diversion program for Indigenous people who live in Toronto and are accused of criminal behaviour. The project provides justice alternatives and brings these individuals before men and women who are trained to deal with criminal law issues from an Indigenous legal perspective and who represent a cross-section of Toronto's Indigenous population. In performing their work, the Community Council focuses on consensually developing a plan to allow the accused person to take responsibility for his or her actions. The council also develops plans to address the root causes of the individual's problem and to facilitate reintegration into the community in a positive way. The people at ALST believe the Community Council concept builds upon the way justice was delivered in Indigenous communities in Central and Eastern Canada for centuries before the arrival of Europeans to North America. As such, the initiative is a current example of Indigenous legal traditions in the present context. ALST also does impressive work in attempting to introduce Indigenous perspectives in test case litigation, law reform advocacy, and for individuals before the courts in the Toronto area.[59]

While some Indigenous peoples use circles to conduct their legal affairs, others prefer gatherings such as feasts and other large public assemblies to encourage discussion and resolution of issues. Feast structures are particularly prominent amongst societies in the Pacific Northwest region, including the Haida, Tsimshian, Salish, Heiltsuk, Tlingit, Nuu-chah-nulth, Nisga'a,

59 ALST also works with the Gladue (Aboriginal Persons) Court, which sits all day Tuesdays and Fridays in Courtroom 126 at the Old City Hall Courts in Toronto. The court derives its name from the 1999 decision of the Supreme Court of Canada, *R. v. Gladue*, [1999] 1 S.C.R. 688, that set out the parameters of section 718.2(e) of the *Criminal Code* regarding the sentencing of offenders, and in particular, Aboriginal offenders. At present, the Court only hears cases from Aboriginal people whose matters are going through the Old City Hall Courts; charges cannot be brought into the Gladue Court from other Toronto Courts. The Court accepts guilty pleas, sentences offenders, and does bail hearings. Eventually it is anticipated that the Court will also take on trials as well. ALST has three staff, Gladue Caseworkers who write reports at the request of defence counsel, the Crown counsel or the judge on the life circumstances of an Aboriginal offender. These reports also contain recommendations that the court can consider in sentencing in light of the circumstances of the offender. These Gladue Reports (as they are often called) can be made for Aboriginal offenders in any court in Toronto as well as for Aboriginal offenders in the Hamilton and Brantford area. When I visited with ALST along with Dawnis Kennedy, we were of the opinion that it was the most successful and sophisticated legal clinic dealing with Aboriginal issues of which we were aware. ALST has an Aboriginal Courtworker Program to explain legal rights and obligations to their clients. Courtworkers assist in securing legal counsel, finding interpreters if they are needed, and also assist with pre-sentence reports, bail hearings, and referrals. The ALST Clinic serves people in a variety of areas including: housing problems and tenant rights, Ontario Works and Ontario Disability Support Plan, *Indian Act* matters, Canada Pension Disability applications, Employment Insurance and Employment Standards, Police Complaints, Criminal Injuries Compensation, Human Rights issues, and referrals to lawyers on other matters including criminal and family law. The clinic is also involved in law reform, community organizing, public legal education, and test case litigation. They do an impressive amount of work in changing the law and its interpretation as it relates to Aboriginal peoples in Canada, particularly in an urban context.

ALST has made it a priority to become involved in test case litigation. In some cases, this means bringing cases forward on behalf of individuals or groups. In other cases, ALST intervenes in cases that have been brought by other parties. In an intervention, ALST's main concern is that the perspectives of Aboriginal people, particularly urban Aboriginal people, are brought to the attention of the court. Some of the matters in which it has intervened are the leading cases affecting urban Aboriginal people's rights in the Criminal Justice system. ALST has filed factums and made representations before the Supreme Court of Canada in the following cases: *Corbière* (granted non-reserve resident voting rights), *Gladue* (recognized special circumstances of Aboriginal offenders in sentencing), *Golden* (strip searches could not be routine police practice), *Powley* (recognition of Métis rights for first time at the Supreme Court), *Sauvé* (denial of prisoner's voting rights violated Charter), *Wells* (further clarification of the *Gladue* case), and *Williams* (identified racism as a problem faced by Aboriginal people in getting a fair trial).

Finally, ASLT involves itself in Law Reform work in the areas of policing, youth criminal justice, the International Convention of the Elimination of All Forms of Racial Discrimination, Legal Aid, section 718 (e) of the *Criminal Code* (Aboriginal considerations in sentencing), and inquests.

Gitksan, Wet'suwet'en, and Kwakwaka'wakw.[60] They contain elaborate protocols to engage communities in important celebrations and decision-making issues.[61] Some of these feasts are best known as potlatches. While the Canadian government unsuccessfully tried to abolish them in the late nineteenth and early twentieth centuries, they have remained an important legal tradition within most West Coast Indigenous societies.[62] Some of these feasts deal with property law disputes and build upon debate and discussion to sort out boundary issues. Gitksan Elder Johnny David explained that such disputes could arise from 'one person crossing the boundary of another person's and when that happened, they usually talked about it and that was the end of the problem.'[63] If informal discussions were unsuccessful, a potlatch process could be initiated as follows: 'They [c]ould invite each other to a feast and gifts would be distributed, and the person who crossed over a boundary would be spoken to by the chiefs and after that happened, the problem was solved and it never occurred again.'[64] Hereditary chiefs direct the proceedings with guidance from the Elders, and the disputants build consensus under this structure by talking to one another through narrative, dance, music, and gift-giving. These deliberations help to create a legal resolution that aims for reconciliation between the parties so that they walk away as friends.[65] Other feasts can deal with family law issues,[66] commercial disputes, or criminal law matters.[67] There is tremendous potential for the continued operation and development of feasting structures and other large gatherings to develop law through the exercise of Indigenous deliberative practices.

One particularly poignant example of feasting as an exercise of law was brought to my attention by former graduate student Perry Shawna. Perry

60 Uuli Steltzer, *A Haida Potlatch* (Vancouver: Douglas and McIntyre, 1984); Margaret Seguin and Margaret Halpin, eds., *Potlatch at Gitsegukla* (Vancouver: UBC Press, 2000); Pamela Amoss, *Coast Salish Spirit Dancing: The Survival of an Ancestral Religion* (Seattle: University of Washington Press, 1978); A. Jonaitis, D. Cole, I. Jacknis, and W. Suttles, *Chiefly Feasts: The Enduring Kwakiutl Potlatch* (Seattle: University of Washington Press, 1994); Sergei Kan, *Symbolic Immortality: The Tlingit Potlatch of the Nineteenth Century* (Washington: Smithsonian Institution Press, 1989); Christopher Bracken, *The Potlatch Papers: A Colonial Case History* (Chicago: University of Chicago Press, 1997); Antonia Mills, *Eagle Down Is Our Law: Witsuwit'en Law, Feasts and Land Claims* (Vancouver: UBC Press, 1994); Dale Hunt, '"We Are All Different, Still Living Under the Same Culture": A Kwakwakw'wakw Perspective on Dispute Resolution and Relationship Building' (Master's in Dispute Resolution, University of Victoria, BC, 2005).

61 For example, the Gitksan and Wet'suwet'en are organized into Houses and Clans in which hereditary chiefs preside over the allocation, administration, and control of traditional lands. Within House structures the chiefs pass on important histories, songs, crests, lands, ranks, and properties from one generation to the next. The passage of these legal, political, social, and economic entitlements is performed and witnessed through Feasts. These Feasts substantiate the territories' relationships. A hosting House serves food, distributes gifts, announces the House's successors to the names of deceased chiefs, describes the territory, raises totem poles, and tells the oral history of the House. Chiefs from other Houses witness the actions of the Feast, and at the end of the proceedings validate the decisions and declarations of the Host House. As such, the Feast is an important 'institution through which the people [have] governed themselves' and it confirms the relationship between each House and its territories. See John Borrows, *Recovering Canada: The Resurgence of Indigenous Law* (Toronto: University of Toronto Press, 2002), 79–80.

62 Douglas Cole and Ira Chaikin, *An Iron Hand Upon the People: The Law against the Potlatch on the Northwest Coast* (Vancouver: Douglas and McIntyre, 1990).

63 Antonia Mills, ed., *Hang Onto These Words: Johnny David's Delgamuukw Evidence* (Toronto: University of Toronto Press, 2005), 360.

64 Ibid., 361.

65 Jo-Anne Fiske and Betty Patrick, *Cis Dideen Kat, When the Plumes Rise: The Way of the Lake Babine Nation* (Vancouver: UBC Press, 2000), 101.

66 Warner Adam, Travis Holyk, and Parry Shawana, 'Whu Neeh Nee (Guiders of Our People): Carrier Sekani First Nations Family Law Alternative Dispute Resolution' (paper presented at the 6th International Conference on Restorative Justice, 1 June 2003), retrieved 5 July 2007 from www.sfu.ca/cfrj/fulltext/adam.pdf.

67 Phil Lucas, producer/director/writer, *Voyage of Rediscovery*, The National Film Board of Canada, 1993, 25 min., video 2 of First Nations, *The Circle Unbroken.*

worked with the Carrier Sekani Family Services Agency (CSFS) for over sixteen years until his untimely death by heart attack. Before teaching at the University of Northern British Columbia and pursuing his LL.M. with me at the University of Victoria, Perry worked with CSFS to offer community-based, professional, and culturally appropriate child and family services to the eleven First Nations communities located to the north-east of Prince George in British Columbia.[68] While Perry was at CSFS, he worked with others to ensure that Carrier Sekani laws and values were followed in reuniting Carrier Sekani children with their communities. During his tenure, the Society implemented the procedures and principles underlying the feast or *bahlats* structure to welcome back children and adults previously removed from their communities. In developing these feasts, there was much discussion, debate, and consultation. Wide-ranging dialogue was needed to ensure that the appropriate people were being recognized for their efforts in helping the children of the community. There was also a great deal of attention paid to learning and following proper legal process at the feasting event. While the welcome home feast was not a *bahlats* in the strict way of gathering community members, *bahlats* values provided the main inspiration for the event. CSFS is now researching and developing a framework to deal with family conflict through the use of Carrier Sekani legal traditions.[69] This process also involves deliberation and discussion through feasting and other large community gatherings.

Of course, besides circles and feasting, there are also other ways in which Indigenous peoples might gather together to develop their laws through persuasion, council, and debate. For example, the Haudenosaunee of the eastern Great Lakes build and maintain their Great Law of Peace on the consensus and agreement of six different nations. While this legal tradition will be discussed in greater detail in the next chapter, it is sufficient at this point to note that structured deliberation is central to making binding legal decisions. For example, past and future generations are considered and consulted as a formal part of their society's deliberations. A council of fifty chiefs chosen by clan mothers takes account of the community's concerns. They administer confederacy business through a deliberative process by repeatedly passing ideas across a longhouse fire to explore and analyse them before taking action. This system also allows any Iroquois nation of the Haudenosaunee Confederacy to request a meeting of the council.[70] Clan mothers, youth, and others can also greatly influence decisions through their involvement in bringing matters to council for discussion and resolution.[71] Unanimity is most often necessary for the adoption of council decisions within the longhouse system of government, which demonstrates the importance of debate and persuasion for making law within Haudenosaunee legal traditions. The reinvigoration of Haudenosaunee law is one of the reasons the Canadian and Ontario governments have had to work differently with the Six Nations community near Brantford, Ontario in recent years, and their laws'

68 Wet'suwet'en, Burns Lake Band, Cheslatta Carrier Nation, Stellat'en, Naudleh Whu'ten, Takla lake, Nee Tahi Buhn, Saik'uz, Lake Babine Nation, Skin Tyee (formerly a part of Nee Tahi Buhn), and Yekochee.

69 Warner Adam, Travis Holyk, and Parry Shawana, 'Whu Neeh Nee (Guiders of Our People): Carrier Sekani First Nations Family Law Alternative Dispute Resolution' (paper presented at the 6th International Conference on Restorative Justice, 1 June 2003), retrieved 5 July 2007 from www.sfu.ca/cfrj/fulltext/adam.pdf.

70 Ibid., 109–10.

71 John Hurley, *Children or Brethren: Aboriginal Rights in Colonial Iroquoia* (Saskatoon: Native Law Centre, 1985), 40.

influence was especially evident in the disputes concerning subdivision land in the Caledonia dispute in 2006–9.[72]

Today, perhaps the most visible example of Indigenous legal tradition developed through deliberation and persuasive debate occurs in band council settings. Although the full expression of their laws is constrained by the harsh overlay of non-Indigenous rules under the *Indian Act*, bands often, though sometimes inconsistently, use traditional legal teachings to conduct their business and regulate their communities. The strictures created by the federal *Indian Act* do create problems because they unnecessarily restrict and occupy jurisdictional space and thus hinder healthier law-making procedures and patterns. Indigenous law-making power through deliberation under the *Indian Act* is thus a poor reflection of what would be possible if this restrictive legislation were repealed. The *Indian Act*'s constraints could lead to concerns that band councils cannot properly claim to administer Indigenous legal traditions in the contemporary context because they are a creation of the Canadian government and therefore only function as a non-Indigenous law-making body. While it is true that band councils may owe some of their life to the federal government, it must also be acknowledged that many continue to be recreated through community participation.

I have known many *Indian Act* elected chiefs and councillors who reference their own First Nation's legal values in debating and making decisions under its structures. Furthermore, many so-called Indian bands pre-existed the *Indian Act* and find their inherent governmental power in their pre-Confederation authority. In that respect, they are not a product of the *Indian Act*. In fact, in my own family, my great-grandfather was both a hereditary chief and an elected chief under the *Indian Act*.[73] Thus, some band councils are well situated to apply Indigenous legal traditions and have a long history of implementing their own community's procedures and principles in their decision-making, despite the *Indian Act*'s strictures. Other band councils, such as those found on the Six Nations reserve in Ontario, have very little legitimacy in administering Indigenous legal traditions because the government's imposition of the band council has never been broadly accepted by their community.

Indian bands can also operate on a customary basis. Section 2(1) of the *Indian Act* defines an Indian 'band' as a 'body of Indians.'[74] Regulations under the *Indian Act* set out procedures for conducting band council meetings,[75] although section 2(1) of the *Indian Act* also states that an Indian band council can be 'chosen according to the custom of the band.' One in three Indian bands in Canada has chosen to organize their political affairs in accordance with their own customs. The fact that Indian bands continue to function under a degree of their own inherent authority demonstrates that, rather than extinguishing Indian governance, the *Indian Act* could be interpreted as explicitly recognizing and affirming pre-existing law-making powers. Despite the potential for the *Indian Act*'s band council structure to allow for the exercise of Indigenous customs, further steps should be taken to remove First Nations from the *Indian Act*'s suffocating embrace. Operating as a custom

72 See *Henco Industries Ltd. v. Haudenosaunee Six Nations Confederacy Council* (2006), 273 D.L.R. (4th) 284 (Ont. C.A.); 1536412 *Ontario Ltd v. Haudenosaunee Confederacy Chiefs Council et al.* (2008) CanLII 28041 (Ont. S.C.) Court file No.: CV-08-82; Date: 2008-06-10.

73 John Borrows, 'A Genealogy of Law: Inherent Sovereignty and First Nations Self-Government' (1992) 30 *Osgoode Hall Law Journal* 2 291–354.

74 *Indian Act*, R.S.C. 1985, c. I-5.

75 *Indian Band Council Procedures Regulations*, C.R.C. 1978, c. 950.

band under the *Indian Act* does not adequately facilitate the growth and development of Indigenous law because the surrounding legislative framework largely assumes a relatively low level of decision-making ability and authority. More First Nations must escape from the *Indian Act* to increase their law-making powers in accordance with their own priorities. Nevertheless, in studying Indigenous legal traditions in Canada, one cannot overlook the fact that band councils are a rich source of Indigenous law, despite the problems that exist.

These examples demonstrate that many Indigenous legal traditions develop in a deliberative fashion, through councils, circles, feasts, and other informal and formal meetings and gatherings. Some of the great civilizations in early northern North America were built on a very generous notion of participation in the law-making functions of society. Many Indigenous societies today continue to encourage very broad participation across their citizenry and might be regarded as being radically egalitarian. Some societies are so generous and liberal in extending personal liberties to their members that every being has a legal right and practical opportunity to assist in the development of their laws. At the same time, it should be noted that other Indigenous communities may, at points, severely restrict participation as a result of rules related to status, heredity, special accomplishment, or Canadian legal impediment.

Rules related to the scope of disclosure and participation must be understood in order to effectively understand deliberation within Indigenous legal traditions. Just as cabinet discussions in a parliamentary democracy may be privileged, some Indigenous legal procedures can be analogously limited. Some of these limits exist because selected Indigenous laws require special position, ceremonial recognition, and hard work to receive them.[76] Others may have limited application or reception because of their hereditary nature. These limits may lead a few to devalue Indigenous law as being secretive, non-transparent, or undemocratic within its deliberative processes. However, before jumping to such conclusions, one must remember the pragmatic limits that also surround other Canadian legal traditions. Sometimes, restrictions on participation are important in preserving the orderly and peaceful flow of our law's development. At other times, a high degree of specialization is necessary in order to understand, produce, or practise law. In this regard, Canadian legal process may be considered somewhat analogous to the special positions, ceremonies, and hard work required by some Indigenous legal traditions. On a more sobering note, the substantial resources, societal position, or family connections required for Canadians to receive legal education, practise law, or become a judge may not be far removed from the hereditary privileges in some Indigenous societies. Indigenous legal traditions are not alone in requiring special ceremonies, hard work, and family connections. Fortunately, even most hereditary positions within Indigenous law also require more of the individual recipient of power than simply being born into the right family. When one balances the radically

76 Sometimes Indigenous laws find their articulation in ceremony. Ceremonies often consist of formalized rituals that enable its participants to directly participate in law. Each group created its own distinctive ceremonies and formalities to renew, celebrate, transfer, or abandon their legal relationships. As such, the ceremonies of the Potlatch on the West Coast produced entirely different legal relationships from those of the Sundance on the prairies, or the Midewiwin and False Face societies of central Canada. The stories told in the Big Houses of the Salish fundamentally differ from those told in the teepees of the Assinaboine, and these could be very different again from those spoken in the longhouses of the Haudenosaunee, or in the lodges of the Mi'kmaq. Some ceremonies required special initiation in order to participate, thus creating a realm of sacred knowledge with some traditions. Each group's ceremonies and stories varied according to its history, material circumstances, spiritual alignment, and social structure.

egalitarian nature of many Indigenous communities with the more limited hereditary roles currently found within them, most observers would quickly understand that heredity alone does not mean much without that person's own hard work and good reputation. Thus, family status may not in itself be either a help or hindrance to participating in the creation of law within Indigenous communities, and thus should not be a reason to defeat fuller deliberation.

The points made in the past few paragraphs demonstrate that many criticisms related to the scope of disclosure and participation within Indigenous societies can be successfully addressed if widespread deliberation remains the heart and focus of a community's legal system. In such cases, the form of deliberation (hereditary office, etc.) would have to give way to the substance (persuasion, choice, etc.) of what a community's tradition protected in order for them to act consistently with their laws. However, to fairly and even-handedly evaluate questions of participation within Indigenous legal traditions, it is also crucial to observe that certain Indigenous legal traditions were, and continue to be, decidedly undemocratic and thereby restrictive of deliberation. Such traditions are far from encouraging an individual's free, uncoerced, and unfettered involvement in the life of the community. When this is the case, these traditions should be renounced and discarded. Fortunately, this has generally taken place. For example, in the past some Indigenous societies practised slavery, and placed numerous limitations on personal rights and freedoms.[77] As in other countries, Indigenous peoples have forsaken slavery and it is clear that this practice has no relevance to their contemporary legal traditions. While the past existence of slavery demonstrates a high degree of social and legal organization, it no longer restricts any Indigenous person in Canada from participating in the formulation and application of their laws. Any remnants of such odious and abhorrent past traditions have long since been repudiated and abandoned, because they are inconsistent with contemporary norms and legal procedures of Indigenous, Canadian, and international legal communities. Where restrictions on deliberation do occur, slavery is rarely, if ever, at the root of such injustice within contemporary Indigenous communities.

Where participation in the creation of Indigenous law is restricted in inappropriate ways, it is usually because some powerful individual or group has used positivistic law to usurp authority from a community. This issue will be discussed in the next section and is hopefully implicit throughout this text because my intolerance for such behaviour is one of the most important reasons for writing this book. In all that is contained herein, I am attempting to show that legitimate and orderly ways can be drawn upon to restrain such people from inappropriately using laws found within our own traditions. At the same time, I am also writing this book because, unfortunately, one of the most profound sources of restrictions on broader participation within Indigenous legal regimes today is Canadian law itself.[78] The attitude of most lawyers, judges, and parliamentarians towards Indigenous law prevents its growth. That is, Indigenous law is regarded as secondrate or incomplete, if it is given any regard at all. For example, one Chief Justice of a provincial Court of Appeal said to me in a personal conversation: 'You say Indigenous law exists; I don't believe it for a moment.' Jurispathic attitudes can 'kill diverse legal traditions' if they are

77 Leland Donald, *Aboriginal Slavery in the Northwest Coast of North America* (Berkeley: University of California Press, 1997).

78 It is also my view that Canadian law as currently formulated and practised also restricts Indigenous peoples' participation in the creation of Canadian law.

falsely regarded as competing with the state.[79] Furthermore, Canada's legislatures have not been very responsive or supportive of Indigenous legal orders. The *Indian Act*, passed in 1876 to assimilate and manipulate Indigenous legal traditions, severely restricts rules on participation.[80] It has also caused some First Nations to abandon specific legal traditions; others have subverted its precepts or incorporated them within their legal orders.[81] Additionally, Canadian governments have restricted the general franchise for many Aboriginal people, thus affecting the deliberative aspect of their legal traditions.[82] When Canadian interferences with Indigenous legal traditions are curbed, Indigenous laws can better facilitate Indigenous participation in their own legal systems, as well as ensuring broader participation within Canadian and international legal debates. Indigenous peoples themselves can also take significant steps to cast aside traditions that interfere with deliberation, persuasion and wide-ranging participation in the creation of their laws.

D. Positivistic Law

Another source of Indigenous law can be found in the proclamations, rules, regulations, codes, teachings, and axioms that are regarded as binding or regulating people's behaviour.[83] The laws to which I refer are somewhat distinct from those above because they do not necessarily depend on appeals to the Creator, the environment, or deliberative processes to possess their force. Legal traditions in this mode have weight because proclamations are made by a person or group regarded by a sufficient number of people within a community as authoritative. Individuals who are seen to possess such power may be hereditary chiefs, clan mothers, headmen, sachems, or band leaders. Their laws may be regarded as positivistic because they rely more on the authority and intelligence of those who issue them than on the notion of creation, nature, or community deliberation. Philosopher John Austin referred to legal positivism as being based upon command. He said that those who have binding legal authority are those who are 'determinate rational being[s] or bod[ies] that the other rational beings are in the habit of obeying.'[84] Rationality is, of course, present in every community and laws flowing from trusted individuals and groups are given due regard as a result. In an Indigenous context, positivistic laws may be formally proclaimed in feast halls, council houses, wampum readings, band council chambers, and other such public settings. In announcing these laws, ancient and contemporary legal ideas can mingle together and become the basis for bylaws, statutes, conventions, and protocols.

---

79 Robert Cover, 'The Supreme Court, 1982 Term—Foreword: Nomos and Narrative' (1983) 97 *Harvard Law Review* 1 at 40–44.

80 John Tobias, 'Protection, Civilization, Assimilation: An Outline History of Canada's Indian Policy,' in *As Long as the Sun Shines and Water Flows: A Reader in Canadian Native Studies*, ed. Ian Getty and Antoine Lussier (Vancouver: University of British Columbia Press, 1990), 29.

81 *Indian Act*, R.S.C. 1985, c. I-5. See John Borrows, 'A Genealogy of Law: Inherent Sovereignty and First Nations Self-Government' (1992) 30 *Osgoode Hall Law Journal* 2 at 291–354.

82 Indians could not vote for the first seventy-five years of Confederation. See, for example, British Columbia's *Qualification and Registration of Voters Amendment Act*, 1872, s. 13. Indians did not generally enjoy federal voting rights until 1960, when the federal franchise was finally extended to them without qualification. The provinces extended the franchise to Indians at different dates: British Columbia 1949, Manitoba 1952, Ontario 1954, Saskatchewan 1960, Prince Edward Island and New Brunswick 1963, Alberta 1965, Quebec 1969. The Inuit were excluded from the federal franchise in 1934 but had the vote restored to them in 1950. Métis were always considered citizens able to vote in federal and provincial elections.

83 Indigenous law creates relationships between people by addressing the consequences of their actions. Arthur Ripstein, 'Justice and Responsibility' (2004) 17 *Canadian Journal of Law and Jurisprudence* 361–86.

84 John Austin, *Lectures on Jurisprudence and the Philosophy of Positive Law* (St Clair Shores, MI: Scholarly Press, 1977), 88.

Some positivistic Indigenous legal traditions may once have been explicitly connected to a larger normative system, but the reasons underlying their original adoption might have been deliberately abandoned or forgotten as circumstances changed. Thus, laws that once drew their authority from deliberation or creation may now be followed for different reasons—because some group or individual has garnered enough power (through respect or fear) that others will now follow their pronouncements without considering the reasons behind the law's development. I have met a few of these First Nations leaders and groups in my travels throughout Canada, and they have managed to effectively regulate their communities by drawing law from this source. In these experiences, I have seen some wonderful people lead with excellent results because of their kindness, knowledge, and care for their communities. Unfortunately, I have also witnessed some leaders who 'command' almost exclusively from their own narrow material interests, without proper motive or beneficial effect.

I must confess that positivistic law as a source of authority (without a broader justification for its use) prompts greater concern for me than the other sources we have been discussing. My concern about statutes and commands not only relates to Indigenous legal traditions; I see problems with the over-reliance on this source within common law and civil law traditions too. My worry is that if a prominent leader or group rules through this form of law for too long, without the restraining influences found in the other sources identified to this point, this could lead to great corruption. The exercise of positivistic law potentially places too much authority in the hands of powerful individuals or popular majorities without other checks, balances, or measurement against a broader normative base. In time, the exercise of legal traditions through positivistic law could lead to abusive domination if the person or group in authority does not submit to other normative legal considerations. Thus, while positivistic law is a legal tradition with force in Indigenous, common law, and civil law communities, my hope is that it will constantly be tempered by other factors to ensure that those who proclaim law do not become a source of oppression to those who follow them. If Indigenous peoples who are governed through positivistic law recognize that they can place their traditions on a broader footing, they may be more inclined to choose those traditions which further facilitate freedom and dignity, while still maintaining crucial connections to their past. Fortunately, in my view, it is rare to see positivistic law existing within Indigenous communities without other sources of law being studied and followed. In fact, Indigenous legal traditions are most often criticized for not having a so-called recognizable sovereign who can pronounce laws and command obedience to them. This, while not strictly true, does demonstrate their decentralized operation.[85]

When positivistic laws operate without being couched in persuasion, deliberation, or a sound understanding of nature and what is sacred, Indigenous peoples may be left with legal traditions that sound like a chronicle of 'dos and don'ts.' Such laws are somewhat like commandments or codes from which much of the context for their development is no longer remembered or considered irrelevant. Examples of these types of laws might be: 'don't swim in that part of the stream,' 'don't walk on that part of the glacier,' 'when you take something from that place, you must leave something there from another place,' 'make sure you walk around the perimeter of an area four times before you leave.' These laws are called

85 Tim Schouls, *Shifting Boundaries: Aboriginal Identity, Pluralist Theory, and the Politics of Self-Government* (Vancouver: UBC Press, 2003).

positivistic in my formulation because they may be followed by people with little understanding of why they are binding, beyond their trust in or fear of the individual or group who gave them the rules.[86]

Along with traditions fashioned through deliberation, Indigenous laws formulated in a positivistic manner might be most recognizable to people schooled in other legal traditions. Most would probably recognize a leader or party's commands or rules as a type of law, and many can relate to the idea that sometimes such rules do not seem to have much relationship to reason or morality. Many societies often obey such laws because they are regarded as necessary to the proper maintenance of order within their jurisdictions.[87] When someone breaks a law, our concern is not usually whether the law-breaker was persuaded at some point to support the law but that they had failed to obey it. When we know someone is flaunting the law, we may not immediately care whether that person sees the law as being in harmony with some broader sacred, natural, or deliberative source. Rather, when a person acts contrary to the law, most people who witness the disobedience are more concerned about their own safety and self-interest, and with that of their neighbours.

Thus, when people feel threatened by illegal activity, they may not immediately be concerned about larger questions of legitimacy surrounding the law. Therefore, in understanding positivistic law's legitimacy, it is important to remind ourselves that such power flows from a leader or group's claim or endowment of reason and responsibility. If there are disquieting concerns with a person's use of tradition, that person could be removed without offending other legal traditions that may flow from deliberation, nature, or the community's sense of the sacred. The narrow base for legitimacy on which positivistic power rests provides some measure of protection to Indigenous peoples who may be in the grip of an autocratic leader. If the law in question is merely a product of a powerful person or group's misdirected preferences, then that law can be changed, or the person can be removed, without any perceived natural or divine consequences. Such removal will also hopefully strengthen the deliberative capacities and processes within a community. This is not to underestimate the political upheaval that could occur if a community, whose laws rest on proclamation alone, sought to remove their leader. It is, however, to acknowledge that bigger underlying normative changes would not necessarily be required if power largely rested on personality or preference alone. Thus, since the major consequence of disobedience in regard to positivistic laws would usually be a change in the political alignment of the group, going against positivistic rules would not typically be seen as a breach of sacred or natural law, and therefore would not directly challenge the deliberative consensus of the larger group. Thus, if an Elder named chief or clan mother suffers from a loss of reputation, people could cease to follow their rules without dire consequences. A respected person or group's fall from community favour does not necessarily create a crisis in the theory of law as would be the case if someone violated the other forms of law developed in this chapter. The person who loses credibility is often merely replaced by someone else who can fill the leadership vacuum. Alternatively, if no one immediately arises to fill the role left by the formerly powerful person, other sources of law, such as deliberation or custom, could fill the void.

86 When laws flow from this source, people might merely obey an injunction because those who continue to proclaim it are regarded with a measure of respect. Of course, obedience might even be given for less healthy reasons, such as the fear of a negative consequence if they fall out of favour with those who are regarded as the law-makers within a community.

87 Robert Cover, 'Violence and the Word' (1986) 95 *Yale Law Journal* 1601.

On occasion, however, the consequences of a leader's loss of reputation may be more complex and the subject of much greater conflict. This could be the case if the formerly respected person or group were to make claims that they were the only ones able to understand, interpret, or proclaim sacred or natural law, or were somehow indispensable to the process of law developed through deliberative sources. No one person should be granted this degree of authority, but most legal systems struggle to contain powerful groups and individuals who proclaim the infallibility, necessity, or inevitability of their rules. In such cases, there could be a struggle to separate the leader's personality from their expression of the other legal sources followed by the community. It might be difficult to disentangle a powerful group's claims to authority from laws flowing from the Creator, nature, or from the functioning of a deliberative council. The challenge of separating political power from legal sources should not be underestimated, because the sources of law identified in this chapter are not as discrete as they might appear. For instance, leaders will sometimes attempt to align their positivistic proclamations with a normative system, such as has been described in the preceding sections. In categorizing discrete sources of Indigenous law, I hope to show that appeals to authority can be based on ideas much broader than those often attributed to Indigenous legal traditions. However, just as critical legal scholars have appropriately attacked claims that purport to separate law from politics,[88] Indigenous legal traditions themselves are also enmeshed with political considerations, as is the case in other legal systems.[89] While this chapter only attempts to identify sources of law that are more distinct from the community's norms because they more firmly rest on the force of an individual personality or group, on the ground, application tends to be messier in mingling the practice of politics and law. Thus, there is always the danger that changes in leadership or group dynamics may make it more difficult to abandon rules that seem, at first glance, to be tied to a person's or group's will-to-power through their proclamations.

Therefore, while we must be attentive to the relationship between law and politics within Indigenous legal traditions, these dynamics should also not lead us to overestimate the problem of leadership conflict or change within Indigenous legal systems where positivistic law is in force. Indigenous people affected by the waning of a certain set of rules closely associated with one powerful person or group would still have many other options to which they could turn in ensuring their affairs remained ordered through the law. The availability of appeals to the Creator, the environment, and reasoned consensus or custom greatly assists communities when an individual or group's proclaimed rules or formerly binding teachings become less compelling for reasons related to their reputations.

E. Customary Law

The final source of law discussed in this chapter relates to the variety of Indigenous legal

88 Robert A. Williams Jr., 'Taking Rights Aggressively: The Perils and Promise of Critical Legal Theory for People of Color' (1987) 5 *Law and Inequality* 103; Duncan Kennedy, *Legal Education and the Reproduction of Hierarchy: A Polemic Against the System: A Critical Edition* (New York: New York University Press, 2004).

89 Andree Lajoie, Henry Quillnan, Rod Macdonald, and Guy Rocher, 'Legal Pluralism at Kahnawake,' in *Aboriginality and Governance: A Multidisciplinary Perspective*, ed. Gordon Christie (Penticton, BC: Theytus Books, 2006), 239.

traditions often referred to as custom.[90] Custom is the label that most people would likely give Indigenous law if they were unfamiliar with the complexity of these societies' social organization.[91] Of course, customary law is not peculiar to Indigenous societies.[92] The common law, civil law, and international law also rely on custom as a source of binding obligation for those subject to their operation.[93] Customary law can be defined as those practices developed through repetitive patterns of social interaction that are accepted as binding on those who participate in them.[94] Customary laws are often inductive, meaning that observations of specific behaviour often lead to general conclusions about how to act; as a result, the obligations they produce are regularly implied from a society's surrounding context.[95] An effective way of learning custom would involve examining or living specific routines and procedures associated with conduct within a community and talking to people about why they felt obliged to act in a particular manner. Such an investigation might lead one to conclude that customary law rests heavily on an individual's unspoken agreement about how rights and obligations will be regulated between community members. The communally layered and individually intuitive nature of this legal form means that disputes are often regulated through social pressures that distribute incentives and disincentives to act or refrain from acting in certain ways. Since customary laws are not always as explicit as other forms of law, their recognition, interpretation, and enforcement is often initially more difficult to achieve when other sources of law intervene. However, this does not mean that customary law should give way to other sources of Indigenous legal tradition. Customary law can be a creative source of law in its own right, and in its proper context can be very effective in producing strong and healthy community relationships.

Indigenous customary law in Canada has been most strongly recognized in the context of marriage and family relationships. In *Casimel v. I.C.B.C.*, the British Columbia Court of Appeal held that a seventy-seven-year-old woman and a ninety-nine-year-old man had legally adopted their daughter's thirty-year-old son according to Carrier law and, thus, when he died, were entitled to death benefits as dependent parents under the

90 'The body of rules, whether proceeding from formal enactment or from custom, which a particular state or community recognizes as binding on its members or subjects,' *Oxford English Dictionary*, 2nd ed. (Oxford: Clarendon Press, 1989), 712. Articles commenting on First Nations law include Bradford Morse and Gordon Woodman, eds., *Indigenous Law and the State* (Providence, RI: Foris, 1988); Michael Coyle, 'Traditional Indian Justice in Ontario: A Role for the Present?' (1986) 24 *Osgoode Hall Law Journal* 605. For a contrary view, see Roger F. McDonnell, 'Contextualizing the Investigation of Customary Law in Contemporary Native Communities' (1992) 34 *Canadian Journal of Criminology* 299; *Delgamuukw v. British Columbia* (1991), 79 D.L.R. (4th) 185 (B.C.S.C.) at 455: 'What the Gitksan and Wet'suwet'en witness[es] describe as law is really a most uncertain and highly flexible set of customs which are frequently not followed by the Indians themselves.' For criticism of this view, see Michael Asch, 'Errors in Delgamuukw: An Anthropological Perspective,' in *Aboriginal Title in British Columbia: Delgamuukw v. The Queen*, ed. Frank Cassidy (Lantzville, BC: Oolichan Books, 1992), 221. For a fuller description of Wet'suwet'en law, see Antonia Mills, *Eagle Down Is Our Law: Witsuwit'en Law, Feasts and Land Claims* (Vancouver: UBC Press, 1994).

91 For further information about Indigenous diversity in Canada, see Tim Schouls, *Shifting Boundaries: Aboriginal Identity, Pluralist Theory, and the Politics of Self-Government* (Vancouver: UBC Press, 2003).

92 The laws of England largely operated through custom until precedent and consolidation took place through the 1700s. Patrick Glenn, 'The Common Law in Canada' (1995) *Canadian Bar Review* 261. Even today, the common law method uses customs and traditions to fill gaps when interpreting written rules, *Reference re Secession of Quebec*, [1998] 2 S.C.R. 217.

93 Rudolf B. Schleinger et al., *Comparative Law*, 4th ed. (New York: Foundation Press, 1980), 669–70, 690–94; Stephen McCaffrey, *Understanding International Law* (Newark, NJ: LexisNexis, 2006), 44–55.

94 General definitions of customary law can be found in J. Brierly, *The Law of Nations*, 4th ed. (Gloucestershire, UK: Clarendon Press, 1949), 60; *Black's Law Dictionary*, 6th ed. (St Paul, MN: West Publishing, 1990), 384.

95 Gerald Postema, 'Implicit Law,' in *Rediscovering Fuller: Essays on Implicit Law and Institutional Design*, ed. Willem Witteveen and Wibren Van der Burg (Amsterdam: Amsterdam University Press, 1999), 255.

province's *Insurance Act*.[96] This case rested upon the finding that Carrier law allowed grandparents to be considered as full parents in their customary regime, and that natural parents were no longer considered to possess the rights or obligations of a parent under this system.[97] Furthermore, the court held that neither Canadian common law, nor federal or provincial statute, nor constitutional law abrogated Carrier customary law. In summarizing the reasons for upholding Carrier legal tradition, Justice Lambert wrote: 'I conclude that there is a well-established body of authority in Canada for the proposition that the status conferred by aboriginal customary adoption will be recognized by the courts for the purposes of application of the principles of the common law and the provisions of statute law to the persons whose status is established by customary adoption.'[98] There are numerous other examples of Canadian courts and legislatures recognizing Indigenous peoples' family law customs.[99] Customary law can also be found in matters related to Indigenous governance,[100] land,[101] and resource use.[102]

Another example of the recognition of Indigenous customary law is found in recent land claim agreements signed throughout the country. These agreements are significant because they implement an extensive array of Indigenous customs across Canada. For example, the *Labrador Inuit Land Claims Agreement* (LILCA), which applies to a large area of coastal Labrador, acknowledges that Inuit law will be a significant source of authority in the region.[103] The extension of custom is possible because LILCA creates a central government that is controlled by the Inuit and enables this government to pass binding laws that are constitutionally protected under section 35(1) of the *Constitution Act, 1982*.[104] The central Inuit government, called Nunatsiavut, works with local Inuit governments and individuals, and operates in accordance with the *Labrador Inuit Constitution* (LIC). The LIC, which was approved by Inuit electors in an April 2002 referendum, proclaims that 'Labrador Inuit customary law is the underlying law of the Labrador Inuit and of Nunatsiavut for all matters within the jurisdiction or authority of the Nunatsiavut Assembly.'[105] Furthermore, LILCA also accepts that Inuit customary law will have force throughout the region and that 'Inuit Law' means a law of the Inuit Central Government, which includes an Inuit customary law proclaimed, published,

96 (1993) 106 D.L.R. (4th) 720 (B.C.C.A.).
97 Ibid., para. 13.
98 Ibid., para. 42.
99 *R. v. Nan-E-Quis-A-Ka* (1889), 1 Terr. L.R. 211; 2 C.N.L.C. 368 (N.W.T.S.C.); *R. v. Bear's Shin Bone* (1899), 4 Terr. L.R. 173 (N.W.T.S.C.); *Re Noah Estate* (1961), 32 D.L.R. (2d) 185 (N.W.T.S.C.); *Re Katie's Adoption Petition* (1961), 32 D.L.R. (2d) 686 (N.W.T.T.C.); *Re Beaulieu's Petition* (1969), 3 D.L.R. (3d) 479 (N.W.T.T.C.); *Re Deborah*, (1972), 27 D.L.R. (3d) 225 (N.W.T.S.C.); *Aboriginal Custom Adoption Recognition Act*, S.N.W.T. 1994, c. 26. For further commentary, see Professor Norman Zlotkin, 'Judicial Recognition of 314 Notes to pages 51–52 Aboriginal Customary Law in Canada: Selected Marriage and Adoption Cases' [1984] 4 C.N.L.R 1.
100 Subsection 2(1) of the *Indian Act* defines the 'council of the band' as being chosen either by the procedures set out in section 74 of the act or according to the custom of the band. Section 2(1)(b) states 'in the case of a band to which section 74 does not apply, the council chosen according to the custom of the band, or, where there is no council, the chief of the band chosen according to the custom of the band.'
101 *R. v. Delgamuukw*, [1997] 3 S.C.R. 1010, para. 141.
102 *R. v. Van der Peet*, [1996] 2 S.C.R. 507, para. 46.
103 *Labrador Inuit Land Claims Agreement Act*, S.N.L. 2004, c. L-3.1; *Labrador Inuit Land Claims Agreement Act*, S.C. 2005, c. 27.
104 See section 3 of the *Labrador Inuit Land Claims Agreement Act*, S.C. 2005, c. 27. See also *Labrador Inuit Land Claims Agreement*, Chapter 2, 2.1.1., schedule A to the *Labrador Inuit Land Claims Agreement Act*, S.N.L. 2004, c. L-3.1.
105 Section 9.1.2 of the *Labrador Inuit Constitution*, retrieved 11 September 2007 from www.nunatsiavut.com/pdfs/Constitution.pdf.

and registered in accordance with part 17.5.[106] To supplement this explanation of LILCA's grant of law-making authority, the *Labrador Inuit Constitution* defines customary law in the following terms: 'The customs, traditions, observances, practices and beliefs of the Inuit of Labrador which, despite changes over time, continue to be accepted by Labrador Inuit as establishing standards or procedures that are to be respected by Labrador Inuit are the customary laws of the Labrador Inuit and are referred to as Labrador Inuit customary law.'[107] The continued development of custom alongside Inuit positivistic law demonstrates its importance as a source of law to the Indigenous peoples of this area.

To help keep each source of law vibrant and strong, there are detailed provisions within the *Labrador Inuit Constitution* and *Labrador Inuit Land Claims Agreement* dealing with the interaction of customary law and positivistic Inuit and Canadian law. For example, the LIC includes a *Charter of Rights and Responsibilities*, which contains provisions relating to equality, dignity, security of the person, personal integrity, religious observance, freedom of expression, elections, freedom of movement, private land rights, freedom of trade, fair labour practices, collective bargaining, environment, rights of children, water, health care, social services, education, language, culture, housing, access to information, right to administrative actions, and access to court.[108] This extensive list of protections illustrates the scope of Inuit law's potential impact on the people to whom the LILCA will apply. It is also noteworthy that the *Inuit Charter* shows that Inuit people regard rights and freedoms as an important part of their legal regime and do not consider such rights as being necessarily contrary to their own customary laws. In fact, the *Labrador Inuit Constitution* goes so far as to proclaim, 'The Labrador Inuit Charter of Rights and Responsibilities does not deny the existence of any other rights or freedoms of Labrador Inuit, including those that are recognized or confirmed by Labrador Inuit customary law to the extent that those rights and freedoms are consistent with the Labrador Inuit Charter of Rights and Responsibilities.'[109] The idea here is that Inuit customary law might help to facilitate rights and freedoms within Nunatsiavut communities and should not be regarded as preventing their protection and extension. Nevertheless, while there is a lively confidence about the general harmonization of customary law with Charter rights and responsibilities, there is also an acknowledgment that sometimes the application of both legal sources might conflict. Therefore, the LIC contains provisions relating to the relationship between customary laws and *Inuit Charter* rights in the event of an inconsistency; section 9.1.3 of the LIC states that the *Inuit Charter* prevails in such circumstances. In addition, the LIC also provides rules for the application of Inuit customary law alongside other Inuit laws passed by the central and local governments. In fact, Inuit customary law is given paramountcy over laws passed by the Nunatsiavut government, unless that law is expressly extinguished by them or contrary to their Charter.[110]

---

106 *Labrador Inuit Land Claims Agreement*, Chapter 1, 1.1.1.

107 Part 9.1 of the *Labrador Inuit Constitution*, retrieved 11 September 2007 from www.nunatsiavut.com/pdfs/Constitution.pdf.

108 There are no criminal justice protections within the Constitution because the *Labrador Inuit Land Claims Agreement* does not include general criminal justice jurisdiction as part of the Nunatsiavut government; see Part 17.28.2 of the *Agreement*.

109 Part 2.2.3. of the *Labrador Inuit Constitution*, retrieved 11 September 2007 from www.nunatsiavut.com/pdfs/Constitution.pdf.

110 Section 9.1.4 of the *Labrador Inuit Constitution* states:

If a Labrador Inuit customary law applies to a matter for which an Inuit law has been made:

(a) both laws are equally operative to the extent that they do not conflict with each other; and

(b) Labrador Inuit customary law will prevail to the extent of any conflict with an Inuit law unless the Inuit law expressly extinguishes, replaces or varies the Labrador Inuit customary law.

Other interesting provisions dealing with customary law within the *Labrador Inuit Constitution* include provisions for the Nunatsiavut Assembly to make laws for the codification and recognition of Inuit customary law.[111] This provision complements section 17.5 of the *Labrador Inuit Land Claims Agreement*, which states that the Nunatsiavut Government shall 'maintain a public registry of the Labrador Inuit Constitution, Inuit Laws, including Inuit customary laws in respect of matters within the jurisdiction of the Nunatsiavut Government and Bylaws.'[112] Furthermore, LILCA also provides guidance about how Inuit customary law can be recognized and proved if it has not been codified by the assembly. Thus, LILCA gives power to any judicial or administrative authority to establish customary law as a question of fact in any proceeding where the existence and content of such law may be relevant.[113] In time, this provision is bound to inspire a host of new interpretations concerning custom through Labrador as the Inuit court and various tribunals set up under LILCA more fully detail their ancient law's contemporary scope and content.

Section 9.1.7 of the *Labrador Inuit Constitution* even provides procedures to assist decision-makers with the task of proving custom. It reads:

> 9.1.7 A person alleging the existence or content of Labrador Inuit customary law under subsection 9.1.6(b) must prove the existence and the content of the Inuit customary law on the balance of probabilities and for that purpose may introduce:
>
> (a) the oral and written traditions, observances and practices of the Labrador Inuit, an Inuit Community or a relevant group of Labrador Inuit;
>
> (b) the opinions of Labrador Inuit elders or other persons who have special knowledge or experience of Inuit customary law in relation to the matter or would be likely to have such knowledge or experience if such law existed;
>
> (c) evidence of the consensus of the Labrador Inuit or community or group of Labrador Inuit, as appropriate; and
>
> (d) any other evidence that is relevant.

This procedure, which allows decision-makers to come to conclusions about the proof of Inuit customary law, will likely prove to be an important source for identifying binding legal traditions that have not been previously committed to writing within the territory covered by the *Labrador Inuit Land Claims Agreement*.

---

111 Part 9.1.5 of the *Labrador Inuit Constitution*, retrieved 11 September 2007 from www.nunatsiavut.com/pdfs/Constitution.pdf.

112 *Labrador Inuit Land Claims Agreement*, Chapter 17.5.1., schedule A to the *Labrador Inuit Land Claims Agreement Act*, S.N.L. 2004, c. L-3.1.

113 The *Labrador Inuit Constitution* states:
Labrador Inuit customary law may be recognized by any judicial or administrative authority and in any proceeding the existence and content of any Labrador Inuit customary law may be established:
(a) if the Labrador Inuit customary law has been codified under section 9.1.5, with reference to the code; or
(b) as a question of fact in relation to the specific matter or matter at issue in the proceeding.
Part 9.1.6 of the *Labrador Inuit Constitution*, retrieved 11 September 2007 from www.nunatsiavut.com/pdfs/Constitution.pdf.

F. Conclusion

It should be noted that the distinctions between the different sources of law outlined in this chapter can be defined too formally and separate from one another. In the real world, Indigenous legal traditions usually involve the interaction of two or more of the sources described above. In fact, in practice it would be hard to separate them from one another. Furthermore, even in the somewhat artificial way they are presented in this chapter, it is easy to see how the sources of law would change as Indigenous communities worked with them. For example, some aspects of customary law could become positivistic if codification is undertaken. Positivistic law could take on a deliberative source if debate occurs about the appropriateness of rules derived from custom. Similarly, sacred law might influence natural law, if people relate to the Creator through natural processes. Once again, my point in making the distinctions using these classifications (sacred, natural, deliberative, positivistic, and customary) is to illustrate the complex nature of Indigenous law. I am attempting to highlight the fact that Indigenous peoples have choices when they turn to their laws for answers. While complexity and choice might make working with the law appear more complicated, it should also provide greater opportunities for those interested in recognizing, interpreting, enforcing, and implementing these laws. Understanding that a source of law is natural, deliberative, positivistic, or customary might help those people who think of Indigenous legal traditions as static to see a much greater space for their application and development in modern Canada. If Indigenous legal traditions are going to expand and be a creative source of authority in Canada, we must reject the view that Indigenous law lies at the bottom of the legal hierarchy, labelled as simply customary. While it is true that many Indigenous laws are customary, this chapter has illustrated that they are much more as well. If understood in this broader light, Indigenous legal traditions can be regarded as living systems of law, open to human choice and agency, within the context of the communities who will use them.

One of the ways Indigenous societies can best keep their legal traditions alive and connected to broader normative bases is by continuing to emphasize the oral transmission of their laws. While Indigenous peoples have been no strangers to recording their laws on paper throughout the past century, many Indigenous societies prefer to express their legal principles through oral tradition to maintain flexibility and relevance amidst changing circumstances. For many Indigenous societies, the spoken word ensures the law's vitality because it sustains connections to their community's underlying cultural foundations. It also ensures that laws remain connected to a living community. This is in contrast with views of the written word, which causes some Indigenous people to fear that law will become disconnected from their lived experiences and ordinary understandings if it is reduced to paper. While most contemporary legal systems rely upon the printed word to communicate important rules, oral tradition is also an accepted part of the common law and civil law,[114] and has a long and distinguished history within Indigenous legal traditions.[115] There is no reason why oral traditions cannot remain strong even as Indigenous peoples write them down, as long as such writing is regarded as supplementary to its existence in the hearts, minds, actions, and voices of the people to whom such laws apply.

---

114 *Quebec Secession Reference*, [1998] 2 S.C.R. 217 at para. 49; John Merryman, John Henry Merryman, and Rogelio Pérez-Perdomo, eds., *The Civil Law Tradition: An Introduction to the Legal Systems of Europe and Latin America* (Palo Alto, CA: Stanford University Press, 2003), 112–24.

115 For more general information about Indigenous oral traditions, see Peter Nabakov, *A Forest of Time: American Indian Ways of History* (Cambridge: Cambridge University Press, 2004).

For many Indigenous people, the oral transmission of law is an important protection against narrowing influences because it allows for a stronger weaving of the past and the present. The spoken word is given pride of place because the transmission of law in orally-based legal systems is bound up with face-to-face persuasion, reason, the configuration of language, political structures, kinship, clan, economic systems, social relations, intellectual methodologies, morality, ideology, and the physical world. These factors assist powerful individuals and groups in knitting legal memories more tightly in their adherents' minds, keeping the laws living in places other than dusty old books full of overly technical rules. Rather than by being hoarded by a professionalized legal elite, laws can be transmitted through memorized speech, historical gossip, personal reminiscences, formalized group accounts, representations of origins and genesis, genealogies, epics, tales, proverbs, and sayings.[116]

Furthermore, oral recitation is also an important legal principle within Indigenous communities because it allows issues from non-Indigenous systems to be incorporated with flexibility. As noted above, one must take care not to assume that oral proclamations of law will contain no references to ideas from other cultures and legal systems. Since oral communications necessarily take place in a contemporary context, Indigenous proclamations will be intermixed with ideas from other sources. They may be lodged in commentaries relating to stories, songs, ceremonies, feasts, dances, scrolls, totems, button blankets, wampum belts, et cetera. Clues to their historic existence and to the way in which they are applied may be found in missionaries' journals, government reports, settlers' correspondence, the research of anthropologists or other academics, newspaper articles, or fur trade records. These sources can be valuable, though extreme care must be used in drawing implications from them: their creators may have an incomplete understanding of the cultures they observed, as well as potential self-interest or bias.

Nevertheless, all of these strands of oral law, whether ancient or more recently incorporated, can be woven together and reinforced by mnemonic devices or other cultural practices, which also encourage broader participation and normative links. Memory aids which may record legal ideas can include wampum belts, masks, totem poles, medicine bundles, culturally modified trees, birch bark scrolls, petroglyphs, button blankets, land forms, and crests. These mnemonic devices can be supplemented by practices which include such complex customs as pre-hearing preparations, ceremonial repetition, the appointment of witnesses, dances, feasts, songs, poems, the use of testing, and the use and importance of place and geographic space. The existence of these formalities and processes can help to ensure that certain legal traditions are accredited within a community. It is very rare to see oral tradition standing alone to communicate significant legal obligations; oral tradition is often best given its meaning through the larger cultural experiences that surround such proclamations. Thus, oral tradition often blends the sources of law discussed in this chapter—sacred, natural, deliberative, positivistic, and customary—and keeps Indigenous legal traditions alive and growing.

116 This list is taken from Jan Vansina, *Oral Tradition as History* (Madison: University of Wisconsin Press, 1985), 13–27.

17

Raymond D. Austin

from *Navajo Courts and Navajo Common Law: A Tradition of Tribal Self-Governance*

[*Ed. note*: Austin refers to other chapters of the book from which this excerpt is taken; these are not included here, but the references have been retained for interested readers.]

Foundational Diné Law Principles

Returning to Traditional Navajo Laws and Methods

While the Navajo Nation courts have been using customary precepts to decide cases since the creation of the Navajo courts in 1958, the Navajo Nation Council has been slow to enact laws and policies based on Navajo philosophy and the Navajo way of doing things. Although the Navajo courts had been using Navajo common law for quite some time, it was not until the 1980s that use of Navajo common law became official court policy through reinstatement of Navajo traditional peacemaking. Nonetheless, once it became widely known that the Navajo courts were emphasizing use of Navajo normative precepts, the rest of the Navajo Nation government had no choice but to also take up the challenge. This chapter traces the methods the Navajo Nation judges and Navajo Nation Council have used in their attempts to right the imbalance in Navajo Nation law.

IMBALANCE IN NAVAJO LAW AND THE RESPONSE

There is an obvious imbalance in all of Navajo Nation law. Adopted Anglo-American law makes up a significant portion of the twenty-six titles that compose the Navajo Nation Code and the regulations that guide the departments of the Navajo Nation government. In comparison, Navajo common law appears primarily in the written decisions of the Navajo Nation courts. Although the Navajo code matches any state code in terms of subjects covered and complexity, traditional Navajos and a significant percentage of the Navajo population would find their Nation's laws perplexing. Diné custom, tradition, language, and culture have only on rare occasions made their way into the code. Very little Navajo common law in the code confirms, first, that the Navajo people did not participate in the initial creation of their government[1] (or they would have insisted on incorporating Navajo ways of doing things), and, second, that non-Indian lawyers with little or no knowledge of Navajo culture, language, customs, or traditions drafted most of the statutory laws.

Moreover, shortly after the Navajo Nation established its court system in 1958, the Navajo Tribal Council simply adopted many provisions

1 As discussed in chapter 1, Secretary of the Interior Albert Bacon Fall established the original Navajo Tribal government primarily to serve the economic interests of exploitative non-Indian mineral companies. Secretary Fall's reasons for creating the Navajo Tribal Council arguably conform to Professor Derrick Bell's interest convergence dilemma theory. Bell's theory holds that "minority rights are only recognized by the dominant society when that society perceives that it is in its own best interests to do so" (Robert A. Williams, Jr., *Like a Loaded Weapon* [Minneapolis: University of Minnesota Press, 2005], xxxiii). The challenge for Indian nation leaders is to convince American policy makers and judges that it is in the country's interests that tribes "govern their reservation homelands and those who enter them by their own laws, customs, and traditions, even when these are incommensurable with the dominant society's values and ways of doing things" (ibid., xxxv).

of the then existing Bureau of Indian Affairs Law and Order Code as Navajo Nation statutory law.[2] The law-and-order regulations promulgated by the Bureau of Indian Affairs for the Court of Indian Offenses are the original sources for the initial Navajo statutory laws on crimes, domestic relations, and courts. Although the Navajo Tribal Council intended to adopt the Bureau's regulations as Navajo law on a temporary basis, many of the adopted provisions remained in the code into the 1980s or became the source of laws presently found in the Navajo Nation Code.

As a necessary exercise of self-government and nation building, contemporary officials of the Navajo Nation must provide sufficient space for traditional Diné ways within a Navajo Nation government that is overly saturated with Western models and laws. Traditional Navajo ways, including philosophy, language, customs, traditions, and sense of place, must significantly influence all aspects of government for the Navajo Nation to maintain its distinct group character, continue its culture, develop a culturally compatible economy, and maintain its sovereign Indian nation status. The same things can be said generally of other American Indian tribes and nations.

Research reveals that Indian nations that employ tribal customs and traditions in the governing process exercise effective sovereignty.[3] Effective sovereignty is integral to preserving distinct group character and independent Indian nationhood. "Distinct," as used here, refers to an Indian nation that uses a good amount of its customary ways to govern and in the process distinguishes itself from the governing ways of the United States and the states of the union. Indian customary ways, including those of the Navajo people, have roots in tribal culture, language, spirituality, and sense of place.

For much of the twentieth century, the federal government implemented its Indian assimilation and termination policies through the Bureau of Indian Affairs. These policies did not support use of traditional Navajo ways in the Western-style Navajo Nation government. The federal government abandoned in practice its termination policy in 1961,[4] but two more decades passed before the political environment became suitable for the Navajo judges to endorse use of customary law ways in the Navajo Nation courts.[5] Although Navajo judges had used customary law and justice methods since the days of the Navajo Court of Indian Offenses, it was not until 1982 that

2 See Navajo Tribal Council Resolution No. CJA-1-59 (January 6, 1959) (titled "Adopting as tribal law the law and order regulations of the Department of the Interior on a temporary basis").

3 Cultural match, which means that the tribe's culture, including customs and traditions, should match its institutions, is one of the components of the Nation-Building Model. The other components are "stable institutions and policies, fair and effective dispute resolution, separation of politics from business management, [and] a competent bureaucracy" (Stephen Cornell and Joseph P. Kalt, "Sovereignty and Nation-Building: The Development Challenge in Indian Country Today," *American Indian Culture and Research Journal* 22 [1998]: 196, 201–05).

4 The goals of the termination policy were to abolish Indian reservations and make the lands taxable and severable, end the tribal–federal relationship, and end the special services that the federal government provides to Indian nations. Although termination in practice was abandoned in 1961, it was not until President Richard M. Nixon called for a new federal policy of self-determination for Indian tribes in 1970 that the termination policy was officially ended. See Stephen Cornell, *The Return of the Native* (New York: Oxford University Press, 1988), 123–25.

5 See Resolution of the Judicial Conference of the Navajo Nation (April 23, 1982). Copy of resolution in James W. Zion and Nelson McCabe, *Navajo Peacemaker Court Manual* (1982). In 1991, the Navajo Nation Supreme Court declared Navajo common law as the law of preference in the Navajo Nation courts. *Navajo Nation v. Platero*, 6 Nav. Rptr. 422 (Nav. Sup. Ct. 1991).

traditional Navajo justice ways became official court policy.[6]

The 1980s began with general consensus among Navajo judges that the Navajo Nation needed an alternative to the Western form of adjudication because of the incompatibility of this system with Navajo ways of life. While reviewing public concerns about the Navajo court system, court officials discovered several problems caused by the inherent incompatibility between traditional Navajo justice ways and Western-style litigation in the Navajo courts. These problems are summarized as follows: (1) The litigious system could not resolve certain kinds of problems in Navajo communities; (2) Navajos complained that the Western form of adjudication was too expensive and time-consuming; (3) Western methods of adjudication confused and frustrated Navajo litigants; and (4) The confrontational style of Western adjudication contravened traditional Navajo justice procedures, which used "talking things out" and consensus to resolve disputes.[7]

The Navajo judges turned to traditional Navajo justice ways for a dispute resolution method that would remedy the problems raised by the public—a method that "would be inexpensive, rapid, simple, and meet the standards of Navajo tradition."[8] Traditional Diné peacemaking was the answer. The judges revived traditional peacemaking and turned it into the Navajo Peacemaker Court in 1982.

The Navajo Peacemaker Court (now called Navajo Peacemaking Division), a traditionally derived dispute resolution system, has surpassed all expectations and is now an essential Navajo justice institution. Navajo peacemaking comports with indigenous justice ways and, as such, is studied around the world as a model of indigenous justice. Several years of experience show that Navajo peacemaking works best when it invokes traditional procedures and *Diné bibee haz´áanii* (Navajo common law).

Diné Bibee Haz´áanii *and Fundamental Laws*

The Navajo Nation Council is a legislative body that enacts laws. In pre-Council days, the traditional Navajo leaders mediated disputes, sometimes using precedent and stern lectures on the norms, but they did not make laws for the whole Navajo people. Traditional Navajos believe in the interconnectedness of all things, so they do not see law as a set of rules detached from daily life. Each day traditional Navajos live their laws with their spirituality, and to traditionalists, any attempt at distinguishing Diné law from spirituality is an improbable undertaking. All spiritual concepts and practices (what non-Indians call religion) are intertwined with the secular into the Diné Life Way, which, according to the Diné Fundamental Laws, is holistic.[9] Norms that produce desirable conditions that include probity, peace, order, and positive relationships are

6 Navajo common law has been a mainstay in the decision making of the Navajo Nation courts since 1959. The Navajo Nation Judicial Branch published the first volume containing Navajo court decisions in 1979. The first reported decision concerns Navajo custom: whether a Navajo custom marriage between two Navajos that lacks a marriage license is a valid marriage. *In re Marriage of Daw*, 1 Nav. Rptr. 1 (Nav. Sup. Ct. 1969). The Navajo judges of the Navajo Court of Indian Offenses also applied customs and used traditional Navajo dispute resolution methods. In 1959, the Navajo Tribal Council converted the old Court of Indian Offenses' choice of law regulation, which had allowed use of Indian customs in decision making, into Navajo Nation law. Navajo Tribal Council Resolution No. CJA-1-59 (January 6, 1959) (codified at 7 N.N.C. § 204 (2005)). See chapter 2, note 23 for the regulation that applied in the Navajo Court of Indian Offenses.

7 Zion and McCabe, *Navajo Peacemaker Court Manual*, 2–3.

8 Ibid., 3.

9 Navajo Nation Council Resolution No. CN-69-2002, Whereas Cl. 6 (November 1, 2002). See also Dan Vicenti, Leonard B. Jimson, Stephen Conn, and M.J.L. Kellogg, *Diné Bibee Haz´áanii* (Ramah, N.Mex.: Ramah High School Press, 1972): "The white man did not understand Navajo law because Navajo people did not call it law, but, rather, religion" (104).

common knowledge among traditional Navajos. In the traditional Navajo world, positive values sustain a condition called *hózhǫ́*—a state where everything is properly situated and existing and functioning in harmonious relationship with everything else (discussed in chapter 3). [*Ed. note*: chapter 3 is not included in the excerpt provided here.]

Traditional Navajos understand *Diné bibee haz'áanii* as values, norms, customs, and traditions that are transmitted orally across generations and which produce and maintain right relations, right relationships, and desirable outcomes in Navajo society. In the modern Navajo world, the term *Diné bibee haz'áanii* is understood as Navajo statutory law, administrative regulations, court-made law, and Navajo common law (values, norms, customs, and traditions). Thus, the standard translation of *bee haz'áanii* is law and that is how the Navajo courts have described the term.

In 1990, the Navajo Nation Supreme Court explained the legal aspects and legal understanding of the word *bee haz'áanii* in *Bennett v. Navajo Board of Election Supervisors*:

> The Navajo word for "law" is *bee-haz'áanii*. While we hear that word popularly used in the sense of laws enacted by the Navajo Nation Council ... it actually refers to higher law. It means something which is "way at the top"; something written in stone so to speak; something which is absolutely there; and, something like the Anglo concept of natural law. In other words, Navajos believe in a higher law, and as it is expressed in Navajo, there is a concept similar to the idea of unwritten constitutional law.[10]

The Supreme Court went on to explain that Navajo higher law includes "fundamental customs and traditions, as well as substantive rights found in the Treaty of 1868, the Navajo Nation Bill of Rights, the Judicial Reform Act of 1985, and the Title Two Amendments of 1989."[11] Although the Supreme Court did not identify any fundamental customs and traditions that would constitute higher law, Navajo thinking would place the doctrines of *hózhǫ́*, *k'é*, and *k'éí* into that category.

These three doctrines are not basic legal principles in the sense that they can be applied directly to legal questions in litigation. They essentially describe conditions generated through law when we speak of them in the legal context. They also describe other conditions, as, for example, when they are spoken of in the spiritual context. The three fundamental Navajo doctrines are like the Anglo concept of natural law.[12] They are also Diné philosophical doctrines. They are integral to the Navajo Creation Scripture and Journey Narratives and undergird, along with other doctrines, Navajo culture (including customs, traditions, and philosophy), language, spirituality, sense of place, and identity.

Although the modern Navajo conception of *bee haz'áanii* put forth by the Supreme Court provides sufficient understanding of law as applied in the Navajo Nation courts, there remains the core conception of the term that merits elaboration. At its most basic understanding (i.e., how a traditional Navajo might describe the concept), the term *bee haz'áanii* can be glossed in English as "by it which a certain state/

10 *Bennett v. Navajo Board of Election Supervisors*, 6 Nav. Rptr. 319, 324 (Nav. Sup. Ct. 1990).

11 Ibid.

12 Natural law is defined as a philosophical system of law and moral principles purportedly deriving from a universalized conception of human nature or divine justice rather than human institutions; also, moral law embodied in principles of right and wrong (Black's Law Dictionary, 7th ed. [1999], 1049).

condition exists." In the main, the state or condition is *hózhǫ́* and the "it" represents the animating norms, customs, and traditions (or customary laws) that produce or maintain that state. The desired condition, especially when relationships are considered, can also be *k´é* (a person's positive relationship with everything) or *k´éí* (a person's positive relationship with relatives). Under a traditional Diné analysis, law functions as the demiurge that produces or maintains the state of *hózhǫ́* (or *k´é* or *k´éí*). An act that does not disrupt *hózhǫ́* is called *bee haz´ą́* (meaning an act permitted, or, literally, "maintains a positive condition") and that term means "legal act" when used in the legal sense.

As the Navajo Nation Supreme Court said in *Bennett*, the term *bee haz´áanii* includes laws enacted by the Navajo Nation Council. In 2002, the Navajo Nation Council incorporated traditional Navajo norms and values into the Navajo Nation Code as "the fundamental laws of the Diné"[13] to guide all aspects of government operations and interactions among government officials and among government officials and the public. Moreover, because traditional Navajo knowledge is fading among the Navajo people, particularly the young people, the Diné fundamental laws were codified so they could be used to educate the Navajo populace and thereby perpetuate Navajo culture.[14] A group of traditionalists, who were selected for their fluency in Navajo philosophy, language, culture, spirituality, and sense of place, scrutinized the Navajo Creation Scripture and Journey Narratives and identified several foundational postulates that were appropriate for codification. The fundamental laws are intended to guide the Navajo Nation courts and leaders of the Navajo Nation when they make decisions, laws, and policies for the Navajo Nation. Nonetheless, without a firm grounding in the Navajo Creation Scripture and Journey Narratives, the fundamental laws are difficult to understand and apply in the legal context.

The Diné fundamental laws form four sections in Title One of the Navajo Nation Code: (1) Traditional Law (*Diyin Bits´ą́ą́dę́ę́´ Bee Haz´áanii*—laws of the Great Spirit); (2) Customary Law (*Diyin Dine´é Bits´ą́ą́dę́ę́´ Bee Haz´áanii*—laws of the Holy Beings); (3) Natural Law (*Nahasdzáán dóó Yádiłhił Bits´ ą́ą́dę́ę́ Bee Haz´áanii*—laws of Mother Earth and Father Heaven); and (4) Common Law (*Diyin Nohookáá Diné Bibee Haz´áanii*—laws of the Diné).[15] Several readings of the laws are recommended to glean foundational doctrines (including *hózhǫ́*, *k´é*, and *k´éí*) and certain customs and traditions because they are not expressly mentioned in the provisions that comprise the sections. Since the sections that constitute the fundamental laws were recently codified, the Navajo Nation Supreme Court has not had much opportunity to discuss them. Thus, the following short and general synopsis of the fundamental laws is offered as a precursor to further discussions of these laws.

Although the words *hózhǫ́*, *k´é*, and *k´éí* do not appear in the sections that make up the fundamental laws, the three doctrines nonetheless inform its provisions. The provision in section

13 Navajo Nation Council Resolution No. CN-69-2002 (November 1, 2002).

14 Ibid.

15 Those who call American Indian philosophy primitive have never done the hard task of explaining Diné epistemology by going to its substratum to abstract subtle features. Navajo philosophy rivals any philosophy in the world. The concepts that comprise Navajo epistemology (called the Diné Way of Knowledge in this book) are highly developed, complex, and difficult to translate into English. For these reasons, and because I am using my traditional education and knowledge to explain traditional concepts, my translation of the Diné Fundamental Laws differs from those in the Navajo Nation Code. The difference in translation does not mean that those in the Code are wrong. The difference results from lack of English words that accurately describe Navajo concepts that have much broader meaning and application than Anglo-American legal concepts.

203(A) that speaks to the people's right to choose their leaders is used here to illustrate this point.[16] Participatory democracy, a concept central to traditional Navajo governance, flourishes when the Navajo people choose their leaders freely and work with them to solve problems. The *k´é* and *k´éí* doctrines come in to guide discussions (which is participatory democracy in action) anytime the people and their leaders use the principle of "talking things out" to address and solve community problems. Harmony (*hózhǫ́*) is restored when the people working with their leaders solve community problems using consensual decision making. This example also demonstrates that the fundamental laws serve as mechanisms through which *hózhǫ́*, *k´é*, and *k´éí* are maintained.

Section 201, which declares the foundation of Diné law, also shows that the three concepts inform the fundamental laws. This section, restated, says the Navajos are people of the Great Covenant, created in their ancestors' image, and connected to all things in creation.[17] Section 201 declares these Navajo beliefs: the interconnectedness and interdependence of everything in creation (i.e., Diné connected to Holy Beings, which includes the sacred and spiritual, by covenant); Diné connected to their ancestors through likeness; and Diné connected to all elements in creation (past, present, and future) through *k´é* and *k´éí*, such that when everything is in its proper place and functioning in harmony, there is *hózhǫ́*. The part written in the Navajo language in section 201 describes important aspects of the process used to create the universe, which is also the same process that produced the primordial conditions of *hózhǫ́*, *k´é*, and *k´éí*; the three are integral to the interconnectedness concept.

Navajos believe that foundational laws like *hózhǫ́*, *k´é*, and *k´éí* have sources in spirituality. The Diné Fundamental Laws contain this view:

> The Diné have always been guided and protected by the immutable laws provided by the Diyin [Great Spirit], the Diyin Dine´é [Holy Beings], Nahasdzáán [Mother Earth] and Yádiłhił [Father Heaven]; these laws have not only provided sanctuary for the Diné Life Way but have guided, sustained and protected the Diné as they journeyed upon and off the sacred lands upon which they were placed since time immemorial.[18]

Traditional Navajo philosophy holds that the Holy Beings established the foundational doctrines that drive the Diné Life Way. Thus, the Diné Fundamental Laws enunciate the traditional view that spirituality is the source of foundational principles. The customs and traditions that come from the foundational principles would also have spiritual sources by way of the primary doctrines. A study of Navajo common law should respect the traditional Navajo understanding that spirituality underlies Diné foundational laws.[19]

---

16 1 N.N.C. §§ 203(A)–(J) (2005). This section speaks to the people's right to choose their leaders; that Navajo leaders should be ethical and law-abiding; that the government is composed of four branches (with specified duties)—executive, legislative, judicial, and national security; that Navajo culture, spirituality, and language should be preserved; and that the Navajo Nation respects all religions and honors religious freedom.

17 1 N.N.C. § 201 (2005). When they created the original Diné, the Holy Beings established foundational laws that the Diné people were directed to follow. This mandate is likely part of the covenant referred to at section 201.

18 Navajo Nation Council Resolution No. CN-69-2002, Preamble: Whereas Cl. No. 2 (November 1, 2002). These are the closest English translations of these terms: *Diyin* means the Creator; *Diyin Dine´é* means the Holy Beings; and *Nahasdzáán* and *Yah diłhił* mean the Earth and the Heavens, respectively.

19 The spiritual origins of Navajo traditional law are briefly discussed in Robert Yazzie, "'Life Comes from It': Navajo Justice Concepts," *New Mexico Law Review* 24 (1994): 175–76.

The view that fundamental Navajo doctrines have spiritual sources does not cause uneasiness among modern Navajo lawmakers when they enact laws for the Navajo people and Navajo homelands. The Navajo Nation Council has tremendous leeway and flexibility to make laws, but those laws should not contravene the primordial principles. The following example illustrates this limitation: Suppose the Navajo Nation Council enacted a law making English the official language of the Navajo Nation. How would a Navajo Nation court analyze this issue on a challenge? The Navajo Creation Scripture and Journey Narratives teaches that the Diné language formed from the Creator's thought process and turned into sound (called the First Word), the sound then became language, and the Holy Beings made the Navajo language a component of Diné identity.[20] Using these accounts, a Council-enacted law that made English the official language of the Navajo Nation would profane the Diné language and Diné identity, both of which connect Navajos to the Holy Beings.

Navajo judges sometimes resort to general propositions that underlie Navajo culture to guide the litigation process. These general propositions would include *hózhǫ́*, *k´é*, and *k´éí*, and others such as "The Navajo language is sacred" and "Words are powerful." These same principles also apply during peacemaking to heal participants and restore them to harmonious relationships with each other and their kin and community. A twentieth-century American anthropologist, E. Adamson Hoebel, calls similar general propositions social postulates.[21] The Navajo Nation courts prefer to call the extant Navajo social postulates, and the norms, values, customs, and traditions of the Navajo people, Navajo common law. In 1987, the Navajo Nation Supreme Court proclaimed that the customs and traditions that Navajos understand as law are collectively Navajo common law:

> Because established Navajo customs and traditions have the force of law, this Court agrees with the Window Rock District Court in announcing its preference for the term "Navajo common law" rather than "custom," as that term properly emphasizes the fact that Navajo custom and tradition *is* law, and more accurately reflects the similarity in the treatment of custom between Navajo and English common law. (emphasis in original)[22]

Although the Navajo Nation courts do not need statutory authorization to use Navajo common law, the Navajo Nation Code has provided such authority in the form of a choice of law statute since 1959. The statute that authorizes use of Navajo common law in the courts has changed little since its predecessor, a regulation of the Court of Indian Offenses, was adopted as a

20 See the Declaration of the Foundation of Diné Law, codified at 1 N.N.C. § 201 (2005) (Diné language is one aspect of Diné identity), Navajo Nation Council Resolution No. CN-69-2002 (November 1, 2002).

21 E. Adamson Hoebel, *The Law of Primitive Man: A Study of Comparative Legal Dynamics*, 5th printing (New York: Atheneum Press, 1974), 12–17.

22 *In re Estate of Belone*, 5 Nav. Rptr. 161, 165 (Nav. Sup. Ct. 1987); see also *Navajo Nation v. Platero*, 6 Nav. Rptr. 422, 424 (Nav. Sup. Ct. 1987). The Window Rock District Court decisions from that time that describe customs and traditions as Navajo common law are *In re Estate of Apachee*, 4 Nav. Rptr. 178, 179–81 (Window Rock Dist. Ct. 1983) and *Tome v. Navajo Nation*, 4 Nav. Rptr. 159, 160–61 (Window Rock Dist. Ct. 1983) (Navajo common law consists of Navajo customs, traditions, and usages and is binding on the Navajo Nation courts). The Navajo Nation Council and the Navajo Nation courts do not use the same terminology to identify Diné fundamental customs and traditions. See 1 N.N.C. §§ 202–06 (2005), Navajo Nation Council Resolution No. CN-69-2002 (November 1, 2002).

Navajo statute in 1959.[23] The current choice of law statute requires the Navajo courts to apply Navajo statutes and regulations to legal matters first; requires use of Navajo common law to interpret Navajo statutes and regulations; and requires application of Navajo common law to legal matters that are not addressed by Navajo statutes and regulations.[24] Navajo Nation Supreme Court decisions hold that the Navajo Nation courts must follow the requirements set forth in the Diné Fundamental Laws.[25]

Finding and Using Navajo Common Law in Litigation

Navajo common law is not difficult to find and understand. Navajo court opinions are published in the *Navajo Reporter*[26] and the *Indian Law Reporter* and are available through VersusLaw, a commercial online legal research source. The written decisions of the Navajo Nation courts contain generous amounts of Navajo common law with appropriate explanations. Legal and nonlegal literature on the Navajo courts and Navajo culture also contains Navajo common law. Relevant customs and traditions that do not appear in the written decisions of the Navajo Nation courts or are not codified in the Navajo Nation Code remain within the domain of Navajo oral tradition, but even these are readily available through knowledgeable people, usually elders. When working with unwritten Navajo common law, experienced legal advocates locate people knowledgeable on customs and traditions, elicit the relevant common law, interpret it, and introduce it into litigation. The Navajo Nation Supreme Court underscored the preeminence of customs and traditions in Navajo jurisprudence when it declared Navajo common law as the law of preference in the Navajo Nation courts.[27] The stakes are indeed high because Navajo common law can trump or alter predisposed expectations premised on Anglo-American legal outcomes. For example, in *Ben v. Burbank*,[28] the Navajo Nation Supreme Court used the *k´é* doctrine to reject the argument that the statute of limitations had run out on an oral contract claim.

Navajo elders, ceremonial practitioners, peacemakers, retired Navajo Nation judges, and Navajos who live a traditional Navajo lifestyle are normally well versed in Navajo customary precepts. Beyond the written materials, the precepts that comprise Navajo common law are present

23 The law-and-order regulation for the Navajo Court of Indian Offenses that became Navajo statutory law stated: "In all civil cases the Court of Indian Offenses shall apply any laws of the United States that may be applicable, any authorized regulations of the Interior Department, and any ordinances or customs of the tribe, not prohibited by such Federal laws." See section 2, "Law Applicable in Civil Actions," *Federal Register* 3 (May 18, 1938), 1135. The term "Courts of the Navajo Tribe" replaced "Court of Indian Offenses" when the Navajo Tribal Council adopted the Bureau of Indian Affairs regulation as Navajo law in 1959. The 1985 amendment reads as follows: "In all cases the Courts of the Navajo Nation shall apply any laws of the United States that may be applicable and any laws and customs of the Navajo Nation not prohibited by applicable federal laws." 7 N.N.C. § 204 (1985). The 1985 amendment dropped the word *civil* from the term "civil cases."

24 The current statutory authorization, 7 N.N.C. § 204(A) (2005), states: "In all cases the courts of the Navajo Nation shall first apply applicable Navajo Nation statutory laws and regulations to resolve matters in dispute before the courts. The courts shall utilize Diné bi beenahaz´aanii (Navajo Traditional, Customary, Natural or Common Law) to guide the interpretation of Navajo Nation statutory laws and regulations. The courts shall also utilize Diné bi beenahaz´aanii whenever Navajo Nation statutes or regulations are silent on matters in dispute before the courts."

25 *Navajo Housing Authority v. Bluffview Resident Management Corp.*, 8 Nav. Rptr. 402, 414 (Nav. Sup. Ct. 2003); *Fort Defiance Housing Corp. v. Lowe*, 8 Nav. Rptr. 463 (Nav. Sup. Ct. 2004); *Judy v. White*, 8 Nav. Rptr. 510 (Nav. Sup. Ct. 2004).

26 The eight published volumes of the *Navajo Reporter* contain opinions from 1969 through 2005. Opinions beginning in January 2006 are in loose-leaf form. The books can be purchased from the Navajo Nation Supreme Court, P.O. Box 520, Window Rock, Navajo Nation, AZ 86515.

27 *Navajo Nation v. Platero*, 6 Nav. Rptr. 422, 424 (Nav. Sup. Ct. 1991). The U.S. Supreme Court recognizes the right of the Navajo Nation courts to use Navajo common law. *United States v. Wheeler*, 435 U.S. 313 (1978).

28 7 Nav. Rptr. 222 (Nav. Sup. Ct. 1996). The *Ben v. Burbank* case is discussed at the end of chapter 4.

in traditional lore, maxims, stories, ceremonies, prayers, songs, and the Navajo language. While working with Navajo common law, it is important to heed the Navajo Nation Supreme Court's caveats: (1) understand the customs and traditions; then decide how they would apply to an issue; (2) customs and traditions may vary from place to place on the Navajo Nation; (3) some customs and traditions may have fallen into desuetude; and (4) parties to a case may not follow customs and traditions.[29]

Although a party may not practice customs or traditions, when any is pleaded in the initial pleadings or anytime thereafter, it becomes relevant and can be considered by the judge and those litigating.[30] Moreover, not all Navajo customs are law,[31] and the individual contributing common-law knowledge may refuse to testify on custom in open court owing to its sacred nature or object on other grounds. Participants should understand that the adversarial process is not a traditional Navajo method of dispute resolution. An in camera disclosure of a sacred custom is a possible solution. Problems sometimes arise when litigants attempt to introduce Indian common law into tribal, state, and federal courts, but under most circumstances any problem can be alleviated through respectful discussion and understanding.

Legal practitioners who are not familiar with Navajo culture, including language, etiquette, and spiritual beliefs and practices, would do well to associate with a court advocate or attorney who is Navajo and a member of the Navajo Nation Bar Association.[32] The Navajo legal practitioner can help locate sources of Navajo common law, including knowledgeable persons, and advise on introducing customs into court proceedings. Although being Navajo alone does not guarantee knowledge of Navajo common law, Navajo legal counselors are usually culturally embedded. They know Navajo spiritual and social practices, can speak the Navajo language, and possess an experienced insider's view of Navajo court practice. Navajo judges, several of whom are former court advocates, know of the indispensability of Navajo court advocates to law practice on the Navajo Nation:

> Navajo advocates are familiar with the customs and traditions of their people. They can speak the tribal language, thereby communicating with those seeking legal help who rely upon their native tongue. An understanding of the Navajo life-style and culture is indispensable to the practice of law within the Navajo Nation, and Navajo advocates advance the development of

---

29 *Lente v. Notah*, 3 Nav. Rptr. 72, 80 (Nav. Sup. Ct. 1982).

30 *In re Estate of Belone*, 5 Nav. Rptr. 161, 163–64 (Nav. Sup. Ct. 1987); *Judy v. White*, 8 Nav. Rptr. 510, 535–36 (Nav. Sup. Ct. 2004).

31 Custom "is a practice and not an opinion.... Custom is what men *do*, not what they think" (emphasis in original). *Lente v. Notah*, 3 Nav. Rptr. 72, 80 (1982). According to Hoebel, customs that are law meet the following criterion: "A social norm is legal if its neglect or infraction is regularly met, in threat or in fact, by the application of physical force by an individual or group possessing the socially recognized privilege of so acting" (Hoebel, *Law of Primitive Man*, 28). Thus, a handshake, although a Navajo custom, is not law.

32 For example, a common etiquette is to wait at least five minutes before knocking on the door when visiting a Navajo family. The time allows the family to prepare for the visitor's welcome. When Navajos still lived in hogans, the delay was used to prepare a place for the visitor on the west side of the hogan.

The Navajo Nation Bar Association, with headquarters in Window Rock, Navajo Nation (Arizona), has more than 450 Navajo and non-Navajo members who practice law on the Navajo Nation. Bar members who are not state-licensed attorneys (both Navajos and non-Navajos) are called court advocates. *Tafoya v. Navajo Nation Bar Association*, 6 Nav. Rptr. 141 (Nav. Sup. Ct. 1989); *In re Practice of Law in the Courts of the Navajo Nation by Avalos*, 6 Nav. Rptr. 191 (Nav. Sup. Ct. 1990); see also *Alderman v. Navajo Nation Bar Association*, 6 Nav. Rptr. 188 (Nav. Sup. Ct. 1990) (the Navajo Nation Supreme Court has ultimate authority over law practice on the Navajo Nation).

> a modern judicial system which retains traditional legal norms.[33]

The Navajo Nation Supreme Court set parameters for locating, pleading, and proving Navajo common law in the Navajo Nation courts in *In re Estate of Belone*.[34] First, the Supreme Court established that when "a claim relies on Navajo custom, the custom must be alleged, and the pleading must state generally how that custom supports the claim."[35] This rule gives the opposing party notice and an opportunity to challenge the common-law claim. In *Judy v. White*, the Navajo Nation Supreme Court ruled that the Diné Fundamental Laws "expand[ed] the *Belone* rule beyond the initial pleading requirement.... Thus, the failure to raise [Navajo common law] in the initial pleading will not lead to exclusion of the claim."[36] Navajo common law can be raised after the initial pleadings have been filed, but the opposing party must still be provided notice that a Navajo common-law claim has been pleaded. The court should still exercise its discretion to guard against late filings of common-law claims that delay proceedings, hamper the rights of litigants, or otherwise cause prejudicial problems.

Second, in addition to oral sources, Navajo common law can be found in written Navajo court opinions, Judicial Branch Solicitor opinions, and literature and studies on Navajo culture, including those by social scientists, legal scholars, attorneys, and Navajo judges.[37] Navajo judges have expressed generally that writings on Navajo culture by Navajo authors are more accurate than those by non-Indian authors, very likely because Navajo authors are embedded in their own culture. For example, the trial judge in the case of *In re Estate of Apachee* stated that materials written by Navajos on Navajo culture are more reliable than those by non-Navajos because Navajos "are the most accurate commentators on themselves."[38] This observation, however, was made in 1983. There are now non-Navajo authors who have interpreted, analyzed, and discussed Navajo culture and philosophy very well in their books.

Third, Navajo common law can be introduced and proved in court through an expert witness.[39] The *Estate of Belone* decision provides general guidelines on qualifying an expert witness on Navajo common law and admitting expert testimony. The trial court exercises "sound discretion" over the qualifying of a witness as an expert and over admitting expert testimony on Navajo common law.[40] If the claimed custom or tradition is not disputed, the trial court "need not avail itself of experts in Navajo culture" and admit it as evidence subject to relevancy.[41] The party desiring to use an expert witness must satisfy the trial court that expert testimony on Navajo common law is "relevant to the issue before the court" and will

33 *Tafoya v. Navajo Nation Bar Association*, 6 Nav. Rptr. 141, 143 (Nav. Sup. Ct. 1989).
34 5 Nav. Rptr. 161 (Nav. Sup. Ct. 1987).
35 *In re Estate of Belone*, 5 Nav. Rptr. 161, 164 (Nav. Sup. Ct. 1987). A party who pleads custom gives notice to all parties and the court that custom will be used in the case.
36 8 Nav. Rptr. 510, 535–36 (Nav. Sup. Ct. 2004).
37 *In re Estate of Belone*, 5 Nav. Rptr. 161, 165 (Nav. Sup. Ct. 1987).
38 4 Nav. Rptr. 178, 180 (Window Rock Dist. Ct. 1983).
39 *In re Estate of Belone*, 5 Nav. Rptr. 161, 165 (Nav. Sup. Ct. 1987).
40 Ibid., 166–67.
41 Ibid., 165.

help the judge or jury understand the custom or tradition.[42]

A witness must be qualified as an expert on Navajo customs and traditions before offering evidence in that area. Evidence of a witness's qualification to testify as an expert on Navajo common law may come from (1) readings on customs, (2) practicing customs, or (3) understanding of customs derived from oral education, living a traditional lifestyle, long-term interest in and acquisition of traditional knowledge, or reputation as a person well versed in traditional knowledge.[43] If litigants dispute the proffered Navajo custom or tradition, the court may hold a pretrial conference with three experts who will use the traditional Navajo civil procedure of talking things out and identify the appropriate custom to be applied in the case.[44] In the interests of fairness, each side should select an expert and the court can appoint the third expert. The litigants can attend the pretrial conference, but their participation will be "limited to asking questions to clarify the expert witnesses' conclusions."[45] Navajo statutory law authorizes Navajo judges to seek out knowledgeable individuals to clarify questions on Navajo common law: "To determine the appropriate utilization and interpretation of Diné bi beenahaz´aanii, the court shall request, as it deems necessary, advice from Navajo individuals widely recognized as being knowledgeable about Diné bi beenahaz´aanii."[46]

The Navajo Nation Supreme Court's guidelines in the *Estate of Belone* opinion supplement the trial court's broad discretion over the qualifying of experts and admitting expert testimony on Navajo common law.[47] On appeal, the Supreme Court will review for abuse of discretion—that is, to determine if the proper procedures (the *Estate of Belone* guidelines) on qualifying experts on relevant Navajo common law were followed.[48] Thus, a record must be made of the evidence used to qualify a witness as an expert on Navajo common law.[49] The de novo standard of review should also apply to issues brought before the Navajo Nation Supreme Court that challenge the trial court's application of the proffered Navajo common law.

The notion that a select person can be elevated above others and called "expert" on Navajo ways would not sit well with most traditional Navajos. True, there are Navajos, particularly ceremonial practitioners, who possess vast amounts of traditional knowledge, but they hardly consider themselves experts, because many elderly Navajos and Navajos who have been exposed to the traditional lifestyle know many of the same

42 Ibid. The Supreme Court stated that the trial court must be satisfied that "use of an expert witness is proper," *In re Estate of Belone*, 5 Nav. Rptr. at 166, which, when interpreted in light of the "sound discretion" standard, would mean that the expert's testimony would help the judge or jury (1) understand the custom, or (2) identify the custom that is applicable, or (3) determine how the custom should be applied. In addition, the second full paragraph on page 166 in *In re Estate of Belone* is general background information on expert witnesses. The guidelines for use of experts in the Navajo Nation courts are set forth on page 167 in *In re Estate of Belone*, beginning with the first full paragraph.

43 Ibid., 167.

44 Ibid.

45 Ibid. This limitation arises from the Court's concern that parties may attempt to manipulate experts to benefit their own interests, which is not in keeping with the traditional Navajo civil procedure of "talking things out" and making decisions by consensus.

46 7 N.N.C. § 204(B) (2005). The predecessor to this provision comes from the 1938 regulations for the Navajo Court of Indian Offenses: "Where any doubt arises as to the customs and usages of the tribe the court may request the advice of counselors familiar with these customs and usages." See section 2, "Law Applicable in Civil Actions," *Federal Register* 3 (May 18, 1938): 1136.

47 *In re Estate of Belone*, 5 Nav. Rptr. 161, 166, 167 (Nav. Sup. Ct. 1987).

48 The Court said, on appeal, it will "review, as a matter of law, whether the district court followed the proper procedure in determining the expert witness's qualifications as regards the custom or tradition applicable to the specific circumstances and locale involved" (ibid., 167). The words at the end of the quote ("locale involved") imply that Navajo custom can be unique to a place.

49 Ibid.

general concepts. The Navajo Nation Supreme Court should revisit the *Estate of Belone* case and reexamine its guidelines on raising and admitting Navajo common law. Any modifications should comport with traditional Navajo thinking and ways of doing things.

The abuse of discretion standard that the Navajo Nation Supreme Court announced in *Estate of Belone* allows for flexible use of Navajo common law, but the overall process on qualifying experts and admitting expert testimony is more a practice of exclusion of evidence, rather than of inclusion, when considered in light of traditional Navajo justice ways. Traditional justice allows discussion of matters that go beyond what would be considered relevant under modern Navajo rules of evidence. Use of formal evidentiary rules to filter witnesses and proffered evidence may be useful to adversarial litigation, but the filtering process under the guise of relevancy is wholly incompatible with traditional Diné justice, which values equality, talking things out, and free-flowing oral discourse.

The American litigation practice (in state, federal, and Navajo courts) of trimming evidence to relevancy through evidentiary rules does damage to the broad perspectives contained in Navajo customs and traditions by straining them of meaning and significance. When stripped of meaning through the evidentiary process, the value or norm carries little credibility with court judges, especially non-Indian state and federal judges. Traditional Navajo values, norms, and doctrines encompass broad perspectives that do not do well in an American form of courts (i.e., state, federal, and Navajo courts) where adversarial competition is used to find the "truth" by constraining evidence to narrow concepts. The same may hold true for other American Indian and indigenous customs and traditions.

Finally, most of the traditional normative precepts that make up the modern body of Navajo common law have been identified and developed through the legal doctrine of judicial notice. Navajo judges using the judicial notice doctrine to accept Navajo common law is not a recent phenomenon. Navajo judges have made use of the doctrine since the early days of the Navajo Court of Indian Offenses. When use of customs and traditions in Navajo court litigation became standard practice, judicial notice of Navajo common law also became standard procedure for the Navajo judges.

Modern Navajo court judges rely on the doctrine of judicial notice to identify unwritten customs and traditions and incorporate them into their decisions.[50] The trial court also has discretion to accept an undisputed custom or tradition under the doctrine of judicial notice. Once they have been applied, previously unwritten customs and traditions become part of a unique body of written Navajo common law. In 1983, after Navajo judges had been using the doctrine of judicial notice for nearly a century, a Navajo trial court established written guidelines for use of the doctrine in litigation.[51] The trial court proclaimed that judicial notice can be taken of normative precepts that are generally known within the community or can be found in accurate sources.[52] The accurate sources can be well-researched materials on Navajo culture, language, spirituality, and other areas and do not have to be written by Navajo authors.

The Navajo Nation Supreme Court adopted the trial court's standards on taking judicial notice of Navajo common law in *Estate of Belone*.[53] In addition to the standards, the

50 Ibid., 165–66.
51 *Apache v. Republic National Life Insurance Co.*, 3 Nav. Rptr. 250 (Window Rock Dist. Ct. 1983).
52 Ibid., 252.
53 5 Nav. Rptr. 161, 165 (Nav. Sup. Ct. 1987).

Supreme Court declared that if a trial court takes judicial notice of Navajo common law, "it must clearly set forth in its order the custom on which it is relying, so that the basis for its decision is clear" in case of appellate review.[54] The Supreme Court also instructed that a Navajo trial court can take judicial notice of normative precepts as adjudicative facts.[55]

The modern guidelines on the judicial notice doctrine that the Supreme Court established in *Estate of Belone* and the pragmatic use of the doctrine by Navajo judges since the days of the Navajo Court of Indian Offenses illustrate ingenious ways of incorporating Navajo common law into adversarial litigation in the Western-style Navajo Nation courts. Now that the foundational doctrines that comprise the Diné Fundamental Laws are in place, the pace of development of Navajo common law should quicken. Although the Navajo Nation courts make extensive use of American court procedures and doctrines, they continue to focus on the traditional norm of restoring disputants to the desired state of *hózhǫ́*(peace, harmony, and balance), much like the traditional Diné peacemakers of yesteryear.

[...]

K´é (Kinship Unity through Positive Values)

[...]

K´é in the Navajo Nation Courts

When the Navajo Nation judiciary adopted the Navajo Nation Code of Judicial Conduct on November 1, 1991, the judges made sure that Navajo common law, including the doctrines of *hózhǫ́*, *k´é*, and *k´éí*, would be used not only in the decision making of the Navajo Nation courts, but also in the daily administration of judicial business:

> A longstanding objective of the Navajo Nation courts is to preserve the customs and traditions of the Navajo people. They are embodied in the Navajo common law, and it is a source for many of the provisions of the [Navajo judicial] code.... While the Navajo Nation courts generally follow the state model of justice ... that system is alien to the Navajo common law. Traditional Navajo justice methods rely upon adjusting the differences of equals, in mediation and the free discussion of problems, to resolve them by consent. It does not rely upon a superior decision-maker, who imposes decisions upon others. It does not use coercion or force, and is instead based upon an agreed need for harmony in the community.[15] ...
>
> Under certain circumstances the [Navajo judicial] code may apply to other members of the court staff, and particularly those who advise or counsel a judge or justice. In particular, the Canons apply to law clerks, attorneys to the courts, paralegals, court administrators, and others who are in close and constant working relationship with a judge or justice. The principles apply, because these officials are identified with judges and justices in the eye of the Navajo public.[16]

One month after the judges approved the Navajo judicial code, the Navajo Nation Supreme Court

54 Ibid., 165–66.
55 Ibid., 165.
15 Preamble, Navajo Nation Code of Judicial Conduct.
16 Application of the Code, Navajo Nation Code of Judicial Conduct.

declared Navajo common law as the law of preference in the Navajo Nation courts.[17] At the time of these declarations, the Navajo Nation courts were handling several cases generated by what Navajos have come to call "the turmoil," a 1989 political power struggle between supporters of suspended Chairman Peter MacDonald Sr. and those in opposition. The 1989 events generated heated and ample public debate, but the judges were most impressed by traditional Navajos who decried the extent to which Navajo leaders had strayed from the teachings that emphasize *hózhǫ́*, *k´é*, and *k´éí*. The turmoil caused Navajos to fight Navajos on the same ground where their ancestors had sought the blessings of the Holy Beings after their release from imprisonment at Fort Sumner more than a hundred years earlier. Most important, the judges saw the turmoil as a lesson that the Navajo courts have a duty to use Navajo common law.

THE COURTS' DUTY TO USE NAVAJO COMMON LAW

The discussions on the early drafts of the Navajo judicial code united the judges in a spirit of collegiality that essentially focused the judiciary on revitalizing dormant customary precepts. The Navajo judges began encouraging each other during their quarterly meetings to use the *hózhǫ́*, *k´é*, and *k´éí* doctrines and other traditional principles in decision making and court administration. Quarterly judicial conferences are held every three months during which judges and staff discuss court policy and planning, fiscal matters, court administration, changes to court rules, judges and staff training, and other topics important to the Navajo Nation courts and American Indian tribal courts in general. During the court system's annual conferences in the 1990s, the Navajo Nation Chief Justice encouraged judicial branch employees, including judges, attorneys, peacemakers, and court staff, to incorporate *k´é* values (friendliness, cooperation, kindness, kinship terms, etc.) into their work and interactions with each other and the public. The Navajo Nation Court System is now at a juncture where traditional principles are not only mainstays in the courts' decision making, but serve as the foundation from which the judicial branch of the Navajo Nation government operates.

Navajo Nation judges know their decisions must be informed by the *hózhǫ́*, *k´é*, and *k´éí* doctrines. Canon One of the judicial code advises the Navajo judges to decide cases within the four sacred mountains, the four mountains located at cardinal directions and that mark the boundaries of ancient Navajoland.[18] This is the land the Navajos believe the Holy Beings promised to them for their home and perpetual possession. Navajos believe the Holy Beings placed everything they would need to prosper and grow on the lands within the Four Sacred Mountains. Navajos believe the mountains are "beings" blessed with divine power, so they contain all knowledge and spiritual blessings that are essential to the Diné Life Way.

Navajo judges are instructed to "apply Navajo concepts and procedures of justice, including the principles of maintaining harmony, establishing order, respecting freedom, and talking things out in free discussion."[19]. The judicial code advises Navajo judges, as successors to the traditional peacemakers, to follow *k´é* rules by treating litigants as if they were relatives. Navajo society, of course, revolves around kinship:

> This value [treat people like relatives] requires judges, as *Hozhoji´ Naat´aah*

17 *Navajo Nation v. Platero*, 6 Nav. Rptr. 422, 424 (Nav. Sup. Ct. 1991).

18 Canon One, Principle, Navajo Nation Code of Judicial Conduct. The Navajo Four Sacred Mountains are Mount Blanca in Colorado; Mount Taylor in New Mexico; San Francisco Peaks in Arizona; and Mount Hesperus in Colorado.

19 Ibid.

> (peace leaders), to treat everyone equally and fairly. Navajos believe in equality and horizontal, person-to-person relationships as part of their concept of justice. Obligations toward relatives extend to everyone, because that is a means of not only stressing personal equality, but creating solidarity ...
>
> The procedure of Navajo justice is people talking out their problems for a consensual resolution of them. A judge should encourage free discussion of the problem before the court, within the limits of reasonable rules of procedure and evidence. A judge should not encourage or permit aggressive behavior, including the badgering of witnesses, rudeness, the infliction of intentional humiliation or embarrassment, or any other conduct which obstructs the right to a full and fair hearing.[20]

Borrowing from traditional dispute resolution practice, a Navajo judge can assume a peacemaker's role at opportune stages of litigation and employ *k´é* to encourage parties to reach consensus on disputed points. A judge can "use the pretrial conference, sentencing hearing, or post-judgment proceeding to encourage the parties to reach consensus regarding their dispute."[21] Because coercion has no place in peacemaking, the judge as peacemaker cannot force parties to settle issues. Even the Navajo Nation Supreme Court has on occasion used *k´é* to encourage parties with cases pending before it to settle their disputes amicably in the interests of community harmony, healing relationships, and maintaining kinship unity.

The Navajo Nation Supreme Court consistently proclaims that the Navajo Nation courts "serve the purpose of bringing people in dispute back into harmony" with their relatives and community.[22] The harmony theme is diffused throughout the judicial code, but is explicitly set forth under Canon One:

> Injustice, in the sense of evil or wrongdoing, is the result of disharmony. One of the goals of justice is to return people and their community to harmony in the resolution of a dispute. The judge must promote harmony between litigants, achieve harmony through assuring reasonable restitution to victims, and foster harmony by providing the means for offenders or wrongdoers to return to their communities. That is achieved through free discussion, conciliation, consensus, and guidance from the judge.[23]

Navajo judges know that although the Navajo judicial code contains a set of ethics principles based on normative precepts, it has other unstated goals: (1) to encourage the judges to use traditional Navajo thinking when deciding cases; (2) to set forth foundational customary principles, including *hózhǫ́*, *k´é*, and *k´éí*, "talking things out," *nályééh* (restitution), *naat´áah* (leadership), and consensus, for active and future judges to know, apply, and develop; (3) to instill in court employees important traditional values pertinent to their work; and (4) to declare that Navajo common law, culture, spirituality, language, sense of

20 Canon One, Considerations No. 3 (Judicial Attitudes), No. 4 (Coercion), and No. 6 ("Fair Play"), Navajo Nation Code of Judicial Conduct.

21 Canon Three, Consideration No. 1 ("The Judge as Mediator"), Navajo Nation Code of Judicial Conduct.

22 *In re Mental Health Services of Bizardi*, 8 Nav. Rptr. 593, 597 (Nav. Sup. Ct. 2004).

23 Canon One, Consideration No. 1 ("Harmony"), Navajo Nation Code of Judicial Conduct.

place, and identity compose the foundation from which the entire Navajo Nation Court System operates.[24]

THE RULE ON ADOPTING BILAGÁANA LAW

The solid emphasis on use of Navajo common law in the Navajo Nation courts does not mean that non-Navajo law is excluded or given less importance in Navajo jurisprudence. Just as the structure of the Navajo Nation Court System replicates the Anglo-American court model, state and federal laws have guided many decisions of the Navajo courts.[25] The Navajo Nation Supreme Court, however, has advised caution and careful deliberation before the Navajo Nation courts adopt foreign legal concepts.[26] After the Navajo Nation Council passed the Diné Fundamental Laws in November 2002, the Navajo Nation Supreme Court established a rule on adoption of non-Navajo law, particularly the rule on adoption of *bilagáana* law (Anglo-American law), which requires compatibility of the foreign law with fundamental Navajo values before its application to an issue:

> In the absence of [Navajo] statutory law, we first and foremost consider *Diné Bi Beenaaz´áanii* (Navajo Fundamental Law). We also consider other ways of dealing with a problem, including approaches in *bilagáana* legal thought such as the Restatements when consistent with fundamental Navajo legal principles, particularly in situations involving adopted concepts. (citations and parenthetical information omitted)[27]

The Navajo word for American white people is *bilagáana*, but the rule on adoption of *bilagáana* law would apply to all non-Navajo laws, including those of the states, federal government, other Indian nations, and international laws.

The Navajo Nation Supreme Court in *Goldtooth v. Naa Tsis´Aan Community School, Inc.* found the non-Navajo concept of apparent authority consistent with Navajo values and joined it with the Navajo principle of *naat´áanii* (traditional leader) to rule that the school's executive director, as *naat´áanii*, had apparent authority to bind the principal (the school board) to an employment contract.[28] The Court said the executive director's (as *naat´áanii*) "words carry great weight"; thus, when the director told the employee that his contract was renewed, his words bound the school board, "absent clear

24 The Navajo people are masters of cultural integration—taking foreign concepts, tweaking them with Navajo ingenuity, and making them their own. For example, the Navajo Nation Court System, while modeled on the Anglo-American form of adjudication, uses Navajo common law in its decisions. Another example is the integration of members of other Indian tribes into the Navajo population and giving them clan names.

25 The Navajo Nation Supreme Court, while addressing the issue of whether a New Mexico statute that exempted certain property from execution in state court should be applied by the Navajo Nation courts, stated as follows: "The Navajo judicial system, as is the federal judicial system, is an independent system for administering justice to those who come within its jurisdiction. That being the case, the Navajo Courts ... follow Navajo policies as to how the Navajo Courts should be run. (We do not, as do the federal courts, consider the policy of providing substantially the same outcome as the state courts. Our policy is often to *not* provide the same outcome in order to protect Navajo interests and cultural values)" (citation omitted) (emphasis in original). *Johnson v. Dixon*, 4 Nav. R. 108, 110 (1983).

26 *In re Validation of Marriage of Francisco*, 6 Nav. Rptr. 134, 139–40 (Nav. Sup. Ct. 1989) ("As a sovereign Indian nation that is constantly developing, the Navajo Nation must be forever cautious about state or foreign law infringing on Navajo Nation sovereignty").

27 *Goldtooth v. Naa Tsis´Aan Community School, Inc.*, 8 Nav. Rptr. 682, 691 (Nav. Sup. Ct. 2005).

28 Ibid., 692; see also *Kesoli v. Anderson Security Agency*, 8 Nav. Rptr. 724 (Nav. Sup. Ct. 2005) (a supervisor employed by a private security company is a naat´áanii, so he must be careful with his words; thus, when he "shouted" at subordinates, he committed "harassment" [unprofessional conduct according to company policy], which justified his firing).

guidance from the [school board that the director's] authority was limited."[29] The Supreme Court's use of *naat´áanii* to find a binding contract comes from norms that associate a traditional leader with strong persuasive ability through skilled use of *k´é* values, and whose words the people respect and follow. The Court's finding of a binding employment contract also furthers the goal of returning disputants to harmony (*hózhǫ́*).[30]

The Navajo Nation Supreme Court confirmed that it will consider and "adopt *bilagáana* legal principles, if consistent with fundamental Navajo principles," in *Etsitty v. Diné Bii Association for Disabled Citizens, Inc.*[31] The Court adopted the "control test" in employment law, which the New Mexico courts use to distinguish between employees and independent contractors.[32] The Court added new factors to the "control test" to "foster harmony by honoring the expectations of the parties under the Navajo principle of *k´é*, a consideration absent from *bilagáana* legal thought."[33] The *Goldtooth* and *Etsitty* cases disclose methods that the Navajo courts use to conjoin traditional Navajo and non-Navajo concepts to form new Navajo law that they apply to issues, without losing focus of the ultimate goal of returning parties to harmony.

In a criminal case involving Miranda rights, the Navajo Nation Supreme Court spoke at length about Navajo and non-Navajo statutes containing similar language on similar topics and whether non-Navajo sources should inform interpretation of those Navajo statutes, particularly similar provisions in the Navajo Nation Bill of Rights and the Indian Civil Rights Act:[34]

> In interpreting the Navajo Bill of Rights and the Indian Civil Rights Act, as with other statutes that contain ambiguous language, we first and foremost make sure that such interpretation is consistent with the Fundamental Laws of the Diné. That the Navajo Nation Council explicitly adopts language from outside sources, or that a statute contains similar language, does not, without more, mean the Council intended us to ignore fundamental Diné principles in giving meaning to such provisions. Indeed, Navajo understanding of the English words adopted in statutes may differ from the accepted Anglo understanding. Further, the Indian Civil Rights Act does not require our application of federal interpretations, but only mandates the application of similar language. (citations and parenthetical information omitted) ...
>
> While we are not required to apply federal interpretations, we nonetheless consider them in our analysis. We consider all ways of thinking and possible approaches to a problem, including federal law approaches, and we weigh their underlying values and effects to decide what is best for our people. We have applied federal interpretations,

---

29 *Goldtooth v. Naa Tsis´Aan Community School, Inc.*, 8 Nav. Rptr. 682, 692 (Nav. Sup. Ct. 2005).
30 Ibid., 691.
31 8 Nav. Rptr. 743, 750 (Nav. Sup. Ct. 2005).
32 Ibid., 749–50.
33 Ibid., 750.
34 *Navajo Nation v. Rodriguez*, 8 Nav. Rptr. 604 (Nav. Sup. Ct. 2004). Despite the similarity of language on the right against self-incrimination in the Navajo Nation Bill of Rights and the Indian Civil Rights Act, the Navajo Nation Bill of Rights does not track its federal counterpart. The Navajo Nation Bill of Rights was passed in 1967, and the Indian Civil Rights Act was passed in 1968. If anything, the Navajo Nation Bill of Rights borrows language from the U.S. Bill of Rights.

> but have augmented them with Navajo values, often providing broader rights than that provided in the equivalent federal provision. Our consideration of outside interpretations is especially important for issues involving our modern Navajo government, which includes institutions such as police, jails, and courts that track state and federal government structures not present in traditional Navajo society. (citations and parenthetical information omitted)[35]

After setting forth instructions, the Navajo Nation Supreme Court adopted the minimum requirements of Miranda because it was consistent with Navajo values.[36] The Court identified individual freedom, which prohibits coerced confessions, as one of those values: "Our Navajo Bill of Rights [specifically, the right against self-incrimination], as informed by the Navajo value of individual freedom, prohibits coerced confessions."[37] The Court also identified respect in Navajo relationships as another value. This value requires clear and concise communication so that "the meaning of our words and the effect of our actions based on those words" can be understood.[38] These two values come from the *k'é* doctrine; thus, they require respect and truthfulness in relationships, not only among individuals, but also between Navajo leaders (officials) and the people. For example, the Supreme Court stated that the method the police officer used to coerce a confession, threatening the defendant with a prison term of sixty years and a fine of more than a million dollars, "does not conform with the ways people should interact [in relationships; that is, government official and citizen]."[39]

The Navajo Nation Supreme Court does not require the Navajo trial courts to adopt non-Navajo law wholly even after satisfactory compliance with the rule on adoption of *bilagáana* law. Foreign law can be modified to meet the Navajo cultural context, it can be joined with Navajo common law, or it can guide the process for crafting new law, including setting the extent of its reach. In some cases, non-Navajo law and Navajo common law may synthesize to form new law. The following sections show the Navajo Nation courts at work using Navajo common law and Anglo-American law to create a unique corpus of Navajo law.

PRINCIPLE OF *NAAT'ÁÁH NABIK'ÍYÁTI'* (PARTICIPATORY DEMOCRACY)

The Navajo belief that the people as a whole can make law is consistent with the universal relations doctrine. According to this doctrine, the entire universe is composed of a community of relatives. The Navajos consider all the multifarious elements that compose the universe as basically equal because they compose the web of universal relations; all relations must be in harmony and balance for the universe to be in a state of *hózhǫ́*. Thus, Navajo concepts of equality and

35 Ibid., 613–14.
36 Ibid., 614.
37 Ibid., 613.
38 Ibid., 615. The Court added to Miranda rights the requirement that a standardized "advice of rights" form given to a suspect to sign as a waiver of rights must be explained in detail so that the suspect understands the rights he is waiving. The requirement of clear and concise communication falls within the principle of *íishjání ádoolnííł*, which is discussed after the next section and in *Rough Rock Community School v. Navajo Nation*, 7 Nav. Rptr. 168, 174–75 (Nav. Sup. Ct. 1995).
39 *Navajo Nation v. Rodriguez*, 8 Nav. Rptr. 604, 610, 613, 615–16 (Nav. Sup. Ct. 2004). To buttress its position, the Court also said that "a police badge cannot eliminate an officer's duty to act towards others in compliance with the principles of *hazhó'ógo*." The word *hazhó'ógo*, when applied to contacts between an authority figure and a non-authority figure, suggests that the government official should observe *k'é* rules when dealing with a member of the community.

egalitarianism derive from the belief that harmony and balance sustain the web of universal relations.

The Navajo Nation Supreme Court explained the egalitarian concept, a principle necessary for participatory democracy, within the context of dispute resolution in *Downey v. Bigman*: "One of the major differences between Western principles of adjudication and Navajo legal procedure as participatory democracy is that it is essentially egalitarian. Egalitarianism is the fundamental principle of participatory democracy. The egalitarian principle is the ability of the people as a whole to make law."[40] Thus participatory democracy, from the traditional Navajo view, means that the people have a right to participate equally and fully with their leaders in all processes of government, including discussions leading to consensual decision making and policy making. The traditional Navajo form of government is therefore a pure democracy.

The *Nidáá´* ceremony, which was mentioned earlier in this chapter, under "Kin Giving, Sharing, and Support," provided the perfect forum for participatory democracy at the local level in more traditional days. The public portion of the ceremony provided an open forum so anyone could discuss issues affecting tribe, community, and families. Leaders were summoned to listen to local concerns so they could act on them during Navajo Nation Council sessions. The open forum also provided a perfect opportunity for people to evaluate the effectiveness of locally elected officials and delegates to the Navajo Nation Council. The adoption of Western ways has caused the local open forums provided by major ceremonies to fall into desuetude.

The doctrine of participatory democracy informed Navajo views of political liberty in *Bennett v. Navajo Board of Election Supervisors*,[41] where a candidate for the Office of Navajo Nation President was disqualified for failure to meet the statutory requirement of previous service as an elected Navajo government official or as an employee of a "Navajo tribal organization." While holding the statute void for vagueness, the Navajo Nation Supreme Court identified and discussed values that foster Navajo political liberty, which is part of the doctrine of participatory democracy:

> Navajo *beehaz´aanii* speaks to political liberty, and we apply Navajo common law rather than the Anglo concept of political liberty. In Navajo tradition, government and governing was a matter of the consensus of the people, and Navajos had a participatory democracy. It was, in fact, one of the purest democracies in human history. Long before the United States of America extended the privilege and right to vote to those who did not own property and to women, all Navajos participated in public decisions. Therefore, there is a strong and fundamental tradition that any Navajo can participate in the processes of government, and no person who is not otherwise disqualified by a reasonable law can be prohibited from holding office.[42]

Because participatory democracy underlies the traditional Navajo political system, modern Navajo leaders must continue to uphold its standards to guarantee the Navajo people their fundamental right to participate in decisions affecting their Nation, communities, and

40 7 Nav. Rptr. 176, 177 (Nav. Sup. Ct. 1995).
41 6 Nav. Rptr. 319 (Nav. Sup. Ct. 1990).
42 Ibid., 325.

families. Navajo participatory democracy works because the "talking things out process" allows free-flowing discussion of values and concepts that lead to consensus in an atmosphere of *k´é*. The case of *Rough Rock Community School v. Navajo Nation* demonstrates how participatory democracy works.[43]

In *Rough Rock* the Navajo Nation Supreme Court was asked to decide whether the Education Committee of the Navajo Nation Council had complied with a statutory requirement of "consultation" with local school boards before drafting an apportionment plan for school-board elections. The Court found that the Education Committee had not followed the dictates of *k´é*, which motivate participatory democracy, and thereby had violated the statutory consultation requirement:

> The statutory requirement of "consultation" should have been strictly adhered to since the apportionment plan was being developed for the local schools and the communities they serve. Navajo common law speaks to consultation as giving participants ample freedom to speak, be heard, and opportunity to present written comments. The Navajo doctrine of *k´e* underlies all transactions between and among Navajos, and it likewise frames our view of consultation under the Election Code. Consultation is far more than giving unilateral testimony under oath for a limited number of minutes. It must encompass complete discussion of Navajo values, concepts, and diversity of opinion in an atmosphere of *k´e* (including equality and respect), ultimately leading to a consensual solution. This is the heart of Navajo due process embedded in Navajo participatory democracy. (citation omitted)[44]

Along the same line, the Navajo Nation Supreme Court reminded the Navajo Nation Council of its duty to uphold the standards of participatory democracy in *Judy v. White*,[45] a case concerning a pay increase that the Navajo Nation Council gave itself without first seeking the approval of the Navajo electorate:

> Through time, our traditional form of participatory democracy has given way to non-Navajo formality; this flexibility is necessary to accommodate the ever-changing face of Navajo governance and its attendant complexities. But the acceptance of formality does not circumscribe the absolute right of the Navajo citizen to complain about the manner in which he or she is governed. We have said before that participatory democracy does not come from the non-Navajo, and today we aver that it also does not come from the [Navajo Nation] Council. It comes from a deeper, more profound system of governance: the Navajo People's traditional communal governance. Whether governance occurred at a public meeting place, a windmill, someone's homestead, the final day of a traditional ceremony or at a chapter meeting, the root of that process comes from the Diné Life Way. Our narratives on the Diné Life Way are replete with

43 7 Nav. Rptr. 313 (Nav. Sup. Ct. 1998).
44 Ibid., 317–18.
45 8 Nav. Rptr. 510 (Nav. Sup. Ct. 2004).

> allusions to communal or participatory governance. Nowhere in our life journey narratives is there any indication that one was denied the privilege to speak, nor shunned for asking.[46]

These cases illustrate that Navajo participatory democracy relies on rules that permit free-flowing discourse leading to group consensus in a milieu of *k´é* among participants. The values that create an environment of *k´é* are, of course, respect, kindness, friendliness, cooperation, use of kinship terms, and other positive values that promote free-flowing discussion and consensual decision making. The Navajo Nation Supreme Court summed up well the constituent values of Navajo participatory democracy in *Downey v. Bigman*:

> Navajo participatory democracy guarantees participants their fundamental right to speak on an issue, and discussion continues until the participants reach consensus. In this sense, decisions are a product of agreement among the community rather than a select few. Status, wealth and age are not determinants of whether a person may participate in the decision-making process. Furthermore, no one is pressured to agree to a certain solution, and persuasion, not coercion, is the vehicle for prompting decisions. Participatory democracy is evident throughout many sectors of Navajo society, including government operations, the chapter meeting, and peacemaking.[47]

The rules that facilitate Navajo participatory democracy are "talking things out," persuasion, and consensus. The "talking things out" (*nabik´íyáti´*) and consensus rules merit further elaboration. The "talking things out" rule protects a person's fundamental right to speak freely on an issue and enables discussion until unanimity on solution results. Duties, responsibilities, obligations, relations, and potential solutions to problems are easily identified when participants engage in free-flowing discussion. Consensual solutions and ways to maintain them are also identified during free-flowing discussion. Thus, the "talking things out" and consensus rules work in unison so that dialogue leads to agreed-upon solutions.

Although achieving consensus on a solution does not present much of a problem in peacemaking sessions, it can become difficult to achieve consensus during community meetings (i.e., local chapter governance), especially if the group is quite large and viewpoints are diverse. To prevent stalemates, community members now vote on solutions to community issues after full discussion, with the majority carrying the day. During a peacemaking session, the "talking things out" rule gives all participants an opportunity to speak on every aspect of an issue, which ensures consideration of all arguments, claims, and proposals expressed. Compromise is a necessary element of "talking things out" in peacemaking, and that assures that the views of all participants, especially minority views, are considered equally.

The "talking things out" rule and its related values of persuasion and consensus may appear incompatible with the adversarial process, particularly during the course of a trial, but they work well during settlement negotiations, pretrial

46 Ibid., 531; *Duncan v. Shiprock District Court,* 8 Nav. Rptr. 581, 592–93 (Nav. Sup. Ct. 2004) (community participation in dispute resolution is an exercise in Navajo ways of governance and reinforces Navajo collective identity).

47 7 Nav. Rptr. 176, 177 (Nav. Sup. Ct. 1995); *In re Mental Health Services of Bizardi,* 8 Nav. Rptr. 593, 597 (Nav. Sup. Ct. 2004) ("talking things out" with respect under the doctrine of *k´é* restores parties to *hózhǫ́*).

conferences, sentencing hearings, or postjudgment proceedings. During different stages of trial, the three rules can be used to encourage parties to settle cases, narrow issues, or agree on undisputed facts. The procedural and evidentiary rules that control litigation unfortunately limit "talking things out," because Anglo-American-model court rules are designed to restrict, rather than promote, free-flowing dialogue. The Navajo Nation courts provide an alternative to rigid court proceedings by allowing parties to transfer disputes to the Navajo Peacemaking Division, where problems and solutions can be "talked out" in free-flowing discussion in an environment of *k´é*.

[...]

FREE SPEECH

In *Judy v. White*, the Navajo Nation Supreme Court introduced the traditional Navajo concept of "community free speech" (different from individual free speech), a right inherent in the Diné Life Way (*Diné bi´í´ool´įįł*) and central to the "community voice" concept:

> It is without question that in recognizing and giving formality to the Navajo People's fundamental principles and tenets of the *Diné bi´ó´ool´įįł*, or the Diné Life Way, the Council conceded that despite its statutory pronouncements, there exists a deeper, more profound system of governance. It is abhorrent to the Diné Life Way to violate the right of a community member to speak or to express his or her view or to challenge an injury, whether tangible or intangible. This right is protected to such an extent that the right to speak to an issue ... belongs to the community as a whole, and any member of that community may speak.[107]

The principle of community free speech justified legal standing for the Navajo citizens challenging a resolution passed by the Navajo Nation Council in the *Judy* case. The Supreme Court has not addressed the extent to which the Navajo Nation courts should recognize fundamental "community" rights, but *Judy* shows that the Court acknowledges that such rights exist in Navajo culture. Whether the Navajo Nation courts should also recognize "community" due process, "community" equality, and other "community" rights will be addressed in due time. Moreover, because Navajo philosophy recognizes other "beings" besides human beings, the Navajo Nation Supreme Court will have to address at some point whether nonhuman "beings" have rights that require protection (e.g., do trees have standing and rights under Navajo common law?).

The Navajo Nation Supreme Court addressed the individual right to free speech in *Navajo Nation v. Crockett*,[108] a case that pitted three fired employees against their former employer, a Navajo Nation-owned business enterprise. The enterprise fired the employees after they copied confidential business records without authorization and disclosed them at a meeting of Navajo officials where they also charged enterprise officials with mismanagement and misconduct.[109] The terminated employees sued, alleging, among other theories, that their rights to free speech were violated.[110] The Court held that under the facts of the case, where the employees voiced concerns (similar to whistle-blowing) about job safety, undue Bureau

107 8 Nav. Rptr. 510, 531 (Nav. Sup. Ct. 2004).
108 7 Nav. Rptr. 237 (Nav. Sup. Ct. 1996).
109 Ibid.
110 Ibid., 237–38.

of Indian Affairs interference in contracts, and misconduct and malfeasance by company officials, the employees' rights to free speech were indeed violated.[111] The Supreme Court declared that free speech rights are embedded in Navajo customs and traditions, particularly the *k´é* principle, and then explained how those customs and traditions regulate speech in Navajo society:

> [A]n individual has a fundamental right to express his or her mind by way of the spoken word and/or actions. As a matter of Navajo tradition and custom, people speak with caution and respect, choosing their words carefully to avoid harm to others. This is nothing more than freedom with responsibility, a fundamental Navajo traditional principle ...
>
> Furthermore, speech should be delivered with respect and honesty. This requirement arises from the concept of *k´e*, which is the "glue" that creates and binds relationships between people. To avoid disruptions of relationships, Navajo common law mandates that controversies and arguments be resolved by "talking things out." This process of "talking things out," called *hoozhoojigo*, allows each member of the group to cooperate and talk about how to resolve a problem.[112]

The *hazhó´ógo* principle (freedom with responsibility) substantiates the Supreme Court's assertion in the preceding quotation that, as a matter of Navajo common law, "people speak with caution and respect, choosing their words carefully to avoid harm to others." This statement also describes the "words are powerful" principle. Traditional Navajos believe that knowledge is power—this means that knowledge formed as thought, which is expressed through language (i.e., everyday spoken Navajo, or ceremonial language, or symbols), which in turn is expressed through words or symbols, can be used to coerce, control, destroy, manipulate, or persuade. The process through which the goal is achieved follows this pattern: knowledge precedes thought; thought precedes language; and language precedes words; thus, a word, as the ultimate manifestation of knowledge, is sacred and powerful. The beliefs that "words are sacred" and "words are powerful" (two separate but related concepts) apply especially during a ceremony.

The Navajo Nation Supreme Court applied the principle of "words are sacred" in *Kesoli v. Anderson Security Agency*,[113] an employment termination case involving a supervisor for a private security company who was fired for unprofessional conduct—shouting at his subordinates. The Court held that the supervisor's unprofessional conduct constituted "harassment" and thus satisfied the "just cause" standard for his termination under the Navajo Preference in Employment Act.[114] The supervisor's shouting equated to harassment under Navajo common law because "[w]ords are sacred and never frivolous in Navajo thinking, and are not to be used to offend or intimidate," particularly where the actor is a supervisor or a *naat´áanii* (leader).[115] The Court said a *naat´áanii* has a "responsibility to conduct

111 Ibid., 242.

112 Ibid., 240–41.

113 8 Nav. Rptr. 724 (Nav. Sup. Ct. 2005).

114 Ibid., 729; NPEA, 15 N.N.C. § 604(B)(8) (2005) ("All employers shall not penalize, discipline, discharge nor take any adverse action against any Navajo employee without just cause").

115 *Kesoli v. Anderson Security Agency*, 8 Nav. Rptr. 724, 732 (Nav. Sup. Ct. 2005); *Goldtooth v. Naa Tsis´ Aan Community School, Inc.*, 8 Nav. Rptr. 682 (Nav. Sup. Ct. 2005) (identifying the school's executive director as *naat´áanii*).

himself thoughtfully and carefully with respect for his employees under the principle of *hazhó'ógo*, including utilizing *k'e*" to deal with subordinates.[116] The *Kesoli* case applied the *hazhó'ógo* principle in a nongovernmental context by casting the company official as a *naat'áanii* and then applying the "words are sacred" principle to the supervisor's conduct. Like the police officer in *Navajo Nation v. Rodriguez*,[117] the supervisor should have used *k'é* norms when interacting with subordinates. In addition, because the Court took the *naat'áanii* principle from the political or governing context and applied it to a supervisor in a private employment dispute, it will have to address the extent to which the characteristics demanded of political leaders should be applied to supervisors in the private sector.

The "words are sacred" principle is also used to construe contract terms. In *Office of Navajo Labor Relations, ex rel. Bailon v. Central Consolidated School District No. 22*,[118] the state school district argued that the Navajo Nation waived its right to force it to grant employment preference to Navajo workers in a lease the parties signed that allowed the state to build a school on Navajo lands. The state also argued that it would be in violation of state antidiscrimination laws if it gave employment preference to Navajos. The Navajo Nation Supreme Court had to construe two provisions in the lease to decide the case. In the first provision, the state promised to give employment preference to Navajos without limitation. In the second provision, the state agreed to comply with Navajo law "as long as those [Navajo] laws, regulations, and ordinances do not conflict with state or federal law."[119] The Court used standard contract interpretation rules to hold that the first provision, as the more specific provision, controlled the second general provision. In its analysis, the Court stated that the standard contract interpretation rules were "consistent with the Navajo common law principle that every word is powerful, sacred, and never frivolous. Under this principle, a contracting party cannot give their word in one section and take it back in the next."[120] Thus, when the state gave its explicit promise to grant Navajos employment preference at the school, it could not take its promise back in a subsequent provision that stated general terms.

The Navajo Nation Supreme Court acknowledged that the Navajo people recognize some traditional limitations on the content of speech in *Navajo Nation v. Crockett* when it said certain statements "reciting oral traditions are prohibited during specific times of the year."[121] The most well-known prohibition on speech confines the traditional narratives on the Hero Twins' journey to visit the Father and their subsequent battlefield exploits to the winter season (from the first frost to about the spring equinox). A prohibition on discussing the property of a deceased during the four-day mourning period is also a limitation on the content of speech. In more traditional days, a deceased person could only be spoken of in the past tense. Offensive and sacrilegious words are

116 *Kesoli v. Anderson Security Agency*, 8 Nav. Rptr. 724, 732 (Nav. Sup. Ct. 2005).

117 8 Nav. Rptr. 604 (Nav. Sup. Ct. 2004).

118 8 Nav. Rptr. 501 (Nav. Sup. Ct. 2004). See also *Smith v. Navajo Nation Department of Head Start*, 8 Nav. Rptr. 709, 714–15 (Nav. Sup. Ct. 2005) (words in a contract [a personnel manual] are sacred and never frivolous; thus, a provision in a personnel manual that allows an employer to terminate a worker for her failure to report that she is not coming to work will be enforced). Up to now, the court has not specifically applied the "words are powerful" principle to a legal issue.

119 8 Nav. Rptr. 501, 504 (Nav. Sup. Ct. 2004).

120 Ibid., 505–06.

121 7 Nav. Rptr. 237, 240–41 (Nav. Sup. Ct. 1996).

prohibited within the immediate vicinity or inside the ceremonial hogan during a ceremony.[122] The Supreme Court also declared that traditional control on speech requires "a disgruntled person [to] speak directly with the person's [the person causing the discomfort] relative about his or her concerns before seeking other avenues of redress with strangers."[123] The area of traditional limitations on speech is still in its nascent stage, but in Navajo culture the limitations are usually observed because "words are powerful." The Navajo Nation Supreme Court has not had much opportunity to analyze free speech issues so far. [...]

Study Questions

1. Does the combination of state laws and customary norms always present conflicts that need to be resolved? Or is there a sense in which such combinations might be better understood as in need of management or co-existence? Is such management or co-existence possible?
2. What are some of the merits, and what are some of the limitations, in understanding law purely in terms of the modern sovereign state?
3. Are there particular forms of recognition of Indigenous law that are more appropriate in countries such as Canada and the United States? How can central governments recognize Indigenous legal orders without re-creating relationships of colonization?
4. What are the similarities and differences between Indigenous natural law theories, of the kinds depicted by Borrows and Austin, and the Western natural law theories of St. Thomas Aquinas and John Finnis?

Further Readings

Paul Berman, *Global Legal Pluralism: A Jurisprudence of Law Beyond Borders.* New York: Cambridge UP, 2012.

John Borrows, *Drawing Out Law: A Spirit's Guide.* Toronto: U of Toronto P, 2010.

Glen Sean Coulthard, *Red Skin, White Masks: Rejecting the Colonial Politics of Recognition.* Minneapolis: U of Minnesota P, 2014.

Patricia Monture-Angus, *Journeying Forward: Dreaming First Nations' Independence.* Halifax: Fernwood, 1999.

Leanne Simpson, *Dancing on our Turtle's Back: Stories of Nishnaabeg Re-creation, Resurgence, and a New Emergence.* Winnipeg: Arbeiter Ring, 2011.

122 These four (Hero Twins, deceased's property and identity, and ceremony) traditional limitations on speech come from my personal knowledge of Navajo culture.

123 *Navajo Nation v. Crockett*, 7 Nav. Rptr. 237, 241 (Nav. Sup. Ct. 1996).

Brian Tamanaha, "Understanding Legal Pluralism: Past to Present, Local to Global," *Sydney Law Review* 30 (2008): 375–411.
William Twining, *General Jurisprudence: Understanding Law from a Global Perspective.* Cambridge, UK: Cambridge UP, 2009.

SECTION 6

Law and Individual Liberty

Introduction

The chapters in this section examine legal limits on individual freedoms. We often hear in films or on television that "It's a free country so I'll do what I want," and we may desire a great deal of individual freedom. Yet even a very little experience soon shows that we cannot have both unlimited individual freedom and the benefits of social life. Some freedoms must be limited for the sake of group coordination in the use of some shared resource, as occurs when we all accept the rule that in North America cars are to be driven on the right side of the road. In other situations, it appears that certain limits on individual freedoms are necessary to preserve the good of the group against the few who will not "play fairly" according to the rules of the group, as we see in rules against riding public transportation without paying. And in still other situations, it seems that an individual's freedom must be limited for the sake of the individual, as when, for example, a friend who is seriously emotionally distressed or under the influence of drugs or alcohol asks us to give them the keys to the vehicle they left with us for safekeeping. We are familiar with a wide range of limits on individual freedoms, and the justification for many of these limits is plain to see. But how are we certain that we have arrived at the right balance between individual freedom and social good? And who is to say when we are justified in limiting a person's freedom "for her own good"? The authors of the selections in this chapter offer arguments about the minimum freedoms necessary for a free individual and a good society, and ways to justify limiting individuals' freedoms for their own or their society's good.

1. Mill's On Liberty

This section begins with an excerpt from John Stuart Mill's *On Liberty*. Mill (1806–73) lived at the height of the power of the British Empire, and participated vigorously in the intellectual life of the day. He was educated rigorously at home by his famous father, James Mill, who was known for his own writings and his association with Jeremy Bentham, the social philosopher and advocate of the moral theory called Utilitarianism. Mill grew up in an atmosphere of boisterous debate over contemporary politics and ways to improve society, and he soon became a leading intellectual voice as he entered his adult career of writing, working for the British East India Company, and serving as a Member of Parliament. By the time Mill's *On Liberty* was published in 1859 he was well-established as one of the keenest minds of the day.

The excerpt from *On Liberty* included here focuses on the freedom or liberty of the individual, and the appropriate limits on laws which interfere with liberty. Here we will focus on three elements of that discussion: autonomy, what has been called the "harm principle," and the idea of paternalism. This introduction will not examine the specific freedoms Mill thinks essential to autonomous persons. Those freedoms are so widespread in the law and culture of the Western world that Mill's arguments will likely seem very familiar.

The term "autonomy" is derived from two Ancient Greek words, *auto*, which means "self," and *nomos*, which means "law" or "rule." For a person to be autonomous is to be self-ruling, and your autonomy as a person is your ability to make choices and to carry out those choices in practice. For Mill, preservation of individuals' autonomy is fundamentally important to the best society, in which all or nearly all persons can find happiness through making and carrying out their own life-plans. We need individual freedom, according to Mill, because we find happiness in various ways, and we are not good judges of what will make one another happiest. Nor are we generally good guardians of other persons' best interests. As Mill argues, the individual person "is the person most interested in his well-being: the interest which any other person, except in cases of strong personal attachment, can have in it, is trifling, compared with that which he himself has."[1] Finally, it seems that there is something valuable about the freedom to choose how we wish, as individuals, to live. Simply having the freedom to choose is an important aspect of being an independent human being with a unique personal identity and a unique life-plan—including those plans for new ways of living which run contrary to currently accepted ways of living.

If we recognize the desirability of a society in which all or nearly all persons can find happiness, Mill suggests, we must protect as strongly as possible the freedom of individuals to make and carry out their own life-plans. The only acceptable legal limit on freedom is the requirement that our actions do not harm others—and in this requirement we find the harm principle. Mill supposes that "the only freedom worth the name, is that of pursuing our own good in our own way, so long as we do not attempt to deprive others of theirs, or impede their efforts to obtain it."[2] We are only justified, then, in interfering with others' liberties in order to protect ourselves from their impeding our exercise of our liberties. Mill famously asserts that "The sole end for which mankind are warranted, individually or collectively, in interfering with the liberty of action of any of their number, is self-protection."[3] Whatever else an individual chooses to do is the private concern of that person. We may still criticize persons' private practices, but we may not interfere except when those private practices harm others and in that way are no longer merely private.

When we deny that others know what is really good for them and make decisions on their behalf for their own good, we act in a paternal manner. "Paternalism" is derived from the Latin *pater*, meaning "father," and can be intuitively understood as an excess of the sort of concern parents have for their children. For reasons including the assertion that no one knows better than the individual person what will make that person happy, Mill supposes that paternalistic limits on individual freedom are not justified. We are only justified in limiting freedoms when their use harms others.

The harm principle is very controversial, so it is worth returning to it for a moment to discuss a few of the problems you will see as you progress through the selections in this section. Many critics have suggested that it is not possible to distinguish, as Mill does, between an individual's "self-regarding" actions, whose consequences affect only the individual, and "other-regarding" actions, whose consequences affect others beyond the individual. It is not possible, the critics claim, to simply separate all actions into one of these two categories. An action which initially appears

---

1 *On Liberty*, Chapter IV.
2 *On Liberty*, Chapter I.
3 *On Liberty*, Chapter I.

to be self-regarding may in the longer term have other-regarding consequences, as a person who abuses alcohol may come to depend on the goodwill and resources of others. Other problems arise from the difficulty of explaining precisely what counts as "harm." Clearly, there are harms beyond the obvious physical harms we may suffer at the hands of others. False statements about a person's competence or trustworthiness may harm that person's reputation and ability to make a living. Or, conduct may harm valuable institutions which are not persons, yet may nonetheless be damaged. Finally, and perhaps most controversially, persons exposed to certain false or distorted views may come to believe and act on those false views, with harmful consequences to themselves and others. Yet somewhere among these setbacks to persons and institutions there must be room for what is offensive or distasteful, but not harmful and not reasonably limited by law. Certain art or politicians' speeches may be in stunningly bad taste, yet still part of the ordinary rough-and-tumble of competing ideas in a free society which values diversity and new ideas for improvements in living. Even these few examples show that the idea of "harm" is far more complex than our daily use of the term might reveal.

2. H.L.A. Hart and Lord Devlin on Legal Moralism

If you have read Sections 1 and 2 on the nature of law, you will be aware that the relation between law and morality is a matter of enduring controversy and confusion. One area of controversy is the question of "legal moralism." Roughly, legal moralism concerns whether the law does in fact or ought to enforce moral standards—either the conclusions of moral philosophy or the social norms of a society. The famous Hart-Devlin debate involves questions about the nature and purpose of law, and the nature and role of morality in law.

In Section 2, a brief sketch of H.L.A. Hart was offered, so we will proceed directly to Lord Devlin. Patrick Devlin was a senior judge in England, well known also for his writing in jurisprudence. The debate between Hart and Devlin arose out of Devlin's arguments in a lecture later published as *The Enforcement of Morals*, from which our selection is taken. In his lecture in 1959, Devlin disputed the conclusion of the Wolfenden Report of 1957, which contained the results of a committee investigation into homosexuality and prostitution. The writers of that report recommended to the United Kingdom Parliament that the English law prohibiting homosexual behavior between consenting adults in private should be repealed.[4] According to the writers of the report, such private conduct is not the proper concern of the criminal law. The proper concern of the criminal law is to protect individual citizens. Devlin criticized the findings of the report, and argued for a much different conclusion: the proper concern of the criminal law is to protect society, and that concern may require prohibition of immoral acts, even those carried out in private and with no outward, other-regarding effects. Let us examine more closely some important parts of the reasoning behind Devlin's view, before turning to Hart's response.

2.1 MORALITY IN THE CRIMINAL LAW

According to Devlin, moral purposes may be found in a large number of criminal laws, and this fact is simply a mirror of the further fact that a society requires a shared morality in order to survive. More importantly, the moral purpose of the criminal law is not limited to laws aimed at protecting individuals from other individuals'

4 This debate over homosexuality may seem to be merely a part of ancient history. It is worth considering, however, that significant political groups in the USA, Canada, and the UK vigorously deny the right to freedom from discrimination on the basis of sexual orientation.

conduct. Rather, the criminal law serves to protect certain accepted social values which make up the moral fabric of an enduring society. To illustrate his claim, Devlin points to the legal fact that no one can consent to being murdered. At first glance, it seems to be a very good thing that a murderer cannot defend herself in court by claiming that the victim consented. On the other hand, however, it seems that this rejection of the possibility of consenting to murder does not exist simply to protect prospective murder victims. In many jurisdictions, the legal rejection of the possibility of consenting to murder makes it impossible for terminally ill persons who need help in dying by suicide to receive help. The person who helps will likely be charged and found guilty of murder, regardless of the fact that the "victim" consented to her murder. The law, in rejecting the "consent" defense, may refuse to permit assisted suicide, despite the fact that assisted suicide is self-regarding and may be carried out privately without offense or harm to others. The law, Devlin claims, plainly has the purpose of advancing the moral principle of respect for human life, and will not tolerate immoral lack of respect for human life, even in private, self-regarding conduct. We leave it to you to consider whether Devlin's argument is supported or weakened by the fact that the law in some jurisdictions such as Canada now permits medical assistance in dying.

2.2 MORALITY AND PRESERVATION OF SOCIETY

Devlin argues that a society requires agreement on moral values. As Devlin puts it, "... society means a community of ideas; without shared ideas on politics, morals, and ethics, no society can exist." If a society comes to lack shared acceptance of a group of ideas, that society will not survive. Devlin explains, "If men and women try to create a society in which there is no fundamental agreement about good and evil they will fail; if, having based it on common agreement, the agreement goes, the society will disintegrate."[5] Unfortunately, Devlin does not point to any examples of a society disintegrating under the weight of disagreement about what is good and evil, but the general thread of his argument can still be understood: societies need morality if they are to avoid chaos. Yet, as you will see in Hart's criticisms, Devlin's argument appears to be incomplete. He does not specify clearly just what a society is. Nor does he explain how a change in public morality can be tolerated by a system which requires agreement in order to survive.

2.3 WHAT MORALITY SHOULD THE CRIMINAL LAW ENFORCE?

Devlin offers an account of morality which diverges significantly from what you may have learned in a course in moral philosophy. According to Devlin, the public morality of England is composed of its Christian heritage, and the standard of the "reasonable man" or "right minded man" as developed by the courts. What is morally right or morally wrong, for the purposes of the courts, is what the reasonable man, in England, views as morally right or morally wrong.

Devlin accepts without question the historical role of the established church in the formation of English morality. By "established church" Devlin means the Church of England, also called the Anglican Church, tied constitutionally to the government of England. This situation is unfamiliar to the context of Canadian and American law where separation of church and state is more clearly drawn. Yet Devlin's view need not be rejected in Canada and the USA simply because the church does not play the same role in public life. Devlin simply points to the church as a source of moral values, and Christian moral views are very often used in the same way in Canada and the USA, as

5 "Morals and the Criminal Law."

standards for criticism and evaluation. Given this understanding of the historical and contemporary importance of Christian values in Canada and the USA, Devlin's assertion that the law needs the church may be understood as the claim that the law needs some set of accepted moral values as its underpinning. Devlin argues that "... the law must base itself on Christian morals and to the limit of its ability enforce them, not simply because they are the morals which are taught by the established Church—on these points the law recognizes the right to dissent—but for the compelling reason that without the help of Christian teaching the law will fail."[6]

We may now assemble the full train of Devlin's argument against repeal of the law prohibiting homosexual activities conducted in private between consenting adults. The criminal law is and has long been concerned to enforce the moral standards which must be maintained if English society is to survive. For better or for worse, English society and the historical interpretation of Christian values has resulted in a public morality which feels repugnance toward the very idea of homosexual activities—even those activities conducted in private between consenting adults. Even an atheist who rejects the existence of the Christian God may recognize that this view is in fact held in England, and the atheist may also recognize that this view is part of the moral fabric which binds English society. Homosexual activities are therefore justifiably made illegal, according to Devlin, because they are a threat to the public morality which preserves English society, and they are the sort of activities which are properly controlled by law.

3. Hart's Response

Let us turn now to Hart's criticism of Devlin. In *Law, Liberty and Morality*, the short book from which our excerpt is taken, Hart challenges the arguments of Lord Devlin and a famous judge and writer of the Victorian era, James Fitzjames Stephen. This introduction and our excerpt will not be concerned with Stephen's arguments, since the core of the debate is between Hart and Devlin.

3.1 MORAL CRITICISM OF SOCIAL INSTITUTIONS

Hart's main dispute with Devlin concerns Devlin's claim that a society is justified in taking whatever measures are required for its continued existence. Yet, Hart argues, it is surely still possible to argue that certain societies pursue such horrible goals that it is better for that society to collapse. It seems, then, that the activity in which Devlin participates as he offers his argument is an activity at two levels: an argument about the measures the society of England ought to take to preserve itself, and an argument that preservation of a society is a worthwhile goal. Devlin has begun a legitimate critical activity which Hart may join on the same basis: on the assumption that it is possible to reason about the nature and limits of the steps societies ought to take to govern themselves.

The nature of this critical activity can be explained further by Hart's distinction between "positive" morality, "the morality actually accepted and shared by a given social group," and "critical" morality, the "general moral principles used in the criticism of actual social institutions including positive morality." In our common activity of critical discussion of social institutions such as law, we readily understand the difference between the social norms of some group and what on reflection we suppose are the standards by which that group's norms may be evaluated. We understand, for example, that North American social standards or "positive morality" regarding premarital sex have changed dramatically between 1950 and now. We use standards

6 "Morals and the Criminal Law."

of critical morality when we discuss whether these changes reflect a general worsening of moral character among North Americans, or perhaps instead a badly needed loosening of misguided restrictions.

3.2 JUSTIFYING LEGAL MORALISM

What does reasoning according to the standards of critical morality have to do with legal enforcement of morality? According to Hart, the legal moralism Devlin proposes needs to be carefully justified, because it proposes to punish certain conduct with a variety of significant punishments, and because it limits freedom of choice and the happiness which freedom of choice has the potential to produce. As Hart explains, "This is of particular importance in the case of laws enforcing a sexual morality. They may create misery of a quite special degree ... [since] suppression of sexual impulses generally is something which affects the development or balances of the individual's emotional life, happiness, and personality."[7] If Devlin proposes such miserable penalties against immoral behavior, Devlin must show that this behavior really is so seriously wrong as to justify the harshness of the proposed punishments.

3.3 MORAL PURPOSES IN THE CRIMINAL LAW

Devlin argues that it is justifiable to prohibit and punish even private, self-regarding immorality, on the grounds that it threatens the fabric of society. And he asserts that the law already contains measures whose only purpose is to enforce a moral principle. An important part of Hart's argument disputes this assertion. It is an error, Hart supposes, to think that laws such as those prohibiting the possibility of consenting to one's own murder can only be understood as enforcing a moral principle (perhaps the principle of respect for life). It is more plausible to understand such laws as instances of paternalism, where individuals are protected against themselves and their weaknesses as human beings. Regardless of whether such paternalism is good or bad, paternalism itself is quite different from enforcement of a particular principle of morality. Devlin's assertion that the criminal law serves only to enforce moral principles seems to be an exaggeration, since many laws which appear to involve enforcement of moral principles are in fact instances of paternalism or legal advancement of other goals.

3.4 SHARED MORALITY AND SOCIETY

Finally, let us consider Hart's criticism of Devlin's idea that a society requires a shared morality for survival, and is justified in prohibiting even private conduct which weakens that shared morality. Hart observes that Devlin provides little evidence that a society tends to be worse off when private, self-regarding conduct strays from that society's positive morality. In particular, Hart claims, tolerance of homosexual activity conducted in private between consenting adults does not seem to have led to a moral breakdown in those European societies which tolerate it. Further, Hart claims, there are problems with Devlin's understanding of the idea of "society" as meaning "a group whose members hold in common a shared morality." If a society is simply a shared morality, Devlin cannot explain shifts in a society's morality without also admitting that the original society has changed and has been replaced by a new society corresponding to the changed morality. Yet this view runs contrary to our ordinary observation that a society may remain the same society despite changes in its positive morality.

Let us sum up Hart's argument. Devlin has failed to distinguish between positive and critical morality, and has left open the possibility that a society might be justified in following standards

7 *Law, Liberty and Morality.*

of morality which are terribly immoral according to the standards of critical morality. Such a society might inflict painful punishment on persons whose actions are seen to be immoral yet are plainly self-regarding. Contrary to Devlin's assertion that English criminal law enforces moral principles of this sort in order to preserve English society, such criminal laws seem to serve other purposes, such as paternalistic intervention to protect persons from themselves. Finally, tolerance of activities Devlin construes as immoral does not seem to lead to moral chaos of the sort Devlin predicts.

What is the end of this debate? It is not easy to see whether Hart or Devlin won. Devlin's argument has likely not survived Hart's criticisms without a scratch. Nor, however, has Hart offered a complete defense of Mill's distinction between other-regarding action which is justifiably limited by law, and self-regarding action which is properly the private business of individual persons and no one else. The problems Hart and Devlin engage are sufficiently complex that it is very difficult to determine what an acceptable final solution might consist of. Yet these problems *require* that we at least attempt to provide answers if we are to avoid mistaken toleration or unjustified punishment of persons for what they really ought to be free to do.

18

John Stuart Mill

from *On Liberty*

The object of this Essay is to assert one very simple principle, as entitled to govern absolutely the dealings of society with the individual in the way of compulsion and control, whether the means used be physical force in the form of legal penalties, or the moral coercion of public opinion. That principle is, that the sole end for which mankind are warranted, individually or collectively, in interfering with the liberty of action of any of their number, is self-protection. That the only purpose for which power can be rightfully exercised over any member of a civilized community, against his will, is to prevent harm to others. His own good, either physical or moral, is not a sufficient warrant. He cannot rightfully be compelled to do or forbear because it will be better for him to do so, because it will make him happier, because, in the opinions of others, to do so would be wise, or even right. These are good reasons for remonstrating with him, or reasoning with him, or persuading him, or entreating him, but not for compelling him, or visiting him with any evil in case he do otherwise. To justify that, the conduct from which it is desired to deter him, must be calculated to produce evil to some one else. The only part of the conduct of any one, for which he is amenable to society, is that which concerns others. In the part which merely concerns himself, his independence is, of right, absolute. Over himself, over his own body and mind, the individual is sovereign.

It is, perhaps, hardly necessary to say that this doctrine is meant to apply only to human beings in the maturity of their faculties. We are not speaking of children, or of young persons below the age which the law may fix as that of manhood or womanhood. Those who are still in a state to require being taken care of by others, must be protected against their own actions as well as against external injury. For the same reason, we may leave out of consideration those backward states of society in which the race itself may be considered as in its nonage. The early difficulties in the way of spontaneous progress are so great, that there is seldom any choice of means for overcoming them; and a ruler full of the spirit of improvement is warranted in the use of any expedients that will attain an end, perhaps otherwise unattainable. Despotism is a legitimate mode of government in dealing with barbarians, provided the end be their improvement, and the means justified by actually effecting that end. Liberty, as a principle, has no application to any state of things anterior to the time when mankind have become capable of being improved by free and equal discussion. Until then, there is nothing for them but implicit obedience to an Akbar or a Charlemagne, if they are so fortunate as to find one. But as soon as mankind have attained the capacity of being guided to their own improvement by conviction or persuasion (a period long since reached in all nations with whom we need here concern ourselves), compulsion, either in the direct form or in that of pains and penalties for non-compliance, is no longer admissible as a means to their own good, and justifiable only for the security of others.

It is proper to state that I forgo any advantage which could be derived to my argument from the idea of abstract right, as a thing independent of utility. I regard utility as the ultimate appeal on all ethical questions; but it must be utility in the largest sense, grounded on the permanent interests of man as a progressive being. Those interests, I contend, authorize the subjection of individual spontaneity to external control, only in respect to those actions of each, which concern the interest of other people. If any one does an act hurtful to others, there is a prima facie case for punishing him, by law, or, where legal penalties are not safely applicable, by general disapprobation. There are also many positive acts for the benefit of others, which he may rightfully be compelled to perform; such as, to give evidence in a court of justice; to bear his fair share in the common defence, or in any other joint work necessary to the interest of the society of which he enjoys the protection; and to perform certain acts of individual beneficence, such as saving a fellow creature's life or interposing to protect the defenceless against ill-usage, things which whenever it is obviously a man's duty to do, he may rightfully be made responsible to society for not doing. A person may cause evil to others not only by his actions but by his inaction, and in either case he is justly accountable to them for the injury. The latter case, it is true, requires a much more cautious exercise of compulsion than the former. To make any one answerable for doing evil to others, is the rule; to make him answerable for not preventing evil, is, comparatively speaking, the exception. Yet there are many cases clear enough and grave enough to justify that exception. In all things which regard the external relations of the individual, he is *de jure* amenable to those whose interests are concerned, and if need be, to society as their protector. There are often good reasons for not holding him to the responsibility; but these reasons must arise from the special expediencies of the case: either because it is a kind of case in which he is on the whole likely to act better, when left to his own discretion, than when controlled in any way in which society have it in their power to control him; or because the attempt to exercise control would produce other evils, greater than those which it would prevent. When such reasons as these preclude the enforcement of responsibility, the conscience of the agent himself should step into the vacant judgement-seat, and protect those interests of others which have no external protection; judging himself all the more rigidly, because the case does not admit of his being made accountable to the judgement of his fellow creatures.

But there is a sphere of action in which society, as distinguished from the individual, has, if any, only an indirect interest; comprehending all that portion of a person's life and conduct which affects only himself, or if it also affects others, only with their free, voluntary, and undeceived consent and participation. When I say only himself, I mean directly, and in the first instance: for whatever affects himself, may affect others through himself; and the objection which may be grounded on this contingency will receive consideration in the sequel. This, then, is the appropriate region of human liberty. It comprises, first, the inward domain of consciousness; demanding liberty of conscience, in the most comprehensive sense; liberty of thought and feeling; absolute freedom of opinion and sentiment on all subjects, practical or speculative, scientific, moral, or theological. The liberty of expressing and publishing opinions may seem to fall under a different principle, since it belongs to that part of the conduct of an individual which concerns other people; but, being almost of as much importance as the liberty of thought itself, and resting in great part on the same reasons, is practically inseparable from it. Secondly, the principle requires liberty of tastes and pursuits; of framing the plan of our life to suit our own character; of doing as we like, subject to such consequences as may follow: without impediment from our fellow creatures, so long as what we do does not harm them, even though they should think our conduct foolish, perverse, or wrong. Thirdly, from this liberty of each individual, follows the liberty, within the same limits, of combination among individuals; freedom to unite, for any purpose not involving harm to others: the persons combining being supposed to be of full age, and not forced or deceived.

No society in which these liberties are not, on the whole, respected, is free, whatever may be its form of government and none is completely free in which they do not exist absolute and unqualified. The only freedom which deserves the name, is that of pursuing our own good in our own way, so long as we do not attempt to deprive others of theirs, or impede their efforts to obtain it. Each is the proper guardian of his own health, whether bodily, or mental and spiritual. Mankind are greater gainers by suffering each other to live as seems good to themselves, than by compelling each to live as seems good to the rest.

...

Of the Limits to the Authority of Society Over the Individual

What, then, is the rightful limit to the sovereignty of the individual over himself? Where does the authority of society begin? How much of human life should be assigned to individuality, and how much to society?

Each will receive its proper share, if each has that which more particularly concerns it. To individuality should belong the part of life in which it is chiefly the individual that is interested; to society, the part which chiefly interests society.

Though society is not founded on a contract, and though no good purpose is answered by inventing a contract in order to deduce social obligations from it, every one who receives the protection of society owes a return for the benefit, and the fact of living in society renders it indispensable that each should be bound to observe a certain line of conduct towards the rest. This conduct consists, first, in not injuring the interests of one another; or rather certain interests, which, either by express legal provision or by tacit understanding, ought to be considered as rights; and secondly, in each person's bearing his share (to be fixed on some equitable principle) of the labours and sacrifices incurred for defending the society or its members from injury and molestation. These conditions society is justified in enforcing at all costs to those who endeavour to withhold fulfilment. Nor is this all that society may do. The acts of an individual may be hurtful to others, or wanting in due consideration for their welfare, without going the length of violating any of their constituted rights. The offender may then be justly punished by opinion, though not by law. As soon as any part of a person's conduct affects prejudicially the interests of others, society has jurisdiction over it, and the question whether the general welfare will or will not be promoted by interfering with it, becomes open to discussion. But there is no room for entertaining any such question when a person's conduct affects the interests of no persons besides himself, or needs not affect them unless they like (all the persons concerned being of full age, and the ordinary amount of understanding). In all such cases there should be perfect freedom, legal and social, to do the action and stand the consequences.

It would be a great misunderstanding of this doctrine to suppose that it is one of selfish indifference, which pretends that human beings have no business with each other's conduct in life, and that they should not concern themselves about the well-doing or well-being of one another, unless their own interest is involved. Instead of any diminution, there is need of a great increase of disinterested exertion to promote the good of others. But disinterested benevolence can find other instruments to persuade people to their good, than whips and scourges, either of the literal or the metaphorical sort. I am the last person to undervalue the self-regarding virtues; they are only second in importance, if even second, to the social. It is equally the business of education to cultivate both. But even education works by conviction and persuasion as well as by compulsion, and it is by the former only that, when the period of education is past, the self-regarding virtues should be inculcated. Human beings owe to each other help to distinguish the better from the worse, and encouragement to choose the former and avoid the latter. They should be for ever stimulating each other to increased exercise of their higher faculties, and increased direction of their feelings and aims towards wise instead of foolish, elevating instead of degrading, objects and contemplations. But neither one person, nor any number of persons, is warranted in saying to another human creature of ripe years, that he shall not do with his life for his own benefit what he chooses to do with it. He is the person most interested in his own well-being: the interest which any other person, except in cases of strong personal attachment, can have in it, is trifling, compared with that which he himself has; the interest which society has in him individually (except as to his conduct to others) is fractional, and altogether indirect: while, with respect to his own feelings and circumstances, the most ordinary man or woman has means of knowledge immeasurably surpassing those that can be possessed by any one else. The interference of society to overrule his judgement and purposes in what only regards himself, must be grounded on general presumptions; which may be altogether wrong, and even if right, are as likely as not to be misapplied to individual cases, by persons no better acquainted with the circumstances of such cases than those are who look at them merely from without. In this department, therefore, of human affairs, individuality has its proper field of action. In the conduct of human beings towards one another, it is necessary that general rules should for the most part be observed, in order that people may know what they have to expect; but in each person's own concerns, his individual spontaneity is entitled to free exercise. Considerations to aid his judgement, exhortations to strengthen his will, may be offered to him, even obtruded on him, by others but he himself is the final judge. All errors which he is likely to commit against advice and warning, are far outweighed by the evil of allowing others to constrain him to what they deem his good.

I do not mean that the feelings with which a person is regarded by others, ought not to be in any way affected by his self-regarding qualities or deficiencies. This is neither possible nor desirable. If he is eminent in any of the qualities which conduce to his own good he is, so far, a proper object of admiration. He is much the nearer to the ideal perfection of human nature. If he is grossly deficient in those qualities a sentiment the opposite of admiration will follow. There is a degree of folly, and a degree of what may be called (though the phrase is not unobjectionable) lowness or depravation of taste, which, though it cannot justify doing harm to the person who manifests it, renders him necessarily and properly a subject of distaste, or, in extreme cases, even of contempt: a person could not have the opposite qualities in due strength without entertaining these feelings. Though doing no wrong to any one, a person may so act as to compel us to judge him, and feel to him, as a fool, or as a being of an inferior order: and since this judgement and feeling are a fact which he would prefer to avoid, it is doing him a service to warn him of it beforehand, as of any other disagreeable consequence to which he exposes himself. It would be well, indeed, if this good office were much more freely rendered than the common notions of politeness at present permit, and if one person could honestly point out to another that he thinks him in fault, without being considered unmannerly or presuming. We have a right, also, in various ways, to act upon our unfavourable opinion of any one, not to the oppression of his individuality, but in the exercise of ours. We are not bound, for example, to seek his society; we have a right to avoid it (though not to parade the avoidance), for we have a right to choose the society most acceptable to us. We have a right, and it may be our duty, to caution others against him, if we think his example or conversation likely to have a pernicious effect on those with whom he associates. We may give others a preference over him in optional good offices, except those which tend to his improvement. In these various modes a person may suffer very severe penalties at the hands of others, for faults which directly concern only himself; but he suffers these penalties only in so far as they are the natural, and, as it were, the spontaneous consequences of the faults themselves, not because they are purposely inflicted on him for the sake of punishment. A person who shows rashness, obstinacy, self-conceit—who cannot live within moderate means—who cannot restrain himself from hurtful indulgences—who pursues animal pleasures at the expense of those of feeling and intellect—must expect to be lowered in the opinion of others, and to have a less share of their favourable sentiments; but of this he has no right to complain, unless he has merited their favour by special excellence in his social relations, and has thus established a title to their good offices, which is not affected by his demerits towards himself.

What I contend for is, that the inconveniences which are strictly inseparable from the unfavourable judgement of others, are the only ones to which a person should ever be subjected for that portion of his conduct and character which concerns his own good, but which does not affect the interests of others in their relations with him. Acts injurious to others require a totally different treatment. Encroachment on their rights; infliction on them of any loss or damage not justified by his own rights; falsehood or duplicity in dealing with them; unfair or ungenerous use of advantages over them; even selfish abstinence from defending them against injury—these are fit objects of moral reprobation, and, in grave cases, of moral retribution and punishment. And not only these acts, but the dispositions which lead to them, are properly immoral, and fit subjects of disapprobation which may rise to abhorrence. Cruelty of disposition; malice and ill nature; that most anti-social and odious of all passions, envy; dissimulation and insincerity; irascibility on insufficient cause, and resentment disproportioned to the provocation; the love of domineering over others; the desire to engross more than one's share of advantages (the *pleonexia* of the Greeks); the pride which derives gratification from the abasement of others; the egotism which thinks self and its concerns more important than everything else, and decides all doubtful questions in its own favour; these are moral vices, and constitute a bad and odious moral character: unlike the self-regarding faults previously mentioned, which are not properly immoralities, and to whatever pitch they may be carried do not constitute wickedness. They may be proofs of any amount of folly, or want of personal dignity and self-respect; but they are only a subject of moral reprobation when they involve a breach of duty to others, for whose sake the individual is bound to have care for himself. What are called duties to ourselves are not socially obligatory, unless circumstances render them at the same time duties to others. The term duty to oneself, when it means any thing more than prudence, means self-respect or self-development; and for none of these is any one accountable to his fellow creatures, because for none of them is it for the good of mankind that he be held accountable to them.

The distinction between the loss of consideration which a person may rightly incur by defect of prudence or of personal dignity, and the reprobation which is due to him for an offence against the rights of others, is not a merely nominal distinction. It makes a vast difference both in our feelings and in our conduct towards him, whether he displeases us in things in which we think we have a right to control him, or in things in which we know that we have not. If he displeases us, we may express our distaste, and we may stand aloof from a person as well as from a thing that displeases us; but we shall not therefore feel called on to make his life uncomfortable. We shall reflect that he already bears, or will bear, the whole penalty of his error; if he spoils his life by mismanagement, we shall not, for that reason, desire to spoil it still further: instead of wishing to punish him, we shall rather endeavour to alleviate his punishment, by showing him how he may avoid or cure the evils his conduct tends to bring upon him. He may be to us an object of pity, perhaps of dislike, but not of anger or resentment; we shall not treat him like an enemy of society: the worst we shall think ourselves justified in doing is leaving him to himself, if we do not interfere benevolently by showing interest or concern for him. It is far otherwise if he has infringed the rules necessary for the protection of his fellow creatures, individually or collectively. The evil consequences of his acts do not then fall on himself, but on others; and society, as the protector of all its members, must retaliate on him; must inflict pain on him for the express purpose of punishment, and must take care that it be sufficiently severe. In the one case, he is an offender at our bar, and we are called on not only to sit in judgement on him, but, in one shape or another, to execute our own sentence; in the other case, it is not our part to inflict any suffering on him, except what may incidentally follow from our using the same liberty in the regulation of our own affairs, which we allow to him in his.

The distinction here pointed out between the part of a person's life which concerns only himself, and that which concerns others, many persons will refuse to admit. How (it may be asked) can any part of the conduct of a member of society be a matter of indifference to the other members? No person is an entirely isolated being; it is impossible for a person to do anything seriously or permanently hurtful to himself, without mischief reaching at least to his near connexions, and often far beyond them. If he injures his property, he does harm to those who directly or indirectly derived support from it, and usually diminishes, by a greater or less amount, the general resources of the community. If he deteriorates his bodily or mental faculties, he not only brings evil upon all who depended on him for any portion of their happiness, but disqualifies himself for rendering the services which he owes to his fellow creatures generally; perhaps becomes a burden on their affection or benevolence; and if such conduct were very frequent, hardly any offence that is committed would detract more from the general sum of good. Finally, if by his vices or follies a person does no direct harm to others, he is nevertheless (it may be said) injurious by his example; and ought to be compelled to control himself, for the sake of those whom the sight or knowledge of his conduct might corrupt or mislead.

And even (it will be added) if the consequences of misconduct could be confined to the vicious or thoughtless individual, ought society to abandon to their own guidance those who are manifestly unfit for it? If protection against themselves is confessedly due to children and persons under age, is not society equally bound to afford it to persons of mature years who are equally incapable of self-government? If gambling, or drunkenness, or incontinence, or idleness, or uncleanliness, are as injurious to happiness, and as great a hindrance to improvement, as many or most of the acts prohibited by law, why (it may be asked) should not law, so far as is consistent with practicability and social convenience, endeavour to repress these also? And as a supplement to the unavoidable imperfections of law, ought not opinion at least to organize a powerful police against those vices, and visit rigidly with social penalties those who are known to practise them? There is no question here (it may be said) about restricting individuality, or impeding the trial of new and original experiments in living. The only things it is sought to prevent are things which have been tried and condemned from the beginning of the world until now; things which experience has shown not to be useful or suitable to any person's individuality. There must be some length of time and amount of experience, after which a moral or prudential truth may be regarded as established: and it is merely desired to prevent generation after generation from falling over the same precipice which has been fatal to their predecessors.

I fully admit that the mischief which a person does to himself may seriously affect, both through their sympathies and their interests, those nearly connected with him, and in a minor degree, society at large. When, by conduct of this sort, a person is led to violate a distinct and assignable obligation to any other person or persons, the case is taken out of the self-regarding class, and becomes amenable to moral disapprobation in the proven sense of the term. If, for example, a man, through intemperance or extravagance, becomes unable to pay his debts, or, having undertaken the moral responsibility of a family, becomes from the same cause incapable of supporting or educating them, he is deservedly reprobated, and might be justly punished; but it is for the breach of duty to his family or creditors, not for the extravagance. If the resources which ought to have been devoted to them had been diverted from them for the most prudent investment, the moral culpability would have been the same. George Barnwell murdered his uncle to get money for his mistress, but if he had done it to set himself up in business, he would equally have been hanged. Again, in the frequent case of a man who causes grief to his family by addiction to bad habits, he deserves reproach for his unkindness or ingratitude; but so he may for cultivating habits not in themselves vicious, if they are painful to those with whom he passes his life, or who from personal ties are dependent on him for their comfort. Whoever fails in the consideration generally due to the interests and feelings of others, not being compelled by some more imperative duty, or justified by allowable self-preference, is a subject of moral disapprobation for that failure, but not for the cause of it, nor for the errors, merely personal to himself, which may have remotely led to it. In like manner, when a person disables himself, by conduct purely self-regarding, from the performance of some definite duty incumbent on him to the public, he is guilty of a social offence. No person ought to be punished simply for being drunk; but a soldier or a policeman should be punished for being drunk on duty. Whenever, in short, there is a definite damage, or a definite risk of damage, either to an individual or to the public, the case is taken out of the province of liberty, and placed in that of morality or law.

But with regard to the merely contingent, or, as it may be called, constructive, injury which a person causes to society, by conduct which neither violates any specific duty to the public, nor occasions perceptible hurt to any assignable individual except himself; the inconvenience is one which society can afford to bear, for the sake of the greater good of human freedom. If grown persons are to be punished for not taking proper care of themselves, I would rather it were for their own sake, than under pretence of preventing them from impairing their capacity of rendering to society benefits which society does not pretend it has a right to exact. But I cannot consent to argue the point as if society had no means of bringing its weaker members up to its ordinary standard of rational conduct, except waiting till they do something irrational, and then punishing them, legally or morally, for it. Society has had absolute power over them during all the early portion of their existence: it has had the whole period of childhood and nonage in which to try whether it could make them capable of rational conduct in life. The existing generation is master both of the training and the entire circumstances of the generation to come; it cannot indeed make them perfectly wise and good, because it is itself so lamentably deficient in goodness and wisdom; and its best efforts are not always, in individual cases, its most successful ones; but it is perfectly well able to make the rising generation, as a whole, as good as, and a little better than, itself. If society lets any considerable number of its members grow up mere children, incapable of being acted on by rational consideration of distant motives, society has itself to blame for the consequences. Armed not only with all the powers of education, but with the ascendancy which the authority of a received opinion always exercises over the minds who are least fitted to judge for themselves; and aided by the *natural* penalties which cannot be prevented from falling on those who incur the distaste or the contempt of those who know them; let not society pretend that it needs, besides all this, the power to issue commands and enforce obedience in the personal concerns of individuals, in which, on all principles of justice and policy, the decision ought to rest with those who are to abide the consequences. Nor is there anything which tends more to discredit and frustrate the better means of influencing conduct, than a resort to the worse. If there be among those whom it is attempted to coerce into prudence or temperance, any of the material of which vigorous and independent characters are made, they will infallibly rebel against the yoke. No such person will ever feel that others have a right to control him in his concerns, such as they have to prevent him from injuring them in theirs; and it easily comes to be considered a mark of spirit and courage to fly in the face of such usurped authority, and do with ostentation the exact opposite of what it enjoins; as in the fashion of grossness which succeeded, in the time of Charles II, to the fanatical moral intolerance of the Puritans. With respect to what is said of the necessity of protecting society from the bad example set to others by the vicious or the self-indulgent; it is true that bad example may have a pernicious effect, especially the example of doing wrong to others with impunity to the wrong-doer. But we are now speaking of conduct which, while it does no wrong to others, is supposed to do great harm to the agent himself: and I do not see how those who believe this, can think otherwise than that the example, on the whole, must be more salutary than hurtful, since, if it displays the misconduct, it displays also the painful or degrading consequences which, if the conduct is justly censured, must be supposed to be in all or most cases attendant on it.

But the strongest of all the arguments against the interference of the public with purely personal conduct, is that when it does interfere, the odds are that it interferes wrongly, and in the wrong place. On questions of social morality, of duty to others, the opinion of the public, that is, of an overruling majority, though often wrong, is likely to be still oftener right; because on such questions they are only required to judge of their own interests; of the manner in which some mode of conduct, if allowed to be practised, would affect themselves. But the opinion of a similar majority, imposed as a law on the minority, on questions of self-regarding conduct, is quite as likely to be wrong as right; for in these cases public opinion means, at the best, some people's opinion of what is good or bad for other people while very often it does not even mean that; the public, with the most perfect indifference, passing over the pleasure or convenience of those whose conduct they censure, and considering only their own preference. There are many who consider as an injury to themselves any conduct which they have a distaste for, and resent it as an outrage to their feelings; as a religious bigot, when charged with disregarding the religious feelings of others, has been known to retort that they disregard his feelings, by persisting in their abominable worship or creed. But there is no parity between the feeling of a person for his own opinion, and the feeling of another who is offended at his holding it; no more than between the desire of a thief to take a purse, and the desire of the right owner to keep it. And a person's taste is as much his own peculiar concern as his opinion or his purse. It is easy for any one to imagine an ideal public, which leaves the freedom and choice of individuals in all uncertain matters undisturbed, and only requires them to abstain from modes of conduct which universal experience has condemned. But where has there been seen a public which set any such limit to its censorship? Or when does the public trouble itself about universal experience? In its interferences with personal conduct it is seldom thinking of anything but the enormity of acting or feeling differently from itself; and this standard of judgement, thinly disguised, is held up to mankind as the dictate of religion and philosophy, by nine-tenths of all moralists and speculative writers. These teach that things are right because they are right; because we feel them to be so. They tell us to search in our own minds and hearts for laws of conduct binding on ourselves and on all others. What can the poor public do but apply these instructions, and make their own personal feelings of good and evil, if they are tolerably unanimous in them, obligatory on all the world?

The evil here pointed out is not one which exists only in theory; and it may perhaps be expected that I should specify the instances in which the public of this age and country improperly invests its own preferences with the character of moral laws. I am not writing an essay on the aberrations of existing moral feeling. That is too weighty a subject to be discussed parenthetically, and by way of illustration. Yet examples are necessary, to show that the principle I maintain is of serious and practical moment, and that I am not endeavouring to erect a barrier against imaginary evils. And it is not difficult to show, by abundant instances, that to extend the bounds of what may be called moral police, until it encroaches on the most unquestionably legitimate liberty of the individual, is one of the most universal of all human propensities.

As a first instance, consider the antipathies which men cherish on no better grounds than that persons whose religious opinions are different from theirs, do not practise their religious observances, especially their religious abstinences. To cite a rather trivial example, nothing in the creed or practice of Christians does more to envenom the hatred of Mohammedans against them, than the fact of their eating pork. There are few acts which Christians and Europeans regard with more unaffected disgust, than Mussulmans regard this particular mode of satisfying hunger. It is, in the first place, an offence against their religion; but this circumstance by no means explains either the degree or the kind of their repugnance; for wine also is forbidden by their religion, and to partake of it is by all Mussulmans accounted wrong, but not disgusting. Their aversion to the flesh of the "unclean beast" is, on the contrary, of that peculiar character, resembling an instinctive antipathy, which the idea of uncleanliness, when once it thoroughly sinks into the feelings, seems always to excite even in those whose personal habits are anything but scrupulously cleanly, and of which the sentiment of religious impurity, so intense in the Hindoos, is a remarkable example. Suppose now that in a people, of whom the majority were Mussulmans, that majority should insist upon not permitting pork to be eaten within the limits of the country. This would be nothing new in Mohammedan countries.[8] Would it be a legitimate exercise of the moral authority of public opinion? And if not, why not? The practise is really revolting to such a public. They also sincerely think that it is forbidden and abhorred by the Deity. Neither could the prohibition be censured as religious persecution. It might be religious in its origin, but it would not be persecution for religion, since nobody's religion makes it a duty to eat pork. The only tenable ground of condemnation would be, that with the personal tastes and self-regarding concerns of individuals the public has no business to interfere.

To come somewhat nearer home: the majority of Spaniards consider it a gross impiety, offensive in the highest degree to the Supreme Being, to worship him in any other manner than the Roman Catholic; and no other public worship is lawful on Spanish soil. The people of all Southern Europe look upon a married clergy as not only irreligious but unchaste, indecent, gross, disgusting. What do Protestants think of these perfectly sincere feelings, and of the attempt to enforce them against non-Catholics? Yet, if mankind are justified in interfering with each other's liberty in things which do not concern the interests of others, on what principle is it possible consistently to exclude these cases? Or who can blame people for desiring to suppress what they regard as a scandal in the sight of God and man? No stronger case can be shown for prohibiting anything which is regarded as a personal immorality, than is made out for suppressing these practices in the eyes of those who regard them as impieties; and unless we are willing to adopt the logic of persecutors, and to say that we may persecute others because we are right, and that they must not persecute us because they are wrong, we must beware of admitting a principle of which we should resent as a gross injustice the application to ourselves.

The preceding instances may be objected to, although unreasonably, as drawn from contingencies impossible among us: opinion, in this country, not being likely to enforce abstinence from meats, or to interfere with people for worshipping, and for either marrying or not marrying, according to their creed or inclination. The next example, however, shall be taken from an interference with liberty which we have by no means passed

8 The case of the Bombay Parsees is a curious instance in point. When this industrious and enterprising tribe, the descendants of the Persian fire-worshippers, flying from their native country before the Caliphs, arrived in Western India, they were admitted to toleration by the Hindoo sovereigns, on condition of not eating beef. When those regions afterwards fell under the dominion of Mohammedan conquerors, the Parsees obtained from them a continuance of indulgence, on condition of refraining from pork. What was at first obedience to authority became a second nature, and the Parsees to this day abstain both from beef and pork. Though not required by their religion, the double abstinence has had time to grow into a custom of their tribe; and custom, in the East, is a religion.

all danger of. Wherever the Puritans have been sufficiently powerful, as in New England, and in Great Britain at the time of the Commonwealth, they have endeavoured, with considerable success, to put down all public, and nearly all private, amusements: especially music, dancing, public games, or other assemblages for purposes of diversion, and the theatre. There are still in this country large bodies of persons by whose notions of morality and religion these recreations are condemned; and those persons belonging chiefly to the middle class, who are the ascendant power in the present social and political condition of the kingdom, it is by no means impossible that persons of these sentiments may at some time or other command a majority in Parliament. How will the remaining portion of the community like to have the amusements that shall be permitted to them regulated by the religious and moral sentiments of the stricter Calvinists and Methodists? Would they not, with considerable peremptoriness, desire these intrusively pious members of society to mind their own business? This is precisely what should be said to every government and every public, who have the pretension that no person shall enjoy any pleasure which they think wrong. But if the principle of the pretension be admitted, no one can reasonably object to its being acted on in the sense of the majority, or other preponderating power in the country; and all persons must be ready to conform to the idea of a Christian commonwealth, as understood by the early settlers in New England, if a religious profession similar to theirs should ever succeed in regaining its lost ground, as religions supposed to be declining have so often been known to do.

To imagine another contingency, perhaps more likely to be realized than the one last mentioned. There is confessedly a strong tendency in the modern world towards a democratic constitution of society, accompanied or not by popular political institutions. It is affirmed that in the country where this tendency is most completely realized—where both society and the government are most democratic—the United States—the feeling of the majority, to whom any appearance of a more showy or costly style of living than they can hope to rival is disagreeable, operates as a tolerably effectual sumptuary law, and that in many parts of the Union it is really difficult for a person possessing a very large income, to find any mode of spending it, which will not incur popular disapprobation. Though such statements as these are doubtless much exaggerated as a representation of existing facts, the state of things they describe is not only a conceivable and possible, but a probable result of democratic feeling, combined with the notion that the public has a right to a veto on the manner in which individuals shall spend their incomes. We have only further to suppose a considerable diffusion of Socialist opinions, and it may become infamous in the eyes of the majority to possess more property than some very small amount, or any income not earned by manual labour. Opinions similar in principle to these, already prevail widely among the artisan class, and weigh oppressively on those who are amenable to the opinion chiefly of that class, namely, its own members. It is known that the bad workmen who form the majority of the operatives in many branches of industry, are decidedly of opinion that bad workmen ought to receive the same wages as good, and that no one ought to be allowed, through piecework or otherwise, to earn by superior skill or industry more than others can without it. And they employ a moral police, which occasionally becomes a physical one, to deter skillful workmen from receiving, and employers from giving, a larger remuneration for a more useful service. If the public have any jurisdiction over private concerns, I cannot see that these people are in fault, or that any individual's particular public can be blamed for asserting the same authority over his individual conduct, which the general public asserts over people in general.

But, without dwelling upon supposititious cases, there are, in our own day, gross usurpations upon the liberty of private life actually practised, and still greater ones threatened with some expectation of success, and opinions propounded which assert an unlimited right in the public not only to prohibit by law everything which it thinks wrong, but in order to get at what it thinks wrong, to prohibit any number of things which it admits to be innocent.

Under the name of preventing intemperance, the people of one English colony, and of nearly half the United States, have been interdicted by law from making any use whatever of fermented drinks, except for medical purposes: for prohibition of the sale is in fact, as it is intended to be, prohibition of their use. And though the impracticability of executing the law has caused its repeal in several of the States which had adopted it, including the one from which it derives its name, an attempt has notwithstanding been commenced, and is prosecuted with considerable zeal by many of the professed philanthropists, to agitate for a similar law in this country. The association, or "Alliance" as it terms itself, which has been formed for this purpose has acquired some notoriety through the publicity given to a correspondence between its Secretary and one of the very few English public men who hold that a politician's opinions ought to be founded on principles. Lord Stanley's share in this correspondence is calculated to strengthen the hopes already built on him, by those who know how rare such qualities as are manifested in some of his public appearances, unhappily are among those who figure in political life. The organ of the Alliance, who would "deeply deplore the recognition of any principle which could be wrested to justify bigotry and persecution," undertakes to point out the "broad and impassable barrier" which divides such principles from those of the association. "All matters relating to thought, opinion, conscience, appear to me," he says, "to be without the sphere of legislation; all pertaining to social act, habit, relation, subject only to a discretionary power vested in the State itself, and not in the individual, to be within it." No mention is made of a third class, different from either of these, viz. acts and habits which are not social, but individual; although it is to this class, surely, that the act of drinking fermented liquors belongs. Selling fermented liquors, however, is trading, and trading is a social act. But the infringement complained of is not on the liberty of the seller, but on that of the buyer and consumer; since the State might just as well forbid him to drink wine, as purposely make it impossible for him to obtain it. The Secretary, however, says, "I claim, as a citizen, a right to legislate whenever my social rights are invaded by the social act of another." And now for the definition of these "social rights." "If anything invades my social rights, certainly the traffic in strong drink does. It destroys my primary right of security, by constantly creating and stimulating social disorder. It invades any right of equality, by deriving a profit from the creation of a misery I am taxed to support. It impedes my right to free moral and intellectual development by surrounding my path with dangers, and by weakening and demoralizing society, from which I have a right to claim mutual aid and intercourse." A theory of "social rights," the like of which probably never before found its way into distinct language: being nothing short of this—that it is the absolute social right of every individual, that every other individual shall act in every respect exactly as he ought; that whosoever fails thereof in the smallest particular, violates my social right, and entitles me to demand from the legislature the removal of the grievance. So monstrous a principle is far more dangerous than any single interference with liberty; there is no violation of liberty which it would not justify; it acknowledges no right to any freedom whatever, except perhaps to that of holding opinions in secret, without ever disclosing them: for, the moment an opinion which I consider noxious passes any one's lips, it invades all the "social rights" attributed to me by the Alliance. The doctrine ascribes to all mankind a vested interest in each other's moral, intellectual, and even physical perfection, to be defined by each claimant according to his own standard.

Another important example of illegitimate interference with the rightful liberty of the individual, not simply threatened, but long since carried into triumphant effect, is Sabbatarian legislation. Without doubt, abstinence on one day in the week, so far as the exigencies of life permit, from the usual daily occupation, though in no respect religiously binding on any except Jews, is a highly beneficial custom. And inasmuch as this custom cannot be observed without a general consent to that effect among the industrious classes, therefore, in so far as some persons by working may impose the same necessity on others, it may be allowable and right that the law should guarantee to each the observance by others of the custom, by suspending the greater operations of industry on a particular day. But this justification, grounded on the direct interest which others have in each individual's observance of the practice, does not apply to the self-chosen occupations in which a person may think fit to employ his leisure; nor does it hold good, in the smallest degree, for legal restrictions on amusements. It is true that the amusement of some is the day's work of others; but the pleasure, not to say the useful recreation, of many, is worth the labour of a few, provided the occupation is freely chosen, and can be freely resigned. The operatives are perfectly right in thinking that if all worked on Sunday, seven days' work would have to be given for six days' wages: but so long as the great mass of employments are suspended, the small number who for the enjoyment of others must still work, obtain a proportional increase of earnings; and they are not obliged to follow those occupations, if they prefer leisure to emolument. If a further remedy is sought, it might be found in the establishment by custom of a holiday on some other day of the week for those particular classes of persons. The only ground, therefore, on which restrictions on Sunday amusements can be defended, must be that they are religiously wrong; a motive of legislation which never can be too earnestly protested against. "Deorum injuriae Diis curae." It remains to be proved that society or any of its officers holds a commission from on high to avenge any supposed offence to Omnipotence, which is not also a wrong to our fellow creatures. The notion that it is one man's duty that another should be religious, was the foundation of all the religious persecutions ever perpetrated, and if admitted, would fully justify them. Though the feeling which breaks out in the repeated attempts to stop railway travelling on Sunday, in the resistance to the opening of Museums, and the like, has not the cruelty of the old persecutors, the state of mind indicated by it is fundamentally the same. It is a determination not to tolerate others in doing what is permitted by their religion, because it is not permitted by the persecutor's religion. It is a belief that God not only abominates the act of the misbeliever, but will not hold us guiltless if we leave him unmolested.

I cannot refrain from adding to these examples of the little account commonly made of human liberty, the language of downright persecution which breaks out from the press of this country, whenever it feels called on to notice the remarkable phenomenon of Mormonism. Much might be said on the unexpected and instructive fact, that an alleged new revelation, and a religion founded on it, the product of palpable imposture, not even supported by the *prestige* of extraordinary qualities in its founder, is believed by hundreds of thousands, and has been made the foundation of a society, in the age of newspapers, railways, and the electric telegraph. What here concerns us is, that this religion, like other and better religions, has its martyrs; that its prophet and founder was, for his teaching, put to death by a mob; that others of its adherents lost their lives by the same lawless violence; that they were forcibly expelled, in a body, from the country in which they first grew up; while, now that they have been chased into a solitary recess in the midst of a desert, many in this country openly declare that it would be right (only that it is not convenient) to send an expedition against them, and compel them by force to conform to the opinions of other people. The article of the Mormonite doctrine which is the chief provocative to the antipathy which thus breaks through the ordinary restraints of religious tolerance, is its sanction of polygamy; which, though permitted to Mohammedans, and Hindoos, and Chinese, seems to excite unquenchable animosity when practised by persons who speak English, and profess to be a kind of Christians. No one has a deeper disapprobation than I have of this Mormon institution; both for other reasons, and because, far from being in any way countenanced by the principle of liberty, it is a direct infraction of that principle, being a mere riveting of the chains of one-half of the community, and an emancipation of the other from reciprocity of obligation towards them. Still, it must be remembered that this relation is as much voluntary on the part of the women concerned in it, and who may be deemed the sufferers by it, as is the case with any other form of the marriage institution; and however surprising this fact may appear, it has its explanation in the common ideas and customs of the world, which teaching women to think marriage the one thing needful, make it intelligible that many a woman should prefer being one of several wives, to not being a wife at all. Other countries are not asked to recognize such unions, or release any portion of their inhabitants from their own laws on the score of Mormonite opinions. But when the dissentients have conceded to the hostile sentiments of others, far more than could justly be demanded; when they have left the countries to which their doctrines were unacceptable, and established themselves in a remote corner of the earth, which they have been the first to render habitable to human beings; it is difficult to see on what principles but those of tyranny they can be prevented from living there under what laws they please, provided they commit no aggression on other nations, and allow perfect freedom of departure to those who are dissatisfied with their ways. A recent writer, in some respects of considerable merit, proposes (to use his own words) not a crusade, but a *civilizade*, against this polygamous community, to put an end to what seems to him a retrograde step in civilization. It also appears so to me, but I am not aware that any community has a right to force another to be civilized. So long as the sufferers by the bad law do not invoke assistance from other communities, I cannot admit that persons entirely unconnected with them ought to step in and require that a condition of things with which all who are directly interested appear to be satisfied, should be put an end to because it is a scandal to persons some thousands of miles distant, who have no part or concern in it. Let them send missionaries, if they please, to preach against it; and let them, by any fair means (of which silencing the teachers is not one), oppose the progress of similar doctrines among their own people. If civilization has got the better of barbarism when barbarism had the world to itself, it is too much to profess to be afraid lest barbarism, after having been fairly got under, should revive and conquer civilization. A civilization that can thus succumb to its vanquished enemy, must first have become so degenerate, that neither its appointed priests and teachers, nor anybody else, has the capacity, or will take the trouble, to stand up for it. If this be so, the sooner such a civilization receives notice to quit, the better. It can only go on from bad to worse, until destroyed and regenerated (like the Western Empire) by energetic barbarians.

19
Patrick Devlin

"Morals and the Criminal Law,"* from *The Enforcement of Morals*

The Report of the Committee on Homosexual Offences and Prostitution, generally known as the Wolfenden Report, is recognized to be an excellent study of two very difficult legal and social problems. But it has also a particular claim to the respect of those interested in jurisprudence; it does what law reformers so rarely do; it sets out clearly and carefully what in relation to its subjects it considers the function of the law to be.[1] Statutory additions to the criminal law are too often made on the simple principle that "there ought to be a law against it." The greater part of the law relating to sexual offences is the creation of statute and it is difficult to ascertain any logical relationship between it and the moral ideas which most of us uphold. Adultery, fornication, and prostitution are not, as the Report[2] points out, criminal offences: homosexuality between males is a criminal offence, but between females it is not. Incest was not an offence until it was declared so by statute only fifty years ago. Does the legislature select these offences haphazardly or are there some principles which can be used to determine what part of the moral law should be embodied in the criminal? There is, for example, being now considered a proposal to make A.I.D., that is, the practice of artificial insemination of a woman with the seed of a man who is not her husband, a criminal offence; if, as is usually the case, the woman is married, this is in substance, if not in form, adultery. Ought it to be made punishable when adultery is not? This sort of question is of practical importance, for a law that appears to be arbitrary and illogical, in the end and after the wave of moral indignation that has put it on the statute book subsides, forfeits respect. As a practical question it arises more frequently in the field of sexual morals than in any other, but there is no special answer to be found in that field. The inquiry must be general and fundamental. What is the connexion between crime and sin and to what extent, if at all, should the criminal law of England concern itself with the enforcement of morals and punish sin or immorality as such?

The statements of principle in the Wolfenden Report provide an admirable and modern starting-point for such an inquiry. In the course of my examination of them I shall find matter for criticism. If my criticisms are sound, it must not be imagined that they point to any shortcomings in the Report. Its authors were not, as I am trying to do, composing a paper on the jurisprudence of morality; they were evolving a working formula to use for reaching a number of practical conclusions. I do not intend to express any opinion one way or the other about these; that would be outside the scope of a lecture on jurisprudence. I am concerned only with general principles; the statement of these in the Report illuminates the entry into the subject and I hope that its authors

* Maccabaean Lecture in Jurisprudence read at the British Academy on 18 March 1959 and printed in the *Proceedings of the British Academy*, vol. xlv, under the title "The Enforcement of Morals."

1 The Committee's "statement of juristic philosophy" (to quote Lord Pakenham) was considered by him in a debate in the House of Lords on 4 December 1957, reported in *Hansard Lords Debates*, vol. ccvi at 738; and also in the same debate by the Archbishop of Canterbury at 753 and Lord Denning at 806. The subject has also been considered by Mr. J.E. Hall Williams in the *Law Quarterly Review*, January 1958, vol. lxxiv, p.76.

2 Para. 14.

will forgive me if I carry the lamp with me into places where it was not intended to go.

Early in the Report[3] the Committee put forward:

> Our own formulation of the function of the criminal law so far as it concerns the subjects of this enquiry. In this field, its function, as we see it, is to preserve public order and decency, to protect the citizen from what is offensive or injurious, and to provide sufficient safeguards against exploitation and corruption of others, particularly those who are specially vulnerable because they are young, weak in body or mind, inexperienced, or in a state of special physical, official or economic dependence.
>
> It is not, in our view, the function of the law to intervene in the private lives of citizens, or to seek to enforce any particular pattern of behaviour, further than is necessary to carry out the purposes we have outlined.

The Committee preface their most important recommendation[4]

> that homosexual behaviour between consenting adults in private should no longer be a criminal offence, [by stating the argument[5]] which we believe to be decisive, namely, the importance which society and the law ought to give to individual freedom of choice and action in matters of private morality. Unless a deliberate attempt is to be made by society, acting through the agency of the law, to equate the sphere of crime with that of sin, there must remain a realm of private morality and immorality which is, in brief and crude terms, not the law's business. To say this is not to condone or encourage private immorality.

Similar statements of principle are set out in the chapters of the Report which deal with prostitution. No case can be sustained, the Report says, for attempting to make prostitution itself illegal.[6] The Committee refer to the general reasons already given and add: "We are agreed that private immorality should not be the concern of the criminal law except in the special circumstances therein mentioned." They quote[7] with approval the report of the Street Offences Committee,[8] which says: "As a general proposition it will be universally accepted that the law is not concerned with private morals or with ethical sanctions." It will be observed that the emphasis is on *private* immorality. By this is meant immorality which is not offensive or injurious to the public in the ways defined or described in the first passage which I quoted. In other words, no act of immorality should be made a criminal offence unless it is accompanied by some other feature such as indecency, corruption, or exploitation. This is clearly brought out in relation to prostitution: "It is not the duty of the law to concern itself with immorality as such ... it should confine itself to those activities which offend against public order

3 Para. 13.
4 Para. 62.
5 Para. 61.
6 Para. 224.
7 Para. 227.
8 Cmd. 3231 (1928).

and decency or expose the ordinary citizen to what is offensive or injurious."[9]

These statements of principle are naturally restricted to the subject-matter of the Report. But they are made in general terms and there seems to be no reason why, if they are valid, they should not be applied to the criminal law in general. They separate very decisively crime from sin, the divine law from the secular, and the moral from the criminal. They do not signify any lack of support for the law, moral or criminal, and they do not represent an attitude that can be called either religious or irreligious. There are many schools of thought among those who may think that morals are not the law's business. There is first of all the agnostic or free-thinker. He does not of course disbelieve in morals, nor in sin if it be given the wider of the two meanings assigned to it in the *Oxford English Dictionary* where it is defined as "transgression against divine law or the principles of morality." He cannot accept the divine law; that does not mean that he might not view with suspicion any departure from moral principles that have for generations been accepted by the society in which he lives; but in the end he judges for himself. Then there is the deeply religious person who feels that the criminal law is sometimes more of a hindrance than a help in the sphere of morality, and that the reform of the sinner—at any rate when he injures only himself—should be a spiritual rather than a temporal work. Then there is the man who without any strong feeling cannot see why, where there is freedom in religious belief, there should not logically be freedom in morality as well. All these are powerfully allied against the equating of crime with sin.

I must disclose at the outset that I have as a judge an interest in the result of the inquiry which I am seeking to make as a jurisprudent. As a judge who administers the criminal law and who has often to pass sentence in a criminal court, I should feel handicapped in my task if I thought that I was addressing an audience which had no sense of sin or which thought of crime as something quite different. Ought one, for example, in passing sentence upon a female abortionist to treat her simply as if she were an unlicensed midwife? If not, why not? But if so, is all the panoply of the law erected over a set of social regulations? I must admit that I begin with a feeling that a complete separation of crime from sin (I use the term throughout this lecture in the wider meaning) would not be good for the moral law and might be disastrous for the criminal. But can this sort of feeling be justified as a matter of jurisprudence? And if it be a right feeling, how should the relationship between the criminal and the moral law be stated? Is there a good theoretical basis for it, or is it just a practical working alliance, or is it a bit of both? That is the problem which I want to examine, and I shall begin by considering the standpoint of the strict logician. It can be supported by cogent arguments, some of which I believe to be unanswerable and which I put as follows.

Morals and religion are inextricably joined—the moral standards generally accepted in Western civilization being those belonging to Christianity. Outside Christendom other standards derive from other religions. None of these moral codes can claim any validity except by virtue of the religion on which it is based. Old Testament morals differ in some respects from New Testament morals. Even within Christianity there are differences. Some hold that contraception is an immoral practice and that a man who has carnal knowledge of another woman while his wife is alive is in all circumstances a fornicator; others, including most of the English-speaking world, deny both these propositions. Between the great religions of the world, of

9 Para. 257.

which Christianity is only one, there are much wider differences. It may or may not be right for the State to adopt one of these religions as the truth, to found itself upon its doctrines, and to deny to any of its citizens the liberty to practise any other. If it does, it is logical that it should use the secular law wherever it thinks it necessary to enforce the divine. If it does not, it is illogical that it should concern itself with morals as such. But if it leaves matters of religion to private judgement, it should logically leave matters of morals also. A State which refuses to enforce Christian beliefs has lost the right to enforce Christian morals.

If this view is sound, it means that the criminal law cannot justify any of its provisions by reference to the moral law. It cannot say, for example, that murder and theft are prohibited because they are immoral or sinful. The State must justify in some other way the punishments which it imposes on wrongdoers and a function for the criminal law independent of morals must be found. This is not difficult to do. The smooth functioning of society and the preservation of order require that a number of activities should be regulated. The rules that are made for that purpose and are enforced by the criminal law are often designed simply to achieve uniformity and convenience and rarely involve any choice between good and evil. Rules that impose a speed limit or prevent obstruction on the highway have nothing to do with morals. Since so much of the criminal law is composed of rules of this sort, why bring morals into it at all? Why not define the function of the criminal law in simple terms as the preservation of order and decency and the protection of the lives and property of citizens, and elaborate those terms in relation to any particular subject in the way in which it is done in the Wolfenden Report? The criminal law in carrying out these objects will undoubtedly overlap the moral law. Crimes of violence are morally wrong and they are also offences against good order; therefore they offend against both laws. But this is simply because the two laws in pursuit of different objectives happen to cover the same area. Such is the argument.

Is the argument consistent or inconsistent with the fundamental principles of English criminal law as it exists today? That is the first way of testing it, though by no means a conclusive one. In the field of jurisprudence one is at liberty to overturn even fundamental conceptions if they are theoretically unsound. But to see how the argument fares under the existing law is a good starting-point.

It is true that for many centuries the criminal law was much concerned with keeping the peace and little, if at all, with sexual morals. But it would be wrong to infer from that that it had no moral content or that it would ever have tolerated the idea of a man being left to judge for himself in matters of morals. The criminal law of England has from the very first concerned itself with moral principles. A simple way of testing this point is to consider the attitude which the criminal law adopts towards consent.

Subject to certain exceptions inherent in the nature of particular crimes, the criminal law has never permitted consent of the victim to be used as a defence. In rape, for example, consent negatives an essential element. But consent of the victim is no defence to a charge of murder. It is not a defence to any form of assault that the victim thought his punishment well deserved and submitted to it; to make a good defence the accused must prove that the law gave him the right to chastise and that he exercised it reasonably. Likewise, the victim may not forgive the aggressor and require the prosecution to desist; the right to enter a *nolle prosequi* belongs to the Attorney-General alone.

Now, if the law existed for the protection of the individual, there would be no reason why he should avail himself of it if he did not want it. The reason why a man may not consent to the commission of an offence against himself beforehand or forgive it afterwards is because it is an offence against society. It is not that society is physically injured; that would be impossible. Nor need any individual be shocked, corrupted, or exploited; everything may be done in private. Nor can it be explained on the practical ground that a violent man is a potential danger to others in the community who have therefore a direct interest in his apprehension and punishment as being necessary to their own protection. That would be true of a man whom the victim is prepared to forgive but not of one who gets his consent first; a murderer who acts only upon the consent, and maybe the request, of his victim is no menace to others, but he does threaten one of the great moral principles upon which society is based, that is, the sanctity of human life. There is only one explanation of what has hitherto been accepted as the basis of the criminal law and that is that there are certain standards of behaviour or moral principles which society requires to be observed; and the breach of them is an offence not merely against the person who is injured but against society as a whole.

Thus, if the criminal law were to be reformed so as to eliminate from it everything that was not designed to preserve order and decency or to protect citizens (including the protection of youth from corruption), it would overturn a fundamental principle. It would also end a number of specific crimes. Euthanasia or the killing of another at his own request, suicide, attempted suicide and suicide pacts, duelling, abortion, incest between brother and sister, are all acts which can be done in private and without offence to others and need not involve the corruption or exploitation of others. Many people think that the law on some of these subjects is in need of reform, but no one hitherto has gone so far as to suggest that they should all be left outside the criminal law as matters of private morality. They can be brought within it only as a matter of moral principle. It must be remembered also that although there is much immorality that is not punished by the law, there is none that is condoned by the law. The law will not allow its processes to be used by those engaged in immorality of any sort. For example, a house may not be let for immoral purposes; the lease is invalid and would not be enforced. But if what goes on inside there is a matter of private morality and not the law's business, why does the law inquire into it at all?

I think it is clear that the criminal law as we know it is based upon moral principle. In a number of crimes its function is simply to enforce a moral principle and nothing else. The law, both criminal and civil, claims to be able to speak about morality and immorality generally. Where does it get its authority to do this and how does it settle the moral principles which it enforces? Undoubtedly, as a matter of history, it derived both from Christian teaching. But I think that the strict logician is right when he says that the law can no longer rely on doctrines in which citizens are entitled to disbelieve. It is necessary therefore to look for some other source.

In jurisprudence, as I have said, everything is thrown open to discussion and, in the belief that they cover the whole field, I have framed three interrogatories addressed to myself to answer:

1. Has society the right to pass judgement at all on matters of morals? Ought there, in other words, to be a public morality, or are morals always a matter for private judgement?

2. If society has the right to pass judgement, has it also the right to use the weapon of the law to enforce it?

3. If so, ought it to use that weapon in all cases or only in some; and if only in some, on what principles should it distinguish?

I shall begin with the first interrogatory and consider what is meant by the right of society to pass a moral judgement, that is, a judgement about what is good and what is evil. The fact that a majority of people may disapprove of a practice does not of itself make it a matter for society as a whole. Nine men out of ten may disapprove of what the tenth man is doing and still say that it is not their business. There is a case for a collective judgement (as distinct from a large number of individual opinions which sensible people may even refrain from pronouncing at all if it is upon somebody else's private affairs) only if society is affected. Without a collective judgement there can be no case at all for intervention. Let me take as an illustration the Englishman's attitude to religion as it is now and as it has been in the past. His attitude now is that a man's religion is his private affair; he may think of another man's religion that it is right or wrong, true or untrue, but not that it is good or bad. In earlier times that was not so; a man was denied the right to practise what was thought of as heresy, and heresy was thought of as destructive of society.

The language used in the passages I have quoted from the Wolfenden Report suggests the view that there ought not to be a collective judgement about immorality *per se*. Is this what is meant by "private morality" and "individual freedom of choice and action"? Some people sincerely believe that homosexuality is neither immoral nor unnatural. Is the "freedom of choice and action" that is offered to the individual, freedom to decide for himself what is moral or immoral, society remaining neutral; or is it freedom to be immoral if he wants to be? The language of the Report may be open to question, but the conclusions at which the Committee arrive answer this question unambiguously. If society is not prepared to say that homosexuality is morally wrong, there would be no basis for a law protecting youth from "corruption" or punishing a man for living on the "immoral" earnings of a homosexual prostitute, as the Report recommends.[10] This attitude the Committee make even clearer when they come to deal with prostitution. In truth, the Report takes it for granted that there is in existence a public morality which condemns homosexuality and prostitution. What the Report seems to mean by private morality might perhaps be better described as private behaviour in matters of morals.

This view—that there is such a thing as public morality—can also be justified by *a priori* argument. What makes a society of any sort is community of ideas, not only political ideas but also ideas about the way its members should behave and govern their lives; these latter ideas are its morals. Every society has a moral structure as well as a political one: or rather, since that might suggest two independent systems, I should say that the structure of every society is made up both of politics and morals. Take, for example, the institution of marriage. Whether a man should be allowed to take more than one wife is something about which every society has to make up its mind one way or the other. In England we believe in the Christian idea of marriage and therefore adopt monogamy as a moral principle. Consequently the Christian institution of marriage has become the basis of family life and so part of the structure of our society. It is there not because it is Christian. It has got there because it is Christian, but it remains there because it is built into the house in which we live and could not be removed without bringing it down. The great majority of those who live in

10 Para. 76.

this country accept it because it is the Christian idea of marriage and for them the only true one. But a non-Christian is bound by it, not because it is part of Christianity but because, rightly or wrongly, it has been adopted by the society in which he lives. It would be useless for him to stage a debate designed to prove that polygamy was theologically more correct and socially preferable; if he wants to live in the house, he must accept it as built in the way in which it is.

We see this more clearly if we think of ideas or institutions that are purely political. Society cannot tolerate rebellion; it will not allow argument about the rightness of the cause. Historians a century later may say that the rebels were right and the Government was wrong and a percipient and conscientious subject of the State may think so at the time. But it is not a matter which can be left to individual judgement.

The institution of marriage is a good example for my purpose because it bridges the division, if there is one, between politics and morals. Marriage is part of the structure of our society and it is also the basis of a moral code which condemns fornication and adultery. The institution of marriage would be gravely threatened if individual judgements were permitted about the morality of adultery; on these points there must be a public morality. But public morality is not to be confined to those moral principles which support institutions such as marriage. People do not think of monogamy as something which has to be supported because our society has chosen to organize itself upon it; they think of it as something that is good in itself and offering a good way of life and that it is for that reason that our society has adopted it. I return to the statement that I have already made, that society means a community of ideas; without shared ideas on politics, morals, and ethics no society can exist. Each one of us has ideas about what is good and what is evil; they cannot be kept private from the society in which we live. If men and women try to create a society in which there is no fundamental agreement about good and evil they will fail; if, having based it on common agreement, the agreement goes, the society will disintegrate. For society is not something that is kept together physically; it is held by the invisible bonds of common thought. If the bonds were too far relaxed the members would drift apart. A common morality is part of the bondage. The bondage is part of the price of society; and mankind, which needs society, must pay its price.

Common lawyers used to say that Christianity was part of the law of the land. That was never more than a piece of rhetoric as Lord Sumner said in *Bowman v. The Secular Society*.[11] What lay behind it was the notion which I have been seeking to expound, namely that morals—and up till a century or so ago no one thought it worth distinguishing between religion and morals—were necessary to the temporal order. In 1675 Chief Justice Hale said: "To say that religion is a cheat is to dissolve all those obligations whereby civil society is preserved."[12] In 1797 Mr. Justice Ashurst said of blasphemy that it was "not only an offence against God but against all law and government from its tendency to dissolve all the bonds and obligations of civil society."[13] By 1908 Mr. Justice Phillimore was able to say: "A man is free to think, to speak and to teach what he pleases as to religious matters, but not as to morals."[14]

You may think that I have taken far too long in contending that there is such a thing as public morality, a proposition which most people

11 (1917), A.C. 406, at 457.
12 *Taylor's Case*, 1 Vent. 293.
13 *R. v. Williams*, 26 St. Tr. 653, at 715.
14 *R. v. Boulter*, 72 J.P. 188.

would readily accept, and may have left myself too little time to discuss the next question which to many minds may cause greater difficulty: to what extent should society use the law to enforce its moral judgements? But I believe that the answer to the first question determines the way in which the second should be approached and may indeed very nearly dictate the answer to the second question. If society has no right to make judgements on morals, the law must find some special justification for entering the field of morality: if homosexuality and prostitution are not in themselves wrong, then the onus is very clearly on the lawgiver who wants to frame a law against certain aspects of them to justify the exceptional treatment. But if society has the right to make a judgement and has it on the basis that a recognized morality is as necessary to society as, say, a recognized government, then society may use the law to preserve morality in the same way as it uses it to safeguard anything else that is essential to its existence. If therefore the first proposition is securely established with all its implications, society has a prima facie right to legislate against immorality as such.

The Wolfenden Report, notwithstanding that it seems to admit the right of society to condemn homosexuality and prostitution as immoral, requires special circumstances to be shown to justify the intervention of the law. I think that this is wrong in principle and that any attempt to approach my second interrogatory on these lines is bound to break down. I think that the attempt by the Committee does break down and that this is shown by the fact that it has to define or describe its special circumstances so widely that they can be supported only if it is accepted that the law *is* concerned with immorality as such.

The widest of the special circumstances are described as the provision of "sufficient" safeguards against exploitation and corruption of others, particularly those who are specially vulnerable because they are young, weak in body or mind, inexperienced, or in a state of special physical, official or economic dependence.[15] The corruption of youth is a well-recognized ground for intervention by the State and for the purpose of any legislation the young can easily be defined. But if similar protection were to be extended to every other citizen, there would be no limit to the reach of the law. The "corruption and exploitation of others" is so wide that it could be used to cover any sort of immorality which involves, as most do, the co-operation of another person. Even if the phrase is taken as limited to the categories that are particularized as "specially vulnerable," it is so elastic as to be practically no restriction. This is not merely a matter of words. For if the words used are stretched almost beyond breaking-point, they still are not wide enough to cover the recommendations which the Committee make about prostitution.

Prostitution is not in itself illegal and the Committee do not think that it ought to be made so.[16] If prostitution is private immorality and not the law's business, what concern has the law with the ponce or the brothel-keeper or the householder who permits habitual prostitution? The Report recommends that the laws which make these activities criminal offences should be maintained or strengthened and brings them (so far as it goes into principle; with regard to brothels it says simply that the law rightly frowns on them) under the head of exploitation.[17] There may be cases of exploitation in this trade, as there are or used to be in

15 Para. 13.
16 Paras. 224, 285, and 318.
17 Paras. 302 and 320.

many others, but in general a ponce exploits a prostitute no more than an impresario exploits an actress. The Report finds that "the great majority of prostitutes are women whose psychological makeup is such that they choose this life because they find in it a style of living which is to them easier, freer and more profitable than would be provided by any other occupation.... In the main the association between prostitute and ponce is voluntary and operates to mutual advantage."[18] The Committee would agree that this could not be called exploitation in the ordinary sense. They say: "It is in our view an over-simplification to think that those who live on the earnings of prostitution are exploiting the prostitute as such. What they are really exploiting is the whole complex of the relationship between prostitute and customer; they are, in effect, exploiting the human weaknesses which cause the customer to seek the prostitute and the prostitute to meet the demand."[19]

All sexual immorality involves the exploitation of human weaknesses. The prostitute exploits the lust of her customers and the customer the moral weakness of the prostitute. If the exploitation of human weaknesses is considered to create a special circumstance, there is virtually no field of morality which can be defined in such a way as to exclude the law.

I think, therefore, that it is not possible to set theoretical limits to the power of the State to legislate against immorality. It is not possible to settle in advance exceptions to the general rule or to define inflexibly areas of morality into which the law is in no circumstances to be allowed to enter. Society is entitled by means of its laws to protect itself from dangers, whether from within or without. Here again I think that the political parallel is legitimate. The law of treason is directed against aiding the king's enemies and against sedition from within. The justification for this is that established government is necessary for the existence of society and therefore its safety against violent overthrow must be secured. But an established morality is as necessary as good government to the welfare of society. Societies disintegrate from within more frequently than they are broken up by external pressures. There is disintegration when no common morality is observed and history shows that the loosening of moral bonds is often the first stage of disintegration, so that society is justified in taking the same steps to preserve its moral code as it does to preserve its government and other essential

18 Para. 223.
19 Para. 306.

institutions.[20] The suppression of vice is as much the law's business as the suppression of subversive activities; it is no more possible to define a sphere of private morality than it is to define one of private subversive activity. It is wrong to talk of private morality or of the law not being concerned with immorality as such or to try to set rigid bounds to the part which the law may play in the suppression of vice. There are no theoretical limits to the power of the State to legislate against treason and sedition, and likewise I think there can be no theoretical limits to legislation against immorality. You may argue that if a man's sins affect only himself it cannot be the concern of society. If he chooses to get drunk every night in the privacy of his own home, is any one except himself the worse, for it? But suppose a quarter or a half of the population got drunk every night, what sort of society would it be? You cannot set a theoretical limit to the number of people who can get drunk before society is entitled to legislate against drunkenness. The same may be said of gambling. The Royal Commission on Betting, Lotteries, and Gaming took as their test the character of the citizen as a member of society. They said: "Our concern with the ethical significance of gambling is confined to the effect which it may have on the character of the gambler as a member of society. If we were convinced that whatever the degree of gambling this effect must be harmful we should be inclined to think that it was the duty of the state to restrict gambling to the greatest extent practicable."[21]

In what circumstances the State should exercise its power is the third of the interrogatories I have framed. But before I get to it I must raise

20 It is somewhere about this point in the argument that Professor Hart in *Law, Liberty and Morality* discerns a proposition which he describes as central to my thought. He states the proposition and his objection to it as follows (p. 51). "He appears to move from the acceptable proposition that *some* shared morality is essential to the existence of any society [this I take to be the proposition on p. 12] to the unacceptable proposition that a society is identical with its morality as that is at any given moment of its history, so that a change in its morality is tantamount to the destruction of a society. The former proposition might be even accepted as a necessary rather than an empirical truth depending on a quite plausible definition of society as a body of men who hold certain moral views in common. But the latter proposition is absurd. Taken strictly, it would prevent us saying that the morality of a given society had changed, and would compel us instead to say that one society had disappeared and another one taken its place. But it is only on this absurd criterion of what it is for the same society to continue to exist that it could be asserted without evidence that any deviation from a society's shared morality threatens its existence." In conclusion (p. 82) Professor Hart condemns the whole thesis in the lecture as based on "a confused definition of what a society is."

I do not assert that *any* deviation from a society's shared morality threatens its existence any more than I assert that *any* subversive activity threatens its existence. I assert that they are both activities which are capable in their nature of threatening the existence of society so that neither can be put beyond the law.

For the rest, the objection appears to me to be all a matter of words. I would venture to assert, for example, that you cannot have a game without rules and that if there were no rules there would be no game. If I am asked whether that means that the game is "identical" with the rules, I would be willing for the question to be answered either way in the belief that the answer would lead to nowhere. If I am asked whether a change in the rules means that one game has disappeared and another has taken its place, I would reply probably not, but that it would depend on the extent of the change.

Likewise I should venture to assert that there cannot be a contract without terms. Does this mean that an "amended" contract is a "new" contract in the eyes of the law? I once listened to an argument by an ingenious counsel that a contract, because of the substitution of one clause for another, had "ceased to have effect" within the meaning of a statutory provision. The judge did not accept the argument; but if most of the fundamental terms had been changed, I dare say he would have done.

The proposition that I make in the text is that if (as I understand Professor Hart to agree, at any rate for the purposes of the argument) you cannot have a society without "morality," the law can be used to enforce morality as something that is essential to a society. I cannot see why this proposition (whether it is right or wrong) should mean that morality can never be changed without the destruction of society. If morality is changed, the law can be changed. Professor Hart refers (p. 72) to the proposition as "the use of legal punishment to freeze into immobility the morality dominant at a particular time in a society's existence." One might as well say that the inclusion of a penal section into a statute prohibiting certain acts freezes the whole statute into immobility and prevents the prohibitions from ever being modified.

These points are elaborated in the sixth lecture at pp. 115–16.

21 (1951) Cmd. 8190, para. 159.

a point which might have been brought up in any one of the three. How are the moral judgements of society to be ascertained? By leaving it until now, I can ask it in the more limited form that is now sufficient for my purpose. How is the law-maker to ascertain the moral judgements of society? It is surely not enough that they should be reached by the opinion of the majority; it would be too much to require the individual assent of every citizen. English law has evolved and regularly uses a standard which does not depend on the counting of heads. It is that of the reasonable man. He is not to be confused with the rational man. He is not expected to reason about anything and his judgement may be largely a matter of feeling. It is the viewpoint of the man in the street—or to use an archaism familiar to all lawyers—the man in the Clapham omnibus. He might also be called the right-minded man. For my purpose I should like to call him the man in the jury box, for the moral judgement of society must be something about which any twelve men or women drawn at random might after discussion be expected to be unanimous. This was the standard the judges applied in the days before Parliament was as active as it is now and when they laid down rules of public policy. They did not think of themselves as making law but simply as stating principles which every right-minded person would accept as valid. It is what Pollock called "practical morality," which is based not on theological or philosophical foundations but "in the mass of continuous experience half-consciously or unconsciously accumulated and embodied in the morality of common sense." He called it also "a certain way of thinking on questions of morality which we expect to find in a reasonable civilized man or a reasonable Englishman, taken at random."[22]

Immorality then, for the purpose of the law, is what every right-minded person presumed to consider to be immoral. Any immorality is capable of affecting society injuriously and in effect to a greater or lesser extent it usually does; this is what gives the law its *locus standi*. It cannot be shut out. But—and this brings me to the third question—the individual has a *locus standi* too; he cannot be expected to surrender to the judgement of society the whole conduct of his life. It is the old and familiar question of striking a balance between the rights and interests of society and those of the individual. This is something which the law is constantly doing in matters large and small. To take a very down-to-earth example, let me consider the right of the individual whose house adjoins the highway to have access to it; that means in these days the right to have vehicles stationary in the highway, sometimes for a considerable time if there is a lot of loading or unloading. There are many cases in which the courts have had to balance the private right of access against the public right to use the highway without obstruction. It cannot be done by carving up the highway into public and private areas. It is done by recognizing that each have rights over the whole; that if each were to exercise their rights to the full, they would come into conflict; and therefore that the rights of each must be curtailed so as to ensure as far as possible that the essential needs of each are safeguarded.

I do not think that one can talk sensibly of a public and private morality any more than one can of a public or private highway. Morality is a sphere in which there is a public interest and a private interest, often in conflict, and the problem is to reconcile the two. This does not mean that it is impossible to put forward any general statements about how in our society the balance ought to be struck. Such statements cannot of their nature be rigid or precise; they would not be designed to circumscribe the operation of the lawmaking power but to guide those who have

22 *Essays in Jurisprudence and Ethics* (1882), Macmillan, pp. 278 and 353.

to apply it. While every decision which a court of law makes when it balances the public against the private interest is an *ad hoc* decision, the cases contain statements of principle to which the court should have regard when it reaches its decision. In the same way it is possible to make general statements of principle which it may be thought the legislature should bear in mind when it is considering the enactment of laws enforcing morals.

I believe that most people would agree upon the chief of these elastic principles. There must be toleration of the maximum individual freedom that is consistent with the integrity of society. It cannot be said that this is a principle that runs all through the criminal law. Much of the criminal law that is regulatory in character—the part of it that deals with *malum prohibitum* rather than *malum in se*—is based upon the opposite principle, that is, that the choice of the individual must give way to the convenience of the many. But in all matters of conscience the principle I have stated is generally held to prevail. It is not confined to thought and speech; it extends to action, as is shown by the recognition of the right to conscientious objection in war-time; this example shows also that conscience will be respected even in times of national danger. The principle appears to me to be peculiarly appropriate to all questions of morals. Nothing should be punished by the law that does not lie beyond the limits of tolerance. It is not nearly enough to say that a majority dislike a practice; there must be a real feeling of reprobation. Those who are dissatisfied with the present law on homosexuality often say that the opponents of reform are swayed simply by disgust. If that were so it would be wrong, but I do not think one can ignore disgust if it is deeply felt and not manufactured. Its presence is a good indication that the bounds of toleration are being reached. Not everything is to be tolerated. No society can do without intolerance, indignation, and disgust;[23] they are the forces behind the moral law, and indeed it can be argued that if they or something like them are not present, the feelings of society cannot be weighty enough to deprive the individual of freedom of choice. I suppose that there is hardly anyone nowadays who would not be disgusted by the thought of deliberate cruelty to animals. No one proposes to relegate that or any other form of sadism to the realm of private morality or to allow it to be practised in public or in private. It would be possible no doubt to point out that until a comparatively short while ago nobody thought very much of cruelty to animals and also that pity and kindliness and the unwillingness to inflict pain are virtues more generally esteemed now than they have ever been in the past. But matters of this sort are not determined by rational argument. Every moral judgement, unless it claims a divine source, is simply a feeling that no right-minded man could behave in any other way without admitting that he was doing wrong. It is the power of a common sense and not the power of reason that is behind the judgements of society. But before a society can put a practice beyond the limits of tolerance there must be a deliberate judgement that the practice is injurious to society. There is, for example, a general abhorrence of homosexuality. We should ask ourselves in the first instance whether, looking at it calmly and dispassionately, we regard it as a vice so abominable that its mere presence is an offence. If that is the genuine feeling of the society in which we live, I do not see how society can be denied the right to eradicate it. Our feeling may not be so intense as that. We may feel about it that, if confined, it is tolerable, but that if it spread it might be gravely injurious; it is in this way that most societies look upon fornication, seeing it as a natural weakness which must be kept within bounds

23 These words, which have been much criticized, are considered again in the Preface at p. viii.

but which cannot be rooted out. It becomes then a question of balance, the danger to society in one scale and the extent of the restriction in the other. On this sort of point the value of an investigation by such a body as the Wolfenden Committee and of its conclusions is manifest.

The limits of tolerance shift. This is supplementary to what I have been saying but of sufficient importance in itself to deserve statement as a separate principle which law-makers have to bear in mind. I suppose that moral standards do not shift; so far as they come from divine revelation they do not, and I am willing to assume that the moral judgements made by a society always remain good for that society. But the extent to which society will tolerate—I mean tolerate, not approve—departures from moral standards varies from generation to generation. It may be that over-all tolerance is always increasing. The pressure of the human mind, always seeking greater freedom of thought, is outwards against the bonds of society forcing their gradual relaxation. It may be that history is a tale of contraction and expansion and that all developed societies are on their way to dissolution. I must not speak of things I do not know; and anyway as a practical matter no society is willing to make provision for its own decay. I return therefore to the simple and observable fact that in matters of morals the limits of tolerance shift. Laws, especially those which are based on morals, are less easily moved. It follows as another good working principle that in any new matter of morals the law should be slow to act. By the next generation the swell of indignation may have abated and the law be left without the strong backing which it needs. But it is then difficult to alter the law without giving the impression that moral judgement is being weakened. This is now one of the factors that is strongly militating against any alteration to the law on homosexuality.

A third elastic principle must be advanced more tentatively. It is that as far as possible privacy should be respected. This is not an idea that has ever been made explicit in the criminal law. Acts or words done or said in public or in private are all brought within its scope without distinction in principle. But there goes with this a strong reluctance on the part of judges and legislators to sanction invasions of privacy in the detection of crime. The police have no more right to trespass than the ordinary citizen has; there is no general right of search; to this extent an Englishman's home is still his castle. The Government is extremely careful in the exercise even of those powers which it claims to be undisputed. Telephone tapping and interference with the mails afford a good illustration of this. A Committee of three Privy Councillors who recently inquired[24] into these activities found that the Home Secretary and his predecessors had already formulated strict rules governing the exercise of these powers and the Committee were able to recommend that they should be continued to be exercised substantially on the same terms. But they reported that the power was "regarded with general disfavour."

This indicates a general sentiment that the right to privacy is something to be put in the balance against the enforcement of the law. Ought the same sort of consideration to play any part in the formation of the law? Clearly only in a very limited number of cases. When the help of the law is invoked by an injured citizen, privacy must be irrelevant; the individual cannot ask that his right to privacy should be measured against injury criminally done to another. But when all who are involved in the deed are consenting parties and the injury is done to morals, the public interest in the moral order can be balanced against the claims of privacy. The restriction on police powers of investigation goes further than the

24 (1957) Cmd. 283.

affording of a parallel; it means that the detection of crime committed in private and when there is no complaint is bound to be rather haphazard and this is an additional reason for moderation. These considerations do not justify the exclusion of all private immorality from the scope of the law. I think that, as I have already suggested, the test of "private behaviour" should be substituted for "private morality" and the influence of the factor should be reduced from that of a definite limitation to that of a matter to be taken into account. Since the gravity of the crime is also a proper consideration, a distinction might well be made in the case of homosexuality between the lesser acts of indecency and the full offence, which on the principles of the Wolfenden Report it would be illogical to do.

The last and the biggest thing to be remembered is that the law is concerned with the minimum and not with the maximum; there is much in the Sermon on the Mount that would be out of place in the Ten Commandments. We all recognize the gap between the moral law and the law of the land. No man is worth much who regulates his conduct with the sole object of escaping punishment, and every worthy society sets for its members standards which are above those of the law. We recognize the existence of such higher standards when we use expressions such as "moral obligation" and "morally bound." The distinction was well put in the judgement of African elders in a family dispute: "We have power to make you divide the crops, for this is our law, and we will see this is done. But we have not power to make you behave like an upright man."[25]

It can only be because this point is so obvious that it is so frequently ignored. Discussion among law-makers, both professional and amateur, is too often limited to what is right or wrong and good or bad for society. There is a failure to keep separate the two questions I have earlier posed—the question of society's right to pass a moral judgement and the question of whether the arm of the law should be used to enforce the judgement. The criminal law is not a statement of how people ought to behave; it is a statement of what will happen to them if they do not behave; good citizens are not expected to come within reach of it or to set their sights by it, and every enactment should be framed accordingly.

The arm of the law is an instrument to be used by society, and the decision about what particular cases it should be used in is essentially a practical one. Since it is an instrument, it is wise before deciding to use it to have regard to the tools with which it can be fitted and to the machinery which operates it. Its tools are fines, imprisonment, or lesser forms of supervision (such as Borstal and probation) and—not to be ignored—the degradation that often follows upon the publication of the crime. Are any of these suited to the job of dealing with sexual immorality? The fact that there is so much immorality which has never been brought within the law shows that there can be no general rule. It is a matter for decision in each case; but in the case of homosexuality the Wolfenden Report rightly has regard to the views of those who are experienced in dealing with this sort of crime and to those of the clergy who are the natural guardians of public morals.

The machinery which sets the criminal law in motion ends with the verdict and the sentence; and a verdict is given either by magistrates or by a jury. As a general rule, whenever a crime is sufficiently serious to justify a maximum punishment of more than three months, the accused has the right to the verdict of a jury. The result is that magistrates administer mostly what I have called the regulatory part of the law. They deal extensively with drunkenness, gambling,

25 A case in the Saa-Katengo Kuta at Lialiu, August 1942, quoted in *The Judicial Process among the Barotse of Northern Rhodesia* by Max Gluckman, Manchester UP, 1955, p. 172.

and prostitution, which are matters of morals or close to them, but not with any of the graver moral offences. They are more responsive than juries to the ideas of the legislature; it may not be accidental that the Wolfenden Report, in recommending increased penalties for solicitation, did not go above the limit of three months. Juries tend to dilute the decrees of Parliament with their own ideas of what should be punishable. Their province of course is fact and not law, and I do not mean that they often deliberately disregard the law. But if they think it is too stringent, they sometimes take a very merciful view of the facts. Let me take one example out of many that could be given. It is an offence to have carnal knowledge of a girl under the age of sixteen years. Consent on her part is no defence; if she did not consent, it would of course amount to rape. The law makes special provision for the situation when a boy and girl are near in age. If a man under twenty-four can prove that he had reasonable cause to believe that the girl was over the age of sixteen years, he has a good defence. The law regards the offence as sufficiently serious to make it one that is triable only by a judge at assizes. "Reasonable cause" means not merely that the boy honestly believed that the girl was over sixteen but also that he must have had reasonable grounds for his belief. In theory it ought not to be an easy defence to make out but in fact it is extremely rare for anyone who advances it to be convicted. The fact is that the girl is often as much to blame as the boy. The object of the law, as judges repeatedly tell juries, is to protect young girls against themselves; but juries are not impressed.

The part that the jury plays in the enforcement of the criminal law, the fact that no grave offence against morals is punishable without their verdict, these are of great importance in relation to the statements of principle that I have been making. They turn what might otherwise be pure exhortation to the legislature into something like rules that the lawmakers cannot safely ignore. The man in the jury box is not just an expression; he is an active reality. It will not in the long run work to make laws about morality that are not acceptable to him.

This then is how I believe my third interrogatory should be answered—not by the formulation of hard and fast rules, but by a judgement in each case taking into account the sort of factors I have been mentioning. The line that divides the criminal law from the moral is not determinable by the application of any clear-cut principle. It is like a line that divides land and sea, a coastline of irregularities and indentations. There are gaps and promontories, such as adultery and fornication, which the law has for centuries left substantially untouched. Adultery of the sort that breaks up marriage seems to me to be just as harmful to the social fabric as homosexuality or bigamy. The only ground for putting it outside the criminal law is that a law which made it a crime would be too difficult to enforce; it is too generally regarded as a human weakness not suitably punished by imprisonment. All that the law can do with fornication is to act against its worst manifestations; there is a general abhorrence of the commercialization of vice, and that sentiment gives strength to the law against brothels and immoral earnings. There is no logic to be found in this. The boundary between the criminal law and the moral law is fixed by balancing in the case of each particular crime the pros and cons of legal enforcement in accordance with the sort of considerations I have been outlining. The fact that adultery, fornication, and lesbianism are untouched by the criminal law does not prove that homosexuality ought not to be touched. The error of jurisprudence in the Wolfenden Report is caused by the search for some single principle to explain the division between crime and sin. The Report finds it in the principle that the criminal law exists for the protection of individuals; on this principle fornication in private between consenting adults is outside the law and thus it becomes logically indefensible to bring homosexuality between consenting adults in private within it. But the true principle is that the law exists for the protection of society. It does not discharge its function by protecting the individual from injury, annoyance, corruption, and exploitation; the law must protect also the institutions and the community of ideas, political and moral, without which people cannot live together. Society cannot ignore the morality of the individual any more than it can his loyalty; it flourishes on both and without either it dies.

I have said that the morals which underly the law must be derived from the sense of right and wrong which resides in the community as a whole; it does not matter whence the community of thought comes, whether from one body of doctrine or another or from the knowledge of good and evil which no man is without. If the reasonable man believes that a practice is immoral and believes also—no matter whether the belief is right or wrong, so be it that it is honest and dispassionate—that no right-minded member of his society could think otherwise, then for the purpose of the law it is immoral. This, you may say, makes immorality a question of fact—what the law would consider as self-evident fact no doubt, but still with no higher authority than any other doctrine of public policy. I think that that is so, and indeed the law does not distinguish between an act that is immoral and one that is contrary to public policy. But the law has never yet had occasion to inquire into the differences between Christian morals and those which every right-minded member of society is expected to hold. The inquiry would, I believe, be academic. Moralists would find differences; indeed they would find them between different branches of the Christian faith on subjects such as divorce and birth-control. But for the purpose of the limited entry which the law makes into the field of morals, there is no practical difference. It seems to me therefore that the free-thinker and the non-Christian can accept, without offence to his convictions, the fact that Christian morals are the basis of the criminal law and that he can recognize, also without taking offence, that without the support of the churches the moral order, which has its origin in and takes its strength from Christian beliefs, would collapse.

This brings me back in the end to a question I posed at the beginning. What is the relationship between crime and sin, between the Church and the Law? I do not think that you can equate crime with sin. The divine law and the secular have been disunited, but they are brought together again by the need which each has for the other. It is not my function to emphasize the Church's need of the secular law; it can be put tersely by saying that you cannot have a ceiling without a floor. I am very clear about the law's need for the Church. I have spoken of the criminal law as dealing with the minimum standards of human conduct and the moral law with the maximum. The instrument of the criminal law is punishment; those of the moral law are teaching, training, and exhortation. If the whole dead weight of sin were ever to be allowed to fall upon the law, it could not take the strain. If at any point there is a lack of clear and convincing moral teaching, the administration of the law suffers. Let me take as an illustration of this the law on abortion. I believe that a great many people nowadays do not understand why abortion is wrong. If it is right to prevent conception, at what point does it become sinful to prevent birth and why? I doubt if anyone who has not had a theological training would give a satisfactory answer to that question. Many people regard abortion as the next step when by accident birth-control has failed; and many more people are deterred from abortion not because they think it sinful or illegal but because of the difficulty which illegality puts in the way of obtaining it. The law is powerless to deal with abortion *per se*; unless a tragedy occurs or a "professional" abortionist is involved—the parallel between the "professional" in abortions and the "professional" in fornication is quite close—it has to leave it alone. Without one or other of these features the crime is rarely detected; and when detected, the plea *ad misericordiam* is often too strong. The "professional" abortionist is usually the unskilled person who for a small reward helps girls in trouble; the man and the girl involved are essential witnesses for the prosecution and therefore go free; the paid abortionist generally receives a very severe sentence, much more severe than that usually given to the paid assistant in immorality, such as the ponce or the brothel-keeper. The reason is because unskilled abortion endangers life. In a case in 1949,[26] Lord Chief Justice Goddard said: "It is because the unskilful attentions of ignorant people in cases of this kind often result in death that attempts to produce abortion are regarded by the law as very serious offences." This gives the law a twist which disassociates it from morality and, I think, to some extent from sound sense. The act is being punished because it is dangerous, and it is dangerous largely because it is illegal and therefore performed only by the unskilled.

The object of what I have said is not to criticize theology or law in relation to abortion. That is a large subject and beyond my present scope. It is to show what happens to the law in matters of morality about which the community as a whole is not deeply imbued with a sense of sin; the law sags under a weight which it is not constructed to bear and may become permanently warped.

I return now to the main thread of my argument and summarize it. Society cannot live without morals. Its morals are those standards of conduct which the reasonable man approves. A rational man, who is also a good man, may have other standards. If he has no standards at all he is not a good man and need not be further considered. If he has standards, they may be very different; he may, for example, not disapprove of homosexuality or abortion. In that case he will not share in the common morality; but that should not make him deny that it is a social necessity. A rebel may be rational in thinking that he is right but he is irrational if he thinks that society can leave him free to rebel.

A man who concedes that morality is necessary to society must support the use of those instruments without which morality cannot be maintained. The two instruments are those of teaching, which is doctrine, and of enforcement, which is the law. If morals could be taught simply on the basis that they are necessary to society, there would be no social need for religion; it could be left as a purely personal affair. But morality cannot be taught in that way. Loyalty is not taught in that way either. No society has yet solved the problem of how to teach morality without religion. So the law must base itself on Christian morals and to the limit of its ability enforce them, not simply because they are the morals of most of us, nor simply because they are the morals which are taught by the established Church—on these points the law recognizes the right to dissent—but for the compelling reason that without the help of Christian teaching the law will fail.

26 *R. v. Tate*, *The Times*, 22 June 1949.

20
H.L.A. Hart
from *Law, Liberty and Morality*

... Much dissatisfaction has for long been felt in England with the criminal law relating to both prostitution and homosexuality, and in 1954 the committee well known as the Wolfenden Committee was appointed to consider the state of the law. This committee reported[14] in September 1957 and recommended certain changes in the law on both topics. As to homosexuality they recommended by a majority of 12 to 1 that homosexual practices between consenting adults in private should no longer be a crime; as to prostitution they unanimously recommended that, though it should not itself be made illegal, legislation should be passed "to drive it off the streets" on the ground that public soliciting was an offensive nuisance to ordinary citizens. The government eventually introduced legislation[15] to give effect to the Committee's recommendations concerning prostitution but not to that concerning homosexuality, and attempts by private members to introduce legislation modifying the law on this subject have so far failed.

What concerns us here is less the fate of the Wolfenden Committee's recommendations than the principles by which these were supported. These are strikingly similar to those expounded by Mill in his essay *On Liberty*. Thus section 13 of the Committee's Report reads:

> [The] function [of the criminal law], as we see it, is to preserve public order and decency, to protect the citizen from what is offensive or injurious and to provide sufficient safeguards against exploitation or corruption of others, particularly those who are specially vulnerable because they are young, weak in body or mind or inexperienced ...

This conception of the positive functions of the criminal law was the Committee's main ground for its recommendation concerning prostitution that legislation should be passed to suppress the offensive public manifestations of prostitution, but not to make prostitution itself illegal. Its recommendation that the law against homosexual practices between consenting adults in private should be relaxed was based on the principle stated simply in section 61 of the Report as follows: "There must remain a realm of private morality and immorality which is, in brief and crude terms, not the law's business."

It is of some interest that these developments in England have had near counterparts in America. In 1955 the American Law Institute published with its draft Model Penal Code a recommendation that all consensual relations between adults in private should be excluded from the scope of the criminal law. Its grounds were (*inter alia*) that "no harm to the secular interests of the community is involved in atypical sex practice in private between consenting adult partners";[16] and "there is the fundamental question of the protection to which every individual is entitled against state interference in his

14 Report of the Committee on Homosexual Offences and Prostitution (CMD 247) 1957.

15 The Street Offences Act 1959.

16 American Law Institute Model Penal Code, Tentative Draft No. 4, p. 277.

personal affairs when he is not hurting others."[17] This recommendation had been approved by the Advisory Committee of the Institute but rejected by a majority vote of its Council. The issue was therefore referred to the annual meeting of the Institute at Washington in May 1955, and the recommendation, supported by an eloquent speech of the late Justice Learned Hand, was, after a hot debate, accepted by a majority of 35 to 24.[18]

It is perhaps clear from the foregoing that Mill's principles are still very much alive in the criticism of law, whatever their theoretical deficiencies may be. But twice in one hundred years they have been challenged by two masters of the Common Law. The first of these was the great Victorian judge and historian of the Criminal Law, James Fitzjames Stephen. His criticism of Mill is to be found in the sombre and impressive book *Liberty, Equality, Fraternity*,[19] which he wrote as a direct reply to Mill's essay *On Liberty*. It is evident from the tone of this book that Stephen thought he had found crushing arguments against Mill and had demonstrated that the law might justifiably enforce morality as such or, as he said, that the law should be "a persecution of the grosser forms of vice."[20] Nearly a century later, on the publication of the Wolfenden Committee's report, Lord Devlin, now a member of the House of Lords and a most distinguished writer on the criminal law, in his essay on *The Enforcement of Morals*[21] took as his target the Report's contention "that there must be a realm of morality and immorality which is not the law's business" and argued in opposition to it that "the suppression of vice is as much the law's business as the suppression of subversive activities."

Though a century divides these two legal writers, the similarity in the general tone and sometimes in the detail of their arguments is very great. I shall devote the remainder of these lectures to an examination of them. I do this because, though their arguments are at points confused, they certainly still deserve the compliment of rational opposition. They are not only admirably stocked with concrete examples, but they express the considered views of skilled, sophisticated lawyers experienced in the administration of the criminal law. Views such as theirs are still quite widely held especially by lawyers both in England and in this country; it may indeed be that they are more popular, in both countries, than Mill's doctrine of Liberty.

Positive and Critical Morality

Before we consider the detail of these arguments, it is, I think, necessary to appreciate three different but connected features of the question with which we are concerned.

[*Ed. note*: Earlier in his lecture Hart states that his goal is to consider a question which "... concerns the legal enforcement of morality and has been formulated in many different ways: Is the fact that certain conduct is by common standards immoral sufficient to justify making that conduct punishable by law? Is it morally permissible to enforce morality as such? Ought immorality as such be a crime?"]

In all the three formulations given ... it is plain that the question is one *about* morality, but it is important to observe that it is also itself a question of morality. It is the question whether the enforcement *of* morality is morally justified; so morality enters into the question in two ways. The importance of this feature of the question is that it would plainly be no sufficient answer to show that in fact in some society—our own or

17 Ibid., p. 278.
18 An account of the debate is given in *Time*, May 30, 1955, p. 13.
19 2nd edition, London, 1874.
20 Ibid., p. 162.
21 Oxford UP, 1959.

others—it was widely regarded as morally quite right and proper to enforce, by legal punishment, compliance with the accepted morality. No one who seriously debates this question would regard Mill as refuted by the simple demonstration that there are some societies in which the generally shared morality endorses its own enforcement by law, and does so even in those cases where the immorality was thought harmless to others. The existence of societies which condemn association between white and coloured persons as immoral and punish it by law still leaves our question to be argued. It is true that Mill's critics have often made much of the fact that English law does in several instances, apparently with the support of popular morality, punish immorality as such, especially in sexual matters; but they have usually admitted that this is where the argument begins, not where it ends. I shall indeed later claim that the play made by some legal writers with what they treat as examples of the legal enforcement of morality "as such" is sometimes confused. But they do not, at any rate, put forward their case as simply proved by pointing to these social facts. Instead they attempt to base their own conclusion that it is morally justifiable to use the criminal law in this way on principles which they believe to be universally applicable, and which they think are either quite obviously rational or will be seen to be so after discussion.

Thus Lord Devlin bases his affirmative answer to the question on the quite general principle that it is permissible for any society to take the steps needed to preserve its own existence as an organized society,[22] and he thinks that immorality—even private sexual immorality—may, like treason, be something which jeopardizes a society's existence. Of course many of us may doubt this general principle, and not merely the suggested analogy with treason. We might wish to argue that whether or not a society is justified in taking steps to preserve itself must depend both on what sort of society it is and what the steps to be taken are. If a society were mainly devoted to the cruel persecution of a racial or religious minority, or if the steps to be taken included hideous tortures, it is arguable that what Lord Devlin terms the "disintegration"[23] of such a society would be morally better than its continued existence, and steps ought not to be taken to preserve it. Nonetheless Lord Devlin's principle that a society may take the steps required to preserve its organized existence is not itself tendered as an item of English popular morality, deriving its cogency from its status as part of our institutions. He puts it forward as a principle, rationally acceptable, to be used in the evaluation or criticism of social institutions generally. And it is surely clear that anyone who holds the question whether a society has the "right" to enforce morality, or whether it is morally permissible for any society to enforce its morality by law, to be discussable at all, must be prepared to deploy some such general principles of critical morality.[24] In asking the question, we are assuming the legitimacy of a standpoint which permits criticism of the institutions of any society, in the light of general principles and knowledge of the facts.

To make this point clear, I would revive the terminology much favoured by the Utilitarians of the last century, which distinguished "positive morality," the morality actually accepted and shared by a given social group, from the general moral principles used in the criticism of actual

22 *The Enforcement of Morals*, pp. 13–14.

23 Ibid., pp. 14–15.

24 Lord Devlin has been criticised for asking the question whether society has a *right* to enforce its judgment in matters of morality on the ground that to talk of "right" in such a context is meaningless. See Graham Hughes, "Morals and the Criminal Law," 71 *Yale L.J.* (1962) at 672. This criticism is mistaken, just because Lord Devlin invokes some general critical principle in support of his affirmative answer to the question.

social institutions including positive morality. We may call such general principles "critical morality" and say that our question is one of critical morality about the legal enforcement of positive morality.

A second feature of our question worth attention is simply that it is a question of *justification*. In asking it we are committed at least to the general critical principle that the use of legal coercion by any society calls for justification as something *prima facie* objectionable to be tolerated only for the sake of some countervailing good. For where there is no *prima facie* objection, wrong, or evil, men do not ask for or give justifications of social practices, though they may ask for and give *explanations* of these practices or may attempt to demonstrate their value.

It is salutary to inquire precisely what it is that is *prima facie* objectionable in the legal enforcement of morality; for the idea of legal enforcement is in fact less simple than is often assumed. It has two different but related aspects. One is the actual punishment of the offender. This characteristically involves depriving him of liberty of movement or of property or of association with family or friends, or the infliction upon him of physical pain or even death. All these are things which are assumed to be wrong to inflict on others without special justification, and in fact they are so regarded by the law and morality of all developed societies. To put it as a lawyer would, these are things which, if they are not justified as sanctions, are delicts or wrongs.

The second aspect of legal enforcement bears on those who may never offend against the law, but are coerced into obedience by the threat of legal punishment. This rather than physical restrictions is what is normally meant in the discussion of political arrangements by restrictions on liberty. Such restrictions, it is to be noted, may be thought of as calling for justification for several quite distinct reasons. The unimpeded exercise by individuals of free choice may be held a value in itself with which it is *prima facie* wrong to interfere; or it may be thought valuable because it enables individuals to experiment—even with living—and to discover things valuable both to themselves and to others. But interference with individual liberty may be thought an evil requiring justification for simpler, utilitarian reasons; for it is itself the infliction of a special form of suffering—often very acute—on those whose desires are frustrated by the fear of punishment. This is of particular importance in the case of laws enforcing a sexual morality. They may create misery of a quite special degree. For both the difficulties involved in the repression of sexual impulses and the consequences of repression are quite different from those involved in the abstention from "ordinary" crime. Unlike sexual impulses, the impulse to steal or to wound or even kill is not, except in a minority of mentally abnormal cases, a recurrent and insistent part of daily life. Resistance to the temptation to commit these crimes is not often, as the suppression of sexual impulses generally is, something which affects the development or balance of the individual's emotional life, happiness, and personality.

Thirdly, the distinction already made, between positive morality and principles of critical morality, may serve to dissipate a certain misunderstanding of the question and to clarify its central point. It is sometimes said that the question is not whether it is morally justifiable to enforce morality as such, but only *which* morality may be enforced. Is it only a utilitarian morality condemning activities which are harmful to others? Or is it a morality which also condemns certain activities whether they are harmful or not? This way of regarding the question misrepresents the character of, at any rate, modern controversy. A utilitarian who insists that the law should only punish activities which are harmful adopts this as a critical principle, and, in so doing, he is quite unconcerned with the question whether a utilitarian morality is or is not already accepted as the positive morality of the society to which he applies his critical principles. If it is so accepted, that is not, in his view, the reason why it should be enforced. It is true that if he is successful in preaching his message to a given society, members of it will then be compelled to behave as utilitarians in certain ways, but these facts do not mean that the vital difference between him and his opponent is only as to the content of the morality to be enforced. For as may be seen from the main criticisms of Mill, the Utilitarian's opponent, who insists that it is morally permissible to enforce morality as such, believes that the mere fact that certain rules or standards of behaviour enjoy the status of a society's positive morality is the reason—or at least part of the reason—which justifies their enforcement by law. No doubt in older controversies the opposed positions were different: the question may have been whether the state could punish only activities causing secular harm or also acts of disobedience to what were believed to be divine commands or prescriptions of Natural Law. But what is crucial to the dispute in its modern form is the significance to be attached to the historical fact that certain conduct, no matter what, is prohibited by a positive morality. The utilitarian denies that this has any significance sufficient to justify its enforcement; his opponent asserts that it has. These are divergent critical principles which do not differ merely over the content of the morality to be enforced, but over a more fundamental and, surely, more interesting issue.

The Use and Abuse of Examples

Both in England and in America the criminal law still contains rules which can only be explained as attempts to enforce morality as such: to suppress practices condemned as immoral by positive morality though they involve nothing that would ordinarily be thought of as harm to other persons. Most of the examples come from the sphere of sexual morals, and in England they include laws against various forms of homosexual behaviour between males, sodomy between persons of different sex even if married, bestiality, incest, living on the earnings of prostitution, keeping a house for prostitution, and also, since the decision in Shaw's case, a conspiracy to corrupt public morals, interpreted to mean, in substance, leading others (in the opinion of a jury) "morally astray." To this list some would add further cases: the laws against abortion, against those forms of bigamy or polygamy which do not involve deception, against suicide and the practice of euthanasia. But, as I shall later argue, the treatment of some of these latter as attempts to enforce morality as such, is a mistake due to the neglect of certain important distinctions....

Paternalism and the Enforcement of Morality

I shall start with an example stressed by Lord Devlin. He points out that,[7] subject to certain exceptions such as rape, the criminal law has never admitted the consent of the victim as a defence. It is not a defence to a charge of murder or a deliberate assault, and this is why euthanasia or mercy killing terminating a man's life at his own request is still murder. This is a rule of criminal law which many now would wish to retain, though they would also wish to object to the legal punishment of offences against positive morality which harm no one. Lord Devlin thinks that these attitudes are inconsistent, for he asserts of the rule under discussion, "There is only one explanation," and this is that "there are certain standards of behaviour or moral principles which society requires to be observed."[8] Among these are the sanctity of human life and presumably (since the rule applies to assaults) the physical

7 *The Enforcement of Morals*, p. 8.
8 Ibid.

integrity of the person. So in the case of this rule and a number of others Lord Devlin claims that the "function" of the criminal law is "to enforce a moral principle and nothing else."[9]

But this argument is not really cogent, for Lord Devlin's statement that "there is only one explanation" is simply not true. The rules excluding the victim's consent as a defence to charges of murder or assault may perfectly well be explained as a piece of paternalism, designed to protect individuals against themselves. Mill no doubt might have protested against a paternalistic policy of using the law to protect even a consenting victim from bodily harm nearly as much as he protested against laws used merely to enforce positive morality; but this does not mean that these two policies are identical. Indeed, Mill himself was very well aware of the difference between them: for in condemning interference with individual liberty except to prevent harm to others he mentions *separate* types of inadequate ground which have been proffered for the use of compulsion. He distinguishes "because it will be better for him" and "because it will make him happier" from "because in the opinion of others it would be right."[10]

Lord Devlin says of the attitude of the criminal law to the victim's consent that if the law existed for the protection of the individual there would be no reason why he should avail himself of it if he did not want it.[11] But paternalism—the protection of people against themselves—is a perfectly coherent policy. Indeed, it seems very strange in mid-twentieth century to insist upon this, for the wane of laissez faire since Mill's day is one of the commonplaces of social history, and instances of paternalism now abound in our law, criminal and civil. The supply of drugs or narcotics, even to adults, except under medical prescription is punishable by the criminal law, and it would seem very dogmatic to say of the law creating this offence that "there is only one explanation," namely, that the law was concerned not with the protection of the would-be purchasers against themselves, but only with the punishment of the seller for his immorality. If, as seems obvious, paternalism is a possible explanation of such laws, it is also possible in the case of the rule excluding the consent of the victim as a defence to a charge of assault. In neither case are we forced to conclude with Lord Devlin that the law's "function is to enforce a moral principle and nothing else."[12]

In Chapter 5 of his essay Mill carried his protests against paternalism to lengths that may now appear to us fantastic. He cites the example of restrictions of the sale of drugs, and criticises them as interferences with the liberty of the would-be purchaser rather than with that of the seller. No doubt if we no longer sympathise with this criticism this is due, in part, to a general decline in the belief that individuals know their own interests best, and to an increased awareness of a great range of factors which diminish the significance to be attached to an apparently free choice or to consent. Choices may be made or consent given without adequate reflection or appreciation of the consequences; or in pursuit of merely transitory desires; or in various predicaments when the judgment is likely to be clouded; or under inner psychological compulsion; or under pressure by others of a kind too subtle to be susceptible of proof in a law court. Underlying Mill's extreme fear of paternalism there perhaps is a conception of what a normal human being is like which now seems not to correspond to the facts. Mill, in fact, endows him with too much of the psychology of a middle-aged man whose

9 Ibid., p. 9.
10 *On Liberty*, Chapter I.
11 *The Enforcement of Morals*, p. 8.
12 See, for other possible explanations of these rules, Hughes, "Morals and the Criminal Law," p. 670.

desires are relatively fixed, not liable to be artificially stimulated by external influences; who knows what he wants and what gives him satisfaction or happiness; and who pursues these things when he can.

Certainly a modification in Mill's principles is required, if they are to accommodate the rule of criminal law under discussion or other instances of paternalism. But the modified principles would not abandon the objection to the use of the criminal law merely to enforce positive morality. They would only have to provide that harming others is something we may still seek to prevent by use of the criminal law, even when the victims consent to or assist in the acts which are harmful to them. The neglect of the distinction between paternalism and what I have termed legal moralism is important as a form of a more general error. It is too often assumed that if a law is not designed to protect one man from another its only rationale can be that it is designed to punish moral wickedness or, in Lord Devlin's words, "to enforce a moral principle." Thus it is often urged that statutes punishing cruelty to animals can only be explained in that way. But it is certainly intelligible, both as an account of the original motives inspiring such legislation and as the specification of an aim widely held to be worth pursuing, to say that the law is here concerned with the *suffering*, albeit only of animals, rather than with the immorality of torturing them.[13] Certainly no one who supports this use of the criminal law is thereby bound in consistency to admit that the law may punish forms of immorality which involve no suffering to any sentient being....

The Moderate and the Extreme Thesis

When we turn from these examples which are certainly disputable to the positive grounds held to justify the legal enforcement of morality it is important to distinguish a moderate and an extreme thesis, though critics of Mill have sometimes moved from one to the other without marking the transition. Lord Devlin seems to me to maintain, for most of his essay, the moderate thesis and Stephen the extreme one.

According to the moderate thesis, a shared morality is the cement of society; without it there would be aggregates of individuals but no society. "A recognized morality" is, in Lord Devlin's words, "as necessary to society's existence as a recognized government,"[26] and though a particular act of immorality may not harm or endanger or corrupt others nor, when done in private, either shock or give offence to others, this does not conclude the matter. For we must not view conduct in isolation from its effect on the moral code: if we remember this, we can see that one who is "no menace to others" nonetheless may by his immoral conduct "threaten one of the great moral principles on which society is based."[27] In this sense the breach of moral principle is an offence "against society as a whole,"[28] and society may use the law to preserve its morality as it uses it to safeguard anything else essential to its existence. This is why "the suppression of vice is as much the law's business as the suppression of subversive activities."[29]

By contrast, the extreme thesis does not look upon a shared morality as of merely instrumental value analogous to ordered government, and it does not justify the punishment of immorality as a step taken, like the punishment of treason,

13 Lord Devlin seems quite unaccountably to ignore this point in his brief reference to cruelty to animals, *The Enforcement of Morals*, p. 17.

26 *The Enforcement of Morals*, p. 13.

27 Ibid., p. 8.

28 Ibid.

29 Ibid., p. 15.

to preserve society from dissolution or collapse. Instead, the enforcement of morality is regarded as a thing of value, even if immoral acts harm no one directly, or indirectly by weakening the moral cement of society. I do not say that it is possible to allot to one or other of these two theses every argument used, but they do, I think, characterise the main critical positions at the root of most arguments, and they incidentally exhibit an ambiguity in the expression "enforcing morality as such." Perhaps the clearest way of distinguishing the two theses is to see that there are always two levels at which we may ask whether some breach of positive morality is harmful. We may ask first, Does this act harm anyone independently of its repercussion on the shared morality of society? And secondly we may ask, Does this act affect the shared morality and thereby weaken society? The moderate thesis requires, if the punishment of the act is to be justified, an affirmative answer at least at the second level. The extreme thesis does not require an affirmative answer at either level.

Lord Devlin appears to defend the moderate thesis. I say "appears" because, though he says that society has the right to enforce a morality as such on the ground that a shared morality is essential to society's existence, it is not at all clear that for him the statement that immorality jeopardizes or weakens society is a statement of empirical fact. It seems sometimes to be an *a priori* assumption, and sometimes a necessary truth and a very odd one. The most important indication that this is so is that, apart from one vague reference to "history" showing that "the loosening of moral bonds is often the first stage of disintegration,"[30] no evidence is produced to show that deviation from accepted sexual morality, even by adults in private, is something which, like treason, threatens the existence of society. No reputable historian has maintained this thesis, and there is indeed much evidence against it. As a proposition of fact it is entitled to no more respect than the Emperor Justinian's statement that homosexuality was the cause of earthquakes.[31] Lord Devlin's belief in it, and his apparent indifference to the question of evidence, are at points traceable to an undiscussed assumption. This is that all morality—sexual morality together with the morality that forbids acts injurious to others such as killing, stealing, and dishonesty—forms a single seamless web, so that those who deviate from any part are likely or perhaps bound to deviate from the whole. It is of course clear (and one of the oldest insights of political theory) that society could not exist without a morality which mirrored and supplemented the law's proscription of conduct injurious to others. But there is again no evidence to support, and much to refute, the theory that those who deviate from conventional sexual morality are in other ways hostile to society.

There seems, however, to be central to Lord Devlin's thought something more interesting, though no more convincing, than the conception of social morality as a seamless web. For he appears to move from the acceptable proposition that *some* shared morality is essential to the existence of any society to the unacceptable proposition that a society is identical[32] with its morality as that is at any given moment of its history, so that a change in its morality is tantamount to the destruction of a society. The former proposition might be even accepted as a necessary rather than an empirical truth depending on a quite plausible definition of society as a body of men who hold certain moral views in common. But the latter proposition is absurd. Taken strictly,

30 *The Enforcement of Morals*, pp. 14–15.
31 *Novels*, 77 Cap. 1 and 141.
32 See, for this important point, Richard Wollheim, "Crime, Sin, and Mr. Justice Devlin," *Encounter*, November 1959, p. 34.

it would prevent us saying that the morality of a given society had changed, and would compel us instead to say that one society had disappeared and another one taken its place. But it is only on this absurd criterion of what it is for the same society to continue to exist that it could be asserted without evidence that any deviation from a society's shared morality threatens its existence.

It is clear that only this tacit identification of a society with its shared morality supports Lord Devlin's denial that there could be such a thing as private immorality and his comparison of sexual immorality, even when it takes place "in private," with treason. No doubt it is true that if deviations from conventional sexual morality are tolerated by the law and come to be known, the conventional morality might change in a permissive direction, though this does not seem to be the case with homosexuality in those European countries where it is not punishable by law. But even if the conventional morality did so change, the society in question would not have been destroyed or "subverted." We should compare such a development not to the violent overthrow of government but to a peaceful constitutional change in its form, consistent not only with the preservation of a society but with its advance.

Conclusion

I have from the beginning assumed that anyone who raises, or is willing to debate, the question whether it is justifiable to enforce morality, accepts the view that the actual institutions of any society, including its positive morality, are open to criticism. Hence the proposition that it is justifiable to enforce morality is, like its negation, a thesis of critical morality requiring for its support some general critical principle. It cannot be established or refuted simply by pointing to the actual practices or morality of a particular society or societies. Lord Devlin, whose thesis I termed the moderate thesis, seems to accept this position, but I have argued that the general critical principle which he deploys, namely, that a society has the right to take any step necessary for its preservation, is inadequate for his purpose. There is no evidence that the preservation of a society requires the enforcement of its morality "as such." His position only appears to escape this criticism by a confused definition of what a society is.

I have also assumed from the beginning that anyone who regards this question as open to discussion necessarily accepts the critical principle, central to all morality, that human misery and the restriction of freedom are evils; for that is why the legal enforcement of morality calls for justification. I then endeavoured to extricate, and to free from ambiguity of statement, the general principles underlying several varieties of the more extreme thesis that the enforcement of morality or its preservation from change were valuable apart from their beneficial consequences in preserving society. These principles in fact invite us to consider as values, for the sake of which we should restrict human freedom and inflict the misery of punishment on human beings, things which seem to belong to the prehistory of morality and to be quite hostile to its general spirit. They include mere outward conformity to moral rules induced simply by fear; the gratification of feelings of hatred for the wrongdoer or his "retributory" punishment, even where there has been no victim to be avenged or to call for justice; the infliction of punishment as a symbol or expression of moral condemnation: the mere insulation from change of any social morality however repressive or barbarous. No doubt I have not *proved* these things not to be values worth their price in human suffering and loss of freedom; it may be enough to have shown what it is that is offered for the price.

Study Questions

1. Can Mill's distinction between self- and other-regarding actions be maintained in contemporary Western society?
2. What dangerous consequences might arise from distinguishing between harmful conduct which may justifiably be legally limited, and merely offensive conduct which does not cause harm and for that reason may not justifiably be legally limited?
3. Even when we know what is in our interests, we often make mistakes as we choose courses of action intended to support those interests. Is our fallibility a good reason for the law to be paternalistic?
4. Is Devlin's argument that a society has the right to legislate against disgusting conduct a good argument? Why or why not?
5. Is Hart's criticism of Devlin's conception of society plausible? What might a society under law be besides a community of shared ideals?
6. To what extent are our liberties dependent on context? Could there be times of emergency when even protection of basic rights and freedoms might need to be relaxed?

Further Readings

Gerald Dworkin, ed., *Morality, Harm, and the Law*. Boulder, CO: Westview P, 1994.
Joel Feinberg, *The Moral Limits of the Criminal Law: Harm to Others*. Oxford: Oxford UP, 1984.
—, *Harm to Self*. Oxford: Oxford UP, 1986.
—, *Offense to Others*. Oxford: Oxford UP, 1986.
—, *Harmless Wrongdoing*. Oxford: Oxford UP, 1988.
Leslie Green, "Should Law Improve Morality?," in *The Germ of Justice: Essays in General Jurisprudence*. Oxford: Oxford UP, 2023.
Rolf Sartorius, ed., *Paternalism*. Minneapolis: U of Minnesota P, 1983.
James Fitzjames Stephen, *Liberty, Equality, Fraternity*. Chicago: U of Chicago P, 1991.
Wayne Sumner, *The Hateful and the Obscene: Studies in the Limits of Free Expression*. Toronto: U of Toronto P, 2003.
Jeremy Waldron, "The Right to Do Wrong," in *Liberal Rights: Collected Papers, 1981–1991*. Cambridge: Cambridge UP, 1993.

SECTION 7

Criminal Responsibility and Punishment

Introduction

News and talk of criminal responsibility and punishment are so much a part of our daily lives that it is tempting to suppose that these ideas and their relation are quite simple. Politicians know they can demonstrate their seriousness by promising tough punishments for crime, with little likelihood of opposition. Crime is bad, and punishment is what awaits criminals, so potential criminals should think twice about committing a crime, and if they do commit a crime, they should be unsurprised that they will be subject to unpleasant penalties. On this simple view of criminal responsibility and punishment, if there are questions about these ideas, they are practical questions about how to capture criminals and how to ensure that punishment fits the crime.

The simple view of criminal responsibility and punishment is so attractive that it is easy to overlook the fact that it is accompanied by a set of nagging worries and doubts. Those doubts are closely connected to the way criminal conduct is identified and punished. The seriousness of a criminal conviction as a denunciation or condemnation of conduct is reflected in the nature of the maximum penalties for criminal wrongdoing: imprisonment, or in the most serious cases in some jurisdictions, death. The seriousness of criminal conviction is also reflected in the standard of proof required for conviction. A person accused of a serious crime is generally required to be shown to be guilty beyond reasonable doubt, a higher standard than that found in civil suits where the plaintiff need only show that it is more probable than not that the respondent breached their legal obligations to the plaintiff. In the political cultures of countries inheriting the structures of the English common law system, individual freedom to make and carry out a life plan has long been at the heart of a range of special rights and procedural protections designed to limit individual liberty as little as possible, and only when necessary. The association of serious punishment with a high standard of proof is then reflected in the concern that our understanding of what a crime is must be very clear if we are to avoid the terrible harm done by a wrongful conviction, whether wrong because the wrong person is found guilty, or wrong because the conviction does not give a correct account of what the convicted person actually did. In considering the dangers of a system that may in wrongful conviction administer punishment we cannot undo, we come to the larger question of just how to ensure that punishment of individuals can be meaningfully isolated to those individuals in ways safeguarding individuals from becoming little more than emblems of the state's ability to wield power against individuals. It is one thing to design a criminal justice system, after all, and quite another to operate it exactly as designed, without error or failure. Can systems be operated with acceptable types and amounts of error? Or should we reconsider how we punish wrongdoing in systems of criminal law so subject to human error and bias that we cannot justify the human cost of error?

The readings in this section demonstrate reasoning regarding a range of worries and doubts regarding the simple view of criminal responsibility and attempts. Our investigation begins not with the relation between a given crime and its punishment, but rather in what might be called the 'beginning' or 'interior' of those crimes committed voluntarily and intentionally. Our first excerpt is from *Criminal Attempts*, by Professor R. Antony Duff, investigating the difficult question of how far intention, or what someone "meant to do," must be put into action before a crime occurs. In the second selection Professor Heidi Hurd explores some of the difficulties liberal democracies face in imposing more severe punishments for criminal offences committed on the basis of hate or prejudice. The section concludes with a selection in which Professor Jeffrie Murphy argues that the best available theory justifying the institution of punishment may nonetheless have no applicability in the common law systems of contemporary societies, given their deep and enduring material inequality. The remainder of this introduction discusses some of the main ideas found in these readings.

1. Professor R.A. Duff on Intentions and Actions

In the excerpt we provide from *Criminal Attempts*, Duff is concerned with how we may best characterize the most serious type of voluntary, intentional criminal wrongdoing in a way which captures those who are genuinely guilty, and guards against wrongful conviction of those who ought not to bear liability-responsibility for some situation, or ought to bear a lesser degree of liability-responsibility.

1.1 *MENS REA* AND *ACTUS REUS*

A large number of serious crimes are understood in terms of two elements: intention and conduct. A crime of this type consists of the *intention* to commit an action which is prohibited by criminal law, and completion of the prohibited *conduct*. Two Latin terms are commonly used to capture these two ideas. The idea of intention or "guilty mind" is contained in the term *mens rea* and the idea of conduct is contained in the term *actus reus*. So, for example, the crime of murder requires both the intention to kill and the completed conduct in which a person is actually killed. This apparently simple way of analyzing and categorizing the components of the crime of murder is in fact part of a very complex understanding of voluntary, intentional criminal wrongdoing. More must be added to this picture if it is to provide useful analysis of less straightforward situations where, e.g., it is uncertain just what the killer intended, or the killer's gun jammed and so the intended victim was not killed. Much of Duff's discussion is concerned with these difficult problems in less straightforward situations such as criminal attempts in which the *actus reus* is incomplete. When we talk of crimes composed of *mens rea* and *actus reus*, we know that we are concerned with crimes where the accused "meant to do it," but *what* did they have to mean or intend in order for us to hold them liable, and *how much* of "it" must they do? Is the *actus reus* simply *evidence* of a defect of character which the criminal law properly aims to identify and punish? Or does the *actus reus* in fact *constitute* or *make up* the wrong done in a crime? We must find a way to state precisely how intentions mix with actions in an "inculpatory" or "guilt-producing" way and how other information might be "exculpatory" or "guilt-excusing."

1.2 SUBJECTIVISM AND OBJECTIVISM

The subjectivist approach claims that the wrong done in a crime is found in intention, or what a wrongdoer "meant to do." Supporters of the subjectivist position often point out that this view matches our sense that what is wrong about a crime is the *willingness* to commit some action prohibited by criminal law. We can see this in our reluctance to excuse from liability a person who intends to commit a crime, yet fails to do so out of bad luck. We are not keen, for example, to excuse the would-be poisoner Bob who slips lethal poison into Aunt Ethel's tea, yet fails in his plan because Fluffy the greedy poodle slurps her owner's tea and saves Aunt Ethel. Bob *meant* to kill his Aunt Ethel, and were it not for the greedy and unthinking intervention of Fluffy, Bob would have succeeded. Bob ought to bear liability for his attempt, we might think, in the same way that murderers who do not suffer bad luck bear liability for murder. Bob's bad luck does not change the fact that he meant to kill his Aunt Ethel.

Supporters of the objectivist approach reject subjectivism on various grounds. Objectivists argue that although intentions matter, the actual consequences of intended actions must also be taken into account when holding someone liable for wrongdoing. Objectivists complain that while the subjectivists' goal of excluding the role of luck from understanding wrongdoing is laudable, there are insurmountable practical difficulties in understanding criminal wrongdoing as occurring "in the head" or in intentions only, regardless of how the intended plan works out in practice. How, objectivists ask, can subjectivists determine reliably what someone intended, when we cannot simply peer into heads to see what thoughts are in them? How can subjectivists show that Bob really intended to poison his aunt and did not, as he claims, merely mistake poison for sugar in Aunt Ethel's badly organized kitchen cupboard? And if a crime consists in intention regardless of completion of the plan, at what point are intentions so plainly criminal that we can be confident that the would-be criminal is beyond turning back? These practical problems of assessing action cannot be overcome, objectivists charge. The only fair way to match crime to punishment is to hold people liable for what actually followed from their intentions.

In our excerpt, Duff explores two ways subjectivists have tried to solve the problems objectivists have raised, while preserving the subjectivist goal of excluding luck from determinations of liability-responsibility for criminal wrongdoing.

1.3 THE "CHOICE" VERSION OF SUBJECTIVISM

The choice version of subjectivism understands persons as essentially free-willed, rational individuals whose freedom allows them to make decisions and to change those decisions. Even while in the midst of carrying out a particular plan of action, a free-willed person might decide at the last moment to withhold from completing that action. If we are to have proper respect for a person's freedom to stop short of criminal wrongdoing, we must avoid judging an action as even an attempted crime until it is quite plain from the context that the actor really *chose* to carry out that particular action. On the choice version of subjectivism, criminal wrongdoing consists in a seamless flow of intention into action, to a point at which there can be no denying an actor's choice to carry out a course of action which happens to be prohibited by criminal law.

As Duff observes, this does not explain fully the relationship between intention, action, and wrongdoing. The practical need for a usable understanding of this sort of wrongdoing requires that we be able to specify how far Christine the would-be kidnapper must progress in her preparatory actions before we are justified in ascribing to her the choice to kidnap Mike. Perhaps we are not justified in arresting Christine for attempted kidnapping on the evidence of the friend from whom Christine borrowed a getaway van, with the explanation that she was off to kidnap Mike. This might be merely an expression of an intention, or a joke in poor taste. But must we wait until the last possible moment before Christine has forcibly taken Mike to the van and has pressed the accelerator to complete her escape plan, leaving Christine every possible opportunity to re-think and call off her plan (a *locus poenitentiae*, in the commonly used Latin phrase)? When does an intention become more than just an idea, and become evidence of a choice made by the wrongdoer? If the choice version of subjectivism is to be a plausible explanation of criminal wrongdoing, it must offer an answer to these questions. In our selection Duff examines some of the answers.

1.4 THE "CHARACTER" VERSION OF SUBJECTIVISM

The character version of subjectivism understands persons as having settled character traits or dispositions which are revealed in action. An intention to commit a crime is an expression of a particular character trait, and the action following from the intention is merely evidence of the undesirable character trait the criminal law aims to discourage. The character version of subjectivism solves the problem the choice theorist encounters when trying to decide whether a person's actions have gone beyond the possibility of a change of mind and withholding from completion of the crime. The character theorist understands action as evidence of a disposition to disobey the law, so whether the action is completed is immaterial to a finding of at least some degree of criminal liability. Both a criminal attempt and a completed crime reveal the character trait the criminal law seeks to limit.

As attractive as the character version of subjectivism may be, it, too, comes with certain problems. Supporters of the character argument must explain *what* action shows that a person has a *specific* character trait, and we must be given an account of how to regard persons who have undesirable character traits but do not act on those traits. Should criminal law aim to punish *defects of character*, even those that do not in fact result in criminal wrongdoing? Or should these weaknesses be regarded as nothing more than the cause of *actions* which, *if* committed, deserve punishment? Duff argues that both choice and character versions of subjectivism contain problems which cannot be overcome. In the remainder of his book, beyond the selection included here, Duff argues that we ought to understand the sort of crimes people meant to do in terms of subjective intentions *and* objective effects of wrongdoing. It is for you to decide whether one of these versions of subjectivism is adequate, or whether Duff's further alternative might need to be pursued if the criminal law is to be rational and fair.

2. Hate Crime Legislation

The next selection in this section is written by American law professor Heidi Hurd. Hurd accepts the distinction between choice and character theories of criminal responsibility, yet she maintains that liberal-democratic societies must adopt a choice theory of criminal responsibility, since only a choice theory of responsibility adequately respects the liberty and autonomy of individuals. In her argument reproduced here, Hurd explores one implication of choice theory for communities that experience racial, ethnic, or religious conflict.

As Hurd recognizes, when liberal democracies and indeed any prevailing political culture chooses to use law to protect individual and group liberties to construct and carry out life plans, provision must be made for resolution of conflicts arising as some life plans prove incompatible with others. Consider, for example, the conflict that arises when some persons refuse on the basis of conscience to join fellow-citizens in taking up arms in defense of the state. Responses to conflict range from constraints on the time and place in which certain choices are carried out, to criminalization and severe punishment for conduct going beyond mere conflict in exercise of freedoms to conduct amounting to abuse of freedoms. One example of what many regard as a justified legal limit on freedoms may be seen in the way criminal laws prohibit or provide additional penalties for offenses motivated by hatred or prejudice. There is considerable debate regarding just what ought to count as an act motivated by hatred or prejudice, but there is general agreement that both ideas capture actions expressing irrational rejection of fundamental, often constitutionally-protected legal commitments to the equality of individuals and their chosen ways of life. Commitments to political equality may be seen in the way liberal democracies protect the freedom of individuals to choose and practice their own religion, and to associate with whomever they choose, to name just two fundamental liberal-democratic values.

Hurd agrees with the view that hate and prejudice are serious social ills justifiably limited by criminal law, yet she rejects the further argument that hate crimes deserve more severe punishment. As she explains the implications of accepting the choice theory, Hurd argues that hate or prejudice are character traits or dispositions of individuals. More importantly, Hurd claims, they are character traits or dispositions which are largely beyond the control of rational, free-willed actors. Since punishment ought to be reserved for aspects of an action within the actor's control, an actor's hatred or prejudice expressed in commission of a crime cannot be a reason to increase the severity of punishment. According to Hurd, hate crimes ought to be punished with the same severity as crimes not committed out of hate or prejudice.

As you consider Hurd's argument, you may find yourself wondering about other implications of acceptance of the choice theory. For example, you may wish to investigate the consequences of accepting Hurd's claim that hate and prejudice are largely beyond the control and rationality of agents. If Hurd is right that those who commit hate crimes should not be subject to increased punishment, could the reasons for this view support a still stronger conclusion, that these persons should be punished less severely or perhaps even excused, since irrational hatred or prejudice interfered with their capacity to make a reasoned choice of a course of action? Or should we think that the very fact of this question arising is a reason to reconsider the choice theory on the grounds that it results in absurd consequences? In other words, if accepting the full consequences of the choice theory means we let those who commit hate crimes escape full criminal responsibility for their actions, should we treat this conclusion as reason for rejecting the choice theory, and look elsewhere to better understand criminal responsibility? We might look, for example, to a character theory of criminal responsibility, or even an objectivist theory, since both provide an account of the relatively greater harm of hate crimes justifying relatively more severe punishments for such crimes. As you evaluate each theory and seek the best understanding of criminal responsibility, the question of identification and punishment of hate crime will serve as an important test of each theory's merits.

3. The Fairness of Punishment

In the final chapter of this section we turn to a well-known article in the philosophy of punishment, by Jeffrie Murphy. Murphy presents a version of 'retributivism', a theory which supposes that the only way that punishment can be justified is on the grounds of desert: that guilt deserves punishment. Guilt of course means that the wrongdoer to be punished is not just causally connected to particular conduct, but is more importantly morally responsible for their conduct so is worthy of being blamed for their wrongdoing and deserving punishment. Recall here the importance criminal law theorists in the common law tradition have attached to the nature of the intentions contained in the *mens rea* element of serious crimes constituted by both a mental element and a conduct element. The retributivist theory gives voice to the sense that while the harmful consequences of crime are important, what is more concerning is the wrongdoer's willingness to do wrong. Punishment justified as retribution seeks to reach into a wrongdoer's intention and identity to mark for rejection by the state on behalf of its citizens that part of a wrongdoer's choosing against the standards of personal performance as a human, made visible in the expectations the state communicates in its criminal law. Sophisticated retributivist theories tie the justification of punishment of individual criminal acts to a supporting general account of the justification of the use of state power to constrain individuals subject to state law. We find, for example, the famous philosopher Immanuel Kant arguing that the only way in which the laws can be justifiably imposed upon us—including criminal laws and associated forms of punishment—is if we can demonstrate that those laws, and their consequences, are somehow up to us. On this view, justified laws might come labeled as products of the state, but really, they are a product of our rational and autonomous selves since they simply enact in a formal way what rational and autonomous selves should choose as the rules of life. For retributivists such as Kant, the state's use of coercion to punish wrongdoers is justified as completion of a sequence of intentions and events arriving as a unified whole in the life of the rational, autonomous chooser, as willful choice to engage in prohibited conduct includes understanding that the prohibition signals inseparable connection of the act with punishment. This sense of an intrinsic link between choice and punishment is usefully illustrated in a term once used by H.L.A. Hart, as he described the criminal law as a 'choosing system': the criminal chooses the wrongful conduct and in so doing chooses the punishment that comes with it, much like ordering a dish from a restaurant menu is both a choice of a dish and choice to purchase the dish at the stipulated price.

Retributivists since Kant have remained committed to the basic idea that punishment is to be justified on the basis of desert, but have developed and explained the idea in different ways. In the selection provided here, Murphy articulates the idea of desert in terms of a balance of benefits and burden. We all benefit from the social order which is achieved through law, but realization of that benefit requires us to accept at the same time the burden of obeying the law and accepting the restrictions it places on our conduct, especially when we might wish to break the law out of self-interest. Achievement of balance between benefits and burdens is a hallmark of a fair and just society. Criminal responsibility, and punishment, are then understood against this backdrop of fairness. Someone who willingly breaks the law has through their conduct decided to upset the balance, and to accept the benefit of others following the law while choosing to relieve themselves of the burden to do likewise. This 'unfair advantage', Murphy argues, is then in need of correction, so the lawbreaker is justifiably given an extra burden in the form of punishment to re-establish the balance of benefit and burden delivering fairness.

While Murphy accepts the theoretical justification of punishment that retributivism supplies in the abstract, he sees a decisive problem with its application in practice. He argues that retributivism can only be justifiably enacted in practice where there is a current state of equal distribution of benefits and burdens, across differences such as economic status, social class, race, and other characteristics of persons and groups. In the absence of such equality, Murphy argues, it is difficult to show that punishment of crime is justified as rejection of a criminal's gaining unfair advantage over others. In situations where inequality is evident, a criminal actor who is in a sense starting from behind in a position of deprivation having suffered prior lack of fair treatment might not gain advantage so much as just reduce persistent disadvantage. What, then, is being punished when a disadvantaged criminal's crime makes them just a little less disadvantaged? Murphy offers this example to illustrate the problem basic social inequality poses for retributivist theories of punishment:

> Consider one example: a man has been convicted of armed robbery. On investigation, we learn that he is an impoverished black whose whole life has been

> one of frustrating alienation from the prevailing socio-economic structure—no job, no transportation if he could get a job, substandard education for his children, terrible housing and inadequate health care for his whole family, condescending-tardy-inadequate welfare payments, harassment by the police but no real protection by them against the dangers in his community, and near total exclusion from the political process. Learning all this, would we still want to talk—as many do—of his suffering punishment under the rubric of "paying a debt to society"? Surely not. Debt for what?

Murphy adds to this perspective observation of some ingrained values and dispositions characteristic of capitalist societies in which we find some of the most glaring forms of inequality. These values and dispositions, tied to expressions such as 'making it' and 'getting ahead', include selfishness, competitiveness, accumulation and greed. If these are the values and dispositions which are prized in our society, what sense does it make to suppose that people who commit crimes to achieve more for themselves (including so-called 'white-collar' crimes) are really acting in deviant ways, i.e., against the norms of their society? How is it anything other than arbitrary or merely self-serving conduct on the part of the powerful to declare some exercises of benefiting at others' expense to be wrong and worthy of punishment conveyed by the state, while other benefiting at others' expense is unobjectionable and even admirable 'getting ahead'?

Murphy is careful to qualify his arguments, recognizing that there is a great deal of variation in the conditions of criminal behavior. Not all forms or instances of criminal conduct are the same. Beyond recognition of variation in conditions, forms and instances of criminal conduct, there is nonetheless an underlying challenge needing to be addressed by any response to Murphy's skepticism regarding the justification of punishment for criminal wrongdoing: is it possible for there to be fair or just punishments in an unfair or unjust world? And if the current state of the world weighs against hoping for fair or just punishment, are we close enough to a fair or just world that any punishment can justifiably be imposed on anyone?

21
R.A. Duff

"Choice, Character, and Action," from *Criminal Attempts**

[*Ed. note*: some of the footnotes in the original chapter have been omitted for the purposes of this excerpt.]

... Disagreements between subjectivists and objectivists can best be understood as concerning the proper criteria for action-ascriptions. Both sides agree that a person should be held

* Duff, R.A. From *Criminal Attempts*, Clarendon Press, 1997. (pp. 147–50, 165–68, 173–80, 183–92).

criminally liable for, and only for, what can properly be ascribed to her as an agent—for what can properly be described as *hers*; she is justly convicted, and punished, only in so far as an action matching the law's definition of an offence can properly be ascribed to her. Subjectivists then argue that the criteria of action-ascription must be "subjective": actions which are to be ascribed to the agent must be described in "subjective" terms. Objectivists, by contrast, argue that what is mine as an agent cannot be identified in purely "subjective" terms; it must be described in partly "objective" terms. What we then need is some account of what such "subjective" or "objective" terms are; and different versions of subjectivism and of objectivism are distinguished in part by the different accounts which they offer. We will also, of course, need some account of *why* these are the appropriate terms in which to identify the actions that can be ascribed to an agent.

...

Subjectivism I: Culpability and Choice

Any subjectivist account of criminal liability must explain what the "subjective," on which criminal liability is to depend, consists in. In its broadest sense, the "subjective" consists in the person's psychological states and attributes. However, not *every* aspect of a person's psychology will be relevant to her criminal liability: we need an account of just which aspects of the "subjective" are relevant.

Two forms of subjectivism have dominated recent discussion: one focuses on the idea of "choice," the other on that of "character." I begin with the former.

6.1 CHOICE, INTENTION, AND BELIEF

Criminal liability, on this subjectivist account, should be determined by *choice*. The actions which can properly be ascribed to me, for which I should be held liable, are those that I choose to do.

Choice, Control, and Chance

Why is choice so important? One answer is that a system of criminal law which makes liability depend on choice respects individual freedom, and maximizes citizens' control over their own lives. If we know that we will be liable to criminal sanctions only if we choose to break the law, we have the power to determine for ourselves whether or not we will be subject to those sanctions. Another answer, which reveals the Kantian inspiration of this form of subjectivism, is that I should be criminally liable only for that for which I can properly be held responsible and culpable; that I am responsible and culpable only for that which I control; and that I control only that which I choose to do or to bring about, my actions *qua* chosen.

This line of argument is often buttressed by a contrast between "choice" and "chance." I control my choices, my actions *qua* chosen: but what happens independently of my choices, and so outside my control, is a matter of chance or luck; and such matters should not affect my criminal liability, since they cannot affect my culpability. Thus a "fully subjective principle" of criminal liability "draws a straight line through the vicissitudes of life and the vagaries of fortune, minimising the influence of chance and keeping as close as possible to the defendant's choice and to what lay within her control."[5] If, on the other hand, we assign liability "according to how things turned out," we improperly "attribute significance to chance rather than choice."[6]

What is choice? A minimal notion of choice can be defined in terms of intention and belief. I choose to bring about those results which I

5 *Ashworth Attempts*, 742.
6 Ashworth, "Sharpening," 82.

intend to bring about, or believe that I will bring about; I choose to take a risk of bringing about those results that I believe my action might bring about. This gives us two "basic principles of criminal liability": the "intent principle," that agents ought to be "held liable for what they intended to do, and not according to what actually did or did not occur"; and the "belief principle," that we must judge them "on the basis of what they believed they were doing, not on the basis of actual facts and circumstances which were not known to them at the time."[8]

This is not to say that agents are to be held liable *merely* for their intentions and beliefs. We are liable for what we *do*, not for our bare intentions or beliefs. The point is rather that a properly subjective description of my actions *qua* chosen, of the actions that can properly be ascribed to me, must describe those actions in terms of the intentions and beliefs with which they are done.

Exculpation and Inculpation

The intent and belief principles are meant, at least, to specify *necessary* conditions of criminal liability. As such, they often play an *exculpatory* role, to exempt from liability those who might otherwise be held liable. So someone who does not realize that her action might damage another's property should not be convicted of criminal damage, even if it "in fact creates an obvious risk" of such damage: she has not chosen to damage or risk damaging another's property. A man who honestly but mistakenly believes that the woman with whom he has intercourse consents to it should not be convicted of rape, even if that belief is quite unreasonable: for he has not chosen to have, or to take a risk of having, intercourse without her consent.

Even in this role, these principles are of course controversial. They preclude liability for negligence, since a negligent agent does not choose to take or create the risk as to which he is negligent. They also require us to define recklessness, as an appropriate type of criminal fault, in terms of *conscious* risk-taking: but some would argue that an agent's criminal recklessness can be displayed in his very failure to notice the risk that he is taking or creating.

Our present concern, however, is with the more ambitious role that these principles may be given as *inculpatory* principles, specifying *sufficient* conditions of criminal liability. This is the role which they play in subjectivist accounts of criminal attempts: they render criminally liable some who might be otherwise not liable at all, or liable only to a lesser degree. An otherwise innocent action may be transformed into a criminal attempt by the fact that it was done "with intent to commit an offence": that it actualized a choice to commit an offence. The fact of failure in a criminal attempt does not by itself entitle the defendant to any lighter sentence than she would have received had it succeeded: for in making the attempt she chose to commit an offence; it is that choice, rather than the attempt's success or failure, which should determine her liability.

Why should choice play this more ambitious, inculpatory role? A concern to maximize citizens' control over their own lives requires only an exculpatory principle of choice: that they should *not* find themselves criminally liable for what they did not choose to do. The answer seems to be that we must give choice this inculpatory role if we are to take seriously the relation of choice to culpability, the importance of "minimising the influence of chance" on criminal liability, and the demand of justice that we "treat like cases alike." If two people each actualize a choice to commit murder, by trying to kill another person, they are equally culpable, equally deserving of punishment; the fact that one fails, or even that her attempt is inevitably doomed to failure by some

8 Ashworth, "Belief," 7: for the "belief principle," see Cross, "Centenary Reflections on Prince's Case," 540.

kind of impossibility, cannot be allowed to reduce or negate her criminal liability. There is "no relevant moral difference" as far as their respective culpability is concerned between the would-be killer who succeeds and one who fails: since the former is properly held liable as having chosen to murder, so also must the latter.

Can "Choice" Be Sufficient for Liability?

The belief and intent principles do not, as they stand, specify sufficient conditions of liability: for those who act under exculpatory kinds of duress, or as a result of exculpatory mental disorder, might, in the minimal sense defined by those principles, "choose" to act as they do. Nor indeed do they really "minimis[e] the influence of chance" on criminal liability. They make "outcome-luck," "luck in the way our actions and projects turn out,"[18] irrelevant: if I am liable for all and only what I intend to do or believe myself to be doing, my liability will be unaffected by the success or failure of my actions, or by the truth or falsity of my beliefs about the results that they will or might bring about. However, there are other kinds of luck that bear on our actions.[19] It is a matter of "constitutive" luck that I have become the kind of person who would choose to commit a crime; it is a matter of "situational" luck that I find myself in a situation in which I am tempted or have the opportunity to commit a crime, or am not prevented from attempting to commit it. These are matters of "luck," in so far as they depend on factors outside my control, factors which can be said to make the difference between me and someone who does not attempt to commit a crime.

To solve these difficulties we need either a richer account of "choice" or an account of the preconditions of responsible choice. Such an account must enable us to say either that the person acting under exculpatory duress or mental disorder does not in the relevant sense "choose" to act as he does, or that in his case some essential precondition of responsible choice is absent. It must also allow us to insist that, whatever role might be played by "constitutive" and "situational" luck, it is still up to the agent (if those preconditions are satisfied) to choose how she will act in the situations in which she finds herself. It will thus need to be an account of "free will," as consisting in the capacity for choice; and of choice as a rational capacity which manifests our freedom as responsible agents.

I will not discuss here the form that this account might take, save to note that its development might require us to attend to the ways in which an agent's "choices" are connected to broader aspects of her character. However, given some such account, a subjectivist can then argue that whilst "outcome-luck" should indeed be irrelevant to criminal liability, we need not in the same way try to discount the influences of other types of luck: for once those types of luck have played their part, the agent still must and (if she has the capacity for rational choice which defines responsible agency) can choose how she will act, and can therefore be properly held responsible for her choice. Outcome-luck, however, helps to determine the actual results of our choices; and that is why it must still be discounted.

...

6.4 THE CONDUCT ELEMENT IN ATTEMPTS

To see what kind of conduct element subjectivists might specify for attempts, we must ask why they should require any such element, and what significance it has for them.

The Significance of Conduct

Fletcher thinks that on "the subjective theory" the conduct element serves a purely evidential function. For the core of liability is "the intention

18 Nagel, "Moral Luck," 28; see Ashworth, "Taking the Consequences."

19 See Nagel, *op cit.*; Feinberg, "Problematic Responsibility in Law and Morals."

to violate a legally protected interest"; and "any act whatever" that justifies an inference to such a (firm) intention will then suffice for liability. Such a theory, he objects, subverts the principle of legality, which requires that liability be founded on an act which "violate[s some] preannounced standard," and "objectively conforms to criteria specified in advance."[94]

Some subjectivists do give the act-requirement such an evidential function: not only those who take the basis of criminal liability to be an agent's dangerous disposition as revealed in his conduct, but also some who take it to be the firm *intention* to commit an offence, whether such an intention is seen as constitutive of culpability or as indicative of future dangerousness.

Intention is of course logically related to action: to intend to do X is to be disposed to do X unless something intervenes. Sometimes, indeed, intentions have no existence independent of action: action flows directly from the agent's perception of her situation, without any intervening process of intention-formation. However, there is often a gap between intention and action: an agent might intend to do X, but find no opportunity to do it, or be prevented from doing it. Someone can thus have a firm criminal intention which he has not yet put into action; he is criminally culpable, but the law should not convict him until he takes some active steps to carry that intention out. For only action provides reliable public evidence of his intention (evidence that he would have committed the crime if he could); and not to require such evidence would encourage intrusively oppressive policing and unreliable convictions.

This rationale for the act-requirement grounds it in considerations *external* to the agent's criminal culpability. A person who has the kind of firm criminal intention which constitutes criminal culpability escapes liability if she has, for whatever reason, not (yet) actualized it. She avoids liability, not because she is not someone whom the law should ideally aim to convict (she has the kind of culpability which concerns the law), but because for other reasons (to protect citizens against oppressive policing and unreliable convictions) the law should be so formulated that she avoids liability.

The "choice" version of subjectivism, however, is more plausibly read as making the conduct element *constitutive* of criminal culpability—of the particular kind of culpability which properly concerns the criminal law. What makes an agent criminally culpable, what constitutes him as a criminal, is not a bare criminal intention, but the *choice* to put that intention into effect; and choice is necessarily actualized in action. Someone who has formed a bare future intention to commit a crime has not yet, in this sense, "chosen" to commit the crime, since he must still choose to put (and could still choose not to put) that intention into effect; only in taking that further step does he define himself as a criminal. The conduct which constitutes the conduct element of an attempt is, therefore, not merely evidence of some underlying criminal culpability that does not itself necessarily involve action: it partly constitutes *criminal* culpability. On this view the act requirement is *internal* to the basic conception of criminal culpability.

Why, though, should we take this view, since someone who forms a bare criminal intention is surely already culpable? Part of the answer is that to take choice seriously as the basis of criminal liability is to take seriously our status as responsible autonomous agents: this requires the law to respect, and as far as possible to allow us to exercise, our capacity to determine our own actions; to leave us to decide for ourselves to abandon (or, therefore, to persist in) even our intended criminal

94 *Fletcher*, esp. 118–20, 157–59: for criticism, see Schulhofer's Review of *Fletcher*; Weinreb, "Manifest Criminality, Criminal Intent, and the 'Metamorphosis of Larceny'"; Galloway, "Patterns of Trying."

enterprises. Another part of the answer is that the culpability of someone who puts her criminal intention into action differs categorically from that of one who has yet to do so. The former has committed herself to the crime in a way that the latter has not; she has spurned one significant *locus poenitentiae*, in moving from (mere or bare) intention to action; she has embarked on doing harm.

This version of subjectivism, we should notice, accords with the "principle of legality," in that agents will be criminally liable only for actions which violate a "preannounced standard." It does not, admittedly, require some action which "objectively conforms to criteria specified in advance," if that means an action which can be recognized as potentially criminal independently of knowledge of the agent's intentions or beliefs: for it may be only her intentions and beliefs which render her apparently innocent action criminal, as an attempt. However, it is not clear why we should take *this* to be a requirement of the principle of legality.

What Kind of Conduct?

We still need to know what *kind* of conduct a criminal attempt should require on this account: how far should the intending criminal have progressed in actualizing his intention if he is to be criminally liable for an attempt?

The "fully subjective principle," Ashworth thinks, requires only "a minimal *actus reus*"; "the doing of any overt act with the necessary intention." Any more stringent act-requirement must be justified by other considerations which outweigh that principle: in particular, considerations of "individual rights and freedom from interference," and of leaving intending criminals a *locus poenitentiae*.[106]

Now the subjective principle is indeed *consistent* with a "first act" test for attempts, since an agent makes himself culpable, in a way that can properly concern the criminal law, as soon as he begins to put a criminal intention into action. However, it does not *require* us to adopt that test. There is a real difference in criminal culpability between one who has only just embarked on a criminal enterprise, and one who has come close to completing it. Someone who is still in the early stages of a criminal enterprise is less culpable (culpably responsible for less) than someone who has completed her criminal attempt: for she has not yet chosen to progress beyond the stage of mere preparation; she has not to the same extent actualized a criminal intention; nor has she, therefore, to the same degree actualized her potential criminal culpability. Since the subjectivist principle presumably does not require us to criminalize anyone who is, *to any degree*, culpable in a way which could concern the criminal law, some narrower specification of the conduct element in attempts would thus not compromise a subjectivist's "basic principles of culpability and of equality of treatment":[107] for it would distinguish more culpable from less culpable conduct.

Furthermore, a desire to leave the agent a *locus poenitentiae* is *internal* to the subjective principle, not a consideration which must be weighed against that principle: it is an implication of taking choice seriously. This might seem to favour a "last act" test for attempts: for only then has the agent fully actualized his criminal choice, and spurned every *locus poenitentiae*. Subjectivists can deal with this, however, by distinguishing complete, "last act," attempts from incomplete attempts, at least at the sentencing stage, and perhaps also at the stage of conviction. They can still criminalize incomplete attempts, as marking at least a partial actualization of a criminal choice which makes the agent criminally culpable.

106 *Ashworth Attempts*, 750–51.
107 *Ashworth Attempts*, 757.

Of course, this does not tell us just where we should draw the line between "mere preparation" and incomplete attempt. Nor can the "choice" principle answer that question: subjectivists could favour, with equal consistency, either a "substantial step" test[111] or the "more than merely preparatory act" test.[112] Ashworth is therefore right to argue that we must appeal to considerations other than "the fully subjective principle" to decide just how narrowly, or broadly, the conduct element should be defined. However, this is not a matter of weighing the subjective principle *against* such other considerations: it is rather a matter of deciding, in the light of those other considerations, just how that principle should be applied.

No matter how the conduct element in attempts is specified, subjectivists must of course insist that that specification be applied to the agent's conduct as *she* conceived it: to her actions as described in terms of her own intentions and beliefs. An action of "handling non-stolen goods," or of "administering an innoxious substance," is in fact neither "proximate" to nor "a substantial step" towards the offence of handling stolen goods or of administering a noxious thing.[113] However, an action of "handling stolen goods," or of "administering a noxious thing," clearly satisfies such tests; and if that is what the agent believed she was doing, that is how we must describe her action when we ask whether it constituted a criminal attempt.[114]

However, this is not to say that whether she is guilty of an attempt depends on whether she believed that her conduct satisfied whatever test the law specifies for the conduct element in attempts (that it was, for instance, "more than merely preparatory"). For even if the question of whether her conduct satisfied that test is a question of "fact" for the jury, rather than one of "law" for the judge,[115] that "fact" is not included in the "facts as she believed them to be" on which she is to be judged. The specification and application of any test for the conduct element in attempts involve an essentially normative judgment: about how far an agent must have progressed in a criminal enterprise to be properly convicted of an attempt. That judgement might fail to be made by the legislature, the judge, or the jury—but not by the defendant herself.

...

Subjectivism II: Character and Action

The previous chapter focused on that form of subjectivism which takes "choice" to be the key determinant of criminal liability. I am responsible, and should therefore be criminally liable, for and only for what I choose to do, since it is through my choices that I actualize myself as a free and responsible agent; thus the "subjective," on which criminal liability should depend, consists in choice, which can itself be minimally defined in terms of intention and belief.

We must now turn to a different form of subjectivism which bases criminal liability on "character," rather than on "choice." This is still a subjectivist theory: it founds liability on what is "subjective" to the agent, rather than on the actual, "objective" nature or results of her conduct. However, it offers a different account of those "subjective" grounds of liability: to explicate that account, we can begin by looking again at a problem faced by the "choice" theorist.

7.1 FROM "CHOICE" TO "CHARACTER"

The problem for the "choice" theorist was that the "belief" and "intent" principles, which give

111 See *Ashworth Attempts*, 753.
112 See *Law Com. 102*, para 2.49; above, ch. 2, at n. 186.
113 See e.g., *Haughton v. Smith* 119751 AC 476, 499–500 (Lord Reid).
114 As both the 1981 Act and the *Model Penal Code* make clear.
115 See Criminal Attempts Act 1981, s 4(3); above, ch. 2, at nn. 186–88.

more precise content to the doctrine that criminal liability should be determined by choice, do not specify *sufficient* conditions of liability, since someone could in that sense "choose" to commit a crime but still not be criminally liable. To meet that problem, the theorist must provide a richer account, either of "choice" or of the preconditions of free, responsible choice. That account must allow us to say of one who acts under exculpatory duress or mental disorder either that he does not in the appropriate sense "choose" to act as he does; or that an essential precondition of responsible choice is lacking. This is one route into something like a "character-based" conception of liability, since a plausible account of how or why such conditions as duress and mental disorder should exculpate will have to refer to the ways in which the agent's immediate "choice" is connected to, or disconnected from, the deeper structures of attitudes and concerns that constitute his character.

Duress as an Excuse

We can sketch this argument by considering duress as an excuse. Someone commits perjury because she is threatened with serious physical injury if she refuses to do so.[6] That duress might not be such as to *justify* her action. Nor is her action *involuntary*: she knows that she is giving false evidence, and "chooses" to do so, to avoid the threatened injury. None the less, she can be excused if her "will" was "overborne" by the threat;[7] or if "a person of reasonable firmness in [her] situation would have been unable to resist" it.[8] If we now ask what it means for someone to be "unable" to resist a threat, we might notice that other accounts of duress do not use that term. They say instead that duress can excuse only if the threat was such that "a sober person of reasonable firmness sharing the characteristics of the defendant" would have acted as she did:[9] the threat must be "one which in all the circumstances (including any of her personal circumstances that affect its gravity) [s]he cannot reasonably be expected to resist,"[10] or which "human nature could not be expected to resist."[11]

These accounts imply that the notion of being "able" or "unable" to resist a threat is a normative one. In asking whether a defendant could "reasonably be expected" to resist this threat, we are asking about a normative, not a factual, expectation: that is, the question is not whether we could reasonably *predict* that she would resist the threat, but whether we can reasonably *demand* that she resist it; and the answer to that question is to be found by asking whether someone of "reasonable firmness" would have resisted it. The imagined person of "reasonable firmness" (the "reasonable person," we might say more simply) thus plays a *criterial*, not an *evidential*, role: that such a person would have resisted that threat is not merely (weak) evidence that this defendant was in fact "able" to resist it; it proves that this defendant was at fault in not resisting that threat.

A "sober person of reasonable firmness" is someone with a reasonable or proper regard for the law and the values it protects, and a reasonable or proper degree of courage: what is "reasonable" here is what we can reasonably expect or demand of citizens. To say that such a person would have resisted a particular threat is thus to say that anyone with the kind of regard for the

6 See Hudson and Taylor [1971] 2 QB 202.
7 Ibid., 206.
8 *Model Penal Code*, s2.09(1). See also Aristotle, *Nicomachean Ethics*, III.1, 1110a23–6, on actions done "under pressure which overstrains human nature and which no one could withstand."
9 Graham [1982] 74 Cr App. R. 235, 241.
10 *1989 Draft Code*, cl 42(3)(b).
11 Stratton (1779) 1 Doug KB 239.

law and its values, and the degree of courage that can properly be demanded of any citizen, would have resisted it. From this it follows that someone who gives in to that threat lacks either that reasonable regard for the law and its values, or that reasonable degree of courage, and is thus justly condemned. On the other hand, to say that such a person would have given in is to say that (even) someone with a proper regard for the law and its values, and with a proper degree of courage, would have given in: in which case this defendant's giving in did not display a lack or failing for which she can properly be condemned.

Of course, it remains to be asked whether a reasonable person "*sharing the characteristics of the defendant*" would have withstood that threat, and we must thus determine which of this defendant's characteristics to ascribe to the "reasonable person." None the less, we can at least now see how to tackle that task: we should ascribe to the reasonable person any of the defendant's actual characteristics that affected her response to the threat, *other than* characteristics which involve either some lack of reasonable regard for the law and its values, or a lack of reasonable courage. So we ascribe to the reasonable person, for instance, this defendant's pathological fear of spiders, but not her unusual (non-pathological) lack of concern for the property rights of others.

From "Choice" to "Character"

This account of the defence of duress suggests that criminal liability does depend partly on "character," and not purely on "choice." We must look behind the defendant's immediate choice to give in to the threat, to those attitudes or concerns (a disregard for the law and its values; an excess concern for one's own safety; cowardice) which her choice did or did not manifest: but these are aspects of her character.

I think that similar conclusions would emerge from an account of other defences, such as mental disorder or provocation. The agent is to be excused because, although his criminal action was intentional, indeed "chosen," it did not manifest that kind of disregard for, or indifference to, the interests and rights of others, or the law and its values, for which agents are properly condemned. We must, therefore, attend not merely to his actions or choices themselves, but to their connection with, or disconnection from, that deeper set of attitudes and concerns which partly constitute his character.

This argument is one aspect of a wider critique of the "choice" conception of criminal liability: that it offers no adequate account of what it is to be a responsible agent, or of what makes an action mine as its responsible agent. What matters is not simply whether an action is "chosen," but how that choice is related to the agent's attitudes and concerns, her conceptions of value and of reasons for action; and these are aspects of her character. This reflects a more general critique of the (roughly) Kantian conception of moral agency and moral worth as residing in "the will," which sometimes inspires "choice" theorists. The moral character of a person's actions, the critic argues, and her moral standing as the agent of those actions, depend not solely or primarily upon what she "chooses" to do, but on those structures of attitudes, motives, and values from which action and choice flow—on the character which her actions manifest.

What kind of account of criminal liability could emerge from such anti-Kantian thoughts about moral agency and worth? We must question more closely what a "character" theorist takes to be the proper ground of criminal liability.

7.2 CHARACTER AND CRIMINAL LIABILITY

The criminal process should properly focus, the "character" theorist argues, not on the particular action for which the defendant is formally convicted, but on some character trait which that criminal action revealed. He is properly convicted if and because his action warranted an inference to some undesirable character trait. If he is acquitted because he lacked the requisite fault element, or had some further defence, this is because the inference from criminal action to undesirable character trait was blocked.

D breaks *V*'s window and is charged with criminal damage. If he broke the window intentionally or recklessly, without lawful excuse, he merits conviction: we can infer from his conduct an undesirable character trait that merits condemnation and punishment. That trait might be described as "the absence of an adequate aversion" to infringing the property rights of others;[16] or as a "practical attitude" of "hostility or indifference towards, or rejection of, either that particular norm [prohibiting criminal damage] or the standards of the criminal law in general."[17]

If, however, he acted without the requisite fault element or has some suitable defence, then he merits acquittal: for no inference to any undesirable character trait is warranted. If he reasonably did not realize that what he was doing might damage another's property, we cannot infer any undesirable character trait from his action. If he broke the window intentionally but under duress (a threat of serious injury if he refused to do so), we can infer something about his character: that he values his own physical safety more than property; or that he lacks the courage to resist such a threat. However, if we think that a person of "reasonable firmness" would have given in to that threat, we cannot infer a *defective* character trait: we cannot infer that he had less regard for the property rights of others or for the law's norms, or less courage in relation to those rights and norms, than we can reasonably expect any citizen to have.

This sketch raises various questions. Most immediately, what are character traits? What kinds of character trait should make a person criminally liable? Why should the law focus on "character"?

Character Traits

Character traits are relatively stable patterns of thought, emotion, and action. They are analysed dispositionally: as dispositions to act in certain ways, to be motivated or affected by certain kinds of consideration, to think in certain ways. Thus the character trait of generosity involves a disposition to give (either money or other goods, such as time), especially to those in need, and even when the giving involves real deprivation. It also involves a disposition to be motivated to give by the other's need—rather than, for instance, by a desire for reward—and to be moved to sympathy by another's need. Generosity also involves a disposition to notice and attend to others' needs as reasons for action to help them. Meanness, by contrast, involves the absence of such dispositions (for some character traits must be understood in such essentially negative terms): a mean person is not disposed to be motivated to act, or to be moved to sympathy, by the needs of others; nor is he disposed even to notice their needs or to see them as a source of reasons for action. His meanness might also involve more positive dispositions: his thoughts, his attention, his deliberations and motivations are structured by an excessive concern to preserve his own money or other goods.

A person's character traits embody her settled values, concerns, and attitudes. We can thus see several reasons why the criminal law should be concerned with character, in particular with those aspects of character which constitute virtues or vices. First, what the law demands of us is not simply a set of discrete acts, but certain dispositions: of obedience to its rules, and of respect for the values it protects. This demands

16 See Brandt, 174.
17 Lacey, 76.

particular character traits: *dispositions* of thought, attitude, and motivation which enable us to respond appropriately to the law. Secondly, in so far as punishment has any corrective aim, what justifies punishment must be something about the offender that requires correction: this cannot be the particular past action or choice for which he was convicted; it must be an underlying, continuing character trait, revealed by his action. Thirdly, what makes my actions "mine," as their responsible agent, is their relationship to my character: they are mine to the extent that they flow from my character: the relationship between action and character is thus crucial if I am to be justly condemned and punished for what I do.

Identifying Criminal Character Traits

The suggestion that the criminal law should focus on "character" is likely to provoke familiar liberal anxieties. The deep structures of thought and motivation which constitute our *moral* characters are certainly proper objects of moral appraisal; and a concern with each other's moral character is proper in close personal relationships, between friends and within families. However, it is surely not the proper task of the criminal law to detect and punish moral vice, or to take such interest in citizens' moral characters. Its proper task is to declare and enforce the fairly minimal standards of conduct which are necessary for any social life: most obviously, to forbid and to prevent those kinds of conduct which harm or might harm the central interests which the law should protect. The law can properly demand that we conform our conduct to its requirements, and punish us if we wilfully fail to do so. But it should not seek to pry into the inner reaches of our characters; for the primary goal of punishment should be rational deterrence, and/or the censure of wrongful conduct, not moral correction or reform.

A "character" conception of criminal liability can certainly be related to a more communitarian account of the proper nature and purposes of the criminal law: one which portrays the law, being the law of a moral community, as having a proper interest in the moral character of its citizens. "Character" theorists, though, more usually meet such liberal worries by limiting the extent of the law's interest in character. It is not properly interested in every aspect of citizens' moral characters, but only in those character traits that are defective or undesirable because they are liable to lead to familiar types of criminal conduct: types of conduct which, liberals would agree, should be criminal because they are likely to infringe rights or injure interests which the law should protect. The law is not a general moral inquisitor; it is concerned only with dangerous character traits which are liable to produce obviously harmful conduct.

There are, however, psychological attributes which might result in conduct that harms the legally protected interests of others, but which we would not count as "defective character traits" warranting criminal liability. For example, the conduct of one who "systematically, characteristically makes unreasonable mistakes, causing danger to the interests of others" *might* reveal "a genuine practical indifference to the interests protected by the criminal law"[24] which is criminally culpable. On the other hand, it might reflect a purely cognitive deficiency in intelligence, which is surely not criminally culpable. Someone who is seriously mentally disordered might have dispositions of thought and motivation that are dangerous because they are liable to lead to criminal conduct: but should he be criminally liable?

Bayles argues that mentally disordered criminals *should* be convicted: for their conduct is "good evidence of an undesirable character trait justifying a social response" (although that "social response" need not be punishment, since other

24 Lacey, 66.

responses "may be more effective and appropriate").[25] However, this is to abandon any attempt to justify a "character" theory of *criminal liability*: it destroys the distinction, vital to any system of law and punishment, between condemning and punishing responsible wrong-doers for their crimes, and diagnosing and treating those who are dangerous to themselves or to others. "Character" theorists who want to rationalize something like our existing structures of criminal law and punishment must be able to rationalize this central distinction.

They can do this by reminding us first that defects of *character* are defects of attitude or motivation. Lack of intelligence is thus not a defective character trait warranting liability, so long as it involves, not a lack of appropriate motivation, but a cognitive deficiency inhibiting the actualization of that respect for the rights and interests of others which a well-meaning but stupid person does have. They can argue, secondly, that mental disorder does not involve a kind of "defective character trait" which merits criminal liability. For character, as an object of moral or legal criticism, consists in a person's *rational* dispositions of thought, feeling, and motivation—those which reflect an intelligible conception of reality and value. It is, though, a defining feature of mental disorder that it involves *non*-rational, or rationally unintelligible, patterns of thought, feeling, and motivation. This means that we cannot engage with the mentally disordered person in a critical discussion of his conduct or of what motivated it. We cannot then hold him morally responsible or criminally liable, since moral criticism and criminal condemnation are (or should be) modes of communication with a rational agent about her intelligible attitudes and actions.

We now have a clearer idea of the kinds of character trait which are, on this account, the proper concern of the criminal law. We do not yet know enough about the relationship between such character traits and the particular kinds of action which are the immediate focus of the criminal process: about why, if criminal liability is founded on defective character traits, it should formally depend on whether the defendant committed a specified type of action. Before tackling that central question, we can ask what implications the "character" conception of liability might have for the law of attempts....

...

7.4 CHARACTER, ACTION, AND LIABILITY

"Character" theorists who see the purpose of punishing attempts as being to neutralize "dangerous individuals," or to apply "corrective sanctions" to a defendant's "anti-social disposition" should favour a broad specification of the conduct element in attempts. For their concern is not with whether the defendant's particular actions were themselves "dangerously proximate" to the completed crime, or whether she had spurned some significant *locus poenitentiae*: it is with whether she had provided adequate evidence of her dangerousness or "anti-social disposition"; and, the *Model Penal Code* argues, that concern is satisfied if her actions constituted "a substantial step" towards the commission of the crime, or were "strongly corroborative of [her] criminal purpose."[52]

Why, though, should action be required at all: why should the law not convict and punish anyone who can be shown to have the relevant type of "anti-social disposition," whether or not it has yet been actualized in a criminal enterprise? Or, if action should be required, why require more than a "first act," since "any act done for the purpose of

25 Bayles, 17–18.
52 S 5.01 (1)(c)–(2).

committing a crime is an act that demonstrates dangerousness"?[53]

Justifying the "Act Requirement"

One obvious rationale for a substantial act requirement is that only conduct going beyond a "first act" provides sufficient *evidence* of the defendant's "anti-social disposition," especially if his disposition must involve some "firmness of criminal purpose": evidence, that is, which is reasonably reliable, and obtainable by reasonably non-oppressive and non-intrusive means. To subject people to punishment without such evidence would invite oppressively intrusive modes of police investigation, and risk convicting too many innocents.[54]

This justification of the act requirement for attempts (and for criminal liability generally) grounds it in considerations *external* to the agent's criminality: a person might have an "anti-social disposition" which requires "corrective sanction," but escape liability because a law which allowed for her conviction would also have other unacceptable implications. It thus portrays the connection between antisocial disposition or undesirable character trait and criminal conduct as *contingent*: it could be true that someone has a dangerous character trait, or a criminally antisocial disposition, though she has never yet exhibited it in criminal conduct.

Now some theorists argue that the relationship between character and action is generally contingent: someone could *be* courageous, although she has never *acted* courageously, if she has never faced a situation calling for courage.[56] As a *general* claim about the relationship between character and action, I think this is mistaken: a courageous person is not merely someone who *would* behave courageously, but someone who *does* behave courageously; if someone has never yet faced a situation calling for courage, the point is not that we might not know whether she is courageous, but that there is as yet no fact of the matter to be known. However, it might be more plausible as a claim about the relationship between *criminal* character and *criminal* conduct.

First, it could surely be true (and knowable) that someone has a criminal trait (a trait such that he would, in certain likely circumstances, attempt to commit a crime), although he has as yet done nothing criminal: the kind of dishonesty which would motivate theft or fraud, for instance, could be clearly manifested in non-criminal types of dishonest behaviour. Secondly, if (for the reasons indicated above) anything more than a "first act" is specified as the conduct element in attempts, an intending criminal could have begun to manifest his criminal disposition in conduct which is not yet criminal, because it does not yet constitute a "substantial step" towards the crime. Thus, even if the general connection between character traits and action is logical or constitutive, rather than contingent, that between *criminal* character traits (those that should attract criminal liability) and *criminal* action (conduct that the law defines as criminal) is contingent; and the reasons for having an act requirement at all, or for requiring more than a "first act," are indeed external to the underlying conception of criminal liability.

The force of the first of these arguments depends partly on whether there is any substantive, pre-legal difference between what the law defines as criminal and what it defines as non-criminal. Is the manifested disposition to engage in non-criminal kinds of dishonest conduct already a disposition to engage in *criminally*

53 Commentary to s 5.01, 326.

54 See *Model Penal Code*, Commentary to s5.01, 326–31. See also Bayles, 19; Brandt, 189. The force of such an argument depends, of course, on large empirical claims about the likely costs and benefits of a law which did not include an "act requirement"—claims which it is not easy to assess.

56 For instance, Brandt, "Traits of Character: A Conceptual Analysis," 26; Moore, 41.

dishonest conduct; or could we argue that, given the substantial moral difference between criminal and non-criminal types of dishonesty, one who manifests a disposition to non-criminal kinds of dishonesty does not yet or thereby manifest a *criminally* dishonest disposition? It also depends on what significance we should attach to a disposition to break the law as such, as distinct from a disposition to engage in conduct which the law in fact prohibits. However, the second argument seems to be strong enough by itself to establish the desired conclusion: that the connection between criminal conduct and criminal character trait is indeed contingent and evidential. Nor should this seem startling: for many legal rules, substantive as well as procedural, aim not so much to define criminality as to protect citizens against mistaken convictions and oppressive policing; and such rules will typically allow some who are indeed criminal to escape liability.

"Choice" theorists, and others, might still be unhappy with this account of the act requirement, since it still implies that offenders are punished essentially for what they *are*—whereas a system of law which is to respect its citizens as responsible agents should surely punish them only for what they *do*. There is, though, another question for the "character" theorist to answer: why should one criminal action be *sufficient*, as well as *necessary*, for criminal liability?

How Can One Criminal Action Be Sufficient?

If what makes a person criminally liable is a settled or lasting disposition (for that is what requires correction), and if the relationship between criminal disposition and criminal action is contingent: how can one criminal action alone suffice to establish the existence of a criminal disposition? For on this account, someone could surely commit one criminal action without having a settled criminal disposition: before convicting and punishing a defendant who was proved to have committed a criminal action (with the usually appropriate fault element), courts should therefore have to determine whether that one action really did manifest an undesirably dangerous disposition, and exempt her from criminal liability if it did not.

It is not enough simply to say that, while the "attitudes" which constitute the various orthodox types of criminal fault might indeed be "fleeting," the law operates with "a general presumption that the combination of behaviour and attitude indicates an undesirable character trait":[60] we need to know what justifies that presumption. Nor is it enough to say that this admittedly artificial presumption protects the defendant "against a free-ranging inquiry of the state into his moral worth."[61] The purpose of such an inquiry would be to determine whether the inference to an undesirable character trait (for which the defendant's criminal conduct provided strong grounds) could be rebutted, thus exempting him from liability; and any defendant who objected to this (possibly exculpating) inquiry could avoid it by pleading guilty.

Lacey argues that courts should indeed often "look more broadly at the defendant's attitudes as manifested in other relevant areas of behaviour" to establish "the inference from action to disposition"; and implies that defendants should not be held criminally liable for "out of character" actions in which their "settled dispositions" are not "centrally expressed."[62] "Choice" theorists might reply that the mere fact that a crime was "out of character" for a defendant surely should not exempt her from conviction and punishment; if the "character" theory would exempt her, that theory is unacceptable.

60 Bayles, 10.
61 Fletcher, 801.
62 Lacey, 75, 68 ("it is unfair to hold people responsible" for "out of character" actions).

To clarify this issue, however, we must ask more carefully just what it is for a crime to be "out of character."

A trusted employee steals a large sum from his employer; this is his first and only act of criminal dishonesty. What might lead us to count this action as "out of character"? Would it also incline us to acquit him of theft?

The mere fact that he had not previously stolen does not render his action out of character. Perhaps this was the first opportunity he had to steal without (he thought) being detected: even if he was not actually waiting for such an opportunity, in taking it he showed himself to be criminally dishonest—disposed to steal if an opportunity arose.

Perhaps his action was weak-willed, rather than whole-heartedly larcenous: on this one occasion he gave in to the temptation to do what he knew was wrong, and now bitterly repents it. Lacey implies that such weak-willed actions are "out of character." Actions should attract liability (i.e., are "in character") only when they are "genuinely expressive of the agent's relevant disposition"; only if they are actions "with which the agent truly identifies, and can call her own":[64] but my weak-willed actions flow from motives or dispositions which I *disown* (that is what makes them *weak-willed*). None the less, we surely are morally, and must be criminally, liable for weak-willed actions, and they do reflect relevant character traits: a lack of commitment to the values they infringe; weakness in the face of temptation.[65]

Perhaps the theft was motivated by some change in his situation which provoked a change in his attitudes. A sudden need of money, or the discovery that his employer had been exploiting him, led him to think (as he had not previously thought) that such theft was morally permissible, or induced a new willingness to steal. Whether this change of attitude is lasting or temporary however, he must surely still be criminally liable (unless those circumstances *justified* his action); and his action was still "in character," as reflecting attitudes and values which intelligibly developed his existing character.

We might, though, give a different account: of the devastating effect on an honest man of suddenly desperate need (for money to get treatment for his seriously ill child), or of perceived injustice (being made redundant, for no good reason that he could see, from a job to which he had devoted himself for twenty years). We might now ascribe his theft not to vice (greed, a lack of respect for others' rights), nor to weakness of will (failing to resist temptation that an honest person would resist), but to emotional disturbance: his anxiety, his rage, was such that it impaired his capacity to guide his actions by the values to which he was truly committed. His action still reveals something about him: that he is a person who breaks down in this way in such a situation. However, if we think that he should be excused (and this thought is more plausible in this case), we might say that his action was "out of character": it did not show him to be really dishonest, or manifest a culpably dishonest character.

I think that some such account must be given if we are to portray his theft as "out of character" in any way which could plausibly bear on his criminal liability. One thing that this suggests is that the controversy between "choice" and "character" theorists over "out of character" actions is spurious. For the "choice" theorist should surely say that in this case the thief did not "freely choose" to do wrong, since his capacity for free, responsible choice (to guide his actions by a rational conception of the good) was impaired. Then, however, it could never be the case that an agent "freely chooses to do wrong" (i.e., he has the

64 Lacey, 77; contrast Moore, 42–43 on "narrow" and "broad" views of character.

65 See Aristotle, *Nicomachean Ethics* I13, II–III, VI–VII.

capacity and a fair opportunity not to so choose), and yet the action is "out of character" for that agent:[67] criminal actions which a "character" theorist could plausibly excuse as being "out of character" are precisely those that "choice" theorists would excuse as being not "freely chosen."

Criminal Action as Constitutive of Criminal Character

The preceding discussion also suggests that we should see criminal actions as *constitutive* of, and not merely as evidence for, the kinds of "character trait" or "disposition" which should concern the criminal law. A single act of theft, committed by someone who is not mentally disordered or acting under an exculpating kind of pressure, is *logically sufficient* for criminal liability: that is, it is sufficient not because it provides empirically adequate evidence for a settled disposition which is likely to issue in further thefts (for it suffices to convict a weak-willed thief who we are sure will not steal again), but because it defines the agent as a dishonest thief. We do not make a contingent *inference* from this dishonest action to a distinct character trait or disposition that caused it: the action itself is constitutive of the thief's criminal dishonesty, since it manifests his dishonest willingness to steal—to *act* thus is to *be* dishonest. By contrast, what makes a person's action "out of character," in the relevant sense, is not just its inconsistency with the settled dispositions he has displayed in other contexts, but that it does not reveal "character" at all: it does not display the valuational and motivational structure of attitudes and practical reasoning in which "character," as an object of moral appraisal, consists.

Of course the attitudes, the structures of value and motivation, that we can see displayed in the thief's action, and cannot see displayed in "out of character" action, are not merely fleeting aspects of a person's psychology. This is the element of truth in the "character" theory: that the actions for which a person is convicted and punished must be "hers"; they must be suitably related to attitudes or motives which are aspects of her continuing identity as a person. This is not to say that she is convicted and punished *for* those character traits, *rather than* for the actions in which they are manifested: for what properly concerns the criminal law, I am arguing, are the agent's practical attitudes *as manifested in and constituted by* her criminal actions.

But if one (non-disordered, non-excused) criminal action is thus logically or constitutively, rather than merely evidentially, sufficient for criminal liability, we might also say that criminal action should be constitutively, rather than merely evidentially, necessary for criminal liability. That is, the "act" requirement is not just an evidential requirement grounded in considerations external to the basic conception of criminal liability: rather, it is only by criminal action that an agent constitutes herself as criminally culpable. We might know of someone who has not yet committed theft that she is *potentially* a thief: given the dispositions or character traits that she has already manifested, we can predict confidently that in certain likely circumstances she will or would commit theft. She is, however, not yet a thief; nor does she yet, on this account, *actually* have a criminally dishonest character: only by committing theft does she constitute herself as a thief, and her character as criminally dishonest.

Why should we accept such an account of the notion of a criminal character trait or disposition (a character trait or disposition of a kind warranting criminal liability), instead of the simpler view that it is a trait or disposition which will predictably result in criminal conduct, but need not logically yet have done so?

One answer is that if the law is to treat its citizens as rational and responsible agents (as it

67 Moore, 51.

should), it must be an "enterprise of subjecting human conduct to the governance of rules,"[70] not just of controlling their conduct by whatever means might be economically effective. That is, it should seek to guide their conduct by giving them good reasons to obey its legitimate requirements, thus treating them as rational agents who are susceptible to rational persuasion—who can recognize and act in accordance with the reasons for action that it provides. However, this also requires that it should subject them to criminal sanctions only if or when they have definitively refused to recognize or to act in accordance with those reasons: for if they were to be made liable to sanctions because of what they *would* do or *might* do, rather than because of what they have actually done, they would no longer be treated as rational agents who can, and should therefore be allowed to, determine their own conduct. We may be certain that someone *will* break the law, that he will not be dissuaded from doing so by the reasons which the law offers him: but we must still treat him as someone who could be rationally persuaded to obey, even at the last moment.

If we take criminal conduct to be merely evidence of a kind of disposition which should attract criminal liability, and if dispositions should attract liability because they are likely to result in criminally harmful conduct (and so require correction), then people are being held criminally liable and punished because of what they will or might do, and are therefore not being treated as responsible agents. By contrast, this alternative account respects the citizens' capacities for rational and responsible agency: it holds them criminally liable only when they actually engage in criminal conduct, not because only then do we have appropriate evidence of their dangerous disposition, but because only then do they constitute, or actualize, themselves as having a criminal character.

"Choice" v. "Character": A False Dichotomy?

It might seem that I am trying to import central elements of the "choice" conception into the "character" conception: although I have not talked explicitly about leaving citizens free to "choose" for themselves whether to break the law, the argument sketched above obviously has close affinities with the kinds of argument that could be offered by a "choice" theorist for a restrictive specification of the conduct element in attempts. The account suggested here, which makes criminal action both necessary and sufficient for criminal liability because it is constitutive of criminality, is certainly at odds with the perspective of many "character" theorists, whose concern is precisely with the agent's "dangerousness" as evidenced but not constituted by her conduct. It also differs from the "choice" conception, however, in that it takes action, and the practical attitudes which actions manifest, rather than "choice," to be the proper foundation of liability.

Indeed, an account which takes "action," rather than "character" or "choice," as the proper basis of criminal liability can claim to dissolve the conflict between "choice" and "character" conceptions of liability, by arguing that each of those two conceptions captures but also distorts part of the truth.

A "character" conception expresses a significant truth about *who* can be held criminally liable: that only moral agents, whose actions exhibit the structures of thought, attitude, and motivation that constitute "character," should be held liable. For only such agents are responsible for, as the authors of, their actions; so only they can be called to answer for their wrongful actions through the criminal process of trial and punishment, to accept those actions as theirs, and to repent them. It also reminds us that actions can be criminally wrongful not merely because they reflect some wrongful *choice*, but because of the *attitudes* that they manifest: an attitude of

70 Fuller, *The Morality of Law*, 122.

disrespect for, or indifference to, the rights and interests of others, for instance. However, it distorts these truths by portraying the connection between action and character as contingent and inferential, and by suggesting that offenders are liable for (because of) their attitudes or dispositions, *rather than* for their actions. We should say instead that offenders are liable for their actions *as manifesting* the kinds of practical attitude which properly concern the criminal law; that those attitudes are constituted, not merely evidenced, by the actions which display them.

The "choice" conception expresses a significant truth about *that for which* agents can properly be held liable: they should be called to answer, and be convicted and punished, for their actions, not for what they "are" in so far as that is distinct from what they "do." It distorts that truth, though, by defining "action" in terms of "choice": it fails to allow for the ways in which "choices" can be understood as responsible or culpable only in virtue of their relation to "character"; and it wrongly supposes that *only* choice can ground criminal liability.

The "character" theorist might say that we are criminally liable for what we *are*, rather than for what we *do*; "choice" theorists will respond that we should be liable for what we (choose to) *do*, rather than for what we *are*. This is a spurious contrast: in the eyes of the criminal law what a person "is" consists in what she "does"; her criminal character is constituted by the character of her actions alone. The law is indeed interested in "character," and not merely in "choice": but what it is interested in is the character of our actions, not in "character" as distinct from action.

These points can be briefly illustrated by looking at recklessness as a species of criminal fault. "Choice" theorists insist that recklessness must be defined in terms of *conscious* risk-taking: I choose to take or to create only those risks which I realize that I am taking or creating. A critic might respond that recklessness should rather be understood as a species of culpable indifference to the rights and interests of others: an indifference which might be displayed in an agent's very failure to notice the obvious risk that her action creates; and a "character" theorist might argue that that indifference is an undesirable or dangerous character trait which we can empirically infer from her conduct. But that would be a mistake: the kind of "indifference" which properly concerns the criminal law is *practical* indifference, an indifference *in action* (not in feeling as distinct from action); and such indifference is displayed only in actively taking or creating an unreasonable risk of causing harm.

I will say more later about *why* we should take action to be the proper basis of criminal liability. We must turn now to a further question about the concept of "action" as it should figure in this context. Both "choice" and "character" conceptions of criminal liability are subjectivist: they hold that liability should be determined, not by the "objective" aspects of the agent's action (its actual impact on the world), but by its "subjective" dimension—by the intentions and beliefs with which he acted, or by the attitudes or dispositions which his action revealed. The actions which we ascribe to an agent, in assigning criminal liability, should therefore be identified and described in subjective terms: their objective aspects, their actual circumstances and consequences, are irrelevant. By contrast, "objectivist" theories of liability argue that the actions which are to be ascribed to agents, for which they are to be criminally liable, cannot be identified in such purely subjective terms: that "action," in this as in other contexts, must be understood (in part) objectively. We must now see what such an objectivist claim involves ...

Works Cited in Notes

American Law Institute, *Model Penal Code* (text and commentaries; Philadelphia: American Law Institute, 1985).

Aristotle, *Nicomachean Ethics* (trans. Ross; Oxford: OUP, 1980).

Ashworth, A.J., "Sharpening the Subjective Element in Criminal Liability," in R.A. Duff and N.E. Simmonds (eds.), *Philosophy and the Criminal Law* (Wiesbaden: Franz Steiner, 1984), 79–89.

—. "Belief, Intent and Criminal Liability," in J. Eekelaar and J. Bell (eds.), *Oxford Essays in Jurisprudence*, 3rd Series (Oxford: OUP, 1987), 1–31.

—. "Taking the Consequences," in S. Shute, J. Gardener, J. Horder (eds.), *Action and Value in Criminal Law* (Oxford: OUP, 1993), 107–24.

—. *Principles of Criminal Law* (2nd ed.; Oxford: OUP, 1995).

Bayles, A.C., "Character, Purpose and Criminal Responsibility," *Law and Philosophy* 1 (1982), 5–20.

Brandt, R.B., "Traits of Character: A Conceptual Analysis," *American Philosophical Quarterly* 7 (1970), 23–37.

—. "A Motivational Theory of Excuses in the Criminal Law," in J. Pennock and J. Chapman (eds.), *Criminal Justice* (New York: New York UP, 1985), 165–98.

Cross, R., "Centenary Reflections on Prince's Case," *Law Quarterly Review* 91 (1975), 540–53.

Feinberg, J., "Problematic Responsibility in Law and Morals," in Feinberg, *Doing and Deserving* (Princeton: Princeton UP, 1970), 25–37.

Fletcher, G., *Rethinking Criminal Law* (Boston: Little Brown, 1978).

—. "Constructing a Theory of Impossible Attempts," in P. Fitzgerald (ed.), *Crime, Justice and Codification* (Toronto: Carswell, 1986), 87–113.

Fuller, L., *The Morality of Law* (2nd ed.; New Haven: Yale UP, 1969).

Galloway, D., "Patterns of Trying: A Critique of Fletcher on Criminal Attempts," *Queen's L J* 7 (1982), 232–52.

Hudson, S., *Human Character and Morality* (London: Routledge, 1986).

Lacey, N., *State Punishment* (London: Routledge, 1988).

—. "A Clear Concept of Intention: Elusive or Illusory?," *Modern L R* 56 (1993), 621–42.

—, Wells, C., and Meure, D., *Reconstructing Criminal Law* (London: Weidenfeld & Nicolson, 1990).

Law Commission, Working Paper No. 102, *Attempt and Impossibility in Relation to Attempt, Conspiracy and Incitement* (London: HMSO, 1985).

—. No. 177, *A Criminal Code for England and Wales*: Vol. 1, Report and Draft Criminal Code Bill; Vol. 2, Commentary (London: HMSO, 1989).

Moore, M.S., "Choice. Character and Excuse," *Social Philosophy and Policy* 7 (1990), 29–58.

—. *Act and Crime* (Oxford: OUP, 1993).

Nagel, T., "Moral Luck," in Nagel, *Moral Questions* (Cambridge: CUP, 1979), 24–38.

Schulhofer, S.J., Review of Fletcher, *Rethinking Criminal Law*, *California L R* 68 (1980), 181–201.

Weinreb, L., "Manifest Criminality, Criminal Intent, and the 'Metamorphosis of Larceny,'" *Yale L J* 90 (1980), 294–318.

Abbreviations

The following abbreviations are used for frequently cited books, reports etc.

Ashworth Attempts
A.J. Ashworth, "Criminal Attempts and the Role of Resulting Harm under the Code, and in the Common Law."

Ashworth Principles
A.J. Ashworth, *Principles of Criminal Law* (2nd ed.).

Fletcher
G. Fletcher, *Rethinking Criminal Law*.

Law Com. 102
Law Commission No.102 *Attempt, and Impossibility in Relation to Attempt, Conspiracy and Incitement* (1980).

1989 Draft Code
Law Commission No.177 *A Criminal Code for England and Wales* (1989): Vol. 1, Report and Draft Criminal Code Bill; Vol. 2, Commentary.

Model Penal Code[35]
American Law Institute, *Model Penal Code* (text and commentaries).

35 Produced by the Law Commission, after considering responses to the *1985 Draft Code*.

22

Heidi M. Hurd

"Why Liberals Should Hate 'Hate Crime Legislation'"

Two justifications are commonly advanced for the increased penalty clauses of hate and bias crime legislation. First, it is said that because hate and bias crimes victimize whole communities of people, they constitute greater wrongs than do otherwise-motivated crimes. Just as a murderer should be punished more than a thief because it is a greater wrong to cause a loss of life than to cause a loss of property, so too, someone who victimizes another because of her religion should be punished more than someone who victimizes another out of jealousy because it is a greater wrong to do something that terrorizes an entire religious community than to do something that terrorizes only a single individual.

Second, it is argued that hate and bias crimes reflect significantly greater culpability on the part of their perpetrators. Just as premeditated murders should be punished far more than negligent homicides because those who plan others' deaths are far more culpable than those who inadvertently cause them, so too, crimes committed as a result of racial hatred or gender bias should be punished far more than crimes committed for other reasons because bigotry is far more culpable than, say, greed.

It is this latter justification for hate crime legislation with which I am concerned. I shall leave to social scientists the empirical question of whether crimes perpetrated as a result of hatred or bias do in fact cause more secondary harm to communities than do otherwise-motivated crimes. And I shall leave for another time both the philosophical question of whether such secondary harms, if greater, are of a sort that should merit special legal concern, and the doctrinal question of whether hate crime statutes as presently drafted would meet that concern. In this contribution I shall focus solely on the legitimacy of justifying hate crime statutes on the basis that hatred and bias constitute uniquely culpable mental states that merit increased punishment. As I shall argue, if hatred and bias are construed as *mens rea* elements, then they are alien to traditional criminal law principles. What is worse, they are alien for profound moral and political reasons: to criminalize hatred and bias is to move from an act-centered theory of criminal punishment to a character-centered theory, and so, to move from a liberal theory of legislation to a perfectionist theory. In short, when political liberals appreciate just how and why hate crime legislation is different from all other sorts of criminal legislation, they should philosophically loathe legislation that targets hate crimes.

I. Three Differences between Hate/Bias Crimes and All Other Crimes

If hate and bias crime legislation construes hate and bias as *mens rea* requirements, then there are three important differences between hate and bias crimes and virtually all other sorts of crimes with which the criminal law is concerned. And these differences, it seems to me, are both practically and philosophically profound. First, hate/bias crimes are concerned with defendants' motivations for action in a way that no other crimes have ever been concerned. Second, the motivations with which they are concerned are emotional states that attend actions (rather than future states of affairs to which actions are instrumental means). And finally, the emotional states with which these crimes are concerned constitute standing character traits rather than occurrent mental states (such as intentions, purposes, choices, etc.). In this Part, I shall make out these three differences, and by so doing I shall demonstrate that the additional penalties that are imposed on defendants who are found guilty of hate/bias crimes constitute, in the end, punishments for bad character.

A. THE DOCTRINAL NOVELTY OF HATRED AND BIAS AS *MENS REA* ELEMENTS

The standard means of measuring culpability in criminal law has long been via a very spare set of mental states. Most criminal statutes require factfinders to answer one of the following questions: Did the defendant purposefully commit the *actus reus* of the offense? Did he knowingly commit it? Was he consciously aware of a substantial and unjustifiable risk that he would commit it—i.e., was he reckless with regard to doing the legally-prohibited deed? Or should he have been consciously aware of the risk that he would commit the offense—i.e., was he negligent with regard to it? None of these inquiries require (or permit) consideration of the reasons for which the defendant acted or the background motivations with which he performed his actions. Inasmuch as hate and bias crimes increase penalties because of particular motivations, they commit fact-finders to discovering altogether novel *mens rea*.

Let me make clear just how true this is by briefly exploring three sets of doctrines that might be thought to provide precedents for the motivational *mens rea* of hate crimes. First, it has traditionally been true that if a defendant acts as a result of good or, at least, exculpatory, motivations, that fact has entered into the analysis of the defendant's responsibility at the level of the defenses. For example, defendants who reasonably believe that they are choosing the lesser of two evils or adopting proportionate means of defending against culpable aggressors will be relieved of legal liability by the justifications of necessity and self-defense. If a defendant kills as a result of being provoked into passion in circumstances in which a reasonable person might be inclined to act rashly, then the provocation/passion doctrine will reduce his liability from murder to voluntary manslaughter. So good, or at least exculpatory, motivations have traditionally been rewarded by defining defenses in ways that fully or partially exonerate persons for well-motivated or understandably ill-motivated conduct.

In contrast to these doctrines, however, hate/bias crimes require courts to consider *bad, or inculpatory*, motivations as bases for enhancing penalties for wrongdoing. The defense doctrines that exculpate defendants from liability for well-motivated (or understandably ill-motivated) conduct are thus disanalogous to the new *mens rea* doctrines created by hate and bias crimes.

Consider, now, two doctrines that seemingly enhance defendants' punishment as a result of finding particularly vicious reasons for action. First, in a number of jurisdictions defendants who premeditate and deliberate about their killings will be eligible for far more severe punishment than are defendants who kill impulsively. Does the premeditation/deliberation doctrine commit fact-finders to a motivational inquiry that provides a precedent for the *mens rea* analysis required by hate and bias crimes? The answer is clearly "no." To determine that a defendant premeditated and deliberated about a killing is to find that he formed the purpose to kill after datable mental calculations about whether and how to kill. While a defendant's motivation for killing may provide evidence that he thought about killing, a finding that a defendant premeditated a killing is ultimately of a different sort than a finding that he killed for a particular reason or while in a particular emotional state.

Consider, finally, the possible precedent for hate crimes provided by so-called "specific intent crimes." Specific intent crimes are crimes that require defendants to commit prohibited actions with certain *further* purposes. Thus, for example, burglary is a specific intent crime because to be guilty of it, a defendant must break and enter with some further intention, say to steal, rape, or kill. Such a crime appears to have a motivational *mens rea* requirement, because to assess liability, fact-finders must ask *why* the defendant did what he did, not just whether he did what he did purposefully (and perhaps, as a result of deliberating about it).[1]

Yet specific intentions take as their objects future states of affairs—states of affairs that constitute reasons for action. In contrast, hatred constitutes an emotional state within which a defendant acts, and bias constitutes a disposition to make and act upon false judgments about others. As I shall argue in the next section, these differences both *are* differences and they make a moral difference.

B. HATE AND BIAS ARE EMOTIONAL STATES, NOT REASONS FOR ACTION

Specific intentions constitute goals—future states of affairs that provide reasons for action. To break and enter so as to get money, or so as to subject another to sexual intercourse, or so as to kill someone is not (necessarily or intrinsically) to act on an emotion; it is rather to act so as to obtain what one perceives as a future good. In contrast, hatred and prejudice, while being distinct from one another, are not goals. Hatred constitutes an emotional state within which a defendant acts. While we speak of emotions as "motivating" actions—saying such things as "he lashed out in anger," or "she flew into a jealous rage"—we do not take them to be ends to which actors seek means. (Indeed, when we reference a defendant's emotional state we are very often explaining why her powers of practical reasoning were partially suspended so as to make her less able to pursue her goals effectively.) And while hatred may require bias, and bias may commonly cause hatred, bias does not require hatred. One who is biased or prejudiced against others possesses false beliefs that are "dispositional" in nature. Such beliefs constitute standing dispositions to draw particular (false) conclusions about particular persons in particular situations without more particular information. It is because prejudices constitute sets of dispositional beliefs that we think of them as "motivational." They induce discriminatory actions by moving actors to make certain (false) factual assumptions about others within the course of practical reasoning.

Two responses might be made to this argument that hate/bias crimes are unique in punishing defendants for their emotions and (dispositional) beliefs. First, it might be argued that people who act out of hatred toward, or a belief in the inferiority of, say, Muslims in their community, are seeking by their actions the future state of affairs in which there are no Muslims in their neighborhood. Such an argument collapses emotions and dispositional beliefs into specific intentions, and thus allows advocates of hate/bias crimes to maintain that the *mens rea* of such crimes are no different than the *mens rea* of traditional specific intent crimes.[2]

While there is nothing conceptually amiss about this move, it seems to me that this argument grossly over-intellectualizes emotions and dispositional beliefs. While a straight defendant who manifests hatred toward a gay neighbor, or who treats him as inferior, might, upon reflection, answer "yes" to the question, "Would you

1 Paul Robinson, for example, has defended the claim that specific intent crimes provide adequate precedent for hate crimes (although he goes on to argue that while hate crimes enjoy such precedents, the use of hate motivation is not necessarily the best criterion for defining the harms that hate crimes seek to punish). See Paul H. Robinson, "Hate Crimes: Crimes of Motive, Character, or Group Terror?," *Annual Survey of American Law 1992–93* (1992), pp. 606–09.

2 For a version of this collapse see Kent Greenawalt, "Reflections on Justifications for Defining Crimes by the Category of the Victim," *1992/93 Annual Survey of American Law*, pp. 6120–6125.

prefer a world in which there are no gays?" this does not mean that at the time of his action he entertained a conscious belief of this sort, or any desire that his actions contribute to such a state of affairs. He could simply have been manifesting a visceral emotion that had not (yet) been given propositional content, or a (dispositional) belief from which he had drawn no conclusions concerning ideal future states of affairs. That we theoreticians can identify future states of affairs with which defendants' emotions and beliefs appear consistent is neither here nor there. The question is whether we have reasons to attribute intentions about such future states to persons who do not subjectively experience them. In my view, nothing is gained by so doing (except the doctrinal advantage that comes to those who may then analogize hate/bias crimes to specific intent crimes) and much may be lost.

First, brute emotions, dispositional beliefs, and specific intentions are experienced differently, and it obfuscates their phenomenological distinctness to collapse them into a single category. Second, these felt differences are very likely to be morally relevant. We may have better control over one category of mental states than over others. Or we may be more (or less) culpable for harboring one category of mental states over others (regardless of our control over these states). Or the law may be better able to affect our possession of one category of mental states over others (assuming, for example, that we have control over all of them, but that some are more responsive to external incentives than others). For these and other reasons, we are likely to slur morally relevant differences between actors if we translate the emotions and dispositional beliefs experienced by some into the sorts of goals that constitute reasons for actions for others.

The second argument that might be advanced to dispute my claim that hate/bias crimes invoke new and novel *mens rea* requirements takes its leave from the fact that many hate/bias crime statutes do not use the language of hate or bias at all. Instead, for example, many hate/bias crime statutes simply require fact-finders to find that the defendant picked his victim *because of* the victim's race, ethnicity, religion, gender, sexual orientation, etc. It might plausibly be said, therefore, that these statutes do not criminalize *any* emotional or belief states (whatever the merits of so doing might be).

It would seem, however, that when hate/bias crimes are defined without reference to hate or bias, their language ill-fits both the occasions on which they are used and the purpose for which they are enacted (if, that is, their purpose is to punish defendants in proportion to their culpability). Suppose, for example, that a defendant picks a black victim because he wants to kill someone, and given the bright lighting, the dark color of his victim's skin allows the defendant to see and take aim at that victim better than at surrounding white prospects. Or suppose that a defendant simply wants to steal from someone who was unlikely to put up a serious fight, and so for that reason he chooses to mug a woman rather than a man. While in these cases the defendants choose their victims because of their race and gender, these are not paradigm cases of hate/bias crimes, nor would they be prosecuted as such—for they do not reflect actions done out of hatred for, or prejudice against, particular communities of people. Indeed, were these hate crimes, virtually all rapes would be hate crimes, as would be all crimes committed by persons who used their victims' race, religion, ethnicity, disability, etc., as proxies for other criteria (such as wealth, physical weakness, philosophical pacifism, etc.).

If legislators of hate/bias crime legislation do not intend for the above sorts of cases to be prosecuted as hate/bias crimes, and if prosecutors and courts do not invoke hate/bias crime statutes in cases of this sort (as they surely do not), then the practical implications of hate/bias crime legislation—even hate/bias crime legislation that does not reference hate or bias—is to punish defendants for hate and bias. In investigating the defensibility of hate/bias crime legislation, therefore, we are entitled to proceed by inquiring into the implications of requiring fact-finders to find not just that a defendant used a victim's membership in a group as the principle criterion for selecting that person, but that the defendant victimized that person out of hatred toward, or prejudice against, a group of which the victim was a member. In short, we are entitled to inquire into the morality of legislation whose language matches its point and practice.

Before we turn squarely to the morality of such legislation, let us make explicit the third difference that has emerged between the *mens rea* of hate/ bias crimes and the *mens rea* of other crimes. For it is this difference that makes the moral difference between traditional criminal legislation and hate crime legislation.

C. HATRED AND BIAS ARE STANDING CHARACTER TRAITS, NOT OCCURRENT MENTAL STATES

The mental states with which hate and bias crimes are concerned are not occurrent states of mind—they are, rather, dispositions possessed over time. While one can form a purpose or fix on a desired goal in a moment's time, it is hard to conceive of what it would mean to hate or be prejudiced against a group only momentarily (and were it possible, it would be hard to imagine why the law would deem such momentary mental states uniquely culpable). Rather, to harbor hatred or bias towards a particular group appears to be a (bad or vicious) character trait—that is, a disposition to act in ways that subjugate members of the group when opportunities to do so without recrimination present themselves. Character traits are both dispositions toward certain sorts of actions and dispositions towards certain sorts of mental states. To be cowardly, for example, is to be disposed to feel fear in (often mildly) threatening circumstances and to flee from its source. Character traits may be a product of nature, nurture, or some combination of the two. In some cases, cowardliness, kindness, and greediness appear so integral to actors' personalities as to make one suspect that these traits are "in the genes." In other cases, these virtues and vices appear to be learned—the product of years of fortunate or unfortunate parenting, schooling, peer pressures, and life experiences.

It is fully possible for one to feel hatred toward particular persons (because, for example, of certain things that they have done), without being a "hateful" person—that is, without being disposed to feel hatred towards groups of persons generally, or towards the offending persons in particular. It is also possible for one to leap to unjustified conclusions about particular persons (because, for example, one lacks the time or ability to gather further important information about them) without being a "biased" person—that is, without being disposed to assume that such persons possess certain attributes solely by virtue of their membership in certain groups (e.g., racial, ethnic, or religious groups). Thus, hatred and bias (in the sense of drawing ill-informed conclusions about persons) are not, as a general matter, dispositional.

But hatred and bias towards whole groups of persons (particularly groups defined by such morally irrelevant criteria as race, ethnicity, gender, age, religion, or disability) *does* appear dispositional. To experience the felt passion of hatred whenever one encounters (or even thinks about) a member of a particular group appears to reflect a standing disposition (whether learned or innate), not a momentary or occurrent emotion. And to regularly draw conclusions and reason from assumptions about the character and deeds of particular persons based solely on their membership in larger groups appears to be similarly dispositional. Thus, for example, to be a racist is to be disposed to believe that members of another race are inferior, and to act in ways that subjugate such persons. To be a chauvinist is to be disposed to believe that women are inferior, and to act in ways that oppress them. To be homophobic is to be disposed to feel revulsion when one encounters persons who are homosexual, and to act in ways that deny them equal status and benefits within the community.

There is thus a significant difference between the sorts of mental states (intentions concerning future states of affairs) that are targeted by specific intent crimes and the sorts of mental states (emotions and beliefs) that are targeted by hate/bias crimes. While one's intentions are often a product of certain aspects of one's character, one may form an intention to do an act (say, to steal) without being disposed to do such an act (i.e., without being a greedy or thieving person). But one cannot hate or be prejudiced against Asians and women without being a racist and a sexist—that is, without being disposed to feel antipathy whenever one is confronted with members of that race and sex, or without being disposed to believe derogatory things about them and to act in ways that oppress them (when capacities and opportunities permit). In punishing defendants for the intentions with which they act, then, specific intent crimes do not punish defendants for having bad character. But in punishing defendants for hating or being prejudiced against their victims because of their victims' membership in particular groups, hate/bias crimes necessarily punish defendants for having bad character. In fact, their enhanced penalties punish defendants *solely* for their bad character.[3]

If hate/bias crime legislation punishes persons for bad character, as it does if it enhances defendants' punishment for criminal wrongdoing when it is perpetrated because of certain emotions or (dispositional) beliefs, then such legislation is, at least prima facie, morally and politically troubling. In the next section, let us turn to the questions that advocates of hate/bias crime legislation must answer in order to defend the moral and political legitimacy of criminalizing bad character.

II. The Moral and Political Implications of Criminalizing Vicious Character Traits

If I am right that hate crime legislation punishes persons for bad character, then hate and bias crime statutes have some surprising implications and raise some very important political questions. Let me pose three such questions, and say why the answers that one gives may have profound implications for the future of American criminal law.

A. CAN WE CHOOSE OUR EMOTIONS OR WILL OUR BELIEFS?

Most of us are pretty confident that would-be defendants can choose not to rape, steal, and kill. But it seems less clear to what degree people can will away, or choose not to have, particular character traits, and specifically, particular emotions and beliefs. At the moment that a defendant is about to throw a rock through his neighbor's window, we are reasonably sure that he can will to do otherwise; but at that moment, can he will away his hatred of his neighbor as a Jew? Can one simply decide not to be selfish, or greedy, or narcissistic? I suspect that anyone who can is not very selfish, greedy or narcissistic! Can one simply refuse to believe things that one has long been disposed to believe? Surely not by an act of will alone. Certainly one can gather more information about others so as to make more discriminating, and thus less discriminatory judgments about them. But it is in the nature of bias for one to believe that no further information is required so as to make informed judgments about others.

3 This is assuming, as I am, that hate/bias crimes enhance punishments for otherwise punishable acts because of the subjective emotional or belief states within which the defendant acted (i.e., because of the defendant's relative culpability for those acts).

And it is unclear how one could simply will a change in one's epistemic standards.

Persons can, with mixed success, *indirectly* alter aspects of their character by choosing to subject themselves to experiences that promise to be character building. People clearly spend enormous amounts of money in therapy to change themselves for the better. And people can, again with imperfect reliability, alter their characters by repeatedly putting themselves in circumstances that challenge them to behave in ways that, over time, affect their beliefs, emotional reactions, and dispositional responses. For example, someone might not be able to will away his disdain for the poor; but he might be able to rid himself of that disdain by moving to the ghetto and volunteering his time to help those in need, so that over time his disdain fades to pity, and then to admiration for the hardiness required to persevere in poverty.

Perhaps by punishing people particularly harshly when they do bad deeds out of hatred for, or bias against, their victims' race, ethnicity, religion, sexual orientation, etc., we will motivate people to take actions that will indirectly alter, over time, their emotional responses to such characteristics.[4] And perhaps those who do not pursue available avenues for dispositional change deserve punishment for their bad character—not because they chose their character, but because they failed to will actions that might have caused their character to be other than it is.

But while character can be indirectly affected by willed actions, and so is not immutable, one's ability to affect it indirectly is clearly imperfect. And, most importantly, such indirect measures are just that: indirect, and hence, non-immediate. We cannot abandon our emotions and (dispositional) beliefs the way that we can abandon our goals—i.e., simply by choice. Thus, criminal legislation that targets emotions and (dispositional) beliefs targets things that are not fully or readily within defendants' immediate control. And if law ought not to punish us for things that we cannot autonomously affect, then hate and bias crime legislation is suspect for doing just that.

B. ARE HATRED AND PREJUDICE WORSE THAN OTHER EMOTIONAL STATES THAT OFTEN ACCOMPANY CRIMINAL ACTIONS?

I am in fact quite sympathetic to the view that moral culpability is largely a function of character—of the beliefs that guide us and the emotions that attend our actions (notwithstanding their inelastic nature). But hatred and bias towards particular groups are but two of many culpable dispositions. Are they the worst of the bunch? Are they so rotten as to justify special criminal attention? How does hate compare to greed, jealousy, revenge, sadism, or cowardliness? If hate and bias crimes are going to remain unique among crimes in picking out emotional and dispositional motivations as bases for increased punishment, then it must be possible either (1) to defend the claim that, say, racial hatred or gender bias is morally worse than greed, jealousy, and revenge, or (2) to advance some reason to think that such hatred and bias are uniquely responsive to criminal sanctions in a way that greed, jealousy, and vengeance are not. I think it unlikely that hate crime advocates can sustain either of these arguments, although both may have more promise than some critics have supposed.

It is true that "motives cannot be readily ranked by their degree of culpability,"[5] and this confounds any easy defense of the first claim. One critic suggests that this is because all motivations to assault persons, for example, share a

---

4 I do not embrace a utilitarian theory of punishment, so if this were the point of hate/bias crimes, my objections to them would exceed those articulated in this paper.

5 Alon Harel and Gideon Parchomovsky, "On Hate and Equality," *Yale Law Journal* 109 (1999), pp. 507, 513.

common denominator, i.e., the motive to humiliate, and this makes them all equally culpable.[6] But this explanation is implausible: someone who renders another unconscious so as to pick his pocket is not necessarily subjectively intending to humiliate his victim, and someone who enjoys embarrassing others is clearly not as culpable as someone who enjoys inflicting physical torture on others, even though both may be said to be motivated by a desire to humiliate. Others have suggested, conversely, that the reason that motivations cannot be clearly ranked is because they are so different as to be incommensurable.[7] I find this suggestion equally implausible, not only because the concept of incommensurability is by itself troublesome. If all culpable motivations were incommensurable, there would be no easy cases of comparison. But there clearly are. A young girl who feels a need to publicly display her affection for her boyfriend (by, say, graffiting "Sally loves John" on a washroom wall in a manner that constitutes technical destruction of property) is clearly not as culpable as the sadist who seeks to prolong the torture of a child over days.

In my view, the likely reason that motives (goals, emotions, and dispositional beliefs) resist cardinal classifications and even ordinal rankings is that they are highly fact-sensitive. Just as the determination that someone was negligent turns on a detailed appreciation of the circumstances in which she acted and the information reasonably available to her, so the evaluation of someone's motives for action requires an appreciation of the nature and the relative weight of an inevitably complex set of goals, emotions, and (dispositional) beliefs, as well as an overall assessment of the merit of their combination. As such, it appears difficult to say that particular motivations, say racial prejudice or religious hatred, are categorically worse than other motivations, say pedophilia or sadism: as between some persons they probably are; as between others they probably are not.

Those who resort to the second means of defending the unique status of hate and bias crimes must advance reasons to think that racism, sexism, and homophobia can be more readily purged by the criminal law than can other vices. Some might maintain that racism, sexism, and homophobia are learned, while sadism, vengeance, and jealousy are not. They thus might argue that racism, sexism, and homophobia can be unlearned in a way that these other dispositions cannot. Perhaps this is so. Even if one believes that the genesis of group hatred and prejudice is environmental, whereas the genesis of other vices is genetic or otherwise innate, one would need reasons to believe that learned dispositions are less immutable than unlearned ones before criminalizing the former but not the latter. And one would need further proof that racists, sexists, and homophobes will more quickly, effectively, or cheaply unlearn their vices when threatened with enhanced criminal liability, than when educated or coerced in other (non-legal, or at least non-criminal) ways. If advocates of hate/bias crime legislation are unable to defend either the claim that hate and bias are more culpable than other motivations or the thesis that hate and bias are uniquely susceptible to coercion by criminal penalties, then they have but two avenues of argument available to them. They must either (1) admit and defend the fact that hate/bias crime legislation arbitrarily picks out for extra punishment a set of mental states that are a subset of a larger class of equally vicious states, or (2) convince theorists and legislators to generalize hate/bias crime legislation by radically revising traditional culpability doctrines so as in every case to

6 See Jeffrie G. Murphy, "Bias Crimes: What Do Haters Deserve?" *Criminal Justice Ethics* 11 (1992), pp. 20, 23.
7 Harel and Parchomovsky, "On Hate and Equality," *supra*, note 5, at p. 513 [p. 000, note 000].

take into account, and dish out punishment in proportion to, the culpable emotional and (dispositional) belief states that motivated a defendant to commit a criminal deed—from racial bias to jealousy to road rage.

The first line of argument is a dangerous one, for it implies that the criminal law both does not and need not treat like cases alike. Equally culpable defendants who commit equally wrongful acts (for example, one who throws a rock as a result of vengeance and one who throws a rock as a result of racial hatred) can justifiably be punished unequally. While like cases must be judged alike, on pain of irrationality, the argument here is that like cases need not be punished alike. Those who would make such a claim clearly cannot think that equality of treatment is much of a moral value. They must believe that so long as someone is not punished *more than* he deserves, he cannot complain that he is punished more than someone of equal culpability and wrongdoing. The success of such an argument, however, turns on the success with which proponents can defeat the formidable arguments advanced in the vast literature on equality for the proposition that it is a serious injustice to punish equally culpable persons unequally when they have committed equally wrongful deeds.

It might be most tempting, in the end, for advocates of hate and bias crime legislation to argue that the traditional criminal law *mens rea* concepts ought to be revolutionized in accordance with the model provided by contemporary hate and bias crime statutes. On such an argument, hate and bias crimes ought not to remain unique in punishing the motivations with which defendants act; rather, in all cases, fact-finders ought to assess defendants' motivations (including the emotions attendant upon their actions and the (dispositional) beliefs that might have informed their practical reasoning), and punish defendants proportionate to the viciousness of their character as manifested in their deeds.

This suggestion brings me to the third moral problem that confronts those who advocate hate/bias crime legislation in particular, and criminal legislation that targets emotions and (dispositional) beliefs in general.

C. SHOULD THE CRIMINAL LAW PUNISH PERSONS FOR BAD CHARACTER?

Inasmuch as hate crime legislation ultimately punishes persons for standing traits of character, it is best explained by, and most at home within, what is called a "character theory of the criminal law"—a theory that takes the proper goals of criminal law to be the punishment of vice and the cultivation of virtue. Now these are distinctively *non-liberal* goals.

Political liberals traditionally license the state to enforce the Right, but not the Good. They maintain that the state must limit the use of its power to constructing and protecting a fair framework of cooperation, defined as a system of rights that allows all citizens maximal equal liberty to pursue their own unique conceptions of the good life. Common to contemporary liberalism is the claim that reasonable people do not now agree, and may never be able to agree, on a singular conception of what it means to live a good life. At most, they can agree, in principle, to disagree, and they can agree, in practice, to peaceable institutional means by which to disagree. Inasmuch as state action is both theoretically unjust and practically impotent unless it can command the agreement (if only hypothetically) of reasonable persons, state action is illegitimate if it pursues a particular conception of the good life.[8]

Liberals have long believed that theories that construe certain character traits as virtuous or vicious belong to the province of the Good, rather than the Right. There are several reasons for this. First, it appears that one person's vice is another person's virtue. That is, the vices and virtues of character are not among the things about which reasonable people agree, whatever else they believe. Reasonable people can seemingly disagree over whether persons should experience a love of God, or deep loyalty to friends and family over strangers, or a driving sense of professional ambition, or an exceptionless commitment to keeping promises or telling the truth.

Second, as we have already discussed, vice and virtue appear only indirectly responsive to choice. Out of deference to the fact that persons' liberty to pursue their own conceptions of the good life is chilled by threats of strict liability, liberals typically predicate moral and legal responsibility on matters of choice. Because persons cannot choose their character traits, but can affect them only indirectly and imperfectly, virtues and vices have appeared to liberals to be inappropriate candidates for praise and blame, rewards and punishments.

Third, persons can seemingly peaceably co-exist without settling the question of the sorts of character traits that persons ought to cultivate or suppress. Indeed, until the enactment of hate/bias crimes, our criminal law was testament to the fact that we could meaningfully assess actors' culpability without resolving inevitable disputes over the sorts of traits that people should cultivate. While people no doubt disagree about the relative culpability of acts of spite, jealousy, vengeance, and racism, few have disagreed that purposeful harms are more culpable than harms committed only knowingly; and that harms committed knowingly are more culpable than harms committed recklessly or negligently. Inasmuch as contemporary liberalism is wedded to the view that our peaceable co-existence requires the state to limit its scope to matters upon which we can agree, it is committed to the view that our old ways are better than our new ones—that hate/bias crime legislation exceeds the proper bounds of state action, as would any attempt to radically revise *mens rea* doctrines so as to use state power to affect people's moral character.[9]

Character theories of the criminal law are most naturally at home with perfectionist political theories. The willingness to use the criminal law to punish people for bad character and to encourage people to cultivate good character is at least closely compatible with, if not required by, the perfectionist directive to use the power of the state to affect individual virtue when possible. Those who advocate the enactment of legislation that punishes racism, sexism, homophobia, and so forth, should thus be wise to align themselves politically with those who view the inculcation of virtue and the elimination of vice as legitimate state goals.

Even still, those who are willing, in principle, to criminalize certain aspects of character must honor what Joseph Raz calls "the morality of freedom." While a political perfectionist, Raz has powerfully insisted that in many instances what is good (virtuous) for persons is a product of what they autonomously chose to do and to

8 For the already classic statement of contemporary liberalism, see John Rawls, *Political Liberalism* (New York: Columbia UP, 1993). For one critique of this political vision, see Heidi M. Hurd, "The Levitation of Liberalism," *Yale Law Journal* 105 (1995), pp. 795–824.

9 Paul Robinson has interestingly argued that if the criminal law does not permit the punishment of bad character as it is expressed in vicious actions, those who are convinced that moral blameworthiness resides primarily in character may eventually force it to permit the punishment of bad character alone. In the interests of preserving an act-oriented system of criminal responsibility, we may do well to permit character-based penalty enhancements. Robinson, "Hate Crimes," *supra*, note 41, at 611 [p. 000, note 000].

believe. Hence, a legislator who seeks to pursue a perfectionist agenda must be careful to preserve a significant arena in which persons can make their own choices about what is good. Inasmuch as many persons come to make virtuous choices only by making a certain number of vicious ones, the state must tolerate a certain number of vices in order to maximize the moral virtues that derive from exercises of liberty.[10]

Thus, not only must those who are willing to criminalize hate and bias meet the challenges of contemporary liberalism generally, but they must be confident that in enacting such legislation, they are not inhibiting the liberty to be bad that is necessary to the cultivation of good. Our long reluctance to prohibit associations that devote themselves to racist, sexist, homophobic, and other intolerant agendas suggests that such associations, while not themselves of moral worth, may be among those unfortunate things that we must tolerate in order to maximize pursuits that are of moral worth. They may contribute to an important marketplace of ideas (if only by revealing how ugly some ideas can be); or they may be such that we must tolerate them on pain of chilling other associations that are of moral worth; or the precedent set by prohibiting them may motivate legislators to prohibit other associations that are in fact quite worthy. Whatever explains our historical commitment to tolerating the non-violent activities of pornographers, anti-Semites, neo-Nazis, the Ku Klux Klan, and other sexist, racist, homophobic, and religiously intolerant groups, may be a good reason for perfectionists to conclude that the vices of group hatred and prejudice are not best repressed by criminalizing them.

In conclusion, if hate and bias have become new conditions of legal culpability, then hate/bias crime legislation has worked important changes in both our criminal law doctrine and our political presuppositions. No longer is character immune from criminal sanctions; no longer is virtue and vice outside the scope of state action. The law now regulates not only what we do, but who we are. Perhaps this is for the better. Perhaps the law is too effective a tool for accomplishing personal improvement to deny its use to those who can show that such evils as racism, sexism, homophobia, and other forms of hatred and bias can be reduced without significant costs to aspects of character that we value. But the burden remains on those who would operate on people's personalities with the state's most powerful instrument to assure us that they will excise only what is diseased.

---

10 For his defense of the morality of freedom, see Joseph Raz, *The Morality of Freedom* (Oxford: Clarendon P, 1986), chs. 14 and 15.

23

Jeffrie G. Murphy

"Marxism and Retribution"*

Punishment in general has been defended as a means either of ameliorating or of intimidating. Now what right have you to punish me for the amelioration or intimidation of others? And besides there is history—there is such a thing as statistics—which prove with the most complete evidence that since Cain the world has been neither intimidated nor ameliorated by punishment. Quite the contrary. From the point of view of abstract right, there is only one theory of punishment which recognizes human dignity in the abstract, and that is the theory of Kant, especially in the more rigid formula given to it by Hegel. Hegel says: "Punishment is the right of the criminal. It is an act of his own will. The violation of right has been proclaimed by the criminal as his own right. His crime is the negation of right. Punishment is the negation of this negation, and consequently an affirmation of right, solicited and forced upon the criminal by himself."

There is no doubt something specious in this formula, inasmuch as Hegel, instead of looking upon the criminal as the mere object, the slave of justice, elevates him to the position of a free and self-determined being. Looking, however, more closely into the matter, we discover that German idealism here, as in most other instances, has but given a transcendental sanction to the rules of existing society. Is it not a delusion to substitute for the individual with his real motives, with multifarious social circumstances pressing upon him, the abstraction of "free will"—one among the many qualities of man for man himself? ... Is there not a necessity for deeply reflecting upon an alteration of the system that breeds these crimes, instead of glorifying the hangman who executes a lot of criminals to make room only for the supply of new ones?

Karl Marx, "Capital Punishment,"
New York Daily Tribune, *18 February 1853*[1]

Philosophers have written at great length about the moral problems involved in punishing the innocent—particularly as these problems raise obstacles to an acceptance of the moral theory of Utilitarianism. Punishment of an innocent man

* An earlier version of this essay was delivered to the Third Annual Colloquium in Philosophy ("The Philosophy of Punishment") at the University of Dayton in October, 1972. I am grateful to the Department of Philosophy at the University of Dayton for inviting me to participate and to a number of persons at the Colloquium for the useful discussion on my paper at the time. I am also grateful to Anthony D. Woozley of the University of Virginia and to two of my colleagues, Robert M. Hamish and Francis V. Raab, for helping me to clarify the expression of my views.

1 In a sense, my paper may be viewed as an elaborate commentary on this one passage, excerpted from a discussion generally concerned with the efficacy of capital punishment in eliminating crime. For in this passage, Marx (to the surprise of many I should think) expresses a certain admiration for the classical retributive theory of punishment. Also (again surprisingly) he expresses this admiration in a kind of language he normally avoids—i.e., the moral language of rights and justice. He then, of course, goes on to reject the applicability of that theory. But the question that initially perplexed me is the following: what is the explanation of Marx's ambivalence concerning the retributive theory; why is he both attracted and repelled by it? (This ambivalence is not shared, for example, by utilitarians—who feel nothing but repulsion when the retributive theory is even mentioned.) Now except for some very brief passages in *The Holy Family,* Marx himself has nothing more to say on the topic of punishment beyond what is contained in this brief *Daily Tribune* article. Thus my essay is in no sense an exercise in textual scholarship (there are not enough texts) but is rather an attempt to construct an assessment of punishment, Marxist at least in spirit, that might account for the ambivalence found in the quoted passage. My main outside help comes, not from Marx himself, but from the writings of the Marxist criminologist Willem Bonger.

in order to bring about good social consequences is, at the very least, not always clearly wrong on utilitarian principles. This being so, utilitarian principles are then to be condemned by any morality that may be called Kantian in character. For punishing an innocent man, in Kantian language, involves using that man as a mere means or instrument to some social good and is thus not to treat him as an end in himself, in accord with his dignity or worth as a person.

The Kantian position on the issue of punishing the innocent, and the many ways in which the utilitarian might try to accommodate that position, constitute extremely well-worn ground in contemporary moral and legal philosophy.[2] I do not propose to wear the ground further by adding additional comments on the issue here. What I do want to point out, however, is something which seems to me quite obvious but which philosophical commentators on punishment have almost universally failed to see—namely, that problems of the very same kind and seriousness arise for the utilitarian theory with respect to the punishment of the guilty. For a utilitarian theory of punishment (Bentham's is a paradigm) must involve justifying punishment in terms of its social results—e.g., deterrence, incapacitation, and rehabilitation. And thus even a guilty man is, on this theory, being punished because of the instrumental value the action of punishment will have in the future. He is being used as a means to some future good—e.g., the deterrence of others. Thus those of a Kantian persuasion, who see the importance of worrying about the treatment of persons as mere means, must, it would seem, object just as strenuously to the punishment of the guilty on utilitarian grounds as to the punishment of the innocent. Indeed the former worry, in some respects, seems more serious. For a utilitarian can perhaps refine his theory in such a way that it does not commit him to the punishment of the innocent. However, if he is to approve of punishment at all, he must approve of punishing the guilty in at least some cases. This makes the worry about punishing the guilty formidable indeed, and it is odd that this has gone generally unnoticed.[3] It has generally been assumed that if the utilitarian theory can just avoid entailing the permissibility of punishing the innocent, then all objections of a Kantian character to the theory will have been met. This seems to me simply not to be the case.

What the utilitarian theory really cannot capture, I would suggest, is the notion of persons having rights. And it is just this notion that is central to any Kantian outlook on morality. Any Kantian can certainly agree that punishing persons (guilty or innocent) may have either good or bad or indifferent consequences and that insofar as the consequences (whether in a particular case or for an institution) are good, this is something in favor of punishment. But the Kantian will maintain that this consequential outlook, important as it may be, leaves out of consideration entirely that which is most morally crucial—namely, the question of rights. Even if punishment of a person would have good consequences, what gives us (i.e., society) the moral right to inflict it? If we have such a right, what is its origin or derivation? What social circumstances must be present for it to be applicable? What does this right to punish tell us about the status of the person to be punished—e.g., how are we to analyze his rights, the sense in which he must deserve to be punished, his obligations in the matter? It is this family of questions which any Kantian must regard as morally central and which the utilitarian cannot easily accommodate

2 Many of the leading articles on this topic have been reprinted in *The Philosophy of Punishment*, ed. H.B. Acton (London, 1969). Those papers not included are cited in Acton's excellent bibliography.

3 One writer who has noticed this is Richard Wasserstrom. See his "Why Punish the Guilty?" *Princeton University Magazine* 20 (1964), pp. 14–19.

into his theory. And it is surely this aspect of Kant's and Hegel's retributivism, this seeing of rights as basic, which appeals to Marx in the quoted passage. As Marx himself puts it: "What right have you to punish me for the amelioration or intimidation of others?" And he further praises Hegel for seeing that punishment, if justified, must involve respecting the rights of the person to be punished.[4] Thus Marx, like Kant, seems prepared to draw the important distinction between (a) what it would be good to do on grounds of utility and (b) what we have a right to do. Since we do not always have the right to do what it would be good to do, this distinction is of the greatest moral importance; and missing the distinction is the Achilles heel of all forms of Utilitarianism. For consider the following example: A Jehovah's Witness needs a blood transfusion in order to live; but, because of his (we can agree absurd) religious belief that such transfusions are against God's commands, he instructs his doctor not to give him one. Here is a case where it would seem to be good or for the best to give the transfusion and yet, at the very least, it is highly doubtful that the doctor has a right to give it. This kind of distinction is elementary, and any theory which misses it is morally degenerate.[5]

To move specifically to the topic of punishment: How exactly does retributivism (of a Kantian or Hegelian variety) respect the rights of persons? Is Marx really correct on this? I believe that he is. I believe that retributivism can be formulated in such a way that it is the only morally defensible theory of punishment. I also believe that arguments, which may be regarded as Marxist at least in spirit, can be formulated which show that social conditions as they obtain in most societies make this form of retributivism largely inapplicable within those societies. As Marx says, in those societies retributivism functions merely to provide a "transcendental sanction" for the status quo. If this is so, then the only morally defensible theory of punishment is largely inapplicable in modern societies. The consequence: modern societies largely lack the moral right to punish.[6] The upshot is that a Kantian moral theory (which in general seems to me correct) and a Marxist analysis of society (which, if properly qualified, also seems to me correct) produces a radical and not merely reformist attack not merely on the scope and manner of punishment in our society but on the institution of punishment itself. Institutions of punishment constitute what Bernard Harrison has called structural injustices[7] and are, in the absence of a major social change, to be resisted by all who take human rights to be morally serious—i.e., regard them as genuine action guides and not merely as rhetorical devices which allow people to morally sanctify

4 Marx normally avoids the language of rights and justice because he regards such language to be corrupted by bourgeois ideology. However, if we think very broadly of what an appeal to rights involves—namely, a protest against unjustified coercion—there is no reason why Marx may not legitimately avail himself on occasion of this way of speaking. For there is surely at least some moral overlap between Marx's protests against exploitation and the evils of a division of labor, for example, and the claims that people have a right not to be used solely for the benefit of others and a right to self-determination.

5 I do not mean to suggest that under no conceivable circumstances would the doctor be justified in giving the transfusion even though, in one clear sense, he had no right to do it. If, for example, the Jehovah's Witness was a key man whose survival was necessary to prevent the outbreak of a destructive war, we might well regard the transfusion as on the whole justified. However, even in such a case, a morally sensitive man would have to regretfully realize that he was sacrificing an important principle. Such a realization would be impossible (because inconsistent) for a utilitarian, for his theory admits only one principle—namely, do that which on the whole maximizes utility. An occupational disease of utilitarians is a blindness to the possibility of genuine moral dilemmas—i.e., a blindness to the possibility that important moral principles can conflict in ways that are not obviously resolvable by a rational decision procedure.

6 I qualify my thesis by the word "largely" to show at this point my realization, explored in more detail later, that no single theory can account for all criminal behavior.

7 Bernard Harrison, "Violence and the Rule of Law," in *Violence*, ed. Jerome A. Shaffer (New York, 1971), pp. 139–76.

institutions which in fact can only be defended on grounds of social expediency.

Stating all of this is one thing and proving it, of course, is another. Whether I can ever do this is doubtful. That I cannot do it in one brief article is certain. I cannot, for example, here defend in detail my belief that a generally Kantian outlook on moral matters is correct.[8] Thus I shall content myself for the present with attempting to render at least plausible two major claims involved in the view that I have outlined thus far: (1) that a retributive theory, in spite of the bad press that it has received, is a morally credible theory of punishment—that it can be, H.L.A. Hart to the contrary,[9] a reasonable general justifying aim of punishment; and (2) that a Marxist analysis of a society can undercut the practical applicability of that theory.

The Right of the State to Punish

It is strong evidence of the influence of a utilitarian outlook in moral and legal matters that discussions of punishment no longer involve a consideration of the right of anyone to inflict it. Yet in the eighteenth and nineteenth centuries, this tended to be regarded as the central aspect of the problem meriting philosophical consideration. Kant, Hegel, Bosanquet, Green—all tended to entitle their chapters on punishment along the lines explicitly used by Green: "The Right of the State to Punish."[10] This is not just a matter of terminology but reflects, I think, something of deeper philosophical substance. These theorists, unlike the utilitarian, did not view man as primarily a maximizer of personal satisfactions—a maximizer of individual utilities. They were inclined, in various ways, to adopt a different model of man—man as a free or spontaneous creator, man as autonomous. (Marx, it may be noted, is much more in line with this tradition than with the utilitarian outlook.)[11] This being so, these theorists were inclined to view punishment (a certain kind of coercion by the state) as not merely a causal contributor to pain and suffering, but rather as presenting at least a prima facie challenge to the values of autonomy and personal dignity and self-realization—the very values which, in their view, the state existed to nurture. The problem as they saw it, therefore, was that of reconciling punishment as state coercion with the value of individual autonomy. (This is an instance of the more general problem which Robert Paul Wolff has called the central problem of political philosophy—namely, how is individual moral autonomy to be reconciled with legitimate political authority?)[12] This kind of problem, which I am inclined to agree is quite basic, cannot even be formulated intelligibly from a utilitarian perspective. Thus the utilitarian cannot even see the relevance of Marx's charge: Even if punishment has wonderful social consequences, what gives anyone the right to inflict it on me?

Now one fairly typical way in which others acquire rights over us is by our own consent. If a neighbor locks up my liquor cabinet to protect me against my tendencies to drink too heavily, I might well regard this as a presumptuous interference with my own freedom, no matter how good the result intended or accomplished. He had no right to do it and indeed violated my rights in doing it. If, on the other hand, I had asked him to do this or had given my free consent

---

8 I have made a start toward such a defense in my "The Killing of the Innocent," forthcoming in *The Monist* 57, no. 4 (October 1973).

9 H.L.A. Hart, "Prolegomenon to the Principles of Punishment," from *Punishment and Responsibility* (Oxford, 1968), pp. 1–27.

10 Thomas Hill Green, *Lectures on the Principles of Political Obligation* (1885), (Ann Arbor, 1967), pp. 180–205.

11 For an elaboration of this point, see Steven Lukes, "Alienation and Anomie," in *Philosophy, Politics and Society* (Third Series), ed. Peter Laslett and W.G. Runciman (Oxford, 1967), pp. 134–56.

12 Robert Paul Wolff, *In Defense of Anarchism* (New York, 1970).

to his suggestion that he do it, the same sort of objection on my part would be quite out of order. I had given him the right to do it, and he had the right to do it. In doing it, he violated no rights of mine—even if, at the time of his doing it, I did not desire or want the action to be performed. Here then we seem to have a case where my autonomy may be regarded as intact even though a desire of mine is thwarted. For there is a sense in which the thwarting of the desire can be imputed to me (my choice or decision) and not to the arbitrary intervention of another.

How does this apply to our problem? The answer, I think, is obvious. What is needed, in order to reconcile my undesired suffering of punishment at the hands of the state with my autonomy (and thus with the state's right to punish me), is a political theory which makes the state's decision to punish me in some sense my own decision. If I have willed my own punishment (consented to it, agreed to it) then—even if at the time I happen not to desire it—it can be said that my autonomy and dignity remain intact. Theories of the General Will and Social Contract theories are two such theories which attempt this reconciliation of autonomy with legitimate state authority (including the right or authority of the state to punish). Since Kant's theory happens to incorporate elements of both, it will be useful to take it for our sample.

Moral Rights and the Retributive Theory of Punishment

To justify government or the state is necessarily to justify at least some coercion.[13] This poses a problem for someone, like Kant, who maintains that human freedom is the ultimate or most sacred moral value. Kant's own attempt to justify the state, expressed in his doctrine of the *moral title* (*Befugnis*),[14] involves an argument that coercion is justified only in so far as it is used to prevent invasions against freedom. Freedom itself is the only value which can be used to limit freedom, for the appeal to any other value (e.g., utility) would undermine the ultimate status of the value of freedom. Thus Kant attempts to establish the claim that some forms of coercion (as opposed to violence) are morally permissible because, contrary to appearance, they are really consistent with rational freedom. The argument, in broad outline, goes in the following way. Coercion may keep people from doing what they desire or want to do on a particular occasion and is thus prima facie wrong. However, such coercion can be shown to be morally justified (and thus not absolutely wrong) if it can be established that the coercion is such that it could have been rationally willed even by the person whose desire is interfered with:

> Accordingly, when it is said that a creditor has a right to demand from his debtor the payment of a debt, this does not mean that he can *persuade* the debtor that his own reason itself obligates him to this performance; on the contrary, to say that he has such a right means only that the use of coercion to make anyone do this is entirely compatible with everyone's freedom,

---

13 In this section, I have adapted some of my previously published material: *Kant: The Philosophy of Right* (London, 1970), pp. 109–12 and 140–44; "Three Mistakes About Retributivism," *Analysis* (April 1971): 166–69; and "Kant's Theory of Criminal Punishment," in *Proceedings of the Third International Kant Congress*, ed. Lewis White Beck (Dordrecht, 1972), pp. 434–41. I am perfectly aware that Kant's views on the issues to be considered here are often obscure and inconsistent—e.g., the analysis of "willing one's own punishment" which I shall later quote from Kant occurs in a passage the primary purpose of which is to argue that the idea of "willing one's own punishment" makes no sense! My present objective, however, is not to attempt accurate Kant scholarship. My goal is rather to build upon some remarks of Kant's which I find philosophically suggestive.

14 Immanuel Kant, *The Metaphysical Elements of Justice* (1797), trans. John Ladd (Indianapolis, 1965), pp. 35ff.

> *including the freedom of the debtor*, in accordance with universal laws.[15]

Like Rousseau, Kant thinks that it is only in a context governed by social practice (particularly civil government and its Rule of Law) that this can make sense. Laws may require of a person some action that he does not desire to perform. This is not a violent invasion of his freedom, however, if it can be shown that in some antecedent position of choice (what John Rawls calls "the original position"),[16] he would have been rational to adopt a Rule of Law (and thus run the risk of having some of his desires thwarted) rather than some other alternative arrangement like the classical State of Nature. This is, indeed, the only sense that Kant is able to make of classical Social Contract theories. Such theories are to be viewed, not as historical fantasies, but as ideal models of rational decision. For what these theories actually claim is that the only coercive institutions that are morally justified are those which a group of rational beings could agree to adopt in a position of having to pick social institutions to govern their relations:

> The contract, which is called *contractus originarius*, or *pactum sociale* ... need not be assumed to be a fact, indeed it is not [even possible as such. To suppose that would be like insisting] that before anyone would be bound to respect such a civic constitution, it be proved first of all from history that a people, whose rights and obligations we have entered into as their descendants, had *once upon a time* executed such an act and had left a reliable document or instrument, either orally or in writing, concerning this contract. Instead, this contract is a *mere idea* of reason which has undoubted practical reality; namely, to oblige every legislator to give us laws in such a manner that the laws *could* have originated from the united will of the entire people and to regard every subject in so far as he is a citizen as though he had consented to such [an expression of the general] will. This is the testing stone of the rightness of every publicly-known law, for if a law were such that it was impossible for an entire people to give consent to it (as for example a law that a certain class of subjects, by inheritance, should have the privilege of the *status of lords*), then such a law is unjust. On the other hand, if there is a mere *possibility* that a people might consent to a (certain) law, then it is a duty to consider that the law is just even though at the moment the people might be in such a position or have a point of view that would result in their refusing to give their consent to it if asked.[17]

> The problem of organizing a state, however hard it may seem, can be solved even for a race of devils, if only they are intelligent. The problem is: "Given a multiple of rational beings requiring universal laws for their preservation, but each of whom is secretly inclined to exempt himself from them, to establish a constitution in such

15 *Ibid.*, p. 37.

16 John Rawls, "Justice as Fairness," *The Philosophical Review* 67 (1958): 164–94; and *A Theory of Justice* (Cambridge, Mass., 1971), especially pp. 17–22.

17 Immanuel Kant, "Concerning the Common Saying: This May be True in Theory but Does Not Apply in Practice (1793)," in *The Philosophy of Kant*, ed. and trans. Carl J. Friedrich (New York, 1949), pp. 421–22.

> a way that, although their private intentions conflict, they check each other, with the result that their public conduct is the same as if they had no such intentions."[18]

Though Kant's doctrine is superficially similar to Mill's later self-protection principle, the substance is really quite different. For though Kant in some general sense argues that coercion is justified only to prevent harm to others, he understands by "harm" only certain invasions of freedom and not simply disutility. Also, his defense of the principle is not grounded, as is Mill's, on its utility. Rather it is to be regarded as a principle of justice, by which Kant means a principle that rational beings could adopt in a situation of mutual choice:

> The concept [of justice] applies only to the relationship of a will to another person's will, not to his wishes or desires (or even just his needs) which are the concern of acts of benevolence and charity.... In applying the concept of justice we take into consideration only the form of the relationship between the wills insofar as they are regarded as free, and whether the action of one of them can be conjoined with the freedom of the other in accordance with universal law. Justice is therefore the aggregate of those conditions under which the will of one person can be conjoined with the will of another in accordance with a universal law of freedom.[19]

How does this bear specifically on punishment? Kant, as everyone knows, defends a strong form of a retributive theory of punishment. He holds that guilt merits, and is a sufficient condition for, the infliction of punishment. And this claim has been universally condemned—particularly by utilitarians—as primitive, unenlightened and barbaric.

But why is it so condemned? Typically, the charge is that infliction of punishment on such grounds is nothing but pointless vengeance. But what is meant by the claim that the infliction is "pointless"? If "pointless" is tacitly being analyzed as "disutilitarian," then the whole question is simply being begged. You cannot refute a retributive theory merely by noting that it is a retributive theory and not a utilitarian theory. This is to confuse redescription with refutation and involves an argument whose circularity is not even complicated enough to be interesting.

Why, then, might someone claim that guilt merits punishment? Such a claim might be made for either of two very different reasons. (1) Someone (e.g., a Moral Sense theorist) might maintain that the claim is a primitive and unanalyzable proposition that is morally ultimate—that we can just intuit the "fittingness" of guilt and punishment. (2) It might be maintained that the retributivist claim is demanded by a general theory of political obligation which is more plausible than any alternative theory. Such a theory will typically provide a technical analysis of such concepts as crime and punishment and will thus not regard the retributivist claim as an indisputable primitive. It will be argued for as a kind of theorem within the system.

Kant's theory is of the second sort. He does not opt for retributivism as a bit of intuitive moral knowledge. Rather he offers a theory of

18 Immanuel Kant, *Perpetual Peace* (1795), trans. Lewis White Beck in the Kant anthology *On History* (Indianapolis 1963), p. 112.

19 Immanuel Kant, *The Metaphysical Elements of Justice*, p. 34.

punishment that is based on his general view that political obligation is to be analyzed, quasi-contractually, in terms of reciprocity. If the law is to remain just, it is important to guarantee that those who disobey it will not gain an unfair advantage over those who do obey voluntarily. It is important that no man profit from his own criminal wrongdoing, and a certain kind of "profit" (i.e., not bearing the burden of self-restraint) is intrinsic to criminal wrongdoing. Criminal punishment, then, has as its object the restoration of a proper balance between benefit and obedience. The criminal himself has no complaint, because he has rationally consented to or willed his own punishment. That is, those very rules which he has broken work, when they are obeyed by others, to his own advantage as a citizen. He would have chosen such rules for himself and others in the original position of choice. And, since he derives and voluntarily accepts benefits from their operation, he owes his own obedience as a debt to his fellow-citizens for their sacrifices in maintaining them. If he chooses not to sacrifice by exercising self-restraint and obedience, this is tantamount to his choosing to sacrifice in another way—namely, by paying the prescribed penalty:

> A transgression of the public law that makes him who commits it unfit to be a citizen is called ... a crime....
>
> What kind and what degree of punishment does public legal justice adopt as its principle and standard? None other than the principle of equality (illustrated by the pointer of the scales of justice), that is, the principle of not treating one side more favorably than the other. Accordingly, any undeserved evil that you inflict on someone else among the people is one you do to yourself. If you vilify him, you vilify yourself; if you steal from him, you steal from yourself; if you kill him, you kill yourself....
>
> To say, "I will to be punished if I murder someone" can mean nothing more than, "I submit myself along with everyone else to those laws which, if there are any criminals among the people, will naturally include penal laws."[20]

This analysis of punishment regards it as a debt owed to the law-abiding members of one's community; and, once paid, it allows re-entry into the community of good citizens on equal status.

Now some of the foregoing no doubt sounds implausible or even obscurantist. Since criminals typically desire not to be punished, what can it really mean to say that they have, as rational men, really willed their own punishment? Or that, as Hegel says, they have a right to it? Perhaps a comparison of the traditional retributivist views with those of a contemporary Kantian—John Rawls—will help to make the points clearer.[21] Rawls (like Kant) does not regard the idea of the social contract as an historical fact. It is rather a model of rational decision. Respecting a man's autonomy, at least on one view, is not respecting what he now happens, however uncritically, to desire; rather it is to respect what he desires (or would desire) as a rational man. (On Rawls's view, for example, rational men are said to be unmoved by feelings of envy; and thus it is not regarded as unjust to a person or a violation of his rights, if he is placed in

20 *Ibid.*, pp. 99, 101, and 105, in the order quoted.

21 In addition to the works on justice by Rawls previously cited, the reader should consult the following for Rawls's application of his general theory to the problem of political obligation: John Rawls, "Legal Obligation and the Duty of Fair Play," in *Law and Philosophy*, ed. Sidney Hook (New York, 1964), pp. 3–18. This has been reprinted in my anthology *Civil Disobedience and Violence* (Belmont, Cal., 1971), pp. 39–52. For a direct application of a similar theory to the problem of punishment, see Herbert Morris, "Persons and Punishment," *The Monist* 52, no. 4 (October 1968): 475–501.

a situation where he will envy another's advantage or position. A rational man would object, and thus would never consent to, a practice where another might derive a benefit from a position at his expense. He would not, however, envy the position *simpliciter*, would not regard the position as itself a benefit.) Now on Kant's (and also, I think, on Rawls's) view, a man is genuinely free or autonomous only in so far as he is rational. Thus it is man's rational will that is to be respected.

Now this idea of treating people, not as they in fact say that they want to be treated, but rather in terms of how you think they would, if rational, will to be treated, has obviously dangerous (indeed Fascistic) implications. Surely we want to avoid cramming indignities down the throats of people with the offhand observation that, no matter how much they scream, they are really rationally willing every bit of it. It would be particularly ironic for such arbitrary repression to come under the mask of respecting autonomy. And yet, most of us would agree, the general principle (though subject to abuse) also has important applications—for example, preventing the suicide of a person who, in a state of psychotic depression, wants to kill himself. What we need, then, to make the general view work, is a check on its arbitrary application; and a start toward providing such a check would be in the formulation of a public, objective theory of rationality and rational willing. It is just this, according to both Kant and Rawls, which the social contract theory can provide. On this theory, a man may be said to rationally will X if, and only if, X is called for by a rule that the man would necessarily have adopted in the original position of choice—i.e., in a position of coming together with others to pick rules for the regulation of their mutual affairs. This avoids arbitrariness because, according to Kant and Rawls at any rate, the question of whether such a rule would be picked in such a position is objectively determinable given certain (in their view) noncontroversial assumptions about human nature and rational calculation. Thus I can be said to will my own punishment if, in an antecedent position of choice, I and my fellows would have chosen institutions of punishment as the most rational means of dealing with those who might break the other generally beneficial social rules that had been adopted.

Let us take an analogous example: I may not, in our actual society, desire to treat a certain person fairly—e.g., I may not desire to honor a contract I have made with him because so doing would adversely affect my own self-interest. However, if I am forced to honor the contract by the state, I cannot charge (1) that the state has no right to do this, or (2) that my rights or dignity are being violated by my being coerced into doing it. Indeed, it can be said that I rationally will it since, in the original position, I would have chosen rules of justice (rather than rules of utility) and the principle, "contracts are to be honored," follows from the rules of justice.

Coercion and autonomy are thus reconciled, at least apparently. To use Marx's language, we may say (as Marx did in the quoted passage) that one virtue of the retributive theory, at least as expounded by Kant and Hegel on lines of the General Will and Social Contract theory, is that it manifests at least a formal or abstract respect for rights, dignity, and autonomy. For it at least recognizes the importance of attempting to construe state coercion in such a way that it is a product of each man's rational will. Utilitarian deterrence theory does not even satisfy this formal demand.

The question of primary interest to Marx, of course, is whether this formal respect also involves a material respect; i.e., does the theory have application in concrete fact in the actual social world in which we live? Marx is confident that it does not, and it is to this sort of consideration that I shall now pass.

Alienation and Punishment

What can the philosopher learn from Marx? This question is a part of a more general question: What can philosophy learn from social science? Philosophers, it may be thought, are concerned to offer a priori theories, theories about how certain concepts are to be analyzed and their application justified. And what can the mundane facts that are the object of behavioral science have to do with exalted theories of this sort?

The answer, I think, is that philosophical theories, though not themselves empirical, often have such a character that their intelligibility depends upon certain empirical presuppositions. For example, our moral language presupposes, as Hart has argued,[22] that we are vulnerable creatures—creatures who can harm and be harmed by each other. Also, as I have argued elsewhere,[23] our moral language presupposes that we all share certain psychological characteristics—e.g., sympathy, a sense of justice, and the capacity to feel guilt, shame, regret, and remorse. If these facts were radically different (if, as Hart imagines for example, we all developed crustaceanlike exoskeletons and thus could not harm each other), the old moral language, and the moral theories which employ it, would lack application to the world in which we live. To use a crude example, moral prohibitions against killing presuppose that it is in fact possible for us to kill each other.

Now one of Marx's most important contributions to social philosophy, in my judgment, is simply his insight that philosophical theories are in peril if they are constructed in disregard of the nature of the empirical world to which they are supposed to apply.[24] A theory may be formally correct (i.e., coherent, or true for some possible world) but materially incorrect (i.e., inapplicable to the actual world in which we live). This insight, then, establishes the relevance of empirical research to philosophical theory and is a part, I think, of what Marx meant by "the union of theory and practice." Specifically relevant to the argument I want to develop are the following two related points:

(1) The theories of moral, social, political and legal philosophy presuppose certain empirical propositions about man and society. If these propositions are false, then the theory (even if coherent or formally correct) is materially defective and practically inapplicable. (For example, if persons tempted to engage in criminal conduct do not in fact tend to calculate carefully the consequences of their actions, this renders much of deterrence theory suspect.)

(2) Philosophical theories may put forth as a necessary truth that which is in fact merely an historically conditioned contingency. (For example, Hobbes argued that all men are necessarily selfish and competitive. It is possible, as many Marxists have argued, that Hobbes was really doing nothing more than elevating to the status of a necessary truth the contingent fact that the people around him in the capitalistic society in which he lived were in fact selfish and competitive.)[25]

In outline, then, I want to argue the following: that when Marx challenges the material adequacy

---

22 H.L.A. Hart, *The Concept of Law* (Oxford, 1961), pp. 189–95.

23 Jeffrie G. Murphy, "Moral Death: A Kantian Essay on Psychopathy," *Ethics* 82, no. 4 (July 1972): 284–98.

24 Banal as this point may seem, it could be persuasively argued that all Enlightenment political theory (e.g., that of Hobbes, Locke and Kant) is built upon ignoring it. For example, once we have substantial empirical evidence concerning how democracies really work in fact, how sympathetic can we really be to classical theories for the justification of democracy? For more on this, see C.B. Macpherson, "The Maximization of Democracy," in *Philosophy, Politics and Society* (Third Series), ed. Peter Laslett and W.G. Runciman (Oxford, 1967), pp. 83–103. This article is also relevant to the point raised in note 11 above.

25 This point is well developed in C.B. Macpherson, *The Political Theory of Possessive Individualism* (Oxford, 1962). In a sense, this point affects even the formal correctness of a theory. For it demonstrates an empirical source of corruption in the analyses of the very concepts in the theory.

of the retributive theory of punishment, he is suggesting (a) that it presupposes a certain view of man and society that is false and (b) that key concepts involved in the support of the theory (e.g., the concept of "rationality" in Social Contract theory) are given analyses which, though they purport to be necessary truths, are in fact mere reflections of certain historical circumstances.

In trying to develop this case, I shall draw primarily upon Willem Bonger's *Criminality and Economic Conditions* (1916), one of the few sustained Marxist analyses of crime and punishment.[26] Though I shall not have time here to qualify my support of Bonger in certain necessary ways, let me make clear that I am perfectly aware that his analysis is not the whole story. (No monolithic theory of anything so diverse as criminal behavior could be the whole story.) However, I am convinced that he has discovered part of the story. And my point is simply that insofar as Bonger's Marxist analysis is correct, then to that same degree is the retributive theory of punishment inapplicable in modern societies. (Let me emphasize again exactly how this objection to retributivism differs from those traditionally offered. Traditionally, retributivism has been rejected because it conflicts with the moral theory of its opponent, usually a utilitarian. This is not the kind of objection I want to develop. Indeed, with Marx, I have argued that the retributive theory of punishment grows out of the moral theory—Kantianism—which seems to me generally correct. The objection I want to pursue concerns the empirical falsity of the factual presuppositions of the theory. If the empirical presuppositions of the theory are false, this does indeed render its application immoral. But the immorality consists, not in a conflict with some other moral theory, but immorality in terms of a moral theory that is at least close in spirit to the very moral theory which generates retributivism itself—i.e., a theory of justice.)[27]

To return to Bonger. Put bluntly, his theory is as follows. Criminality has two primary sources: (1) need and deprivation on the part of disadvantaged members of society, and (2) motives of greed and selfishness that are generated and reinforced in competitive capitalistic societies. Thus criminality is economically based—either directly in the case of crimes from need, or indirectly in the case of crimes growing out of motives or psychological states that are encouraged and developed in capitalistic society. In Marx's own language, such an economic system alienates men from themselves and from each other. It alienates men from themselves by creating motives and needs that are not "truly human." It alienates men from their fellows by encouraging a kind of competitiveness that forms an obstacle to the development of genuine communities to replace mere social aggregates.[28] And in Bonger's thought, the concept of community is central. He

26 The writings of Willem Adriaan Bonger (1876–1940), a Dutch criminologist, have fallen into totally unjustified neglect in recent years. Anticipating contemporary sociological theories of crime, he was insisting that criminal behavior is in the province of normal psychology (though abnormal society) at a time when most other writers were viewing criminality as a symptom of psychopathology. His major works are: *Criminality and Economic Conditions* (Boston, 1916); *An Introduction to Criminology* (London, 1936); and *Race and Crime* (New York, 1943).

27 I say "at least in spirit" to avoid begging the controversial question of whether Marx can be said to embrace a theory of justice. Though (as I suggested in note 4) much of Marx's own evaluative rhetoric seems to overlap more traditional appeals to rights and justice (and a total lack of sympathy with anything like Utilitarianism), it must be admitted that he also frequently ridicules at least the terms "rights" and "justice" because of their apparent entrenchment in bourgeois ethics. For an interesting discussion of this issue, see Allen W. Wood, "The Marxian Critique of Justice," *Philosophy & Public Affairs* 1, no. 3 (Spring 1972): 244–82.

28 The importance of community is also, I think, recognized in Gabriel de Tarde's notion of "social similarity" as a condition of criminal responsibility. See his *Penal Philosophy* (Boston, 1912). I have drawn on de Tarde's general account in my "Moral Death: A Kantian Essay on Psychopathy."

argues that moral relations and moral restraint are possible only in genuine communities characterized by bonds of sympathetic identification and mutual aid resting upon a perception of common humanity. All this he includes under the general rubric of reciprocity.[29] In the absence of reciprocity in this rich sense, moral relations among men will break down and criminality will increase.[30] Within bourgeois society, then, crimes are to be regarded as normal, and not psychopathological, acts. That is, they grow out of need, greed, indifference to others, and sometimes even a sense of indignation—all, alas, perfectly typical human motives.

To appreciate the force of Bonger's analysis, it is necessary to read his books and grasp the richness and detail of the evidence he provides for his claims. Here I can but quote a few passages at random to give the reader a tantalizing sample in the hope that he will be encouraged to read further into Bonger's own text:

> The abnormal element in crime is a social, not a biological, element. With the exception of a few special cases, crime lies within the boundaries of normal psychology and physiology....
>
> We clearly see that [the egoistic tendencies of the present economic system and of its consequences] are very strong. Because of these tendencies the social instinct of man is not greatly developed; they have weakened the moral force in man which combats the inclination towards egoistic acts, and hence toward the crimes which are one form of these acts ... Compassion for the misfortunes of others inevitably becomes blunted, and a great part of morality consequently disappears....
>
> As a consequence of the present environment, man has become very egoistic and hence more *capable of crime*, than if the environment had developed the germs of altruism....
>
> There can be no doubt that one of the factors of criminality among the bourgeoisie is bad [moral] education.... The children—speaking of course in a general way—are brought up with the idea that they must succeed, no matter how; the aim of life is presented to them as getting money and shining in the world....
>
> Poverty (taken in the sense of absolute want) kills the social sentiments in man, destroys in fact all relations between men. He who is abandoned by all can no longer have any feeling for those who have left him to his fate....
>
> [Upon perception that the system tends to legalize the egoistic actions of the bourgeoisie and to penalize those of the proletariat], the oppressed resort to means which they would otherwise scorn. As we have seen above, the basis of the social feeling is reciprocity. As soon as this is trodden

29 By "reciprocity" Bonger intends something which includes, but is much richer than, a notion of "fair trading or bargaining" that might initially be read into the term. He also has in mind such things as sympathetic identification with others and tendencies to provide mutual aid. Thus, for Bonger, reciprocity and egoism have a strong tendency to conflict. I mention this lest Bonger's notion of reciprocity be too quickly identified with the more restricted notion found in, for example, Kant and Rawls.

30 It is interesting how greatly Bonger's analysis differs from classical deterrence theory—e.g., that of Bentham. Bentham, who views men as machines driven by desires to attain pleasure and avoid pain, tends to regard terror as the primary restraint against crime. Bonger believes that, at least in a healthy society, moral motives would function as a major restraint against crime. When an environment that destroys moral motivation is created, even terror (as statistics tend to confirm) will not eradicate crime.

> under foot by the ruling class the social sentiments of the oppressed become weak towards them....[31]

The essence of this theory has been summed up by Austin J. Turk. "Criminal behavior," he says, "is almost entirely attributable to the combination of egoism and an environment in which opportunities are not equitably distributed."[32]

No doubt this claim will strike many as extreme and intemperate—a sample of the old-fashioned Marxist rhetoric that sophisticated intellectuals have outgrown. Those who are inclined to react in this way might consider just one sobering fact: of the 1.3 million criminal offenders handled each day by some agency of the United States correctional system, the vast majority (80 percent on some estimates) are members of the lowest 15-percent income level—that percent which is below the "poverty level" as defined by the Social Security Administration.[33] Unless one wants to embrace the belief that all these people are poor because they are bad, it might be well to reconsider Bonger's suggestion that many of them are "bad" because they are poor.[34] At any rate, let us suppose for purposes of discussion that Bonger's picture of the relation between crime and economic conditions is generally accurate. At what points will this challenge the credentials of the contractarian retributive theory as outlined above? I should like to organize my answer to this question around three basic topics:

1. *Rational Choice.* The model of rational choice found in Social Contract theory is egoistic-rational institutions are those that would be agreed to by calculating egoists ("devils" in Kant's more colorful terminology). The obvious question that would be raised by any Marxist is: Why give egoism this special status such that it is built, a priori, into the analysis of the concept of rationality? Is this not simply to regard as necessary that which may be only contingently found in the society around us? Starting from such an analysis, a certain result is inevitable—namely, a transcendental sanction for the status quo. Start with

31 *Introduction to Criminology*, pp. 75–76, and *Criminality and Economic Conditions*, pp. 532, 402, 483–84, 436, and 407, in the order quoted. Bonger explicitly attacks Hobbes: "The adherents of [Hobbes's theory] have studied principally men who live under capitalism, or under civilization; their correct conclusion has been that egoism is the predominant characteristic of these men, and they have adopted the simplest explanation of the phenomenon and say that this trait is inborn." If Hobbists can cite Freud for modern support, Bonger can cite Darwin. For, as Darwin had argued in the *Descent of Man*, men would not have survived as a species if they had not initially had considerably greater social sentiments than Hobbes allows them.

32 Austin J. Turk, in the Introduction to his abridged edition of Bonger's *Criminality and Economic Conditions* (Bloomington, 1969), p. 14.

33 Statistical data on characteristics of offenders in America are drawn primarily from surveys by the Bureau of Census and the National Council on Crime and Delinquency. While there is of course wide disagreement on how such data are to be interpreted, there is no serious disagreement concerning at least the general accuracy of statistics like the one I have cited. Even government publications openly acknowledge a high correlation between crime and socio-economic disadvantages: "From arrest records, probation reports, and prison statistics a 'portrait' of the offender emerges that progressively highlights the disadvantaged character of his life. The offender at the end of the road in prison is likely to be a member of the lowest social and economic groups in the country, poorly educated and perhaps unemployed.... Material failure, then, in a culture firmly oriented toward material success, is the most common denominator of offenders" (*The Challenge of Crime in a Free Society, A Report by the President's Commission on Law Enforcement and Administration of Justice*, U. S. Government Printing Office, Washington, D.C., 1967, pp. 44 and 160). The Marxist implications of this admission have not gone unnoticed by prisoners. See Samuel Jorden, "Prison Reform: In Whose Interest?" *Criminal Law Bulletin* 7, no. 9 (November 1971): 779–87.

34 There are, of course, other factors which enter into an explanation of this statistic. One of them is the fact that economically disadvantaged guilty persons are more likely to wind up arrested or in prison (and thus be reflected in this statistic) than are economically advantaged guilty persons. Thus economic conditions enter into the explanation, not just of criminal behavior, but of society's response to criminal behavior. For a general discussion on the many ways in which crime and poverty are related, see Patricia M. Wald, "Poverty and Criminal Justice," *Task Force Report: The Courts*, U.S. Government Printing Office, Washington, D.C., 1967, pp. 139–51.

a bourgeois model of rationality and you will, of course, wind up defending a bourgeois theory of consent, a bourgeois theory of justice, and a bourgeois theory of punishment.

Though I cannot explore the point in detail here, it seems to me that this Marxist claim may cause some serious problems for Rawls's well-known theory of justice, a theory which I have already used to unpack some of the evaluative support for the retributive theory of punishment. One cannot help suspecting that there is a certain sterility in Rawls's entire project of providing a rational proof for the preferability of a certain conception of justice over all possible alternative evaluative principles, for the description which he gives of the rational contractors in the original position is such as to guarantee that they will come up with his two principles. This would be acceptable if the analysis of rationality presupposed were intuitively obvious or argued for on independent grounds. But it is not. Why, to take just one example, is a desire for wealth a rational trait whereas envy is not? One cannot help feeling that the desired result dictates the premises.[35]

2. *Justice, Benefits, and Community.* The retributive theory claims to be grounded on justice; but is it just to punish people who act out of those very motives that society encourages and reinforces? If Bonger is correct, much criminality is motivated by greed, selfishness, and indifference to one's fellows; but does not the whole society encourage motives of greed and selfishness ("making it," "getting ahead"), and does not the competitive nature of the society alienate men from each other and thereby encourage indifference—even, perhaps, what psychiatrists call psychopathy? The moral problem here is similar to one that arises with respect to some war crimes. When you have trained a man to believe that the enemy is not a genuine human person (but only a gook, or a chink), it does not seem quite fair to punish the man if, in a war situation, he kills indiscriminately. For the psychological trait you have conditioned him to have, like greed, is not one that invites fine moral and legal distinctions. There is something perverse in applying principles that presuppose a sense of community in a society which is structured to destroy genuine community.[36]

Related to this is the whole allocation of benefits in contemporary society. The retributive theory really presupposes what might be called a "gentlemen's club" picture of the relation between man and society—i.e., men are viewed as being part of a community of shared values and rules. The rules benefit all concerned and, as a kind of debt for the benefits derived, each man owes obedience

35 The idea that the principles of justice could be proved as a kind of theorem (Rawls's claim in "Justice as Fairness") seems to be absent, if I understand the work correctly, in Rawls's recent *A Theory of Justice*. In this book, Rawls seems to be content with something less than a decision procedure. He is no longer trying to pull his theory of justice up by its own bootstraps, but now seems concerned simply to exhibit a certain elaborate conception of justice in the belief that it will do a good job of systematizing and ordering most of our considered and reflective intuitions about moral matters. To this, of course, the Marxist will want to say something like the following: "The considered and reflective intuitions current in our society are a product of bourgeois culture, and thus any theory based upon them begs the question against us and in favor of the status quo." I am not sure that this charge cannot be answered, but I am sure that it deserves an answer. Someday Rawls may be remembered, to paraphrase Georg Lukács's description of Thomas Mann, as the last and greatest philosopher of bourgeois liberalism. The virtue of this description is that it perceives the limitations of his outlook in a way consistent with acknowledging his indisputable genius. (None of my remarks here, I should point out, are to be interpreted as denying that our civilization derived major moral benefits from the tradition of bourgeois liberalism. Just because the freedoms and procedures we associate with bourgeois liberalism—speech, press, assembly, due process of law, etc.—are not the only important freedoms and procedures, we are not to conclude with some witless radicals that these freedoms are not terribly important and that the victories of bourgeois revolutions are not worth preserving. My point is much more modest and noncontroversial—namely, that even bourgeois liberalism requires a critique. It is not self-justifying and, in certain very important respects, is not justified at all.)

36 Kant has some doubts about punishing bastard infanticide and dueling on similar grounds. Given the stigma that Kant's society attached to illegitimacy and the halo that the same society placed around military honor, it did not seem totally fair to punish those whose criminality in part grew out of such approved motives. See *Metaphysical Elements of Justice*, pp. 106–07.

to the rules. In the absence of such obedience, he deserves punishment in the sense that he owes payment for the benefits. For, as rational man, he can see that the rules benefit everyone (himself included) and that he would have selected them in the original position of choice.

Now this may not be too far off for certain kinds of criminals—e.g., business executives guilty of tax fraud. (Though even here we might regard their motives of greed to be a function of societal reinforcement.) But to think that it applies to the typical criminal, from the poorer classes, is to live in a world of social and political fantasy. Criminals typically are not members of a shared community of values with their jailers; they suffer from what Marx calls alienation. And they certainly would be hard-pressed to name the benefits for which they are supposed to owe obedience. If justice, as both Kant and Rawls suggest, is based on reciprocity, it is hard to see what these persons are supposed to reciprocate for. Bonger addresses this point in a passage quoted earlier (p. 236): "The oppressed resort to means which they would otherwise scorn.... The basis of social feelings is reciprocity. As soon as this is trodden under foot by the ruling class, the social sentiments of the oppressed become weak towards them."

3. *Voluntary Acceptance.* Central to the Social Contract idea is the claim that we owe allegiance to the law because the benefits we have derived have been voluntarily accepted. This is one place where our autonomy is supposed to come in. That is, having benefited from the Rule of Law when it was possible to leave, I have in a sense consented to it and to its consequences—even my own punishment if I violate the rules. To see how silly the factual presuppositions of this account are, we can do no better than quote a famous passage from David Hume's essay "Of the Original Contract":

> Can we seriously say that a poor peasant or artisan has a free choice to leave his country—when he knows no foreign language or manners, and lives from day to day by the small wages which he acquires? We may as well assert that a man, by remaining in a vessel, freely consents to the dominion of the master, though he was carried on board while asleep, and must leap into the ocean and perish the moment he leaves her.

A banal empirical observation, one may say. But it is through ignoring such banalities that philosophers generate theories which allow them to spread iniquity in the ignorant belief that they are spreading righteousness.

It does, then, seem as if there may be some truth in Marx's claim that the retributive theory, though formally correct, is materially inadequate. At root, the retributive theory fails to acknowledge that criminality is, to a large extent, a phenomenon of economic class. To acknowledge this is to challenge the empirical presupposition of the retributive theory—the presupposition that all men, including criminals, are voluntary participants in a reciprocal system of benefits and that the justice of this arrangement can be derived from some eternal and ahistorical concept of rationality.

The upshot of all this seems rather upsetting, as indeed it is. How can it be the case that everything we are ordinarily inclined to say about punishment (in terms of utility and retribution) can be quite beside the point? To anyone with ordinary language sympathies (one who is inclined to maintain that what is correct to say is a function of what we do say), this will seem madness. Marx will agree that there is madness, all right, but in his view the madness will lie in what we do say—what we say only because of our massive (and often self-deceiving and self-serving) factual ignorance or indifference to the circumstances of the social world in which we live. Just as our whole way of talking about mental phenomena hardened before we knew any neurophysiology—and this leads us astray, so Marx would argue that our whole way of talking about moral and political phenomena hardened before we knew any of the relevant empirical facts about man and society—and this, too, leads us astray. We all suffer from what might be called the *embourgeoisment* of language, and thus part of any revolution will be a linguistic or conceptual revolution. We have grown accustomed to modifying our language or conceptual structures under the impact of empirical discoveries in physics. There is no reason why discoveries in sociology, economics, or psychology could not and should not have the same effect on entrenched patterns of thought and speech. It is important to remember, as Russell remarked, that our language sometimes enshrines the metaphysics of the Stone Age.

Consider one example: a man has been convicted of armed robbery. On investigation, we learn that he is an impoverished black whose whole life has been one of frustrating alienation from the prevailing socio-economic structure—no job, no transportation if he could get a job, substandard education for his children, terrible housing and inadequate health care for his whole family, condescending-tardy-inadequate welfare payments, harassment by the police but no real protection by them against the dangers in his community, and near total exclusion from the political process. Learning all this, would we still want to talk—as many do—of his suffering punishment under the rubric of "paying a debt to society"? Surely not. Debt for what? I do not, of course, pretend that all criminals can be so described. But I do think that this is a closer picture of the typical criminal than the picture that is presupposed in the retributive theory—i.e., the picture of an evil person who, of his own free will, intentionally acts against those just rules of society which he knows, as a rational man, benefit everyone including himself.

But what practical help does all this offer, one may ask. How should we design our punitive practices in the society in which we now live? This is the question we want to ask, and it does not seem to help simply to say that our society is built on deception and inequity. How can Marx help us with our real practical problem? The answer, I think, is that he cannot and obviously does not desire to do so. For Marx would say that we have not focused (as all piecemeal reform fails to focus) on what is truly the real problem. And this is changing the basic social relations. Marx is the last person from whom we can expect advice on how to make our intellectual and moral peace with bourgeois society. And this is surely his attraction and his value.

What does Bonger offer? He suggests, near the end of his book, that in a properly designed society all criminality would be a problem "for the physician rather than the judge." But this surely will not do. The therapeutic state, where prisons are called hospitals and jailers are called psychiatrists, simply raises again all the old problems about the justification of coercion and its reconciliation with autonomy that we faced in worrying about punishment. The only difference is that our coercive practices are now surrounded with a benevolent rhetoric which makes it even harder to raise the important issues. Thus the move to therapy, in my judgment, is only an illusory solution—alienation remains and the problem of reconciling coercion with autonomy remains unsolved. Indeed, if the alternative is having our personalities involuntarily restructured by some state psychiatrist, we might well want to claim the "right to be punished" that Hegel spoke of.[37]

37 This point is pursued in Herbert Morris, "Persons and Punishment." Bonger did not appreciate that "mental illness," like criminality, may also be a phenomenon of social class. On this, see August B. Hollingshead and Frederick C. Redlich, *Social Class and Mental Illness* (New York, 1958). On the general issue of punishment versus therapy, see my *Punishment and Rehabilitation* (Belmont, Cal., forthcoming 1973).

Perhaps, then, we may really be forced seriously to consider a radical proposal. If we think that institutions of punishment are necessary and desirable, and if we are morally sensitive enough to want to be sure that we have the moral right to punish before we inflict it, then we had better first make sure that we have restructured society in such a way that criminals genuinely do correspond to the only model that will render punishment permissible—i.e., make sure that they are autonomous and that they do benefit in the requisite sense. Of course, if we did this, then—if Marx and Bonger are right—crime itself and the need to punish would radically decrease if not disappear entirely.

Study Questions

1. How might a "character" subjectivist respond to the criticism that this understanding of *mens rea* leaves too little room for a potential wrongdoer to withhold from carrying out her intentions?
2. How might a "choice" subjectivist respond to the criticism that this understanding of *mens rea* cannot distinguish adequately between acts done freely and acts which are the product of coercion?
3. Is Hurd correct to think that hatred and bias are not justifiably targeted by increased criminal punishment?
4. Can all forms of criminal behavior be understood as taking an unfair advantage over law-abiding citizens? What might be the limits of this view?

Further Readings

Andrew Ashworth, *Principles of Criminal Law*. 5th. ed. Oxford: Clarendon P, 2006.

Jules Coleman and Allen Buchanan, eds., *In Harm's Way: Essays in Honor of Joel Feinberg*. Cambridge: Cambridge UP, 1994.

R.A. Duff, ed., *Philosophy and the Criminal Law: Principle and Critique*. Cambridge: Cambridge UP, 1998.

Raymond Frey and Christopher Morris, eds., *Liability and Responsibility*. Cambridge: Cambridge UP, 1991.

H.L.A. Hart, *Punishment and Responsibility: Essays in the Philosophy of Law*. 2nd ed. Oxford: Oxford UP, 2008.

Ted Honderich, *Punishment: The Supposed Justifications Revisited*. Ann Arbor, MI: Pluto Press, 2006.

Stephen Shute, John Gardner, and Jeremy Horder, eds., *Action and Value in Criminal Law*. Oxford: Clarendon P, 1995.

Victor Tadros, *Criminal Responsibility*. Oxford: Oxford UP, 2006.

SECTION 8

The Nature of International Law

Introduction

This section explores the idea of international law. Until quite recently, international law was not a central topic of interest for the bulk of legal philosophers. Now, as rapid advances in communications and transport technology make possible more and more interaction between people of different countries, new problems of international relations are arising, and older unresolved problems are acutely in need of solutions. Are there any basic obligations which all countries have whether they like those obligations or not? How can a country be both truly *independent* and yet a subject of *restrictions* imposed by international law? How is international law different from international politics? These and other questions are in urgent need of good answers.

This introduction surveys some facts and terms of international law, and introduces readings from four authors who examine some of the problems we have just noted. The first reading is taken from the work of Hugo Grotius, who is regarded by many as the founder of international law theory. According to Grotius, the existence of international law is rooted in natural law requirements which hold true for all persons, regardless of time, culture, religion, and political or geographic boundaries. Other writers argue that the differences between international law and the law of individual states are so large that international law cannot be viewed as having a legal system at all. In the second reading H.L.A. Hart offers an argument in support of this view. A quite different suggestion is advanced in the third article, "The Politics of International Law," by the Finnish diplomat and law professor Martti Koskenniemi. He argues that international law has a misunderstood political dimension which must be clarified if we are to have an adequate picture of the possibilities and limits of international law. The fourth and final article of the chapter, by socio-legal theorist Roger Cotterrell, presents a challenge to the very framework of thinking about law as a product of individual states or states acting collectively. Professor Cotterrell argues that too many phenomena in a globalized world are simply missed or distorted by such a state-centric view, so the concept of law itself is in need of reconsideration.

1. The Idea of International Law

If asked to define the term "international law" many non-lawyers might respond that it refers to the laws which govern interactions between nations, as the combination of "inter" and "national" suggests. This definition is adequate for everyday purposes, but we need a more sophisticated definition for our philosophical investigation of international law. We must first distinguish "nations" from "states." The term "state" is used in international law to refer to a specific populated territory whose independent government controls activities within the state's boundaries. A nation, by contrast, consists in a people who share a culture, and often a language. Often, but not always, states embody a nation. The term "nation-state" is often used to refer to this situation. For example, the state of Japan is populated by citizens who are in the vast majority culturally Japanese and thus members of the Japanese nation. Other states such as New

Zealand contain more than one nation: the Maori people and, later, mostly British immigrants.

The name for the part of international law which guides relations among independent or "sovereign" states is "public international law." Public international law ordinarily does not apply to the affairs of so-called "states" which are in fact part of a larger union, as is, e.g., the State of Oregon in the USA. While the terms "nation," "state," and "country" are often used in everyday talk as though they all mean the same thing, it is important for our purposes to understand that independent, sovereign *states* are the main subjects of public international law. Private international law, by contrast, is concerned with resolution of disputes which arise when some interaction between private individuals is governed by the laws of more than one state. A judge may be asked, for example, to decide what to do about a disputed contract made in one state for the purpose of having something done in another. The laws of the state where the agreement was made may conflict with the laws of the state where the agreed activity is to be carried out. The judge must decide which state's law applies, and how. This area of law is often called "conflict of laws." The writers whose work is included in this chapter are concerned mostly with public international law, even though they may refer to it simply as "international law." In this introduction, the phrase "international law" is used to mean "public international law." We should also note the apparently unusual use of the term "municipal law" in debates about international law. This term is often used to refer to laws created by cities. Originally, however, it was used by the Romans to refer to the laws of independent, sovereign states. In this introduction, the term "municipal law" will be used in the original, Roman sense to refer to the laws of individual states, e.g., the law of the USA.

The distinction between international law and municipal law is so familiar and so readily demonstrated that it might easily be regarded as a natural or permanent feature of law-governed life. Yet changes in each of international and municipal law are challenging the practical usefulness and conceptual value of the distinction. In this section Professor Cotterrell explores the idea of transnational law as the basis of a better explanation of the law found in what can be described as the social space between what is called international law, and municipal law in states. While there is considerable disagreement as to just what is captured by the idea of transnational law, what is more important is that there appears to be law that is neither straightforwardly state law nor a matter of agreement among states, as might be seen in the law used by commercial communities across states, to name just one frequently cited example of transnational law. As we consider whether an understanding of municipal law and international law is a comprehensive understanding of law, and see reasons for doubt in the claimed rise of transnational law, we should at the same time be aware of arguments found in Section 5: Legal Pluralism and Indigenous Law. The authors whose work we provide ask whether state law is in fact unified in a way making its distinction from transnational or international law helpful to our understanding of law. If what we have called municipal law is in fact a combination of various forms of law extending into forms of transnational law bound up in specific states' relations to one another, and international law is a form of law beyond transnational law, we must revisit our understanding of what international law is and does, and our broader understanding of what we ought to expect from a comprehensive understanding of law. Will investigation of municipal law plus international law deliver a comprehensive understanding? Or is this image of law a mirage, and our understanding of both the ideas of international and municipal law in need of reconsideration, and with them, the idea that already interacting states are as meaningfully sovereign and independent as they sometimes claim? Perhaps international law is simply a mirage obscuring the true complexity of law, comprised of at least state law and intertwining other legal systems such as Indigenous law, and perhaps transnational and further international law? Or are municipal and international law the real core of law and other claimants to our attention as the core of law simply pretenders needing appropriate categorization under one of the two main types of law? We leave answering these questions to you, once you have worked through our explanation of the origin of international law, our introduction to this section's authors, and their work.

2. The Foundations of International Law

International law first grew out of customs established by people of many nations, especially those engaged in international trade. Some of those customs were later formalized in treaties, and other entirely new treaties were made between individual nations and among groups of nations. Much more recently, the formation of the League of Nations (founded in 1920) and its successor, the United Nations (founded in 1945), has produced international bodies which pass resolutions that are often accepted by the international community of states as having binding force. International law is now taken to consist largely in customs, treaties, judicial decisions, general legal principles, and sometimes the resolutions of the United Nations. This web of international norms regulates such matters as borders, war, diplomacy, citizenship, and immigration, and is for the most part accepted by states as binding in their relations to other states. There is, of course, a significant difference between norms being "for the most part accepted," and norms having binding force whether some individual state likes it or not. It is characteristic of municipal law that it binds citizens whether they like it or not, and where this characteristic is absent, we reasonably suspect that law is absent also. Many legal writers have observed the less than regular way in which international law is accepted as binding, and have claimed at various times that international law is not law at all. The written foundations of international law are open for all to see, but in practice the force of these written foundations is often unclear.

There are many reasons why international law is variably effective. Some of those reasons can be found in the structure and institutions of international law. For example, while resolutions passed by the United Nations certainly have great political force, international law still lacks a central, authoritative legislative body. And, while there is an International Court of Justice, it hears only a limited range of disputes. Matters heard before the International Court of Justice are submitted *voluntarily* by the disputing states. (For example, Spain and Canada brought to the International Court of Justice a dispute over fishing rights in the Atlantic Ocean.) It is not unreasonable to view the activity of the court in resolving these sorts of disputes as essentially arbitration or mediation, especially in light of the fact that there is no independent enforcement body for international law. The world community must rely on the wrongdoer to fulfill its obligations when made aware of them, or a group of states may join together to force another state to comply with the standards of international law. (For example, during the time that the Republic of South Africa violated international human rights standards by maintaining a policy of racial separation, the United Nations passed a resolution condemning South Africa, urging that member nations impose various sanctions on South Africa.) These important differences between international law and typical municipal legal systems reasonably lead us to ask whether international law really is law in the ordinary sense of "law," or whether international law is a different form of regulation of international affairs.

3. International Law and Private Individuals

We have marked several differences between municipal and international law, yet the largest difference has not yet been mentioned. Municipal legal systems are deeply concerned with guidance of the lives of *individual citizens*. International law, by contrast, is concerned for the most part with relations among states. Recently, however, there have been very large changes to the way international law operates, as international legal norms are applied increasingly frequently to individual persons. This change is most clearly seen in the development of international human rights law (often called international humanitarian law).

Let us examine the grounds for supposing that the operation of international law has changed fundamentally. In May 1994 a Commission of Experts appointed by the United Nations delivered a wide-ranging report on crimes against humanity committed in the former Yugoslavia. This report formed the background for the trial of certain individuals for acts constituting the crime of genocide. Genocide involves actions "committed with intent to destroy, in whole or in part, a national, ethnical, racial or religious group, as such."[1] Investigations by United Nations officials who travelled to the former Yugoslavia revealed mass graves, and victims reported rape and murder aimed at eliminating specific religious and ethnic groups. These investigations provided the basis for the indictment of persons accused of genocide, crimes against humanity, and war crimes. Between 1993 and 2017, one hundred and sixty-one persons were tried before a UN-authorized International Criminal Tribunal for the Former Yugoslavia in The Hague, Netherlands (www.icty.org). Shortly after the establishment of this tribunal, the United Nations established the International Tribunal for Rwanda (1994–2015) to try individuals accused of crimes against humanity in the African state of Rwanda (https://unictr.irmct.org/).

What made these trials so special is not the crimes they treat. Atrocities committed against civilians are unfortunately quite common in history. Rather, these trials were unusual because they involved the application of international law in international law courts to *individuals* rather than states. With the exception of the war crimes trials at the end of World War II, the trials at The Hague were the first in which individuals were tried for crimes by courts not tied to a specific state. In all other recent instances of crimes against humanity, individual states have taken it upon themselves to prosecute offenders. It is also significant that the persons accused of war crimes were captured and brought to trial without their consent. In the future, it is likely that many trials of this kind will not be held before special tribunals, which are temporary and established to address specific events. Instead, it is likely that many of the issues faced by the tribunals will be taken to the International Criminal Court, which began operations in 2002 (www.icc-cpi.int). One hundred twenty-five states now accept the court's jurisdiction, so the court is an important contributor to international law. Yet some important states (such as the United States of America) have not yet agreed to accept the court. Until the court is universally accepted, its operations may be criticized as falling short of being truly international.

Concerns regarding the International Criminal Court should not distract us from the success of the tribunals we have discussed. These tribunals may even be evidence that international law is becoming a legal system with many of the characteristics we associate with municipal legal systems. But are these developments enough to show that there is an international legal system? Or is the leap from an increase in international legal activity to regarding that activity as creating

1 1948 Convention on the Prevention and Punishment of the Crime of Genocide, Article II.

a system simply mistaken, and what we have is simply a growth of transnational law and, beyond that, a special sort of international politics? The readings included in this chapter begin to answer some of these questions and give you resources for finding your own answers to these questions.

4. Hugo Grotius

The work of Dutch lawyer and diplomat Hugo Grotius (1583–1645) has had an enormous influence on thinking about international law. Grotius is admired in part because of the hard-headed practicality he brought to consideration of law. He is also admired for his attempt to gather the scattered customs, treaties, and unspoken rules of international relations into a *system* truly deserving the title of international law.

The knowledge and experience Grotius brought to his writing was earned both in university and in the very rough world of Dutch diplomacy. Grotius was a star student at the University of Leiden, where he studied law. He then served briefly as a diplomat in a mission to France, then as a historian, and later as a lawyer for the Dutch East India Company. After a trip to England to negotiate international trading rights with competing English companies, Grotius spent time in The Netherlands as a public official, but was eventually forced out of the country to live in Paris with little recognition and less money. In Paris between 1623 and 1624, Grotius wrote the book from which our excerpt is taken, *De Jure Belli Ac Pacis* (*The Law of War and Peace*). After further failed attempts to return to Dutch political life (opponents put a price on his head!), Grotius took up a position as Swedish Ambassador to France. He occupied this position with varying success and was finally dismissed by the Swedish queen. After an unsuccessful appeal in Sweden for re-appointment, Grotius decided to return to Holland and died during the trip.

Grotius's legal philosophy bears the mark of his life. He was a diplomat in the midst of the Dutch struggle to reject Spain's religious and military conquest of what is now Holland, and he witnessed the death and misery which resulted from this conflict. His philosophy of law is the product of a person deeply concerned with suffering and ways to end it. Grotius's legal philosophy is often called a natural law view, but it is far more complex than this simple title indicates. Grotius flings many different types of arguments at the reader. He offers arguments from a natural law position, notes on long-practiced customs, historical arguments which catalogue the views of historically important writers, and religious arguments which appeal to Christian duties. It is not unfair to characterize Grotius as having an argument ready for everyone. The effect is like a garden with so many different types of plants that it is difficult to see any one plant through the tangle of stems and leaves.

Grotius's work has achieved new prominence with the recent renewal of interest in natural law theory. This does not mean, however, that all legal theorists have come to think that Grotius's arguments are plainly true. As you will see, Grotius's view of international law has two parts which are not obviously compatible. The first is the natural law component. Grotius argues that there exist morally justified standards of conduct which apply universally, to all persons in all states. The second part is the human or conventional aspect of law, found in the customs, treaties, and other rules of international law which states have developed in different ways at different times to guide their interaction. Grotius appears to think that there is some natural unity or wholeness to be found in the shared, common features of human and natural law. Precisely what that unity is, or how we are to justify rejecting some part of human law, is not clear. Nonetheless, it is remarkable that Grotius even attempts to find a truly international law which is shared between all states, and not imposed on states by the will of some small group among them. The excerpt included here is Grotius's initial statement of the basic principles underlying the long arguments of *The Law of War and Peace*. In it you will find the richness of Grotius's thought and knowledge of history, and the jumble of ideas which may ultimately be incompatible.

5. H.L.A. Hart

H.L.A. Hart is familiar from earlier chapters of this book as the author of *The Concept of Law*, perhaps the strongest defense yet of the theory of law known as legal positivism. Professor Hart's theory of social rules was explored in Section 2, as was his examination of the relation between law and coercion. This introduction will assume familiarity with the earlier introduction to legal positivism.

In the essay "International Law" included here, Hart argues that international law is something significantly different from what is ordinarily regarded as law. Hart discusses two problems or "sources of doubt"[2] regarding the legal status of international law. The first is a problem about the power of international law to impose binding obligations. Some writers have suggested that the lack of an international enforcement power should count against the legal status of international law. Hart argues that this criticism relies on an unmentioned acceptance of the "command" or "gunman" theory of legal obligation, which Hart took great pains to disprove. To say that international law must have an enforcement body is to accept that international law would not be obeyed if it were not backed up with threats. Yet Hart has argued that where law is said to exist, it is typically accepted for reasons other than fear of threats. If the legal status of international law is to be disputed, Hart suggests, it must be for reasons other than the absence of an enforcement body.

The second source of doubt involves sovereignty. Ordinarily, "sovereign" states are those states which have complete control over their own affairs. The term "sovereign" is also used to refer to the absolute power of some body: a Parliament is said to be sovereign in the sense that no other political body can overrule it. This ordinary understanding of the power of states conflicts with what international law is intended to do: place limits on what states do. Yet even this problem can be overcome, according to Hart. From the fact that there are limitations on a state's or even an individual's behavior, it does not follow that we are wrong to think of the state or individual as an independent thing or person. No state or person exists in complete isolation from others. Our ordinary way of speaking about our own personal independence mirrors this: we may take on obligations or other limitations on what we can do, and yet no one thinks we are not still individual, independent persons. Similarly, a state may have limits on its power through a variety of customary or voluntary agreements with other states, and that state is still thought to be independent in a meaningful sense.

According to Hart's analysis, the trouble which international law has *not* overcome is its lack of a rule of recognition. There is no test or "master" rule generally accepted and used by legal officials of the world to identify binding international laws. There are customs, habits, and multilateral treaties, but there is no clear and accepted way of sorting true from false claims about which customs or habits and so on really are part of international law. It is worth remembering that Hart wrote this in 1961 and did not return in later years to the topic of international law. Hart was conscious of the fact that international law was changing and was careful to note that he did not deny the possibility of international law ever existing. It is for you to assess whether the world of international relations has changed enough to justify the claim that international law exists.

2 *The Concept of Law*, p. 210.

6. Martti Koskenniemi, "The Politics of International Law"

The third article of this section brings us to Martti Koskenniemi's claim that international law is essentially and unavoidably political. Let us begin by trying to understand what Koskenniemi's claim means, before proceeding to examine the reasons he offers in support of this claim.

The title "The Politics of International Law" might seem to promise discussion of how politicians make international law. Koskenniemi's article does not do this. He is interested in a different sort of politics. By his claim that international law is political, Koskenniemi means to contrast the *settled* quality of the Rule of Law with the *unsettled* quality of politics. We often see this distinction in action in municipal legal systems when a problem occurs and a variety of solutions are offered. (Consider, for example, the question of appropriate limits on private ownership of guns.) The air soon grows thick with arguments whose strengths and weaknesses can be very difficult to assess amidst the noise of politics, as one side accuses another of doctoring the facts, or as a movie star's popularity is used to lend weight to a position. It may even appear that several different solutions to the problem are each independently acceptable, or that there is no way to defeat entirely any one of the acceptable proposals. These political arguments often appear to be unending: there appears to be no principled way of proving the superiority of a single option over all others. Yet much of this turmoil comes to an end once a particular solution is made into law. This does not always mean that the best, or even a good, solution is adopted. However, so long as the making, publication, and enforcement of the law is carried out in a procedurally fair way as required by the principles of the Rule of Law, consistently applied law sets a clear and reliable standard which makes certain conduct *non-optional* and makes a previously troublesome area of life much more predictable. With this distinction in hand, we may now state Koskenniemi's main claim more precisely: what is called international law is something quite different from what we ordinarily think of as law under the principles of the Rule of Law. International law is instead a part of the continuing debates of politics. Let us turn to the reasons why Koskenniemi supposes this claim to be true.

Koskenniemi suggests that the main goal in the development of international law has been to separate international law from politics and the wishes of the powerful, and instead to give international law the clarity and stability that is characteristic of the Rule of Law in municipal legal systems. The achievement of this goal requires that states follow the requirements of international law, and treat it as making certain state conduct non-optional. Yet the entire state-system which international law tries to govern is based on the recognition of each state's right to conduct its own affairs as it wishes—according to its own self-interest, or "vital interest," as international lawyers say. Sovereign states are understandably reluctant to give up their independence to international law, which by making certain state conduct non-optional might make a state's conduct predictable to others and so leave it at a significant strategic disadvantage. We are left with a conflict between the aim to achieve the Rule of Law on an international scale, and the unwillingness of states to give up their independence to international law.

Koskenniemi provides an interesting analysis of the result of states' worries that an international Rule of Law might cramp state sovereignty. States have tended to accept as legitimate sources of obligation only those international customs or agreements which either (1) match what states were going to do anyway, or (2) are so vague or idealistic that their meaning and application in any given circumstance can nearly always be challenged and rejected by states which do not wish to comply. International law of the first type is simply pleasant words and handshakes added to what states were going to do anyway, so these standards do not impose obligations. Rather, these standards simply "apologize" for the conduct states were going to undertake (possibly even in the absence of a formal international standard). At the other extreme, Koskenniemi calls "utopian" those international standards which meet the requirements of the Rule of Law, but are unlikely to be carried out in practice by states who consider those norms to be too idealistic, too costly, too risky, or perhaps simply not in those states' self-interest. Both apologist and utopian international standards lack *normative force*: they do not function as norms treated as obligatory and non-optional whether states like those standards or not. The unfortunate result of this situation is a body of international laws which often do not contain any unequivocal guidance as to how to resolve a dispute.

Perhaps the most interesting part of Koskenniemi's argument is his insistence that there is no way to balance the Rule of Law, state sovereignty, and the need for law to be "concrete" and have normative force whether states like it or not. He sketches four attempts to demonstrate how an international Rule of Law can be established without becoming apologist or utopian, and argues that each attempt collapses. We will not discuss the four approaches here. What is important here is why Koskenniemi supposes they each collapse. He argues that each approach, no matter how strong its arguments are, can always be met with sound objections. The result, Koskenniemi suggests, is that the making and interpretation of international standards is always and necessarily a matter of politics. To establish *only* those international standards which will in fact be obeyed is to make a political choice *not* to work for better international standards which might be unpopular and for that reason inconsistently obeyed. The alternative choice also falls into politics. To establish those international standards which meet some broadly accepted goal (e.g., global justice), despite the objections of some states, is to make a political choice to ignore the sovereignty of individual states in favor of the greater value of the Rule of Law. There is no middle road, according to Koskenniemi: the making and interpreting of international law always involves political choices which cannot be successfully defended against all objections.

Koskenniemi's conclusion offers some very interesting observations on the reaction of states to the uncertainty of international law. States have responded to the uncertainty of international standards by employing both apologist and utopian types of argument when resolving a dispute, knowing that either approach on its own is always open to sound criticism. Koskenniemi suggests that states' response to this difficulty leads the international community back to where it began: making and interpreting international standards so each side in a dispute is treated *fairly* as justice requires, according to what lawyers call principles of equity. Of course, justice between states is a political idea, and so states must engage in politics as they decide disputes, offering the best understanding of what fairness requires in any particular instance. It is for you to decide whether Koskenniemi's analysis is accurate, and to assess where this leaves legal theory. Does international law resemble law as integrity, with disputing states trying to understand international law in its morally best light? Or is international law simply a matter of political argument in fancy dress, in which the latest decision of the International Court of Justice is the best guide to what the law is on some matter?

7. Roger Cotterrell, "Transnational Communities and the Concept of Law"

In the fourth article of this section we find an argument which challenges one of the basic presumptions of international law and its theory: that the only law that exists above or beyond state borders is international law, which is created and applied by states or associations of states. Professor Roger Cotterrell, a British socio-legal theorist, argues that such a view of law overlooks the emergence of networks of transnational regulation, which often claim to be or are treated as law. The very expression "transnational" is meant to highlight the nature of such networks and regulation, since "trans" signifies "across" as opposed to "between." So transnational regulation, or transnational law, refers to legal regulation across states but not between states, as we find when private actors or non-state organizations create norms and rules for their interaction across state boundaries. The importance of explanation of such non-state law may already be familiar to you from Brian Tamanaha's article in Section 5, in which he provides a legal pluralist account of life in Micronesia. Like Tamanaha, Cotterrell is generally taken to be advocating a legal pluralist view, as he seeks to illuminate the diverse sources of law present in our globalized world. Cotterrell, like many other legal pluralists, holds that once the possibility of non-state, transnational law is recognized, it is easy to see many examples of transnational orders, sometimes loosely connected to states and sometimes having hardly any connection to states. Transnational orders tend to emerge along with what Cotterrell calls "transnational communities," geographically-dispersed groups of actors interacting on the basis of shared interests or purposes. The emergence of such communities is tied closely to the rise of globalization, the phenomenon of increased global interconnection resulting from the development of pervasive, fast networks of communication and transport. Transnational communities enabled by these networks have created new bodies of legal norms to enable these communities to function beyond state boundaries in matters such as technical standards, human rights, and business practices. Once the existence of transnational orders is demonstrated and acknowledged, legal pluralists argue that such orders become visible nearly everywhere, with varying reach and at diverse scales.

It might be argued that while the existence of non-state, transnational forms of legal order is interesting for various reasons, it remains philosophically uninteresting. A philosophically-focused observer might suggest that recognition of transnational law in addition to recognition of international law amounts only to a recognition that there is more law than previously supposed. An increase in quantity is not, however, in itself of much philosophical interest when it is an increase in the quantity of an already-understood thing. Cotterrell rejects this argument. He argues that the fact of transnational law should motivate rethinking of the concept of law itself. Once we accept that transnational law exists, we should realize that the concept of law which has dominated discussion until now is actually the concept of state law, a much narrower concept than the concept of law we need—one which includes both state and non-state law, including but not limited to international law. The state-centered concept of law so familiar to our thinking has been developed while we have been preoccupied with sovereign states and their relations with each other. Such a concept of law embodies a number of questionable features: it presumes that law always and everywhere claims supreme authority over those within its jurisdiction, that law is composed of hierarchically-ordered institutions and rules, and that law rests on a foundation always traceable back to a sovereign state. Each of these features is challenged by transnational law, which often claims or exerts a relative degree of authority, need not be practiced by hierarchically-ordered institutions or in hierarchically-organized rules, and typically has at most a loose connection to states. In the article reproduced below Cotterrell explains the emergence of forms of transnational regulation and why their characteristics warrant a kind revision to our understanding of what law is. It will be up to you to decide whether legal pluralists such as Cotterrell might simply be attempting to change the subject, or whether they might be successful in showing that a focus on international law alone is detrimental to our understanding of law's role in social life at the regional and global levels.

24

Hugo Grotius

"Prolegomena," from *De Jure Belli Ac Pacis Libri Tres* (1625), in *The Classics of International Law*

1. The municipal law of Rome and of other states has been treated by many, who have undertaken to elucidate it by means of commentaries or to reduce it to a convenient digest. That body of law, however, which is concerned with the mutual relations among states or rulers of states, whether derived from nature, or established by divine ordinances, or having its origin in custom and tacit agreement, few have touched upon. Up to the present time no one has treated it in a comprehensive and systematic manner; yet the welfare of mankind demands that this task be accomplished.

2. Cicero justly characterized as of surpassing worth a knowledge of treaties of alliance, conventions, and understandings of peoples, kings and foreign nations; a knowledge, in short, of the whole law of war and peace. And to this knowledge Euripides gives the preference over an understanding of things divine and human; for he represents Theoclymenus as being thus addressed:

> For you, who know the fate of men and gods,
> What is, what shall be, shameful would it be
>
> To know not what is just.

3. Such a work is all the more necessary because in our day, as in former times, there is no lack of men who view this branch of law with contempt as having no reality outside of an empty name. On the lips of men quite generally is the saying of Euphemus, which Thucydides quotes,[1] that in the case of a king or imperial city nothing is unjust which is expedient. Of like implication is the statement that for those whom fortune favours might makes right, and that the administration of a state cannot be carried on without injustice.

Furthermore, the controversies which arise between peoples or kings generally have Mars as their arbiter. That war is irreconcilable with all law is a view held not alone by the ignorant populace; expressions are often let slip by well-informed and thoughtful men which lend countenance to such a view. Nothing is more common than the assertion of antagonism between law and arms. Thus Ennius says:

1 The words are in Book VI [xxxv]. The same thought is found in Book V [V. lxxxix], where the Athenians, who at the same time of speaking were very powerful, thus address the Melians: "According to human standards those arrangements are accounted just which are settled when the necessity on both sides is equal; as for the rest, the more powerful do all they can, the more weak endure."

> Not on grounds of right is battle joined,
>
> But rather with the sword do men
>
> Seek to enforce their claims.

Horace, too, describes the savage temper of Achilles in this wise:

> Laws, he declares, were not for him ordained;
>
> By dint of arms he claims all for himself.

Another poet depicts another military leader as commencing war with the words:

> Here peace and violated laws I leave behind.

Antigonus when advanced in years ridiculed a man who brought to him a treatise on justice when he was engaged in besieging cities that did not belong to him. Marius declared that the din of arms made it impossible for him to hear the voice of the laws.[2] Even Pompey, whose expression of countenance was so mild, dared to say: "When I am in arms, am I to think of laws?"[3]

4. Among Christian writers a similar thought finds frequent expression. A single quotation from Tertullian may serve in place of many: "Deception, harshness, and injustice are the regular business of battles." They who so think will no doubt wish to confront us with this passage in Comedy:

> These things uncertain should you, by reason's aid,
>
> Try to make certain, no more would you gain
>
> Than if you tried by reason to go mad.

5. Since our discussion concerning law will have been undertaken in vain if there is no law, in order to open the way for a favourable reception of our work and at the same time to fortify it against attacks, this very serious error must be briefly refuted. In order that we may not be obliged to deal with a crowd of opponents, let us assign to them a pleader. And whom should we choose in preference to Carneades? For he had attained to so perfect a mastery of the peculiar tenet of his Academy that he was able to devote the power of his eloquence to the service of falsehood not less readily than to that of truth. [*Ed. note*: The Athenian philosopher and noted skeptic Carneades (214–129 BCE) was famous for his moral relativism.]

Carneades, then, having undertaken to hold a brief against justice, in particular against that phase of justice with which we are concerned, was able to muster no argument stronger than this, that, for reasons of expediency, men imposed upon themselves laws, which vary according to customs, and among the same peoples often undergo changes as times change; moreover that

2 In Plutarch Lysander displaying his sword says [*Apothegms, Lysander*, iii = 190 E]: "He who is master of this is in the best position to discuss questions relating to boundaries between countries."

In the same author Caesar declares [*Caesar*, xxxv = 725 B]: "The time for arms is not the time for laws."

Similarly Seneca, *On Benefits*, IV. xxxviii [IV. xxxvii]: "At times, especially in time of war, kings make many grants with their eyes shut. One just man cannot satisfy so many passionate desires of men in arms; no one can at the same time act the part of a good man and good commander."

3 This view-point of Pompey in relation to the Mamertines Plutarch expresses thus [*Pompey*, x = 623 D]: "Will you not stop quoting laws to us who are girt with swords?" Curtius says in Book IX [IX. iv. 7]: "Even to such a degree does war reverse the laws of nature."

there is no law of nature, because all creatures, men as well as animals, are impelled by nature toward ends advantageous to themselves; that, consequently, there is no justice, or, if such there be, it is supreme folly, since one does violence to his own interests if he consults the advantage of others.

6. What the philosopher here says, and the poet reaffirms in verse,

> And just from unjust Nature cannot
> know,

must not for one moment be admitted. Man is, to be sure, an animal, but an animal of a superior kind, much farther removed from all other animals than the different kinds of animals are from one another; evidence on this point may be found in the many traits peculiar to the human species. But among the traits characteristic of man is an impelling desire for society, that is, for the social life—not of any and every sort, but peaceful, and organized according to the measure of his intelligence, with those who are of his own kind; this social trend the Stoics called "sociableness."[4] Stated as a universal truth, therefore, the assertion that every animal is impelled by nature to seek only its own good cannot be conceded.

7. Some of the other animals, in fact, do in a way restrain the appetency for that which is good for themselves alone, to the advantage, now of their offspring, now of other animals of the same species.[5] This aspect of their behaviour has its origin, we believe, in some extrinsic intelligent principle, because with regard to other actions, which involve no more difficulty than those referred to, a like degree of intelligence is not manifest in them. The same thing must be said

4 Chrysostom, *On Romans*, Homily XXXI [Homily V, i, on chap. i, verse 31]: "We men have by nature a kind of fellowship with men; why not, when even wild beasts in their relation to one another have something similar?"

See also the same author, *On Ephesians*, chap. i [Homily I], where he explains that the seeds of virtue have been implanted in us by nature. The emperor Marcus Aurelius, a philosopher of parts, said [V. xvi]: "It was long ago made clear that we were born for fellowship. Is it not evident that the lower exist for the sake of the higher, and the higher for one another's sake?"

5 There is an old proverb, "Dogs do not eat the flesh of dogs." Says Juvenal [*Sat.* xv. 163, 159]:

> Tigress with ravening tigress keeps the peace;
> The wild beast spares its spotted kin.

There is a fine passage of Philo, in his commentary on the Fifth Commandment, which he who will may read in Greek. As it is somewhat long, I shall here quote it only once and in Latin [Philo, *On the Ten Commandments*, xxiii, in English as follows]:

"Men, be ye at least imitators of dumb brutes. They, trained through kindness, know how to repay in turn. Dogs defend our homes; they even suffer death for their masters, if danger has suddenly come upon them. It is said that shepherd dogs go in advance of their flocks, fighting till death, if need be, that they may protect the shepherds from hurt. Of things disgraceful is not the most disgraceful this, that in return of kindness man should be outdone by a dog, the gentlest creature by the most fierce?

"But if we fail to draw our proper lesson from the things of earth, let us pass to the realm of winged creatures that make voyage through the air, that from them we may learn our duty. Aged storks, unable to fly, stay in their nests. Their offspring fly, so to say, over lands and seas, seeking sustenance in all places for their parents; these, in consideration of their age, deservedly enjoy quiet, abundance, even comforts. And the younger storks console themselves for the irksomeness of their voyaging with the consciousness of their discharge of filial duty and the expectation of similar treatment on the part of their offspring, when they too have grown old. Thus they pay back, at the time when needed, the debt they owe, returning what they have received; for from others they cannot obtain sustenance either at the beginning of life, when they are small, or, when they have become old, at life's end. From no other teacher than nature herself have they learned to care for the aged, just as they themselves were cared for when they were young.

"Should not they who do not take care of their parents have reason to hide themselves for very shame when they hear this—they that neglect those whom alone, or above all others, they ought to help, especially when by so doing they are not really called upon to give, but merely to return what they owe? Children have as their own nothing to which their parents do not possess a prior claim; their parents have either given them what they have or have furnished to them the means of acquisition."

In regard to the extraordinary care of doves for their young, see Porphyry, *On Abstaining from Animal Food*, Book III; concerning the regard of the parrot-fish and lizard-fish for their kind, see Cassiodorus, [*Variae*] XI. xl.

of children. In children, even before their training has begun, some disposition to do good to others appears, as Plutarch sagely observed; thus sympathy for others comes out spontaneously at that age. The mature man in fact has knowledge which prompts him to similar actions under similar conditions,[6] together with an impelling desire for society, for the gratification of which he alone among animals possesses a special instrument, speech. He has also been endowed with the faculty of knowing and of acting in accordance with general principles. Whatever accords with that faculty is not common to all animals, but peculiar to the nature of man.

8. This maintenance of the social order,[7] which we have roughly sketched, and which is consonant with human intelligence, is the source of law properly so called. To this sphere of law belong the abstaining from that which is another's,[8] the restoration to another of anything of his which we may have, together with any gain which we may have received from it; the obligation to fulfil promises, the making good of a loss incurred through our fault, and the inflicting of penalties upon men according to their deserts.

9. From this signification of the word law there has flowed another and more extended meaning. Since over other animals man has the advantage of possessing not only a strong bent towards social life, of which we have spoken, but also a power of discrimination which enables him to decide what things are agreeable or harmful (as to both things present and things to come), and what can lead to either alternative: in such things it is meet for the nature of man, within the limitations of human intelligence, to follow the direction of a well-tempered judgement, being neither led astray by fear or the allurement of immediate pleasure, nor carried away by rash impulse. Whatever is clearly at variance with such judgement is understood to be contrary also to the law of nature, that is, to the nature of man.

10. To this exercise of judgement belongs moreover the rational allotment[9] to each man, or to each social group, of those things which are properly theirs, in such a way as to give the

6 Marcus Aurelius, Book IX [IX. xlii]: "Man was born to benefit others"; also [IX. ix]: "It would be easier to find a thing of earth out of relation with the earth than a human being wholly cut off from human kind." The same author in Book X [X. ii]: "That which has the use of reason necessarily also craves civic life."

Nicetas of Chonae [*On Isaac Angelus*, III. ix]: "Nature has ingrained in us, and implanted in our souls, a feeling for our kin." And what Augustine says, *On Christian Doctrine*, III. xiv.

7 Seneca, *On Benefits*, Book IV, chap. xviii: "That the warm feeling of a kindly heart is in itself desirable you may know from this, that ingratitude is something which in itself men ought to flee from, since nothing so dismembers and destroys the harmonious union of the human race as does this fault. Upon what other resource, pray tell, can we rely for safety, than mutual aid through reciprocal services? This alone it is, this interchange of kindnesses, which makes our life well equipped, and well fortified against sudden attacks.

"Imagine ourselves as isolated individuals, what are we? The prey, the victims of brute beasts—blood most cheap, and easiest to ravage; for to all other animals strength sufficient for their own protection has been given. The beasts that are born to wander and to pass segregate lives are provided with weapons; man is girt round about with weakness. Him no strength of claws or teeth makes formidable to others. To man [deity] gave two resources, reason and society; exposed as he was to danger from all other creatures, these resources rendered him the most powerful of all. Thus he who in isolation could not be the equal of any creature, is become the master of the world.

"It was society which gave to man dominion over all other living creatures; man, born for the land, society transferred to a sovereignty of a different nature, bidding him exercise dominion over the sea also. Society has checked the violence of disease, has provided succour for old age, has given comfort against sorrows. It makes us brave because it can be invoked against Fortune. Take this away and you will destroy the sense of oneness in the human race, by which life is sustained. It is, in fact, taken away, if you shall cause that an ungrateful heart is not to be avoided on its own account."

8 Porphyry, *On Abstaining from Animal Food*, Book III [III. xxiv]: "Justice consists in the abstaining from what belongs to others, and in doing no harm to those who do no harm."

9 Ambrose treats this subject in his first book *On Duties* [I. xxx].

preference now to him who is more wise over the less wise, now to a kinsman rather than to a stranger, now to a poor man rather than to a man of means, as the conduct of each or the nature of the thing suggests. Long ago the view came to be held by many, that this discriminating allotment is a part of law, properly and strictly so called; nevertheless law, properly defined, has a far different nature, because its essence lies in leaving to another that which belongs to him, or in fulfilling our obligations to him.

11. What we have been saying would have a degree of validity even if we should concede that which cannot be conceded without the utmost wickedness, that there is no God, or that the affairs of men are of no concern to Him. The very opposite of this view has been implanted in us partly by reason, partly by unbroken tradition, and confirmed by many proofs as well as by miracles attested by all ages. Hence it follows that we must without exception render obedience to God as our Creator, to Whom we owe all that we are and have; especially since, in manifold ways, He has shown Himself supremely good and supremely powerful, so that to those who obey Him He is able to give supremely great rewards, even rewards that are eternal, since He Himself is eternal. We ought, moreover, to believe that He has willed to give rewards, and all the more should we cherish such a belief if He has so promised in plain words; that He has done this, we Christians believe, convinced by the indubitable assurance of testimonies.

12. Herein, then, is another source of law besides the source in nature, that is, the free will of God,[10] to which beyond all cavil our reason tells us we must render obedience. But the law of nature of which we have spoken, comprising alike that which relates to the social life of man and that which is so called in a larger sense, proceeding as it does from the essential traits implanted in man, can nevertheless rightly be attributed to God,[11] because of His having willed that such traits exist in us. In this sense, too, Chrysippus and the Stoics used to say that the origin of law should be sought in no other source than Jupiter himself; and from the name Jupiter[12] the Latin word for law (*ius*) was probably derived.

13. There is an additional consideration in that, by means of the laws which He has given, God has made those fundamental traits more manifest, even to those who possess feebler reasoning powers; and He has forbidden us to yield to impulses drawing us in opposite directions—affecting now our own interest, now the interest of others—in an effort to control more effectively our more violent impulses and to restrain them within proper limits.

14. But sacred history, besides enjoining rules of conduct, in no slight degree reinforces man's inclination towards sociableness by teaching that all men are sprung from the same first parents. In this sense we can rightly affirm also that which Florentinus asserted from another point of view, that a blood-relationship has been established among us by nature; consequently it is wrong for a man to set a snare for a fellow-man. Among

10 Hence, in the judgement of Marcus Aurelius, Book IX [IX. i]: "He who commits injustice is guilty of impiety."

11 Chrysostom, *On First Corinthians*, xi 3 [Homily XXVI. iii]: "When I say nature I mean God, for He is the creator of nature." Chrysippus in his third book *On the Gods* [Plutarch, *On the Contradictions of the Stoics*, ix = *Morals*, 1035c]: "No other beginning or origin of justice can be found than in Jupiter and common nature; from that source must the beginning be traced when men undertake to treat of good and evil."

12 Unless perhaps it would be more true to say that the Latin word for "right," *ius* is derived, by the process of cutting down, from the word for "command," *iussum*, forming *ius*, genitive *iusis*, just as the word for "bone," *os*, was shortened from *ossum*; *iusis* afterwards becoming *iuris*, as *Papirii* was formed from *Papisii*, in regard to which see Cicero, *Letters*, Book IX. xxi.

mankind generally one's parents are as it were divinities,[13] and to them is owed an obedience which, if not unlimited, is nevertheless of an altogether special kind.

15. Again, since it is a rule of the law of nature to abide by pacts (for it was necessary that among men there be some method of obligating themselves one to another, and no other natural method can be imagined), out of this source the bodies of municipal law have arisen. For those who had associated themselves with some group, or had subjected themselves to a man or to men, had either expressly promised, or from the nature of the transaction must be understood impliedly to have promised, that they would conform to that which should have been determined, in the one case by the majority, in the other by those upon whom authority had been conferred.

16. What is said, therefore, in accordance with the view not only of Carneades but also of others, that

> Expediency is, as it were, the mother
>
> Of what is just and fair,[14]

is not true, if we wish to speak accurately. For the very nature of man, which even if we had no lack of anything would lead us into the mutual relations of society, is the mother of the law of nature. But the mother of municipal law is that obligation which arises from mutual consent; and since this obligation derives its force from the law of nature, nature may be considered, so to say, the great-grand-mother of municipal law.

The law of nature nevertheless has the reinforcement of expediency; for the Author of nature willed that as individuals we should be weak, and should lack many things needed in order to live properly, to the end that we might be the more constrained to cultivate the social life. But expediency afforded an opportunity also for municipal law, since that kind of association of which we have spoken, and subjection to authority, have their roots in expediency. From this it follows that those who prescribe laws for others in so doing are accustomed to have, or ought to have, some advantage in view.

17. But just as the laws of each state have in view the advantage of that state, so by mutual consent it has become possible that certain laws should originate as between all states, or a great many states; and it is apparent that the laws thus originating had in view the advantage, not of particular states, but of the great society of states. And this is what is called the law of nations, whenever we distinguish that term from the law of nature.

This division of law Carneades passed over altogether. For he divided all law into the law of nature and the law of particular countries. Nevertheless if undertaking to treat of the body of law which is maintained between states—for he added a statement in regard to war and things acquired by means of war—he would surely have been obliged to make mention of this law.

18. Wrongly, moreover, does Carneades ridicule justice as folly. For since, by his own admission, the national who in his own country obeys its laws is not foolish, even though, out of regard

13 Hierodes, in his commentary on the *Golden Verse* [rather *How parents should be treated*, quoted by Stobaeus, *Anthology*, tit lxxix. 53], calls parents "gods upon earth"; Philo, *On the Ten Commandments* [chap. xxiii], "visible gods, who imitate the Unbegotten God in giving life." Next after the relationship between God and man comes the relationship between parent and child; Jerome, *Letters*, xcii [cxvii. 2]. Parents are the likenesses of gods; Plato, *Laws*, Book XI [XI. 11]. Honour is due to parents as to gods; Aristotle, *Nicomachean Ethics* Book IX, chap. ii.

14 In regard to this passage Acron, or some other ancient interpreter of Horace [*Sat* I. iii. 98]: "The poet is writing in opposition to the teachings of the Stoics. He wishes to show that justice does not have its origin in nature but is born of expediency." For the opposite view see Augustine's argument, *On Christian Doctrine*, Book III, chap. xiv.

for that law, he may be obliged to forgo certain things advantageous for himself, so that nation is not foolish which does not press its own advantage to the point of disregarding the laws common to nations. The reason in either case is the same. For just as the national, who violates the law of his country in order to obtain an immediate advantage,[15] breaks down that by which the advantages of himself and his posterity are for all future time assured, so the state which transgresses the laws of nature and of nations cuts away also the bulwarks which safeguard its own future peace. Even if no advantage were to be contemplated from the keeping of the law, it would be a mark of wisdom, not of folly, to allow ourselves to be drawn towards that to which we feel that our nature leads.

19. Wherefore, in general, it is by no means true that

> You must confess that laws were framed
>
> From fear of the unjust,[16]

a thought which in Plato some one explains thus, that laws were invented from fear of receiving injury, and that men are constrained by a kind of force to cultivate justice. For that relates only to the institutions and laws which have been devised to facilitate the enforcement of right; as when many persons in themselves weak, in order that they might not be overwhelmed by the more powerful, leagued themselves together to establish tribunals and by combined force to maintain these, that as a united whole they might prevail against those with whom as individuals they could not cope.

And in this sense we may readily admit also the truth of the saying that right is that which is acceptable to the stronger; so that we may understand that law falls of its outward effect unless it has a sanction behind it. In this way Solon accomplished very great results, as he himself used to declare,

> By joining force and law together,
>
> Under a like bond.

20. Nevertheless law, even though without a sanction, is not entirely void of effect. For justice brings peace of conscience, while injustice causes torments and anguish, such as Plato describes, in the breast of tyrants. Justice is approved, and injustice condemned, by the common agreement of good men. But, most important of all, in God injustice finds an enemy, justice a protector. He reserves His judgements for the life after this, yet in such a way that He often causes their effects to become manifest even in this life, as history teaches by numerous examples.

21. Many hold, in fact, that the standard of justice which they insist upon in the case of individuals within the state is inapplicable to a nation or the ruler of a nation. The reason for the error lies in this, first of all, that in respect to law they have in view nothing except the advantage which accrues from it, such advantage being apparent in the case of citizens who, taken singly, are powerless to protect themselves. But great states, since they seem to contain in themselves all things required for the adequate protection of life, seem not to have need of that virtue which looks toward the outside, and is called justice.

---

15 This comparison Marcus Aurelius pertinently uses in Book IX [IX. xxiii]: "Every act of thine that has no relation, direct or indirect, to the common interest, rends thy life and does not suffer it to be one; such an act is not less productive of disintegration than he is who creates a dissension among a people." The same author, Book XI [XI. viii]: "A man cut off from a single fellow man cannot but be considered as out of fellowship with the whole human race." In effect, as the same Antoninus says [VI. liv]: "What is advantageous to the swarm is advantageous to the bee."

16 As Ovid says [*Metamorphoses*, VIII. 59]: "Strong is the cause when arms the cause maintain."

22. But, not to repeat what I have said, that law is not founded on expediency alone, there is no state so powerful that it may not some time need the help of others outside itself, either for purposes of trade, or even to ward off the forces of many foreign nations united against it. In consequence we see that even the most powerful peoples and sovereigns seek alliances, which are quite devoid of significance according to the point of view of those who confine law within the boundaries of states. Most true is the saying, that all things are uncertain the moment men depart from law.

23. If no association of men can be maintained without law, as Aristotle showed by his remarkable illustration drawn from brigands,[17] surely also that association which binds together the human race, or binds many nations together, has need of law; this was perceived by him who said that shameful deeds ought not to be committed even for the sake of one's country. Aristotle takes sharply to task[18] those who, while unwilling to allow any one to exercise authority over themselves except in accordance with law, yet are quite indifferent as to whether foreigners are treated according to law or not.

24. That same Pompey, whom I just now quoted for the opposite view, corrected the statement which a king of Sparta had made, that that state is the most fortunate whose boundaries are fixed by spear and sword; he declared that that state is truly fortunate which has justice for its boundary line. On this point he might have invoked the authority of another king of Sparta, who gave the preference to justice over bravery in war,[19] using this argument, that bravery ought to be directed by a kind of justice, but if all men were just they would have no need for bravery in war.

Bravery itself the Stoics defined as virtue fighting on behalf of equity. Themistius in his address to Valens argues with eloquence that kings who measure up to the rule of wisdom make account not only of the nation which has been committed to them, but of the whole human race, and that they are, as he himself says, not "friends of the Macedonians" alone, or

17 Chrysostom, *On Ephesians*, chap iv [Homily IX. iii]: "But how does it happen, some one will say, that brigands live on terms of peace? And when? Tell me, I pray. This happens, in fact, when they are not acting as brigands; for if, in dividing up their loot, they did not observe the precepts of justice and make an equitable apportionment, you would see them engaged in strifes and battles among themselves."

Plutarch [*Pyrrhus*, ix = 388 A] quotes the saying of Pyrrhus, that he would leave his kingdom to that one of his children who should have the sharpest sword, declaring that this has the same implication as the verse of Euripides in the *Phoenician Maidens* [line 68]:

That they with gory steel the house divide.

He adds, moreover, the noble sentiment: "So inimical to the social order, and ruthless, is the determination to possess more than is one's own!"

Cicero, *Letters*, XI. xvi [*Ad Fam.* IX. xvi. 3]: "All things are uncertain when one departs from law." Polybius, Book IV [IV. xxix. 4]: "This above all other causes breaks up the private organizations of criminals and thieves, that they cease to deal fairly with one another; in fine, that good faith among them has perished."

18 Plutarch, *Agesilaus* [xxxvii = 617 D]: "In their conception of honour the Lacedaemonians assign the first place to the advantage of their country; they neither know nor learn any other kind of right than that which they think will advance the interests of Sparta."

In regard to the same Lacedaemonians the Athenians declared, in Thucydides, Book V [V. cv]: "In relations with one another and according to their conception of civil rights they are most strict in their practice of virtue. But with respect to others, though many considerations bearing upon the subject might be brought forward, he will state the fact in a word who will say that in their view what is agreeable is honourable, what is advantageous is just."

19 Hearing that the king of the Persians was called great, Agesilaus remarked: "Wherein is he greater than I, if he is not more just?" The saying is quoted by Plutarch [*Apophthegms*, *Agesilaus*, lxiii = *Morals*, 213 C].

"friends of the Romans"[20] but "friends of mankind." The name of Minos[21] became odious to future ages for no other reason than this, that he limited his fair-dealing to the boundaries of his realm.

25. Least of all should that be admitted which some people imagine, that in war all laws are in abeyance. On the contrary war ought not to be undertaken except for the enforcement of rights; when once undertaken, it should be carried on only within the bounds of law and good faith. Demosthenes well said that war is directed against those who cannot be held in check by judicial processes. For judgements are efficacious against those who feel that they are too weak to resist; against those who are equally strong, or think that they are, wars are undertaken. But in order that wars may be justified, they must be carried on with not less scrupulousness than judicial processes are wont to be.

26. Let the laws be silent, then, in the midst of arms, but only the laws of the State, those that the courts are concerned with, that are adapted only to a state of peace; not those other laws, which are of perpetual validity and suited to all times. It was exceedingly well said by Dio of Prusa, that between enemies written laws, that is, laws of particular states, are not in force, but that unwritten laws[22] are in force, that is, those which nature prescribes, or the agreement of nations has established. This, is set forth by that ancient formula of the Romans, "I think that those things ought to be sought by means of a war that is blameless and righteous."

The ancient Romans, as Varro noted, were slow in undertaking war, and permitted themselves no licence in that matter, because they held the view that a war ought not to be waged except when free from reproach. Camillus said that wars should be carried on justly no less than bravely; Scipio Africanus, that the Roman people commenced and ended wars justly. In another passage you may read: "War has its laws no less than peace." Still another writer admires Fabricius as a great man who maintained his probity in war—a thing most difficult—and believed that even in relation to an enemy there is such a thing as wrongdoing.

27. The historians in many a passage reveal how great in war is the influence of the

20 Marcus Aurelius exceedingly well remarks [VI. xliv]: "As Antoninus, my city and country are Rome; as a man, the world." Porphyry, *On Abstaining from Animal Food*, Book III [III. xxvii]:

"He who is guided by reason keeps himself blameless in relation to his fellow-citizens, likewise also in relation to strangers and men in general; the more submissive to reason, the more godlike a man is."

21 In regard to Minos there is a verse of an ancient poet:

Under the yoke of Minos all the island groaned.

On this point see Cyril, *Against Julian*, Book VI.

22 Thus King Alphonse, being asked whether he owed a greater debt to books or to arms, said that from books he had learned both the practice and laws of arms Plutarch [*Camillus*, x = 134 B]: "Among good men certain laws even of war are recognized, and a victory ought not to be striven for in such a way as not to spurn an advantage arising from wicked and impious actions."

consciousness that one has justice on his side;[23] they often attribute victory chiefly to this cause. Hence the proverbs, that a soldier's strength is broken or increased by his cause; that he who has taken up arms unjustly rarely comes back in safety; that hope is the comrade of a good cause; and others of the same purport.

No one ought to be disturbed, furthermore, by the successful outcome of unjust enterprises. For it is enough that the fairness of the cause exerts a certain influence, even a strong influence upon actions, although the effect of that influence, as happens in human affairs, is often nullified by the interference of other causes. Even for winning friendships, of which for many reasons nations as well as individuals have need, a reputation for having undertaken war not rashly nor unjustly, and of having waged it in a manner above reproach, is exceedingly efficacious. No one readily allies himself with those in whom he believes that there is only a slight regard for law, for the right, and for good faith.

28. Fully convinced, by the considerations which I have advanced, that there is a common law among nations, which is valid alike for war and in war, I have had many and weighty reasons for undertaking to write upon this subject. Throughout the Christian world I observed a lack of restraint in relation to war, such as even barbarous races should be ashamed of; I observed that men rush to arms for slight causes, or no cause at all, and that when arms have once been taken up there is no longer any respect for law, divine or human; it is as if, in accordance with a general decree, frenzy had openly been let loose for the committing of all crimes.

29. Confronted with such utter ruthlessness many men, who very furthest from being bad men, have come to the point of forbidding all use of arms to the Christian,[24] whose rule of conduct above everything else comprises the duty of loving all men. To this opinion sometimes John Ferus and my fellow-countryman Erasmus seem to incline, men who have the utmost devotion to

23 Pompey well says in Appian [*Civil Wars*, II. viii. 51]: "We ought to trust in the gods and in the cause of a war which has been undertaken with the honourable and just purpose of defending the institutions of our country." In the same author Cassius [*Civil Wars*, IV. xii. 97]: "In wars the greatest hope lies in the justice of the cause." Josephus, *Antiquities of the Jews*, Book XV [XV. v. 3]: "God is with those who have right on their side."

Procopius has a number of passages of similar import. One is in the speech of Belisarius, after he had started on his expedition to Africa [*Vandalic War*, I. xii. 21]: "Bravery is not going to give the victory, unless it has justice as a fellow-soldier." Another is in the speech of the same general before the battle not far from Carthage [I. xii. 19]. A third is in the address of the Lombards to the Herulians, where the following words, as corrected by me, are found [*Gothic War*, II. xiv]:

"We call to witness God, the slightest manifestation of whose power is equal to all human strength. He, as may well be believed, making account of the causes of war, will give to each side the outcome of battle which each deserves." This saying was soon afterward confirmed by a wonderful occurrence.

In the same author Totila thus addresses the Goths [*Gothic War*, III. viii]: "It cannot, it cannot happen, I say, that they who resort to violence and injustice can win renown in fighting; but as the life of each is, such the fortune of war that falls to his lot." Soon after the taking of Rome Totila made another speech bearing on the same point [*Gothic War*, III. xxi].

Agathias, Book II [*Histories*, II. i]: "Injustice and forgetfulness of God are to be shunned always, and, are harmful, above all, in war and in time of battle." This statement he elsewhere proves by the notable illustrations of Darius, Xerxes, and the Athenians in Sicily [*Histories*, II. x]. See also the speech of Crispinus to the people of Aquileia, in Herodian, Book VIII [*Histories*, VIII. iii. 5, 6].

In Thucydides, Book VII [VII. xviii], we find the Lacedaemonians reckoning the disasters which they had suffered in Pylus and elsewhere as due to themselves, because they had refused a settlement by arbitration which had been offered them. But as afterward the Athenians, having committed many wicked deeds, refused arbitration, a hope of greater success in their operations revived in the Lacedaemonians.

24 Tertullian, *On the Resurrection of the Flesh* [chap. xvi]: "The sword which has become bloodstained honourably in war, and thus has been employed in man-killing of a better sort."

peace in both Church and State; but their purpose, as I take it, is, when things have gone in one direction, to force them in the opposite direction, as we are accustomed to do, that they may come back to a true middle ground. But the very effort of pressing too hard in the opposite direction is often so far from being helpful that it does harm, because in such arguments the detection of what is extreme is easy, and results in weakening the influence of other statements which are well within the bounds of truth. For both extremes therefore a remedy must be found, that men may not believe either that nothing is allowable, or that everything is.

30. At the same time through devotion to study in private life I have wished—as the only course now open to me, undeservedly forced out from my native land, which had been graced by so many of my labours—to contribute somewhat to the philosophy of the law, which previously, in public service, I practised with the utmost degree of probity of which I was capable. Many heretofore have purposed to give to this subject a well-ordered presentation; no one has succeeded. And in fact such a result cannot be accomplished unless—a point which until now has not been sufficiently kept in view—those elements which come from positive law are properly separated from those which arise from nature. For the principles of the law of nature, since they are always the same, can easily be brought into a systematic form; but the elements of positive law, since they often undergo change and are different in different places, are outside the domain of systematic treatment, just as other notions of particular things are.

31. If now those who have consecrated themselves to true justice should undertake to treat the parts of the natural and unchangeable philosophy of law, after having removed all that has its origin in the free will of man; if one, for example, should treat legislation, another taxation, another the administration of justice, another the determination of motives, another the proving of facts, then by assembling all these parts a body of jurisprudence could be made up.

32. What procedure we think should be followed we have shown by deed rather than by words in this work, which treats by far the noblest part of jurisprudence.

...

40. In order to prove the existence of this law of nature, I have, furthermore, availed myself of the testimony of philosophers,[25] historians, poets, finally also of orators. Not that confidence is to be reposed in them without discrimination; for they were accustomed to serve the interests of their sect, their subject, or their cause. But when many at different times, and in different places, affirm the same thing as certain, that ought to be referred to a universal cause; and this cause, in the lines of inquiry which we are following, must be either a correct conclusion drawn from the principles of nature, or common consent. The former points to the law of nature; the latter, to the law of nations.

The distinction between these kinds of law is not to be drawn from the testimonies themselves (for writers everywhere confuse the terms law of nature and law of nations), but from the character of the matter. For whatever cannot be deduced from certain principles by a sure process of reasoning, and yet is clearly observed everywhere, must have its origin in the free will of man.

---

25 Why should not one avail himself of the testimony of the philosophers, when Alexander Severus constantly read Cicero *On the Commonwealth* and *On Duties*? [Lampridius, *Alexander Severus*, xxx2.]

25
H.L.A. Hart
"International Law," from *The Concept of Law**

1. Sources of Doubt

The idea of a union of primary and secondary rules to which so important a place has been assigned in this book may be regarded as a mean between juristic extremes. For legal theory has sought the key to the understanding of law sometimes in the simple idea of an order backed by threats and sometimes in the complex idea of morality. With both of these law has certainly many affinities and connections; yet, as we have seen, there is a perennial danger of exaggerating these and of obscuring the special features which distinguish law from other means of social control. It is a virtue of the idea which we have taken as central that it permits us to see the multiple relationships between law, coercion, and morality for what they are, and to consider afresh in what, if any, sense these are necessary.

Though the idea of the union of primary and secondary rules has these virtues, and though it would accord with usage to treat the existence of this characteristic union of rules as a sufficient condition for the application of the expression "legal system," we have not claimed that the word "law" must be defined in its terms. It is because we make no such claim to identify or regulate in this way the use of words like "law" or "legal," that this book [*The Concept of Law*] is offered as an elucidation of the *concept* of law, rather than a definition of "law" which might naturally be expected to provide a rule or rules for the use of these expressions. Consistently with this aim, we investigated ... the claim made in the German cases, that the title of valid law should be withheld from certain rules on account of their moral iniquity, even though they belonged to an existing system of primary and secondary rules. In the end we rejected this claim; but we did so, not because it conflicted with the view that rules belonging to such a system must be called "law," nor because it conflicted with the weight of usage. Instead we criticized the attempt to narrow the class of valid laws by the extrusion of what was morally iniquitous, on the ground that to do this did not advance or clarify either theoretical inquiries or moral deliberation. For these purposes, the broader concept which is consistent with so much usage and which would permit us to regard rules however morally iniquitous as law, proved on examination to be adequate.

International law presents us with the converse case. For, though it is consistent with the usage of the last 150 years to use the expression "law" here, the absence of an international legislature, courts with compulsory jurisdiction, and centrally organized sanctions have inspired misgivings, at any rate in the breasts of legal theorists. The absence of these institutions means that the rules for states resemble that simple form of social structure, consisting only of primary rules of obligation, which, when we find it among societies of individuals, we are accustomed to contrast with a developed legal system. It is indeed arguable, as we shall show, that international law not only lacks the secondary rules of change and adjudication which provide for legislature and courts,

* Hart, H.L.A. From Chapter X: "International Law" (pp. 213–32); of *The Concept of Law*, Oxford University Press, 1961.

but also a unifying rule of recognition specifying "sources" of law and providing general criteria for the identification of its rules. These differences are indeed striking and the question "Is international law really law?" can hardly be put aside. But in this case also, we shall neither dismiss the doubts, which many feel, with a simple reminder of the existing usage; nor shall we simply confirm them on the footing that the existence of a union of primary and secondary rules is a necessary as well as a sufficient condition for the proper use of the expression "legal system." Instead we shall inquire into the detailed character of the doubts which have been felt, and, as in the German case, we shall ask whether the common wider usage that speaks of "international law" is likely to obstruct any practical or theoretical aim.

Though we shall devote to it only a single chapter some writers have proposed an even shorter treatment for this question concerning the character of international law. To them it has seemed that the question "Is international law really law?" has only arisen or survived, because a trivial question about the meaning of words has been mistaken for a serious question about the nature of things: since the facts which differentiate international law from municipal law are clear and well known, the only question to be settled is whether we should observe the existing convention or depart from it; and this is a matter for each person to settle for himself. But this short way with the question is surely too short. It is true that among the reasons which have led theorists to hesitate over the extension of the word "law" to international law, a too simple, and indeed absurd view, of what justifies the application of the same word to many different things has played some part. The variety of types of principle which commonly guide the extension of general classifying terms has too often been ignored in jurisprudence. None the less, the sources of doubt about international law are deeper, and more interesting than these mistaken views—about the use of words. Moreover, the two alternatives offered by this short way with the question ("Shall we observe the existing convention or shall we depart from it?") are not exhaustive; for, besides them, there is the alternative of making explicit and examining the principles that have in fact guided the existing usage.

The short way suggested would indeed be appropriate if we were dealing with a proper name. If someone were to ask whether the place called "London" is *really* London, all we could do would be to remind him of the convention and leave him to abide by it or choose another name to suit his taste. It would be absurd, in such a case, to ask on what principle London was so called and whether this principle was acceptable. This would be absurd because, whereas the allotment of proper names rests *only* on an *ad hoc* convention, the extension of the general terms of any serious discipline is never without its principle or rationale, though it may not be obvious what that is. When as, in the present case, the extension is queried by those who in effect say, "We know that it is called law, but is it really law?," what is demanded—no doubt obscurely—is that the principle be made explicit and its credentials inspected.

We shall consider two principal sources of doubt concerning the legal character of international law and, with them, the steps which theorists have taken to meet these doubts. Both forms of doubt arise from an adverse comparison of international law with municipal law, which is taken as the clear, standard example of what law is. The first has its roots deep in the conception of law as fundamentally a matter of orders backed by threats and contrasts the character of the *rules* of international law with those of municipal law. The second form of doubt springs from the obscure belief that states are fundamentally incapable of being the subjects of legal obligation, and contrasts the character of the *subjects* of international law with those of municipal law.

2. Obligations and Sanctions

The doubts which we shall consider are often expressed in the opening chapters of books on international law in the form of the question "How can international law be binding?" Yet there is something very confusing in this favourite form of question; and before we can deal with it we must face a prior question to which the answer is by no means clear. This prior question is: what is meant by saying of a whole system of law that it is "binding"? The statement that a particular rule of a system is binding on a particular person is one familiar to lawyers and tolerably clear in meaning. We may paraphrase it by the assertion that the rule in question is a valid rule, and under it the person in question has some obligation or duty. Besides this, there are some situations in which more general statements of this form are made. We may be doubtful in certain circumstances whether one legal system or another applies to a particular person. Such doubts may arise in the conflict of laws or in public international law. We may ask, in the former case, whether French or English Law is binding on a particular person as regards a particular transaction, and in the latter case we may ask whether the inhabitants of, for example, enemy-occupied Belgium, were bound by what the exiled government claimed was Belgian law or by the ordinances of the occupying power. But in both these cases, the questions are questions of law which arise *within* some system of law (municipal or international) and are settled by reference to the rules or principles of that system. They do not call in question the general character of the rules, but only their scope or applicability in given circumstances to particular persons or transactions. Plainly the question, "Is international law binding?" and its congeners "How can international law be binding?" or "What makes international law binding?" are questions of a different order. They express a doubt not about the applicability, but about the general legal status of international law: this doubt would be more candidly expressed in the form "Can such rules as these be meaningfully and truthfully said ever to give rise to obligations?" As the discussions in the books show, one source of doubt on this point is simply the absence from the system of centrally organized sanctions. This is one point of adverse comparison with municipal law, the rules of which are taken to be unquestionably "binding" and to be paradigms of legal obligation. From this stage the further argument is simple: if for this reason the rules of international law are not "binding," it is surely indefensible to take seriously their classification as law; for however tolerant the modes of common speech may be, this is too great a difference to be overlooked. All speculation about the nature of law begins from the assumption that its existence at least makes certain conduct obligatory.

In considering this argument we shall give it the benefit of every doubt concerning the facts of the international system. We shall take it that neither Article 16 of the Covenant of the League of Nations nor Chapter VII of the United Nations Charter introduced into international law anything which can be equated with the sanctions of municipal law. In spite of the Korean war and of whatever moral may be drawn from the Suez incident, we shall suppose that, whenever their use is of importance, the law enforcement provisions of the Charter are likely to be paralysed by the veto and must be said to exist only on paper.

To argue that international law is not binding because of its lack of organized sanctions is tacitly to accept the analysis of obligation contained in the theory that law is essentially a matter of orders backed by threats. This theory, as we have seen, identifies "having an obligation" or "being bound" with "likely to suffer the sanction or punishment threatened for disobedience." Yet, as we have argued, this identification distorts the role played in all legal thought and discourse of the ideas of obligation and duty. Even in municipal law, where there are effective organized sanctions, we must distinguish, for the variety of reasons given in Chapter III [of *The Concept of Law*], the meaning of the external predictive statement "I (you) are likely to suffer for disobedience," from the internal normative statement "I (you) have an obligation to act thus" which assesses a particular person's situation from the point of view of rules accepted as guiding standards of behaviour. It is true that not all rules give rise to obligations or duties; and it is also true that the rules which do so generally call for some sacrifice of private interests, and are generally supported by serious demands for conformity and insistent criticism of deviations. Yet once we free ourselves from the predictive analysis and its parent conception of law as essentially an order backed by threats, there seems no good reason for limiting the normative idea of obligation to rules supported by organized sanctions.

We must, however, consider another form of the argument, more plausible because it is not committed to definition of obligation in terms of the likelihood of threatened sanctions. The sceptic may point out that there are in a municipal system, as we have ourselves stressed, certain provisions which are justifiably called necessary; among these are primary rules of obligation, prohibiting the free use of violence, and rules providing for the official use of force as a sanction for these and other rules. If such rules and organized sanctions supporting them are in this sense necessary for municipal law, are they not equally so for international law? That they are may be maintained without insisting that this follows from the very meaning of words like "binding" or "obligation."

The answer to the argument in this form is to be found in those elementary truths about human beings and their environment which constitute the enduring psychological and physical setting of municipal law. In societies of individuals, approximately equal in physical strength and vulnerability, physical sanctions are both necessary and possible. They are required in order that those who would voluntarily submit to the restraints of law shall not be mere victims of malefactors who would, in the absence of such sanctions, reap the advantages of respect for law on the part of others, without respecting it themselves. Among individuals living in close proximity to each other, opportunities for injuring others, by guile, if not by open attack, are so great, and the chances of escape so considerable, that no mere natural deterrents could in any but the simplest forms of society be adequate to restrain those too wicked, too stupid, or too weak to obey the law. Yet, because of the same fact of approximate equality and the patent advantages of submission to a system of restraints, no combination of malefactors is likely to exceed in strength those who would voluntarily cooperate in its maintenance. In these circumstances, which constitute the background of municipal law, sanctions may successfully be used against malefactors with relatively small risks, and the threat of them will add much to whatever natural deterrents there may be. But, just because the simple truisms which hold good for individuals do not hold good for states, and the factual background to international law is so different from that of municipal law, there is neither a similar necessity for sanctions (desirable though it may be that international law should be supported by them) nor a similar prospect of their safe and efficacious use.

This is so because aggression between states is very unlike that between individuals. The use of violence between states must be public, and though there is no international police force, there can be very little certainty that it will remain a matter between aggressor and victim, as a murder or theft, in the absence of a police force, might. To initiate a war is, even for the strongest power, to risk much for an outcome which is rarely predictable with reasonable confidence. On the other hand, because of the inequality of states, there can be no standing assurance that the combined strength of those on the side of international order is likely to preponderate over the powers tempted to aggression. Hence the organization and use of sanctions may involve fearful risks and the threat of them add little to the natural deterrents. Against this very different background of fact, international law has developed in a form different from that of municipal law. In a population of a modern state, if there were no organized repression and punishment of crime, violence and theft would be hourly expected; but for states, long years of peace have intervened between disastrous wars. These years of peace are only rationally to be expected, given the risks and stakes of war and the mutual needs of states; but they are worth regulating by rules which differ from those of municipal law in (among other things) not providing for their enforcement by any central organ. Yet what these rules require is thought and spoken of as obligatory; there is general pressure for conformity to the rules; claims and admissions are based on them and their breach is held to justify not only insistent demands for compensation, but reprisals and counter-measures. When the rules are disregarded, it is not on the footing that they are not binding; instead efforts are made to conceal the facts. It may of course be said that such rules are efficacious only so far as they concern issues over which states are unwilling to fight. This may be so, and may reflect adversely on the importance of the system and its value to humanity. Yet that even so much may be secured shows that no simple deduction can be made from the necessity of organized sanctions to municipal law, in its setting of physical and psychological facts, to the conclusion that without them international law, in its very different setting, imposes no obligations, is not "binding," and so not worth the title of "law."

3. Obligation and the Sovereignty of States

Great Britain, Belgium, Greece, Soviet Russia have rights and obligations under international law and so are among its subjects. They are random examples of states which the layman would think of as independent and the lawyer would recognize as "sovereign." One of the most persistent sources of perplexity about the obligatory character of international law has been the difficulty felt in accepting or explaining the fact that a state which is sovereign may also be "bound" by, or have an obligation under, international law. This form of scepticism is, in a sense, more extreme than the objection that international law is not binding because it lacks sanctions. For whereas that would be met if one day international law were reinforced by a system of sanctions, the present objection is based on a radical inconsistency, said or felt to exist, in the conception of a state which is at once sovereign and subject to law.

Examination of this objection involves a scrutiny of the notion of sovereignty, applied not to a legislature or to some other element or person *within* a state, but to a state itself. Whenever the word "sovereign" appears in jurisprudence, there is a tendency to associate with it the idea of a person above the law whose word is law for his inferiors or subjects. We have seen ... how bad a guide this seductive notion is to the structure of a municipal legal system; but it has been an even more potent source of confusion in the theory of international law. It is, of course, *possible* to think of a state along such lines, as if it were a species of Superman—a Being inherently lawless but the source of law for its subjects. From the sixteenth century onwards, the symbolical identification of state and monarch ("L'état c'est moi") may have encouraged this idea which has been the dubious inspiration of much political as well as legal theory. But it is important for the understanding of international law to shake off these associations. The expression "a state" is not the name of some person or thing inherently or "by nature" outside the law; it is a way of referring to two facts: first, that a population inhabiting a territory lives under that form of ordered government provided by a legal system with its characteristic structure of legislature, courts, and primary rules; and, secondly, that the government enjoys a vaguely defined degree of independence.

The word "state" has certainly its own large area of vagueness but what has been said will suffice to display its central meaning. States such as Great Britain or Brazil, the United States or Italy, again to take random examples, possess a very large measure of independence from both legal and factual control by any authorities or persons outside their borders, and would rank as "sovereign states" in international law. On the other hand, individual states which are members of a federal union, such as the United States, are subject in many different ways to the authority and control of the federal government and constitution. Yet the independence which even these federated states retain is large if we compare it with the position, say, of an English county, of which the word "state" would not be used at all. A county may have a local council discharging, for its area, some of the functions of a legislature, but its meagre powers are subordinate to those of Parliament and, except in certain minor respects, the area of the county is subject to the same laws and government as the rest of the country.

Between these extremes there are many different types and degrees of dependence (and so of independence) between territorial units which possess an ordered government. Colonies, protectorates, suzerainties, trust territories, confederations, present fascinating problems of classification from this point of view. In most cases the dependence of one unit on another is expressed in legal forms, so that what is law in the territory of the dependent unit will, at least on certain issues, ultimately depend on law-making operations in the other.

In some cases, however, the legal system of the dependent territory may not reflect its dependence. This may be so either because it is merely formally independent and the territory is in fact governed, through puppets, from outside; or it may be so because the dependent territory has a real autonomy over its internal but not its external affairs, and its dependence on another country in external affairs does not require expression as part of its domestic law. Dependence of one territorial unit on another in these various ways is not, however, the only form in which its independence may be limited. The limiting factor may be not the power or authority of another such unit, but an international authority affecting units which are alike independent of each other. It is possible to imagine many different forms of international authority and correspondingly many different limitations on the independence of states. The possibilities include, among many others, a world legislature on the model of the British Parliament, possessing legally unlimited powers to regulate the internal and external affairs of all; a federal legislature on the model of Congress, with legal competence only over specified matters or one limited by guarantees of specific rights of the constituent units; a regime in which the only form of legal control consists of rules generally accepted as applicable to all; and finally a regime in which the only form of obligation recognized is contractual or self-imposed, so that a state's independence is legally limited only by its own act.

It is salutary to consider this range of possibilities because merely to realize that there are many possible forms and degrees of dependence and independence, is a step towards answering the claim that because states are sovereign they "*cannot*" be subject to or bound by international law or "*can*" only be bound by some specific form of international law. For the word "sovereign" means here no more than "independent"; and, like the latter, is negative in force: a sovereign state is one *not* subject to certain types of control, and its sovereignty is that area of conduct in which it is autonomous. Some measure of autonomy is imported, as we have seen, by the very meaning of the word state but the contention that this "*must*" be unlimited or "*can*" only be limited by certain types of obligation is at best the assertion of a claim that states ought to be free of all other restraints, and at worst is an unreasoned dogma. For if in fact we find that there exists among states a given form of international authority, the sovereignty of states is to that extent limited, and it has just that extent which the rules allow. Hence we can only know which states are sovereign, and what the extent of their sovereignty is, when we know what the rules are; just as we can only know whether an Englishman or an American is free and the extent of his freedom when we know what English or American law is. The rules of international law are indeed vague and conflicting on many points, so that doubt about the area of independence left to states is far greater than that concerning the extent of a citizen's freedom under municipal law. None the less, these difficulties do not validate the *a priori* argument which attempts to deduce the general character of international law from an absolute sovereignty, which is assumed, without reference to international law, to belong to states.

It is worth observing that an uncritical use of the idea of sovereignty has spread similar confusion in the theory both of municipal and international law, and demands in both a similar corrective. Under its influence, we are led to believe that there *must* in every municipal legal system be a sovereign legislator subject to no legal limitations; just as we are led to believe that international law *must* be of a certain character because states are sovereign and incapable of legal limitation save by themselves. In both cases, belief in the necessary existence of the legally unlimited sovereign prejudges a question which we can only answer when we examine the actual rules. The question for municipal law is: what is the extent of the supreme legislative authority recognized in this system? For international law it is: what is the maximum area of autonomy which the rules allow to states?

Thus the simplest answer to the present objection is that it inverts the order in which questions must be considered. There is no way of knowing what sovereignty states have, till we know what the forms of international law are and whether or not they are mere empty forms. Much juristic debate has been confused because this principle has been ignored, and it is profitable to consider in its light those theories of international law which are known as "voluntarist" or theories of "autolimitation." These attempted to reconcile the (absolute) sovereignty of states with the existence of binding rules of international law, by treating all international obligations as self-imposed like the obligation which arises from a promise. Such theories are in fact the counterpart in international law of the social contract theories of political science. The latter sought to explain the facts that individuals, "naturally" free and independent, were yet bound by municipal law, by treating the obligation to obey the law as one arising from a contract which those bound had made with each other, and in some cases with their rulers. We shall not consider here the well-known objections to this theory when taken literally, nor its value when taken merely as an illuminating analogy. Instead we shall draw from its history a threefold argument against the voluntarist theories of international law.

First, these theories fail completely to explain how it is known that states "*can*" only be bound by self-imposed obligations, or why this view of their sovereignty should be accepted, in advance of any examination of the actual character of international law. Is there anything more to support it besides the fact that it has often been repeated? Secondly, there is something incoherent in the argument designed to show that states, because of their sovereignty, *can* only be subject to or bound by rules which they have imposed upon themselves. In some very extreme forms of "auto-limitation" theory, a state's agreement or treaty engagements are treated as mere declarations of its proposed future conduct, and failure to perform is not considered to be a breach of any obligation.

This, though very much at variance with the facts, has at least the merit of consistency: it is the simple theory that the absolute sovereignty of states is inconsistent with obligation of any kind, so that, like Parliament, a state cannot bind itself. The less extreme view that a state may impose obligations on itself by promise, agreement, or treaty is not, however, consistent with the theory that states are subject only to rules which they have thus imposed on themselves. For, in order that words, spoken or written, should in certain circumstances function as a promise, agreement, or treaty, and so give rise to obligations and confer rights which others may claim, *rules* must already exist providing that a state is bound to do whatever it undertakes by appropriate words to do. Such rules presupposed in the very notion of a self-imposed obligation obviously cannot derive *their* obligatory status from a self-imposed obligation to obey them.

It is true that every specific *action* which a given state was bound to do might in theory derive its obligatory character from a promise; none the less this could only be the case if the *rule* that promises, &c., create obligations is applicable to the state independently of any promise. In any society, whether composed of individuals or states, what is necessary and sufficient, in order that the words of a promise, agreement, or treaty should give rise to obligations, is that rules providing for this and specifying a procedure for these self-binding operations should be generally, though they need not be universally, acknowledged. Where they are acknowledged the individual or state who wittingly uses these procedures is bound thereby, whether he or it chooses to be bound or not. Hence, even this most voluntary form of social obligation involves some rules which are binding independently of the choice of the party bound by them, and this, in the case of states, is inconsistent with the supposition that their sovereignty demands freedom from all such rules.

Thirdly there are the facts. We must distinguish the *a priori* claim just criticized, that states *can* only be bound by self-imposed obligations, from the claim that though they could be bound in other ways under a different system, in fact no other form of obligation for states exists under the present rules of international law. It is, of course, possible that the system might be one of this wholly consensual form, and both assertions and repudiations of this view of its character are to be found in the writings of jurists, in the opinions of judges, even of international courts, and in the declarations of states. Only a dispassionate survey of the actual practice of states can show whether this view is correct or not. It is true that modern international law is very largely treaty law, and elaborate attempts have been made to show that rules which appear to be binding on states without their prior consent do in fact rest on consent, though this may have been given only "tacitly" or has to be "inferred." Though not all are fictions, some at least of these attempts to reduce to one the forms of international obligation excite the same suspicion as the notion of a "tacit command" which, as we have seen, was designed to perform a similar, though more obviously spurious, simplification of municipal law.

A detailed scrutiny of the claim that all international obligation arises from the consent of the party bound, cannot be undertaken here, but two clear and important exceptions to this doctrine must be noticed. The first is the case of a new state. It has never been doubted that when a new, independent state emerges into existence, as did Iraq in 1932, and Israel in 1948, it is bound by the general obligations of international law including, among others, the rules that give binding force to treaties. Here the attempt to rest the new state's international obligations on a "tacit" or "inferred" consent seems wholly threadbare. The second case is that of a state acquiring territory or undergoing some other change, which brings with it, for the first time, the incidence of obligations under rules which previously it had no opportunity either to observe or break, and to which it had no occasion to give or withhold consent. If a state, previously without access to the sea, acquires maritime territory, it is clear that this is enough to make it subject to all the rules of international law relating to the territorial waters and the high seas. Besides these, there are more debatable cases, mainly relating to the effect on non-parties of general or multilateral treaties; but these two important exceptions are enough to justify the suspicion that the general theory that all international obligation is self-imposed has been inspired by too much abstract dogma and too little respect for the facts.

4. International Law and Morality

In Chapter V [of *The Concept of Law*] we considered the simple form of social structure which consists of primary rules of obligation alone, and we saw that, for all but the smallest, most tightly knit and isolated societies, it suffered from grave defects. Such a regime must be static, its rules altering only by the slow processes of growth and decay; the identification of the rules must be uncertain; and the ascertainment of the fact of their violation in particular cases, and the application of social pressure to offenders must be haphazard, time-wasting, and weak. We found it illuminating to conceive the secondary rules of recognition, change, and adjudication characteristic of municipal law as different though related remedies for these different defects.

In form, international law resembles such a regime of primary rules, even though the content of its often elaborate rules are very unlike those of a primitive society, and many of its concepts, methods, and techniques are the same as those of modern municipal law. Very often jurists have thought that these formal differences between international and municipal law can best be expressed by classifying the former as "morality." Yet it seems clear that to mark the difference in this way is to invite confusion.

Sometimes insistence that the rules governing the relations between states are only moral rules, is inspired by the old dogmatism, that any form of social structure that is not reducible to orders backed by threats can only be a form of "morality." It is, of course, possible to use the word "morality" in this very comprehensive way; so used, it provides a conceptual wastepaper basket into which will go the rules of games, clubs, etiquette, the fundamental provisions of constitutional law and international law, together with rules and principles which we ordinarily think of as moral ones, such as the common prohibitions of cruelty, dishonesty, or lying. The objection to this procedure is that between what is thus classed together as "morality" there are such important differences of both form and social function, that no conceivable purpose, practical or theoretical, could be served by so crude a classification. Within the category of morality thus artificially widened, we should have to mark out afresh the old distinctions which it blurs.

In the particular case of international law there are a number of different reasons for resisting the classification of its rules as "morality." The first is that states often reproach each other for immoral conduct or praise themselves or others for living up to the standard of international morality. No doubt *one* of the virtues which states may show or fail to show is that of abiding by international law, but that does not mean that that law is morality. In fact the appraisal of states' conduct in terms of morality is recognizably different from the formulation of claims, demands, and the acknowledgements of rights and obligations under the rules of international law. In Chapter V we listed certain features which might be taken as defining characteristics of social morality: among them was the distinctive form of moral pressure by which moral rules are primarily supported. This consists not of appeals to fear or threats of retaliation or demands for compensation, but of appeals to conscience, made in the expectation that once the person addressed is reminded of the moral principle at stake, he may be led by guilt or shame to respect it and make amends.

Claims under international law are not couched in such terms though of course, as in municipal law, they may be joined with a moral appeal. What predominate in the arguments, often technical, which states address to each other over disputed matters of international law, are references to precedents, treaties, and juristic writings; often no mention is made of moral right or wrong, good or bad. Hence the claim that the Peking Government has or has not a right under international law to expel the Nationalist forces from Formosa is very different from the question whether this is fair, just, or a morally good or bad thing to do, and is backed by characteristically different arguments. No doubt in the relations between states there are half-way houses between what is clearly law and what is clearly morality, analogous to the standards of politeness and courtesy recognized in private life. Such is the sphere of international "comity" exemplified in the privilege extended to diplomatic envoys of receiving goods intended for personal use free of duty.

A more important ground of distinction is the following. The rules of international law, like those of municipal law, are often morally quite indifferent. A rule may exist because it is convenient or necessary to have some clear fixed rule about the subjects with which it is concerned, but not because any moral importance is attached to the particular rule. It may well be but one of a large number of possible rules, any one of which would have done equally well. Hence legal rules, municipal and international, commonly contain much specific detail, and draw arbitrary distinctions, which would be unintelligible as elements in moral rules or principles. It is true that we must not be dogmatic about the possible content of social morality: as we saw in Chapter V the morality of a social group may contain much by way of injunction which may appear absurd or superstitious when viewed in the light of modern knowledge. So it is possible, though difficult, to imagine that men with general beliefs very different from ours, might come to attach *moral* importance to driving on the left instead of the right of the road or could come to feel moral guilt if they broke a promise witnessed by two witnesses, but no such guilt if it was witnessed by one. Though such strange moralities are possible, it yet remains true that a morality cannot (logically) contain rules which are generally held by those who subscribe to them to be in no way preferable to alternatives and of no intrinsic importance. Law, however, though it also contains much that is of moral importance, can and does contain just such rules, and the arbitrary distinctions, formalities, and highly specific detail which would be most difficult to understand as part of morality, are consequently natural and easily comprehensible features of law. For one of the typical functions of law, unlike morality, is to introduce just these elements in order to maximize certainty and predictability and to facilitate the proof or assessments of claims. Regard for forms and detail carried to excess, has earned for law the reproaches of "formalism" and "legalism"; yet it is important to remember that these vices are exaggerations of some of the law's distinctive qualities.

It is for this reason that just as we expect a municipal legal system, but not morality, to tell us how many witnesses a validly executed will must have, so we expect international law, but not morality, to tell us such things as the number of days a belligerent vessel may stay for refuelling or repairs in a neutral port; the width of territorial waters; the methods to be used in their measurement. All these things are necessary and desirable provisions for *legal rules* to make, but so long as the sense is retained that such rules may equally well take any of several forms, or are important only as one among many possible means to specific ends, they remain distinct from rules which have the status in individual or social life characteristic of morality. Of course not all the rules of international law are of this formal, or arbitrary, or morally neutral kind. The point is only that legal rules *can* and moral rules *cannot* be of this kind.

The difference in character between international law and anything which we naturally think of as morality has another aspect. Though the effect of a law requiring or proscribing certain practices might ultimately be to bring about changes in the morality of a group, the notion of a legislature making or repealing moral rules is, as we saw in Chapter VII, an absurd one. A legislature cannot introduce a new rule and give it the status of a moral rule by its *fiat*, just as it cannot, by the same means, give a rule the status of a tradition, though the reasons why this is so may not be the same in the two cases. Accordingly morality does not merely lack or happen not to have a legislature; the very idea of change by human legislative *fiat* is repugnant to the idea of morality. This is so because we conceive of morality as the ultimate standard by which human actions (legislative or otherwise) are evaluated. The contrast with international law is clear. There is nothing in the nature or function of international law which is similarly inconsistent with the idea that the rules might be subject to legislative change; the lack of a legislature is just a lack which many think of as a defect one day to be repaired.

Finally we must notice a parallel in the theory of international law between the argument, criticized in Chapter V, that even if particular rules of municipal law may conflict with morality, none the less the system as a whole must rest on a generally diffused conviction that there is a moral obligation to obey its rules, though this may be overridden in special exceptional cases. It has often been said in the discussion of the "foundations" of international law, that in the last resort, the rules of international law *must* rest on the conviction of states that there is a moral obligation to obey them; yet, if this means more than that the obligations which they recognize are not enforceable by officially organized sanctions, there seems no reason to accept it. Of course it is possible to think of circumstances which would certainly justify our saying that a state considered some course of conduct required by international law morally obligatory, and acted for that reason. It might, for example, continue to perform the obligations of an onerous treaty because of the manifest harm to humanity that would follow if confidence in treaties was severely shaken, or because of the sense that it was only fair to shoulder the irksome burdens of a code from which it, in its turn, had profited in the past when the burden fell on others. Precisely whose motives, thoughts and feelings on such matters of moral conviction are to be attributed to the state is a question which need not detain us here.

But though there *may* be such a sense of moral obligation it is difficult to see why or in what sense it *must* exist as a condition of the existence of international law. It is clear that in the practice of states certain rules are regularly respected even at the cost of certain sacrifices; claims are formulated by reference to them; breaches of the rules expose the offender to serious criticism and are held to justify claims for compensation or retaliation. These, surely, are all the elements required to support the statement that there exist among states rules imposing obligations upon them. The proof that "binding" rules in any society exist, is simply that they are thought of, spoken of, and function as such. What more is required by way of "foundations" and why, if more is required, must it be a foundation of moral obligation? It is, of course, true that rules could not exist or function in the relations between states unless a preponderant majority accepted the rules and voluntarily cooperated in maintaining them. It is true also that the pressure exercised on those who break or threaten to break the rules is often relatively weak, and has usually been decentralized or unorganized. But as in the case of individuals, who voluntarily accept the far more strongly coercive system of municipal law, the motives for voluntarily supporting such a system may be extremely diverse. It may well be that any form of legal order is at its healthiest when there is a generally diffused sense that it is morally obligatory to conform to it. None the less, adherence to law may not be motivated by it, but by calculations of long-term interest, or by the wish to continue a tradition or by disinterested concern for others. There seems no good reason for identifying any of these as a necessary condition of the existence of law either among individuals or states.

5. Analogies of Form and Content

To the innocent eye, the formal structure of international law lacking a legislature, courts with compulsory jurisdiction and officially organized sanctions, appears very different from that of municipal law. It resembles, as we have said, in form though not at all in content, a simple regime of primary or customary law. Yet some theorists, in their anxiety to defend against the sceptic the title of international law to be called "law," have succumbed to the temptation to minimize these formal differences, and to exaggerate the analogies which can be found in international law to legislation or other desirable formal features of municipal law. Thus, it has been claimed that war, ending with a treaty whereby the defeated power cedes territory, or assumes obligations, or accepts some diminished form of independence, is essentially a legislative act; for, like legislation, it is an imposed legal change. Few would now be impressed by this analogy, or think that it helped to show that international law had an equal title with municipal law to be called "law"; for one of the salient differences between municipal and international law is that the former usually does not, and the latter does, recognize the validity of agreements extorted by violence.

A variety of other, more respectable analogies have been stressed by those who consider the title of "law" to depend on them. The fact that in almost all cases the judgment of the International Court and its predecessor, the Permanent Court of International Justice, have been duly carried out by the parties, has often been emphasized as if this somehow offset the fact that, in contrast with municipal courts, no state can be brought before these international tribunals without its prior consent. Analogies have also been found between the use of force, legally regulated and officially administered, as a sanction in municipal law and "decentralized sanctions," i.e., the resort to war or forceful retaliation by a state which claims that its rights under international law have been violated by another. That there is some analogy is plain; but its significance must be assessed in the light of the equally plain fact that, whereas a municipal court has a compulsory jurisdiction to investigate the rights and wrongs of "self help" and to punish a wrongful resort to it, no international court has a similar jurisdiction.

Some of these dubious analogies may be considered to have been much strengthened by the obligations which states have assumed under the United Nations Charter. But, again, any assessment of their strength is worth little if it ignores the extent to which the law enforcement provisions of the Charter, admirable on paper, have been paralysed by the veto and the ideological divisions and alliances of the great powers. The reply, sometimes made, that the law-enforcement provisions of municipal law *might* also be paralysed by a general strike is scarcely convincing; for in our comparison between municipal law and international law we are concerned with what exists in fact, and here the facts are undeniably different.

There is, however, one suggested formal analogy between international and municipal law which deserves some scrutiny here. Kelsen and many modern theorists insist that, like municipal law, international law possesses and indeed must possess a "basic norm," or what we have termed a rule of recognition, by reference to which the validity of the other rules of the system is assessed, and in virtue of which the rules constitute a single system. The opposed view is that this analogy of structure is false: international law simply consists of a *set* of separate primary rules of obligation which are not united in this manner. It is, in the usual terminology of international lawyers, a set of customary rules of which the rule giving binding force to treaties is one. It is notorious that those who have embarked on the task have found very great difficulties in formulating the "basic norm" of international law. Candidates for this position include the principle *pacta sunt servanda*. This has, however, been abandoned by most theorists, since it seems incompatible with the fact that not all obligations under international law arise from "*pacta*," however widely that term is construed. So it has been replaced by something less familiar: the so-called rule that "States should behave as they customarily behave."

We shall not discuss the merits of these and other rival formulations of the basic norm of international law; instead we shall question the assumption that it must contain such an element. Here the first and perhaps the last question to ask is: why should we make this *a priori* assumption (for that is what it is) and so prejudge the actual character of the rules of international law? For it is surely conceivable (and perhaps has often been the case) that a society may live by rules imposing obligations on its members as "binding," even though they are regarded simply as a set of separate rules, not unified by or deriving their validity from any more basic rule. It is plain that the mere existence of rules does not involve the existence of such a basic rule. In most modern societies there are rules of etiquette, and, though we do not think of them as imposing obligations, we may well talk of such rules as existing; yet we would not look for, nor could we find, a basic rule of etiquette from which the validity of the separate rules was derivable. Such rules do not form a system but a mere set, and, of course, the inconveniences of this form of social control, where matters more important than those of etiquette are at stake, are considerable. They have already been described in Chapter V. Yet if rules are in fact accepted as standards of conduct, and supported with appropriate forms of social pressure distinctive of obligatory rules, nothing more is required to show that they are binding rules, even though, in this simple form of social structure, we have not something which we do have in municipal law: namely a way of demonstrating the validity of individual rules by reference to some ultimate rule of the system.

There are of course a number of questions which we can ask about rules which constitute not a system but a simple set. We can, for example, ask questions about their historical origin, or questions concerning the causal influences that have fostered the growth of the rules. We can also ask questions about the value of the rules to those who live by them, and whether they regard themselves as morally bound to obey them or obey from some other motive. But we cannot ask in the simpler case one kind of question which we can ask concerning the rules of a system enriched, as municipal law is, by a basic norm or secondary rule of recognition. In the simpler case we cannot ask: "From what ultimate provision of the system do the separate rules derive their validity or 'binding force'?" For there is no such provision and need be none. It is, therefore, a mistake to suppose that a basic rule or rule of recognition is a generally necessary condition of the existence of rules of obligation or "binding" rules. This is not a necessity, but a luxury, found in advanced social systems whose members not merely come to accept separate rules piecemeal, but are committed to the acceptance in advance of general classes of rule, marked out by general criteria of validity. In the simpler form of society we must wait and see whether a rule gets accepted as a rule or not; in a system with a basic rule of recognition we can say before a rule is actually made, that it *will* be valid *if* it conforms to the requirements of the rule of recognition.

The same point may be presented in a different form. When such a rule of recognition is added to the simple set of separate rules, it not only brings with it the advantages of system and ease of identification, but it makes possible for the first time a new form of statement. These are internal statements about the validity of the rules; for we can now ask in a new sense, "What provision of the system makes this rule binding?" or, in Kelsen's language, "What, within the system, is the reason of its validity?" The answers to these new questions are provided by the basic rule of recognition. But though, in the simpler structure, the validity of the rules cannot thus be demonstrated by reference to any more basic rule, this does not mean that there is some question about the rules or their binding force or validity which is left unexplained. It is not the case that there is some mystery as to why the rules in such a simple social structure are binding, which a basic rule, if only we could find it, would resolve. The rules of the simple structure are, like the basic rule of the more advanced systems, binding if they are accepted and function as such. These simple truths about different forms of social structure can, however, easily be obscured by the obstinate search for unity and system where these desirable elements are not in fact to be found.

There is indeed something comic in the efforts made to fashion a basic rule for the most simple forms of social structure which exist without one. It is as if we were to insist that a naked savage *must* really be dressed in some invisible variety of modern dress. Unfortunately, there is also here a standing possibility of confusion. We may be persuaded to treat as a basic rule, something which is an empty repetition of the mere fact that the society concerned (whether of individuals or states) observes certain standards of conduct as obligatory rules. This is surely the status of the strange basic norm which has been suggested for international law: "States should behave as they have customarily behaved." For it says nothing more than that those who accept certain rules must also observe a rule that the rules ought to be observed. This is a mere useless reduplication of the fact that a set of rules are accepted by states as binding rules.

Again once we emancipate ourselves from the assumption that international law *must* contain a basic rule, the question to be faced is one of fact. What is the actual character of the rules as they function in the relations between states? Different interpretations of the phenomena to be observed are of course possible; but it is submitted that there is no basic rule providing general criteria of validity for the rules of international law, and that the rules which are in fact operative constitute not a system but a set of rules, among which are the rules providing for the binding force of treaties. It is true that, on many important matters, the relations between states are regulated by multilateral treaties, and it is sometimes argued that these may bind states that are not parties. If this were generally recognized, such treaties would in fact be legislative enactments and international law would have distinct criteria of validity for its rules. A basic rule of recognition could then be formulated which would represent an actual feature of the system and would be more than an empty restatement of the fact that a set of rules are in fact observed by states. Perhaps international law is at present in a stage of transition towards acceptance of this and other forms which would bring it nearer in structure to a municipal system. If, and when, this transition is completed the formal analogies, which at present seem thin and even delusive, would acquire substance, and the sceptic's last doubts about the legal "quality" of international law may then be laid to rest. Till this stage is reached the analogies are surely those of function and content, not of form. Those of function emerge most clearly when we reflect on the ways in which international law differs from morality, some of which we examined in the last section. The analogies of content consist in the range of principles, concepts, and methods which are common to both municipal and international law, and make the lawyers' technique freely transferable from the one to the other. Bentham, the inventor of the expression "international law," defended it simply by saying that it was "sufficiently analogous"[1] to municipal law. To this, two comments are perhaps worth adding. First, that the analogy is one of content not of form: secondly, that, in this analogy of content, no other social rules are so close to municipal law as those of international law.

26
Martti Koskenniemi
"The Politics of International Law"*

I. The Flight from Politics

It may be a matter of some controversy among historians as to when one should date the beginning of the modern states-system.[1] Less open to debate, however, is that somehow the idea of such a system is historically as well as conceptually linked with that of an international Rule of Law. In a system whose units are assumed to serve no higher purpose than their own interests and which assumes the perfect equality of those interests, the Rule of Law seems indeed the sole thinkable principle of organization—short of the *bellum omnium*. Since the publication of Emmerich de Vattel's *Droit des gens ou principes de loi naturelle appliqués a la conduite et aux affaires des nations et des souverains* (1758), jurists have written about international matters by assuming that the liberal principles of the Enlightenment and their logical corollary, the Rule of Law, could be extended to apply in the organization of international society just as they had been used in the domestic one.[2]

1 *Principles of Morals and Legislation*, XVII. 25, n. I.

* Koskenniemi, Martti. "The Politics of International Law," *European Journal of International Law*, 1.1 (1990): 4–32. https://doi.org/10.1093/oxfordjournals.ejil.a035781.

1 For example, A.F. von der Heydte: *Geburistunde des souveränen Staates* (1952) suggests the turn of the 14th century, 41–43, while F.H. Hinsley: *Power and the Pursuit of Peace* (1962), 153, argues that one cannot properly speak of a states-system until the 18th century.

2 The analogy is explicit in J.J. Rousseau: *The Social Contract* (trans. and intro. by Maurice Cranston) (1986) Bk. I Ch. 7 at 63; J. Locke, *Two Treatises on Government* (intro. by W.S. Carpenter) (1984) Second Treatise, sect. 183 at 211. For commentary, see, e.g., P. Vinogradoff, *Historical Types of International Law* (1920) 55–57; E.D. Dickinson, *The Equality of States in International Law* (1920) 29–31, 49–50, 97–98, 111–13. See also M. Walzer, *Just and Unjust Wars* (1980) 58–63; C.L. Beitz, *Political Theory and International Relations* (1979) 74. For useful analysis of the effect of the analogy to the conception of a state's (territorial) rights, see A. Carty, *The Decay of International Law?* (1986) 44–46, 55–56.

Notwithstanding the historical difficulty with dates and origins, the connexion between the Rule of Law and the principles of the Enlightenment appear evident. Of the latter, none seems more important than that of the subjectivity of value.[3] Hobbes writes:

> For one calleth wisdom what another calleth fear and one cruelty what another justice; and prodigality what another magnanimity ... And therefrom such names can never be ground for any ratiocination.[4]

However much later liberals may have disliked Hobbes's substantive conclusions or his political realism, the one thing which unites them with Hobbes is their criticism of relying upon natural principles to justify political authority. Appealing to principles which would preexist man and be discoverable only through faith or *recta ratio* was to appeal to abstract and unverifiable maximums which only camouflaged the subjective preferences of the speaker. It was premised on utopian ideals which were constantly used as apologies for tyranny. From the simple denial of the existence of principles of natural justice—or at least of our capacity to know them—follow the three liberal principles of social organization: freedom, equality and the Rule of Law. If man is not born to a world of pre-existing norms, then he is born free; if there are no antecedent principles establishing the relative worths of individuals, the individuals must be assumed equal. And finally, freedom and equality are guaranteed only if social constraint is governed by public, verifiable and determining rules: "A free people obey but it does not serve; it has magistrates but not masters; it obeys nothing but the laws, and thanks to the force of laws, it does not obey men."[5]

The fight for an international Rule of Law is a fight against politics, understood as a matter of furthering subjective desires and leading into an international anarchy. Though some measure of politics is inevitable, it should be constrained by non-political rules: "... the health of the political realm is maintained by conscientious objection to the political."[6]

The diplomatic history of the 19th century is a history of such a fight. Since the Vienna Congress of 1814–15 and the defeat of Napoleon, the relations between European powers were no longer built on one power's search for primacy but on a general pursuit of the maintenance of the balance of power, guaranteed by complicated legal procedures and alliances.[7] As contemporaries increasingly saw Europe as a "system" of independent and equal political communities (instead of a *respublica Christiana*) they began to assume that the governing principles needed to become neutral and objective—that is, legal.

The legal scholarship of the 19th century interpreted and systematized diplomatic practice into legal rules. It assumed that the behavior of European states was determined and explicable by reference to a body of (European) public law. The plausibility of this assumption relied on the procedural character of that law. Containing mainly rules concerning diplomatic and consular contacts, procedures for attaining statehood,

3 My discussion of this principle is influenced by R.M. Unger, *Knowledge and Politics* (1975) 76–81, and A. MacIntyre, *After Virtue; A Study in Moral Theory* (2nd ed.) (1985) 6–35.

4 T. Hobbes, *Leviathan* (ed. and intro. by C.B. Macpherson) (1982) Ch. 4, at 109–10.

5 J.J. Rousseau, *Œuvres complètes*, Pléiade (Vol. III sect. 841–42) quoted by Cranston (Introduction to J.J. Rousseau, *The Social Contract*, *supra* note 2, at 32).

6 Wight, "Western Values in International Relations," in Butterfield, Wight, *Diplomatic Investigations: Essays in the Theory of International Politics* (1966) 122.

7 See, e.g., F.H. Hinsley, *supra* note 1, at 186–271.

territory or neutral status, it did not severely restrict the ends which European sovereigns attempted to pursue. In particular, it renounced theories of the just war: war became now one political procedure among others.[8] Though the professional lawyers of the 19th century did speak about justice in the conduct of the sovereigns' affairs, they no longer thought of justice as material principles. Woolsey put the matter adroitly:

> By justice, however, we intend not justice objective, but as it appears to the party concerned or, at least, as it is claimed to exist. From the independence of nations it results that each has a right to hold and make good its own view of right in its own affairs.[9]

Though 20th-century lawyers have not looked too kindly upon the scholarship of the preceding century, they never rejected the ideal of the Rule of Law. On the contrary, the reconstructive scholarship which emerged first from the catastrophe of World War I and then in the 1950s and 1960s accused the pre-war doctrines of *not going far enough* to uphold the Rule of Law. Wherever attempts by jurists to construct a solid framework of public law had faltered, it had done so not because of some defect in the liberal assumptions behind this project but because jurists had deviated from them.

The vision of a Rule of Law between states (which re-emerged most recently in United Nations General Assembly Resolution 44/23 [15 November 1989] declaring the period 1990–99 as the "United Nations Decade of International Law") is yet another reformulation of the liberal impulse to escape politics. So strong is the grip of this vision that the representative of the Soviet Union at the same session of the General Assembly explained that in his view to restructure the basis of international relations there was a need to "arrive at a comprehensive international strategy for establishing the primacy of law in relations between states."[10]

Throughout the present century, reconstructive doctrines have claimed that what merits criticism is the corruption of the Rule of Law either in the narrow chauvinism of diplomats or the speculative utopias of an academic elite. If only the Rule of Law can be fortified to exclude these contrasting distortions, then at least the jurist's part in the construction of a just world order has been adequately executed.

In this article, however, I shall extend the criticism of the liberal idea of the *Rechtstaat*, a commonplace in late modern western society,[11] into its international counterpart. I shall attempt to show that our inherited ideal of a World Order based on the Rule of Law thinly hides from sight the fact that social conflict must still be solved by political means and that even though there may exist a common legal rhetoric among international lawyers, that rhetoric must, *for reasons internal to the ideal itself*, rely on essentially contested—political—principles to justify outcomes to international disputes.[12]

---

8 See, e.g., H. Wheaton, *Elements of International Law* (Text of 1866 with Notes, Carnegie Endowment, Classics of International Law, No. 19) (1936) 313–14.

9 T.D. Woolsey, *Introduction to the Study of International Law; Designed as an Aid in Teaching, and in Historical Studies* (5th ed.) (1879) 183.

10 "Memorandum: On Enhancing the Role of International Law," UN Doc.A/44/585 (2 October 1989).

11 For the ensuing text, particularly relevant are criticisms stressing the *internal* tensions of liberal theory. See generally Unger, *supra* note 3, at 63–103 and, e.g., A. Levine, *Liberal Democracy: A Critique of Its Theory* (1981) 16–32; Fishkin, "Liberal Theory and the Problem of Justification," *NOMOS XXVIII* at 207–31.

12 This article is a condensed version of some of the themes in M. Koskenniemi, *From Apology to Utopia: The Structure of International Legal Argument* (1989).

II. The Content of the Rule of Law: Concreteness and Normativity

Organizing society through legal rules is premised on the assumption that these rules are objective in some sense that political ideas, views, or preferences are not. To show that international law is objective—that is, independent from international politics—the legal mind fights a battle on two fronts. On the one hand, it aims to ensure the *concreteness* of the law by distancing it from theories of natural justice. On the other hand, it aims to guarantee the *normativity* of the law by creating distance between it and actual state behaviour, will, or interest. Law enjoys independence from politics only if both of these conditions are simultaneously present.

The requirement of concreteness results from the liberal principle of the subjectivity of value. To avoid political subjectivism and illegitimate constraint,[13] we must base law on something concrete—on the actual (verifiable) behaviour, will and interest of the members of society-states. The modern view is a *social conception of law*.[14] For it, law is not a natural but an artificial creation, a reflexion of social circumstances.

According to the requirement of normativity, law should be applied regardless of the political preferences of legal subjects. In particular, it should be applicable even against a state which opposes its application to itself. As international lawyers have had the occasion to point out, legal rules whose content or application depends on the will of the legal subject for whom they are valid are not proper legal rules at all but apologies for the legal subject's political interest.[15]

Stated in such a fashion, I believe that the requirements of legal objectivity *vis-à-vis* political subjectivity are met. For if the law could be verified or justified only by reference to somebody's views on what the law *should* be like (i.e., theories of justice), it would coincide with their political opinions. Similarly, if we could apply the law against those states which accept it, then it would coincide with those states' political views.

This argumentative structure, however, which forces jurists to prove that their law is valid because concrete and normative in the above sense, both creates and destroys itself. For it is impossible to prove that a rule, principle or doctrine (in short, an argument) is both concrete and normative simultaneously. The two requirements *cancel each other*. An argument about concreteness is an argument about the closeness of a particular rule, principle or doctrine to state practice. But the closer to state practice an argument is, the less normative and the more political it seems. The more it seems just another apology for existing power. An argument about normativity, on the other hand, is an argument which intends to demonstrate the rule's distance from state will and practice. The more normative a rule, the more political it seems because the less it is possible to argue it by reference to social context. It seems utopian and—like theories of natural justice—manipulable at will.

The dynamics of international legal argument are provided by the constant effort of lawyers to show that their law is either concrete or normative and their becoming thus vulnerable to the charge that such law is in fact political because apologist or utopian. Different doctrinal and practical controversies turn on transformations of this dilemma. It lies behind such dichotomies as "positivism"/"naturalism," "consent"/"justice," "autonomy"/"community," "process"/"rule," etc., and explains why these and other oppositions

13 For a typical argument stressing the political character of natural law, see, e.g., S. Sur, *L'interprétation en droit international public* (1974) 25–32 or J.H.W. Verzijl, *International Law in Historical Perspective* (Vol. I) (1968) 391–93.

14 "C'est à une conception fonctionnelle de pouvoir, à une conception sociale du droit que s'attache notre enseignement," De Visscher, "Cours général de principes de droit international public," 86 *RCDI* (1954) 451.

15 See, e.g., H. Lauterpacht, *The Function of Law in the International Community* (1933) 189 and *passim*.

keep recurring and do not seem soluble in a permanent way. They recur because it seems possible to defend one's legal argument only by showing either its closeness to, or its distance from, state practice. They seem insoluble because both argumentative strategies are vulnerable to what appear like valid criticisms, compelled by the system itself.[16]

This provides an argumentative structure which is capable of providing a valid criticism of each substantive position but which itself cannot justify any. The fact that positions are constantly taken and solutions justified by lawyers, demonstrates that the structure does not possess the kind of distance from politics for which the Rule of Law once seemed necessary. It seems possible to adopt a position only by a political choice: a choice which must ultimately defend itself in terms of a conception of justice.

III. Doctrinal Structures

Two criticisms are often advanced against international law. One group of critics has accused international law of being too political in the sense of being too dependent on states' political power. Another group has argued that the law is too political because founded on speculative utopias. The standard point about the non-existence of legislative machineries, compulsory adjudication and enforcement procedures captures both criticisms. From one perspective, this criticism highlights the infinite flexibility of international law, its character as a manipulable facade for power politics. From another perspective, the criticism stresses the moralistic character of international law, its distance from the realities of power politics. According to the former criticism, international law is too *apologetic* to be taken seriously in the construction of international order. According to the latter, it is too *utopian* to the identical effect.

International lawyers have had difficulty answering these criticisms. The more reconstructive doctrines have attempted to prove the normativity of the law, its autonomy from politics, the more they have become vulnerable to the charge of utopianism. The more they have insisted on the close connexion between international law and state behaviour, the less normative their doctrines have appeared. Let me outline the four positions which modern international lawyers have taken to prove the relevance of their norms and doctrines. These are mutually exclusive and logically exhaustive positions and account for a full explanation of the possibilities of doctrinal argument.

Many of the doctrines which emerged from the ashes of legal scholarship at the close of World War I explained the failure of pre-war international doctrines by reference to their apologist character. Particular objects of criticism were "absolutist" doctrines of sovereignty, expressed in particular in the *Selbstverpflichtunglehre*, doctrines stressing the legal significance of the balance of power or delimiting the legal functions to matters which were unrelated to questions of "honour" or "vital interest." Writings by Hersch Lauterpacht, Alfred Verdross and Hans Kelsen among others, created an extremely influential interpretation of the mistakes of prewar doctrines.[17] By associating the failure of those doctrines with their excessive closeness to state policy and national interest and by advocating the autonomy of international legal rules, these jurists led the way to the establishment of what could be called a *rule approach* to international law, stressing the law's normativity, its capacity to oppose state policy as the key to its constraining relevance.

16 For an alternative but similar type of exposition, see D. Kennedy, *International Legal Structure* (1987).

17 Lauterpacht, *supra* note 15; A. Verdross, *Die Verfassung der Völkerrechtsgemeinschaft* (1926); H. Kelsen, *Das Problem der Souveränität und die Theorie des Völkerrechts* (1920).

This approach insists on an objective, formal test of pedigree (sources) which will tell which standards qualify as legal rules and which do not. If a rule meets this test, then it is binding. Though there is disagreement between rule approach lawyers over what constitutes the proper test, there is no dispute about its importance. The distinctions between hard and soft law, rules and principles, regular norms and *jus cogens*, for instance, are suspect: these only betray political distinctions with which the lawyer should not be too concerned.[18] Two well-known criticisms have been directed against the rule approach. First, it has remained unable to exclude the influence of political considerations from its assumed tests of pedigree. To concede that rules are sometimes hard to find while their content remains, to adopt H.L.A. Hart's expression "relatively indeterminate"[19] is to undermine the autonomy which the rule approach stressed. Second, the very desire for autonomy seems suspect. A pure theory of law, the assumption of a *Völkerrechtsgemeinschaft* or the ideal of the wholeness of law—a central assumption in most rule approach writing[20]—may only betray forms of irrelevant doctrinal utopianism. They achieve logical consistency at the cost of applicability in the real world of state practice.

The second major position in contemporary scholarship uses these criticisms to establish itself. A major continental interpretation of the mistakes of 19th-century lawyers and diplomats explains them as a result of naive utopianism: an unwarranted belief in the viability of the Congress system, with its ideas of legality and collective intervention. It failed because it had not been able to keep up with the politics of emergent nationalism and the increasing pace of social and technological change. Lawyers such as Nicolas Politis or Georges Scelle stressed the need to link international law much more closely to the social—even biological—necessities of international life.[21] Roscoe Pound's programmatic writings laid the basis for the contemporary formulation of this approach by criticizing the attempt to think of international law in terms of abstract rules. It was, rather, to be thought of "in terms of social ends."[22]

According to this approach—*the policy approach*—international law can only be relevant if it is firmly based in the social context of international policy. Rules are only trends of past decision which may or may not correspond to social necessities. "Binding force" is a juristic illusion. Standards are, in fact, more or less effective and it is their effectiveness—their capacity to further social goals—which is the relevant question, not their formal "validity."[23] But this approach is just as vulnerable to well-founded criticisms as the rule approach. By emphasizing the law's concreteness, it will ultimately do away with its constraining force altogether. If law is only

---

18 This approach is best illustrated in G. Schwarzenberger, *The Inductive Approach to International Law* (1965). Many of its points are forcefully made in Weil, "Towards Relative Normativity in International Law," 77 *AJIL* (1983) 413–42. For further references on this and the other approaches, see Koskenniemi, *supra* note 12, at 154–86.

19 H.L.A. Hart, *The Concept of Law* (1961) 132.

20 See, e.g., Lauterpacht, "Some Observations on the Prohibition of 'Non liquet' and the Completeness of Law," *Symbolae Verzijl* (1958) 196–221, and the "realist" criticism by Stone, "Non-Liquet and the Function of Law in the International Community," XXV *BYUL* (1959) 124–61.

21 G. Scelle, *Précis de droit des gens. Principes et systématique I–II* (1932, 1936); N. Politis, *Les nouvelles tendances du droit international* (1927).

22 Pound, "Philosophical Theory and International Law," I *Bibliotheca Visseiana* (1923) 1–90.

23 The contemporary formulation of this approach is perhaps clearest in McDougal, "International Law, Power and Policy: A Contemporary Perspective," 82 *RCDI* (1953) 133–259. For useful analysis, see B. Rosenthal, *L'étude de l'œuvre de Myres Smith McDougal en matière du droit international public* (1970).

what is effective, then by definition, it becomes an apology for the interests of the powerful. If, as Myres McDougal does, this consequence is avoided by postulating some "goal values" whose legal importance is independent of considerations of effectiveness, then the (reformed) policy approach becomes vulnerable to criticisms which it originally voiced against the rule approach. In particular, it appears to assume an illegitimate naturalism which—as critics stressing the liberal principle of the subjectivity of value have noted—is in constant danger of becoming just an apology of some states' policies.[24]

The rule and the policy approaches are two contrasting ways of trying to establish the relevance of international law in the face of what appear as well-founded criticisms. The former does this by stressing the law's normativity, but fails to be convincing because it lacks concreteness. The latter builds upon the concreteness of international law, but loses the normativity, the binding force of its law. It is hardly surprising, then, that some lawyers have occupied the two remaining positions: they have either assumed that international law can neither be seen as normatively controlling nor widely applied in practice (the sceptical position), or have continued writing as if both the law's binding force as well as its correspondence with developments in international practice were a matter of course (idealist position). The former ends in cynicism, the latter in contradiction.[25]

The late modern mainstream often situates itself between the rule and the policy approaches. In Richard Falk's words, the task of an adequate doctrine is to establish:

> [an] intermediate position, one that maintains the distinctiveness of the legal order while managing to be responsive to the extra-legal setting of politics, history and morality.[26]

But such a movement towards pragmatic eclecticism seems self-defeating. There is no space between the four positions: rule approach, policy approach, scepticism and idealism. Middle-of-the-road doctrines may seem credible only insofar as their arguments, doctrines or norms are not contested. But as soon as disagreement emerges, such doctrines, too, must defend their positions either by showing their autonomous binding force, or by demonstrating their close relationship with what states actually do. At this point, they become vulnerable to the charge of being either utopian or apologist.

The result is a curiously incoherent doctrinal structure in which each position is *ad hoc* and therefore survives only. Mainstream doctrine retreats into general statements about the need to "combine" concreteness and normativity, realism and idealism, which bear no consequence to its normative conclusion. It then advances, emphasizing the contextuality of each solution—thus undermining its own emphasis on the general and impartial character of its system.

A doctrine's own contradictions force it into an impoverished and unreflective pragmatism. On the one hand, the "idealist" illusion is preserved that law can and does play a role in the organization of social life among states. On the other, the "realist" criticisms have been accepted and the law is seen as distinctly secondary to power and politics. Modern doctrine, as Philip

24 For such criticisms, see, e.g., Allott, "Language, Method and the Nature of International Law," 45 *BYIL* (1971) 123–25; Boyle, "Ideals and Things: International Legal Scholarship and the Prison-House of Language," 26 *Harvard Journal Int'l Law* (1985) 349; and Fitzmaurice, "vae Victis or Woe to the Negotiators!," 65 *AJIL* (1971) 370–73.

25 For references, see Koskenniemi, *supra* note 12, at 167–70, 178–86.

26 Falk, "The Interplay of Westphalia and Charter Conceptions of the International Legal Order," in R. Falk, Black (eds.), *The Future of the International Legal Order* (Vol. I) (1969) 34–35.

Allott has shown, uses a mixture of positivistic and naturalistic, consensualistic and non-consensualistic, teleological, practical, political, logical and factual arguments in happy confusion, unaware of its internal contradictions.[27] The style survives because we recognize in it the liberal doctrine within which we have been accustomed to press our political arguments.

A final point is in order. Both of the main positions reviewed, as well as their combinations, remain distinctly modern. Each refuses to develop its concept of law in terms of some material theory of justice. Each assumes that law is an artificial, human creation which comes about through social processes and that an adequate concept of law is one which provides a reliable description of those processes. Moreover, each bases its claim to superiority *vis-à-vis* the other on that very description. The point at which they diverge is their theory on how to interpret those processes, how to understand what goes on in social life in terms of law-creation and law-application.

The difficulty in choosing between a rule and a policy approach is the difficulty of defending the set of criteria which these put forward to disentangle "law" from other aspects of state behaviour. For the rule approach lawyer, the relevant criteria are provided by his theory of sources. For the policy approach, the corresponding criteria are provided by his theory of "base-values," authority or some constellation of national or global interest and need. Because it is these criteria which claim to provide the correct description of social processes, they cannot be defended without circularity in terms of social processes themselves.[28] To decide on the better approach, one would have to base oneself on some non-descriptive (non-social) theory about significance or about the relative justice of the types of law rendered by the two—or any alternative—matrices.[29] Such a decision would, under the social conception of law and the principle of the subjectivity of value, be one which would seem to have no claim for objective correctness at all. It would be a political decision.

IV. Substantive Structures

It is possible to depict the tension between the demands for normativity and concreteness in two contrasting methods of explaining the origin of the law's substance. From the perspective of concreteness, this substance comes about as a consequence of the fact of sovereignty of the state. One aspect of sovereignty is the liberty to "legislate" international norms which bind oneself. Wherever particular norms have not been thus established, the metaprinciple of sovereign liberty—the "Lotus principle"—remains valid.

It is equally possible to understand the law as a consequence of the functioning of normative criteria for law-emergence. From the perspective of normativity, there must be assumed criteria—"sources"—which allow us to distinguish between the fact of the existence and behaviour of certain centres of power (states) and the law. In this sense, all international legal substance is dependent on the content of those criteria. These explanations seem radically conflicting and appear to provide exhaustive but incompatible methods for elucidating the origin and character of international law. Indeed, much of the dispute between "idealists" and "realists," or the rule and policy approaches, seems captured in this contrast, reflected also in the organization

27 Allott, *supra* note 24, at 100–05, 113.

28 The point about conceptual matrices, scientific theories, "paradigms," interests of knowledge or prejudices, if not strictly determining what we can know of the social world at least significantly influencing our perception, is a common theme in much modern epistemology. See further Koskenniemi, *supra* note 12, at 466–71.

29 On choosing significant features for description, see, e.g., J. Finnis, *Natural Law and Natural Rights* (1980) 3, 9–18. See also MacIntyre, "The Indispensability of Political Theory," in Miller, Siedentop, *The Nature of Political Theory* (1983) 19–33.

of the substance of standard textbooks. One style consists of preceding the law's substance with an analysis of the character of statehood and that of the international order—the "political foundations." Another starts out by listing the sources of international law and lets the law's substance follow therefrom.

Despite their initially contrasting outlook, both "methods" rely on each other. "Realist" doctrines use criteria to distinguish between law and coercion which fall short of a doctrine of sources only by not bearing that name. "Idealist" programmes look at state practice to defend the relevance of their sources and to verify the content of the law they support.[30] The fact that the available outlooks provide identical substantive systems and both remain vulnerable to well-rehearsed arguments further explains the late modern turn to doctrinal pragmatism.

In the practice of international dispute resolution the lack of a satisfactory explanation for the origin of legal rules has led lawyers to abandon seeking justification for solving interpretative controversies from any of the suggested explanations. Behind ritualistic references to well-known rules and principles of international law (the content of which remains a constant object of dispute), legal practice has increasingly resorted to solving disputes by a contextual criterion—an effort towards an equitable balance. Though this has seemed to work well, the question arises as to whether such practice can be adequately explained in terms of the Rule of Law.

A. SOVEREIGNTY

There is a body of doctrine which addresses itself to the questions: what are the character and normative consequences of statehood? It deals with such themes as the acquisition and loss of statehood, the justification and extent (limits) of territorial sovereignty, the rights of states, the delimitation of competing jurisdictions, etc. The rhetorical importance of this doctrine has varied, but its urgency within the liberal doctrine remains unchallenged. In some ways, sovereignty doctrine plays a role analogous to that played by individual liberty in legitimation discourse. It explains a critical character of legal subjects and sets down basic conditions within which the relations between legal subjects must be organized.

The character and consequences of sovereign statehood might, however, be explained from different perspectives. One explanation holds sovereignty as basic in the sense that it is simply imposed upon the law by the world of facts. Sovereignty and together with it a set of territorial rights and duties are something external to the law, something the law must recognize but which it cannot control. I shall call this the "pure fact view."[31] Another explanation holds sovereignty and everything associated with it as one part of the law's substance, determined and constantly determinable within the legal system, just like any other norms. This might be called the "legal" view.[32]

Normative argument within the different realism of sovereignty doctrine uses the contrast between these explanations to constitute itself. One party argues in terms of pure facts (of effectiveness, for example) while the other makes its point by reference to a criterion external to facts (general recognition, for example). But neither position is sustainable alone. Relying on the pure fact of power is apologist.[33] Relying on a criterion independent of effectiveness is both abstract and

30 Compare also Kennedy, *supra* note 16.

31 G. Jellinek, *Allgemeine Staatslehre* (3. Aufl.) (1925) 337, 364–67 and, e.g., Korowicz, "Some Present Problems of Sovereignty," 112 *RCDI* (1961) 102.

32 See, e.g., Verdross, *supra* note 17, at 35 and, e.g., Rousseau, "Principes de droit international public," 93 *RCDI* (1958) 394.

33 See, e.g., H. Lauterpacht, *International Law* (Vol. I) (1979) 341–44.

question-begging.[34] It is question-begging as it merely raises the further question about whose interpretation of the criterion or its application should be given precedence. A defendable argument seems compelled to make both points: it must assume that sovereign rights are somehow matters of pure fact as well as of some criterion external to those facts themselves.

The development of the positions of Norway and Denmark during the *Eastern Greenland* case (1933) illustrates this. Originally, Norway based its rights to the disputed territory on its effective occupation. Relying on the views of other states would have violated Norway's sovereign equality. Denmark based its own claim on general recognition and challenged Norwegian title on the absence of such recognition. As the title was to be valid *erga omnes*, it could not be dependent on Norway's acts. In their subsequent arguments both states replied assuming their adversary's first position: Norway argued that its occupation was sanctioned by a generally recognized rule which based title on occupation. Denmark aimed to show that Norway in fact could not have occupied the territory because it had already been effectively occupied by Denmark.[35]

Neither claim could be preferred by simply preferring the "pure fact" or the "criterion" of general recognition because both states argued both points. Consequently, the Court affirmed both argumentative tracks. To support its view that Denmark had sovereignty it argued from Danish occupation as well as general recognition and denied both in respect of Norway.[36] To reach this conclusion, the Court had to make interpretations about the facts (effective occupation) as well as the law (the extent of general recognition) which, however, were external to the applicable facts and the law and which were difficult to justify against Norway's conflicting sovereign interpretation of them. The crucial point in the judgement was the Court's discussion of the famous "Ihlen declaration," which allowed the Court to protect Norwegian sovereignty by denying its possession in reference to the construction according to which Norway itself had already "recognized" Danish sovereignty in Eastern Greenland.[37]

The same structure can be detected in all territorial disputes. In each, the "pure fact" and "legal" approaches dissolve into each other in a way which makes it impossible for the court or tribunal to solve the case by merely choosing one over the other. There are two difficulties. First, the need to make both points loses the initial sense of both: the pure fact view was premised on the assumption that the law follows from what facts say. The legal view assumed that the sense of facts was to be determined by rules. In argument, both points claim to defer, or *overrule* each other. To assume that they could be valid (determining) simultaneously makes both meaningless. Second, that the "pure fact" and the "legal" approaches show themselves indeterminate compels the decision-maker to look closer into the relevant "facts" and the relevant "legal" criterion. Decisions turn on contextual interpretations about the facts and the law—interpretations which, by definition, can no longer be justified by reference to those facts or criteria themselves.

Late modern practice of solving sovereignty disputes pays hardly more than lip-service to the traditional bases of territorial entitlement. Deciding such questions is now thought of in

34 See, e.g., *Island of Palmas* case, II *UNRIAA* at 839, 843–46.

35 These points are belaboured at length in the written proceedings. See PCIJ, *Eastern Greenland* case, Ser.C.62 and C.63 and the parties' oral arguments, C.66. For more detailed analysis, see Koskenniemi, *supra* note 12, at 251–53.

36 PCIJ, *Eastern Greenland* case, Ser.A.53 at 45–62.

37 *Id.* at 64–74.

terms of trying to establish the most equitable solution.[38] The point is that the various interpretations and pragmatic considerations, as well as the final appreciation of the equity of the proposed solution, cannot be justified by reference to legal rules. On the contrary, recourse to the kind of justice involved in such appreciation can only mean, from the perspective of the Rule of Law, capitulation to arbitrariness or undermining the principle of the subjectivity of value, required in the pursuit of a Rule of Law. Let me take another example. It was often argued that the existence of states is a "matter of fact" and that "recognition" was only "declaratory" and not "constitutive" of statehood. If states were created by an external act of recognition, this would introduce for existing states a political right to decide which entities shall enjoy the status of legal subjects. This conflicts with the principles of self-determination and equality—both following from the rejection of a natural law.[39]

Yet, even such an apparently realistic and democratic view needed to assume the existence of some kind of pre-existing criteria whereby it could be ascertained whether statehood was present in some entity or not. The problem was never really that anyone would have seriously contested that the emergence of states was a factual, sociological process. The problem was—and remains—that people view the normative consequences of social process through different criteria and arrive at irreconcilable conclusions even when using the same criteria.

There is, though, a measure of common agreement on a matter as important as statehood. But it has very little to do with factual power or effectiveness. Rhodesia, Transkei and Taiwan were never regarded as states, whereas Tuvalu and Monaco were. But to explain these "anomalies"—as well as other apparently puzzling cases of statehood—simply by reference to the "constitutive" view is equally unsatisfactory. The original objections against the imperialistic character of this theory remain valid. Lauterpacht's middle-of-the-road position about a *duty* to recognize when the legal criteria have been fulfilled remains question-begging:[40] if a state refuses to recognize an entity because it says that this fulfilled the relevant criteria, there is little point to insist upon the existence of the duty. The matter turns on the interpretation of either the factual circumstances or the content of the relevant norm. The real problem is that it is impossible, within liberal premises, to overrule any participant interpretation in a legitimate fashion. Under those premises norms are "auto-interpretative" and each state must be presumed to have the liberty to interpret the sense of factual events around it.[41]

These anomalies of statehood as well as the resurgence of the time-honoured practice of non-recognition after the *Namibia* Opinion (1971) suggest that the attainment of statehood territorial title—at least if the matter is of some importance—has a relationship to what is decided externally.[42] But they also show that to believe that such decision can be understood as "following a rule" requires either a rule or an imagination so flexible that neither the legal nor the pure fact view can take much credit in trying to establish itself upon it.

If the presence of the quality of sovereignty in some entity is difficult to explain in terms of pure

38 See ICJ, *Burkina Faso—Mali Frontier* case, Reports (1986) 567–68 (para. 28) and *infra* note 47.

39 The classic remains Ti-Chiang Chen, *The International Law of Recognition* (1951). See also Kato, "Recognition in International Law: Some Thoughts on Traditional Theory, Attitudes of and Practice by African States," 10 *IJIL* (1970) 299–323.

40 H. Lauterpacht, *Recognition in International Law* (1948).

41 For a useful restatement of this (liberal) point, see Bin Cheng, Custom, "The Future of General State Practice in a Divided World," in Macdonald, Johnston (eds.) *The Structure and Process of International Law*, at 513, 519–23.

42 ICJ, *Namibia* case, Reports (1971) 51, 54 (paras. 112, 117, 119).

facts or legal rules, it is even more trying to do this in respect of the consequences of sovereignty. That the boundaries of domestic jurisdiction are shifting, and that "sovereignty" has seemed compatible with a state's hermetic isolation as well as extensive integration, indicates that whatever rights or liberties this quality may entail is, as the Permanent Court of International Justice observed, a "relative matter"—dependent on the content of the state's obligations at any given time.[43] In other words nothing determinate follows from sovereignty as a matter of "pure fact"—on the contrary, the content of sovereignty seems determinable only once we know what obligations the state has.

Lawyers adopting the "legal view" sometimes believe that the above conclusion fully vindicates their position. "Sovereignty" is not a matter outside but within the law, a convenient shorthand for the rights, liberties and competences which the law has allocated to the state—and which can be retrieved at any time.[44] To solve a sovereignty dispute it suffices only to look at the body of legal rules, and see if the state has the capacity which it claims by a legislative allocation.

The problem with such a conclusion, however, is that on most areas of state conduct no definite legislative act can be found which would establish the state's competence to act in some particular way. Moreover, and here is another paradox, the most important rules of general application seem to be precisely those rules which lay down the right of exclusive jurisdiction, self-determination, non-intervention and—sovereignty. It is not only that if sovereignty were reduced to a non-normative abstraction, then international law would appear as a huge *lacuna*, we would also lack a connected explanation, an interpretative principle to solve differences of opinion about the content or application of the few particular rules which we could then discern.

In most areas of non-treaty-related state conduct, specific obligations are, or can be, plausibly made to seem either ambiguous or lacking. In such case, the state's sovereignty—its initial liberty—will reemerge as a normative principle in its own right: in the absence of clear prohibitions, the state must be assumed free. This principle—the *Lotus* principle[45]—is not only a convenient rule of thumb. It encapsulates the assumption that the mere fact of statehood has a normative sense (right of self-determination) and that in the absence of unambiguous legislative prohibitions any attempt to overrule the liberty inherent in statehood can only appear as illegitimate constraint.

The difficulty with the *Lotus* principle is twofold. First, all the rules and principles are more or less indeterminate in their content. If the mere fact of the existence of differing interpretations were sufficient to trigger the presumption of liberty, then the binding force of most rules would seem an illusion. The even more important difficulty is useless if the case involves a *conflict* of liberties. But if it is assumed—as is inevitable if the idea of a material natural law is discarded—that the liberties of one state are delimited by those of another, then any dispute about the rights or obligations of two or more states can be conceptualized in terms of a conflict of their liberties and, consequently, would not seem soluble by simply preferring "liberty"—because we would not know which state's liberty to prefer.

At that point, legal practice breaks from the argumentative cycle by recourse to equity—an undifferentiated sense of justice.

Continental shelf disputes are one example. The International Court of Justice (ICJ), as is

43 PCIJ, *Nationality Decrees* case, Ser.B.4. at 24.

44 Schwarzenberger, "The Forms of Sovereignty," 10 *CLP* (1957) 284; Hart, *supra* note 19, at 218.

45 PCIJ, *Lotus* case, Ser.A.10 at 30. See further Koskenniemi, *supra* note 12, at 220–23.

well-known, started out with the assumption that the entitlement to continental shelf was a matter of giving effect to the coastal state's *ab initio* and *ipso facto* right. It was not a matter of "abstract justice" but of (objective) fact.[46] But this view has proved unhelpful. Which facts are relevant—the decisive problem—is decided by the Court *ad hoc* and it is not inscribed in some transcendental code *ex ante*. Later delimitations have even ceased paying lip-service to the *ipso facto/ab initio* theory and seen "arriving at an equitable result" as its proper task.[47] The history of the argument in continental shelf cases is the history of the Court first noting the lack, or at least the ambiguity of the relevant rule, it then making appeal to a pure fact (*ipso facto*) view; then abandoning that view (because no "fact" can be normative without an anterior criterion) in favour of a legal view (equity *infra legem*[48] as the correct rule) and the whole cycle ending in the content of that rule being dispersed into justice—a justice which can, under the principle of subjective value and the Rule of Law, only be seen as arbitrary.[49]

Transboundary pollution, to take another example, involves the juxtaposition of the freedoms of the source-state and the target-state: on the one hand, there is the former's sovereign right to exploit its natural resources in accordance with its own environmental policies; on the other hand, there is the victim's sole right to decide what acts shall take place in its territories.[50] The former's liberty to pursue economically beneficial uses of its territory is contrasted with the latter's liberty to enjoy a pure environment. The conflict is insoluble by simply preferring "liberty," or some right inscribed in the very notion of sovereignty. Balancing seems inevitable in order to reach a decision.[51]

A similar structure manifests itself everywhere within sovereignty doctrine. While sovereignty immunity is usually stated either in terms of the (pure fact of) sovereignty or a systematic necessity for international communication, legal practice tends to construct the foreign sovereign's exemption from local jurisdiction by balancing the two sovereigns' interests vis-à-vis each other.[52] The same seems true in cases dealing with the determination of the allowable reach of a state's extraterritorial jurisdiction.[53] The law on uses of international watercourses[54] and fishery resources,[55] as well as conflicts concerning foreign investment between the home state and the host state,[56] entails the drawing of a boundary between the two sovereigns, a determination of the extent of their sovereign liberty. In the absence of any determinate rules, and being unable to prefer one sovereign over another, legal

46 ICJ, *North Sea Continental Shelf* cases, Reports (1969) 22–23 (paras. 19–20).

47 ICJ, *Tunisia-Libya Continental Shelf* case, Reports (1982) 59 (para. 70); *Gulf of Maine* case, Reports (1984) 312 (para. 155); *Libya-Malta Continental Shelf* case, Reports (1985) 38–39 (para. 49). See further Koskenniemi, *supra* note 12, at 223–32.

48 ICJ, *North Sea Continental Shelf* cases, Reports (1969) 20–22 (paras. 15–20).

49 For this criticism, see, e.g., Gros. *diss.op.* ICJ, *Tunisia-Libya Continental Shelf case*, Reports (1982) 151–56 and *Gulf of Maine* case, Reports (1984) 378–80.

50 See Principle 21, UN Conference on the Human Environment, Stockholm 5–16 June 1972, UN Doc. A/CONF.48/14.

51 See, e.g., Koskenniemi, "International Pollution in the System of International Law," 17 *Oikeustiede-Jurisprudentia* (1984) 152–64; Lammers, "Balancing the Equities: International Environmental Law," *RCDI Coll.* (1984) 153–65.

52 Crawford, "International Law and Foreign Sovereigns, Distinguishing Immune Transactions," 54 *BYIL* (1983) 114–18.

53 Meng, "Völkerrechtliche Zulässigkeit und Grenzen der wirtschaftsverwaltungsrechtlichen Hoheitsakte mit Auslandswirkung," 44 *ZaOeRV* (1984) 675–783; Lowe, "The Problem of Extraterritorial Jurisdiction: Economic Sovereignty and the Search for a Solution," 34 *ICLQ* (1985) 730.

54 Schwebel, "Third Report on the Non-Navigational Uses of International Watercourses," *YILC* (1982/II/1) 75–100.

55 *Fisheries Jurisdiction* cases, ICJ Reports (1974) 30 (paras. 69–70).

56 *The LIAMCO Award*, 20 ILM (1981) 76–77 (paras. 150–51).

practice has turned to equity in order to justify the delimitation of the two sovereignties vis-à-vis each other.

The substance of the law under sovereignty doctrines has dispersed into a generalized call for equitable solutions or "balancing" whenever conflicts arise. Standard academic justifications of state rights, either as a consequence of the pure fact of statehood or as laid down in legislative enactments, have no application. Nor can they have application because neither "facts" nor "rules" are self-evident in the way Enlightenment lawyers once believed. The facts which are assumed to establish title do not appear "automatically" but are the result of choosing a criterion from which facts may be invested with normative significance.[57] But rules, too, are always subject to interpretation. In order to link itself to something tangible, interpretation should refer back to some kind of facts. To establish the sense of facts, we must take the perspective of a rule; to decide interpretative controversies about the rule, we must—under the social conception—look at facts. Hence the late modern silence about theoretical justifications and the leap to *ad hoc* compromise.

B. SOURCES

Despite its original emphasis on actual power, the doctrine of sovereignty seemed unworkable because of the abstract and arbitrary way in which its normative content was determined. It is possible to make a fresh start and imagine that international law might just as well be described not as consequence of statehood but through a set of normative criteria—sources—for law-creation and identification.

Not surprisingly, sources doctrine is riddled with dualisms which express in different ways the conflicting pull of the demands for concreteness and normativity. The very doctrine is often understood from two perspectives: as a description of the social processes whereby states create law (concreteness) and as a methodology for verifying the law's content independently of political opinions (normativity). By integrating both explanations, sources doctrine can maintain its apparent objectivity. On the one hand, something would not be law merely as a result of its content but as a result of a social process. On the other hand, the existence of sources as a constraining methodology creates the needed distance between it and whatever states might will at any one moment.

Though there is no major disagreement among international lawyers about the correct enumeration of sources (treaties, custom, general principles), the rhetorical force of sources ("binding force") is explained from contrasting perspectives. Their importance is sometimes linked with their capacity to reflect state will (consensualism). At other times, such binding force is linked with the relationship of sources arguments with what is "just," "reasonable," "in accordance with good faith," or some other non-consensual metaphor.

Standard disputes about the content or application of international legal norms use the contradiction between consent and justice based explanations. One party argues in terms of consent, the other in terms of what is just (reasonable, etc.). But neither argument is fully justifiable alone. A purely consensual argument cannot ultimately justify the application of a norm against non-consenting states (apologism). An argument relying only on a notion of justice violates the principle of the subjectivity of value (utopianism). Therefore, they must rely on each other. Arguments about consent must explain

57 "In the realm of law there is no fact in itself, no immediately evident fact; there are only facts ascertained by the competent authorities in a procedure determined by law." H. Kelsen, *Principles of International Law* (ed. and rev. by R.M. Tucker) (1966) 388.

the relevance and content of consent in terms of what seems just. Arguments about justice must demonstrate their correctness by reference to what states have consented to. Because these movements (consent to justice; justice to consent) make the originally opposing positions look the same, no solution can be made by simply choosing one. A solution now seems possible only by either deciding what is it that states "really" will or what the content of justice "really" is. Neither question, however, is answerable on the premises of the Rule of Law.[58]

For the modern lawyer, it is very difficult to envisage, let alone to justify, a law which would divorce itself from what states think or will to be the law. The apparent necessity of consensualism seems grounded in the very criticism of natural norms as superstition. Yet, the criticisms against full consensualism—its logical circularity, its distance from experience, its inherent apologism—are well-known.[59] Consensualism cannot justify the application of a norm against a state which opposes such application unless it creates distance between the norm and the relevant state's momentary will. It has been explained, for example, that though law emerges from consent, it does not need every state's consent all the time, that a general agreement, a *volonté générale* or a *Vereinbarung* is sufficient to apply the norm.[60]

But these explanations violate the principle of sovereign equality—they fail to explain why a state should be bound by what another state wills. This can, of course, be explained from some concept of social necessity. But in such case we have already moved away from pure consensualism and face the difficulty of explaining the legal status of the assumed necessity and why it should support one norm instead of another.

A more common strategy is to explain that the state has originally consented (by means of recognition, acquiescence, by not protesting or by "tacitly" agreeing) although it now denies it has. Such an argument is extremely important in liberal legitimation discourse. It allows defending social constraint in a consensual fashion while allowing the application of constraint against a state which denies it consent.[61] But even this argument fails to be convincing because it must ultimately explain itself either in a fully consensual or fully non-consensual way and thereby become vulnerable to the objections about apologism or utopianism.

Why should a state be bound by an argument according to which it has consented, albeit "tacitly"? If the reason is stated in terms of respecting its own consent, then we have to explain why we can know better than the state itself what it has consented to. Even consensualists usually concede that such knowledge is not open to external observers. But even if it were possible to "know better," such an argument is not really defensible within the premises of the Rule of Law. It contains the unpleasant implication that we could no longer rely on the expressed will of the legal subject. It would lose the principal justification behind democratic legislation and justify the establishment of a Leviathan—the one who knows best what everyone "really" wills. It is a strategy for introducing authoritarian opinions in democratic disguise.

Tacit consent theorists usually explain that the question is not of "real" but of "presumed" will. But what then allows the application of the presumption against a state denying that it had ever consented to anything like it? At this point the tacit consent lawyer must move from

58 See also Kennedy, *supra* note 16, at 11–107.

59 Koskenniemi, *supra* note 12, at 270–73.

60 For the classic, see H. Triepel, *Völkerrecht und Landesrecht* (1899) 27, 51–53.

61 See, e.g., the argument in A. Bleckmann, *Grundprobleme und Methoden des Völkerrechts* (1982) 81, 184–89. On the tacit consent construction generally, see Koskenniemi, *supra* note 12, at 284–91.

consensualism to non-consensualism. Tacit consent—or the presumption of consent—binds because it is "just" or in accordance with reasonableness or good faith, or it protects legitimate expectations or the like.[62] Now the difficulty lies in defending the assumed non-consensual position. But under the principle of subjective value, justice cannot be discussed in a non-arbitrary way.[63] Were this otherwise, the Rule of Law would be pointless if not harmful. One might, of course, say that a notion of reasonableness is justified because the state in question has itself accepted it. But this defence will re-emerge the problem of how it is possible to oppose a consensual justification against a state denying its validity. And so on, ad infinitum.

In the *Gulf of Maine* case (1984), Canada argued that the United States was bound to a certain line of delimitation as it had not protested against its *de facto* use. Relying on absence of protest reflected, Canada explained, on the one hand, US consent to be bound and, on the other hand, gave expression to good faith and equity. It argued in terms of consent as well as justice. The Chamber of the Court accepted both explanations. It started out with the latter, non-consensual one. What is common to acquiescence and estoppel is that: "... both follow from the fundamental principle of good faith and equity."[64]

Had it followed this understanding, it should, because not *all* silence creates norms, have had to enter a discussion of whether or not the conditions of good faith or equity were present to bind the United States now. But there was no such discussion. This is understandable, as arguing from non-consensual justice seems so subjective. Instead, it moved to a consensual understanding of relying on absence of protest and went on to discuss whether the "Hoffmann letter" was evidence of United States acceptance of the Canadian equidistance. It was not: "... facts invoked by Canada do not warrant the conclusion that the US Government thereby recognized the median line ..."[65]

In other words, the United States was not bound because there was no subjective intent to be (regardless of considerations of good faith or equity). How did the Court arrive at this conclusion? This would have been apologist and a violation of Canadian sovereignty. The Chamber's conclusion did not concern lack of "real" intent but rather of "constructive" US intent. On what principles was that construction based? Mainly on inconsistency in the facts and on the low governmental status of the authorities involved.[66] But what justified this choice of relevant facts and their ensuing interpretation? What made the Court's construction better than the Canadian one? The argument stops here. The principles of construction were left undiscussed.

In theory, the Chamber could have used two principles of construction: 1) a construction is justified if it corresponds to intent; 2) a construction is justified if it reflects non-consensual justice. These are exclusive justifications. But neither was open to the Chamber. The former was excluded by the previous argument which ruled out the possibility of knowing real US intent and using it against Canada. The latter was excluded because it would have involved arguing in a fully non-consensual way against Canadian non-consensual justifications. This would have assumed the correctness of an objective justice and would have conflicted with the Chamber's previous refusal to think of acquiescence-estoppel in a fully non-consensual way. The Chamber simply

62 See, e.g., J.P. Muller, *Vertrauenschutz im Völkerrecht* (1970); A. Martin, *L'estoppel en droit international public* (1979).
63 "[L]e principe de bonne foi est un principe moral et rien de plus." E. Zoller, *La bonne foi en droit international public* (1977) 345.
64 *Gulf of Maine* case, ICJ Reports (1984) 305 (para. 130).
65 *Id.* at 307 (para. 138).
66 *Id.*

took another interpretation of US conduct than Canada. Why it was better was not discussed as it could not have been discussed. The decision was, on its own premises, undetermined by legal argument.

An identical argumentative structure is present in treaty interpretation. Particular interpretations are traced back either to party will or to some idea of good faith, reasonableness, etc.[67] Because "real" party will cannot be identified and justifiably opposed to a party denying such intent, and because the content of what is a just interpretation cannot be determined in a legal way, late modern doctrines usually concede the aesthetic, impressionistic character of the interpretative process.[68] Controversial points about party will clash against equally controversial points about the justice of particular interpretations.

In the case *Concerning the Interpretation of the Algerian Declaration of 19 January 1981*, the Iran-United States Claims Tribunal was to decide whether Article II of the Claims Settlement Declaration included a right for Iran to press claims against United States' nationals. The majority held that it could not be so interpreted. A "clear formulation" of that Article excluded Iranian claims from the Tribunal's jurisdiction. This clear formulation had authority because it was clearest evidence of Party consent.[69] The minority argued that a literal construction failed to give effect to the settlement's reciprocal character. According to the minority, reciprocity had been the very basis on which Iran had entered the agreement. By excluding reciprocity, the majority had violated Iranian consent and unjustifiably preferred the justice of literality to the justice of reciprocity.[70] Both sides invoke consent and justice but are unable to address each others' views directly. Neither side argues on the basis of "real consent." But while the majority sees consent manifested in the text, the minority sees consent in reciprocity. Both sides say their interpretative principle is better as it better reflects consent. But deciding the dispute on these arguments would require a means of knowing consent independently of its manifestations—a possibility excluded as reference was made to manifestations because of the assumption that real consent could not be known. Moreover, neither can the two sides argue that their justice—the justice of literality or the justice of reciprocity—is better without arguing from a theory of justice which seems indefensible under the Rule of Law. Ultimately, both interpretations are unargued. A doctrine which excludes arguments from "knowing better" and natural justice has no means to decide on the superiority of conflicting interpretations.

Attempts to explain why states should be bound by unilateral declarations meet with similar problems. In the first place, as the ICJ observed in the *Nuclear Tests* case (1974) such statements might be held binding "(w)hen it is the intention of the state making the declaration that it should become bound according to its terms."[71] However, their binding force cannot be fully consensual because then the state could be freed simply by a further act of will. Therefore, the Court also noted that "(o)ne of the principles governing the creation and performance of legal obligations ... is the principle of good faith ... Thus interested states may take cognizance of unilateral declarations and place confidence in them, and are entitled to require that the obligation thus created be respected."[72]

67 For this contrast generally, see, e.g., Zoller, *supra* note 63, at 205–44.
68 Sur, *supra* note 13. See also McDougal, *supra* note 23 at 149–57.
69 Iran–United States Claims Tribunal, "Interpretation of the Algerian Declaration of 19th January 1981," 62 *ILR* (1982) 599–600.
70 *Id.* at 603–06.
71 *Nuclear Tests* cases, ICJ Reports (1974) 267 (para. 43).
72 *Id.* at 268 (para. 46).

Now the declaring state is bound regardless of its will, by the simple fact of the statement and others' reliance.

The necessity of making both arguments seems evident. The Court's first—consensual—argument justified holding France bound by its statements. But it was also threatening because it implied that France could modify or terminate this obligation at will. This would violate the wills and sovereignty of the Applicants (Australia and New Zealand). The second—non-consensual—argument about good faith and legitimate expectations was needed to protect the latter. The decision was consensualist and non-consensualist at the same time. It allowed basing the applicable norm on protecting the sovereignty of each state involved. Simultaneously, it seemed to give effect to what justice seemed to require.

But the decision remains also vulnerable from each perspective. How could the Court base its norm on French consent in face of French denial of such consent? It leaves unexplained how it can protect the Applicants' reliance, as they denied having relied. And it leaves unexplained its theory of justice which says that these statements and actions in these circumstances bind because that is in accordance with good faith.

The structure, importance and weaknesses of tacit consent is nowhere more visible than in the orthodox argument about customary international law.

According to this argument, binding custom exists if there is a material practice of states to that effect and that practice is motivated by the belief that it is obligatory. This "two-element theory" gives expression to the principle of liberal sociology for which the meaning—law or not law—of social action lies neither in its external appearance nor in what someone thinks about but is a combination of the two: an external (material) and an internal (psychological) element.[73] The function of the former element is to ensure that custom can be ascertained without having to rely on states' momentary, political views. The point of the latter is to distinguish custom from coercion.

The problem with the two-element theory is that neither element can be identified independently of the other. Hence, they cannot be used to prevent the appearance of Mr. Hyde in each other.

Modern lawyers have rejected fully materialistic explanations of custom as apologist, incapable of distinguishing between factual constraint and law. If the possibility is excluded that this distinction can be made by the justice of the relevant behaviour, then it can only be made by reference to the psychological element, the *opinio juris*. But, as many students of the ICJ jurisprudence have shown, there are no independently applicable criteria for ascertaining the presence of the *opinio juris*. The ICJ has simply inferred its presence or absence from the extent and intensity of the material practice it has studied.[74] Moreover, it does not even seem possible to assume the existence of such criteria and that the opinion thus received could be opposed to a non-consenting state. That would be an argument about knowing better. In other words, though it seems possible to distinguish "custom" from what is actually effective only by recourse to what states believe, such beliefs do not seem capable of identification regardless of what is actually effective.

One might try to avoid the above circularity by assuming that some types of behaviour are by their character—"intrinsically"—such as to

73 See Hart, *supra* note 19, at 91. For discussion, see Koskenniemi, "The Normative Force of Habit: International Custom and Social Theory," 1 *Finnish Yearbook of International Law* (forthcoming).

74 See, e.g., M. Sørensen, *Les sources du droit international* (1946) 108–11; Virally, "The Sources of International Law," in Sørensen (ed.), *Manual of Public International Law* (1968) 134–35; H. Günther, *Zur Entstehung von Völkergewohnheitsrecht* (1970) 70. See further, Koskenniemi, *supra* note 12, at 380–81.

generate (or not to generate) normative custom. But attempts to single out lists of such types have been unsuccessful. A "flexible" concept of material practice has emerged: any act or statement may count as custom-generating practice if only the states wish so.[75] (Indeed, any other conclusion would manifest an illegitimate naturalism and violate the principles of liberal sociology: it would fail to have regard to the "internal aspect.") Using this criterion (what it is that states wish), however, would assume that we can know the opinion independently of the act in which it is expressed. But this possibility was already excluded by our previous argument about the need to look at material practice in the first place. Indeed, were it so that we could know state intentions regardless of what states do, the whole two-element theory would become unnecessary: we could simply apply those intentions. Custom would coalesce with (informal) agreement. (In which case, of course, we would face the difficulty of having to interpret the content embedded in any such agreement by further reference to the parties' "real" wills or to some notion of justice, as explained above.)

Customary law doctrine remains indeterminate because it is circular. It assumes behaviour to be evidence of states' intentions (*opinio juris*) and the latter to be evidence of what behaviour is relevant as custom. To avoid apologism (relying on the state's present will), it looks at the psychological element from the perspective of the material; to avoid utopianism (making the distinction between binding and nonbinding usages by reference to what is just), it looks at the material element from the perspective of the psychological. It can occupy neither position in a permanent way without becoming vulnerable to criticism compelled by the other. The very assumptions behind customary international law provide the mechanism for its self-destruction.

For late modern international practice the standard theory is increasingly a camouflage for what is really an attempt to understand custom in terms of a bilateralized equity. The ICJ, for instance, has always been somewhat ambiguous as to the character of the rules of non-written law which it has discerned. The Court's argument about the relevant custom in the *Anglo-Norwegian Fisheries* (1951) as well as *Fisheries Jurisdiction* (1974) cases already looked upon the matter more in terms of the relevant interest at stake than trying to find some general rule to "apply."[76] The several maritime boundary cases further extended this move. The judgement in the *U.S. Military and Paramilitary Activities* case (1986) did not even seriously attempt to justify its four customary rules—non-use of force, non-intervention, respect for sovereignty and especially the relevant humanitarian rules—in terms of material practice and the opinio juris.[77]

Many have been dissatisfied with the modern strategy of arguing every imaginable non-written standard as "custom." Sir Robert Jennings, among others, has noted that what we tend to call custom: "is not only not customary law: it does not even faintly resemble a customary law."[78] But if a non-written standard is not arguable in terms of material practices or beliefs relating to such practices then it can only exist as natural law—being defensible only by reference to the political importance of its content. In fact, much ICJ practice in the relevant respect remains *ex cathedra*: the Court has "instituted a system of decision-making in which the conclusion reached is determined by the application of rules largely

75 See, e.g., Ferrari-Bravo, "La coutume internationale dans la pratique des Etats," 192 *RCDI* (1985) 243, 261 and Koskenniemi, *supra* note 12, at 383–84.
76 *Anglo-Norwegian* case, ICJ Reports (1951) 133. *Fisheries Jurisdiction* cases, Reports (1974) 30–33 (paras. 69–79).
77 *US Military and Paramilitary Activities* case, ICJ Reports (1986) 97–115 (paras. 183–220).
78 Jennings, "The Identification of International Law," in Cheng (ed.), *International Law, Teaching and Practice* (1982) 5.

treated as self-evident."[79] To be sure, often there is consensus on such rules, for instance, on the "elementary considerations of humanity" invoked by the Court in the *Corfu Channel* case (1949). But the problem is clearly less to explain why people who agree are bound than why also those should be who do not and how one should argue if interpretative controversies arise.

V. The Politics of International Law

The idea of an international Rule of Law has been a credible one because to strive for it implies no commitment regarding the content of the norms thereby established or the character of the society advanced. It was possible for 19th-century European powers to start thinking of their relationships in terms of legal rules because they formalized inter-sovereign relationships and no sovereign needed to feel that his substantive policies were excluded by them [sic]. It was possible for the UN General Assembly to accept by consensus the Declaration on the "Decade for International Law" for precisely those same reasons. This is strikingly highlighted by the fact that the Decade contained no substantive programme. The declaration merely calls for the promotion of respect for the principles of international law and the peaceful settlement of disputes and for the encouragement of the development and dissemination of international law. For what purpose the law was to be put or what kinds of rules it should promote is not addressed by it.

Modern international law is an elaborate framework for deferring substantive resolution elsewhere: into further procedure, interpretation, equity, context, and so on. The 1982 Law of the Sea Convention is the typical example: in place of a list of do's and don't's it establishes a framework for delimiting sovereign powers and allocating jurisdictions—assuming that the substantive problems of the uses of the sea can be best dealt with through allocating decision-power elsewhere, into context and usually by reference to "equitable principles."[80] The success of international law depends on this formality; this refusal to set down determining rules or ready-made resolutions to future conflict. Though there is a distinctly legal "process"—and in this sense a relatively autonomous and coherent system which can be abstracted in academic treatises—there are no determining legal standards. Let me explain this somewhat schematically.

The Rule of Law constitutes an attempt to provide communal life without giving up individual autonomy. Communal life is, of course, needed to check individualism from leading either into anarchy or tyranny. Individualism is needed because otherwise it would remain objectionable for those who feel that the kind of community provided by it does not meet their political criteria. From their perspective, the law's communitarian pretensions would turn out as totalitarian apologies.[81]

The law aims to fulfil its double task by becoming formal: by endorsing neither particular communitarian ideals nor particular sovereign policies. Or, conversely, an acceptable legal rule, argument or doctrine is one which can explain itself both from the perspective of enhancing community (because it would otherwise seem apologist) as well as safeguarding sovereignty (because its implications would otherwise remain totalitarian). The problem is that as soon as any of these justifications are advanced to support *some particular kind of communal existence or*

79 Kearney, "Sources of Law and the International Court of Justice," in Gross (ed.), *The Future of the International Court of Justice* (Vol. I) (1976) 653.

80 See generally, Allott, "Power Sharing in the Law of the Sea," 77 *AJIL* (1983)1–30; Kennedy, *supra* note 16, at 201–45.

81 See further the seminal article by Kennedy, "The Structure of Blackstone's Commentaries," 18 *Buffalo L.R.* (1979) 205.

some determined limit for sovereign autonomy, they are vulnerable from an opposing substantive perspective. So, while an advocate justifies his preferred substantive outcome by its capacity to support community, it becomes simultaneously possible for his counterpart—not sharing the same communal ideal—to challenge the very justification as totalitarian. Correspondingly, a rule, principle or solution justified by recourse to the way it protects sovereignty may—for someone drawing the limits of "sovereignty" differently—be objected as furthering egoism and anarchy.

Take the case of transfrontier pollution. Noxious fumes flow from state A into the territory of state B. State A refers to its "sovereign right to use its natural resources in accordance with its national policies." State B argues that A has to put a stop to the pollution. It interprets A's position to be an egoistic one while it makes its own argument seem communitarian. It might refer to a norm of "non-harmful use of territory," for example, and justify this by reference to analogies from rules concerning international rivers and natural resources as well as precedents and General Assembly resolutions.[82]

State A can now retort by saying that norms cannot be opposed to it in such a totalitarian fashion. A is bound only by norms which it has accepted. It has never accepted the analogies drawn by B. This would force B either to argue that its preferred norm binds irrespective of acceptance—in which case it stands to lose as its argument would seem utopian—or to change ground so as to make its position seem protective of sovereignty as well. State B might now argue that the pollution violates its own freedom and constitutes an interference in its internal affairs as Australia did in the *Nuclear Tests* case.[83] B's position would now seem both communitarian (in respect to A) and individualistic (in respect to B itself).

To counter this last argument by B, A needs to make a communitarian point. It may argue that there is a norm about friendly neighbourliness, for example such as that observed in the *Lake Lanoux* case (1957), which requires that states tolerate minor inconveniences which result from legitimate uses of neighbouring states' territories.[84] B cannot demand complete territorial integrity. A's position is now both individualistic (in respect of A itself) and communitarian (in respect of B).

The argument could be continued. Both parties could support the communitarian strand in their positions by referring to equity, general principles and the like, to deny the autonomy (egoism) of the other. And they could support the sovereignty-based arguments by further emphasis on their independence, consent, territorial integrity, self-determination, etc. to counter their adversary's communitarian (totalitarian) arguments. As a result, the case cannot be decided by simply preferring autonomy to community or vice-versa. Both arguments support both positions. The case cannot be solved by reference to any of the available concepts (sovereignty, non-harmful use of territory, territorial integrity, independence, good neighbourliness, equity, etc.) as each of the concepts may be so construed as to support either one of the claims. And the constructions have no legally determined preference. A court could say that one of the positions is better as a matter of equity, for example. Or it might attempt to "balance" the claims. But in justifying its conception of what is equitable, the court will have to assume a theory of justice—a

82 For both arguments, see Principle 21 of the Stockholm Declaration, *supra* note 50 and further Koskenniemi, *supra* note 51, at 100–03.

83 *Nuclear Tests* cases, ICJ Pleadings I at 14.

84 *Lake Lanoux* case, XII UNRIAA at 316.

theory, however, which it cannot justify by further reference to the legal concepts themselves.

Another example concerns the relations between a foreign investor and the host state. The view which emphasizes individualism, separation and consent may be put forward to support the host state's sovereignty—its right to nationalize the corporation without "full, prompt and adequate" compensation. But the same position can equally well be derived from communitarian points about justice, equality or solidarity or the binding character of the new international economic order, for example.[85] The home state's case may be argued in a similar way, by laying emphasis on that state's freedom, individuality and consent—as expressed in the acquired rights doctrine—or the non-consensually binding character of the *pacta sunt servanda* norm, good faith or other convenient conceptions of justice. To make a choice, the problem-solver should simply have to prefer one of the sovereignties—in which case sovereign equality is overruled—or it should use another theory of justice (or equity) which it cannot, however, justify by reference to the Rule of Law.[86]

The relationship between the principles of self-determination and territorial integrity, both having been enshrined in countless UN General Assembly Resolutions, has remained a puzzle.[87] The problem, as we now can understand it, is that neither of the conflicting principles can be preferred because they are ultimately the same. When a people call for territorial integrity, they call for respect for their identity as a self-determining entity and vice-versa. In order to solve the conflict, one should need an external principle about which types of human association entail this respect and which do not. And this seems to involve arguing on the basis of contested, political views about the type of organization the law should materially aim at.

The formality of international law makes it possible for each state to read its substantive conception of world society as well as its view of the extent of sovereign freedom into legal concepts and categories. This is no externally introduced distortion in the law. It is a necessary consequence of a view which holds that there is no naturally existing "good life," no limit to sovereign freedom which would exist by force of some historical necessity. If this kind of naturalism is rejected—and since the Enlightenment, everybody has had good reason to reject it—then to impose any substantive conception of communal life or limits of sovereignty can appear only as illegitimate constraint—preferring one state's politics to those of another.

It is impossible to make substantive decisions within the law which would imply no political choice. The late modern turn to equity in the different realms of international law is, in this sense, a healthy admission of something that is anyway there: in the end, legitimizing or criticizing state behaviour is not a matter of applying formally neutral rules but depends on what one regards as politically right, or just.

Conclusion

Theorists of the present often explain our postmodern condition as a result of a tragedy of losses. For international lawyers, the Enlightenment signified loss of faith in a natural order among peoples, nations and sovereigns. To contain political

85 Both justifications for this right may be read, for example, from the Charter of Economic Rights and Duties of States, UNGA Res. 3281 (XXIX) (12 December 1974).

86 "A solution therefore should recognize the home state's and the host state's sovereign right to the investment concerned and should endeavour to find an equitable balance between them." Seidi-Hohenveldem, "International Economic Law: General Course on Public International Law," 198 *RCDI* (1986) 54.

87 See UNGA Res. 1514 (XV) 14 December 1960; 2625 (XXV) 24 October 1970 and comments, e.g., in M. Pomerance, *Self-Determination in Law and Practice: The New Doctrine in the United Nations*, 43–47 and *passim*.

subjectivism, 19th- and 20th-century jurists put their faith variably on logic and texts, history and power to find a secure, objective foothold. Each attempt led to disappointment. One's use of logic depended on what political axioms were inserted as the premises. Texts, facts and history were capable of being interpreted in the most varied ways. In making his interpretations the jurist was always forced to rely on conceptual matrices which could no longer be defended by the texts, facts or histories to which they provided meaning. They were—and are—arenas of political struggle.

But the way back to Victoria's or Suarez's unquestioning faith is not open to us. We cannot simply start assuming that politics—justice and equity—could be discussed so that in the end everyone should agree. This teaches us a lesson. Because the world—including lawyers' views about it—is conflictual, any grand design for a "world order" will always remain suspect. Any legal rule, principle or world order project will only seem acceptable when stated in an abstract and formal fashion. When it is applied, it will have overruled some interpretation, some collective experience, and appear apologist.

Social theorists have documented a recent modern turn in national societies away from the Rechtstaat into a society in which social conflict is increasingly met with flexible, contextually determined standards and compromises.[88] The turn away from general principles and formal rules into contextually determined equity may reflect a similar turn in the development of international legal thought and practice. There is every reason to take this turn seriously—though this may mean that lawyers have to re-think their professional self-image. For issues of contextual justice cannot be solved by the application of ready-made rules or principles. Their solution requires venturing into fields such as politics, social and economic casuistry which were formally delimited beyond the point at which legal argument was supposed to stop in order to remain "legal." To be sure, we shall remain uncertain. Resolutions based on political acceptability cannot be made with the kind of certainty post-Enlightenment lawyers once hoped to attain. And yet, it is only by their remaining so which will prevent their use as apologies for tyranny.

27
Roger Cotterrell
"Transnational Communities and the Concept of Law"

This article's concern is with globalisation and the concept of law. It asks: What is the significance of globalisation for legal theory's attempts to analyse the nature of law? Putting matters differently: Is it necessary to conceptualise law in new ways because of changes in the conditions and forms of regulation brought about by processes associated with globalisation?

To invoke "globalisation," however, is always problematic. To refer to it is to indicate a vast and indeterminate topic. Most often the term is taken to encompass a range of (possibly interrelated)

88 See, e.g., R.M. Unger, *Law in Modern Society: Toward a Criticism of Social Theory* (1976); T. O'Hagan, *The End of Law?* (1984).

changes in the nature of (i) transnational economic (commercial, financial, etc.) relations, (ii) population movements between countries, (iii) cultural influences, commitments and bonds, and (iv) processes of global communication. More specifically, it usually refers to claims about the increasing intensity and scale of these relations, movements and processes, and to a sense of the compression of global space and time, so that the transnational effects of events, situations and actions arise more quickly, directly and powerfully than in the past. But the idea of globalisation embraces so much, and entails such huge claims about social and economic forces and the movements of history, that it is hard to grapple with.

It is also widely seen as weighed down with valuations positive or negative.[1] Attempted descriptions of phenomena associated with globalization usually carry with them arguments or assumptions about the causes of these phenomena. They are seen, for example, sometimes as the product of inevitable, almost natural forces (a global "invisible hand"), or as the result of more deliberate political, economic, cultural or other strategies (often seen as imperialistic). And judgments are made about the consequences of globalisation. There are important differences in the typical connotations of Anglo-American usage of "globalisation" and French usage of "*mondialisation*" and the valuations frequently associated with each term (Arnaud 2004, chap. 1)—especially when viewed from within the cultural contexts that inform the other term. A range of other concepts also exists to try to grasp the scale and meaning of transnational developments: for example, "world system" (Wallerstein 1974), "world polity" (Meyer 1987), "world society" (Luhmann 1982), "world risk society" (Beck 1999), "postnational constellation" (Habermas 2001, chap. 4) and "cosmopolitanism" (Habermas 1999, chap. 7), each with its own intellectual orientations, each attempting to grasp aspects of the "freeing up" and "speeding up" of economic, political and cultural influences, with resulting opportunities and dangers.

However, the vast research horizons opened up by the globalization literature are not this article's direct concern. It is not necessary to engage in debates about the nature and meaning of globalisation in order to suggest implications for legal theory of some of the regulatory phenomena associated with it—that is, for theory aiming to explain the general nature of law. We need only recognise the many new or newly prominent kinds of transnational regulation, transnational legal aspirations and transnational regulatory problems to identify conceptual problems that contemporary legal theory faces. By transnational regulation is meant here regulation that applies to (or is intended to affect directly) non-state actors (individuals, groups, corporate bodies) and is not restricted within the jurisdictional limits of a single nation state. Some of this regulation is indisputably law. But some of it raises difficult issues about what "law" should be taken to mean in transnational contexts. How should legal theory understand the field of transnational law?

1. Varieties of Transnational Regulation

Francis Snyder and others have written illuminatingly about what they call "global legal pluralism" (e.g., Snyder 1999; 2004; Perez 2003).[2] For Snyder, "pluralism" here indicates a transnational arena in which many different kinds of law exist. These include the familiar constitutions, legislation, treaties, and case law produced and

1 Cf. Salah 2002, 1, seeing "*mondialisation*" as "simultaneously, a descriptive concept, an explanatory principle and a positive and irreversible orientation of individual and collective actions."

2 The term is useful in so far as it suggests the diversity and polycentricity of transnational regulation, not necessarily implying any single globalising process in relation to law, any emerging unified global legal regime, any homogeneity of transnational regulation, or any theoretical presuppositions about the form or scope of this regulation.

enforced by nation states; the rules and institutions of public international law; the relatively "hard" (elaborately formulated and officially enforced) law created by transnational structures such as the European Union and the World Trade Organisation;[3] but also many kinds of "soft" (not so formulated or enforced) law or regulation varying in authoritativeness, precision and regulatory effectiveness and produced from public and private sources (e.g., Schäfer 2006; Qureshi 1999, 22–24). Snyder notes "a startling variety of new legal forms and regimes," "a variety of institutions, norms and dispute resolution processes located, and produced, at different structured sites around the world" (Snyder 2004, 624; 1999, 342). There is a "global legal playing field" (surely far from level), including "a novel regime for governing global economic networks"; but the many sites of global legal pluralism "do not make up a legal system" (Snyder 1999, 343, 372, 374). There is no uniform jurisdictional reference point, no single discursive arena in which legal reasoning takes place. Instead, regimes of different kinds (state, interstate and trans-state, public and private, official and unofficial) intersect, conflict, compete, and overlap.

As Snyder has shown, for example, in studying the international toy industry (ibid.), industries organised on a transnational basis typically produce extensive regulation governing the relationships of actors who wish to operate in the particular commercial field. Whether or not this kind of regulation, often created by or on behalf of the leading multinational corporate players in the field, is considered law, it is often undoubtedly what Eugen Ehrlich (2002) famously termed "living law"—that is, practically recognised, operative social norms governing relationships, establishing mutual understandings, claiming authority, defining obligations and entitlements, and often preventing disputes.

Many lawyers will wish to differentiate carefully between these various types of regulation, seeking to reserve the label "law" for some but not others. Most will want, for example, to distinguish sharply between public and private sources of regulation, often refusing the title "law" to products of the latter, or to regulation lacking official institutionalisation. They will tend to assume a hierarchy of regulatory types and sources. They will usually treat regulation produced by the law-making agencies of the state, according to what legal positivists see as "pedigree tests" of the legal, as "most fully" law. Generally, now, lawyers recognise international law between states as law, either because nation states and national legal systems provide the authority by which international law is created or recognised, or because international law as a body of doctrine has a degree of historical stability, managed by international institutions and, broadly, understood by states as linking them in an international community. But the institutionalisation of international legal doctrine is still limited by comparison with that of the most stable and developed municipal legal systems. So, international law, in this traditional conception, tends to be seen as "not a system but a set of rules" analogous in content and function (but not form) with those of nation-state legal systems (Hart 1994, 236–37).

2. Limits of Methodological Nationalism

This way of ordering the terrain of law is, however, coming to seem out of touch with reality in important respects. It is founded on what some social scientists call "methodological nationalism"

3 The WTO's website http://www.wto.org declares: "The WTO's agreements, negotiated and signed by a large majority of the world's trading nations, and ratified in their parliaments [...] are the legal ground-rules for international commerce [...] The agreements were negotiated and signed by governments. But their purpose is to help producers of goods and services, exporters, and importers conduct their business."

(Beck and Sznaider 2006). This is the idea that the basic focus of social (including legal) analysis is the politically organised society of the nation state, and that all meaningful concepts of social analysis presuppose this nation-state point of ultimate reference. Leading sociologists now advocate discarding "a nation-state definition of society and politics" and replacing it with a "cosmopolitan outlook" (ibid., 2). This will entail constructing an entirely new set of concepts with which to study transnational social phenomena (again including law). One reason why Ulrich Beck and Natan Sznaider talk of cosmopolitanism rather than globalisation in this context is to reject the idea that what must be taken into account now are solely external processes—a tide of globalisation enveloping and transforming local environments (ibid., 9). They argue that it is necessary to think also of innumerable local experiences and individual perceptions, of people changing their relations to and understandings of others no less than being changed by externally operating forces. What is at issue is not just a new perspective of globalisation, but a multiplicity of perspectives and standpoints.

If we translate this insight into the agenda of legal theory, it means that legal theory's task is not just to analyse, from its traditional standpoints, a range of new transnational legal phenomena. The task is rather to rethink legal theory in a situation in which it is slowly losing its basic modern reference points, the firmly defined jurisdiction of the nation state and the politically organised national society as the terrain from which all legal phenomena can be observed and evaluated. Perhaps, indeed, there can no longer be a single legal reference point to provide the basis for juristic thought.

Indications of this changing situation are now familiar. Legal experience in national legal systems is clearly being changed by such matters as the impact of European law, the influence of international human rights norms and aspirations, extraterritorial law enforcement and legal influences, and transnational commercial norms and practices. The matter can be regarded as one of confrontation and interaction between legal or regulatory regimes, regarded as "internal" or "external" according to various criteria. But it is also a matter of shifting perspectives involving a disorientation and renegotiation of legal and social experience.

Much western legal thinking has presupposed, until recently, a juridically-unified, regulated population—whether thought of as subjects (e.g., Hobbes, Bentham, Austin), citizens with powers and duties (e.g., Hart) or members of a community inspiring or creating its law (e.g., Dworkin, and classical English common law thought). But some of the most perceptive and socially-observant forms of legal philosophy in the Anglophone world have, more recently, been developing various versions of a "jurisprudence of difference" (Cotterrell 2003, chap. 8) that recognizes structured distinctions (by gender, race, ethnicity, religion, class, physical capacity, sexual orientation, etc.) among law's regulated population and its professional interpreters. These distinctions can produce different experiences and views of law. Law can thereby be given different meanings, making it a different phenomenon for different people. Assumptions about a single juristic standpoint from which law is to be observed and interpreted are undermined.

If this kind of thinking is applied to the transnational arena (something which has so far not been done very much) it makes sense to see law's regulated population and its interpreters not just in terms of a national jurisdiction, and still less in terms of some kind of homogeneous national community (which the jurisprudence of difference suggests may not exist in any meaningful sense) but in terms of transnational communities of many kinds. The many different kinds of transnational regulation which now exist, or are developing, relate to the interests, experiences, allegiances and values associated with transnational networks of community: for example, transnational business and financial networks; networks established and sustained by NGOs and social movements in environmental and human rights fields; networks of production and distribution in particular transnational industries (like that described in Snyder's toy industry study); networks facilitated by co-operation between states such as the EU, NAFTA, MERCOSUR; and professional networks such as those involved in international commercial arbitration or transnational legal practice. Inside one network of community, ideas about law or regulation may appear in very different ways from the way they appear in a different network. And, equally, perceptions of the way different regimes of regulation relate may vary.

3. Sources of Legal Authority

Orthodox juristic thinking may be ill-equipped to deal with this regulatory variety and its diverse regulated populations. A main reason may be the need in this thinking always to try to identify stable and—as far as possible—uncontroversial structures of legal authority. If much legal philosophy has been concerned to demonstrate the systemic unity of law, a major reason has been that it has tried to meet lawyers' need for a clear specification of the location of legal authority and the criteria of legal validity (see, generally, Cotterrell 2003). It has often sought law's criteria of validity and hallmarks of authority in a demonstration of its systematic character or the hierarchical structure of legal rules or norms. For all its originality, Kelsen's (1961, 363–88) explanation of the relationship between national and international law is typical in this respect. He claims that both of these necessarily form part of the same system. Either international law is authorised by the norms of national law (and so exists as an extension of it) or national law is subsumed in the system of international law—the basic norm of international law ultimately authorising the production of national legal norms as valid law. But the price paid for such a clear solution of the authority-validity puzzle is that a diversity of valid, competing legal systems or legal regimes, co-existing in the same social environment yet not integrated, cannot be envisaged.[4]

The existence of transnational communities, combined in complex networks and requiring particular kinds of regulation, makes it necessary to think differently. Hart's claim that international law is not a system but only a set of rules is an implicit criticism of Kelsen. Even eminent international lawyers—perhaps committed, like Kelsen, to emphasising the systematic quality of this law—note a worrying lack of co-ordination in its current development and serious institutional conflicts or contradictions in its practice and interpretation (e.g., Higgins 2006). In relation to transnational law, regulating the relations of non-state actors in transnational arenas, there seems to be an even more obvious indeterminacy about questions of regulatory authority (Cutler 2003, 62–70) and little coordination. When different regimes of transnational regulation collide, how is their relative authority or validity to be determined? Which rules or regulations should prevail in cases of conflict? There is often no hierarchy but only a plurality of authority. Much transnational law seems free-floating, not tethered to the

4 See Kelsen 1961, 363: "It is logically not possible to assume that simultaneously valid norms belong to different, mutually independent systems."

hierarchical authority structures of nation-state legal systems.[5] Often, its main (potential) sources of authority seem moral rather than political—rooted primarily in the regulatory demands, aspirations and understandings of its particular diverse communal constituencies.

Legal sociologists do not necessarily have juristic concerns with finding clear, uncontroversial sources of legal authority or criteria of legal validity. They are not necessarily disturbed by the idea of many such sources or criteria, competing or remaining fluid or vague. In fact, almost all theoretically sophisticated socio-legal writing on globalisation and law adopts a legal pluralist perspective. What is such a perspective? The term "legal pluralism" normally refers to "a situation in which two or more legal systems coexist in the same social field" (Merry 1988, 870), making independent jurisdictional claims. In other words, these systems have similar or overlapping jurisdictions, so that they compete in their claims to regulate the same social situations.

Lawyers encounter an apparent legal pluralism in relation, for example, to federal legal systems, colonial law, or relations between European Union law and the law of member states. Crucially, however, in these juristically recognised cases, a hierarchy of authority or juridical division of labour between the potentially competing legal regimes is postulated. So, in theory, questions about the applicability of particular laws can be resolved by appeals to established legal criteria that fix the validity, authority and jurisdiction of particular rules. The approach depends on agreement, both about what is to count as law and about the legal relationship between different systems of law. So, it presupposes ultimately a monistic rather than pluralistic conception of legal order—in other words, a seeming plurality of legal systems is to be understood in terms of a larger, overall conception of legal order that unifies this plurality and ultimately defines the structures of legal authority within it.

Jurists are often forced to recognise that this approach may not readily solve all problems in practice. In federal systems there can be ongoing uncertainties about boundaries of jurisdiction between state and federal legal authorities. Elsewhere, difficult problems of jurisdiction and conflicting authority arise, casting some doubt on the normative integrity of legal systems and the juristic security of their authority structures. Extensively discussed contemporary examples are uncertainties about the relations of EU law and state law, or of EU law and WTO law (e.g., Barber 2006, 323ff; Weiler 2000, especially chap. 4). But those adopting the monistic presupposition necessarily assume that all such problems can eventually be conclusively solved through juristic analysis or legislative clarification.

4. Some Approaches to Legal Pluralism

Legal sociologists have often had little hesitation in recognising legal pluralism in situations where no monistic presupposition seems warranted. Snyder's "global legal pluralism," for example, denies any necessary unity of transnational law, and emphasises the great diversity of its independent, often entirely unrelated sites and regimes. The question then arises: What is to count as "law" in this scenario? There seem to be four realistically possible approaches to the conceptualisation of law in legal pluralism:

a. One is the orthodox juristic approach, which (following Kelsen's approach to international

5 For Cutler 2003, 241, old ideas of state-based authority are "incapable of providing contemporary understanding or locating the authority and historical effectivity of transnational merchant law." Strange 1996, 198–99 sees, more generally, the loosening of the "strings that held each of us to the nation-state" as having created "a ramshackle assembly of conflicting sources of authority [...] a world of multiple, diffused authority."

law) has been called, above, monistic. It claims that ultimately there must be a single criterion of law to be applied to the diversity of legal regimes and that this criterion will then determine the relationship between those regimes (and hence the structure of legal authority within and between them).

b. A second approach, which might be called agnostic, avoids any final determination of the criterion of law and merely recognises the interaction of various normative regimes with varying degrees of practical effectiveness and authority. The question of what counts as law might be decided merely for particular purposes in particular contexts but does not need to be addressed as a general matter.

c. A third approach, which can be termed statist, would recognise some regimes as law by reference to particular criteria usually modelled on those applicable to nation-state law, and would see other regimes as merely non-legal regulation.

d. A final approach would be to rethink the concept of law to free it from biases built into it by its almost universal modern association with nation-state law. Such a concept would not be one that purports to reduce the plurality of transnational regulation to a single, unified system (a surely pointless task at the present time). Nor would it treat state law as necessarily expressing the essential contemporary characteristics of law. Instead, it would adopt criteria of the legal that are sufficiently flexible to recognise many different forms of law in currently indeterminate but potentially developing relations with each other.[6]

Let us look at each of these approaches more closely. The monistic approach merely ignores the fact that transnational law does not form a system of any kind and does not have established general criteria of authority or validity of its regulation. There is no reason why, for juristic purposes, transnational regulation cannot be portrayed in terms of a comprehensive normative system, hierarchically ordered. But this would bear scant relation to the actual practice of transnational regulatory regimes. It would be juristic wishful thinking. Globalisation's gift to law, for the moment, is a high degree of juristic chaos and indeterminate foundations of regulatory authority in many transnational fields. Transnational law is a work in progress without a basic norm or rule of recognition, a Hartian system of rules or Kelsenian hierarchy of norms, or any other juristic model of unity and authority.

The second (agnostic) approach, which avoids determination of what is to count as law, except pragmatically for the purposes of particular projects, is adopted by William Twining in his writings on globalization and legal theory—or what he more recently has seen as a return to general jurisprudence (Twining 2000, 249; 2002). He emphasises normative pluralism, rather than legal pluralism, and so deliberately leaves questions about the concept of law to one side (Twining 2003, 201 note, 224, 249–51, 253; 2000, 224–33). For many purposes of socio-legal research this is acceptable. But it leaves juristic questions about legal authority and validity unaddressed, at least when transnational regulatory regimes come into conflict. It bypasses central issues of juristic legal theory. The question "What is transnational law?" remains unanswerable in this approach.

6 Brian Tamanaha has advocated a further approach which he calls *conventionalist*. It amounts to accepting as law "whatever people identify and treat through their social practices as 'law' (or *droit*, *Recht*, etc.)": See Tamanaha 2001, 166. But this surely combines the worst of all worlds: maintaining a definitional concern with what the concept of law should cover, yet removing from the concept so defined all analytical power. Because of this it cannot contribute to legal theory's conceptual concerns with transnational law as identified in the present article.

The third (statist) approach is, in many ways, appealing. It largely leaves intact familiar juristic approaches to the identification and conceptualization of law and considers other normative phenomena by analogy with a basic model of law as state law. One version of this approach is André-Jean Arnaud's. Arnaud (1995; 2004) advocates a legal pluralist approach in considering the terrain of globalisation and law as well as the regulation produced within the framework of the European Union. But he writes of a plurality of "juridical" (not legal) systems, and reserves the term "law" (*droit*) for nation-state law. Juridical systems gain their identity from their relation to (state) legal systems. They consist of alternatives to or extensions of (state) law, or norms in the process of becoming or influencing law, or presenting themselves for consideration for enactment as legal norms. They are especially what Arnaud calls the "*avant dire-droit*" (law prior to its enunciation); norms waiting to be thematised as legal, often produced by campaigning organisations aiming to change law, or in various kinds of social practice that might eventually be formalised or recognised in legal relations (Arnaud 1981, 369–87; 1998; Arnaud and Fariñas-Dulce 1998, 297–304).

This approach is useful and illuminating in many ways, especially as a sophisticated updating of Ehrlich's "living law" concept (for Ehrlich, living law gets its identity mainly as a kind of shadow or parallel of state law, much like Arnaud's *avant dire-droit*). And it makes the powerful claim that the juridical is much wider in scope than state law. But what makes norms juridical except their possible destiny as future rules of state law? Ultimately, the statist approach—in this form—goes beyond the agnostic approach only by making the definite affirmation that state law is, indeed, fully law. Like agnosticism it actually backs away from a commitment to *legal* pluralism because it refuses to attribute legal qualities to norms unless they are part of the law of the state, or will become a part of it. On this juristic view, the state remains the sole source of all that is truly legal. But the interesting implication is that the transnational arena is full of what might be considered, in some way, the "nearly legal."

I should like to suggest that it is only the fourth approach (which now appears as the only *genuinely pluralist* approach to law among these four possibilities) that can be adequate to reflect the variety of transnational regulation and the reality, but also the ambiguities, of its character as law. One of legal theory's most important conceptual problems is to develop a useful pluralist approach to law. Certainly, it might be objected that this has already been achieved: Legal anthropology and legal sociology have produced numerous such approaches, and legal pluralism is a much discussed idea in these fields of research (see, e.g., among a huge literature, Von Benda-Beckmann 2002, Dalberg-Larsen 2000, Merry 1988, Belley 1986). But legal theory needs a genuinely pluralist approach for *juristic* purposes no less than for socio-legal ones.[7]

Juristic legal theory needs to knock away the support on which it has been leaning since the rise of modern legal positivism. That support is the assumption that all law is created by the state or derives authority and validity from its recognition by agencies of the state, and that its guarantee is its enforceability by the state. Clearly, a vast amount of law still relies securely on these conditions that relate it to the state, and it will continue to do so for the foreseeable future. But much regulation lacks these characteristics, wholly or in part. And it is becoming embarrassing to deny some of this regulation the name of law, or to see

7 Autopoiesis theory has been proposed as a basis for a genuine legal pluralism: See Teubner 1992. But its approach is to observe law (perhaps as a plurality of discourses), not to engage juristically with it. For wider criticisms of this theory see Cotterrell 2001.

it as legally insignificant, or as inferior to state legal regulation. A useful pluralist concept of law would be one that can recognise the current (and probably enduring) prominence of state law but not assume that all law must conform to or be measured against the state law model, or exist in inevitable subordination to or dependence on the law of the state.

5. Legal Pluralism inside the Nation State

In the space available it is not possible to do more than comment on a few aspects of how such a pluralist approach might be developed, built on elements already contributed by many writers. One essential is to recognize that the problems of conceptualising transnational regulation are not the only socio-legal developments demanding a pluralist approach in juristic legal theory.

For example, experiences of multiculturalism are relevant. Social groups having shared religious or other beliefs or cultural traditions often express distinctive regulatory aspirations reflecting the nature of their particular social relations of community. These aspirations sometimes inspire demands for an official legal pluralism within the nation state; for more diverse and flexible approaches to legal regulation reflecting the cultural mix of multicultural society (Shadid and Van Koningsveld 2005; Shah 2005; Pearl and Menski 1998, chap. 3; Rohe 2007). The effective rejection or negotiation of this demand and the continued enforcement of a unitary state law depend ultimately on the state's monopoly of coercive power but also on the strength of the moral sources of legitimacy of state law that are to be found in the whole range of networks of community that constitute the "society" of the nation state. But the more fundamental point is that, in these conditions of cultural pluralism, perspectives on law and its bases of authority tend to become increasingly diverse and relativistic, dependent on standpoint; a situation already signalled by the emergence of the jurisprudence of difference, mentioned earlier. Legal thinking requires new concepts and methods, paralleling the "cosmopolitanism outlook" that, as noted above, is now being advocated in social science.

Some writers have also emphasised a plurality of legal sources and structures of legal authority *within* state law itself. Leading positivist legal philosophers now frequently accept that it may not be possible to characterize realistically the source of ultimate authority of a legal system in the idea of a single rule of recognition, however complex its form (Raz 1979, 93–97; see also, e.g., Barber 2006, 316–18). And, from a socio-legal standpoint based on an empirical examination of legal practice, it may seem obvious that serious conflicts and unresolved differences or ambiguities sometimes arise in views of the legal position that are adopted by different state administrative or enforcement agencies, or between different courts (e.g., Dalberg-Larsen 2000, 103–14). These matters, in practice, are not necessarily resolved by formal appeals or final judgments, either because the matters are never raised for resolution or because ambiguities survive after efforts have been made to remove them. Differences in legal practice informed by different understandings of law may remain. Perhaps in the common law world, where much law is created by a plurality of courts, this idea of pluralism in state law is easier to accept than in some continental European civil law contexts where code and legislation provide primary models of law enacted by centralised, unified authorities.

6. Law and Community

Throughout this article an attempt has been made to try to avoid large, perhaps intractable, conceptual issues surrounding globalisation by referring to diverse communities as social sites of law and regulation or even as sources of (moral) legitimacy for this regulation. I also want to suggest that an idea of communities or, more precisely, networks of community as the basis of regulatory systems, aspirations, or problems, may point towards productive ways of conceptualising law in the context of transnational regulatory regimes.

By "community" I mean the existence of relatively stable social relations, where this stability comes from mutual interpersonal trust between those involved in such relations. Law regulates innumerable kinds of social relations. For legal theory an important question is whether there are some fundamental, endlessly recurring regulatory problems associated with particular types of social relations of community. If so, one can generalize about law's problems of regulating community life, while recognizing important differences in the basic types of possible bonds linking people together socially and that these differences will be reflected in basic differences in regulatory problems. So, for example, regulatory problems and possibilities may differ greatly depending on whether social relations of community are based on (i) common or convergent interests or projects, (ii) shared fundamental beliefs or ultimate values, (iii) purely emotional bonds and allegiances, or (iv) common traditions, customs, environments or historical experiences. To regulate co-operation for common projects may, in general terms, be significantly different from regulating to reflect or protect basic beliefs or value commitments held for their own sake; or from regulating merely to make possible co-existence without unacceptable friction in a shared environment. Even more different may be regulatory problems in addressing relationships largely shaped by emotional attachments or rejections.

These, at least, are hypotheses for which Max Weber's classic social theory provides some warrant. Weber (1978, 24–25) saw all social phenomena as built from innumerable combinations of just four basic (pure) types of social action. Correspondingly, one can postulate four basic types of social relations of community that largely mirror Weber's action-types and produce the distinctions just noted between possible bases of communal bonds—instrumental, belief/value-based, affective, and traditional. These basic types of social relations of community are combined in social life in innumerable ways. The combinations can be called networks of community. Legal theory obviously cannot examine all possible kinds of trans-national, national or sub-national networks of community that can exist; it cannot become sociology. But it can explore *general* regulatory problems posed by *basic types* of community and their interaction. In this way it can examine the general characteristics of the law that community life inspires (see, generally, Cotterrell 2006).

As regards the nature of law's authority, legal theory can recognise that this authority has two aspects. It resides partly in law's legitimated power of command (*voluntas*)—often guaranteed by the police and military power of a state—and partly in the principled character (*ratio*) of legal doctrine; that is, in the moral meaningfulness of that doctrine for the communities it regulates.[8] Ultimately law's *voluntas*, too, has to found its legitimacy on some stable relationship with the networks of community that are regulated by law; a relationship of acceptance or at least acquiescence by those involved in such networks.

Thus, in this approach, a task of legal theory is to consider the specifically regulatory aspects of community life so as to consider the forms that law may take and the general problems that face law in expressing the regulatory needs of these types of community as they combine in innumerable ways in the collective life of social networks and groups.

This merely sketches a way of going about things—a direction for developing a pluralistic legal theory. Its most obvious characteristic

8 On *voluntas* and *ratio* see Neumann 1986, 45–46, and Cotterrell 1995, 317–20.

is that it partly detaches the idea of law from the idea of the state, but it does not leave law detached from all specific social reference—for example, as social rules conceived, as in Hart's concept of law, in purely abstract form. It roots law in the practical regulatory requirements of communal life. Hence it opens the possibility for seeing transnational networks of community as producing or inspiring their own law or, at least, being in a position to give or refuse legitimacy to forms of regulation addressed to them or developed with reference to them. One might begin to develop a sense of legal authority and validity as given or refused, in some way, by networks of community that are not restricted to homogeneous nation-state populations (i.e., subjects or citizens of the state).

7. Modelling Transnational Law

How might one begin to set about conceptualising law using such an approach? It would be possible to start from Hart's model of rules. Neil MacCormick (1993), for example, has already explored its applicability beyond the nation state in relation to the European legal order. Combinations of primary and secondary rules, as Hart describes them, might be expected to be found in transnational as in national law. But a meaningful ultimate Hartian rule of recognition will be hard to find for much trans-national regulation and it might be doubted whether the lack of one is enough to settle the question of whether law exists.

To understand law's expansion beyond the hegemony of the state, there is also a need for a realistic and nuanced concept of the state in its relation to law (Belley 1986, 28–31),[9] but, as has long been noted (Raz 1979, 98), Hart's theory does not supply one. Such a concept would need to be one that imports into both juristic and socio-legal analysis a sense of current discussion of the postulated "hollowing out of the state," the reduction or redirection of its regulatory capacities in the face of the expansion of trans-state, interstate and intrastate regulation and regulatory pressures, as well as the possible atrophying or undermining of a strong sense of national public interest.

Clearly, where states exist they have regulatory power, yet the nature and extent of this power surely varies greatly between them. In some cases, both legal and political authority of states might be seen as greater (for example, in the reach of their authority beyond nation-state boundaries) than orthodox theories of state sovereignty postulate. In other cases, this authority might seem much weaker. These matters of variation in the nature and situation of states are extensively documented in social science literature,[10] but little noted in the literature of juristic legal theory when it searches for an ultimate source of legal authority. Such a source (as in Hart's and Kelsen's theories) is often linked to a criterion of effectiveness, but the idea of the "effectiveness" of a legal order—or indeed of a legal norm insofar as this bears on questions of legal authority or validity (Kelsen 1967, 211–14)—surely cries out for re-examination in conditions of legal pluralism where the role of the state as a regulator is a matter of debate.

I think that a useful direction could be to expand Hart's approach in various ways. To focus only on rules—the Hartian "model of rules"—in a concept of law seems too limited to address the great diversity of normative forms that transnational regulation shows. It may be very useful to treat soft (imprecise, negotiated, relatively

9 More generally, and abstractly, it can be said that what is needed is a concept of power as it exists in networks of community (such as, but not limited to, the political society of the nation state) and a focus on how power is organised and exercised politically in regulating such networks.

10 See, e.g., Van Creveld 1999; Strange 1996; Jones 2000; Sur 1997. For detailed debates in a specifically British context see, e.g., Holliday 2000, and literature there cited.

unenforced) law as law for certain purposes and to explore its conceptual relation to "hard" law. It might be best, indeed, to use a concept of law as "doctrine,"[11] that encompasses rules, standards, principles, concepts and values as part of law. There is nothing new in such a suggestion, adopted in various ways by such diverse legal scholars as John Dickinson (1929), Roscoe Pound (1954, 56–59), Karl Llewellyn (1941), and Ronald Dworkin (1977).

It might be good, also, to think not merely in terms of secondary rules but also in terms of the existence of institutionalised *practices* and *agencies* existing specifically for the purpose of creating, interpreting, applying or enforcing doctrine. Law, seen as institutionalised doctrine in this way (Cotterrell 1995, chap. 2), is not an all-or-nothing matter. The existence of law might be—as, for example, Lon Fuller (1969) and Karl Llewellyn (1940) suggested[12]—a matter of degree; regulatory arrangements and systems might be more or less institutionalised, more or less legalised.[13] Not all aspects of creation, interpretation, application, or enforcement of legal doctrine will be institutionalised to the same extent in all legal regimes; indeed, some aspects might not be institutionalised at all.

Hence, in working towards answering questions about the legal authority of different transnational regulatory phenomena it may be possible to develop a useful conception of relative legal authority linked to a notion of degrees of legality. This will not solve jurisdictional disputes or conflicts over authority and legitimacy claims but it may offer a slowly emerging template in terms of which these can be judged. Consistently with the idea of an emerging "cosmopolitan outlook," the emphasis in determining the authority, scope and meaning of regulation will fall increasingly on negotiation and mutual recognition from diverse perspectives and standpoints, rather than on hierarchical juristic determination and observation from some fixed jurisdictional point (which, in fact, for many purposes no longer exists).[14]

Nevertheless, such an approach will surely need to recognise that, for the time being, state law—with its highly institutionalised, elaborately developed legal doctrine and its long established national networks of community—is, for many purposes and from many standpoints, the most authoritative, secure and precisely delineated form of law (cf. Belley 1986, 28–31). But as the institutionalisation of various kinds of transnational regulatory doctrine continues, this superior status may be increasingly challenged. And beyond familiar juristic concerns with legal authority and validity, other questions about regulatory legitimacy remain.

The legitimacy of the law of the nation state has been slowly secured, in the most stable states, over long periods of experimentation with democracy and other forms of government. Through these experiments, ways have been found by which effective claims can be made that the moral authority of the regulated population infuses law. Transnational law requires a similar process of evolution. Its moral legitimacy (which also ultimately underpins any political legitimacy it can secure) lies in the transnational networks of community that, in some way, it has to represent. These remain fluid and in process of formation. It cannot be taken for granted that they will continue to develop and strengthen although at present the indications seem to be that they will. At present, the relationship between transnational

11 The term is not used here in the civil law sense of juristic or judicial exposition of legal ideas.

12 Both Fuller and Llewellyn, unusually among jurists, accept a genuinely (i.e., my fourth) pluralist approach to conceptualising law.

13 See also, as regards degrees of legalisation in international relations, Abbott et al. 2000.

14 On the problems of juristic perspective and standpoint see also Schlag 1991.

communities and the concept of law is hardly explored. Yet this is now one of the most important items to be added to legal theory's agenda of juristic problems. The aim here has been merely to identify certain themes that will surely need to be a central part of the discussion of that item.

References

Abbott, K.W., R.O. Keohane, A. Moravcsik, A.-M. Slaughter, and D. Snidal. 2000. "The Concept of Legalization." *International Organization* 54: 401–19.

Arnaud, A.-J. 1981. *Critique de la raison juridique 1. Où va la sociologie du droit?*. Paris: LGDJ.

Arnaud, A.-J. 1995. "Legal Pluralism and the Building of Europe." In *Legal Polycentricity: Consequences of Pluralism in Law*. Eds. H. Petersen and H. Zahle, 149–69. Aldershot: Dartmouth.

Arnaud, A.-J. 1998. "From Limited Realism to Plural Law: Normative Approach versus Cultural Perspective." *Ratio Juris* 11: 246–58.

Arnaud, A.-J. 2004. *Entre modernité et mondialisation: Leçons d'histoire de la philosophie du droit et de l'État*. 2nd ed. Paris: LGDJ.

Arnaud, A.-J., and M.J. Fariñas-Dulce. 1998. *Introduction à l'analyse sociologique des systèmes juridiques*. Brussels: Bruylant.

Barber, N.W. 2006. "Legal Pluralism and the European Union." *European Law Journal* 12: 306–29.

Beck, U. 1999. *World Risk Society*. Cambridge: Polity.

Beck, U., and N. Sznaider. 2006. "Unpacking Cosmopolitanism for the Social Sciences: A Research Agenda." *British Journal of Sociology* 57: 1–23.

Belley, J.-G. 1986. "L'État et la régulation des sociétés globales. Pour une problématique du pluralisme juridique." *Sociologie et sociétés* 18: 11–32.

Cotterrell, R. 1995. *Law's Community: Legal Theory in Sociological Perspective*. Oxford: Clarendon.

Cotterrell, R. 2001. "The Representation of Law's Autonomy in Autopoiesis Theory." In *Law's New Boundaries: The Consequences of Legal Autopoiesis*. Eds. J. Přibán and D. Nelken, 80–103. Aldershot: Ashgate.

Cotterrell, R. 2003. *The Politics of Jurisprudence: A Critical Introduction to Legal Philosophy*. 2nd ed. Oxford: Oxford UP.

Cotterrell, R. 2006. *Law, Culture and Society: Legal Ideas in the Mirror of Social Theory*. Aldershot: Ashgate.

Cutler, A.C. 2003. *Private Power and Global Authority: Transnational Merchant Law in the Global Political Economy*. Cambridge: Cambridge UP.

Dalberg-Larsen, J. 2000. *The Unity of Law: An Illusion? On Legal Pluralism in Theory and Practice*. Glienicke: Galda & Wilch.

Dickinson, J. 1929. "The Law Behind Law." *Columbia Law Review* 29: 113–46, 285–319.

Dworkin, R. 1977. *Taking Rights Seriously*. Revised ed. London: Duckworth.

Ehrlich, E. 2002. *Fundamental Principles of the Sociology of Law*. Trans. W.L. Moll. New Brunswick, NJ: Transaction.

Fuller, L. 1969. *The Morality of Law*. Revised ed. New Haven, CT: Yale UP.

Habermas, J. 1999. *The Inclusion of the Other: Studies in Political Theory*. Eds. C. Cronin and P. De Greiff. Cambridge: Polity.

Habermas, J. 2001. *The Postnational Constellation: Political Essays*. Trans. M. Pensky. Cambridge: Polity.

Hart, H.L.A. 1994. *The Concept of Law*. 2nd ed. Oxford: Clarendon.

Higgins, R. 2006. "A Babel of Judicial Voices? Ruminations from the Bench." *International and Comparative Law Quarterly* 55: 791–804.

Holliday, I. 2000. "Is the British State Hollowing Out?" *Political Quarterly* 71: 167–76.

Jones, R.J.B. 2000. *The World Turned Upside Down? Globalization and the Future of the State*. Manchester: Manchester UP.

Kelsen, H. 1961. *General Theory of Law and State*. Trans. A. Wedberg. New York, NY: Russell & Russell.

Kelsen, H. 1967. *Pure Theory of Law*. Trans. M. Knight. Berkeley, CA: U of California P.

Llewellyn, K.N. 1940. "The Normative, the Legal, and the Law-Jobs: The Problem of Juristic Method." *Yale Law Journal* 49: 1355–400.

Llewellyn, K.N. 1941. "My Philosophy of Law." In *My Philosophy of Law: Credos of 16 American Scholars*. Ed. A. Kocourek, 183–97. Boston, MA: Boston Law Book Co.

Luhmann, N. 1982. "The World Society as a Social System." *International Journal of General Systems* 8: 131–38.

MacCormick, N. 1993. "Beyond the Sovereign State." *Modern Law Review* 56: 1–18.

Merry, S.E. 1988. "Legal Pluralism." *Law and Society Review* 22: 869–96.

Meyer, J. 1987. "The World Polity and the Authority of the Nation-State." In *Institutional Structure: Constituting State, Society and the Individual*. Eds. G. Thomas, J. Meyer, F. Ramirez, and J. Boli, 41–70. Newbury Park, CA: Sage.

Neumann, F.L. 1986. *The Rule of Law: Political Theory and the Legal System in Modern Society*. Leamington Spa: Berg.

Pearl, D., and W. Menski. 1998. *Muslim Family Law*. 3rd ed. London: Sweet & Maxwell.

Perez, O. 2003. "Normative Creativity and Global Legal Pluralism: Reflections on the Democratic Critique of National Law." *Indiana Journal of Global Legal Studies* 10: 25–64.

Pound, R. 1954. *An Introduction to the Philosophy of Law*. Revised ed. New Haven, CT: Yale UP.

Qureshi, A.H. 1999. *International Economic Law*. London: Sweet & Maxwell.

Raz, J. 1979. *The Authority of Law: Essays on Law and Morality*. Oxford: Clarendon.

Rohe, M. 2007. *Muslim Minorities and the Law in Europe: Chances and Challenges*. New Delhi: Global Media Publications.

Salah, M.M. Md. 2002. *Les contradictions du droit mondialisé*. Paris: PUF.

Schäfer, A. 2006. "Resolving Deadlock: Why International Organisations Introduce Soft Law." *European Law Journal* 12: 194–208.

Schlag, P. 1991. "The Problem of the Subject." *Texas Law Review* 69: 1627–743.

Shadid, W., and P.S. Van Koningsveld. 2005. "Muslim Dress in Europe: Debates on the Headscarf." *Journal of Islamic Studies* 16: 35–61.

Shah, P. 2005. *Legal Pluralism in Conflict: Coping with Cultural Diversity in Law*. London: Glass House.

Snyder, F.G. 1999. "Governing Economic Globalization: Global Legal Pluralism and European Law." *European Law Journal* 5: 334–74.

Snyder, F.G. 2004. "Economic Globalisation and the Law in the Twenty-First Century." In *Blackwell Companion to Law and Society*. Ed. A. Sarat, 624–40. Malden, MA: Blackwell.

Strange, S. 1996. *The Retreat of the State: The Diffusion of Power in the World Economy*. Cambridge: Cambridge UP.

Sur, S. 1997. "The State between Fragmentation and Globalization." *European Journal of International Law* 3: 421–34.

Tamanaha, B.Z. 2001. *A General Jurisprudence of Law and Society*. Oxford: Oxford UP.

Teubner, G. 1992. "The Two Faces of Janus: Rethinking Legal Pluralism." *Cardozo Law Review* 13: 1443–62.

Twining, W.L. 2000. *Globalisation and Legal Theory*. London: Butterworths.

Twining, W.L. 2002. "Reviving General Jurisprudence." In *Transnational Legal Processes: Globalisation and Power Disparities*. Ed. M. Likosky, 3–22. London: Butterworths.

Twining, W.L. 2003. "A Post-Westphalian Conception of Law." *Law and Society Review* 37: 199–257.

Van Creveld, M. 1999. *The Rise and Decline of the State*. Cambridge: Cambridge UP.

Von Benda-Beckmann, F. 2002. "Who's Afraid of Legal Pluralism?" *Journal of Legal Pluralism & Unofficial Law* 47: 37–82.

Wallerstein, I. 1974. *The Modern World System*. New York, NY: Academic P.

Weber, M. 1978. *Economy and Society: An Outline of Interpretive Sociology*. Ed. G. Roth and C. Wittich. Berkeley, CA: U of California P.

Weiler, J.H.H., ed. 2000. *The EU, the WTO and the NAFTA: Towards a Common Law of International Trade*. Oxford: Oxford UP.

Study Questions

1. How might a legal positivist respond to Koskenniemi's claim that legal positivism and natural law theory are locked in an unending battle which neither can win?
2. Why is the tension between "apologist" and "utopian" theories of law irresolvable?
3. Have times changed sufficiently since Hart doubted the existence of a rule of recognition for international law that we can now say such a rule exists?
4. Does Grotius's natural law theory of international law contain any relevant similarities to Finnis's theory? Could Finnis's view of natural law be used to support Grotius's theory of international law?
5. How might Cotterrell respond to the objection that transnational law really isn't law at all, but simply a kind of private agreement among non-state actors? What might be at stake in such a debate?

Further Readings

Barcelona Traction, International Court of Justice Reports, 1970.
Samantha Besson and John Tasioulas, eds., *The Philosophy of International Law*. Oxford: Oxford UP, 2010.
Ian Brownlie, ed., *Basic Documents in International Law*. 5th ed. Oxford: Oxford UP, 2002.
Keith Culver and Michael Giudice, *Legality's Borders*. Oxford: Oxford UP, 2010.
Jack Goldsmith and Eric Posner, *The Limits of International Law*. Oxford: Oxford UP, 2005.
International Criminal Court: www.icc-cpi.int.
International Criminal Tribunal for Rwanda: https://unictr.irmct.org/.
International Criminal Tribunal for the Former Yugoslavia: www.icty.org.
Journal of Philosophy of International Law.
Lotus, Permanent Court of International Justice, Series A, No. 10, 1927.
Neil MacCormick, *Questioning Sovereignty*. Oxford: Oxford UP, 1999.
North Sea Continental Shelf, International Court of Justice Reports, 1969.
Malcolm N. Shaw, *International Law*. 5th ed. Cambridge: Cambridge UP, 2003.
William Twining, *General Jurisprudence*. Cambridge: Cambridge UP, 2009.
United Nations international law homepage: www.un.org/law.

Glossary

This glossary contains legal, Latin, and philosophical terms which occur frequently in legal writing and in philosophical writing about law. This is not a comprehensive glossary: a complete list of philosophical and legal terms would run to several volumes. This glossary is meant to be an introductory reference and guide to help the reader bridge the gap between philosophy and law, and to bridge also some of the gaps among American, British, and Canadian usage. We have tried to offer an accurate yet concise definition of each term. Where strict accuracy relative to the actual law of today in various jurisdictions might require a long explanation of different practices, we have offered a more general definition which explains a main or common sense of the term. If a more precise definition of a term is required, it is best to consult a dictionary of law or philosophy that applies the term to the specific context in which you have found it used.

We have relied extensively on the following excellent resources:

Brian Bix, *A Dictionary of Legal Theory*. Oxford: Oxford UP, 2004.

Bryan A. Garner, ed., *Black's Law Dictionary*. 12th ed. St. Paul, MN: Thomson West, 2024.

Jonathan Law, ed., *A Dictionary of Law*. 10th ed. Oxford: Oxford UP, 2022.

Dennis Patterson, ed., *A Companion to the Philosophy of Law and Legal Theory*. 2nd ed. Oxford: Wiley-Blackwell, 2010.

J.A. Yogis, S.G. Coughlan, and C. Cotter, eds., *Canadian Law Dictionary*. 7th ed. Hauppauge, NY: Barron's Educational Series, 2013.

Ab initio: (Latin) from the beginning.

Accession: the act of joining and accepting the terms of an international agreement (e.g., treaty, convention), typically used to refer to the act of joining an already established agreement.

Accused: in its most general sense, a person charged but not yet convicted of criminal wrongdoing.

Acquit: in contract law, to be released from an obligation; in criminal law, to be not proven guilty and saved from further prosecution for the same crime. Note that acquittal in the criminal courts does not eliminate the possibility of a civil suit treating the same set of events.

Act: 1. intentional conduct. 2. a legislative body's written statement of a legal rule or rules, usually referred to as statute law.

Action: a legal proceeding one party has brought against another in order to have a matter of dispute resolved by a court.

Actus reus: (Latin) the conduct element of criminal wrongdoing. A criminal act is composed of legally prohibited conduct and criminal intention (*mens rea*). Some crimes involve an intentional omission or failure to act.

Adduce: in the context of evidence, to offer or introduce, often in the context of court proceedings specifying how evidence is to be brought to the court for consideration in a given case.

Adjective law: the law specifying the procedures and practices of courts.

Adjudication: a judgment which resolves a legal dispute. A theory of adjudication accounts for what courts do (or ought to do) in order to reach a decision which resolves a legal dispute.

Administrative law: law regarding the powers and obligations of the officials of a legal system.

Affirm: an appellate court's confirmation of a lower court's decision.

Affirmative action: government or non-government organizational policy and practice intended to ensure fair treatment of persons or groups whose representation and participation in some activity has been limited by past policy and practice.

Alternative Dispute Resolution: methods for resolving non-criminal disputes in settings other than court trial before a judge or judges. *See* **Arbitration** and **Mediation**

Amicus curiae: (Latin) friend of the court. A representative of the public interest or some other interest relevant to the disposition of a legal action, yet otherwise unrepresented by the parties to the action. The *amicus curiae* typically presents information to the court in the form of a brief.

Analogy: a comparison of one thing with another, used to show that similar features of the two things compared means there is some respect in which they should receive similar treatment. In legal argument, analogies are often used to support applying law to a new set of facts in the same way as the same law was applied to a relevantly similar prior set of facts.

Analytical jurisprudence: the branch of the philosophy of law concerned mainly with description and explanation of law and legal practices.

Appeal: review by a higher court of the decision of a lower court. Appeals may be granted in order for a higher court to evaluate a party's claim that there is a need to remedy such errors of law as misapplication of law to facts, incorrect directions to a jury, or use of legally unacceptable evidence.

Appellant: the party who appeals a decision. An appeal is typically, though not necessarily, made by the party who is dissatisfied with the decision of the lower court.

Appellate court: *see* **Court of Appeal**

Arbitration: a dispute resolution process conducted outside the court system by an independent person or persons who may have the power to advise how a dispute ought to be resolved, or may have the power to reach a decision the parties are obligated to accept. Arbitration is often proposed in disputes between parties who wish to resolve the dispute more quickly than may be possible in a given court system, or in disputes where the technical or private nature of the dispute motivates the parties to seek a private resolution. Arbitration is often specified in contracts as the means by which parties will resolve disputes regarding the contract. In some situations, some courts have the power to propose that parties resolve a dispute using arbitration. *See* **Alternative Dispute Resolution** and **Mediation**

Arraignment: a legal procedure in which the charge against an accused is read out in court and the accused is asked to enter a plea (usually guilty or not guilty).

Arrest: the legally authorized deprivation of a person's liberty in order to bring a charge against that person.

Attorney: generally, a person legally empowered to act as an agent for another; in the USA, a term used to refer to a lawyer legally authorized to practice law.

Attorney General: in Canada and England, the chief legal officer for the Crown, politically responsible for public prosecution and a source of legal advice to government. Attorneys General are elected members of Parliament or the legislative assembly of the jurisdiction for which each is responsible. In the USA, the US Attorney General is the appointed, non-elected chief legal officer of the federal government who also heads the Department of Justice and advises the government on legal matters. A similar function is performed by the Attorneys General of individual states (elected or appointed, according to individual states' laws).

Bar: 1. the physical or imaginary division in a courtroom between public observers and the judges, lawyers, and persons formally involved in the case at trial. Bar associations comprise members of the legal profession, distinguished from Benchers, the judges who render decisions. 2. prevent. Once a case has been decided by a judge, the fact of that decision bars the parties from bringing the same matter to trial again.

Barrister: in England and Wales and some other common law jurisdictions, a lawyer who argues cases in court. A solicitor is a lawyer who prepares cases and works outside the court in co-operation with barristers. In Canada this distinction is not made, and all lawyers may retain the designation "barrister and solicitor." *See* **Solicitor**

Begging the question: a fallacy (error of *reasoning*), consisting in circular reasoning which assumes what it sets out to prove.

Bellum omnium: (Latin) war of all against all. The state of nature in the absence of the rule of law.

Bench: generally, the court and judges. The physical seat used by judges, or the body of judges as opposed to the lawyers who argue cases and are members of the bar.

Bencher: in England, a judge or senior lawyer who is a member of the group which governs the activities of one of the Inns of Court (legal associations in London which govern the activities of barristers and perform an educational function). In Canada, a member of a provincial law society which governs activities of that law society.

Bill: most generally, a document proposing a law, and brought before a legislative body for consideration and approval.

Bill of Rights: a legislative statement of basic rights and freedoms. In England, refers to the Bill of Rights of 1689. In the USA, the first ten amendments of the United States Constitution. In Canada, the Bill of Rights of 1960 has been largely superseded by the *Charter of Rights and Freedoms* of 1982 which entrenches and protects in a stronger manner the basic rights and freedoms of Canadians.

Breach: to break by action or inaction the requirements of a legal rule.

Breach of contract: failure without legal excuse by a contracting party to comply with certain provisions of a legally acceptable contract.

Brief: in the USA and Canada, a document prepared by a lawyer prior to arguing a case in court. The brief contains the facts of the case, relevant sources of law, and argument showing how the relevant legal rules apply to the facts. In England, a document prepared by a solicitor directing a barrister to argue a case in court.

Bright line: a legal norm whose meaning is so clear that it is easily applied without question as to its relevance and without question as to the meaning of the consequences of its application.

Burden of proof: (Latin: *onus probandi*) generally, the duty of a party to a trial to prove the party's claims about the way a case at trial ought to be resolved. In criminal trials, it is assumed that the accused is innocent until proven guilty, and the prosecution bears the burden of proving the accused guilty beyond reasonable doubt, with certain exceptions.

By-law: local legislation by authorities who are subordinate to some higher authority. Also rules of an association or corporation.

Canon: general term for a rule, especially in the codes of conduct of professional societies.

Canon law: Roman Catholic church law, used also by the Church of England (Anglican Church), governing activities of the church and some activities of church members who are not also members of the clergy.

Case: a legal controversy to be resolved by a court, and more generally the argument offered by each party to the dispute.

Case law: the body of law created by recording the decisions of a court or judge to create a permanent record of how a court or judge applied a particular law or laws to the facts of a dispute brought before the court for resolution.

Causation: questions of causation in law are questions regarding the relation between a prior event and a subsequent event, often for the purpose of determining whether the connection between a person's conduct and its effect has characteristics warranting that person being held responsible for that conduct in a way justifying a finding of criminal guilt or civil responsibility. Courts have found challenges to common sense understanding of causation in many areas of criminal and civil law. Examples of problems of causation in criminal law include questions of how to understand the actions of a person who is sleep-walking or under the influence of drugs. Examples of problems of causation in civil law include questions of how to understand actions serving as the first cause in a chain of action and reaction.

Cause: the reason for some effect, or the reason for bringing a dispute to a court for resolution. Many other legal uses.

Certiorari: (Latin) to be informed. A way of causing a higher court to investigate the decision of a lower court, with the effect of cancelling the practical effects of the lower court's decision. The higher court issues a writ to the lower court, causing the lower court to give to the higher court the records of its reasoning and decision in some matter.

Challenge: 1. to question the legal justification of some state of affairs. 2. the legal right to object to and have a potential juror or jurors removed from a jury. In Canada and the USA, each side to a dispute is allowed a set number of peremptory challenges with which a juror may be disqualified for no stated reason. Peremptory challenges were abolished in the UK by the Criminal Justice Act 1988.

Charge: in criminal law, to formally accuse a person of having committed a specific crime.

Charter: in its most general sense, a foundational document setting out the basic standards according to which a specific wide range of conduct is to be governed. In Canada, an informal way of referring to the *Canadian Charter of Rights and Freedoms*.

Civil action: legal proceeding to resolve a non-criminal dispute over a private or civil right.

Civil law: 1. law concerned with interactions between private individuals and legal persons such as corporations. Concerns rights and remedies in the context of property, family law, contracts, and torts. Distinguished from criminal law, which governs conduct which wrongs society in general. 2. Roman law which formed the basis for civil law in Louisiana, and several states in western Europe. In a form influenced by the Code Napoléon of France, civil law also forms the basis of private law in Quebec.

Civil rights: 1. personal rights protected by law. 2. in American jurisprudence, functionally synonymous with civil liberties. 3. in Canadian jurisprudence, civil rights pertain largely to interpersonal relations, and civil liberties pertain largely to relations between private persons and social institutions.

Code: generally, a systematic assembly of a particular area of law in a particular jurisdiction, e.g., the Criminal Code of Canada.

Comity: an act or more regular practice of courtesy between or among states, conducted not as a matter of exercise of legal rights or legal obligations, but rather as a voluntary demonstration of good will.

Common law: generally, the English precedent-based system of law, inherited by Commonwealth nations and the USA. More specifically, that part of the law developed by the courts in their decisions which extend the customs and principles already in place in the practices of the people. More recently, as unwritten customs have been displaced by court decisions, that part of the law developed by the courts.

Competent: generally, having authority and meeting minimum standards of rationality to take some action.

Conceptual analysis: in legal theory, the activity of developing the clearest possible understanding of concepts such as law, morality, obligation, rights, permissions, responsibility, and punishment. Conceptual analysis proceeds through logically rigorous analysis of the content of concepts, analysis of how application and misapplication of concepts can generate insight or distort understanding of legal practice and social life, and analysis of how concepts are related to one another. Conceptual analysis is less a single method or set of analytical steps than a set of questions whose answers have benefited from reflection on the implications of investigations of logic, language, psychology, sociology, and economics for understanding of legal concepts.

Conflict of laws: the branch of jurisprudence concerned with principled resolution of conflicts which arise when the laws of more than one jurisdiction apply to some matter. Private international law treats the ways in which a court in one jurisdiction chooses to interpret the force of laws of some other jurisdiction.

Congress: the federal legislative body of the USA, comprising the House of Representatives and the Senate.

Consideration: in contract law, the valuable thing given over as payment for some present or promised action. Valid contracts generally require consideration.

Constitution: most simply, the body of written or unwritten norms specifying the nature and basic operations of an organization. Most typically in a legal context, a constitution specifies in writing, or in writing and a body of widely recognized practices, the fundamental and supreme legal norms governing a state's basic social institutions, and the relations of those institutions to members of the state. State constitutions generally specify institutions for law-creation (legislative institutions such as a House of Commons or a Congress), law-application (executive institutions such as the office of president), and law-determination (judicial institutions such as supreme courts). State constitutions often include further explanation of the rights and obligations of citizens relative to fundamental institutions and legal commitments regarding the nature and purpose of the state.

Constitutional conventions: unwritten rules regarding the operation of a constitution, whose weight in practice is not a matter of enforcement by legal officials, but by political expectation and social pressure applied to violators of the rules. Such conventions may be viewed as the unwritten good habits of actors operating constitutional law to serve societies committed to the predictability and stability delivered by shared commitment to the principle of the rule of law.

Constitutional laws: 1. generally, individual laws contributing to specification of the fundamental institutions and legal norms making up the basic law of a state legal system. 2. when framed negatively in reference to "unconstitutional law" or in common expressions exerting that some law or situation is "not constitutional," to assert that some actual or proposed law is invalid in virtue of its failing to comply with standards of legal validity established by an applicable, superior and indeed supreme constitutional law.

Construction: interpretation of an unclear part of some legal standard, typically according to accepted construction rules.

Contra: (Latin) against.

Contra bonos mores: (Latin) against good morals.

Contract: a legally binding agreement which gives the contracting parties specific rights or obligations which may be enforced by the courts should either party fail to comply with the conditions of the contract. Valid contracts are characterized by (1) an offer and (2) acceptance by (3) competent parties who exchange (4) consideration and aim at some (5) legal purpose.

Convention: in the context of international law, a form of international agreement most typically used to identify shared commitment by many states to a particular set of legal norms.

Conveyance: a documented transfer of land between persons.

Conviction: the finding in a criminal trial that, according to the standard set by law, the accused is guilty as charged. Conviction typically also refers to the sentence which results from the finding of guilt.

Corporation: an artificial person treated by the law as a single person even though it may in fact be composed of an individual (corporation sole) or many individuals (corporation aggregate). Corporations may hold legal rights and duties.

Corpus delicti: (Latin) body of a crime. The object or the harm resulting from the *actus reus* of a crime.

Corrective justice: in the context of private law governing interactions between individuals, the idea that when one individual wrongs another, justice is served by the wrongdoer being held liable for the wrong done, generally in a way involving direct compensation of the person who suffered the wrong, in a way proportional to the wrong suffered.

Counsel: 1. generally, advice given from one to another. 2. in the USA, a general term for an attorney. In the UK, a term for a barrister or barristers. In Canada, a general term for lawyers.

Court Martial: a military court in which members of armed forces are tried for offences against service law. In the US, military courts are responsible for trial and punishment of offences against the Uniform Code of Military Justice committed by those properly subject to that code. The service law of the UK consists of a series of acts and further regulations governing each service. The service law of Canada is specified in the National Defence Act 1985.

Court of Appeal: a higher court which reviews a lower court's application of law to a case. Also referred to as "appellate courts" to mark the fact that courts which perform appeal functions need not be explicitly called "Courts of Appeal." Appellate courts evaluate a party's claim that a lower court's resolution of a legal proceeding was in error, for reasons including errors in the conduct of the trial, errors of application of law to facts, and errors in admission of evidence.

Court of first instance: used to refer to the court that first handles a given matter, marking the fact that subsequent courts are handling a matter that has already been a matter of argument before a court, typically in trial followed by appeal of a decision.

Court of King's Bench / Queen's Bench: in the UK, the highest court of common law, forming one division (Queen's Bench Division) of the High Court's three divisions. The other divisions are Chancery and Family. In Canada, this term refers to the trial division of a province's superior or supreme court.

Crime: legally prohibited wrong against society in general.

Crown: in the UK, the office formally held by the reigning monarch as the supreme legal power. In practice, the activities of the crown are in control of the elected government and the civil service. Barring exceptional circumstances, the monarch does not exercise legal powers except on the advice of elected ministers. In Canada, the crown generally refers to the elected government and all subordinate officials.

Crown Attorney: in Canada, a lawyer appointed by an Attorney General to prosecute accused criminals on behalf of the crown. Also called Crown Prosecutor. In the UK, a prosecutor works under a regional Chief Crown Prosecutor.

Culpable: blameworthy. Culpability requires intention, recklessness, or negligence, except in instances of strict liability.

Custom: a long-held practice, standard, or usage in some place which through common acceptance is treated as law.

Damages: compensation awarded a person who has suffered a legal wrong. There are many types of damages.

De facto: (Latin) in fact. Often used to contrast actual practice with formal legal requirements.

De jure: (Latin) by right, as required by law. Often contrasted with *de facto*, "matter of fact" practice.

De novo: (Latin) fresh, new. A trial *de novo* is held as if the matter had not previously been tried.

Decision: used in several senses, often to refer to the formal judgment by a court which resolves a dispute brought before it.

Defamation: public utterance of claims which tend to harm a person's reputation according to the standards of right-thinking persons. In the USA and Canada, spoken defamation is called *slander*, and published or graphic defamation is called *libel*. In England, defamation of short duration is called *slander*, and more permanent defamation is called *libel*.

Defendant: in a criminal trial, the person accused of commission of a crime. In a civil trial, the person sued by the plaintiff.

Defense: in a criminal trial, the legally acceptable reasons presented to the court in an attempt to have the accused found not guilty. In a civil trial, the legally acceptable reasons presented to the court in an attempt to reduce or eliminate the plaintiff's claim against the defendant. Also used to refer to the pleading given the court by a defendant in response to a plaintiff's claim.

Deposition: pre-trial testimony made under oath by a witness in response to spoken or written questions, as part of the process of discovery in which each side gathers evidence for its case. In Canada and the US, depositions are typically taken in the office of the lawyer of one of the parties. In criminal trials in the UK, depositions are taken before the magistrates' court; and in civil trials an examiner of the court (an official) may take depositions.

Devolution: a central government's delegation of limited domestic authority to a regional government. Recent example: establishment of regional governments in Scotland and Wales.

Dicta / dictum: (Latin) words/word. Remarks offered by a judge in the course of resolving a dispute, but not directly connected to the reasons upon which the judge relies in reaching a judgment. *Dicta* usually do not set a binding precedent.

Diligence: many types. Generally, the standard of carefulness reasonably expected of a person in a given situation.

Diminished responsibility: a state of mind excusing a person from full liability for certain crimes whose commission includes a mental element, assessed by a test for the existence of a medical condition creating abnormal mental function. This concept is used as a defense of an accused with varying acceptance and success in various jurisdictions.

Discharge: generally, a release from some obligation.

Discovery: in the context of trials, the pre-trial process by which opposing parties gather information from one another in order to prepare the arguments to be heard before the court.

Discretion: generally, the power of an official to exercise official powers in accordance with the official's best judgment.

Dismiss: to end a legal dispute prior to or during a trial.

Dissent: in a judicial decision, the fact of disagreement by a judge or judges who are in the minority. A dissenting opinion consists of reasons for disagreement with the majority of the court.

Distinguishing a case: the process of giving reasons intended to show that a case differs significantly from an apparently similar case, often to show that application of the same law ought to produce a different result.

Distributive justice: in political theory and ethics focused on legal institutions and law, examination of and advocacy for design and practice aiming to distribute benefits and burdens fairly across individuals and groups, with attention to differences among them.

Docket: generally, a record of a court's activities, including a list of disputes to be heard, and the resolution of the dispute.

Double jeopardy: the legal doctrine that an accused person cannot be tried more than once for the same charge on the same evidence.

Due process: US and Canadian doctrine of fairness in both procedural operation of law and its substantive effects.

Duress: coercive or other threat used to compel action against the actor's will.

Duty: an obligation to act or withhold from a particular course of conduct.

Duty of care: the context- and relationship-specific obligation of one person to take reasonable care not to damage another person or their property.

Eminent domain: American legal doctrine, later adopted in Canada, recognizing a governmental right to take private property for public purposes.

Enlargement: in the context of the European Union, the process of growth of the Union by acceptance of more state members.

Entrenchment: in constitutional law, a special and elevated kind of recognition of rights, liberties, and freedoms which protects these from change by normal legislative means.

Epistemology: the branch of philosophy concerned with the foundations of knowledge and what can be known.

Equity: generally, recourse to considerations of justice or fairness, rather than the strict letter of the law.

Erga omnes: (Latin) against all.

Ergo: (Latin) therefore.

Estoppel: generally, the legal principle that bars or stops party A from denying or alleging that the truth of some matter is different from what A previously represented it to be, and was (usually) taken by B as the truth, so A cannot gain advantage over B through a new, different representation of the truth of some matter. A is bound by A's initial representation of the truth of the matter. Roughly and intuitively stated, you may not change your story now to take advantage of someone else's having relied on your prior story. There are several types of estoppel, whose interpretation must be determined with reference to the specific jurisdiction.

Et al.: (Latin) and others.

Ethics: 1. the branch of philosophy concerned with the nature of the good life and right conduct. 2. in the legal context, often used to refer to standards of professional conduct which apply to members of the legal profession. *See also* **Moral philosophy**

European Parliament: a 720-member body directly elected from member states of the European Union. This Parliament operates as a co-legislator together with the European Council (comprised of heads of state and governments of member states), amending, adopting, or rejecting legislative proposals of the European Commission (which exercises the European Union's executive function). This Parliament has budgetary powers insofar as approval of the European Union budget requires the agreement of the Parliament and the European Council. This Parliament has additional supervisory powers with respect to the European Commission and European Union institutions.

Evidence: legally acceptable matter such as testimony, documents, substantial objects used to prove or disprove the existence of some claimed fact.

Ex officio: (Latin) from office, used to refer to roles held as a consequence of holding an office and not as a result of independent processes.

Ex parte: (Latin) on behalf of one side only.

Ex post facto: (Latin) after the fact.

Exclusionary rules: an element of the law of evidence setting limits on acceptable claims of fact and methods of proof of claimed facts. Often encountered in the context of claims that legal officials have obtained evidence in impermissible ways, so courts should exclude that evidence from consideration at trial.

Exculpatory: legally admissible evidence or other facts which tend to relieve a defendant from legal liability. *See* **Inculpatory**

Excuse: a legally acceptable reason for relief from legal liability. *See* **Exculpatory**

Extradition: the process in which a person is returned to a state in which he or she is to stand trial for a criminal offence. Extradition treaties between states provide for the giving over of fugitives from other states' criminal law.

Factum: (Latin) a fact. In legal practice, written argument making a case, often discussed in the context of seeking permission to appeal a prior court's decision on the basis of an account of relevant facts, the legal basis of an appeal, and statement of the desired outcome of the appeal.

Felony: in the USA, especially serious crimes, contrasted with less serious misdemeanors. In Canada and England this term has largely fallen out of use, and carries on in England only in pre-1967 criminal statutes. Especially serious crimes are now called indictable offences, and less serious crimes are now called summary offences.

Fraud: intentional misrepresentation of the truth of some matter for the purpose of gain.

Gratis: (Latin) free.

Guilty: a plea before the court or a finding by a court that an accused has committed the crime charged.

Habeas Corpus: (Latin) you have the body. A *writ* used in the procedure of judicial determination of the legality of detention of a person. If the detention is illegal, the accused is released.

Hansard: a term used in Britain, Canada, Australia, New Zealand, India, and many Commonwealth countries to refer to official records of specified proceeding in parliaments, especially debates. Hansard records are sometimes used in a legal context to discern the intention of parliamentary lawmakers when application of law created by Parliament is unclear. The word Hansard is the surname of the first official printer of the proceedings of the British Parliament at Westminster.

Hearing: a proceeding held to resolve issues of fact and of law. Can refer to proceedings of courts, or quasi-judicial institutions.

House of Commons: in the UK and Canada, the lower house of Parliament, composed of elected Members of Parliament who serve terms of up to five years.

House of Lords: formerly the highest appellate court in the UK. In 2009 its judicial authority was transferred to the newly created Supreme Court of the UK, in accordance with the *Constitutional Reform Act 2005*.

House of Representatives: one-half of the United States Congress, composed of elected members who serve terms of two years.

Human rights: broadly in moral philosophy, those universal freedoms of all persons and sometimes groups *to* certain circumstances, and freedom *from* certain intervention or prevention of protected action. Debate continues regarding the nature of such rights. Examples of claimed human rights receiving nearly universal agreement and support include a right *to* freedom of conscience, and a freedom *from* torture. In legal contexts, international law and state law contain aspirations to protection of specified human rights, and in many instances, human rights are given robust protection in effectively enforced legislation supported by longstanding custom.

Ibid.: abbreviation for (Latin) *ibidem*: in the same place.

I.e.: abbreviation for (Latin) *Id est*: that is.

Ignorantia legis non excusat: (Latin) ignorance of the law is no excuse.

In camera: (Latin) in private, used to identify aspects of trial or other administrative procedures conducted in a non-public manner excluding observers such as spectators or media reporters. Matters of national security, matters concerning vulnerable persons, and matters of commercial confidentiality are all examples of subjects sometimes treated *in camera* at trial and in other government, business, or association administrative proceedings.

Inculpatory: legally admissible evidence or other facts which tend to incriminate or contribute weight to the case aimed at proving a defendant's legal liability. *See* **Exculpatory**

Indictable offence: In Canada and the UK, a criminal offence involving a matter more serious (e.g., murder) than matters involved in a summary offence (e.g., assault). Typically heard by courts higher than those which deal with less serious summary offences, and typically involving the option of a trial by judge and jury. Distinction no longer clearly evident in Canada. *See also* **Summary offence**, **Felony**

Indictment: a written charge of a serious criminal offence which must be proved before a court.

Indigenous peoples: in general usage in the context of legal and political theory, peoples whose occupation of a territory pre-dates the arrival of invaders or settlers whose social systems displaced or overpowered prior systems in ways leading to persistent unfairness in distribution of power and influence, notwithstanding formal and informal agreements to the contrary. Definitions of Indigenous peoples vary in state law as do legal provisions for their legal status and its relevance to matters such as constitutional recognition of groups and group rights.

Infra: (Latin) below. Indicates a following provision of reference information. See ***Supra***

Injunction: a judicial direction to a specific party to refrain from or to carry out certain conduct.

Intellectual property: generally, a form of duration-limited exclusionary property right enabling the right-holder to exclude others from payment-free use of an idea protected by the right. Forms of copyright vary and are treated state by state in ways interacting with international agreement on intellectual property rights. Forms include copyright, patent, trademark, design, plant breeders' rights, and trade secret.

Inter alia: (Latin) among others.

Intergenerational justice: in political and legal theory, questions and considerations regarding what is owed as a matter of fairness of distribution of benefits and burdens across generations, including consideration of possible duties to prior generations, and duties to future generations notwithstanding present lack of knowledge regarding the characteristics of those future generations.

International Court of Justice: a 15-judge court based in The Hague, in The Netherlands, established by the United Nations as successor to the Permanent Court of International Justice. The International Court of Justice adjudicates disputes between states who voluntarily accept the Court's jurisdiction, and provides non-binding advisory opinions on matters of international law brought before it. The International Court of Justice is not now and has never been a final court of appeal or court of last resort superior to the highest courts of states. The Court does not now and has never held power to direct police or military forces of any state or international body to enforce its decisions, which rely for their effect on disputants having accepted the authority of the Court and in so doing having committed to respect its decisions.

International Criminal Court: a Court sitting in The Hague, in The Netherlands, established in 1998 by a treaty called the Rome Statute. The International Criminal Court's jurisdiction is now accepted by 125 states. States not accepting the jurisdiction of the International Criminal Court include the United States, China, Russia, and India. The International Criminal Court is a permanent body complementary to state courts, providing the international community with a last resort option for investigation and trial of persons accused of committing especially serious crimes. The International Criminal Court has jurisdiction with respect to genocide, and since 2002, crimes against humanity and war crimes, and since 2018, crimes of aggression. As an international court complementary to state courts, the International Criminal Court is not a final court of appeal superior to state courts. The International Criminal Court does not operate or direct a police force, relying instead on operations of police forces in states accepting the Court's jurisdiction. The International Criminal Court holds persons detained under its authority in a prison located within a prison of the International Criminal Court's host country, The Netherlands, and transfers convicted persons to serve their sentences in the prison systems of other countries accepting the Court's jurisdiction.

Invalidation: the nullification, typically by appellate level courts, of legislation, rendering that legislation or some particular legislative provision of no force or effect. *See also* **Striking down**

Ipso facto: (Latin) by the fact.

Judgment: a decision by a court of competent jurisdiction regarding a dispute brought before it.

Judicial review: a practice established for courts to assess the legality or constitutionality of government actions, laws, or policies.

Jurisdiction: 1. the area of law to which a specific court's authority extends. 2. generally, a particular legal system.

Jurist: a person knowledgeable in law.

Jury: a number of persons selected to decide the facts of a case at trial, and to render a verdict. Grand juries traditionally composed of twenty-three persons are still used in the USA to determine whether facts and charges brought by a prosecutor are sufficient for the matter to go to trial. In England and Canada, grand juries are no longer used. Trial juries are typically composed of six or twelve persons.

Jus: (Latin) law or right.

Jus belli: (Latin) law of war.

Jus cogens: (Latin) known law. Refers to the doctrine of public international law which declares invalid any new agreement which conflicts with the overriding, peremptory norms of the widely accepted body of fundamental international legal norms.

Jus gentium: (Latin) law of nations. Refers to international law generally.

Leading case: a particularly important decision which has resolved a dispute in a way which is later relied upon as a strong guide for similar cases.

Leading question: a question which suggests to the witness the answer desired by the questioner, typically a "yes" or "no" answer. Usually allowed only in cross-examination or examination of a witness hostile to the questioner.

Legislation: generally, written law enacted by an authoritative body.

Liability: term broadly used to include obligation, duty, responsibility, in civil and criminal contexts.

Libel: generally, defamation of longer duration, typically printed, written, or graphic as opposed to verbally issued defamation. May include cartoons, sketches, sculpture, films, or audio recordings. *See also* **Defamation**

Limited company: generally, a company created under law limiting the personal liability of members of the company for the company's debts. There are many forms of limited companies.

Litigants: the persons engaged in a civil dispute brought before a court.

Litigation: generally, the activity of bringing a civil dispute before a court for resolution.

Locus poenitentiae: (Latin) place for repentance. An opportunity for a change of mind prior to completion of some act.

Logic: the branch of philosophy concerned with the characteristics of good and bad arguments.

Magna Carta: Latin (great charter). A record of the statement of King John of England in 1215 accepting limits to the power of the King, creating the foundation of the tradition of individual rights that cannot be violated by government, serving over time less as a source of specific legal obligation and more as a noted ancestor of principles in constitutional government in societies inheriting the common law system founded in English law.

Malfeasance: generally, wrongdoing. The term is associated with specific variations in various jurisdictions and should not be viewed as synonymous with the terms misfeasance and non-feasance.

Malum in se: (Latin) evil or wrong in itself. Evil according to the standard of civilized society even in the absence of specific limiting legislation.

Malum prohibitum: (Latin) evil or wrong because it is prohibited.

Martial law: government of civilians by military authorities in a time of emergency.

Material: important, necessary, substantially relevant.

Mediation: a dispute resolution process conducted outside the court system by an independent person employed not to reach a decision but rather to enable the disputing parties to reach a resolution each accepts. See **Alternative Dispute Resolution** and **Arbitration**

Mens rea: (Latin) guilty mind. The mental element of the type of crime which requires for its commission both *mens rea* and the actual criminal conduct, called *actus reus*. The *mens rea* requirement for particular crimes is specified by legislation or precedent as intention, recklessness, or negligence. Strict liability criminal offences have no *mens rea* requirement. *See* **Strict liability**

Mercantile law: the body of law regarding commercial transactions.

Metaphysics: the branch of philosophy which examines the nature of what is real.

Misdemeanor: in the USA, a crime less serious than a felony. Distinction eliminated from English and Canadian law.

Mistrial: a failure of a trial for a fundamental reason.

Moral philosophy: the branch of philosophy which examines the nature of the good life and right conduct. *See also* **Ethics**

Natural justice: generally, principles of procedural fairness which prohibit bias on the part of the judge, and require that both sides to a dispute be heard.

Necessity defense: a defense against a criminal charge on the ground that no alternative legally permissible course of action was available to the defendant.

Negligence: conduct which is assessed careless when measured against the standard of what a reasonable person could be expected to do or not do. Aspect of *mens rea*.

Non-performance: the failure of a contracting party to adhere to the terms of a contract.

Non sequitur: (Latin) it does not follow. A conclusion which does not follow from the premises or reasons given.

Normative jurisprudence: the branch of philosophy of law concerned mainly with evaluation and justification of law and legal practices.

Not guilty: a plea made by the accused to deny charges, and a verdict which indicates that the case against the accused was not proven beyond reasonable doubt.

Nota bene: (Latin) note well. Abbreviated N.B.

Nulla poena sine lege: (Latin) no punishment without law. The principle that no punishment shall be given unless the punishment is set by law.

Obiter dictum: (Latin) said in passing. A reported statement or observation by a judge that does not form part of the reasons for decision in the case at hand, yet conveys how the judge views related matters so contributes to a fuller understanding of a court's view of an area of law.

Offence: generally, a crime.

Ontology: the branch of philosophy which examines questions about the existence of things.

Opinion: a judge's or court's reasons for a decision regarding a dispute.

Overrule: the overturning of a decision in a particular case by the same court or a higher court of the same jurisdiction.

Pacta sunt servanda: (Latin) agreements must be served. General legal principle that what is agreed must be carried out.

Parliamentary sovereignty: legal doctrine that Parliament is supreme and can make or eliminate any law.

Party: persons with a direct interest in a legal proceeding.

Per curiam: (Latin) by the court.

Performance: the carrying out of an obligation, e.g., the terms of a contract.

Perjury: knowingly giving false testimony while under oath to give true testimony.

Person: an individual human or a group of persons such as a corporation or a union.

Plaintiff: a person bringing civil suit or action against another before a court.

Plea bargaining: a practice of negotiating a reduction in charges or sentence in exchange for the accused pleading guilty to agreed charges.

Pleadings: written statements of fact given by each party to the opponent reporting facts used in support of each party's case, used to make plain the issues to be resolved at trial.

Positive law: law actually put into place by an authority for government of a law-governed society.

Positive morality: the actual current moral beliefs of a particular society.

Precedent: legal doctrine by which previously decided cases are authoritative sources for settlement of later similar cases. *See also* ***Stare decisis***

Preponderance of evidence: more probable than not. The standard of proof used in civil law, contrasted with the higher standard of reasonable doubt used in criminal law.

Presumption: a legal requirement or commitment to regarding some fact or situation in a specified way until reason and evidence require revision of the view. For example, the presumption of innocence in criminal law is a starting point to which common law systems are generally committed, yet specified reasons and evidence can show that the presumption cannot be sustained, so it is overwhelmed and replaced by the judgment supported by the contrary reasons and evidence. For an accused to be found guilty beyond reasonable doubt, reasons and evidence must show beyond reasonable doubt that innocence can no longer be presumed. Many additional presumptions exist in law.

Prima facie: (Latin) on its face. On initial appearance or examination.

Private international law: *see* **Conflict of laws**

Private law: law regarding the relations between persons and not relations between persons and the state.

Pro bono: (Latin) for the good. Often used to refer to legal work undertaken by lawyers on an unpaid, voluntary basis.

Proceeding: generally, the form and manner of operations before a court, and the steps in the course of judicial resolution of a dispute.

Prosecutorial discretion: the power of a prosecutor to rely on his or her best judgment as to whether criminal charges ought to be laid.

Public law: law regarding relations between persons and the state, and the composition and operation of the state and its institutions.

Question of fact: a dispute over facts, decided by a jury.

Question of law: a dispute over a matter of law, decided by a judge.

Ratio decidendi: (Latin) reason for decision. The *ratio* of a case binds lower courts by the doctrine of precedent.

Reasonable doubt: the standard of proof used in criminal trial. A person guilty of a crime must be guilty beyond reasonable doubt, according to the standard of the reasonable person.

Rechtsstaat: (German) a state under the rule of law. This complex term expresses the ideal of a state whose nature and existence is intrinsically tied to a commitment to the principles of the rule of law.

Reckless: heedless, rash conduct which is indifferent to the existence of recognized danger. More serious than negligence. Aspect of *mens rea*.

Remedy: a means to enforce a right or to redress violation of a right.

Repeal: a legislative act which eliminates a previous law.

Res ipsa loquitur: (Latin) thing speaks for itself. A part of the law of evidence expressing the idea that the relation between a particular cause and particular effect are so obvious that no further reasons or evidence are needed to establish that a particular cause did indeed result in a particular effect.

Restorative justice: processes and an understanding of justice seeking to achieve at the level of wrongdoer and wronged parties and sometimes their surrounding communities a restoration of relationships to the state prior to wrongdoing, in ways going beyond mere restitution or compensation to include a wrongdoer's acknowledgment of wrongdoing (sometimes public) and corresponding resumption of the wrongdoer's status as a full member of a community.

Reversal: the overturning of the decision of a lower court by a higher court.

Rule of law: an ideal rather than a specific rule. The content of the ideal is a matter of enduring debate. Yet the ideal is often used to identify the aim of societies and legal systems seeking a kind of social stability supported by predictability of members' situations before the law and the supremacy of law over arbitrariness found in rules guided by the personal desires of powerful individuals or groups. Societies seeking to enact the ideal aim for separation of the roles of law-creating legislators from the roles of independent courts and judges, whose application of law is procedurally fair and treats all members of the society and system as equal before the law, with durable rights to challenge violations of procedural fairness or arbitrarily special treatment of some members of the society. While the rule of law may be spoken of as a commitment to a moral ideal, it has been observed that the value of the procedural regularity and predictability promised by the ideal can be achieved in both societies enacting well-justified moral views, and societies enacting poorly-justified moral views.

Senate: in the USA, one-half of the United States Congress (the other half being the House of Representatives). Senators are elected to six-year terms. In Canada, the upper house of Parliament, composed of appointed members who serve until age seventy-five.

Sentence: the punishment given a defendant upon conviction of criminal wrongdoing.

Slander: spoken defamation. *See also* **Defamation**

Slippery slope: in informal logic, also known as argumentation theory, the idea that once some course of action or set of reasons is enacted or endorsed, a further sequence of actions or ideas is inevitably enacted or endorsed, including unintended, often extreme consequences. When it is suggested that action or reasoning leads to a slippery slope, opponents of the suggestion must show that a stopping point is indeed possible, or that the envisioned consequences do not occur. When an actual slippery slope can be identified, potentially unwanted consequences can be identified and sometimes avoided. When a slippery slope is claimed to exist but can be shown to be an illusion, the argument for a slippery slope is said to commit a logical error called a fallacy.

Social construction: refers to human-created ideas as opposed to ideas reflective of some reality fixed by factors beyond human choice and creation. In the context of law, the idea of social construction has been used in explanations seeking to show that law is less a reflection of some natural order of things beyond human creation, and more a product of human choice and decision. For example, ideas and practices such as rights and intellectual property have been invented by humans to advance human interests, and are not external to human practice in the way that the existence of such things as animals, gravity, roads, and bridges are. Even roads, and bridges once imagined then built are things that exist without further human agreement and practice.

Solicitor: in England and Wales and some other common law jurisdictions, a lawyer who prepares cases and works outside the court in co-operation with barristers. In Canada this distinction is not made, and all lawyers may retain the designation "barrister and solicitor." *See also* **Barrister**

Sovereign immunity: legal doctrine which prevents a suit against the government without the consent of the government.

Sovereignty: an ideal expressed in legal theory and practice in various ways, expressing the general idea that a government or people are the supreme authority over the totality of their affairs. In international law, sovereignty often refers to the supreme authority of a state with respect to its territory and population in distinction to the supreme authority of other states with respect to their identity and internal affairs. As an ideal, sovereignty inspires pursuit of a degree of independence generally known to be in tension with the reality of existence as a state. Even new states are presumed to be bound by fundamental international law constraining exercise of their independence, whether or not the new state voluntarily accepts those obligations in some public act of acknowledgment. The life of a state also generally includes limitations on independence created by obligations found in treaties to which states have formally agreed voluntarily even while in many instances those obligations are in effect forced upon the state. It should also be noted that states and other political societies claiming some form of sovereignty depend on recognition by other states and political societies, so are in practice the meaningfulness of claims to sovereignty.

Stare decisis: (Latin) stand by decided matters. The doctrine that courts follow precedent, and lower courts treat decisions of higher courts of the same jurisdiction as binding, and decisions of higher courts in other jurisdictions as only persuasive.

Statute: a written legislative act by an authoritative body.

Strict liability: a type of offence in which responsibility is assigned without a finding of fault. Strict liability offences are typically matters where the value of efficient regulation and nominal penalties outweigh the danger of omitting an assessment of fault.

Striking down: a court decision to invalidate or nullify legislation or some particular legislative provision. *See also* **Invalidation**

Subsidiarity: the principle of European Union law which, together with principles of proportionality and necessity, requires that decisions should be made at the level closest to the citizen whenever possible, thereby balancing the need and importance of local control with the need and importance of shared European laws.

Sui generis: (Latin) of its own kind. Used to identify something truly unique and independent of other kinds with which it might be confused, but once identified as *sui generis* can be understood to need independent analysis and understanding recognizing its standing apart from similar objects or ideas.

Summary offence: In Canada and the UK, a criminal offence involving a matter less serious (e.g., assault) than matters involved in an indictable offence (e.g., murder). Typically heard by a single judge in a lower court for speedy resolution of the charge. *See also* **Indictable offence**, **Felony**

Supra: (Latin) above. Often used in legal writing to indicate that a full reference to some source of information has already been given, and may be found in an earlier part of the work. E.g., *supra* n. 17 means that a fuller reference may be found in note 17 which occurs in the preceding text. See ***Infra***

Testimony: a witness's statement of evidence, given under oath.

Time immemorial: generally, referring to a state of affairs existing since a point in time prior to written or other records of origin. Sometimes used with respect to the existence of a legal norm such as a customary right whose coming into existence has no single point of origin in the legal record. Used additionally in the context of some Indigenous peoples' claim to occupancy of territory prior to purported discovery by later arrivals, and associated claims of continuous practice of norms within and regarding those territories.

Tort: a civil wrong remedied by an award of damages.

Tortfeasor: a person who commits a tort, called a "tortious" act.

Ultra vires: (Latin) outside of or beyond the powers. An action beyond the authorized power of the actor.

Unconstitutional: refers to a law which is inconsistent with the provisions of a constitution.

Viz.: abbreviation for (Latin) *videlicet*: namely.

Volenti non fit injuria: (Latin) no injury or wrong is done to a consenting person. Defense in tort law which claims that plaintiff consented to damage or risk of damage suffered.

Writ: generally, a written court order giving authority and direction to carry out some act.

Wrong: in a legal context, acts whose negative consequences for others as harms to their individual interests or broader social interests are subject to legal control as unlawful. Both criminal and civil law are concerned with wrongs. There are complex debates regarding the relation between moral wrongs and legal wrongs.

Credits

Austin, John. From *The Province of Jurisprudence Determined, Fifth Edition* (1885).

Austin, Raymond D. From *Navajo Courts and Navajo Common Law: A Tradition of Tribal Self-Governance* (pp. 37–51, 94–105, 120–24), University of Minnesota Press, 2009. Copyright © 2009 by the Regents of the University of Minnesota. Reprinted with permission.

Borrows, John. "Sources and Scope of Indigenous Legal Traditions," from *Canada's Indigenous Constitution*. Copyright © 2010 University of Toronto Press Inc. Reprinted with permission of the publisher.

Cotterrell, Roger. "Transnational Communities and the Concept of Law," from *Ratio Juris*, 21.1 (2008): 1–18. https://doi.org/10.1111/j.1467-9337.2007.00377.x. Copyright © 2008 Roger Cotterrell. Reprinted by permission of John Wiley & Sons, Inc., conveyed through Copyright Clearance Center, Inc.

Crenshaw, Kimberlé. "Demarginalizing the Intersection of Race and Sex: A Black Feminist Critique of Antidiscrimination Doctrine, Feminist Theory and Antiracist Politics." Originally appeared in the *University of Chicago Legal Forum*, Vol. 1989. Reprinted with permission from the University of Chicago Legal Forum and the University of Chicago Law School.

Delgado, Richard. "About Your Masthead: A Preliminary Inquiry into the Compatibility of Civil Rights and Civil Liberties," *Harvard Civil Rights-Civil Liberties Law Review*, 39.1 (Winter 2004): 1–15. Used by permission of The Harvard Civil Rights-Civil Liberties Review, conveyed through Copyright Clearance Center, Inc.

Devlin, Patrick. From "The Enforcement of Morals," in *Proceedings of the British Academy*, Vol. XLV, London: The British Academy. Copyright © The British Academy 1959. Reproduced with permission.

Duff, R.A. From *Criminal Attempts* (pp. 147–50, 165–68, 173–80, 183–92), Clarendon Press, 1997. Copyright © 1996, 1997 by Antony Duff. Reproduced with the permission of Oxford Publishing Limited through PLSclear.

Dworkin, Ronald. "Integrity in Law," from *Law's Empire*, published by The Belknap Press of Harvard University Press. Copyright © 1986 by Ronald Dworkin. Also published by Hart Publishing, an imprint of Bloomsbury Publishing Plc. Copyright © 1998 Ronald Dworkin. Used by permission. All rights reserved. "The Model of Rules I," from *Taking Rights Seriously, Second Edition*, published by The Belknap Press of Harvard University Press. Copyright © 1977, 1978 by Ronald Dworkin. Also published by Bloomsbury Academic, an imprint of Bloomsbury Publishing Plc. Copyright © Ronald Dworkin 1977, 1997. Used by permission. All rights reserved.

Finnis, John. From *Natural Law and Natural Rights, First Edition* (pp. 3–4, 18–19, 23–26, 59–60, 100–12, 118–19, 351–62), Oxford University Press, 1980. Copyright © J.M. Finnis 1980. Reproduced with the permission of Oxford Publishing Limited through PLSclear.

Grotius, Hugo. "Prolegomena" (pp. 9–21, 23–24) from *De Jure Belli Ac Pacis Libri Tres* (1625) in *The Classics of International Law*, ed. J.B. Scott. Oxford: Clarendon Press, 1925.

Hart, H.L.A. From Chapter V: "Law as the Union of Primary and Secondary Rules" (pp. 79–96); Chapter VI: "The Foundations of a Legal System" (pp. 97–114); Chapter X: "International Law" (pp. 213–32) of *The Concept of Law*, Oxford University Press, 1961. Copyright © 1961, 1994 Oxford University Press. Reproduced with the permission of Oxford Publishing Limited through PLSclear. "Positivism and the Separation of Law and Morals," *Harvard Law Review*, 71.4 (Feb. 1958): 593–629. https://doi.org/10.2307/1338225. Reprinted by permission of Harvard Law Review, conveyed through Copyright Clearance Center, Inc. From *Law, Liberty and Morality* (pp. 4, 13–26, 30–34, 48–52, 81–83), Stanford University Press, 1972. Copyright © 1963 by the Board of Trustees of the Leland Stanford Junior University. Reprinted with permission. Used by permission of Stanford University Press, conveyed through Copyright Clearance Center, Inc.

Holmes, Oliver Wendell. "The Path of the Law," from *The Common Law* (1897).

Hurd, Heidi. "Why Liberals Should Hate 'Hate Crime Legislation,'" *Law and Philosophy*, 20.2 (Mar. 2001): 215–32. https://doi.org/10.1023/A:1010661127873. Copyright © 2001 Kluwer Academic Publishers. Reprinted by permission of Springer Nature, conveyed through Copyright Clearance Center, Inc.

Koskenniemi, Martti. "The Politics of International Law," *European Journal of International Law*, 1.1 (1990): 4–32. https://doi.org/10.1093/oxfordjournals.ejil.a035781. Copyright © 1990 Oxford University Press. Used with the permission of Oxford University Press, conveyed through Copyright Clearance Center, Inc.

Leiter, Brian. "Constitutional Law, Moral Judgment, and the Supreme Court as Super-Legislature," *Hastings Law Journal*, 66.6 (2015). Reprinted by permission of the author and Hasting Law Journal.

MacKinnon, Catharine A. From *Toward a Feminist Theory of the State*, Harvard University Press, 1989. Copyright © 1989 by Catharine A. MacKinnon. Reprinted by permission of the author.

Mill, John Stuart. From *On Liberty* (pp. 199–211), London: Oxford University Press, 1859.

Murphy, Jeffrie G. "Marxism and Retribution," *Philosophy & Public Affairs*, 2.3 (Spring 1973): 217–43. http://www.jstor.org/stable/2264911. Copyright © 1973 Wiley. Reprinted by permission of John Wiley & Sons, Inc., conveyed through Copyright Clearance Center, Inc.

Smith, M.B.E. "Is There a Prima Facie Obligation to Obey the Law?," *The Yale Law Journal*, 82.5 (Apr. 1973): 950–76. https://doi.org/10.2307/795537. Reprinted with permission.

Smith, Patricia. From Introduction (pp. 3–12), *Feminist Jurisprudence*, ed. Patricia Smith, Oxford University Press. Copyright © 1993 by Oxford University Press, Inc. Reproduced with the permission of Oxford Publishing Limited through PLSclear.

St. Thomas Aquinas. "Treatise on Law," from *Summa Theologica*.

Tamanaha, Brian. "Introduction: Three Themes" (pp. 1–18) from *Legal Pluralism Explained*, Oxford University Press. Copyright © 2021 Brian Z. Tamanaha. Reproduced with the permission of Oxford Publishing Limited through PLSclear.

About the Publisher

The word "broadview" expresses a good deal of the philosophy behind our company. Our focus is very much on the humanities and social sciences—especially literature, writing, and philosophy—but within these fields we are open to a broad range of academic approaches and political viewpoints. We strive in particular to produce high-quality, pedagogically useful books for higher education classrooms—anthologies, editions, sourcebooks, surveys of particular academic fields and sub-fields, and also course texts for subjects such as composition, business communication, and critical thinking. We welcome the perspectives of authors from marginalized and underrepresented groups, and we have a strong commitment to the environment. We publish English-language works and translations from many parts of the world, and our books are available world-wide; we also publish a select list of titles with a specifically Canadian emphasis.

broadview press